The
Meaning
of the
Bible

The Meaning *of the* Bible

*What the Jewish Scriptures and
Christian Old Testament Can Teach Us*

Douglas A. Knight
and Amy-Jill Levine

HarperOne
An Imprint of HarperCollinsPublishers

HarperOne

THE MEANING OF THE BIBLE: *What the Jewish Scriptures and Christian Old Testament Can Teach Us*. Copyright © 2011 by Douglas A. Knight and Amy-Jill Levine. All rights reserved. Printed in the United States of America. No part of this book may be used or reproduced in any manner whatsoever without written permission except in the case of brief quotations embodied in critical articles and reviews. For information address HarperCollins Publishers, 10 East 53rd Street, New York, NY 10022.

HarperCollins books may be purchased for educational, business, or sales promotional use. For information please write: Special Markets Department, HarperCollins Publishers, 10 East 53rd Street, New York, NY 10022.

HarperCollins website: http://www.harpercollins.com
HarperCollins®, ✠ ®, and HarperOne™ are trademarks of
HarperCollins Publishers.

FIRST EDITION

Maps designed by Lauren E. Kohut.

Library of Congress Cataloging-in-Publication Data
Knight, Douglas A.
The meaning of the Bible : what the Jewish scriptures and Christian Old Testament can teach us / by Douglas A. Knight and Amy-Jill Levine.
p. cm.
ISBN 978-0-06-112175-3
1. Bible. O.T.—Criticism, interpretation, etc. I. Levine, Amy-Jill. II. Title.
BS1173.3.K55   2011
221.6'1—dc23   2011017114

11 12 13 14 15 RRD(H) 10 9 8 7 6 5 4 3 2 1

To our families

Catherine Whitehead Snow
Lisa Irene Knight
Jonathan Whitehead Snow

and

Jay Geller
Sarah Elizabeth Geller
Alexander David Geller

Contents

PART 2

PART 3

PART 4

List of Abbreviations

Gk.	Greek
Heb.	Hebrew
Lat.	Latin
BCE	Before the Common Era
CE	Common Era
LXX	Septuagint
MT	Masoretic Text
KJV	King James Version
NEB	New English Bible
NKJV	New King James Version
NRSV	New Revised Standard Version
JPS	Jewish Publication Society (Tanakh)

Introduction

The Bible is many things to many people—an ancient literary master-piece, a cultural artifact, an authoritative scripture for Judaism and Christianity, even a weapon in the culture wars. A library of diverse literary forms including stories, songs, proverbs, laws, and prophecies, the Bible is an enigma to some readers and a delight and inspiration to others. It contains descriptions of horrific violence, strong emotions, and aesthetic beauty; it moves from sometimes incomprehensible legal prescriptions and peculiar customs to lofty poetry, dramatic narratives, and enduring moral and religious principles.

It's also the principal building block of much of Western culture. The Bible's language undergirds how we think and how we speak. It offers the menu of "forbidden fruit," "sour grapes," and "sweet honey in the rock" that many found in the "land of milk and honey." It adores the "apple of my eye," but nevertheless demands in cases of injury an "eye for an eye." "Tender mercies" vie with "spare the rod," although "thy rod and thy staff they comfort me." "To everything there is a season," which is a good thing since there's also a "fly in the ointment" and a "drop in the bucket," both of which can leave us at "wit's end" unless we can read the "handwriting on the wall." The Bible helps us understand John Steinbeck's *East of Eden* and William Faulkner's *Absalom, Absalom,* along with Bette Davis's great performances in *Jezebel* and *The Little Foxes.* Josef Haydn, Jean Sibelius, Aaron Copeland, and Duke Ellington all found ways of expressing what happened "in the beginning"; Igor Stravinsky and Benjamin Britten gave new voice to Genesis 22, Abraham's "binding" of Isaac for sacrifice.

The Bible has always been, and will remain, a source of political idealism and political debate. Consequently, familiarity with the text—including the ability to distinguish what the text says from what people through the centuries have claimed it says—is necessary for those who wish fully to understand the current rhetoric about "biblical values." Some want to post the Ten Commandments in schoolrooms and courthouses; others note, correctly, that the commandments are not identical in the two texts that present them and are even reckoned differently by Jews and Christians; to post only one version would necessarily sanction one particular religious tradition.

Some want the Bible to be required reading in public schools. Although biblical literacy is to be encouraged, such instruction presents problems. Do we tell our students that the world was created in six twenty-four-hour days and that the "sun stood still" (Josh. 10:13) so the Israelites could win a battle, or do we present the accounts as metaphor or myth? Do we state that the prophet Isaiah predicted a "virgin birth" in 7:14, when the Hebrew text says nothing about a virgin? Do we insist that the "suffering servant" of Isaiah 52:13–53:12 is a prediction about Jesus of Nazareth, when elsewhere Isaiah explicitly identifies the servant as the people Israel (49:3)? Should the text be taught as great literature or as the divine Word?

There is also a necessary distinction between asking what the text *says* and determining what the text *means*. The "meaning" of the Bible will be different for every reader who encounters the text; at times, the meaning changes for the same reader, for each time the text is studied new insights can arise. For some readers, the Bible is inerrant, perfect, and the source of all knowledge. For others, it is a repository of a people's culture or a brilliant collection of stories with varying degrees of historicity. For some, it is the source of hope and inspiration; for others, it is a text of colonialism, conquest, slavery, misogyny, and homophobia. What we bring to the text necessarily determines what the text says to us. In turn, the more knowledge we have of the Bible in its original setting and the greater facility we have with the critical approaches to the text, the better we will be able to assess those meanings.

In this book, we attempt to take seriously the various ways the Bible can be and has been understood. We are interested in the theological questions the text raises. As faculty in a divinity school, part of our responsibility is to help those seeking to become priests, ministers, rabbis, and religious educators see how the text has been, can be, and perhaps should be interpreted within the communities of faith. Far too often the Bible, rather than being a rock on which one can stand, becomes a rock thrown to do damage to others. We have too much respect for the text, and for the communities that proclaim it to be *sacred* scripture, to ignore such concerns.

Those with a specific religious stake should find these pages enhancing their knowledge and appreciation of the text.

But as faculty also in a college of arts and science, we are interested in the text's literary brilliance, moral profundity, and clues about ancient history. We attend not only to what the text has meant to religious communities, but also, in fact especially, to what it meant in its own historical and cultural context. It has been said that a text without a context becomes simply a pretext for idiosyncratic interpretation. At the very least, we do think that historical awareness coupled with attention to the meaning of the original language can help in sorting out the acceptability of interpretations.

Each reader will see something distinct in the text, just as religious communities have developed their own lenses for interpretation. The very names for the biblical text show this diversity and demonstrate as well how our vocabulary already betrays our religious influences. For the synagogue, the text is not called the "Jewish scriptures" (the title of the present book is intended to indicate the contents descriptively, without using technical terminology). Instead, it is called the Tanakh, an acronym. The *T* stands for Torah, a Hebrew term for the first five books of the Bible; *N* is for Nevi'im, the term for "prophets"; and the *K* stands for Ketuvim, or "writings" (the remaining books, such as Psalms, Proverbs, Esther, and Job).

For the church, the familiar term is "Old Testament." The term "Christian Old Testament" is redundant; there is no "Jewish Old Testament" or "Muslim Old Testament." Again, however, the label "Christian Old Testament" in our title signals that this present book is looking at this collection of texts not only as an ancient anthology, but also as the sacred, authoritative writings of both church and synagogue.

In the academy, the common term for this collection is "Hebrew Bible," a descriptive rather than confessional name. It generally designates only the books in the Tanakh and does not include all the Old Testament books in the Catholic and Orthodox communions—deuterocanonical Greek texts such as Judith, a fabulous account of a gorgeous widow who chops off the enemy's head, with his own sword no less (see the cover art), and Susanna, what may be the world's first detective story. Whatever term we choose to call this collection will necessarily promote a specific religious or humanistic view. And again, the meaning of the Bible will change for the reader depending on which collection of texts, or canon, is used and indeed on the translation employed.

We often provide the Hebrew or the Greek of the earliest translations where the nuance of the original language matters (e.g., that conflict over the "virginal conception" in Isa. 7:14). Hebrew can be transliterated in multiple ways, a phenomenon perhaps most familiar to English-speakers from the numerous ways of spelling the holiday commemorating the re-dedication of the Jerusalem temple following the Maccabean revolt in the second century BCE. The name of the holiday comes from the Hebrew term for "dedication": Hannukah, Channukah, Chanukah, and Chanuka. The *ch* should be pronounced as in "Bach," but since that sound does not come easily to Americans and since it should not be pronounced like the *ch* in "church," it sometimes becomes replaced by a simple *h* or a *kh*. Similarly, a person's accent or dialect determines the pronunciation and so transliteration of the letter *tav*, the last letter in the Hebrew alphabet. In Ashkenazic (Eastern European, French, German) Hebrew, the *tav*, when it comes at the end of a word, is pronounced like an *s*, as in the term *bas mitzvah* (literally, "daughter of the commandment"). In Sephardic (Iberian, today's Middle Eastern, including Israeli and North African) pronunciation, the letter is pronounced as a *t* (*bat mitzvah*). In some Christian seminaries and other academic settings, the letter is rendered as a *th* to show that it is a dental fricative. Problems enter when the seminarian then inquires about the "*bath mitzvah*," which sounds to many familiar with either Israeli or synagogal pronunciation as if the person is speaking of a commandment to bathe.

Our transliteration follows substantially the phonetic system found both in synagogue contexts and in the teaching of modern Hebrew. Thus the Hebrew letter *bet* can be *b* or *v* depending on the word, and the letter *pe* may be *p* or *f*. For the letter *chet* and some occurrences of *kaf* we write *ch* (the German Ba*ch*). The Hebrew definite article is *ha-* preceding its noun.

Although the Bible has several overarching themes or, perhaps better, general questions, for example, about the relationship between divinity and humanity, the demands of justice, and what it means to live under covenant with God, the texts speak also to different times and places. The historical period described in this collection encompasses well over one thousand years, from the settlement of the land of Canaan, beginning around 1200 BCE, to the middle of the Hellenistic period, around 150 BCE. For the earlier materials from the primeval history (the stories of Adam and Eve and Noah) to the narratives of the ancestors from Abraham,

Sarah, and Hagar to Joseph, we have no clear external markers to confirm the biblical account. Nor have we corroborating historical evidence of the exodus from Egypt or the people's trek through the wilderness. Traceable origins of the biblical narrative begin with the Israelite settlement of the land of Canaan. From this point forward we can begin to correlate what the biblical text says with what can be determined from external sources, including archaeological evidence.

From 1200 on, the Israelites—variously known also as Hebrews, Judahites, Judeans, and Jews as well as Samaritans—inhabited the land. During the biblical period (ca. 1200–150 BCE), the people subsisted as best they could, coalesced in the form of a monarchic state, built cities, were successively conquered and occupied by four massive empires (Assyrian, Babylonian, Persian, and Hellenistic), articulated a set of religious and moral principles, developed a cultural memory, and survived despite frequent tragedies. Whether their survival, compared to the disappearance of neighboring nations such as the Hittites, Assyrians, Edomites, and Canaanites, is due to particular cultural practices such as circumcision and dietary restrictions, to an eventually centralized religious system, to luck or tenacity, to divine intervention, to a theological worldview that allowed for complaint as well as lament (the text turns the theological kvetch into an art form), *to the biblical text itself,* or to a combination of factors cannot be determined in any scientific manner. But survive they did. The Bible is the testament to their experiences, beliefs, and practices.

Today the Bible is available to all readers, a relatively recent phenomenon. The ancient Hebrew text—comprised only of consonants, no vowels, no punctuation—could only be read by those with special training. The general population of ancient Israel and, until relatively recently in human history, the total general population was illiterate. The people learned the biblical stories through teaching in the communities and eventually in both synagogues and churches; knowledge of rituals and codes of behavior was passed down from parent to child. Churches helped teach through religious art, while the synagogue, a relatively recent development in biblical history (David did not go to Hebrew school), promoted literacy.

But availability of the text, whether handwritten or printed, is not quite the same thing as accessibility. All texts need interpretation. Today we have footnotes and glosses, study guides and discussion groups. In the academy, we have various critical tools that aid us in determining when texts were written, what they might have meant to their original audiences, and how their meanings have changed over time. In this volume, we show how these tools function and so equip readers to apply them, artfully and carefully, to a variety of texts.

Some one thousand printed pages in length, depending on the version, the Hebrew Bible/Tanakh/Old Testament can seem formidable to many readers. Some find even the beginning to be a stumbling block. If read as history, the opening chapters conflict with what science tells us. The Bible mentions the birds and the wild creatures, but not the pterodactyl or tyrannosaurus; nor would they easily fit in the ark. Adam and Eve are gardeners, not hunter-gatherers. There was no universal flood; humanity never had a single language; people did not live to be as old as Methuselah (who checked out at 969). And so some readers will shelve the text as a work of fantasy at best, more likely of foolishness, and irrelevant to modern concerns. But the text offers neither foolishness nor fantasy, and it remains relevant today, for it helps us raise the right questions. To find the meaning, or a meaning, of the text requires the critical tools necessary to open and appreciate what it might (still) be saying.

If Genesis and the beginning of Exodus are read as "stories" rather than as "history," they are generally accessible. Readers assimilate the lyrical account of creation, in which everything "was good." They are intrigued with the record of the first humans in the Garden of Eden and the difficulties they face with a tempting snake and an even more tempting tree of knowledge. The accounts of Noah and his ark, the Tower of Babel, the ancestors, the slavery of the people in Egypt, and their exodus—all these make general narrative sense. Then, however, come the law codes, the detailed instructions on how to build the wilderness sanctuary, the commandments for temple sacrifice, and the descriptions of ritual purity. Now well-intentioned readers become confused or, worse, bored, or, worst, disgusted by what can appear to be a retributive system that makes today's religious extremists look enlightened. For such readers, again, critical tools are necessary. *How* to read the Bible is just as important as knowing what the text says. Here again, biblical scholarship can provide numerous keys.

Given that the Bible is an anthology, different readers will find different books more appealing. And given that biblical studies is itself a multifaceted discipline—it draws from literature and sociology, legal theory and archaeology, ethics and psychology, and anything else that might give insight into the text—different studies will emphasize different approaches.

The same holds for us as authors. Unlike the Bible, which was formed with the input of multiple authors over several centuries who produced a text that usually conceals their identities, this book has only two authors who willingly claim their authorship. One of us is more intrigued by law codes, prophetic discourse, and political developments; the other by literary artistry, gender roles, and diaspora existence. One specializes in the Hebrew Bible in its ancient Southwest Asian context from the Middle Bronze Age through the Persian period, and the other is an expert in the Persian, Greco-Roman, and early Jewish contexts of these materials. One of us comes from a Christian background; the other is a member of an Orthodox synagogue. In some cases, we disagree on what a text meant in its original context or what possible meanings it might hold today. In this volume, we combine our interests and our expertise to show our readers the various ways that the texts have been and can be understood, and readers can then apply the same reading strategies to unlock the meanings of other texts.

We began this book by first developing its overall structure and approach, and we then divided the chapters equally between us. Amy-Jill Levine wrote Chapters 2, 5, 6, 8, 9, 10, and 12, and Doug Knight authored Chapters 1, 3, 4, 7, 11, 13, and 14. We largely wrote each chapter separately, discussing issues as needed. After each of us completed a chapter, the other read it and offered questions and suggestions, which the original author then took into consideration in revising the draft. Our offices are next door to each other, we have team-taught classes, we have sat in on each other's lectures, and we have solidified our friendship in working on this project.

The book is therefore a result of a conversation between two scholars with different strengths. Both of us realize we are each shaped by our respective histories and points of view, but we also trust we are sufficiently transparent about our aims and interests. Together we complement and, we hope, correct each other as needed. We have spent our professional lives engaged with ancient history, and we hope you will be as captivated by the Bible as are we.

It is from our experience in teaching this material that we chose the format for this book. Most general treatments of this biblical material take one of three approaches. The most popular is the *chronological,* in which the discussions follow history from the earliest to the latest periods. This approach commends itself because the Bible carries a chronological thrust: creation, period of the ancestors, Egyptian slavery and exodus, journey to

Canaan, possession of the land, history of the monarchy, exile to Babylon, and return.

However, the composition of these stories does not match the chronology. Accounts set in the early period may have a late date of composition. For example, the opening chapter of Genesis, which begins, "In the beginning when God created the heavens and the earth . . . ," was not written "in the beginning" of Israel's history, but likely during or after the Babylonian exile in the sixth century BCE. The story of Adam and Eve, which picks up in Genesis 2:4b, may be an earlier account, perhaps based on an older tradition reaching back several centuries. Therefore, any chronological attempt is doomed to the vagaries of historical reconstruction and speculation.

Some texts resist dating at all. Was the book of Ruth written during the period of the judges, which is when the story is set? Or was it written while David was attempting to solidify his kingship, in order to explain how this Israelite ruler happened to have a Moabite great-grandmother? Or was it written comparatively late, during the time following the Babylonian exile, when some factions of the community, represented by Ezra and Nehemiah, encouraged the divorcing of foreign wives and others wanted to show that foreign wives were not only appropriate, but also divinely sanctioned?

We attempt to date the materials when internal and external markers warrant it, and we draw on archaeological and sociohistorical information to fill out the picture of the text's development and meaning. But the upshot is that very often the specific date, cultural influences, and original form of a particular text cannot be known.

Another approach is a *literary* one, in which one begins with the book of Genesis and moves step by step through the entire literature. Yet again, problems ensue, since the step-by-step trek through the Old Testament goes in different directions than the same trek through the Tanakh, given that the books appear in a different order in each collection. The Tanakh ends both the Torah and the canon itself with an image of the people Israel outside the land of Israel. Deuteronomy concludes with Moses on Mt. Nebo, overlooking the "promised land"; 2 Chronicles ends with the edict of King Cyrus of Persia, which encourages the Jews in exile in Babylon to return home to Israel. The focus on the land is palpable. But the Old Testament ends with the prediction of Malachi concerning the return of the prophet Elijah and the time of the messianic age. The journey for the

Christian canon thus ends with a look toward what would be known as the New Testament.

The book-by-book approach also creates repetition, since, for example, the books of 1–2 Samuel and 1–2 Kings are replayed in the books of 1–2 Chronicles (with, notably, most of the problematic, or juicy contents, such as David and Bathsheba's adultery, omitted; the Bible provides early examples of what today we call spin control). It also eludes the discussion of the sources that were brought together to create the various narratives.

A third approach is *theological,* in which studies attempt to explain the relationship between humanity and divinity as well as the divine nature itself. No one has satisfactorily for all or even most readers found the Bible's theological core, although themes such as "covenant" and "salvation" and "God's holiness" remain popular. In some cases, the theology is complicated, because the deity does not directly appear (the book of Esther here provides the best test case). Given the diversity of texts within the corpus, finding a theological core might be comparable to finding a singular meaning in all of Shakespeare's plays, or in human history, or even in a single life. Moreover, the deity of this text, the one who appears in the middle of the Midianite wilderness by means of a burning bush that is not consumed and self-identifies as "I will be what I will be" to a Hebrew shepherd on the lam for murdering an Egyptian, is too free to be boxed into a systematic theology. And human nature is also too free, too imaginative, and sometimes too cruel to become predictable.

None of these approaches is wrong; each has distinctive and valuable insights. But we've found, in teaching the material through the chronological/historical approach, the literary/canonical approach, and even the theological approach, more problems than benefits. Specifically, we could not both highlight the issues that we, and our students, found to be of greatest concern and provide a comparative basis for how the Bible addresses these issues.

Therefore, in this book we take a *thematic* approach to the Bible. We pursue general topics that appear throughout a variety of texts, and we interpret them in light of other similar occurrences of the same subject. A benefit to this approach, we have found, is that texts that otherwise would mainly be interpreted in light of their own contexts can be brought together, and so dimensions that may not be evident without this comparative examination can be explored. Further, the thematic approach allows us to consider matters of historical context, literary artistry, and theological understanding and to show how the Bible displays these matters in all their glorious diversity.

We begin with the broader biblical story: historical context, literary art, geographical setting. We then turn to the major themes: law and justice, the divine, religious practice, chaos and creation, the search for the meaning of history and the complementary yearning for a homeland, the self-definition of the community, gender and sexuality, politics and economics, diaspora existence, wisdom and cultural critique. For each chapter, we provide both general overviews and specific analyses of select passages. For each, we explain how the approaches we use work, and we offer various strategies for interpretation. The thematic approach allows us to return to certain texts by asking of them different questions—and in the answers we see the diversity of biblical voices, the meanings the text has held and now holds, and the possibilities for the way this ancient collection can still continue to puzzle, to challenge, and to inspire.

Part 1

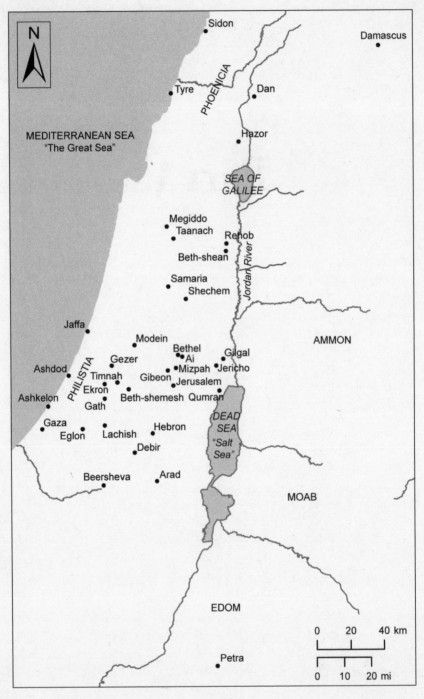

Ancient Israel

Chapter 1

The History of Ancient Israel

For a country of such small size, ancient Israel has had a singular impact on world history. By most standards Israel should have disappeared into oblivion when Babylon conquered it some twenty-five hundred years ago, depriving it of sovereignty and a sizable portion of its population. Yet its memory survived, and its religious and moral traditions grew in standing and significance, influencing both religious movements and secular communities.

Located adjacent to the eastern Mediterranean, Israel in the first millennium BCE had the fortune (and misfortune) of being situated on the land bridge between Egypt to the southwest and Mesopotamia and Asia Minor to the north and northeast. It thus benefited from an influx of ideas, culture, and technology from both directions, but it also suffered from the hostilities and hegemonies originating in those lands. Israel's heritage survived due as much to its openness to new influences as to its firm basis in the particular experiences of its people and their descendants. Other countries and territories—Greece, Roman Italy, Egypt, and China—have had perhaps more wide-ranging influence, but they were all much larger and more geopolitically powerful. No other country Israel's size can claim to have served as the setting for formative events in the origin of three great world religions, Judaism, Christianity, and Islam.

Israel's history lies in the distant past, but our knowledge of it grows continually. In comparison with what we knew just two hundred years ago, our understanding of the culture has advanced to an unprecedented extent. Most of this new knowledge stems from the work of archaeology, which has literally laid bare evidence concealed for the past two millennia. We can now see traces of city walls, residences, monumental buildings, and even tiny villages. Earlier archaeologists sought primarily to unearth the monumental structures of the elite and the powerful, but recent decades have seen a broadening of efforts to learn about the common people in ancient Israel—their habitats, utensils, tools, livelihood, and even diet. As a result, the picture of ancient Israel is much more detailed and nuanced than ever before. Especially significant for historians is the discovery of hundreds of thousands of tablets and documents, ranging in content from inventories to letters to exquisite literature. Relatively few of these writings outside the Hebrew Bible have emerged so far from ancient Israel itself, but adjacent lands supply a wealth of comparative information about political, religious, and everyday features that provides insight into the Israelites' experiences. The coming years and decades promise to multiply this knowledge.

All of this new information has the potential of changing many of our fixed notions about ancient Israel. Until the Enlightenment, people relied on the Bible, as interpreted by religious authorities, to provide the outline of events and personages in Israel's history. In the nineteenth century the beginning of archaeology coincided with a new impetus in biblical scholarship to reconsider the nature of the biblical literature, and the resulting theories brought novel notions about religion and literature, but not much change in the historical outline of the country. The twentieth century, especially its second half, ushered in more radical questions about what many have thought of as historical records. For example, archaeology has not been able to confirm the illustrious story of Joshua's conquest of the land or turn up any unequivocal trace of David and Solomon and their magnificent constructions in Jerusalem.

This absence of material evidence where we might expect it raises new questions about the significance of these texts. Which counts more—that an event actually happened or that we value the meaning attached to it by earlier interpreters of the tradition? For example, for two thousand years people have assumed David and Solomon were real persons who acted as described in the Hebrew Bible. Whether or not they actually existed as portrayed, or existed at all, the figures of David and Solomon have commanded an astounding role in the history of art, literature, thought, politics, justice, warfare, wisdom, and poetry during the past two millennia.

But the "facts" can change as new knowledge emerges. Historians do not now claim absolutely that these two figures did not exist, but only that considerable archaeological effort has not found solid evidence for them. So the new "fact" now is that specialists, despite their efforts using the best available tools, have not uncovered any trace of David or Solomon.

From this example we should learn to be cautious about grand assertions extrapolated from the biblical texts, for the "history" we thought we knew may have changed. Next week archaeologists might reverse this situation again, but for now we can only assert what we know and acknowledge what we do not. Our evolving understanding of this rich cultural history gives us ever new possibilities for rediscovering and appropriating this heritage for our own time.

Reconstructing History

The process of recovering history begins with basic questions about scope and method. In the case of ancient Israel three specific issues stand out. First is the question of the very subject matter of history. The past comprises an unlimited number of events, persons, and circumstances, not all of which may be worthy of inclusion in a history—were it even possible to ascertain them. From among a wealth of details we have to select the ones most suitable to our purposes. To this end, deciding which facets of history we want to explore makes a difference. A religious history of Israel will not be the same as a political history, just as a literary history differs from a social history or a material history from an intellectual history. Each of these types is a fully legitimate undertaking, and later in this chapter we focus primarily on political and social history, with material history (i.e., the tangible findings of archaeologists) also in the picture at key points. Later chapters in the book will deal more explicitly with issues in religious, literary, and intellectual history.

Second, once we have delineated the nature and scope of the project, we must determine the extent to which the Hebrew Bible itself should serve as a source of history. The Bible is not a neutral or objective text—if there even is such a thing. It is a religious text that promotes a point of view, and this perspective affects the ways in which it relates history. For example, the book of Joshua describes the conquest of the land and the attempted extermination of the indigenous Canaanites as being the will of God. Whatever actually happened during that period (did the conquest occur as described?) is one matter; what the biblical writers make of it (do they condemn or praise the actions of Joshua and the people?) may be quite another; and the meaning ascribed to this story by modern readers is yet another. Or again, the history of the monarchy in the books of 1–2 Samuel and 1–2 Kings appraises each king not according to general ruling ability or the country's economic stability or international reputation, but mainly according to the king's faithfulness or unfaithfulness to the worship of "the LORD (YHWH)" alone and secondarily to the king's treatment of the people. Thus King Ahab ranks as extremely evil because he marries the foreigner Jezebel, fosters the worship of Baal, tries to kill the prophet Elijah, and benefits from the judicial murder of Naboth (1 Kings 16:29–22:40). In such cases we can reasonably consider whether the biblical text gives a fair picture of the persons and events or whether the situation is likely to have been more complicated, perhaps even quite different from the biblical account. Religious texts, that is, texts held sacred by a particular community, should not be given a historical "pass"; the same questions and critical standards applied to secular literature should also be applied to sacred literature.

Third, as a result of the special character of the biblical text as a predominantly religious take on history, historians look for additional sources of evidence to fill out the picture or even offer a different perspective. Archaeology has provided most of this "new" knowledge, which falls into the category of "extrabiblical" evidence, that is, evidence stemming from outside the Hebrew Bible itself. Archaeologists conduct their work under controlled conditions and with the participation of experts such as biologists, chemists, paleobotanists, archaeozoologists, architects, engineers, geologists, paleographers, and many others. For example, radiocarbon (carbon–14) analysis has become especially useful in calculating the age of organic remains; it is generally accurate within a range of plus or minus fifty years for material from the ancient Israelite period. Some of the results of these analyses may confirm or question specific details in the Hebrew Bible; most frequently, however, they supplement the general store of knowledge about those ancient people and their life circumstances.

A controversy in recent biblical scholarship demonstrates both the problems and the stakes in history writing. In the 1990s, two camps purportedly faced off against each other, the "maximalists" and the "minimalists." As the disagreement was often depicted in the media, the "maximalist" approach accepts most of the history recorded in the Hebrew Bible as true except for those individual parts that have been definitely proven false (e.g., by archaeology), while the "minimalist" view does not assume that biblical details are historically accurate until they are established as such. For example, in discussing the occupation of the land of Canaan, "maximalists" might assume the accuracy of the story of Joshua's sweeping conquest as told in the book of Joshua and make note of a few exceptions of cities that were not conquered according to archaeological findings. "Minimalists," on the other hand, will not be led by the Joshua story but will begin with archaeological evidence of new settlements in the land at a given period, taking note of any destroyed cities and not concluding that a large military invasion occurred unless physical evidence of it comes to light. The two positions represent very different starting points and conclusions.

In fact, most historians and biblical scholars position themselves somewhere between these two poles, scrutinizing the available evidence and trying to make reasonable decisions in the face of insufficient and often conflicting information. Our strategy, followed in this chapter, is to distinguish between "biblical" and "extrabiblical" evidence, that is, between the historical descriptions and details found in the Hebrew Bible and the writings and findings that have turned up in outside sources from that period. Ideally, both sources of evidence will support each other, but often they do not, and not infrequently they suggest two different sets of events.

These and other issues make up the work of history. Specialists constantly improve their techniques in an effort to increase findings and enhance interpretations. Doing history is part detective work, part genius, and part luck. Watching it all unfold is a captivating process that affords new and surprising ways of understanding the past and the present.

Historical Synopsis

An overview of Israel's history will provide a framework for this book. The accompanying chart lays out three chronological tracks in parallel form for comparison—archaeological periods, political/social entities, and Bible books. Not all archaeologists agree with the time divisions in the first column and give strong reasons for varying them slightly. The century from 1000 to 900 BCE is the most contested, as it designates the period when there was or was not a "united monarchy"—depending on one's assessment of David and Solomon's rule. Thus an alternate proposal downplaying the historical importance of a Davidic and Solomonic kingdom views the Iron I Age as 1150–900 and Iron II as 900–586. We use the breakdown on the chart not because many still follow it but because it provides a convenient way to focus discussion on the Iron IIA period.

The geographical area where most of the biblical history played out has received various names over the years: Canaan, Israel, Judah, Palestine,

Chronologies of Ancient Israel and the Hebrew Bible

Archaeological Periods	Political and Social History	Biblical Chronology (According to the Biblical Texts)
		Genesis 1–11
Middle Bronze 2000–1550 BCE	Various empires and city-states	Genesis 12–50; Job?; 1 Chronicles 1–9 (overall genealogy)
Late Bronze 1550–1200	City-states	Exodus–Deuteronomy
Iron I 1200–1000	Settlement of the land	Joshua; Judges; 1 Samuel 1–8; Ruth
Iron IIA 1000–922	United monarchy	1 Samuel 9–31; 2 Samuel; 1 Kings 1–11; 1 Chronicles 10–2 Chronicles 9; Proverbs; Ecclesiastes; Song of Songs; Psalms (most)
Iron IIB 922–722	Divided monarchy	1 Kings 12–2 Kings 17; 2 Chronicles 10–28; Isaiah; Hosea; Amos; Jonah; Micah
Iron IIC 722–586	Southern kingdom Neo-Assyrian empire	2 Kings 18–25; 2 Chronicles 29–36; Jeremiah; Ezekiel; Daniel 1–4; Nahum; Habakkuk; Zephaniah
Neo-Babylonian 586–539	Babylonian exile	Lamentations; Ezekiel; Daniel 5, 7–8; Obadiah?
Early Persian 539–424	Persian empire Return from exile Rebuilding Jerusalem	Daniel 6, 9–12; Joel?; Haggai; Zechariah; Malachi?; Ezra; Nehemiah; Esther
Late Persian 424–331	Persian empire	
Hellenistic 331–63	Hellenistic empire Maccabean revolt (165) Hasmonean kingdom (140–63)	
Roman 63 BCE–476 CE	Roman empire	
		Isaiah 24–27; Ezekiel 40–48; Zechariah 9–14; Daniel 7–12

Syro-Palestine, or the southern Levant (the Levant is the land area immediately east of the Mediterranean now home to Syria, Lebanon, Israel, Jordan, and the Palestinian territories).

The second column identifies each period's primary type of political power or social structure, centralized during monarchic times, but dispersed during the Iron I, Neo-Babylonian, and Persian periods. Social history encompasses a wide range of phenomena, including settlement patterns, domestic living, regional connections, livelihood, and customs. They are less apparent in this chronology than they will be in the course of discussions throughout the book.

The third column is more complex. Much of the biblical literature purports to describe specific periods in Israel's history, but those literary blocs were in fact written in a later period, perhaps even centuries later. For example, Genesis 12–50 contains stories about the ancestors in the period before the exodus and the final settlement of the land of Canaan, but the literature did not come into existence until much later. This column displays the biblical story line, organizing the books and sections to match the political and social settings they describe, not the period in which the texts were written. Biblical books with little or no clear mention of historical periods are listed where they seem most to fit, and a question mark identifies them as such. For example, Job gives the impression of a setting in the early periods, but it does not explicitly situate itself there.

The following summary of the various periods focuses on historical questions. Later chapters will deal more with the biblical stories, political issues, religious commentary, and critiques from prophets and others. Thus, for example, the portrayals and actions of Abraham and the story of the exodus are saved for later discussion; here we are primarily interested in what is known about the history of those early periods, especially in light of extrabiblical evidence, and whether the biblical accounts fit this history.

The primeval period described in Genesis 1–11 belongs to the category long known as prehistory, that is, the period prior to the introduction of written means for recording information about events, processes, and people. Prehistory does not imply that the period is not historical, only that information about it does not stem from written records but from such other means as archaeology, physical anthropology, geology, biology, genetics, and comparative linguistics. Recorded history normally begins, as it does in ancient Southwest Asia, during the Bronze Age. Consequently, we will treat the material in Genesis 1–11 as a separate theme in Chapter 7.

The Ancestors

Although the Bible opens with the story of creation and the spread of humanity over the earth, history for the Israelites begins primarily with Abraham and his family. Even today, "Abrahamic faiths" has become a common designation for the three monotheistic religions that trace their ancestry to Abraham—Judaism, Christianity, and Islam. Genesis 12–50 contains legendary stories of Abraham and the next three generations, and these ancestors assume the form of culture heroes, founders of the Israelite people and their division into twelve tribes.

The biblical story line follows Abram (Abraham) and his wife, Sarai (Sarah), along with their household, as they migrate from Mesopotamia to Canaan, where they settle after a brief sojourn in Egypt. The main actors form a lineage favoring one male offspring in each generation: Abraham, Sarah, Hagar, Keturah, with children Ishmael, Isaac, and others; Isaac and Rebekah, with children Esau and Jacob; Jacob, Leah, Rachel, Bilhah, and Zilpah, with at least two daughters and twelve sons, the youngest two being Joseph and Benjamin; and Joseph and Asenath, with children Manasseh and Ephraim. The majority of the stories focus on familial matters: marriages, conceptions and births, tensions between family members, accommodations with outsiders, food production, and inheritance. In the process, the narratives cast many of these individuals as progenitors of later groups: Abraham and Hagar's son, Ishmael, is the ancestor of the desert caravaners (Gen. 21:20; 25:12–18; 37:25–27); the (grand)sons of Lot, Abraham's nephew, are Moab and Ben-ammi (the incestuous offspring of Lot and his daughters), the forebears of the Moabites and the Ammonites (19:30–38); Esau's descendants are the Edomites (Gen. 36); and Jacob's sons (exceptions: Levi is ancestor of the Levitical priests, and Joseph's two sons inherit in his place) become eponymous founders of the twelve Israelite tribes.

How much of these stories can be considered historical is a debated issue. Those who deem the ancestors to be real figures as described generally date them to the second millennium BCE, especially the first half, which would place them in the Middle Bronze Age. However, no external source dating from that period explicitly corroborates any of the ancestral figures or the events connected with them. Abraham and family do not appear in any records, inscriptions, letters, legal documents, or other source material. The only ancient information we have about these patriarchs and matriarchs exists in biblical and postbiblical texts, including the New Testament and the Qur'an. The sole recourse available to anyone interested in substantiating the biblical history about the ancestors is to look for circumstantial evidence.

Several types of indirect evidence have appeared. First, we know that groups of people, from single clans to multiple tribes, migrated from one location to another, sometimes traveling substantial distances. A limited form of such relocating is called transhumance, a seasonal movement by pastoralists or nomads to find grazing land for their livestock. Permanent migration on a larger scale is usually triggered by natural or political circumstances or perhaps instigated by a charismatic leader.

The tradition of Abraham and his clan moving from Ur in southern Mesopotamia to Haran in northern Mesopotamia and eventually to the land of Canaan in the southern Levant (Gen. 11:31–12:9) may fit this picture. So may his temporary move to Egypt, and later that of the Jacob clan as well, due to famine in Canaan (Gen. 12:10; 46:1–27). Some historians have dated Abraham's movements to roughly the period 2000–1800 BCE and connected him with the migrations of the Amorites (in Akkadian this group is known as the Amurru) from Mesopotamia to northern Syria. Others have considered the seventeenth–sixteenth centuries BCE more likely for the time of the migrations in Genesis, in light of the relocation of the Hyksos people to Egypt, which seems parallel to the story of the movement of Joseph and Jacob's clan to Egypt. The origin of the Hyksos is uncertain, but they probably stemmed from north of the Levant before they occupied Egypt. Although such migrations during the second millennium BCE appear to make the Hebrew ancestors' movements plausible, the evidence does not go so far as to confirm that *this* specific group, Abraham and his clan, existed and migrated—only that migrations by various people did occur during this period.

A second form of possible extrabiblical evidence is the names of people and places. Various texts in Semitic languages other than Hebrew contain forms of the names Abraham, Jacob, Benjamin, and others. The problem, again, is that mere similarity of names across languages does not prove the existence of Genesis's Abraham or Benjamin. It is as if we were to take references to Ivan, Johan, Johannes, Jan, Juan, Giovanni, Ian, Ion, and Jean as evidence that a specific person named John existed. A few cities such as Beersheva, Bethel, and Ai are also named in Genesis, but they were not in existence until the Iron Age.

The third form of circumstantial evidence takes the form of social customs. Remains of the ancient city of Nuzi, near modern-day Kirkuk in northern Iraq, have yielded several thousand cuneiform tablets from the fifteenth–fourteenth centuries BCE, and many historians cite them for cultural practices parallel to details present in Genesis. Nuzi was populated by Hurrians, a people that probably originated from the area north and west of Mesopotamia and by this point had spread throughout much of the northern Mesopotamian region. Many tablets discovered in private dwellings from that period appear to reflect family customs with parallels in Genesis. For example, it was possible for individuals at Nuzi to adopt an adult to inherit their estate in exchange for caring for them in their old age; Genesis 15:1–4 indicates that the childless Abraham expects to bequeath his holdings to his slave Eliezer. Nuzi tablets record contracts in which a man's wife can be considered his sister, which seems parallel to the stories in Genesis 12, 20, and 26 of the matriarch in jeopardy. Some interpreters also find counterparts in Nuzi to the marriage negotiated in Genesis 24 between Abraham's servant and Abraham's nephew Bethuel, the father of Rebekah. Other documents may elucidate the customs in Genesis of concubinage, of working for the bride-price, and of stipulating the consequences if a man takes a second wife.

Although such speculative parallels between Genesis and Nuzi intrigued historians mainly toward the middle of the twentieth century, today they have been roundly questioned, if not refuted. Customs are too indistinct and diffuse to help with the problem of dating. Furthermore, the largely pastoral society described in Genesis and the urban society reflected in the Nuzi tablets are very different, and we need to be wary of cherry-picking details from the latter in order to corroborate the former. Now historians tend to be much more cautious about using all circumstantial "evidence" when direct lines of influence cannot be traced.

We are left with the biblical picture of the ancestors, but with little or nothing in the way of corroborating extrabiblical evidence from the second millennium BCE. Not even the frequent biblical references to their use of camels (several times in Gen. 24 and elsewhere) can support an early date, as camels did not become domesticated until the latter part of the second millennium BCE. Yet the later Israelites obviously had ancestors of one sort or another. The problem we cannot resolve on the basis of extrabiblical evidence is whether the Israelites had a *single common* ancestral lineage, such as the Hebrew Bible describes, or many lines of descent.

Stymied in substantiating the biblical history, historians have a consolation. If, as is probably the case, these Genesis texts were composed and written no earlier than the monarchic period and quite possibly as late as the postexilic period, then the stories reflect Israelite culture during this later period, even if they do not reveal much about the very early period. We see in them an image of family life, of generational difficulties, of health matters, of more well-to-do landholders (Abraham and family were no subsistence farmers), of the relationship between countryside and city or state, and of tensions between Israelites and outside powers. A text can be historical in more ways than one.

The Exodus

The event best known and most celebrated from the Hebrew Bible is the exodus, and it has also drawn considerable attention from historians. Here we limit ourselves to historical investigations, holding the religious, literary, and ethnic significance of the exodus for later discussions.

The exodus story comprises numerous details that should be open for verification: the presence of a foreign population like the Israelites in ancient Egypt, the building or rebuilding of Egyptian cities in the Delta region (north of today's Cairo), perhaps even forced labor to carry out this construction work, the occurrence of plagues and natural disturbances, a successful escape by slaves or some other large contingent of the population, and a trek through the Sinai wilderness by a massive group of people. We should expect some of these events to appear in the written records of Egypt, and some should also leave material traces. By comparison, a substantial number of inscriptions and artifactual evidence remains from the Hyksos, who invaded and ruled Egypt during the Fifteenth Dynasty, 1650–1550 BCE. However, neither extrabiblical texts nor physical evidence has emerged to substantiate the exodus stories, and historians are again left mainly to look for circumstantial backing or to speculate on the basis of the biblical stories. There is, on the other hand, no evidence that the exodus did *not* happen; it is impossible to prove a historical negative.

Deciding on a plausible time period for the exodus is only the first problem. The story about Solomon's building the Jerusalem temple states that its construction began 480 years after the Israelites escaped from Egypt (1 Kings 6:1), which would put the date of the exodus around 1450 BCE, if, as many think, Solomon's reign began in 970 BCE (more on this subject shortly). However, archaeology and Egyptian sources make a fifteenth-century BCE date for the exodus very unlikely. The city built according to Exodus 1:11 could scarcely have been named Ramesses since no pharaoh by that name ruled until 1295 BCE. Thus the setting most commonly proposed for the exodus is the latter part of the Late Bronze Age, during the thirteenth century BCE.

Exodus 1:8 opens on an ominous note: "Now a new king arose over Egypt, who did not know Joseph." The last in the line of ancestors described at length in Genesis, Joseph had attained a position of high power in Egypt according to the biblical account, and his father's clan enjoyed privileges there—until Joseph's death and the passage of some indeterminate number of years or centuries. Although the book of Exodus does not identify the pharaoh at the time of Israel's servitude or escape, he is usually thought to be Ramesses II (also called Ramesses the Great), who ruled 1279–1212 BCE. Like his father, Sety (or Seti) I, Ramesses conducted massive construction projects, the kind of building that required an enormous number of slaves and labor conscripts, such as is described in Exodus 1.

Biblical history focuses on the oppression experienced by the Israelites and their flight from the country. No Egyptian source from Ramesses's reign, however, refers to the Israelites by name as having been among those forced into labor. Various Semitic groups, sometimes referred to as "Asiatics," appear in Egyptian records from this general period, but none of the terms applies only to Israelites. It could be (and has been) argued that we should not expect the Egyptians to have recorded a low moment in their history when a sizable number of slaves escaped their control and humiliated the Egyptian army, but such an argument, while sound, does not count as verification of the exodus.

The stories describing the events leading up to the Israelites' escape from Egypt provide a masterful, suspenseful account that accomplishes a variety of narrative goals. Moses is lionized as the people's leader, which is especially evident in his repeated escapes from danger: when he auspiciously survives near death at his birth, after he slays an Egyptian, when God seeks to kill him in the wilderness (Exod. 4:24), each time when he ventures into Pharaoh's presence, and when he leads the people in their escape from the Egyptian army. God's power outshines even Moses's distinction in the stories of the ten plagues, which target Egyptian deities directly: Hapy, god of the Nile River; Hekate, the frog goddess; Apis, the bull god; Hathor, the cow goddess; the sun god, Ra (or Re); and Pharaoh, identified with the falcon god, Horus.

Some interpreters have attempted to find naturalistic explanations for all these plagues—an eclipse that caused the darkness, red algae that could make the Nile look like blood, a meteorological anomaly with thunder and hail, a disease among the livestock, a freakish proliferation of frogs, gnats, flies, and locusts, and epidemics causing boils and infant deaths. But the notion that all of these natural disasters happened in short order and on command stretches credulity. An even more imaginative modern scenario has a massive natural phenomenon, a volcanic eruption, give rise both to the plagues and to the sinking of a city, the legendary Atlantis, but there is as much evidence for such an event as there is for an explicit mention of Atlantis in the Bible. The Egyptian magicians, who replicate the first two plagues with their spells, cannot match the rest of Moses's plagues and give up after the second—further underscoring the ineffectuality of Egyptian religion from the Israelites' point of view. Whatever historical details are present in these texts, the stories intend to cast the Israelites and their God in a much better light than the Egyptians and their gods.

The number of escapees from Egypt represents a detail that should have left some material trace, were it an actual occurrence. According to Exodus 12:37, a total of 600,000 "men" (Heb. *gevarim*), with children (this text does not mention the women), fled the country. Numbers 1:45–46 is more specific, reporting that Moses took a census of the people during their wilderness march and counted 603,550 able-bodied, battle-ready men above twenty years of age, not including the Levites. Adding an equal number of women as well as all the children and elderly would put the total number of Israelites in the wilderness around 2 million or more—an incredible number of people to have escaped Egypt and made their way together through the wilderness to the land of Canaan.

Someone once calculated that a crowd of that size, walking four abreast, would stretch all the way from the Delta region in northern Egypt to the southern tip of the Sinai Peninsula and back again. Whether that estimate is accurate or not, it may be more productive to think of a city of 2 million today (e.g., Houston or Stuttgart) and then try to imagine so many people collected in one place and migrating en masse across the desert. Such a vast population group trekking through the peninsula for a period of forty years would have left behind physical evidence, but archaeologists have found nothing. In an effort to make the number more historically plausible, some scholars have suggested that the Hebrew word *elef,* translated as "thousand" in both Exodus 12:37 and Numbers 1:46, should perhaps be translated here as "military unit," maybe with 10–100 persons each. In that case 600,000 soldiers becomes 600 military units, which would total a much smaller number of people.

But this adjustment in translation is only speculative, aimed at accommodating the biblical text to make it plausible. When the story says 600,000, its indirect message is that the Israelites represented an impressive, formidable number; calculations were often inflated in other documents of ancient Southwest Asia as well. If ever a group of Israelites resided in Egypt, were enslaved, and somehow managed to leave—and there is no extrabiblical evidence for any of it—then they more likely numbered no more than a few thousand. Even a group of that size could have viewed their escape from oppression as miraculous, which is the tradition the Bible presents.

One final detail in the story bears mentioning, especially for those who saw the for-its-time-amazing special effects in the 1956 film *The Ten Commandments.* Exodus 14–15 describes the close escape from Pharaoh's army at a site near "Pi-hahirot, between Migdol and the sea, in front of Baal-zephon." Presumably the Nile Delta is meant, but the many attempts to identify the specific location are speculative. The body of water where the crossing and drowning occurred is commonly known as the "Red Sea" (Exod. 13:18; 15:4, 22). The Hebrew phrase, however, is actually the "Sea of Reeds" (*yam suf*), which the Septuagint, the Greek translation of the Hebrew text, rendered as the "Red Sea," located much farther south than the Delta. Again there have been many attempts to pinpoint the specific site, and some historians have gone so far as to claim—unconvincingly— that they have found tracks and chariot wheels underwater that must be the remains of Pharaoh's doomed army. As with the plagues, the religious symbolism is key: in Canaanite mythology, the sea is deified as a god, Yamm (cognate to the Hebrew word for "sea," *yam*), so by splitting the water for the Israelites to pass through YHWH signifies his absolute power over Yamm.

From a historical and literary point of view, Exodus 1–15 is less a factual report than it is a founding narrative, a story of a people's beginning or new stage so significant that it helps to define them. It may well contain descriptions of events that actually occurred, but to date no one has unequivocally substantiated them. Nor should we expect such verification. The story's significance lies in its affirmations about YHWH's liberating power, the people's obedience despite oppression, and the reliable performance of its leaders when they comply with God's directions. And the text turns the story into a song of praise, both a long one attributed to Moses (Exod. 15:1–18) and a concise couplet by his sister, Miriam: "Sing to YHWH, for he has triumphed gloriously; horse and rider he has thrown into the sea" (15:21). The tradition of the exodus preserves this theme of liberation and celebration.

Settlement of the Land

The Hebrew Bible devotes a full third of its great expanse to primeval times, the ancestors, the exodus and wilderness wanderings, and finally the conquest and settlement of the land. It is a subtle alert to the enduring significance attributed to Israel's origins, prior to the founding of the monarchy. The settlement period is also the first period for which substantial extrabiblical information exists to compare with the biblical narratives. Archaeologists have uncovered material remains of numerous cities and villages, and a pattern of demographic changes in the land during this period emerges. As we will see, some of it supports, some of it disputes, and some of it supplements the biblical presentations.

The books of Joshua and Judges provide two different perspectives on the conquest and settlement. According to Deuteronomy 31:1–8, Moses transfers leadership to Joshua before his death, and the book of Joshua opens with Joshua and all the people of Israel poised on the west side of the Jordan River, preparing to invade Canaan. Their first foray is to the city of Jericho, which they conquer in memorable fashion (Josh. 6). Next they stumble badly at Ai when Achan violates the prohibition against taking plunder (Josh. 7). The forces recover and make a full conquest of the rest of the land—first the central highlands, then the kingdoms in the south, and finally the city-states of the north (Josh. 10–12). While slaying their tens of thousands, they reportedly suffer no more than thirty-six Israelite casualties, all at Ai (7:5). The battles fit the model of holy wars, as described in Deuteronomy 20: unwavering allegiance, no personal booty, annihilation of the enemy cities, and killing the enemy or taking them captive. Having conquered the land, Joshua is ready to divide it among the twelve tribes. He spends the next nine chapters doing just that (Josh. 13–21), and the book ends with a pledge of allegiance to YHWH. The conquest is complete, "and YHWH gave them rest on every side" (21:44).

The book of Judges, however, follows immediately with a very different picture, already intimated in Joshua 13:1–6. Jerusalem has not been taken, and there are still Canaanites in the hill country, the southern wilderness, and the lowlands (Judg. 1:8–10, 21). The cities of the Philistines, who settled the coastal area around 1200 BCE, remain, as do many other cities and territories. According to the rest of Judges 1, the Israelites are able to conquer some of these people and compel others to serve as forced labor. Judges 3:4 suggests another reason for YHWH's sparing some regions: "They were for the testing of Israel, to know whether Israel would obey the commandments of YHWH, which he commanded their ancestors by Moses."

What follows is a sad picture of collective recidivism. Some six times the Israelites go through a four-step cycle of apostasy and punishment. First they abandon their exclusive allegiance to YHWH, usually described tersely with the phrase, "The Israelites again did what was evil in the sight of YHWH" (Judg. 3:7, 12; 4:1; 6:1; 10:6; 13:1). Once the vicious cycle begins, God responds by sending an army to conquer them, after which the Israelites cry to God for mercy, and God sends a "judge," a charismatic military leader, to deliver them. And then they rebel again. The book of Judges portrays the people in a perpetual state of disarray, summarized four times with the statement: "In those days there was no king in Israel; all the people did what was right in their own eyes" (21:25, the concluding verse of the book; similar in 17:6; 18:1; 19:1).

Historians have sought to reconcile this biblical history of the settling of the land of Canaan with the archaeological evidence. A beginning point is the stunning 10-foot-tall black granite stele discovered in 1896 by the famed British archaeologist and Egyptologist Flinders Petrie. This remarkable find contains the earliest mention of the name "Israel" in any extrabiblical source. The Egyptian pharaoh Merneptah (1212–1202 BCE), the son of Ramesses II, undertook a military campaign into the southern Levant about 1208 BCE and recorded his victories on the stele, including these lines:

Tehenu is desolated. Hatti is at peace.
Canaan is plundered with all evil.

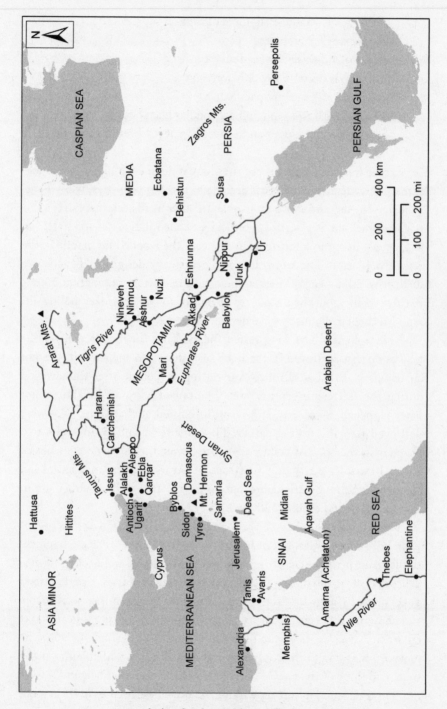

Ancient Southwest Asia and Egypt

Ashkelon is vanquished. Gezer is seized.

Yanoam exists no more.

Israel is laid waste, its seed no more.

Hurru has become a widow for Egypt.

All lands together are pacified.

Everyone who was moving around has been bound

By the King of Upper and Lower Egypt . . . Merneptah.

Except for Israel, all of these sites have a distinctive hieroglyphic feature called a determinative that designates them as countries, while Israel alone has the determinative for people. In other words, Merneptah is identifying Israel not as a settled, politically defined nation or city-state, but as a people living in a territory, in this case the wooded highlands in the southern Levant. The word does not necessarily designate "Israel" as a distinctive ethnic entity since it could include various population groups in that territory, but the people are obviously not yet organized politically. And Merneptah claims to have destroyed them.

Archaeologists have long tested the evidence for the sweeping military campaign portrayed in the book of Joshua, and their results are not encouraging for a Late Bronze Age setting, sometime after Ramesses II during the thirteenth century BCE. The famed battle of Jericho cannot have happened, as no city and no walls existed at that time; they were destroyed several centuries earlier. The same is true of Ai, to which two chapters in the book of Joshua (7–8) are devoted; there is no evidence of a Late Bronze Age city or its destruction. At most, there may have been small, insignificant settlements, but no fortification walls at either site in the general period around 1200 BCE.

The books of Numbers, Joshua, and Judges describe the destruction of a total of sixteen cities, but only three or four of them—Hazor, Lachish, Bethel, and perhaps Debir in the south—reveal any archaeological evidence of destruction during this period. Jerusalem and Dan, also described as conquered (Judg. 1:8; 18:27–29; Josh. 19:47), were minor settlements and show no thirteenth-century destruction layer. These biblical books report that twelve cities were occupied but not destroyed; archaeologists, however, have found that only seven of them had any inhabitants at the time, and three of the twelve (Beth-shemesh, Gezer, and Megiddo) were razed to the ground in this time frame. Another twelve cities in the region, not even mentioned in Joshua or Judges, do show evidence of destruction, though several of them were near the coast and were probably conquered by the Sea Peoples. The bottom line is that fewer than one-third of the reports in Numbers, Joshua, and Judges can be confirmed by archaeology; in most cases these sites give very different material evidence than what the texts claim.

Even if the picture of a sweeping conquest by the Israelites is improbable, archaeologists have uncovered evidence that a new wave of settlements in the land of Canaan commenced during the twelfth century BCE and lasted a good two hundred years, 1200–1000 BCE, the Iron I Age. Several hypotheses try to account for this development: the conquest model, somewhat like that described in the book of Joshua, although with far fewer than 600,000 troops and with mainly sporadic military conflicts; a peaceful-immigration model, according to which a variety of people from around Southwest Asia moved into Canaan because it was largely a political vacuum during this period and outsiders could settle there without significant military opposition; and a peasant-uprising model, in which peasants rebelled against or escaped oppression in the city-states in the valleys and on the coastal plains and settled in the Canaanite highlands away from their tyrants.

A cultural-evolution model may, however, fit the available evidence more plausibly than these three hypotheses. Archaeological surveys show that the population in the land increased dramatically between 1200 and 1000 BCE. Most of these peoples were probably indigenous or from nearby areas, with roots reaching back unknown centuries. The biblical texts refer to numerous ethnic groups already in the vicinity—for example, "the Canaanites, the Hittites, the Amorites, the Perizzites, the Hivites, and the Jebusites" (Judg. 3:5). Texts found at the Egyptian ruins at Amarna in middle Egypt along the Nile (fourteenth century BCE) also name other groups in the southern Levant, especially the Apiru and the Shasu, some of whom may have been pastoralists, Bedouin-type itinerants, or even brigands, as well as the Chupshu (Heb. *chofshi*), free farmers and laborers, mentioned in other sources. Together, all such groups had the opportunity to take advantage of the reduced political pressure during this period, and they settled in communities and made their livelihood from farming and herding. This combination of peoples thus matches the image of a "mixed crowd" escaping Egypt and wandering in the wilderness (Exod. 12:38), except that the convergence of peoples happened mainly during the settlement period, not in the time of the exodus. Their origins were not as important to them as was their autonomy in the Canaanite highlands. Gradually social structures developed, as did their affinity for each other. This shared identity and ethos eventually made it possible for a centralized kingdom to emerge.

By the end of the Iron I period, the people to be known as Israelites eventually came into control of the country. When the process began and who they were at that point is difficult to say, and even Merneptah's stele fails to reveal as much as we may wish. Some hostilities played out, archaeology confirms, but peaceful and gradual settlement of the land, drawing heavily on indigenous populations, predominated. It is possible but speculative that an incipient form of alliance, along the lines of a loose confederacy, developed during this period. We can be certain, though, that sometime between 1000 and 900 BCE the early Israelites' social and political independence gave way to a centralized government.

The Founding of the Monarchy

The move to a monarchy from a decentralized, diffused populace represents one of the most far-reaching, consequential developments in Israel's history. The Bible subtly acknowledges its significance by devoting almost 40 percent more space to the 100-year period of the kingdom's establishment under Saul, David, and Solomon than it does to all 335 years of later monarchic history. As with the earlier periods in Israel's history, however, historians remain divided over the extent to which these narratives serve as reliable sources and how significant the extrabiblical evidence—or lack thereof—rates in comparison.

Although kingdoms throughout the region left behind archives and inscriptions, Israelite kings did not produce such records of their achievements—or at least archaeologists have not yet uncovered them. So historians must decide whether the biblical stories stem from the periods they are describing or, alternatively, whether they are largely the products of later times, perhaps even several centuries later. If the biblical accounts are late, then their use in reconstructing the monarchic period may be very limited. On the other hand, contemporaneous sources from outside Israel may also not be trustworthy since rulers throughout Southwest Asia were prone to record material flattering to themselves. For this reason, each historical assertion in the various records needs to be analyzed on its own terms.

The biblical stories in 1 Samuel 8–10 contain two accounts of the foundation of the monarchy, one basically promonarchic (9:1–10:16) and the other antimonarchic (8:1–22; 10:17–27). They belong to the larger corpus of historical writings in 1–2 Samuel and 1–2 Kings, all of which adopts a very definite position—mostly critical—about the long sequence of monarchs, judging each one according to his or her faithfulness to the worship of YHWH alone. Since this literature belongs to the theme of political and religious critique, we will return to it later in Chapter 13, where it can be compared to other forms of criticism levied especially by the prophets. Here we focus on the question of what can be known about the historical beginning of the monarchy.

The short answer to this question is that we are almost entirely dependent on the biblical account of the reigns of the first three kings, Saul, David, and Solomon. For most of modern times we have assumed that Saul was crowned king around 1020 BCE, that David followed him around 1000 BCE, and that Solomon succeeded his father in 970, reigning until about 922 BCE, at which point the united kingdom split into two parts, the northern kingdom, Israel, and the southern kingdom, Judah. Now, however, some historians and archaeologists are proposing that the monarchy did not begin until around 900 BCE or later, and that the first kingdom started in the north rather than the south. If such is the case, then Saul, David, and Solomon are largely legendary figures. A dramatic shift, indeed.

If tenth-century inscriptions from inside or outside Israel had been found containing mention of any of these three kings by name or even just an allusion to the presence of a monarch in Jerusalem, the situation facing historians would be completely different than it is now. According to the Bible, these kings had substantial influence, especially Solomon, who reportedly extended his territory to include "all the kingdoms from the Euphrates to the land of the Philistines, even to the border of Egypt" (1 Kings 4:21; Tanakh 5:1). Yet no treaties, no victory inscriptions, no land grants, no correspondence, no political marriages, no commercial transactions exist that reference any of them. Perhaps we should not expect such records, but they occur frequently enough in other periods to suggest that their absence from this early period is anomalous, especially for kings of such putative import.

Archaeological evidence of Jerusalem and its buildings contrasts with the biblical stories. The city seems to have been little more than a small settlement with outlying villages. No trace has turned up of Solomon's temple in Jerusalem, traditionally called the First Temple, described at length in 1 Kings 5–6. Since capital cities normally had impressive temples (probably also in Samaria, the capital of Israel, the later northern kingdom), other reasons may explain the Jerusalem temple's absence from the archaeological record. The probable site of the First Temple in Jerusalem is somewhere in the area now known as the Temple Mount, the location today of two prominent mosques as well as the Kotel, or Western Wall, constructed by King Herod the Great in the first century BCE as part of his renovation of the Second Temple. Excavations have largely been disallowed or not completely finished because of conflicting claims over the area. Consequently, for the foreseeable future we cannot expect any information about the presence, size, and features of the First Temple. Some archaeologists speculate that, because of the extensive rebuilding of the Mount by Herod, no evidence may even be extant if an excavation were attempted.

A find in 1993–94 could aid in the quest for the historical David, but the evidence still remains inconclusive. At the site of Tel Dan in northern Israel, near the border with Lebanon, archaeologists discovered three fragments of a basalt inscription in Aramaic containing the word *bytdwd*, normally translated as "house of David" (other proposals are "house of the uncle" or "house of the loved one," since *dwd* or *dod* can also mean "uncle" or "loved one"). The debate over the translation and significance of this inscription continues, but most likely it is the earliest extrabiblical mention of David. Three factors complicate its historical significance, however. First, the fragments should probably be dated around 840 BCE, which puts it some 130 years after the traditional date of David's death—relatively close to his reign but not within living memory. Second, the phrase "house of David" seems to refer to the Davidic dynasty, not directly to David. And third, just this slight mention does not confirm any of the details about David found in the books of Samuel, Kings, and Chronicles. We are left with at best a tantalizing clue about David's historicity, but little more.

For all the power of the biblical stories about Saul, David, and Solomon, no corroborating evidence for any of them exists from extrabiblical sources dating from the late eleventh and tenth centuries BCE, the time when they are thought to have lived. Thus we can say little more than that the monarchy in Israel had its beginning at some indefinite point in history. The biblical stories constitute cultural artifacts in their own right, and external verification of them will be welcome whenever it can occur. But for now historians cannot go much further than to acknowledge both the presence of these stories and the absence of corroborating contemporaneous evidence, both textual and material. The Hebrew Bible alone describes a united monarchy, in which Saul, David, and Solomon appear as larger-than-life figures. Yet *some* factors and *some* figures initiated the centralization of power in the land, and the effort to find its beginning point will and should continue.

From the Divided Kingdom to the Fall of Jerusalem

Whatever may have transpired in Israel during the tenth century, the history of the monarchy from the ninth to the sixth centuries presents its own separate issues. First, during much of this time two separate kingdoms existed in the land. The name "Israel" during this period properly refers only to the northern kingdom, with its capital at Samaria, while Judah, with its capital in Jerusalem, was a separate and distinct state. According to 1 Kings 12, the north seceded when King Rehoboam, Solomon's son and successor, decided to increase taxes and conscriptions. Monarchs in ancient Southwest Asia typically depended on forced labor, called the corvée, to construct palaces, temples, city walls, road systems, and much more, and they conscripted able-bodied men from among the peasants to form labor gangs and work only for their daily food. According to 1 Kings 4:6, one of Solomon's high officials was the superintendent of the corvée. At word that Rehoboam intended to intensify rather than lessen this duty, Jeroboam led the northern tribes in a rebellion to form their own kingdom, with Jeroboam as the first king. As might be expected, subsequent kings in both north and south did not hesitate to recruit workers from among their subjects whenever they wished, and there is no evidence of any difference in this practice between the two countries.

A second problem lies in the nature of the biblical text reporting the monarchic history. As we will discuss in more detail in Chapter 13, the books of 1–2 Kings and 1–2 Chronicles are not neutral in their depictions. All of the kings in Israel are roundly condemned as evil—tyrannical, exploitative, and apostate. Many of their counterparts in Judah rule similarly, but several others are rated highly, even very highly in the cases of kings Hezekiah and Josiah. The biblical history reflects the viewpoint of the south in this assessment of the two monarchies, and we need to take this bias or agenda into consideration when weighing the reports.

The third issue is the witness of written sources from other countries, of which substantially more exist than are available for the earlier periods. The so-called Mesha inscription or Moabite stone, found in southern Jordan and dated toward the end of the ninth century BCE, refers by name to King Omri of Israel. In it King Mesha of Moab, the small kingdom to the east of the Dead Sea, describes Omri's conquest of Moab, attributing Moab's defeat to their god Kemosh's anger against his people, much as YHWH is often angry with the Israelites according to the book of Judges:

> Omri was the king of Israel, and he oppressed Moab for
> many days, for Kemosh was angry with his land. And his
> son succeeded him, and he said—he too—"I will oppress
> Moab!" . . . And Kemosh said to me: "Go, take Nebo from
> Israel!" And I went in the night, and I fought against it
> from the break of dawn until noon, and I took it, and I
> killed [its] whole population, . . . for I had put it to the ban
> (*cherem*) for Ashtar Kemosh.*

The word *cherem*, usually translated as "ban" or "devoted to destruction," is the same term used in Hebrew to designate a holy war, as, for example, in Joshua 6:17, prior to Joshua's attack on Jericho: "The city and all that is in it shall be *devoted* to YHWH *for destruction*." In the Moabite case, Israel is on the receiving end of the holy war.

Neo-Assyrian sources from the ninth, eighth, and seventh centuries BCE also include numerous references to kings and places in the Levant, including both Israel and Judah. They attest to local resistance when the Neo-Assyrian empire sought to establish its hegemony over the larger region. Similar mentions occur in the records of the Neo-Babylonian empire, which followed the Neo-Assyrian. These inscriptions do not corroborate all of the details in the biblical history, since these extrabiblical sources had no interest in doing so, but they provide historians with external information and checkpoints to consider for reconstructing the political and economic affairs in the land.

Point of view is crucial when evaluating sources. When the Hebrew Bible records the impact of imperial forces on Israel and Judah, it does so

---

* William W. Hallo, ed., *The Context of Scripture*, vol. 2, *Monumental Inscriptions from the Biblical World* (Leiden, Boston: Brill, 2003), 37–38.

from the Israelite or Judahite perspective rather than that of the invaders. Predictably, the writings from other countries, such as the victory accounts of the Neo-Assyrian emperors, are similarly slanted in their own favor.

Fourth, Israel and Judah were greatly affected by geopolitical pressures in the region. The countries were invaded and occupied repeatedly, each time becoming small provinces in vast empires extending from Egypt to Greece to the Indus River or beyond. Although not powerful in their own right, Israel and Judah were positioned at a strategically vital spot—en route between Egypt and Mesopotamia, thus directly in the path of traveling merchants and imperial forces intent on expanding their interests. Invasions on a more limited scale also occurred, such as that conducted in the tenth century BCE by Pharaoh Shoshenq I (ca. 946–925 BCE; called Shishak in 1 Kings 11:40; 14:25–28), who caused destruction but did not dominate the land of Israel for long. An inscription on a temple wall in Karnak, Egypt, lists a number of towns in the southern Levant that he claims to have captured during his campaign.

The histories of the two kingdoms proceed in parallel for the first two hundred years since they often interact and are affected by similar outside forces. To show concurrent reigns in the two kingdoms, the following chart lists the thirty-eight kings and one queen who succeeded Saul, David, and Solomon. The dates are often uncertain, especially because of the above-mentioned problem regarding the start of the monarchy; we follow here the dates given in the *HarperCollins Study Bible*. In several cases the Hebrew Bible uses two names for the same king.

The first major empire to affect monarchic history in lasting ways was the Neo-Assyrian. Based in the northern part of Mesopotamia with its capital at Asshur on the Tigris River, the Old Assyrian empire wielded influence in the region during the early part of the second millennium; the so-called Middle Assyrian empire of the latter part of the second millennium was especially powerful and prosperous. The Neo-Assyrian empire controlled ancient Southwest Asia, including the Levant, during much of the tenth through the seventh centuries, and it changed the course of history for both Israel and Judah during the eighth century. Israel, larger, wealthier, and more populous than Judah, allied with the Syrian kingdom of Damascus and others to resist the Neo-Assyrians during the 730s, and the Neo-Assyrian emperor Tiglath-pileser III (744–727) led his army in a punishing attack on these small kingdoms, turning them into vassals. When Israel continued to resist, the Neo-

Chronology of the Kings of the Divided Monarchy

Judah (Southern Kingdom)	Israel (Northern Kingdom)
Davidic Dynasty	
Rehoboam (922–915)	Jeroboam I (922–901)
Abijam / Abijah (915–913)	
Asa (913–873)	Nadab (901–900) [killed by Baasha] Baasha (900–877) Elah (877–876) [killed by Zimri] Zimri (876) [committed suicide] *Omride Dynasty*
Jehoshaphat (873–849)	Omri (876–869) Ahab (869–850) [killed in battle] Ahaziah (850–849)
Jehoram / Joram (849–843/2)	Jehoram / Joram (849–843/2) [killed by Jehu] *Jehu Dynasty*
Ahaziah (843/2) [killed by Jehu]	Jehu (843/2–815)
Athaliah [Omride queen] (843/2–837) [killed by Jehoiada]	
Joash / Jehoash (837–800) [killed by his servants]	Jehoahaz / Joahaz (815–802)
Amaziah (800–783) [killed by conspirators]	Jehoash / Joash (802–786) Jeroboam II (786–746)
Uzziah / Azariah (783–742)	Zechariah (746–745) [killed by Shallum] *End of Jehu Dynasty* Shallum (745) [killed by Menahem]
Jotham (742–735)	Menahem (745–737) Pekahiah (737–736) [killed by Pekah]
Ahaz / Jehoahaz I (735–715)	Pekah (736–732) [killed by Hoshea] Hoshea (732–724) *Fall of Samaria—722/1*
Hezekiah (715–687/6)	
Manasseh (687/6–642)	
Amon (642–640) [killed by his servants]	
Josiah (640–609) [killed in battle]	
Jehoahaz II / Shallum (609)	
Jehoiakim / Eliakim (609–598)	
Jehoiachin / Jeconiah / Coniah (598/7)	
Zedekiah / Mittaniah (597–587/6)	
Fall of Jerusalem—586	

Assyrian emperors Shalmaneser V (726–722) and Sargon II (721–705) invaded the northern kingdom and captured the capital city of Samaria (Samerina in Assyrian) around 722; both emperors claim the victory. The Nimrud Prism, found in 1952–53 and named after the ninth- to eighth-century Neo-Assyrian capital located twenty miles south of today's Mosul, relates Sargon's version of Samaria's fall (words damaged in the inscription are in brackets):

> [The inhabitants of Sa]merina, who agreed [and plotted] with a king [hostile to] me not to do service and not to bring tribute [to Asshur] and who did battle, I fought against them with the power of the great gods, my lords. I counted as spoil 27,280 people, together with their chariots, and gods, in which they trusted. I formed a unit with 200 of [their] chariots for my royal force. I settled the rest of them in the midst of Assyria. I repopulated Samerina more than before. I brought into it people from countries conquered by my hands. I appointed my eunuch as governor over them. And I counted them as Assyrians.*

With that battle the northern kingdom met its end. Attributing the capture to the Israelites' worship of other gods, 2 Kings 17:5–41 also describes the shift of population groups: Israelites were exiled to various parts of the empire, and, in turn, other conquered peoples moved into the region around Samaria. In all likelihood Sargon deported only a portion of the population of the northern kingdom, mostly the rulers and the elites who could have been in a position to organize an uprising against the empire if they were left in their homeland. The tradition of the "lost ten tribes of Israel," still cited today, refers to this forced exile. Many northerners also must have fled to the south because, according to archaeology, the city of Jerusalem doubled in size by the end of the seventh century, from some six thousand inhabitants to about thirteen thousand.

The southern kingdom, Judah, sought a route other than resistance, the northern kingdom's strategy; instead, Judah became a Neo-Assyrian

---

* William W. Hallo, ed., *Context of Scripture*, vol. 2, *Monumental Inscriptions from the Biblical World* (Leiden, Boston: Brill, 2003), 295–96.

vassal for a century, until the time of King Josiah. This status meant that Judah was a province or colony rather than a sovereign nation, and it was required to send tribute regularly to the emperor. King Hezekiah (715–687), judged very favorably in 2 Kings 18–20, complies with Neo-Assyrian expectations, but also seems to strengthen Judah's position. For example, 2 Chronicles 32:30 (similarly 2 Kings 20:20) states that "Hezekiah closed the upper outlet of the waters of Gihon and directed them down to the west side of the city of David." Now called Hezekiah's Tunnel or the Siloam Tunnel and still available for visitors to squeeze through today, this remarkable engineering feat stretches 1,750 feet, a third of a mile, from the Gihon Spring outside the old Jerusalem wall to the Siloam Pool inside the wall. When it was completed, the spring was sealed from view, and a steady supply of water flowed into the city, a vital resource in times of siege. Replacing an earlier channel, the tunnel necessitated cutting through solid rock by two teams working from opposite ends. They left an inscription on the tunnel wall near the Siloam Pool end to describe the final moment of breaking through the rock:

> While the tunnelers were wielding their pickaxes, one
> group toward the other, and while three cubits [ca. 4–5
> feet] remained to be cut through, a voice was heard of one
> man calling to the other, for a fissure was in the rock on
> the right and the left. On the day of the breakthrough,
> the hewers struck, one meeting the other, pickax against
> pickax. And the water flowed from the spring to the pool,
> a distance of 1,200 cubits [ca. 1,800 feet].

Building such a tunnel to protect against siege probably drew the attention of imperial officials, especially since it may have coincided with actions taken by other provinces to revolt following the death of Sargon in 705. The new Neo-Assyrian emperor, Sennacherib (705–681), invaded Judah and many other countries in 701 BCE to bring them in line again. In a lengthy inscription on the beautiful baked-clay Sennacherib Prism (three copies exist, the earliest being the Taylor Prism, found in 1830 in Nineveh, near Mosul), Sennacherib lists numerous cities in the Levant he conquered and claims he removed 200,150 people from Judah—a number that, if true, would have emptied the country. He especially gloats over his victory over King Hezekiah, whom he claims to have trapped in Jerusalem "like a bird in a cage." The account in 2 Kings 18:13–19:37 gives a very different picture; there Hezekiah and the Judahites survive unscathed, Sennacherib's army is decimated, and he himself is assassinated. A possible explanation for the discrepancy may be that Sennacherib invaded Judah twice, the second time in 689 or later when he met with less success. The invasion in 701 also included the siege and eventual capture of Lachish (mentioned in 2 Kings 18:14), about twenty-five miles southwest of Jerusalem and at the time the largest fortified city in Judah after Jerusalem. Sennacherib commemorated the victory with a large relief in his palace in Nineveh, picturing the siege warfare against the Lachish city wall; the relief, some 60 feet by 9 feet, is now in the British Museum.

The seventh century saw the decline of the Neo-Assyrian empire. In Judah Hezekiah was succeeded by his son Manasseh (687–642), whom the Bible describes as one of the worst kings because of his apostasy (2 Kings 21:1–18). The picture of his reign is probably more complicated than this brief summary suggests. On the whole, he served the Neo-Assyrians as a loyal vassal; the emperor Esarhaddon (681–669) mentions "Manasseh, king of Judah" among the many from whom he demanded and received tribute. When the army of emperor Ashurbanipal (669–627) attacked Egypt, some of the troops came from Judah. During Manasseh's reign the countryside recovered agriculturally from losses due to earlier battles, and towns and other settlements reemerged, including several in the southern areas near the desert. Most important, there was peace in Judah.

Despite Ashurbanipal's strong start, the Neo-Assyrian empire on the whole soon began to crumble. The empire was probably too extensive to control, and prolonged wars sapped its strength. Not only did the rulers have to cope with internal intrigues and disaffections; they were also under continual attack along the northern frontier by Cimmerians and Scythian raiders coming from the Caucasus. With Ashurbanipal's death several provinces, including Judah under King Josiah (640–609), began to break free of Neo-Assyrian control.

The Babylonians under Nabopolassar (626–605) constituted the most powerful nation to assert itself, leading to the founding of the Neo-Babylonian empire. Based mainly in central and southern Mesopotamia (on today's map, the area between the Tigris and Euphrates Rivers, roughly from just northwest of Baghdad toward the southeast), the Neo-Babylonians, like their Neo-Assyrian neighbors to the north, could look back on a millennium and more of intermittent political and cultural power. Now, together with the Medes from the west (the general area around Tehran in present-day Iran) they proceeded to dismantle the Neo-Assyrian empire. First the Medes captured Asshur in 614 BCE. Then in 612 the allies razed Nineveh; Assyrian refugees who escaped were next thrown out of Haran in 610. In the meantime, the Egyptians, who under Pharaoh Neco (or Necho) II (610–595) had been increasing in power, marched northward, rolling over Judah en route and killing Josiah at Megiddo in 609. Finally in 605 the Neo-Babylonians under Nebuchadnezzar II (or Nebuchadrezzar; 605–562) won the battle at Carchemish, eliminating the Neo-Assyrian remnants and stopping the Egyptian forces. With Nebuchadnezzar back in Babylon, the Neo-Babylonian army continued southward where they forced Josiah's successor, Jehoiakim (609–598), to become their vassal. Judah hesitated to pay tribute and was invaded in 601 and 598/7.

Of the kings in this period only Jehoiachin is mentioned by name in Neo-Babylonian sources, which is ironic since he ruled for only three months in 598/7, a much shorter time than Josiah, whom the Bible praises. Jehoiachin had the misfortune of sitting on the throne when Nebuchadnezzar sent his army into Jerusalem in 598/7; the Babylonians exiled numerous Judahites and imprisoned the king. Nebuchadnezzar appointed Zedekiah, one of Josiah's sons, to be king, but in 594 Zedekiah aligned himself with the Egyptians in a failed attempt to resist. In 587 the Neo-Babylonian army responded, laying siege to Jerusalem for eighteen months. In 586 they breached the walls, tore down the temple, and sacked the city. King Zedekiah sought to escape but was captured: "They slaughtered the sons of Zedekiah before his eyes, then put out the eyes of Zedekiah; they bound him in fetters and took him to Babylon" (2 Kings 25:7). Jerusalem's fall marked the absolute end to the monarchy and changed life in the land and in the community forever. Second Kings 25 concludes solemnly with a description of the destruction and a notice that the Neo-Babylonians appointed Gedaliah as governor and eventually released King Jehoiachin in 560 after thirty-seven years in prison.

Exile and Return

Following its fall, Jerusalem faced a bleak situation. The Neo-Babylonians plundered and then destroyed large edifices and left the city uninhabitable. The people relocated to more rural settings rather than face the formidable task of rebuilding Jerusalem and other cities such as Lachish.

According to recent archaeological studies, the population in the land declined by upward of 70 percent, with almost all areas affected. The Neo-Babylonians built their provincial capital at Mizpah, some ten miles north of Jerusalem in Benjaminite territory. The resettlement of Jerusalem did not begin until more than a century had passed.

The period from 586 to 538 BCE usually goes by the name "exilic period" or "(Neo-)Babylonian exile." Although these terms may imply that only one exile occurred in Israel's and Judah's history, there were multiple occasions when foreign empires forcibly moved residents to other lands. The first occurred in 722 when the northern kingdom fell and the Neo-Assyrians deported captives from Samaria. Then leading up to the 586 disaster, the Neo-Babylonians invaded and took into exile a number of Judahites, including King Jehoiachin, in 597. The main deportation probably occurred in 586, and an additional group was exiled in 582 after the assassination of the governor Gedaliah, reported in Jeremiah 41.

The number of persons exiled remains uncertain. By no means was the whole population deported. Sargon claims to have taken 27,280 in 722. According to 2 Kings 24:14, the Neo-Babylonians exiled a total of 10,000 in 597 alone, whereas Jeremiah 52:28–30 counts a total of 4,600 for all three exiles together (597, 586, and 582). The lower numbers may be more credible, given the types of people likely to be taken into exile.

It makes little sense to exile people from all classes of a defeated society unless the conquerors had major military needs or massive construction projects at home that required slave labor. More important was keeping laborers in the provinces where they could work the land, raise livestock, mine minerals or metals, cut timber, and produce the other goods and foods needed by the empire. Without a steady stream of products sent to the imperial centers, the empire could not increase in wealth and power. Of equal concern was the possibility of defections or resistance in the provinces, instigated by local leaders with their own interests in play. Consequently the imperial authorities exiled mainly those persons who possessed the skills and experience to lead or help in a resistance movement: the royal family, the harem, officials, the elite of the land, priests, professional warriors, artisans, smiths, and the like (2 Kings 24:14–16). The "poorest of the land" remained in Judah to till the soil (25:12; 24:14).

Finally, there is the question of where the exiles lived in Babylon. Unlike the Neo-Assyrians, who preferred a policy of erasing the identity of those they captured by dispersing them throughout the empire, the Neo-Babylonians resettled their captives as communities in several sites in Babylon, some former agricultural areas, and expected them to be productive there. According to Ezekiel 1:1–3 and 3:15, many were in Tel-abib near the River Chebar (actually more of a canal than a river), not far from the city of Nippur, roughly 120 miles southeast of modern-day Baghdad. Other sites mentioned in Ezra 2:59 and 8:17 are Tel-melah, Tel-harsha, Cherub, Addan, Immer, and Casiphia, but their locations are now unknown. Most specifics about this period are uncertain, but the general picture fits the encouraging letter reportedly sent by the prophet Jeremiah to the exiles in Babylon:

> Build houses and live in them; plant gardens and eat what
> they produce. Take wives and have sons and daughters;
> take wives for your sons, and give your daughters in mar-
> riage, that they may bear sons and daughters; multiply
> there, and do not decrease. But seek the welfare of the
> city where I have sent you into exile, and pray to YHWH
> on its behalf, for in its welfare you will find your welfare.
> (29:5–7)

These exiles were taken forcibly to Babylon, but others from Judah chose on their own to relocate to Egypt, and a community formed at El-ephantine, named after an unusual rock formation on the island in the upper Nile at modern-day Aswan. A considerable number of letters and contracts, written in Aramaic during the fifth century BCE, remain from that community. Jeremiah was taken to Egypt against his will by another group from Judah (Jer. 43), and according to an old tradition he died there.

The Persian and Hellenistic Periods

The Neo-Babylonian empire declined rather quickly as the Persians grew in power on the eastern horizon. Cyrus II of Persia (558–530) began his rise in stages, first by conquering the Medes in 549 BCE and then by taking the kingdom of Lydia, located in today's western Turkey, in 546. The Neo-Babylonian empire had weakened so much that Cyrus was able to take it with relatively little opposition in 539, proclaiming himself the liberator. By capturing Babylon, he implicitly acquired the whole Neo-Babylonian empire as well, but he needed to secure his hold. His imperial strategy for stabilizing his reign differed significantly from that of preceding empires. The Neo-Assyrians had scattered and assimilated their captives around the empire and the Neo-Babylonians had deported them to several sites where they lived together, but the Persians released the exiles remaining from the Neo-Babylonian empire. Quite propagandistic in nature, the Cyrus Cylinder, discovered at Babylon in 1879 and written in Akkadian probably soon after 539, contains a long description of Cyrus's innovative policy, including this passage:

> I returned the (images of) the gods to the sacred centers
> [on the other side of] the Tigris whose sanctuaries had
> been abandoned for a long time, and I let them dwell in
> eternal abodes. I gathered all their inhabitants and re-
> turned (to them) their dwellings.*

Although not the actual edict, Ezra 1:2–4 and 6:2–5 describe the implications of the release for the Judahites in exile, for Cyrus supported not only their return but also the rebuilding of their temple. Small wonder, then, that the Hebrew Bible cites him several times, notably in Isaiah 45:1, where he is called YHWH's "messiah" or "anointed one," and in Isaiah 44:28, which reads: "[YHWH] says of Cyrus: 'He is my shepherd, and he shall carry out all my purpose'; and [YHWH] says of Jerusalem, 'It shall be rebuilt,' and of the temple, 'Your foundation shall be laid.'"

As it did for the exiles from other lands, Cyrus's edict allowed the Judahites in Babylon to return to their homeland, now called Yehud (the Aramaic word for Judah; the Greco-Latin form is Judea), and to rebuild their temple. How many returned and when cannot be determined with any precision. Ezra 2 and Nehemiah 7 set the number of returnees at 42,360 plus 7,337 slaves and 200 (245 in Nehemiah) singers, in addition to all their livestock. The number seems very high, even if it includes several waves. The population that went into exile—4,600 according to Jeremiah 52; 10,000 according to 2 Kings 24—could not have multiplied that much in just two generations. Perhaps we have here another case of exaggerating the numbers in order to enhance the story.

A number of the exiles apparently remained in Babylonia, which vari-

---

* William W. Hallo, ed., *Context of Scripture*, vol. 2, *Monumental Inscriptions from the Biblical World* (Leiden, Boston: Brill, 2003), 315.

ous documents found there from Persian and Hellenistic times confirm. In 1999, three new tablets from a private collection came to light, and one of them, dated around 500 BCE, contains the previously unknown name of a Babylonian town, al-Yahudu, "the city of Judah," presumably named after the homeland of its inhabitants. Another collection of tablets, known as the Murashu Archive, records commercial transactions by a firm located around Nippur between about 450 and 400, and they contain some 2,200 personal names, of which approximately 80 are Jewish names, probably of descendants of the original exiles. Centuries later the community in Babylonia had developed a prominent center of Jewish tradition and study, rivaling a similar center in the land of Israel; from these two centers come the two great Talmuds, the Babylonian and the Jerusalem.

If it is the case, as mentioned in 2 Kings 24–25 and as seems reasonable, that those taken into exile were largely the leaders, the elites, and the skilled workers, then it was their children and grandchildren who returned to Yehud beginning in 538 BCE. They would have been raised to expect the life their parents and grandparents had enjoyed before the fall of Jerusalem, and they then could assume they deserved their parents' standing and properties back in Yehud. Having experienced the Babylonian and then the Persian powers during the exile, they were also well prepared to deal with the Persian administrators in Yehud.

This scenario fits the biblical descriptions of the conflicts between the returnees and those who had remained in Yehud throughout the exilic period, mainly the lower class of laborers and farmers, termed "the people of the land." According to Ezra 6, Darius I, emperor of Persia from 522 to 486, authorized and even funded the rebuilding of the temple in Jerusalem, the "Second Temple," which was completed between 520 and 516. Ezra 4 reports that the returnees rebuffed an overture from "the people of the land," perhaps including Samaritans from the north as well as some settlers from Neo-Assyrian times, to help in rebuilding the temple. These residents later tried to obstruct the building of the city wall and even wrote to the Persian emperor Xerxes (486–465) to urge stoppage. Subsequently, the emperor Artaxerxes I (465–424) commissioned Nehemiah to rebuild the city of Jerusalem (Neh. 2), which he accomplished despite opposition from neighboring territories, including Samaria in the north.

The Persian policy of tolerating traditional practices and institutions in the provinces proved to be a shrewd strategy for currying the allegiance of imperial subjects. Not all of the provinces were compliant, however.

Throughout the Persian empire's two-hundred-year existence many revolts occurred—in Babylon, Bactria, Egypt, Athens, Media, the Levant, and elsewhere—which the army needed to put down. Revolts were relatively common especially during the fifth and fourth centuries BCE under the emperors Xerxes, Artaxerxes I, and their successors. Yehud's history is not well known during some of these reigns, but there is evidence of both new and ongoing settlements as well as the destruction of some sites, presumably by Persian forces.

The end came for the Persian empire with the arrival of Alexander the Great (336–323). In 334, at the young age of twenty-two, Alexander left his homeland, Macedonia, and led his army of thirty-five thousand into the Persian-held region of Asia Minor, present-day Turkey, where he quickly dispatched the initial Persian resistance. In his trek eastward only occasional cities opposed him, and none for long. Darius III (339–331), the last of the Persian emperors, put up fierce resistance at Issus, near the coast where Asia Minor and the Levant meet, and in the end he escaped. Alexander then proceeded directly south, through Syria and Phoenicia to Gaza, which he besieged for two months before it fell. Not much is known about any actions he took in Judea, though it presumably capitulated without resistance. In 332 he marched into Egypt with no difficulty. The next year he was back in the Levant, where he attacked and punished Samaria for rebelling against him. He continued toward Babylon and eventually to the Persian cities of Susa, Persepolis, and Ecbatana, which he conquered in 330, thereby ending the Persian empire and establishing Hellenistic control. After ranging with his army farther north and east, he returned to Babylon, where he died in 323 at the age of thirty-two.

The next several decades demonstrate the contentions, intrigues, power plays, and political murders that followed Alexander's death. By 301 the lines had fairly well formed for the central part of the empire, where two of Alexander's generals were in control: Seleucus I over Babylonia, much of Asia Minor, and Syria; and Ptolemy I over Egypt, Judea, Samaria, and Coele-Syria (a name designating various regions, mostly in present-day Lebanon and southern Syria). Unrest, especially the repeated wars over the northern Levant, continued to unsettle the larger region. The southern Levant remained a part of the Ptolemaic empire for all of the third century BCE. The inhabitants of Judea felt its impact as the Ptolemies, centered in Egypt, drew heavily on them for agricultural products, military conscripts, and slaves.

At this time, it becomes appropriate to use the term "Jew" to designate all who identify themselves with the ethnic and religious trajectory rooted in ancient Israel. The Judean population, defined according to geographical location in the earlier periods and connected to a particular people and, eventually, a recognized ethnic group and culture, began in the postexilic period to be opened to permanent affiliation. That is, it extended its ethnic and geographical identity to include a religious identity.

In about 200 BCE Judea changed hands as the Seleucid empire, with its capital in Antioch (modern-day Antakya, Turkey, near northern Syria), took it from the Ptolemies. After Antiochus IV Epiphanes (175–164) seized the throne, he attempted to hellenize the Jews by turning Jerusalem into a Greek city and forbidding their practice of religious traditions, including Sabbath observance, temple sacrifices according to the ancient rites, and circumcision. He also ordered destruction of all copies of Jewish law, and in 167 he converted the temple into a Greek shrine with an altar to Zeus. Jews considered these acts, above all the establishment of the altar to Zeus in the temple, the ultimate blasphemy, and resistance broke out. Daniel 7–12 reflects this period of 167–164, veiled as an apocalyptic piece set in the time of the Neo-Babylonian and Persian empires.

The military response to Antiochus was led by Mattathias, an elderly priest from the town of Modein, about twenty miles northwest of Jerusalem. Although Antiochus had internal support from the Jewish high-priesthood, he was less interested in establishing a new religion than in adapting the old one to Greek norms. However, according to the portrayal in the book of 1 Maccabees, it is a new religion that the king's officers arriving in Modein sought to institute. Mattathias responded with zeal, killing the first Jew who tried to sacrifice on the altar and slaying the officer as well. He and his sons then fled to the hills, calling on others to join them. After Mattathias died, leadership shifted to one of his sons, Judas Maccabeus ("the hammer"), who together with his brothers became known as the Maccabees. They amassed sufficient support from among the people to engage the Seleucids in battle and stop the effort to crush them. After the Maccabees recaptured most of Jerusalem, the Seleucids abandoned their efforts to control religious practice, and the Jews were able to cleanse and rededicate the temple on the 25th of Kislev (November/December) 164, an event still celebrated as Channukah ("dedication"). They gained further concessions and recognition from the Seleucids, and in 140 BCE

Judea became independent as the Hasmonean kingdom; the name's derivation is uncertain, referring either to an ancestor of Mattathias or to a place named Heshmon or Hashmonah. The Hasmonean kingdom, the last period of Jewish independence and sovereignty in the land for the next two thousand years, continued until 63 BCE, when the Romans under Pompey captured Jerusalem.

The Hellenistic period proved formative for Judaism. Some Jews collaborated with the Hellenists while others resisted their influence. How much of the Hebrew Bible bears the marks of Hellenism is still hotly debated. The book of Ecclesiastes (Qohelet), probably written during the third or second century, may well reflect some Greek influence, as do other texts of the time. Factions among Jews arose as they struggled to appropriate their heritage in their present circumstances. In light of the various movements, it is best to think of "Judaisms" rather than one common Judaism during this period. The community at Qumran on the northwestern shore of the Dead Sea, in operation from the second century BCE to 68 CE, is a good example of one such group.

The history of the Persian and Hellenistic empires is not simply a postscript to the history of Israel, for during these later centuries much of the Hebrew Bible was either written or edited into final form. The events, social circumstances, political conflicts, religious practices, and other factors from this period influenced the biblical text in both content and form, from the views of political leadership to the religious sentiments and rituals. It is too much to say that the Hebrew Bible reflects the thoughts and experiences of the Jews only during the Persian and Hellenistic periods, but at the same time it is too little to say that these Jewish communities were only conduits of early traditions rather than also producers and editors of the biblical literature. A global assertion will not work. Decisions about influences and authorship of the biblical texts need to be reached on a case-by-case basis, and familiarity with the changing circumstances throughout the whole of Israel's history is key to making such judgments.

During the Hellenistic period the Greek language grew in importance in the region of the Levant and Egypt, and many Jews in the diaspora (outside the homeland) were more at home reading and speaking Greek or other languages than Hebrew. Beginning in the third century BCE the Hebrew texts were translated into Greek, probably first among them the Pentateuch (the Torah, or first five books of the Bible). The Ptolemaic capital city of Alexandria, Egypt, is the most likely location for such translation since the city was a center of learning and certainly housed a large Jewish community in need of the text in Greek.

The Historical Time Frame

Reasonable people can disagree about both the starting point and the end point of ancient Israel's history, that is, the period to be considered as the span of ancient Israel's existence. The Bible envisions Abraham as the progenitor of the Hebrew people. It includes lengthy descriptions of Israel's ancestors and experiences in Egyptian slavery before it ushers the people into the land. But this whole presettlement period lacks external verification of the Israelites' presence; only the Bible is witness to these early Israelites. Material evidence outside the literary portrayals does not emerge until about 1200 BCE, when "Israel" is named on an Egyptian stele and when a considerable increase in settlement in the Canaanite highlands begins to become observable in the archaeological record. From that point forward we have to sort through the mixed situation of a detailed biblical account and a spotty collection of external sources, whether inscriptional or archaeological, all the way to Persian and Hellenistic times.

The end point of ancient Israel's history is also indistinct, but for a different reason. From Persian and Hellenistic times, many records from inside and outside the southern Levant exist for our study, but now the problem is the dispersion of the Jews and their position as vassals to overbearing empires, Neo-Babylonian, Persian, Hellenistic, and Roman. At no time after 722 did they possess sovereignty except during the short-lived Hasmonean kingdom of the second and first centuries BCE. The year 150 BCE serves as a reasonable end point, after the event that provoked the last biblical composition, the Seleucid desecration of the Jewish temple in 167 BCE, which prompted the writing of the apocalyptic materials in Daniel 7–12. The Hebrew Bible had not yet reached its final shape by this point, but the bulk of the remaining work on it involved mainly compiling and editing its books into final form, not the creation of new compositions. The deuterocanonical books in the Catholic and Orthodox canons were, however, not yet quite at this stage.

From 1200 to 150 BCE the ancient Israelites lived through most of the experiences and religious developments that became recorded in the

Hebrew Bible. This millennium included momentous events, memorable individuals, intricate processes, and lofty ideas—much more than we may expect of such a small country. The cultural memory that developed was powerful enough to keep its influence alive to this day. We will focus on many of its components and themes during the remainder of the book, revisiting points in this grand history of Israel whenever necessary to see the larger context.

Chapter 2

The Literary Heritage of Ancient Israel

The literary heritage of ancient Israel remains with us today, despite our increasing biblical illiteracy. Our language is peppered with biblical allusions. Our moral values are informed by biblical precepts, for example, "You shall love your neighbor as yourself" (Lev. 19:18). And our political views—from our view of the Middle East to our view of homosexuality—have biblical antecedents. Whether we are a member of a church or synagogue, whether we identify as Jewish, Christian, or neither, we are impacted by the language and values of the Bible.

This impact is, however, selective. The biblical text speaks in multiple voices and even multiple languages. It varies in genre, from poetry to prose, from law to lament. And it varies in opinion. The beauty of the text is that it does not homogenize its views; rather, it offers readers multiple perspectives. Whereas it does sometimes appear to express its mandates clearly— "Thou shalt not kill"; "Thou shalt not commit adultery"—at other times it prompts us to engage with it, as in a conversation or a dance: Does killing an enemy in battle violate that first injunction? How does the text define "adultery"? The narrative does not always agree with the law. The great king David arranged for the deaths of others, and he certainly committed adultery, but he is hailed by Jews, Christians, and Muslims alike. That his character can capture our imagination, and often our admiration, speaks to the literary power of the text.

Anyone can appreciate this literature. When we pick up a Bible and read the opening lines, "In the beginning when God created the heavens and the earth . . ." (Gen. 1:1), we are swept up into the majesty of creation as heaven and earth are separated, humanity comes into being, male and female both appear in the image of the divine, and we hear the command to be fruitful and multiply (the opening commandment is not a "Thou shalt not" but a very emphatic "thou shalt!"). We can read the stories of

Adam and Eve, Noah and the Tower of Babel, Abraham and David, Ruth and Esther. These stories have been appreciated for centuries, without academics butting in to complicate matters.

However, if we look again at these texts and others through the lenses of history, we can see so much more. The stories take on brighter colors, the laws find more profound interpretations. If we understand why these texts were written and how their ancient audiences understood them, we can appreciate them more fully. This informed approach is not the enemy of a faith-based reading; biblical scholarship is not, in our view, a weapon designed to destroy one's religious beliefs. It is, rather, something that can enhance such beliefs. Indeed, if three or four pages of a book or a single lecture based on a rigorous academic understanding of the Bible calls one's faith into question, then that is a faith that needs to be reconsidered. In turn, understanding these texts as they were understood in antiquity can provide all readers, regardless of religious affiliation, insight into ancient history and the genius of the human spirit.

To understand the literary heritage of ancient Israel, we begin with the question of *genre* and therefore the question of how to read this text. If we read Leviticus, Deuteronomy, or today's Congressional Record as narrative rather than as law, we can find many interesting readings, but we will miss the main point of the text. If we read the story of creation as science, as those who promote "creationism" or "intelligent design" are wont to do, we again confuse genre.

Even those who claim to be biblical literalists are nevertheless engaged in the interpretive act. The literalists themselves recognize that poetry is to be understood in a different manner than prose. When literalists read, "Your eyes are doves behind your veil" (Song 4:1), they are not picturing frantic squabs trapped atop a nose. Nor do literalists insist that the earth is a flat rectangle, despite the biblical reference to the "four corners of the earth" (Isa. 11:12).

To determine what a text "says" is, moreover, not always to determine what it "means." We can read the words, but in order to gain a good sense of the meaning we need to do more. We need to understand the genre in which the words are placed, understand their connotations as well as the denotations, and attend to who is speaking to determine if the words are meant literally or figuratively, earnestly or sarcastically, as command or advice or hint. The act of reading is necessarily one of interpretation. That commentaries on the books of the Bible continue to be written demonstrates that the same texts can be interpreted in multiple ways; that religious movements interpret the texts differently shows that more is at stake in the act of interpretation than just a question of aesthetics. To interpret the literary heritage of ancient Israel is in some ways comparable to interpreting Homer or Shakespeare, but because the text is not just script but scripture, the stakes are much higher for many people. If we can see not only how, but why the same text is interpreted in such different ways by different communities, we may even come a bit closer to mutual understanding.

Tanakh or Old Testament or Hebrew Bible?

"What's in a name?" is a question found not in the Bible, but in Shakespeare (*Romeo and Juliet*, act 2, scene 1), but it applies to the text in question. "Old Testament," the most popular designation, was first applied to this collection of books by the North African Christian Tertullian (160–230 CE). The term "testament" translates the Greek word *diathēkē*, which also means "covenant" (the Hebrew would be *berit*, a term known even outside Jewish circles as a reference to the *brit milah*, or the covenant of circumcision; in Yiddish, the term is *bris;* in modern Hebrew, *brit*). The church proclaimed that there were two covenants, an "old" one represented by the scriptures of Israel and a "new one" described in what we call the "New Testament."

The Old Testament begins, as does the Hebrew Bible, with Genesis, Exodus, Leviticus, Numbers, and Deuteronomy. For the Samaritans, and probably for the ancient Sadducees as well, these five books constituted the entire Bible. The common designation for this collection of five books, which could be handwritten on five large scrolls, is the Pentateuch, a Greek term for "five scrolls." In Judaism, this collection is called the Torah, a Hebrew word meaning "instruction," but also translated "law." At this point, Samaritans, Jews, and Christians are in general agreement.

The Christian Old Testament then proceeds in roughly the chronological order of the stories recounted—though probably not the chronological order of the dates when the books were actually written: Joshua, Judges, Ruth, 1–2 Samuel, 1–2 Kings, 1–2 Chronicles, Ezra, Nehemiah, and Esther. Then come works of wisdom: Job, Psalms, Proverbs, Ecclesiastes, and Song of Solomon (Canticles). Finally, it ends with prophecy: Isaiah, Jeremiah, Lamentations, Ezekiel, Daniel, Hosea, Joel, Amos, Obadiah,

Jonah, Micah, Nahum, Habakkuk, Zephaniah, Haggai, Zechariah, and Malachi. Neatly, Malachi, the last book, predicts the coming of that final moment when all history draws to a close: "Lo, I will send you the prophet Elijah before the great and terrible day of YHWH comes. He will turn the hearts of parents to their children and the hearts of children to their parents, so that I will not come and strike the land with a curse" (4:5–6; Tanakh 3:23–24). In some ancient manuscripts, Malachi 4:4 comes last, so the prophetic corpus would not end on this foreboding note.

Ending the canon with Malachi fit the theology for the early church. The role of Elijah, a prophetic messenger who did not die but who was taken up to heaven—the song "Swing Low, Sweet Chariot" is a reference to Elijah's ascension in a whirlwind via a "chariot of fire and horses" (2 Kings 2:11)—was ascribed to John the Baptist (Matt. 17:12), the first-century prophetic figure who baptized Jesus of Nazareth. Thus the Old Testament, ending with Malachi, led neatly into the Gospels.

The synagogue begged to differ. For the Jewish tradition, the term "Old Testament" is inappropriate. "Old Testament" presumes there is a "New Testament," the book containing the four Gospels and Acts, the letters of Paul and others, and Revelation. This collection is not part of the canon of the synagogue. As mentioned earlier, the Jewish designation for this collection of books is Tanakh (or Tanach, or TaNaK), an acronym in which T stands for Torah, N stands for Nevi'im ("Prophets"), and K for Ketuvim ("Writings"). The Prophets include Joshua, Judges, 1–2 Samuel, 1–2 Kings, Isaiah, Jeremiah, Ezekiel, and the "book of the twelve" (Hosea through Malachi). We can see major differences between this order and that of the Old Testament. These differences continue when we get to the Writings: Psalms, Proverbs, and Job; then a subcategory of the five Megillot ("scrolls"; Song of Songs, Ruth, Lamentations, Ecclesiastes, and Esther); and finally Daniel, Ezra-Nehemiah, and 1–2 Chronicles. Daniel, often regarded as the most prophetic of the prophets, is not even grouped among the prophets in the Tanakh.

The order of the volumes tells us about the distinct stories told by the church and the synagogue. For the Christian order, ending with the prophets, the story is one of promise in the Old Testament leading to fulfillment in the New. This reading is confirmed when the New Testament then interprets the Old. It finds in the story of Adam and Eve an account of an irreparable rupture between humanity and divinity that only Jesus can reconcile; it finds in Isaiah's depiction of the suffering servant a prediction of the saving death of Jesus. For the Tanakh, the Prophets are not at the end, but in the middle. For the synagogue, although the events in Eden do create less than ideal conditions for human existence, there is no irreparable breach established that only the sacrifice of Jesus can repair. The human condition is not one of irredeemable sin apart from the Christ; the relationship between God and creation continues.

The Tanakh ends with 2 Chronicles, a text set in the late fifth century BCE when King Cyrus of Persia, having just defeated the Babylonian empire, tells the exiles from Judah who had been displaced from their home by the Babylonian king Nebuchadnezzar fifty years earlier: "YHWH, the God of heaven, has given me all the kingdoms of the earth, and he has charged me to build him a house at Jerusalem, which is in Judah. Whoever is among you of all his people, may YHWH God be with him! Let him go up" (2 Chron. 36:23). The Jewish canon ends not with a prediction of a future fulfillment, but with a look back home.

A few medieval manuscripts of the Tanakh end not with 2 Chronicles, but with Ezra-Nehemiah. This ending too gives a sense of completion rather than of promise and fulfillment. The last line of these combined books of history is "Remember me, O my God, for good" (Neh. 13:31). The Hebrew term for God is Elohim; "good" is *tov*. These terms echo Genesis 1:31, in which Elohim creates the heavens and the earth and all that is in them and sees that "it [is] very good" (*tov*).

The separate terms "Tanakh" and "Old Testament" thus convey different canonical orders and different religious viewpoints. The second term also, for some readers, conveys a negative sense. The term "old" in "Old Testament" is taken to mean "less good," "antiquated," or "surpassed." But in antiquity, what was antique was good; the old was respected—it was seen as precious, the wisdom of the ages—and the new was suspect, the "upstart" or the "neophyte." Today, much of Western culture has a different set of values; we like the new, and we are uncomfortable with the old. Thus, some well-intentioned theologians and biblical scholars, in an effort to remove the negative sense that "Old Testament" could convey and also in an attempt to find a less religiously charged designation for the books in question, proposed "Hebrew Bible" or "Hebrew scriptures." Hence, "Hebrew Bible" courses began to be offered on college campuses. Aside from the few confused students who worried that a course on the Hebrew Bible was taught in Hebrew, the term caught on in the secular world. Some more conservative Christians felt (and still feel) it is a denial of their traditional designation, and they correctly noted that Christians do not negate the Old Testament or consider it of little worth. Some Jews, uncomfortable with the term "Old Testament" for the same reasons as their Christian colleagues, were happy with the shift. Others found "Hebrew Bible" or "Hebrew scriptures" redundant. Since the Jewish canon is in Hebrew (with a bit of Aramaic in Daniel and Ezra-Nehemiah), saying "Hebrew Bible" is like saying "Jewish rabbi." In a Jewish context, "Bible" presupposes "Hebrew" just as "rabbi" presupposes "Jew."

In keeping with current usage, the term generally used in this book for the primary biblical material under discussion is "Hebrew Bible" or simply "Bible." Deuterocanonical texts we discuss will be identified as such.

Every Translator, a Traitor

An Italian proverb, "A translator, a traitor," points to the difficulties inherent in translating material written in one language into another. The literature of ancient Israel is written in Hebrew, with a smattering of the related language Aramaic. In the third century BCE, the Hebrew text began to be formally translated into Greek, the predominant language of the Mediterranean cultures following the conquests of Alexander the Great in 333 BCE. The Greek translation of the Hebrew text, along with the deuterocanonical Greek texts, is called the Septuagint, from a Greek term meaning "seventy," usually abbreviated LXX. As the legend recorded in an ancient text called the *Letter of Aristeas* recounts, Pharaoh Ptolemy II Philadelphus (285–246 BCE) wanted a copy of the scriptures of the Jews for his library, and he requested it of the high priest in Jerusalem, the head of the local government in Jerusalem. The high priest commissioned seventy-two scribes to produce the Greek translation. In a retelling of this legend by the first-century Jewish philosopher Philo of Alexandria (whose works were preserved by the church), the production of this text was miraculous: "They, like men inspired, prophesied, not one saying one thing and another another, but every one of them employed the self-same nouns and verbs, as if some unseen prompter had suggested all their language to them" (*Life of Moses* 2.37). This story, which can legitimately be labeled "apocryphal," shows that for Philo and many other Greek-speaking Jews the Septuagint has as much authority as the Hebrew text.

Despite the fact that Jews translated the Hebrew into Greek and that synagogues throughout antiquity began using the Greek, the Jewish tradition at one point determined that only the Hebrew was to be used. Initially, there was no single version of these books; different copyists produced different texts, and different communities preserved different readings. The Dead Sea Scrolls, which contain parts of all the Hebrew books (with the exception of Esther) as well as Hebrew versions of some of the deuterocanonical books, such as Tobit, attest to numerous variants. It is likely that the Greek translators in some cases, such as for the book of Jeremiah, which is about one-eighth shorter in the Septuagint than in the Hebrew text, worked with versions much different from those of the extant Hebrew manuscripts.

The standardized Hebrew version that was later developed is called the Masoretic text (MT). The name comes from the Hebrew term *masorah*, which signifies "[a chain of] tradition." The term may derive from Ezekiel 20:37, which speaks of the "bond of the covenant" (Heb. *mesoret ha-brit*). The "bond" (or chain) served to protect and to guard. From the sixth through the tenth centuries CE, Jewish scholars known as Masoretes took upon themselves the task of guarding the text from error by standardizing the Hebrew. They added vowels to what was originally only a consonantal text and accents to show phrasing.

Of course, the standardizations differed depending on where the Masoretes were located. The three major headquarters were in Tiberias and Jerusalem in the land of Israel and in Babylonia (modern Iraq). In Tiberias alone there were two major schools, those of Ben Naphtali and Ben Asher. The famous tenth-century Aleppo Codex, which once contained the entire Tanakh but now lacks virtually all of the Torah, derives from the school of Ben Asher, and it was this version that eventually determined the Torah as copied and preserved in synagogues to this day.

In antiquity, despite the fluidity of both various Hebrew versions and various Greek versions, the two traditions came to define certain religious views and eventually became the Bibles of the two heirs of the biblical tradition. The church, rapidly a gentile (i.e., non-Jewish) community whose primary language was Greek, stayed with the Septuagint, and the synagogue kept to the Hebrew. Many of the differences between these two traditions are grounded in the differences between the Hebrew and the Greek texts.

An influential difference can be seen in the rendering of Isaiah 7:14. In the Hebrew Isaiah is addressing Ahaz, the king of Judah, who is in the middle of a political crisis and is debating about joining an international alliance to stave off a border attack. Encouraging the king to stay firm and depend on divine power rather than military alliance, Isaiah states: "Therefore the Lord himself will give you a sign. Look, the young woman is with child and shall bear a son, and shall name him Immanuel. He shall eat curds and honey by the time he knows how to refuse the evil and choose the good. For before the child knows how to refuse the evil and choose the good, the land before whose two kings you are in dread will be deserted" (7:14–16). The sign is a pregnant woman. The Hebrew term used for her is *almah,* which simply means "young woman." Hebrew does have a term for "virgin," *betulah,* but it does not appear in Isaiah 7:14. Since the woman in Isaiah's sign is pregnant, the king, and readers subsequently, would presume that she became pregnant in the normal manner.

When this text was translated into Greek, the term *almah* appeared as *parthenos,* which can mean "virgin" (as in the *Parthenon,* the temple dedicated to the virgin goddess Athena). However, the term in the second century BCE could simply mean young woman or unmarried woman. The LXX of Genesis 34:3 reports that Shechem, who had just had sexual intercourse with Jacob's daughter Dinah, "loved the *parthenos.*" At this point in the story, Dinah is no longer a "virgin," and *parthenos* can simply mean "young woman" (as does the underlying Hebrew, *naʾarah*). The Gospel of Matthew, written toward the end of the first century CE, takes Isaiah in the Greek as speaking about a virgin—for Matthew, this was a perfectly legitimate reading—interprets this "sign" as a miracle, and applies it to the conception of Jesus: "All this took place to fulfill what had been spoken by the Lord through the prophet: 'Look, the virgin shall conceive and bear a son'" (Matt. 1:22–23a). The church, using the Greek, had a virginal conception; the synagogue, using the Hebrew, did not.

The disagreement became sufficiently heated that in the second century a Christian apologist named Justin Martyr (ca. 165) accused the Jews of changing the text. That the Dead Sea Scrolls preserve copies of Isaiah in which the Hebrew reads *almah* shows that Justin's claim was unfounded. Nevertheless, the Jewish community in the late first century, faced with this and other interpretations of the Septuagint by the followers of Jesus, produced two new Greek versions, called after their (presumed) authors Symmachus and Theodotion, that translate the Hebrew in a more literal fashion than did the Septuagint.

Even if we look only at the Hebrew, the problems of translation continue. By adding vowels to the consonantal text, the Masoretes limited the meanings of words. Without the vowels, the text opened up numerous possible meanings, especially puns, although for the most part those who were literate were able to determine meaning from context. Already in the Garden of Eden story the pun is present, thus questioning what sort of paradise it is. The snake is described as *arum*, a Hebrew term usually translated "crafty" (Gen. 3:1). The human couple are described as *arumim* (plural), translated "naked" (3:7, 10, 11). The consonants are the same. The connection between the snake and the people is thus a visual and aural one, and it is fully lost in the English translation.

The Eden story contains a number of other puns in which words having the same root meaning serve different functions. Genesis 2:7 reads, "Then YHWH God formed man from the dust of the ground." Missing in this dry and dusty description is a glorious Hebrew pun. The term for "man" in Hebrew is *adam* (hence the name Adam), and the term for "ground" is *adamah*, or arable soil. The better translation would be "formed a human from the dust of the humus," or, depending on one's opinion of Adam, who is standing next to his wife when she has that conversation with the serpent, "formed a clod from the dust of the clods."

Whereas puns are deliberate wordplays, at times manuscript traditions represent scribal errors or misunderstandings. *Text criticism* is that aspect of interpretation that asks, "What was the original version?" If the Septuagint and the Masoretic text disagree, or if the Masoretic text and a version of one of the Dead Sea Scrolls differ, can we determine the original? The question presumes that there was an original written text, which can probably never be confirmed. We have no original manuscripts of any biblical book. The Bible even mentions books—the "Book of the Wars of YHWH" (Num. 21:14); the "Book of Jashar" (Josh. 10:13); the "Book of the Acts of Solomon" (1 Kings 11:41)—that are, if they ever existed, now lost.

Whether there was a pristine version of any biblical book cannot be known. What a speaker states and what a scribe inscribes may be two different things. Two scribes, hearing the same sentence, may write two different versions of it. At times, a bit of detective work can establish how the different readings originated.

For example, in the book of Jonah, the prophet, who has managed to fall asleep in the hull of a boat despite the violent storm at sea, is awakened from his slumber by the sailors frightened that their boat is about to be destroyed. The gentile sailors suspect that Jonah is to blame for angering the gods. To their query, "Of what people are you?" Jonah responds, "I am a Hebrew" (1:9). The Septuagint, however, reads, "I am a servant of YHWH." The difference, in English, is evident. Here's how it happened.

First, the Hebrew letter *resh*, the equivalent of the English *R*, looks very much like the Hebrew letter *dalet*, the equivalent of English *D*. Second, the little Hebrew letter *yod*, transliterated both as an *I* and a *Y*, can serve as an abbreviation for the name of the deity, for YHWH begins with a *yod*. Finally, it helps to know that the Hebrew letter *bet* (*B*), depending on where it shows up in a word or phrase, sometimes is pronounced like the English *V*. Now to our test case: Jonah, in Hebrew, used the word spelled *ayin-bet-resh-yod*, or to transliterate, *ivri*. The *ayin*, by the way, has no sound in English; it is a glottal stop, or a voiced pharyngeal fricative, or, perhaps most helpful, a silent letter, that can be transliterated variously with an *i* or an *e* or an open parenthesis. The Greek translator read the *resh* as a *dalet* and the *yod* as an abbreviation for YHWH. That reading gives the letters *ayin-bet-dalet* + the abbreviation, or to translate, *eved-Yah*, meaning "a servant of God."

The text-critical problem in Job 13:15 is even more severe: different readings appear depending on which vowels are used and how the words are divided. The problem is exacerbated by the observation that all the possible translations fit the context. Perhaps the writer who first inscribed the text intended for all three possible meanings; they can be found in the Hebrew, but the poor English translator is unable to capture them all. The influential KJV has Job exclaim, "Though he slay me, yet I will trust him." The NEB is a bit less trusting: "If he wishes to slay me, I have nothing to lose." The NRSV is less trusting still: "See, he will kill me; I have no hope." And the Anchor Bible offers the defiant, "He may slay me, I'll not quaver."

Scholars have created various guidelines to help the text critic. Although the guides don't always work perfectly, they are generally helpful. The most frequently cited is: the more difficult the reading, the more likely it is to be original. For example, in Exodus 1:22, the Hebrew (MT) reads: "Then Pharaoh commanded all his people, 'Every son that is born you shall throw into the Nile, but you shall let every daughter live.'" The Septuagint, noting that Pharaoh's command, as worded, would have required the death of the Egyptian sons as well, adds the phrase "to the Hebrews" after "son," and it is the Septuagint that is followed by most English translations in this case. The Hebrew likely is the original, for it is evident why the Septuagint put in the clarification. Yet the Hebrew is not itself necessarily untrue: Pharaoh's original command anticipates the death also of the Egyptian boys, in the tenth plague. The Hebrew offers subtle foreshadowing; the Greek offers technical clarification.

Along with text-critical issues, which are substantially based in variant manuscript traditions, we have the basic problems of translation. Should Song of Solomon 1:5 be translated "I am black, but beautiful," and so indicate that usually darkness of skin and beauty are antithetical? That would be the conclusion drawn from the next verse, "Do not gaze at me because I am dark, because the sun has gazed on me." Unlike elite women who would stay indoors or who would veil in the sunlight, the heroine has allowed herself, or has been forced to be, outside. Or should we read, as does the NRSV, "I am black and beautiful," seeing no contradiction between the terms?

A similar problem concerns the identification of Hagar, Sarah's slave who becomes Abraham's wife and bears his child Ishmael. Should she be identified as a "handmaid" (Gen. 16:1, KJV) or "maidservant" (JPS) or "slave-girl" (NRSV)? The Hebrew term here, *shifchah*, is appropriately translated "female slave" (e.g., Jer. 34:9, NRSV). The terms "handmaid," "maidservant," and "slave-girl" have different connotations: The first sounds comparatively genteel; the second suggests a lower-class role that emphasizes the servant; the third adds a note of infantalism ("girl") as well as makes subservience and lack of freedom explicit. How we translate thus tells us something not only about the text, but about our own cultural concerns.

Literary Conventions

One means by which the biblical text shows its artistry is in wordplay; another is in its use of literary convention. Through repetition of scenes, withholding of motive, subtle shifts in vocabulary, and evocation of external literature, the narrative takes on richness and nuance.

Today, the idea of a literary convention is well known. Genres are one form of convention. If we pick up a paperback with a cover depicting a well-muscled, long-haired man holding in his arms a beautiful woman with impressive décolletage, we can presume we are not reading the Congressional Record or a textbook on quantum mechanics. We can expect to find instead lots of passionate emoting, rapacious barons, daring pirates, high adventure, and moderately chaste sex scenes.

We can locate the conventions in the literature of Israel by noting repeated scenes. For example, in four scenes a man meets a woman at a well. First, in Genesis 24, Abraham's servant encounters the beautiful, hospitable, virginal, and very active (the subject of eleven active verbs in Genesis 24:16–20) Rebekah, the perfect wife for Abraham's son Isaac. Second, in Genesis 29, Rebekah and Isaac's son Jacob, fleeing from his brother Esau, stops by a well, where, along with negotiating with the local men (thus showing his interests in political alliance), he encounters his cousin, the beautiful, virginal, but less active Rachel. Jacob removes a stone from the well and draws the water. But it is love at first sight, and following a number of machinations Jacob and Rachel marry.

In Exodus 2, Moses, fleeing Egypt after having killed a slave master, in complete exhaustion stops by a well. By now readers expect he will meet his future bride, and so he does, as seven daughters of the priest of Midian stop to water their flocks. But here there is no matchmaker like Abraham's servant, and there is no love at first sight, as with Jacob. Moses "saves" the women by driving away the shepherds who attempt to interfere with their obtaining water for their flocks, and the women, having had an easy job for the day, return home. When they return, their father asks why they are early. They reply, "An Egyptian helped us against the shepherds; he even drew water for us and watered our flock." Their father says, "Where is he? Why did you leave the man? Invite him to break bread" (2:18–20). The poor priest is desperate: seven daughters, not a husband in sight, and suddenly an "Egyptian" who can fight off shepherds and help take care of the flock—this is son-in-law material of the best kind. It should not surprise when the next verse reads, "Moses agreed to stay with the man, and he gave Moses his daughter Zipporah in marriage."

Three scenes with wells and three marriages. Each scene portrays different characters, and the matches are arranged in different ways, but the convention is now securely in place. In 1 Samuel, another well scene surfaces, as Saul, a handsome young member of the tribe of Benjamin, goes in search of his father's lost donkeys. As Saul and his servant go up the hill to the town, they meet some girls coming to draw water (9:11). Attractive man, women coming to draw water; we know what to expect. But instead of arranging a marriage, Saul asks the women for advice on where to find the local seer, who can help locate the lost donkeys. The women point Saul in the direction of the seer (who turns out to be the prophet Samuel), and Saul follows their advice. The convention is incomplete; Saul does not fulfill the expectation of marrying one of the women. Thereby the biblical author tells attentive readers that just as Saul did not fulfill the convention of marrying a woman at a well, so he will not complete the task to which he will shortly be appointed; Samuel will anoint the young man to be king over Israel, but Saul will lose Samuel's support and eventually be replaced by David.

The convention of the woman at the well and talk of marriage appears in the New Testament as well. In John 4, Jesus (here the eligible Jewish bachelor) meets a Samaritan woman at a well and, as might be expected, they talk about marriage. However, it turns out that the Samaritan woman has been married five times and is currently living with someone to whom she is not married. She is not ideal "wife" material. And yet a match of sorts does take place, since through her efforts, the people in her village come to believe in Jesus.

Other conventions include the motifs of a husband passing his wife off as his sister (Abraham and Sarah, twice, Gen. 12; 20; Isaac and Rebekah, Gen. 26); the Jew in the court of a foreign king (Joseph in Egypt, Gen. 40–50; Daniel in Babylon and then Persia, Dan. 1–6; Mordecai and Esther in Persia); and the annunciation of a birth. With the annunciation convention, the text moves from pathos to high humor. The first annunciation is to Hagar, who is not an elite or an Israelite insider, but a pregnant Egyptian slave fleeing from her mistress (Gen. 16:11). Then in the second iteration the mistress, Sarah, overhears a prediction that she will have a child. Given that she is postmenopausal, her response is one of laughter and incredulity (18:12).

Next is Rebekah, who suffers from infertility, but then suffers again through a painful pregnancy. To Rebekah, the heavenly messenger helpfully states, "Two nations are in your womb, and two peoples born of you shall be divided; the one shall be stronger than the other, the elder shall serve the younger" (Gen. 25:23). The prediction comes to pass as the younger, Jacob, tricks the elder, Esau, out of his birthright and blessing.

Jacob marries the beautiful Rachel as well as her weak-eyed older sister, Leah. As Jacob had tricked his older brother, so Laban, the father of Rachel and Leah, tricks Jacob by substituting the older daughter for the younger on Jacob's first wedding night (Gen. 29:26). Leah, the less-loved, is loved sufficiently that she continues to have children. Rachel cannot bear her lack of children, and cries to Jacob, "Give me children or I shall die" (30:1). She receives no annunciation; the convention works because here it is expected, but does not appear. Rachel, ironically, predicts her fate: she will die giving birth to her second son, Benjamin.

The next annunciation occurs in Judges 13, the story of the birth of Samson. This version is high comedy. Out of the blue, an angel appears to Mrs. Manoah and states, "Although you are barren, having borne no children, you shall conceive and bear a son." She had expressed no desire for a child; no background on her family is given; no specific worthiness has been manifested on her part or that of her husband. The unexpected continues, as the angel gives the woman prenatal advice: "Now be careful not to drink wine or strong drink, or to eat anything unclean, for you shall conceive and bear a son. No razor is to come on his head, for the boy shall be a nazirite to God from birth. It is he who shall begin to deliver Israel from the hand of the Philistines" (13:4–5).

The woman then tells her husband about what transpired. She does not explicitly state that the man was an angel; her words could suggest, rather, that she found the man attractive and charismatic: "A man of God came to me, and his appearance was like that of an angel of God, most awe-inspiring; I did not ask him where he came from, and he did not tell me his name." Next, she does not exactly report what the angel instructed. She omits the point about the razor coming near his head (that missing razor will reappear when Delilah shaves Samson's head), but she adds a reference to "the day of his death" and thus anticipates his tragic end (13:7).

Manoah, who is not the sharpest Danite in the neighborhood, then prays that the "man of God" will return to teach them what they are to do "concerning the boy who will be born." The request is a bit silly, since the angel had already provided the instruction. But the request is nevertheless fulfilled. The angel comes again to the woman, this time "as she sat in the field." Why was she in the field? The text offers no reason; it simply notes "Manoah was not with her." The woman runs to find her husband, who, upon arriving, demands information about the child. The angel, perhaps exasperated, repeats: "Let the woman give heed to all that I said to her."

Manoah, having no part in the instructions regarding the pregnancy, wants to hold on to the angelic connection, so he invites the angel to lunch ("Allow us to detain you, and prepare a kid for you"). Attentive readers will be reminded of the earlier scene in which Sarah overhears the message that she will become pregnant; in each case the husband had expressed hospitality to heavenly messengers (see Gen. 18). But Manoah is no Abraham, and the angel is not inclined to eat. He instead hints strongly that instead of being worried about lunch, Manoah would do well to offer a sacrifice of thanksgiving. When Manoah does make this sacrifice, the angel leaps into the flame and ascends to heaven. Finally, Manoah realizes he has been talking with an angel. But rather than rejoice, Manoah becomes fearful and exclaims to his wife, "We shall surely die, for we have seen God" (13:22). Mrs. Manoah has to reassure her husband that they are not about to die, because she's pregnant, and to die now would prevent the predictions from coming true. The child is eventually born and, somewhat clueless like his father, will nevertheless begin the process of gaining independence from the Philistines. Yet her reference to his death anticipates the end of his story: blinded, chained, and brought out to amuse his Philistine captors, he destroys them, their temple, and himself in a final act of strength.

By this point in the biblical text, the "annunciation" convention is sufficiently established that its *absence* can also be recognized. Second Kings 4 describes how the "great woman" (4:8; NRSV: "wealthy woman") of Shunem aids the prophet Elisha, to the point of building him a small apartment attached to her house. In gratitude, the prophet asks her if he might reciprocate; he is thinking in political rather than personal terms: "Would you have a word spoken on your behalf to the king or to the commander of the army?" (4:13), but the woman declines. When he then inquires of his servant Gehazi, "What may be done for her?" the servant replies, "Well, she has no son, and her husband is old" (4:14). The plot is already in place. When Elisha then announces to the women, who like Mrs. Manoah had expressed no desire for a child, she doubts him. Sounding like a second Sarah, she exclaims, "No, my lord, O man of God; do not deceive your servant." But, like Sarah, she conceives and bears a son.

The text then draws on the Genesis story again by describing how this son almost dies, and how the prophet, practicing what resembles a form of mouth-to-mouth resuscitation, restores him to life: "Then he got up on the bed and lay upon the child, putting his mouth upon his mouth, his eyes upon his eyes, and his hands upon his hands; and while he lay bent over him, the flesh of the child became warm" (4:34). The boy is a second Isaac: conceived by a woman in her old age, conceived despite doubt, threatened with death, and yet revived. Second Kings thus comments on Genesis, just as Genesis comments on 2 Kings. Each repetition of a convention adds richness to all the texts involved.

Readers of the New Testament should recognize the annunciation convention as well, since it takes its name from the "annunciation" of the angel Gabriel to Mary that she will have a child. This miraculous conception, accomplished through the Holy Spirit and not through any human male involvement, according to the Gospel of Matthew (1:18, 20), is one step more miraculous than a conception by a postmenopausal woman. The Gospel of Luke makes this clear, since this text prefaces the story of Mary with the story of her cousin Elizabeth, an elderly, pious, Jewish woman who has no child. Elizabeth's husband, the priest Zechariah, receives an annunciation from Gabriel, and he and his wife do have a son: John the Baptist.

Characterization

Samson, whose annunciation story involves an aware mother and a less-than-aware father, seems to take after the paternal side of his family. He is given no interior monologue, which should not surprise, and his motives are abundantly clear. With Samson, what we see is what we get. This is not the case with a number of other biblical figures, especially women. The Hebrew text often suppresses the thoughts of the characters, and thus their motives have to be imputed by readers. Here are three examples.

The first case, the famous account of the meeting of David and Bathsheba (2 Sam. 11) raises questions for readers. What did Uriah the Hittite, Bathsheba's husband, know, and when did he know it? It raises as well the same question about Bathsheba, whose motives are also suppressed. The text opens with the narrator's judgmental statement that at the time of the year when kings go out to war, David remained in Jerusalem. However, the affairs to which he was attending were not affairs of state.

Rather than shoring up Jerusalem's economic infrastructure, the great king, "late one afternoon . . . rose from his couch and was walking about on the roof of the king's house, [and] he saw from the roof a woman bathing; the woman was very beautiful" (2 Sam. 11:2). Although aware that Bathsheba is both the daughter and the wife of members of his military, and that the entire military is fighting the Ammonites, David sends messengers to "get" Bathsheba. No Hollywood romance, the relationship is described simply, "She came to him, and he lay with her." The narrator, however, does not tell us what Bathsheba was thinking. Did she know that David took his afternoon constitutional on the palace roof at the same time each day? When he saw her, had she seen him? Had she planned for him to see her? Was her reaction upon being summoned worry (had the king news of her husband's death?), pride (did she think Uriah had acquitted himself heroically in battle?), or satisfaction (got him!)?

This one event leads to conception. That Bathsheba had been purifying herself after the completion of her menstruation indicates that David is the father. Bathsheba sends word to the king that she is pregnant. What she wants him to do, however, remains unstated. Perhaps she wants him to marry her (dispatching her first husband along the way). Perhaps she wants him to pray that she miscarries or find her an abortionist. Perhaps she hopes he will send for her husband, so that Uriah's paternity can be claimed. Perhaps she is panicked and hopes David will know what to do.

David recalls Uriah from the front. But what did Uriah know? The messengers who brought Bathsheba to the palace, the palace functionaries who saw her there, the messengers who brought news of the pregnancy from Bathsheba to David—all knew of the relationship. David greets Uriah warmly, and after a bit of small talk advises him to return to his home to "wash his feet." That in biblical Hebrew "feet" is a euphemism for male genitalia makes David's wish less than innocent. The king even sends a present. But Uriah chooses instead to remain with the "servants of his lord." Informed that Uriah did not go home, David coaxes him, and Uriah refuses: "The ark and Israel and Judah remain in booths; and my lord Joab and the servants of my lord are camping in the open field; shall I then go to my house, to eat and to drink, and to lie with my wife? As you live, and as your soul lives, I will not do such a thing" (2 Sam. 11:11). The third night, David gets Uriah drunk, but the soldier remains in the palace. Does he refuse to return home because of loyalty to his fellow soldiers and to the Israelite tradition of holy war indicated by the presence of the ark in the field? In holy war, men are to be celibate. Or did he realize David's agenda and think to himself that the only way he could retain his honor was to refuse to acquiesce to the plot? Did he suspect his wife of infidelity? Did he realize that by refusing to return home he was signing his death warrant?

A second example of how suppressed emotions and motives, coupled with another good example of a problem in translation, impact how readers understand the text appears in Judges 4, the first recounting of the story of Deborah. Judges 4:4 introduces, as the NRSV puts it, Deborah as "a prophetess, wife of Lappidoth." This is a fine translation, but not the only one. The Hebrew for "wife of Lappidoth," *eshet lapidot*, can also be translated "woman of flames." The words for "wife of" and "woman of" are the same, and there is no Mr. Lappidoth featured in this text. Nor is there any fellow named Lappidoth found elsewhere in the Bible. That Deborah's military companion is a fellow named Barak, which is Hebrew for "lightning," does commend the reference to flames. Then again, perhaps both translations are appropriate.

The question of motive arises when we meet the second woman in the story, Jael, wife of Heber the Kenite. Deborah and Barak have defeated the enemy forces, but their leader, Sisera, escapes on foot. He arrives at Jael's tent, and he expects to be safe there, since Heber had separated himself from his fellow Kenites, relatives of Moses's father-in-law. Jael not only welcomes him to her tent, but also covers him with a blanket and brings him warm milk. Then, when he is fast asleep, "she went softly to him and drove the peg into his temple, until it went down into the ground" (Judg. 4:21). Her motive, however, is not given. Had she disagreed with Heber's decision to separate from Israel (that Heber, like Mr. Lappidoth, never appears in the text should give us some pause)? Did she seek to protect herself from Sisera's attack? Was she sociopathic?

Changes in description, which can indicate changes in motive, also enhance the artistry of biblical narrative. The story of Jael provides a good example. Judges 4 is a narrative description of the military success of Deborah and Barak as well as the demise of Sisera "by the hand of a woman" (in ancient Southwest Asia, an extremely dishonorable way of dying). But the story is recounted again, this time in poetic form, in Judges 5. The "Song of Deborah" is considered by some to be one of the oldest pieces of Hebrew literature in the Bible, though the evidence is shaky. In this song, Deborah celebrates Jael's actions:

> Most blessed of women be Jael,
> the wife of Heber the Kenite,
> of tent-dwelling women most blessed.
> He asked water and she gave him milk,
> she brought him curds in a lordly bowl.
> She put her hand to the tent peg
> and her right hand to the workmen's mallet;
> she struck Sisera a blow,
> she crushed his head,

she shattered and pierced his temple.
He sank, he fell,
he lay still at her feet;
at her feet he sank, he fell;
where he sank, there he fell dead. (5:24–27)

In the prose account, Sisera is lying in bed, asleep from weariness. In the poem, he appears to be standing up. Also, by detailing Sisera's death as sinking, as falling literally "between her feet," the poem adds a sexual component to his death. Finally, the poem develops maternal images. It opens with Deborah identifying herself as a "mother in Israel"; it ends with a depiction of Sisera's mother looking out the window and waiting for her son to return with the spoils of victory; in between is the bad mother, who provides milk and then death. Like the classical Greek narratives—of Oedipus, Electra, Medea—that depict the human concerns of *eros* and *thanatos*, of sex and death, so too the Bible taps into these concerns and, here in poetry, brings them to the surface.

Finally there is Delilah, whose name has echoes of the Hebrew word for "night" (it probably derives from a term meaning "to hang," as in to have loose hair). Samson, whose name reflects the Hebrew *shemesh*, meaning "sun," is eclipsed by this woman with whom he falls in love (Judg. 16:4). The text does not mention how Delilah feels about him. Nor are her motives regarding the betrayal of her lover explicit. Judges 16:5 depicts the "lords of the Philistines" telling Delilah to discover the secret of Samson's strength; in reward, they will each give her "eleven hundred pieces of silver," which is an enormous sum. But given the enmity between Samson and the Philistines and factoring in the death of Samson's first wife at the hands of the Philistines, perhaps Delilah had no choice. She could be betraying Samson out of greed, out of fear for her own life, or for patriotic reasons (she would be regarded as a Philistine heroine), or perhaps she is simply frustrated with her Hebraic Hercules. The Hebrew text remains silent as to her motive.

Adding one more element to the complexity of her characterization is the fact that, although Samson lies to her repeatedly, she never lies to him. Adding another, the text identifies her as living in the "valley of Sorek," which is between Israelite and Philistine territory, but it never makes her ethnicity explicit. She may be, to paraphrase Cher, "a vamp, a scamp, and a bit of a tramp," but she is also a fascinating, ultimately mysterious literary figure for whom the eternal question remains, in the equally immortal words of Tom Jones: "Why, why, why, Delilah?"

Concerns for retelling a story, such as with Judges 4 and 5, combine with the complex portrayal of female characters in Genesis 39, the account of Joseph and Mrs. Potiphar. Joseph, the beloved son of Jacob and Rachel, is sold into slavery in Egypt. The text notes that "Joseph was handsome and good-looking, and after a time his master's wife cast her eyes on Joseph and said, 'Lie with me.'" Joseph refuses, despite her daily invitations. Desperate, she grabs his garment, but he flees, leaving her with his one piece of clothing. At this point, Mrs. Potiphar has to explain why Joseph is naked and his clothes are in her hand. To the servants, she says: "See, my husband has brought among us a Hebrew to insult us! He came in to me to lie with me, and I cried out with a loud voice." Her focus is on Joseph's ethnic identity, and she creates loyalty among the staff by appealing to their common Egyptian identity. When Potiphar returns home, she states: "The Hebrew servant, whom you have brought among us, came in to me to insult me" (39:17). The appeal is one of class: she and the husband are the masters, Joseph, the slave.

There is in this story a literary trail that began with Joseph's long-sleeved tunic or, as the popular but less accurate translation puts it, "coat of many colors." Jacob, showing the sort of favoritism that destroys families and keeps psychiatrists in business, bestowed this coat upon Joseph, his favorite son of his favorite wife. The coat, along with Joseph's reporting of dreams in which his family would bow down to him, prompted envy among his brothers. Throwing Joseph in a pit and eventually selling him to Ishmaelites (thus evoking the memory of the slave Hagar and her son, Ishmael, expelled from Abraham's camp), the brothers dip his coat in the blood of a goat and allow Jacob to believe that Joseph had been killed by a wild animal. The coat serves as false evidence. Now again, the garment in the hands of Mrs. Potiphar serves as false evidence. As Joseph's story continues, his dress will help fool his brothers, who do not recognize him when they come to Egypt in search of food. The connecting clothing brings coherence to the narrative, and satisfaction to readers.

Joseph is thrown in jail. Perhaps Potiphar recognized his wife's obsession or her lies and thus chose not to kill Joseph; death would have been the expected punishment for a slave who attempted to rape his owner's wife. Or perhaps Potiphar also found Joseph attractive. For the biblical text, Mrs. Potiphar gets away with her false accusations. Like Delilah, her fate is not recorded. This gave later interpreters an opening for more stories. The Qur'an devotes an entire section (Sura 12) to Joseph. Islamic legend suggests that Mrs. Potiphar, named Zuleika, loses her wealth and her beauty. She lives alone like a Christian penitent, but she continues to think of Joseph. Upon seeing that she had grown old and ugly, Joseph not only takes pity on her and brings her to his palace; he also prays that she be restored to youth and health. The angel Gabriel restores Zuleika, and she and Joseph then marry.

Another example of subtle changes in description appears in the book of Ruth. In the middle of the night, on the threshing floor, Ruth, the faithful Moabite widow, convinces Boaz, the richest man in town, to marry her (readers will have to wait until Chapter 10, the discussion of sexuality, for full details). Boaz, along with his promises, gives Ruth six measures of barley. When Ruth returns home, barley in hand and marriage in the offing, she tells her mother-in-law, Naomi: "He gave me these six measures of barley, for he said, 'Do not go back to your mother-in-law empty-handed'" (3:17). Boaz had said no such thing—at least it's not in the text.

For a final example of how dialogue contributes to characterization, coupled with the repetition of a scene, we return first to Ruth's great-grandson, King David. Years have passed since he met Bathsheba. David arranged the death of Uriah and married Bathsheba, and the child conceived from that first meeting died. The couple have another child, Solomon. When David is on his deathbed, Bathsheba and the prophet Nathan, who had earlier condemned David for his sins regarding Uriah, approach him. Bathsheba, prompted by Nathan, says to David, "My lord, you swore to your servant by YHWH your God, saying: Your son Solomon shall succeed me as king, and he shall sit on my throne" (1 Kings 1:17). She then reports that Solomon's rival (and David's son) Adonijah has made arrangements to take the throne. Nathan enters and repeats Bathsheba's concerns. David, who is twice described as "old" (1:1, 15), agrees: "As I swore to you by YHWH, the God of Israel, 'Your son Solomon shall succeed me as king, and he shall sit on my throne in my place,' so will I do this day" (1:30). The problem is the text nowhere depicts David as making this promise. Readers will never know if Nathan concocted a plan to preserve his own position of power; if Bathsheba was a dupe or a willing accomplice or a wife faithful to David's wishes; if David remembered a promise, was too incapacitated to remember what he had done, or realized that Solomon would be his best successor and therefore agreed to go along with the ruse.

This story recapitulates Genesis 27, the first account of a bedridden father, a manipulative mother, rival sons, and the question of inheritance. When Isaac was old and could not see, he called his elder son, Esau, and told him to prepare savory food, so that he could bless him before he died (27:1). Overhearing this conversation, Rebekah arranges for Jacob to take his brother's place. Her motives are not entirely clear. She had received the angelic announcement that "the one shall be stronger than the other, the elder shall serve the younger" (25:23). Did she think she was doing God's will by aiding Jacob? If so, why not share the news with Isaac? Perhaps she realized that her older son would not be a fitting leader. A man of the wild, Esau thinks with his stomach. When Jacob convinced Esau to barter his birthright for a bowl of lentil stew, Esau's less than subtle personality came to the fore. As the narrator puts it: "Esau said, 'Let me chow down on that red, red stuff.' . . . And he ate, and drank, and rose, and went and despised, did Esau, the birthright" (25:30, 34).

Rebekah fixes dinner, fetches some of Esau's clothes for Jacob to wear, and covers her younger son's hands and neck with goatskin so that they would feel hairy. Jacob brings the dinner to Isaac, who remarks, "The voice is Jacob's voice, but the hands are the hands of Esau" (Gen. 27:22). After checking several times to make sure the son is Esau, he offers the blessing. Readers knowing of Rebekah's ruse may recall it when Bathsheba comes to David about Solomon. Readers knowing of Jacob's rise to power may associate him with Solomon; they are both figures who use their brains rather than military might to achieve their ends. The repetition of images enhances the complexity of the literature, and thus readers' appreciation.

Different Stories, Different Authors

Shared themes and rhetorical techniques within the biblical narrative do not indicate unity of authorship. Just as television shows can use the same form (the situation comedy, the medical drama, the western, the talk show, the soap opera), but reflect different authors, so too the biblical text, despite connections, offers multiple authors, settings, and viewpoints. To locate these distinctions, biblical studies has developed a number of approaches.

Form criticism, which originated in the late nineteenth century in folklore studies, looks at how the same literary structure takes on different characteristics. For example, the prophets adopt the "woe oracle" form, which characteristically begins, "Woe to you . . . ," and goes on to explain to whom and why. The news is never good. Variants of the form include "Woe to us" (1 Sam. 4:7) and "Woe to me" (Job 10:15).

Another form is an etiology, or a story that explains origins. Why do snakes crawl on their bellies? Genesis 3:14 explains their ancestor was cursed by God for having tricked the woman into eating the forbidden fruit. Why is there a rainbow in the sky? Because God placed his bow (a weapon of war) in the heavens as a sign of the peaceful covenant made with Noah and his descendants that the world will never again be destroyed by flood (Gen. 9:13). Why were there ruins near Bethel, with a "great heap of stones that remains to this day" (Josh. 7:26)? Because Joshua led the Israelite troops to destroy a city called Ai (the name itself means "heap [of ruins]," which suggests that the original name had been lost, along with the original story of the destruction). The heap of stones had its origin in the story of Achan, an Israelite who took booty from Ai when everything was supposed to be dedicated to God (i.e., destroyed). When his treachery was discovered by lottery, Achan, along with his family, his animals, and his goods, was stoned and then burned. The heap of stones remains a warning, and the story a cautionary tale, to any who would take what belongs to God or violate the rules of holy war.

One way of imagining the form-critical approach is to picture a series of houses, all constructed on the same blueprint. The layout of the rooms will be the same, but the colors, the furnishings, and the inhabitants will differ. Another, more faithful to the origins of this method, looks at contemporary urban legends, the modern version of the folktale. These stories are usually passed down from "a friend of a friend," they cannot be verified, they often have a social or moral import, and they are memorable. In one example, a person goes to a local fast-food restaurant, orders a meal, takes a bite, and finds something unpleasant. Then the details appear. The person is a young American bride, the store is a fast-food restaurant, the meal is the extra crispy, and in her mouth she finds her wedding ring that she had accidentally dropped down the sewer the day before. The social import of the story is that young wives should prepare home-cooked meals and one should distrust corporate franchises. A similar story is told in western Europe, the food store is owned by immigrants, and the social import is fear of non-Western neighbors. The social context is, in the German technical terminology of biblical studies, called the *Sitz im Leben,* the "life setting."

In applying the form-critical model to biblical materials, we can see how the stories reflect cultural values. A favorite test case is the story of the flood (Gen. 6–9) or, more broadly, stories of universal destruction and reconstitution. The plot, or form, of these stories is relatively consistent in outline: the earth is to be destroyed, and one hero or family escapes. The differences between the stories then reveal distinct cultural interests. For example, in ancient Southwest Asia, the destruction is caused by flood; this would fit cultures that experienced the flooding of the Nile, the Euphrates, and the Tigris. In British Guiana and Bengal, the destruction is caused by fire; in Zoroastrian records, the cause is a freeze.

The prompt for the destruction also differs. In Iceland the cause is a war between giants. In New Zealand two sages create a rain spell that gets out of hand. In the Bible, "YHWH saw that the wickedness of humankind was great in the earth, and that every inclination of the thoughts of their hearts was only evil continually. And YHWH was sorry that he had made humankind on the earth, and it grieved him to his heart" (Gen. 6:5–6).

The heroes vary from a single man (India), to a man and a coyote (Native American traditions), to a man and a female dog who becomes a woman (Mexico), to Noah and his family. The escape is facilitated by a boat (ancient Southwest Asia and Greece), a woman's hair entangled in a tree (Sumatra), a giant eagle (Philippines), or a very large nutshell (Lithuania).

Flood stories inundated ancient Southwest Asian literature. Sumer told of Ziusudra, king of Shuruppak (ca. 1600 BCE); the Akkadians spoke of Utnapishtim, who appears in the *Epic of Gilgamesh,* tablet 11 (probably from the mid-second millennium BCE, with parts extending another millennium back in time); preserved in cuneiform fragments as well as in Old Babylonian and Neo-Assyrian accounts is the Atrahasis epic (ca. 1700 BCE?). Berossus, the third-century BCE Babylonian historian, records a flood story in his *Babylonaika,* and the Roman poet Ovid (43 BCE–17 CE) recounts the survival of a flood by the Phrygian couple Philemon and Baucis. By looking at the biblical version, especially compared with these other ancient Southwest Asian tales, we can see cross-cultural influence as well as distinct biblical concerns.

According to the Bible, Noah was 600 years old (60×10); according to the Sumerian account, the flood hero Ziusudra was 36,000 years old ($60^2 \times 10$). Both ages are fantastic, which tells us that the genre of these stories is "myth" or "folktale," not objective history. "Myth" here means a story, usually set in the distant past when the normal rules of physics do not apply (i.e., that world is not our world), that offers a summary of a cultural worldview; it explains how life as we do know it came to be; it expresses our hopes and fears. It is true, in the same way that a parable is true. The term is not meant to disparage.

Noah's ark has the dimensions 300 by 50 by 30 cubits (which yields another multiple of 60). In the Babylonian version, which is part of the Gilgamesh epic, the flood hero Utnapishtim builds a boat measuring 120 cubits per side, that is, a cube. The biblical ark has no rudder; Noah is not a skipper, and his fate rests in the hands of God. The interest in his "ark" (Heb. *tevah*) will reappear in the story of the infancy of Moses, when his mother prepares an "ark" (*tevah*, Exod. 2:3, 5; here the term is usually translated "basket"), places the child in it, and sets the ark on the bank of the river. The symbolism is profound: the children of Israel are being drowned in the Nile by orders of Pharaoh, who thinks of himself as divine, and the preservation of the people rests with this one inhabitant of this one little ark.

In the biblical version, Noah preserves on the ark his wife, his three sons and their wives, and all animals, whether "two of each kind" (Gen. 6:19) or "seven pairs of all beasts that are ritually clean, and one pair of all beasts that are not clean" (7:2). In the Babylonian version, Utnapishtim takes on board plants and craftspeople. Utnapishtim weeps when he learns about humanity's destruction, but Noah neither weeps nor pleads on humans' behalf. The Babylonian story displays an interest in urban civilization. In comparison, for the early parts of the biblical narrative, urban culture is treated with ambivalence. The father of musicians and metalworkers is Lamech, the violent descendant of the equally violent Cain (4:17–24). For a final distinction, whereas Utnapishtim and Ziusudra are granted immortality, Noah is neither adventurous nor godlike. He may be "a righteous man, blameless in his generation" (6:9), but, given his generation, this is not much of a compliment.

The biblical account of the flood can be divided into two stories. In one, the animals go on two by two. In the other, only the unclean animals go two by two; the kosher animals go seven by seven. It appears the original version has been edited to fit the concerns of the dietary regulations. This interest in editing introduces another method for approaching the text: *redaction criticism*. Whereas the form critic looks at separate elements of a story, the redaction critic looks at the editorial whole and attempts to determine the style as well as the agenda of the editor. Some scholars think that priestly writers, who were concerned about things such as clean and unclean foods, added the note about the clean animals. Others propose the distinction stems from the J writer (see below, page 222).

The various peoples who comprised Israel—the twelve tribes described in the Torah, the other tribes who joined them such as the Calebites and the Kenites, the resident aliens and the traveling merchants, Canaanite and Philistine neighbors—all told stories, and those stories would have developed as they were passed down orally from one generation to the next, from one town to the next. Eventually, they were compiled by editors and sewn into a narrative whole. At times the seams can be located, and there the hand of the redactor is at work. Redaction criticism, as it developed in the early part of the twentieth century, initially saw these editors as working in somewhat of a cut-and-paste method; rather than creative writers themselves, they were seen more like organizers. Today, however, the artistry of the final form of a text, the "edited" form, is given as much recognition as that of the anterior materials.

The best example of the redactor's art might be the general history that runs from the book of Joshua through the end of 2 Kings. This collection is called the "Deuteronomistic History" because it presents a general view of the way life works based on the teachings of the book of Deuteronomy, namely, the righteous are rewarded and the wicked are punished.

In form criticism, the focus is on structural units and on narratives that were likely passed down through the oral tradition; redaction criticism looks at how the editor put those received stories together. A related approach, *source criticism,* looks at the individual literary sources, which can themselves represent a combination of oral tradition and editorial involvement.

For the Torah, the original view held by both synagogue and church was that Moses wrote the text. For those confused by the notion that Moses would have recorded his own death (Deut. 34:4ff.), the simple explanation was that God dictated the materials and Moses wrote with tears in his eyes. Exodus 24:4 does state that "Moses wrote down all the words of YHWH," Joshua 8:31 speaks of the "book of the law of Moses," and Ezra 6:18 mentions the "book of Moses." The claim for Mosaic authorship appears as well in early Jewish sources, such as the first-century Jewish historian Josephus (*Antiquities* 4) and his slightly older contemporary, the Jewish philosopher Philo of Alexandria (*Life of Moses*). Mark 12:26 and Acts 15:21 also suggest Mosaic authorship.

But even in antiquity, doubts began. A text called *4 Ezra* (or 2 Esdras), which appears in Jerome's Latin translation of the Old Testament (the Vulgate), records that the Torah had been destroyed during the Babylonian raid on Jerusalem in the sixth century BCE and that the prophet Ezra rewrote the text. The Christian philosopher Clement of Alexandria (ca. 150–211/216) insisted that Moses would not state that Noah had gotten drunk (Gen. 9), for that was certainly a lie.

With the Enlightenment, more serious questioning of Mosaic authorship began. Why would Moses, if he were the author, refer to himself in the third person? Why would he continually change the name of the deity (Elohim, YHWH, El Elyon, El Shaddai)? Why would he say that animals were created before humanity (Gen. 1), only to contradict himself and say that humanity was created prior to the animals (Gen. 2)? Why did he give three accounts of how Isaac received his name, with different explanations as to who laughed and why (Gen. 17; 18; 21)? He speaks sometimes of Mt. Sinai (Exod. 19) and other times of Mt. Horeb (Deut. 1)—did he not know where he received the Torah? Is his father-in-law named Jethro, Ruel, or Hobab? Why did he list the Ten Commandments twice and add thirty minor variants (Exod. 20; Deut. 5; see also Exod. 34:14–26, the so-called Ritual Decalogue)?

None of these problems was insurmountable for those who wanted to retain Mosaic authorship. The divine names could reflect different aspects of the deity; the so-called contradictions could be harmonized or explained as poetic license; the repetition of scenes could reflect the author's creativity; and so on. But these problems as well as apparent anachronisms in the Torah, such as references to domesticated camels, and to the Philistines, who did not arrive until about 1200 BCE, well past the date of Moses, suggested a later hand was involved in the editorial process. Discrepancies between what the law code mandated and what the biblical characters did, with no criticism of those actions, also suggested that perhaps the law code was later than the stories. How could Moses not have commented on Jacob's marrying two sisters, when this is forbidden by Leviticus 18:18? Why would Moses note Abraham's marriage to his half sister (Gen. 20:12), given Leviticus 18:9 and Deuteronomy 27:22? Why would Moses say, "At that time the Canaanites were in the land" (Gen. 12:6)? The phrase suggests the perspective of a much later writer.

By 1651, Thomas Hobbes (of *Leviathan* fame) claimed much of the Pentateuch was post-Mosaic; shortly thereafter Baruch Spinoza agreed.

Source criticism developed as multiple scholars suggested multiple sources lying behind the Pentateuch and extending into the Deuteronomistic History. In 1878, the famous German biblical scholar Julius Wellhausen assessed the various sources already suggested and ordered them by date. His Documentary Hypothesis, which still lives on today, albeit with numerous nuances and departures, proposes four major sources. After describing his highly influential proposal here, we will indicate ways in which scholars have changed it in recent years.

The Yawhist or J writer, dating around 900 BCE and working within court circles in Judah, provides narratives such as Genesis 2–3 (Adam and Eve). The hallmark of J is the use of the name YHWH for the deity, and the writing style tends to be direct and colorful. YHWH is described anthropomorphically, walking in the Garden of Eden (Gen. 3), observing construction of the Tower of Babel (Gen. 11), dining in disguise with Abraham (Gen. 18), and ambushing and almost killing Moses (Exod. 4:24–26).

Second is the Elohist or E writer, who identifies the deity as Elohim until Exodus 3, the story of the burning bush. Unlike J, E does not anthropomorphize Elohim, but pictures God as communicating to humans mainly through dreams (e.g., Gen. 20:3). It is the E writer, associated with the northern kingdom, just as J is associated with the southern kingdom, who offers the account of the near sacrifice of Isaac in Genesis 22. Typical of E's style, in Genesis 22:11 an angel stops Abraham from sacrificing Isaac. Since the northern kingdom was destroyed in 722 by the Assyrians, E must antedate that time. Perhaps composed in the early eighth century, the E writer's works were probably combined with J when northern refugees fled south.

The third source, according to Wellhausen's hypothesis, is called D, or the Deuteronomic writer. One of the prompts that called into question Mosaic authorship of the Torah was the account in 2 Kings 22:8–13, in which, during the reign of King Josiah (ca. 620 BCE), workers doing maintenance in the Jerusalem temple discover "the book of the law." The book is verified by the prophet Huldah. Josiah then implements a reform movement based on this book, including reinstituting the celebration of Passover (23:21–23), which had apparently been ignored for three centuries. Factual report, an excuse for religious reform, or a bit of both, this book may be connected to the laws in Deuteronomy 12–26, which are assigned to the D writer. The Deuteronomistic historians, responsible for Joshua,

Judges, 1–2 Samuel, and 1–2 Kings, follow the theological and ethical agenda Deuteronomy establishes.

Josiah began his reforms in the late seventh century BCE. In the early sixth century, Judah was conquered by the Babylonians, and the court, the scribes, the artisans, and many of the retainer class were taken into exile in Babylon. There the priests, in the successful attempt to prevent the people from assimilating, highlighted those practices that would keep them culturally distinct: Sabbath observance, dietary practices, and so on. The source responsible for this legal and cultic material is known as P, for the "priestly" writers. In its classical formulation, the Documentary Hypothesis suggests that these priests eventually combined their materials with those of J, E, and D to produce the full Pentateuch.

The Babylonian exile ended in 538 BCE, after the Persian empire, under Cyrus the Great, conquered the weakened Neo-Babylonian state. Although many of the exiles remained in Babylon (thus forming the beginning of the great Jewish community there that would produce, a millennium later, the Babylonian Talmud), others returned to Judah. There, with the leadership of scribes such as Ezra, they compiled at least the Torah and the Nevi'im and likely an early formal collection of Psalms as well. According to Nehemiah 8:1–3, Ezra assembled the people in Jerusalem and read to them the "book of the law of Moses." Although it is unlikely that this book was the Torah in the shape we now have it, the rudiments of the canon are here falling into place.

Wellhausen's Documentary Hypothesis survived well into the twentieth century, but has come under fire in more recent times. First, some of its early proponents inadvertently discredited the approach by pushing it beyond its reasonable limits. They proposed additional sources besides these four and commenced to divide up the text, even single verses, in a cut-and-paste manner that in the end simply proved implausible. Beginning in the 1970s, others took a different tack by dating the sources much later than Wellhausen suggested. One approach placed J in the sixth century, effectively throwing into confusion the logical sequence Wellhausen developed. Then literary critics began to protest that the repetitions and distinctive literary features highlighted by the source critics were, rather, more likely part of Hebrew narrative style, not an indication of different sources. Finally, the whole scenario of advanced literature arising during monarchic times became suspect, as many scholars came to regard the Persian period (539–331 BCE) and perhaps even the early Hellenistic period

(331–63) as the most likely context for the compilation of traditions and production of the literature. In addition, many interpreters moved away from historically oriented work of this type and instead found more useful the feminist, critical-race, sociohistorical, ideological, postcolonial, deconstructive, and ecological approaches to biblical interpretation.

Wellhausen's great source-critical work and its aftermath illustrate the dynamic character of biblical studies; the various reading strategies that have been applied to the Bible and the diverse results those strategies yield enhance that dynamic character. Each reading remains subject to evaluation, revision, and replacement. The end result is a more nuanced, more varied appreciation of the Hebrew Bible as we know it. Our focus in this volume is heavily but not exclusively historical-critical. We are interested in the Bible as it would have been understood in its original cultural context, but we are well aware how difficult, even impossible, it is to be certain that we know the details of that original context. We are inevitably hampered by difficulties in dating and in determining which reading strategy best provides the answers to the questions we ask. Thus we are also interested in viewing the texts from other perspectives—feminist, sociohistorical, ideological, and reception-historical (the ways in which the biblical text has been interpreted and appropriated by later communities). These methods are, at the base, also historical-critical in a sense, but they go well beyond the approaches taken by Wellhausen and cohorts a century ago.

One more type of biblical criticism fits into the trajectory of source, form, and redaction criticism. Called *canonical criticism,* this approach seeks the unifying themes of the entire collection. Canonical criticism tends, more than the three others, to be invested in a religious concern. Given the biblical anthology, canonical criticism seeks an overarching message. How, within the biblical diversity, is the religious community that holds the text sacred to interpret it? Numerous themes have been proposed as the central motif or uniting factor of the Old Testament (the choice of word is intentional, since canonical criticism has been primarily a Christian endeavor); covenant and law are two popular views. The problem with this endeavor is that it necessarily marginalizes one part of the text and enhances the other, and it also privileges the last voice over the earlier voices, that is, it primarily focuses on the last stages of the text when it finally became authoritative, and it downgrades the centuries and generations of contributors who developed the tradition to the point that it could even become canonized and authoritative. The canonical stage is significant, but no more so than all the stages in the tradition's evolution.

Canonization

The difficulty in dating the canonization of this collection also creates problems with interpretation. The term "canon," from the Greek term for "reed" and suggesting a measuring stick, refers to the collection of books recognized by a particular community as having special import. In antiquity, the "canon" of the Greek-speaking synagogue, the Septuagint in its various forms (for there is no single Greek text tradition), differed from that of Hebrew- and Aramaic-speaking congregations. Although rabbinic legend suggests that the Jewish community established the canon of the synagogue around the year 90 CE at a council in the town of Jamnia, south of present-day Tel Aviv, at that time the "rabbis" did not have the authority over all Jewish communities needed to make such a universal proclamation stick.

More likely, for the Hebrew scriptures, the Septuagint, and even the New Testament, the canonization process was as much, if not more, a matter of popular support than elite mandate. Rabbinic sources note debates, through the second century CE, about the canonicity of at least four books. Esther was debated, since the Hebrew text does not mention God; copies of Esther have not surfaced among the Dead Sea Scrolls, and it is possible that the community that copied these texts also did not consider Esther canonical. Song of Songs was debated because of its eroticism and because, as one legend has it, it was being sung in taverns; it achieves canonical status through its ascription to Solomon and on the allegorical reading that it depicts the deep love between God and Israel. The book of the great prophet Ezekiel received some discussion, because its image of the Jerusalem temple differed both from what Leviticus described and from what the Second Temple actually looked like. And Qohelet/Ecclesiastes was suspect, because of what were considered its fatalistic views. Like the Song of Songs, it also had the benefit of ascription to Solomon.

At least by around 200 CE the texts of the books that eventually became canonized were fairly fixed; that is, their wording was firmly set. However, they were written with only the consonantal letters, as was typical at the time. A few centuries later, the Masoretes, whom we met earlier in this chapter, began the process of meticulously copying and recopying the texts over the next four or five centuries. In the process, they developed a system of vowel points, comprising dots and short lines above, below, or inside the consonantal letters, to designate the vowels. With that essential development, the text became readable without having to rely on the old tradition of memorization and recitation.

The oldest Masoretic manuscript of the whole Hebrew Bible now in existence is the Leningrad Codex B19ᴬ, so named because it has been preserved in the Russian National Library in St. Petersburg (previously Leningrad), Russia, ever since the middle of the nineteenth century. It dates from approximately 1009 CE and now serves as the textual basis used by many scholars. A second and older Hebrew manuscript is the Aleppo Codex, dating from around 920 CE and now preserved in Jerusalem. Called the Keter, or "crown," of Aleppo, this text is superior to the Leningrad, since it stems from the famous ben Asher family of Masoretes. Unfortunately, only about 60 percent of the manuscript is now extant. However, even today, pieces continue to surface.

We thus know that by the tenth and perhaps even ninth century CE the books that comprise the Hebrew Bible were in place. Yet synagogues may well have been reading other texts along with the Hebrew (the Wisdom of Jesus ben Sirach, also known as Ecclesiasticus, a deuterocanonical text, is occasionally cited in rabbinic literature; Jews were also telling the stories of Judith and Susanna). Rabbinic literature shows concern that people are reading more texts than are in the rabbis' canon. *Midrash Qohelet* (12:12) sets a canon of twenty-four books, but notes that others add more.

Although the canon was eventually standardized, not all books received the same emphasis in the communities that held that canon sacred. This matter of emphasis may be inevitable—people choose which texts speak best to them. The synagogue foregrounds the Torah, the church foregrounds the Prophets (and especially those that are cited in the New Testament), and everyone likes the Psalms. Martin Luther downgraded the books of the Apocrypha to "meditative" status, in part because they were not included in the Jewish canon. The synagogue gives the book of Esther its own holiday (Purim); Luther wanted to toss it from the canon; typically, the only time it is cited in churches is on the Sunday dedicated to the woman's group, where the reading is Esther 4:14, "for just such a time as this."

Chapter 3

Land and Settlement

The story is told of twelve spies, each a leader of one of Israel's tribes, whom Moses sends into the land of Canaan, the promised land, to scout out the territory and the people living there (Num. 13–14). The Israelites have been passing through the Sinai Peninsula following their escape from Egypt, and after the theophany at Mt. Sinai they reach the Wilderness of Paran, on the northeastern side of Sinai and directly south of the land of Canaan. There Moses dispatches the spies to reconnoiter Canaan in preparation for their attack on the land. Entering from the south, the spies pass through the Negev desert and move on to Hebron and the wadi Eshcol, where they cut down a branch with a single cluster of grapes so full and weighty it needs to be carried hanging from a pole between two of them—an image used today as the logo for Israel's Ministry of Tourism. Over a period of forty days they continue their reconnaissance through the central highlands and the rest of the land, reaching Rehob in the far north.

Upon their return, the spies make a double report. First, they show the grapes they have brought with them, and they praise the lushness and fertility of the land, which, in their words, "flows with milk and honey." But then they add that the inhabitants of the land are fearsome, living in large fortified cities. Especially threatening are the Anakites, descendants of the giant Nephilim, compared to whom the spies felt like grasshoppers. While one of the spies, Caleb (joined later by Joshua), urges the people to proceed with an attack on the inhabitants, the other spies strike the opposite note, emphasizing that the land of Canaan "is a land that devours its inhabitants" (Num. 13:32). The Israelites become frightened and contemplate a mutiny against Moses (and God). As a result, God punishes them by declaring that none of this generation of Israelites will be allowed to enter the land of Canaan except for Caleb and Joshua. God condemns the people to forty years of wandering in the wilderness, one year for each day the spies were in the land of Canaan.

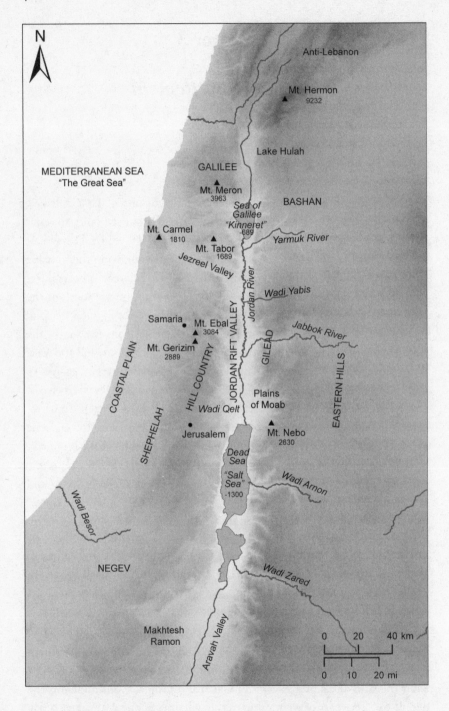

N

Anti-Lebanon

Mt. Hermon
9232

Lake Hulah

MEDITERRANEAN SEA
"The Great Sea"

GALILEE

Mt. Meron
3963

BASHAN

*Sea of
Galilee
"Kinneret"*
-689

Mt. Carmel
1810

Mt. Tabor
1689

Yarmuk River

Jezreel Valley

Jordan River

Wadi Yabis

Samaria

Mt. Ebal
3084

Jabbok River

Mt. Gerizim
2889

GILEAD

JORDAN RIFT VALLEY

EASTERN HILLS

HILL COUNTRY

Wadi Qelt

Plains
of Moab

COASTAL PLAIN

Jerusalem

Mt. Nebo
2630

SHEPHELAH

*Dead
Sea
"Salt
Sea"*
-1300

Wadi Arnon

Wadi Besor

NEGEV

Wadi Zared

Makhtesh
Ramon

Aravah Valley

0   20   40 km

0   10   20 mi

Topography of the Southern Levant

This tantalizing glimpse of the goodness of the land and then the frustrating forty-year delay before the people can experience it serve to underscore the key role played by the land in the Hebrew Bible. It is the object of Abraham's long migration from Ur, located near the Euphrates River and the Persian Gulf. (In the third and second millennia BCE, Ur was much closer to the Gulf than its ruins are now due to silting at the mouth of the Tigris and Euphrates.) According to Genesis, Abraham and his lineage settle in the southern Levant, and his grandson Jacob's generation relocates to Egypt due to famine. A later generation of Israelites conquers the land of Canaan under the leadership of Joshua, where they remain for the rest of the biblical narrative, with the exception of certain segments of the population that are taken away into exile or for other reasons (e.g., political pressures, economic distress, or famine) relocate to other lands such as Egypt or the Philistine region along the Mediterranean coast.

Israel's Environs

The Levant is the immediate context for Israel's history and the Hebrew Bible, even though the biblical texts often call attention to the wider Southwest Asian setting as well. The term "Levant" means "rising," referring to the rising of the sun. Thus from the perspective of the Mediterranean, the sun rises over the eastern shore, which includes the modern lands of Syria, Lebanon, Israel, and Gaza. The Levant is not just the shoreline but all the territory from the Mediterranean to but not including the great desert east of Syria and Jordan. Topographically the Levant includes a considerable variety of land types, from mountains and hill country to sharp escarpments and broad valleys, flowing rivers to seasonal wadis, lush to arid regions, and especially the distinctive Jordan Rift Valley.

The Israelites were only one of many ethnic groups in the region, as the Hebrew Bible recognizes. They shared the southern Levant with a number of other ethnic groups, such as those named by the spies—Anakites, Amalekites, Hittites, Jebusites, Amorites, and Canaanites, many of whom remained in the land even after the monarchy was founded. At the same time, the Israelites—at least those who wrote the Hebrew Bible—were somewhat aware of their larger world as well. Although the average Israelite would scarcely have had the opportunity for foreign travel unless compelled to it in the military or in exile, there were merchants, diplomatic envoys, and other governmental officials who traveled to other areas in the region.

Genesis 10 mentions a wide variety of other ethnic groups, some still recognizable and others no longer identifiable. Cast in the form of a genealogy, it seeks to demonstrate that Noah's offspring repopulated the world known to the Priestly authors of this chapter. Seventy names in the three generations following Noah appear in Genesis 10, and according to the text they become the ancestors, often eponymous, of prominent cultures in the region, among them: Shem, of the Semites; Javan, of the Ionian Greeks; Ashkenaz, of the Scythians; Kittim, of the city of Kition (today's Larnaca, Cyprus); Rodanim, perhaps of the inhabitants of Rhodes; Cush, of the people south of Egypt; Egypt, of the Egyptians; Put, of the people west of Egypt (today Libya); Caphtorim, of the Philistines; Canaan, of the Canaanites, the Amorites, and the Jebusites (the pre-Israelite city-state at Jerusalem); Sheba, of the Sabaeans; Nimrod, of the cities of Asshur, Erech, Akkad, and Nineveh; Sidon, of the Phoenician city bearing this name; Heth, of the Hittites; Elam, of the Elamites (in modern Iran); Asshur, of the Assyrians; Lud, of the Lydians (in modern Turkey); Aram, of the Arameans; and Eber, of the Hebrews. Though it is far from an exhaustive list, the number seventy symbolizes completeness, suggesting that this list represents the entirety of their known world.

Most of these peoples belonged to the general region between the eastern shores of the Mediterranean Sea and the northern coast of the Persian Gulf, in addition to Egypt and adjacent lands. The ancient Israelites had no general term for this region, but in recent centuries the area has gone by a variety of names, the most common being the Near East, the Middle East or Mideast, and the Greater Middle East. All of these terms are basically Eurocentric, reflecting their origin in the nineteenth-century perspective that defined the parts of the world from the standpoint of western Europe and England. At first the Near East denoted the Balkans, Turkey, and some adjacent areas, and Middle East applied to the area from Iran (Persia) through India. The Far East, then, was China, Japan, and Korea. After World War I and the fall of the Ottoman empire, "Middle East" became the dominant term for the area east of the Mediterranean as well as Egypt, although historians and archaeologists continued to use the phrase "ancient Near East." The name "Greater Middle East" appeared in political and financial circles after 2000 to designate the much larger economic area from all of North Africa to Pakistan.

An alternative term, used in this book, is "Southwest Asia," preferable because it avoids political boundaries that can change over time. Instead, it focuses on the geographical land mass of Asia, of which the area often called the Middle East occupies the southwest section. The contemporary political entities included in Southwest Asia are, alphabetically, Bahrain, the island of Cyprus, Iran, Iraq, Israel, Jordan, Kuwait, Lebanon, Oman, the Palestinian Territories, Qatar, Saudi Arabia, Syria, Turkey, United Arab Emirates, and Yemen. Egypt is conventionally grouped with these others even though it is located in northwest Africa.

Sweeping through Southwest Asia is a distinct swath of land known as the "Fertile Crescent," a term coined in 1916 by the American historian and Egyptologist James Henry Breasted. The Fertile Crescent extends in the form of a great arc beginning at the northwestern end of the Persian Gulf, moving northwest through Mesopotamia, then south through the Levant, and with an extension in Egypt's Nile River and Delta. The vast Arabian Desert and Syrian Desert mark the southern and eastern borders of the crescent, and on the northern side lie the Zagros and Taurus mountain chains. West of the Levantine portion is the Mediterranean, and south the Sinai Peninsula.

The "fertile" part of the Fertile Crescent refers above all to the areas around the Tigris, Euphrates, and Nile Rivers, each of which floods annually and waters extensive tracts along its banks. Other smaller rivers bring additional water from the mountainous regions to the lower lands. Extensive irrigation systems in ancient times, as also today, allowed for the arable land to reach well beyond the immediate vicinity of the rivers and sustain crops during low-water periods. Still, the Fertile Crescent was not entirely fertile as substantial semiarid sections break up the pattern, and without human intervention in the form of irrigation canals even some of the lowlands near the rivers would not be productive throughout the year.

Communication and contact followed a network of roads and paths developed over time as a result of economic and political needs. From their base in southern Mesopotamia, the Sumerians in the fourth millennium BCE were, to our knowledge, the first to build an extensive international trade system, using both overland roads and water transport. The network's extent and complexity grew throughout the Early Bronze Age (third millennium BCE) and later stretched from the Persian Gulf all the way to the Mediterranean, Asia Minor, the Levant, and Egypt.

Roads in antiquity fell far short of today's paved highways and transportation infrastructure, but the sheer complexity and utility of the ancient systems represent remarkable achievements of the times. Except for some short lengths for royal purposes near capital cities, especially during the Neo-Assyrian period in the first millennium BCE, the roads were unpaved, but road crews sometimes leveled the ground and demarcated the routes. An allusion to such work occurs in Isaiah 40:3–4, in which the exilic prophet known as Second Isaiah poetically announces the preparation of the road to lead the exiles from Babylon back to the land of Israel: "In the wilderness prepare the way of YHWH, make straight in the desert a highway for our God. Every valley shall be lifted up, and every mountain and hill be made low; the uneven ground shall become level, and the rough places a plain."

Centuries later the Romans greatly enhanced the road system they inherited, instituting more extensive use of paving stones set in a gravel or sand base to allow for easier passage of chariots and troops. Evidence of this road work is still visible in many parts of their realm. For example, the route the Romans followed from Jerusalem down to Jericho is still partly evident, and ruts from their chariots show on some of the bedrock.

By the time ancient Israel arrived on the scene in the late second millennium BCE, the transportation and communication network throughout Southwest Asia was advanced and regularly used. Two primary north–south international routes existed in the Levant: the Via Maris, the Way of the Sea, running from Egypt to northern Syria, where it connected with routes into Mesopotamia and Asia Minor; and the King's Highway (e.g., Num. 20:17), extending from the Gulf of Aqavah in the south, through Jordan, and to Damascus. Another artery ran from Megiddo to Damascus, then to Mari on the Euphrates River, which it followed down to Akkad and Babylon and beyond. Donkeys were the most common pack animals; camels did not become domesticated in the Levant until the latter part of the second millennium BCE. In addition to other strains of travel, bandits remained a constant threat for anyone except armies and well-guarded emissaries.

The Hebrew Bible speaks of persons traveling great distances. Abraham with his family migrates some 1,200 miles from Ur to the land of Canaan; Jacob walks about 600 miles to Haran near the upper Euphrates; Joseph and his father's clan relocate about 350 miles to Egypt. Solomon has cedar logs hauled nearly 200 miles from Lebanon for the temple in Jerusalem. Twice Jeremiah walks 450 miles to the Euphrates and back to bury a linen loincloth in the riverbank to illustrate that the Israelites will be sent there in exile (Jer. 13:1–11). The Israelites whom the Neo-Babylonians take into exile must march some 900 miles to Babylon. After being vomited up by a "big fish," Jonah goes 750 miles to the city of Nineveh. Nehemiah covers some 1,100 miles to make it to Jerusalem from Susa, the capital of the Persian empire.

Travel was an arduous and time-consuming process, especially wherever the terrain proved inhospitable. Trade caravans, which were outfitted for transporting goods in a timely manner, typically managed only fifteen to twenty miles per day. A large, motley group such as the exiles may not have matched even that speed. The trip from Jerusalem to Babylon took them at least two full months of daily walking.

Topography

To survey the topography requires first deciding on the country's borders, which in itself is complicated by two circumstances. First, the territory settled or governed by the Israelites fluctuated continuously; each period brought new borders to Israel's extent. In the premonarchic period the Israelites lived mainly in the Canaanite highlands. With the advent of the monarchy the country's boundaries became more distinct, but they shifted as the monarchs expanded and lost the territory they governed. According to the biblical story, David greatly expanded Saul's petty kingdom, and Solomon outdid David considerably: 1 Kings 4:21–24 (Tanakh 5:1–4) imaginatively pictures the Solomonic kingdom reaching all the way to the Euphrates River, approximately 450 miles by foot from Jerusalem, and including all lands from Syria to Gaza.

The defeat of the northern kingdom, Israel, in 722 BCE by the Assyrians meant the shrinkage of national land by more than 60 percent. After the Babylonian capture of the southern kingdom in 586 BCE, the portion remaining later as the Persian province of Yehud extends to a radius of less than twenty-five miles around the city of Jerusalem. The Israelites suffered a total loss of sovereignty over the land for the rest of biblical history, with the short-lived exception of the Hasmonean kingdom in the second and first centuries BCE. Thus following political history, whether based on biblical or extrabiblical evidence, requires a repeated recalculation of the country's boundaries from one period to the next. For this reason using a geographical term such as the "southern Levant" is in many ways clearer than political or ethnic terms like "Israel" or "Judah." Geography is a constant in a way that politics and identity are not, and a geographical delimitation avoids discriminating among ethnic or political groups within the given territory.

Second, at no single time are the boundaries ever defined clearly enough in the Hebrew Bible for us to determine the size of the country. When Joshua divides the land among the twelve tribes (Josh. 13–21), he includes considerable detail about the borders between tribes in the south, which he keys mainly to landmarks and geographical features, but the lands of some of the tribes in the far north are not clearly marked, and the eastern borders of the two and a half tribes assigned to land on the eastern side of the Jordan River are unmentioned. According to 1 Kings 4:7–19, Solomon divides his kingdom into twelve administrative districts plus Judah, districts that do not follow tribal lines and are even less explicit than Joshua's delineations. The overall extent of the two kingdoms is also indistinct. When modern cartographers draw their maps of any of these periods, they generally appear more confident of their borders and sites than the biblical and other historical data actually warrant.

Aside from the exaggerated projection of Solomon's kingdom, the greatest extent of the Israelites' holdings probably occurred during the relatively brief period of the divided kingdom during the ninth and eighth centuries BCE. We can do little more than venture an approximate area: eight to nine thousand square miles. By way of comparison, other places close to this size include the state of New Jersey, El Salvador, Rwanda, Wales, and the modern state of Israel (excluding Palestinian territories).

The southern Levant is a topographical wonder. Despite its relatively small size, the land offers a variety of landscapes rarely seen within such small confines—beaches and deserts, a snow-covered mountain and one of the saltiest seas on earth, verdant pastures and land suitable mostly for grape vines and olive trees, and in the south a breathtakingly beautiful view of the Makhtesh Ramon, one of the world's largest natural craters and a sight suggestive of a moonscape.

Six topographical regions are discernible in the southern Levant, five of them mentioned in God's command to the Israelites to cease their wilderness wanderings and proceed now to the land of Canaan: "Resume your journey, and go into the hill country of the Amorites as well as into the neighboring regions—the *Aravah*, the *hill country*, the *Shephelah*, the *Negev*, and the *seacoast*—the land of the Canaanites and the Lebanon, as far as the great river, the river Euphrates" (Deut. 1:7).

Lacking in this list is the hill country east of the Jordan River, unless the "hill country" in this verse includes both such landscapes east and west of the Jordan River. All of the regions but the Negev have a north–south orientation; that is, they are longer on a north–south axis than they are wide. For reference during the following descriptions of the physical features of the land, see the accompanying topographical map (page 76).

Coastal Plain. The entire western side of the southern Levant borders on the "Great Sea" (Num. 34:6), the biblical name for the Mediterranean. It is not all beachfront although there are many sandy areas from which the biblical metaphor for innumerable amounts stems (e.g., Abraham's descendants will be "as numerous as the stars of heaven and as the sand that is on the seashore," Gen. 22:17). At the far north the interior highlands end in high cliffs at the water's edge. Farther south rocky land juts into the sea. Mt. Carmel looms over the coast and modern-day Haifa. Continuing south, one comes to plains, some probably quite marshy in ancient times. The coastal plain widens south of Jaffa (or Joppa, modern-day Yafo, on the southern edge of Tel Aviv). The Philistines inhabited this region, taking advantage of the fertile ground farther inland.

Except for the section north of Mt. Carmel, the coast did not provide much in the way of natural harbors for ships. From the second to the first millennium BCE, however, the Philistines built and maintained a thriving port city at Ashkelon in the south, the largest such site during Israel's history. Little evidence remains of significant maritime involvement by the Israelites themselves, though, and their lack of familiarity with seafaring may explain why biblical texts often seem to regard the unfathomable waters with either foreboding or reverence.

Shephelah. Some twenty miles inland from Ashkelon in the south is a topographical region called the Shephelah, a Hebrew word meaning "lowland." Running north–south like the Dead Sea and somewhat larger than it, the Shephelah forms the foothills between the coastal plain and the hill country to the east. Several east–west valleys provide fertile cropland for grains, vines, and trees as well as roads to pass between the coast and the highlands.

This area serves as the setting for a number of biblical stories, such as those of Samson. One particular account refers to the wheat that grows so well in this region (Judg. 15:1–8). After Samson discovers that his Philistine father-in-law has given his wife in marriage to the best man because Samson remained absent for a long period, Samson swears revenge. He catches three hundred foxes, ties them together in pairs, attaches a torch between each pair of tails, lights the torches, and sets the foxes loose in the Philistines' wheat field. They burn not only the wheat, but also the grape vines and olive trees in the vicinity. The Philistines respond by burning to death Samson's wife and her father, and the cycle of revenge continues.

The Hill Country. The geographical region where most of Israel's history and the majority of biblical stories take place is the hill country, sometimes referred to as the highlands. The area runs like a spine down the center of the southern Levant, from Lebanon south to the Galilee highlands, then continuing through the hearts of Israel and Judah, and gradually ending south of Beersheva in the Negev. This landscape is noticeably higher than the coastal plains to the west and especially than the Jordan Rift Valley to the east. It is also an area that receives snow in the cold months—not every year and not masses of snow, but enough to give the highlands a dramatic coloring of white.

This nearly continuous highland area has one major interruption in the north. The Jezreel Valley, dissecting the hill country in an east–west direction just below the Galilee highlands, covers an area upward of thirty miles in length by ten miles in width. At its head in the west, about fifteen miles inland from the Mediterranean, the splendid city of Megiddo—perhaps best known today from its association with the apocalyptic Armageddon, "the mountain of Megiddo"—holds a commanding view over the plain, one of the most fertile areas in the country. At the eastern end the valley descends below sea level en route to the Jordan River.

At 3,963 feet, the hill country's highest point is Mt. Meron, situated in Galilee. Other elevated places in the central and southern parts of the hill country include Mt. Ebal near Shechem (3,084 ft.), the mountain north of Bethel (modern Beitin; 3,333 ft.), and the site north of Hebron (3,350 ft.). These "mountains" stand out clearly from their surroundings, but none of them is particularly high since the land at their bases is well above sea level. For example, today's city of Nablus, located near the site of ancient Shechem, has an elevation of 1,804 feet, which means that Mt. Ebal rises only some 1,500 feet above it. Not exactly an alp, but certainly impressive in this setting nonetheless.

Even though the hill country did not loom above all the surrounding territory as a mountain chain of impressive stature, it figured into the literature of ancient Israel, and probably into the mind-set of the people as well, as an imposing physical and spiritual presence. Walking from the Mediterranean seashore toward the east, one sees in the distance the foothills, and beyond them lie the higher elevations, even if they are not immediately visible. A common phrase in biblical Hebrew, still used today in modern Hebrew, is "to *go up* (*alah*) to Jerusalem," not simply "to go to Jerusalem." Psalms 120–134 form a group of psalms in which each has the subtitle "song of ascents," apparently pilgrimage songs to be recited or sung as Israelites travel to the Jerusalem temple. One begins with the familiar words:

> I lift up my eyes to the hills—
> from where will my help come?
> My help comes from YHWH,
> who made heaven and earth. (Ps. 121:1–2)

These well-known lines are frequently interpreted as an affirmation that help will come from these hills (actually "mountains," Heb. *harim*), YHWH's protectorate and the site of Zion and the Jerusalem temple. Other texts refer to this central hill country as "mountains" (e.g., Deut. 11:11 and especially Ezek. 36:1–12). However, this verse may also have the opposite, ironic meaning: that Israel's help does *not* come from the mountains associated with the Canaanite god Baal.

In other settings the hill country represents a safe haven from disaster, as in the case of the impending destruction of Sodom and Gomorrah when God's angels tell Lot and his family: "Flee for your life; do not look back or stop anywhere in the Plain; flee to the hills, or else you will be consumed" (Gen. 19:17). A similar motivation might underlie the settlement movement of the first Israelites, seeking safety as well as a means for livelihood. They first settled on the eastern side of the central hill country, before later progressing westward and to the north and south, according to archaeologists.

The land in this hill country is not everywhere hospitable for agriculture. The area in the far north is more fertile; the central and southern hill country tends to be rocky, rugged, and dry. Wadis, a form of seasonal waterway, represent a distinctive feature of much of this terrain. An Arabic word, "wadi" has been adopted in English and sometimes in modern Hebrew, though the more common Hebrew term is *nachal*. Wadis have through erosion carved out the ubiquitous hills throughout the highland region, and they carry water down to the desert areas. Occasionally individuals in the lower regions suffer the paradox of a desert drowning if they are caught in a flash flood caused by rains miles away in the hill country. The wadis could also allow for clandestine movements, as in the story of Joshua's troops secretly advancing on the city of Ai in a surprise attack (Josh. 8:1–29).

These hills would not be conducive to much planting, were it not for the strategy practiced in the southern Levant of hillside terracing. Building and maintaining terraces, especially in the rocky terrain of the highlands, is labor-intensive. Each terrace is typically 15–30 feet wide, and the retaining wall ranges between 5 and 10 feet. Such construction must have been a community project since individuals or single families could scarcely have managed it alone and still had time to work the fields. This stair-step pattern of terraces, with the wadis at the bottom where the hills meet, is still widely used in the central hill country.

Once established, the terraces are ideal for olive trees and the sheep and goats that fertilize them as they graze. Other terraces are devoted to grapevines, grains, and other crops. This method of accommodating to the natural conditions of the land provided many of the Israelites with their means for subsistence. Although the early settlers used terraces from the time they first took up residence in the land, they probably did not originate them but adopted them from their predecessors in the region.

Jordan Rift Valley. The fourth topographical region in the southern Levant has a claim to uniqueness, for here lies the Dead Sea, the lowest point of land on the globe's surface as well as the lowest river flowing on land. The whole valley is arguably the most striking part of the country. Walking from Jerusalem in the hill country (2,500 ft.), one can in a single day descend 3,346 feet to reach the city of Jericho in the Jordan Valley, which lies 846 feet below sea level. That walk also affords a dramatic view over the valley floor, part of the Jordan River's course, the Dead Sea to the south, and the Kingdom of Jordan beyond the river.

The Jordan Rift Valley belongs to the northern part of the Great Rift Valley, a geological trench running a total of some 3,700 miles from Mozambique in East Africa to Syria in the northern Levant. Formed by the early movement of two tectonic plates, the Arabian and the African, away from each other, the Great Rift Valley appears like a long scar on the ground when photographed from satellites. From eastern Africa the rift continues northward through the Red Sea and the Gulf of Aqavah before entering the southern Levant en route to Lebanon's Beqaa Valley and eventually Syria.

Befitting its name (*yarad* means "it descends"), the Jordan River starts at its headwaters on the slopes of Mt. Hermon and descends quickly first to Lake Hulah in northern Israel (230 ft. above sea level) and then down a deep gorge and to the Sea of Galilee (689 ft. below sea level). The Hebrew name for the Sea of Galilee is Kinneret (sometimes spelled Chinnereth), probably derived from *kinor*, "lyre," as the lake seems to have the shape of a lyre when viewed from the Galilee heights to the northwest. From the Sea of Galilee to the Dead Sea is 65 miles by air, but the river meanders three times that distance, almost 200 miles total, before reaching its mouth. Today the river seems quite modest in size, as much of its water upstream is diverted to supply human and agricultural needs, but in the time of ancient Israel it was more of a substantial waterway. Mentioned in the Hebrew Bible 182 times, it is the site of numerous episodes and images, from the launch of Joshua's conquest of the land (Josh. 3) and the subsequent construction of a controversial oversized altar (Josh. 22) to the prophet Jeremiah's picture of it as a thick jungle harboring lions (Jer. 49:19).

Like the rest of the Jordan Rift Valley, the Dead Sea basin was created by tectonic plate shifts, here leaving an especially deep gulf. The surface of the Dead Sea lies approximately 1,300 feet below sea level. Measurements vary from year to year for this and the other bodies of water along the Jordan River, and the Dead Sea is currently about 50 feet lower than its surface level in 1990. Its length from north to south has also shortened from forty-five to thirty miles. The Dead Sea's depth surprises most observers—about 1,250 feet.

With a salinity level of approximately 33 percent (ocean water is typically 3.5 percent), the Dead Sea is among the saltiest natural lakes in the world; its name is apt, as no aquatic life can survive in it. The sea has no outlet and, as a result of evaporation over the centuries, not just the salt but a number of other minerals have greatly increased in intensity—bromine, potassium, iodine, magnesium, sulfur, and more. The Romans made use of the water for medicinal purposes, and mud baths and mineral treatments are still available at the spas there today. Swimming is an unusual experience, as the body cannot sink in the heavy water. The first-century CE Jewish historian Josephus reports that the Roman emperor Vespasian, arriving at the Dead Sea, tested these claims by having some of his men who could not swim bound and thrown into the water to see if they would float, which they of course did.

The Hebrew Bible refers to the Dead Sea as the "Salt Sea" or the "Sea of the Aravah" (Aravah means an arid area or desert steppe). Joshua 3:16 uses both: ". . . the water flowing toward the Sea of the Aravah, the Salt Sea," as if the text's audience may not all know it by the same name (see also Deut. 3:17). This region is also said to be the site of Sodom and Gomorrah (Gen. 13:10–13), the cities destroyed by God for their wickedness. According to Genesis 19, Abraham's nephew Lot and his family lived at Sodom but were warned by God's angels to flee, with the explicit instruction that they not look back when the destruction began. Lot's wife looked back and was immediately turned into a pillar of salt—a consequence that fits the Salt Sea locale.

The rift valley stretching all the way from the southern end of the Sea of Galilee down to the Dead Sea and from there south to the Gulf of Aqavah is called the Aravah in the Hebrew Bible (Deut. 3:17 explicitly includes the portion from the Sea of Galilee to the Dead Sea). In today's usage, though, the Aravah applies only to the final portion from the Dead Sea to the Aqavah. This long valley has considerable geological variety. Between the Sea of Galilee and the Dead Sea the rift ranges between 3 miles and 15 miles wide; it is widest shortly before the Jordan River reaches its terminus. According to Joshua 3, it is there on the Plains of Moab, with the Dead Sea immediately to their left, that Joshua musters his troops prior to crossing the river and commencing the conquest of Canaan.

On the western side of the same part of the valley and near the northwest shore of the Dead Sea are the remains of the site occupied by the Qumran community from about 200 BCE to 68 CE. Sometimes connected with the early Jewish movement known as the Essenes—although the literary remains from the community do not claim Essene authorship—the inhabitants made an invaluable contribution to the Bible in their extensive work in copying its texts and interpreting them from their own perspective. Discovered in nearby caves beginning in 1947, with texts continuing to surface today, the Dead Sea Scrolls confirm scholars' suspicion that the biblical texts had not yet been finalized and fixed by this period but still existed in multiple forms, one of them being this Qumran tradition. Inkwells found on the site may well have been the ones used by the scribes who copied these manuscripts and other texts.

Over its distance of about a hundred miles from the southern end of the Dead Sea to the Gulf of Aqavah, the Aravah Valley leaves the Dead Sea's elevation of approximately 1,300 feet below sea level, rises to a high of 655 feet near the halfway point, and descends over the second half to sea level at Aqavah. The kingdom of Edom, with which Israel often interacts in the Hebrew Bible, occupied the southern Aravah Valley and territory to its east.

The Eastern Hills. The eastern side of the Aravah Valley includes the eastern half of the rift. It is not a mirror image of the western hill country, but many similarities between the two exist, including the escarpments that face the valley from both sides. The eastern hills reach an elevation of 4,090 feet above sea level at the midway point between the Sea of Galilee and the Dead Sea. The Golan Heights, on the eastern side of the Sea of Galilee, belong to the Anti-Lebanon or Eastern Lebanon Mountain Range, which rises northward to peak at Mt. Hermon, the highest point (9,232 feet) in the land claimed by Moses, according to Deuteronomy 3:8. Often snow-topped during the year, Mt. Hermon is mentioned several times in the Hebrew Bible, for example, in Joshua 12:1, where it marks the northernmost part of the land conquered by Moses, "from the Wadi Arnon to Mt. Hermon."

Wadis sculpt the landscape of the eastern hills, leading seasonal rains to the valley floor. Several rivers and wadis lead westward into the Jordan River or the Dead Sea—the Yarmuk just south of the Sea of Galilee; the Yabis and the es-Zerqa (the Jabbok) farther to the south; the Zerqa Ma'an (perhaps the Nahaliel) and el-Mojib (the Arnon) into the Dead Sea; and the el-Hesa (probably the Zered) south of the Dead Sea. East of the hilly area the land plateaus and gradually slopes downward to join the Syrian Desert.

On a clear day with the conditions right, the eastern hills are visible all the way from Jerusalem, thirty miles to the west, which may account for the frequent biblical references to the area east of the Jordan. Jacob wrestles the angel at the Jabbok River (Gen. 32:22–32; Tanakh 32:23–33). The prophet Elijah finds safe haven from King Ahab and Queen Jezebel in the wadi Cherith (1 Kings 17:1–6, although some have associated this site with the wadi Qelt leading from Jerusalem down toward Jericho). Many of the names from the eastern hill country occur in connection with the wilderness wanderings or Joshua's division of the land among the tribes. Two and a half of the tribes—Gad, Reuben, and half of Manasseh—receive their allotment on the eastern side of the Jordan River, from the Arnon by the Dead Sea, through the land called Gilead east of the Jordan, to the land of Bashan (the Golan Heights) east of the Sea of Galilee. According to Numbers 32, Moses leads the Israelites in conquering this region and designates it for these tribes, and Joshua carries out the order (Josh. 13). Also in this general area, south of the Dead Sea, lies the ancient city of Petra. Though not mentioned in the Hebrew Bible, the city was founded by the Nabateans, who occupied the area south of the Dead Sea during the last part of the biblical period, from the fourth century BCE through the initial centuries CE. Petra, carved out of the living rock of a cliff east of the Aravah Valley, has rightly fascinated ancient and modern travelers with its beauty and architecture.

Negev. The final distinctive topographical region in the southern Levant lies in the far south. The Negev, meaning "dry or parched ground" in Hebrew, occupies the large expanse south of Beersheva in the hill country, west of the Aravah Valley (the part south of the Dead Sea), north of the Sinai Peninsula, and east of the Mediterranean—a total of about forty-six hundred square miles. Although this whole area is arid, its landscape is extremely varied. In the center are the three main craters, unusual vast depressions with ridges, declines, rock formations, drainage via wadis, and overall rugged terrain, all colored from burnt sienna to black. Although called "craters," they were not formed by meteors but by gradual rain and wind erosion, and scarcely any other such geological structures of their size exist on earth. The largest, the Makhtesh Ramon, is twenty-four miles long, five miles wide, and a thousand feet deep. Hills, wadis, plains, gorges, escarpments, sand dunes, occasional oases, and a palette of earth colors are found throughout the rest of the Negev.

In the Bible the Negev appears often as both real space and symbolic space. Abraham "journeyed on by stages toward the Negev" in his first migration into the land of Canaan (Gen. 12:9), and Isaac made his home there (24:62). Moses's spies enter the land through the Negev (Num. 13:17). It is also the setting for one of the Israelites' rebellions against Moses during their wilderness wanderings, the episode in which God punishes them by sending poisonous snakes against them. According to the story in Numbers 21:4–9, their relief comes when Moses, at God's command, makes a bronze snake on a pole (the *nechushtan* of 2 Kings 18:4), which the people have only to look at to be saved from snakebite—a symbol parallel to Asclepius's rod and serpent much used today as a sign of the healing arts. The Negev is also included among the areas conquered under Joshua (Josh. 10–12) and later David (1 Sam. 30).

As a symbol, the Negev represents divine blessings, as in the words of the psalmist: "Restore our fortunes, O YHWH, like the watercourses in the Negev" (Ps. 126:4). More frequently, though, the prophets cite the Negev as a symbol of ominous devastation. Isaiah has two oracles keyed to the Negev, one to its erratic winds and the other to its dangerous animals. The metaphor in the first refers to the threat ("it" in the quote) coming against the Assyrians or, perhaps, the later Babylonians: "The oracle concerning the wilderness of the sea. As whirlwinds in the Negev sweep on, it comes from the desert, from a terrible land" (Isa. 21:1). In the second case Isaiah criticizes King Hezekiah's effort to obtain help from the Egyptians, predicting that his caravan laden with tribute will be endangered en route to Egypt: "An oracle concerning the animals of the Negev. Through a land of trouble and distress, of lioness and roaring lion, of viper and flying serpent, they carry their riches on the backs of donkeys, and their treasures on the humps of camels, to a people that cannot profit them" (30:6).

With a more positive message, Jeremiah refers explicitly to the Negev as one of the places in the land that will be restored after the exile when the Judeans return from Babylon: "Fields shall be bought for money, and deeds shall be signed and sealed and witnessed, in the land of Benjamin, in the places around Jerusalem, and in the cities of Judah, of the hill country, of the Shephelah, and of the Negev; for I will restore their fortunes, says YHWH" (32:44).

Climate and Water Resources

Scholars have researched evidence about water levels, plant and pollen remains, animal bones, soils and sediments, and so on and have concluded that the climate during biblical times was very similar to the climatic conditions prevailing today. Any climatic differences between ancient and modern times are largely a result of human actions, not the natural climate itself.

In general terms, Israel's climate conforms to its larger Mediterranean or subtropical region. As such there are only two distinct annual seasons, one wet and the other dry. They are often called winter and summer, although they do not quite match those seasons in temperate, four-season regions. Latitudes farther from the equator than Israel experience a greater difference between high and low temperatures than Israel does, while Israel's wet and dry seasons are more extreme than those in the more temperate climates.

Temperatures vary according to the topographical areas, but in general they tend to be higher than, for example, in central Europe. In August, usually the hottest month of the year, the typical daytime temperature ranges from the 80s Fahrenheit on the coast and in the central hill country to the 90s and even over 100 near the Dead Sea and in the Negev. In January the range is generally in the 40s and 50s throughout the country, except near the Dead Sea where it is in the 60s.

An uncomfortable heat source comes occasionally between the seasons—the sirocco, often called by its Arabic name *khamsin,* or in Hebrew *sharav.* The sirocco originates in North Africa, bringing stagnant and hot air as well as fine dust. Temperatures can jump another 15–20 degrees, producing discomfort and even health problems. The word *sharav* occurs only twice in the Hebrew Bible. Isaiah 49:10 uses it to describe the heat stress ("scorching wind") the exiles will *not* have to endure during their trek home, and in Isaiah 35:6–7 the word refers to the torrid ground ("burning sand").

As the humidity levels are much lower in the Jordan Rift Valley (around 37 percent in August) in comparison with the coastal plain (70 percent), the dry heat offers some relief. Simply moving out of the sun and under some shade improves comfort immediately. On the other hand, shade is not always available. The dry season has almost no completely overcast days, and August typically has cloud cover of less than 10 percent. Even the rainy season has fewer cloudy periods than is typical at higher latitudes.

Rainfall rates also differ depending on the topographical region. The Bible speaks of God's promise to "give the rain for [the] land in its season, the early rain and the later rain" (Deut. 11:14–15). Records from recent times show a varied pattern—some years with more rain in the early or late period, other years with rainfall more evenly distributed. For the farmer, the most important dates are the beginning and the end of the rainy period since they determine planting and harvesting. Nonetheless, the annual amount of rain is hardly reliable, as records show that about one-third of the time the rainfall is significantly below average.

Despite the impression that London must surely receive much more rain than the desertlike Jerusalem, the annual total in both is actually quite close—about 23 inches in London and 21 inches in Jerusalem. The two cities, however, receive their rains in very different patterns. The rainfall in London is distributed fairly evenly throughout the year. In Jerusalem on the other hand, almost all of the rain falls in the months of November through March, and nothing in June through September. In a recent year London recorded 153 wet days compared to only 39 days in Jerusalem, while Jerusalem averaged 9 hours of sunlight per day throughout the year compared to 4 hours in London. Almost the same total amounts of rain, only delivered in contrasting ways.

Across the southern Levant precipitation varies considerably. On the coastal plain rainfall ranges from 10 inches in the south to 32 inches in the northern sections. The Shephelah receives about 19 inches. The western hill country, which includes Jerusalem, varies from 40 inches in Galilee in the north to 12 inches in the south. In the Jordan Rift Valley the rainfall north of the Sea of Galilee is about 20 inches, compared to 6 inches at Jericho, north of the Dead Sea, to a parched 2 inches in the Aravah Valley south of the Dead Sea. The eastern hill country approximates the differentials in the western hill country. The Negev's averages range from 10 inches in the north to 4 inches in the central and southern sections. In general terms, the northern part of the Negev and the Jordan Rift Valley around the Dead Sea and the area about halfway to the Sea of Galilee are semiarid, while the southern half of the Negev and the Aravah Valley south of the Dead Sea count as arid desert.

When the rains come, they hit with force. Roughly twenty-five times during the rainy season, cyclonic storms form over the Mediterranean, circulating in a counterclockwise direction as they move eastward toward the Levant. The cyclones strike the coast and the hill country with a torrent of rain and wind, delivering much of the annual precipitation.

Although the climate has not changed appreciably from the biblical period to the present, vegetation has undergone substantial shifts. Deforestation is a prime example. During the second millennium BCE forests covered wide areas of the southern Levant. The entire western hill country down to Hebron as well as much of the coastal area, the Shephelah, and parts of the eastern hill country were forested—not the dense forests with sparse underbrush known elsewhere, but a Mediterranean maquis variant consisting of open woodlands with the trees interspersed with shrubs. Of the trees in these woodlands, the evergreen oak reached a height of 40–50 feet, the deciduous terebinth, 30 feet, and in certain regions the Aleppo (or Jerusalem) pine, 33–66 feet. With the increase in settlements after 1200 BCE, areas were cleared to make room for cropland, and wood was cut for fires, including pottery ovens and smelting furnaces. Joshua commanded

the tribes of Ephraim and Manasseh: "The hill country shall be yours, for
though it is a forest, you shall clear it and possess it to its farthest borders"
(Josh. 17:18). Allowing sheep and goats to graze in wooded areas also
contributed to the decline. Thus human exploitation rather than climate
change over centuries led to deforestation, and rain runoff on the slopes is
a further consequence. In recent decades Israelis have launched a reforesta-
tion campaign to try to reverse this trend.

Settlement of the Land

The settlement period in Israel's history began about 1200 BCE, which also
marks the start of the Iron Age. As discussed in Chapter 1, Israel's history
before this period (the ancestors, the exodus, and the conquest of the land)
is largely unconfirmed by archaeological or other extrabiblical evidence.
This situation begins to change after 1200.

Archaeologists have spent decades conducting extensive surface surveys throughout the southern Levant and have found traces of habitations
everywhere, even in the hard terrain and climate of the Negev and the
Jordan Rift Valley. In the central region of the western hill country only
about 30 small villages have come to light from 1200 BCE, but by 1000
BCE this number explodes to over 250 villages. Other areas have produced
similar findings during this two-hundred-year period, if not at the same
eightfold rate of increase. At least 68 villages were present in Galilee by
year 1000, around 60 in the Jordan Rift Valley, and over 200 east of the
Jordan River. In the western hill country more than half of the villages
were new settlements, not continuations of previous villages.

These villages were typically very small in size and population. Archaeologists have calculated that villages averaged only 0.75–1.5 acres in
size, although some were even smaller. A 1-acre settlement typically contained 20–30 houses, with upward of half of the space devoted to common
usage. A village's population averaged 75–150, though many of those discovered may not have held more than 50 inhabitants each. As this range
suggests, villages were small, certainly smaller than what we today might
call a village. They were also vulnerable to passing armies as well as robber
bands. Ezekiel 38:11–12 describes the defenselessness of settlements without fortification walls.

Villages did not crop up without the proper conditions in place around
them: a reliable water source, ideally within half of a mile; suitable terrain

for building houses; proximity to arable land or pasturage; availability of raw resources for buildings, tools, pottery, and the like; and relative safety. The villages did not congregate only near arable land; they are found in all areas of the country, including the desert fringe. Some were close to cities, and others seemingly as far away from urban pressures as possible. If the countryside was hospitable enough to handle it, two or more villages were frequently close enough to be in sight of each other or within easy walking distance. For the period around 1000 BCE, villages in the central hill country occurred with the frequency of one per four or five square miles, but in the area of the western slopes their density decreased to one per twelve to fifteen square miles. The density increased almost twofold during the centuries of monarchic rule.

Archaeologists estimate the total population west of the Jordan River jumped from around twenty-one thousand in 1150 BCE to around fifty-one thousand in 1000 BCE. Natural fertility cannot explain this increase, as infant mortality rates hover around 50 percent in harsh environmental settings without the availability of modern medicine. A steady influx of people from outside the region is the more likely reason for this growth.

All of these data point to a demographic shift that not only indicates residential patterns during this early period, but also describes the primary settlement model during later centuries. Throughout Israel's history, even when cities were well established, villages always housed the vast majority of the population—between 80 percent and 95 percent of all inhabitants of the southern Levant were villagers. During the eighth century BCE before the fall of the northern kingdom in 722, the country's population reached its peak, totaling some 450,000, of which approximately 350,000 lived in the more arable north and 100,000 in the south. In both regions villagers far outnumbered urbanites.

Yet the cities exercised much more control over the villages than vice versa. The political and economic dimensions of settlement patterns will be a focus of Chapter 11, and here we concentrate primarily on the physical details. Urbanization in Southwest Asia had already had a long history before the Israelites built their first cities. Two major waves in the development of urban centers and cultures were the Early Bronze Age (ca. 3000 BCE and later) and the Middle Bronze Age (2000–1550 BCE). Cities supported the efforts of the Sumerian, Old Babylonian, and Egyptian empires to control vast portions of Southwest Asia and beyond. In each case the cities eventually entered a period of decline, accompanied by the ruralization of their area when agrarians had a better chance to survive without the taxation and conscription practiced by urban powers.

In the southern Levant, this urban decline occurred during the Late Bronze Age, 1550–1200 BCE. Once-strong cities were abandoned or diminished, sometimes leaving only modest settlements, although not all experienced this fate. In the southern coastal region during the twelfth century BCE, the Philistines conquered and rebuilt the Canaanite cities of Ashkelon, Ashdod, Ekron, Gath, and Gaza—the Philistine pentapolis. A few inland urban centers, such as Megiddo and Hazor in the north, Beth-shean in the Jordan River Valley, and Gezer in the Shephelah, survived or were reconstructed in the early Iron Age. Many of these had been city-states, fortified urban centers in each case ruled by a petty king and encompassing a limited area of land, including its feeder villages.

The Israelites did not begin to found cities until after 1000 BCE, probably closer to 900, which coincides with the next archaeological period, Iron II. The two capitals, Samaria in the north and Jerusalem in the south, were complemented by other cities that the government needed to control the larger populace, collect taxes, and conscript peasants into the military and labor gangs. A number of towns also developed to serve the agricultural needs of the people.

Most urban settlements were destroyed by the Neo-Assyrian and later the Neo-Babylonian armies, and beginning in 539 BCE the Persian empire instituted a ruralization policy. A few cities were eventually rebuilt under the Persians, but with no autonomy of their own. Jerusalem, for example, became a small town of about three thousand without much economic or political significance. Reurbanization of the land did not occur until the Hellenistic and Roman periods from the latter part of the fourth century BCE onward. The one constant throughout all of these periods, however, was the village. Individual villages would appear and disappear, but village life itself always remained as the most consistent residential preference or option available for the vast majority of Israelites.

A Land of Milk and Honey

One of the most frequently used phrases to describe the land's goodness and agricultural bounty, "a land flowing with milk and honey," occurs twenty times in the Hebrew Bible. In its first biblical appearance, Moses has just noticed the burning bush in the desert, turns aside to investigate why it is not being consumed, and confronts God instead. In the course of their exchange, God announces:

> I have observed the misery of my people who are in Egypt;
> I have heard their cry on account of their taskmasters.
> Indeed, I know their sufferings, and I have come down to
> deliver them from the Egyptians, and to bring them up
> out of that land to a good and broad land, *a land flowing
> with milk and honey,* to the country of the Canaanites, the
> Hittites, the Amorites, the Perizzites, the Hivites, and the
> Jebusites. (Exod. 3:7–8)

This brief statement emphasizes that the land with its abundance contrasts with Egypt and its miseries, but also that this promised land now belongs to the Canaanites and five other groups. In the Bible the phrase almost always looks forward to a land not yet reached, and it occurs by far most frequently in texts involving Moses or Joshua. The image lures the people forward in their trek through the wilderness. Three prophetic texts also use the phrase to speak of the promise before the people arrive in the land. Jeremiah, for example, refers to the oath that God "swore to your ancestors, to give them a land flowing with milk and honey, as at this day" (11:5; see also 32:22).

The description highlights the fertility of the land: milk and honey are two food products that can be consumed without necessitating the death or inhibiting the growth of their source. When nuts or seeds are used for food, plants will not be generated from them; fruits and vegetables are picked from the earth; meat and eggs indicate the cessation or the prevention of life.

Only twice does the phrase seem to have a problematic twist to it. In one of the rebellions against Moses in the wilderness, Dathan and Abiram complain to Moses: "Is it too little that you have brought us up out of a land flowing with milk and honey to kill us in the wilderness, that you must also lord it over us?" (Num. 16:13). Here Egypt, in contrast to the harsh conditions in the desert, is the "land flowing with milk and honey," parallel to the contrast between the land of Canaan and the severe wilderness. The other unusual use of the phrase comes in Ezekiel:

> Moreover I swore to them in the wilderness that I would
> not bring them into the land that I had given them, *a land*
> *flowing with milk and honey,* the most glorious of all lands,
> because they rejected my ordinances and did not observe
> my statutes, and profaned my sabbaths; for their heart went
> after their idols. (20:15–16)

The tradition is used as a critique of the people's perfidy, threatening to deprive them of this land—which in fact occurs with the exile.

When Moses's spies returned from scouting the land of Canaan, they reported that it "flows with milk and honey" (Num. 13:27). It is a picturesque, compelling, if idealized image, yet perhaps not as excessive as it seems. The land during Israel's early period was more forested and biodiverse than after centuries of use and development. From the perspective of many generations, this space was home. They had settled there, learned to embrace it in all of its vagaries, and knew how to work the soil. The land was the ground of personal histories and cultural memories. It was for them, in the words of Ezekiel 38:12, "the navel of the world," their center of the earth.

Part 2

Chapter 4

Law and Justice

While specific laws governing various dimensions of life and legal process are discussed thematically throughout this book, the present chapter focuses on fundamental questions about the origin and nature of law and justice in ancient Israel and in the Hebrew Bible. Even though the biblical text depicts its laws as stemming from God through Moses to the people, humans are very much in the picture as actors—not only Moses, but also elders, priests, and even the people. The five daughters of Zelophehad, for example, confront Moses about the inheritance custom that disallows daughters as heirs if there are no sons, and they secure a new ruling that privileges daughters in such situations, so long as they marry within the clan of their father's tribe (Num. 27:1–11; 36:1–12; carried out in Josh. 17:3–6). This case of legislation is unusual in the Hebrew Bible, but the role of the elders and the priests in adjudicating possible violations is not.

All laws are socially constructed, the products of human actions and decisions in light of societal, political, economic, religious, and other cultural forces. They emerge in specific historical circumstances under the pressure of distinct forces and in response to particular demands. Special interests affect the enactment of new laws in our own times, and they did in former times as well. However, the institutions in place to create and enforce the laws, whether formal or informal, can vary substantially from society to society. If we imagine a situation lacking our intricate legislative and judiciary systems, we are left with a legal structure quite comparable to that faced by most ancient societies, including ancient Israel. The vast majority of societies in human history did not have a governmental system similar to democratic countries in the modern age, and yet they managed to develop laws to keep their societies orderly and anarchy at bay.

The distinction between positive and natural laws can help to clarify fundamental types of prohibitions and prescriptions. Positive laws are enacted by legislatures or declared binding by a monarch or tyrant. Natural laws, on the other hand, are those that people may believe (and the emphasis here is on *believe*) to be ordained by the divine world, inherent in the nature of the world, or fundamental to human nature. Multiple notions about natural law have emerged since the time of Aristotle. Today, advocates often hold up human rights as prime examples of natural laws or natural rights writ into the very being of human life. Others regard natural law as contrived and postulated. The eighteenth-century British utilitarian philosopher and jurist Jeremy Bentham famously dismissed natural rights as "rhetorical nonsense—nonsense upon stilts." Many will think more highly of rights than did Bentham, but the annoying characteristic of natural laws is that their existence can be advocated but neither proved nor disproved.

This distinction between positive and natural laws is helpful in the analysis of biblical laws since it reflects categories in which we moderns may think, but the distinction does not appear explicitly in the biblical text. The Hebrew Bible regards all the laws included in its pages as having stemmed from God, which—at least according to some definitions—should qualify them as natural laws. However, according to the narrative, the laws of Sinai are given to the people of Israel and apply above all to them, and the Hebrew Bible does not see them as inherent in human beings in general.

The Hebrew Bible has no question about the divine origin of the laws received at Mt. Sinai. God gives them to Moses, who in turn passes them on to the people. God is the ultimate source; Moses is the mediator—a mouthpiece, but one with a temper. As he descends from Mt. Sinai and sees Aaron and the Israelites worshiping the golden calf, Moses dashes to pieces the very two stone tablets on which God had written the laws (Exod. 31:18; 32:15–19). Deuteronomy 10:4 states that God has to rewrite the laws (actually, just the Ten Commandments) on new tablets; Exodus 34:27 says it is Moses who writes at God's dictation.

The law is a substantial component of the Hebrew Bible. Almost a full third of the great expanse of the Pentateuch consists of laws. The early rabbis tallied a total of 613 biblical commandments. The Talmud (*Makkot* 23b) attributes to Rabbi Simlai in the third century CE the statement: "Six

hundred thirteen commandments were revealed to Moses; 365 being prohibitions equal in number to the days of the year, and 248 being mandates
corresponding in number to the bones of the human body."

The rabbis also revered the "oral law," which they believed reached all
the way back to Moses and supplemented the written law of the Torah.
It was eventually recorded in rabbinic literature in the Mishnah, codified
around 200 CE, the later Babylonian and Jerusalem Talmuds, and additional rabbinic writings. Law is the lifeblood of the tradition, the pulse
that is continually checked, discussed, interpreted, and compared with
other parts of the tradition.

Christians are also inheritors of the laws of the Bible. Jesus and Paul
were steeped in them and frequently used them as points of reference in
their teachings. Even at those points where the New Testament and later
Christian theologians declare positions that vary from biblical laws, they
are very much defined in relation to this legal tradition.

Yet to acknowledge the influence of this tradition is not to declare
it natural law—legal principles that all humans should know intuitively.
Even though the biblical text introduces them after humanity is already
created, it does not identify them as human products, thus as positive laws.
The trend in biblical scholarship since the Enlightenment regards them as
human creations, and considerable effort has gone into connecting them
with specific historical contexts and stimuli. The biblical texts contain indications of the Israelites' social world, the political and economic contexts
in which such laws arose. To say that humans influenced the formation of
the laws, even developed them, does not necessarily rule out the divine,
although it does shift the accent from the otherworldly to the this-worldly.
We readily talk about the effect of religion on society, but the impact of
society on religion also needs to be gauged.

The biblical laws can thus be seen as precepts drafted by persons within
ancient Israel, but another whole realm of law from that period was not
recorded—the customary laws that arose to regulate behavior, adjudicate
disputes, and specify penalties or remedies. Such laws flourished among
the wider population, the majority of the population that lived in villages
throughout the country. These laws, though not written and though not
enacted by centralized authorities, nonetheless functioned as positive laws
in their own regions and deserve also to be considered in this discussion of
the laws of ancient Israel.

The Written and the Unwritten

Biblical laws are thus not necessarily identical with the laws that functioned among the ancient Israelites. In some cases the biblical laws may reflect the agenda of the specific elite group writing them and were not even known, let alone practiced, among the people at large. For example, the central priesthoods in Samaria and Jerusalem could have developed their own system of forbidden practices without successfully making the wider public follow them, or the elites in the cities may have had rules for property ownership that did not match the legal customs among villagers. For their own part, various Israelites, especially the mass of peasants living in the villages scattered around the country, probably had their own legal customs that were not preserved in the text. Even trying to determine whether the biblical laws were actually practiced is difficult. At a minimum, the legal texts in the Hebrew Bible represent literature. Rather than being a compendium of actual functioning laws that were applied and enforced among the majority of the population, they exist now in literary dress as part of the larger narrative of the Pentateuch.

Nonetheless, biblical scholars for over a century now have assumed that these texts record actual laws, and they have expended considerable effort to identify and date various groupings of them. They usually name five clusters, each from a separate chronological period and social or religious setting. The whole notion is speculative, yet it is widely shared and is therefore worth reviewing here before we consider another scenario.

The *Covenant Code* refers to Exodus 21:1–23:19 (or perhaps beginning in 20:22). Also called the *Book of the Covenant,* this collection takes its name from the statement shortly after its close: "Then [Moses] took the book of the covenant and read it in the hearing of the people; and they said, 'All that YHWH has spoken we will do, and we will be obedient'" (Exod. 24:7). The Covenant Code is commonly thought to be Israel's oldest assemblage of laws because it seems to fit an agricultural setting and to reflect practices antedating the foundation of the monarchy. The individual laws may have existed in oral form originally, in which case some think they were recorded during the reign of David or Solomon. The laws touch on a range of matters, including marriage, violence, slavery, liability and restitution, social justice, Sabbath and sabbatical year, and the three annual religious festivals.

The *Deuteronomic Code* is usually associated with Deuteronomy 12–26.

The Deuteronomic Code is more diverse than the Covenant Code, treating some of the same issues but additional topics as well: murder, warfare, property, marriage, sexual behavior, inheritance, slavery, judicial witnesses, refuge from blood vengeance, humanitarian protections, political leaders, judges, priests, and more. It is commonly associated with the finding of "the book of the law" according to 2 Kings 22. The laws may have originated in the northern kingdom and been taken to Jerusalem by refugees after Israel fell in 722, where they were then used as the basis of Josiah's sweeping religious reform.

The third collection of laws, generally called the *Holiness Code*, is found in Leviticus 17–26. Its name derives from its frequent injunctions to be holy, both morally and ritually. Some of these laws deal with practices or behavior that in the priests' view can compromise one's sanctity—illicit sexual acts, immorality, blasphemy. Others lay out the proper procedures for sacrifices, observing religious festivals, and honoring the sabbatical and jubilee years of release. These laws may have had a longer history of practice before they were written in the exilic or postexilic period.

The *Priestly Code* is the fourth collection, although unlike the other codes it is not grouped in one place. Instead, these laws are scattered throughout Exodus, Leviticus, and Numbers. The Priestly Code regulates religious behavior, prescribes the proper rituals and cultic paraphernalia, deals with norms regarding purity and impurity, and treats a variety of other matters, mostly but not all explicitly cultic in nature. The term "Priestly Code" is somewhat of a catchall indicating not only the variety in its subject matter but also the dispersion of its laws throughout three books of the Pentateuch. Some of the laws may well date back to monarchic times, but as a group they probably came together in the fifth or fourth century BCE after the exile.

The final collection is the *Ten Commandments*, also called the Decalogue, from the Greek for "ten words," corresponding to the Hebrew phrase *aseret ha-devarim*, "ten words" (Exod. 34:28; Deut. 4:13; 10:4). One of the best known parts of the Bible, it is the smallest of all the legal collections, only sixteen verses in length. On the other hand, it is the only collection to occur twice in the Pentateuch, Exodus 20:2–17 and Deuteronomy 5:6–21, with some variations between them. For example, the reason given for the Sabbath law in Exodus cites God's resting on the seventh day of creation, whereas in Deuteronomy it is God's delivering the people from Egyptian slavery. A similar concise listing of laws, called the Ritual Decalogue (which may be a list of twelve, hence a dodecalogue) appears in Exodus 34:13–26.

The Ten Commandments contains two parts: the first four laws are religious in nature (each contains the phrase "YHWH your God") and the last six focus on social and moral matters. There is a difference between Jewish and Christian traditions, even in enumerating the commandments. For example, Jews count the first commandment as: "I am YHWH your God, who brought you out of the land of Egypt, out of the house of slavery; you shall have no other gods before me" (Exod. 20:2–3), whereas many Christians consider v. 2 background and then begin the count with v. 3 as the first commandment ("You shall have no other gods before me"). The date of composition remains elusive; the Decalogue may be the earliest collection and the basis for the fundamental principles elaborated in other collections, or it may be a late summary of the other legal traditions.

The identification of these five collections and the dates in which each was supposedly compiled is, as mentioned, entirely hypothetical. Second Kings 22 does refer to the "book of the law," but it does not equate it with Deuteronomy 12–26. Exodus 21–23 does contain some agricultural laws (or the urbanites' view of agricultural laws), but they are not limited to only the premonarchic period. The Decalogue consists of ten commandments, but it makes no explicit claim about its relation to all the other laws of the Pentateuch. The Holiness Code and the Priestly Code both contain cultic laws, but the overlap between the two is not explained. There may be a better way to understand biblical law than to posit a chronological scheme for the collections, as is usually maintained.

There are several other questions about these collections that the hypothesis just delineated does not answer—questions that do not spring so much from the biblical text as from our current understandings of how ancient Israelite social systems worked. First, in what sense are these texts "law collections"? It is hard to imagine that someone roamed through the countryside assembling laws about agricultural practices or social standards among the peasants and compiling them into collections. And why consider them "codes"? We know of no legislative body in ancient Israel, nor do we hear of kings issuing bodies of laws. These legal texts, especially taken separately as outlined, fall far short of covering all the legal matters needed in a law code.

Who might have written them in the first place? Literacy at an advanced enough level to render legal nuances was limited in Israelite society to fewer than 5 percent, and probably closer to 1 percent, of the total population, and the ability to write and read was expected only of those, such as scribes and archivists, for whom it was a profession. So if functionaries likely did the writing, did someone else instigate it? The scribes were not likely to have compiled laws on their own, but only at the behest of certain groups or individuals. For whom would they have been written? The wider populace was too illiterate to have had any use for these documents. Their own laws existed in oral form and functioned with full force in that form. The vast majority of the population thus did not need laws to be written. Some other stimulus must have triggered the writing of laws, something other than the Sinai scenario. We need to look elsewhere.

An intriguing episode occurred in the late sixth century BCE that may shed light on the writing of laws—perhaps not exactly the laws as they now exist in the Pentateuch, but some assortment of laws known in postexilic Judea. An ancient papyrus document, called the Demotic Chronicle, was acquired by Napoleon's forces during his 1801 campaign in Egypt; it is currently held in the Bibliothèque Nationale de France. It records a directive from Darius I, the great Persian emperor (522–486 BCE), who sought to secure his rule and reduce the chance of uprising by pursuing a policy of supporting the traditions and institutions of his far-flung provinces. According to the papyrus, Darius sent an order in 519 BCE to his governor in Egypt to write the old traditional laws:

> Let them bring to me the wise men among the warriors,
> priests, and scribes of Egypt, who have assembled from the
> temples, and let them write down the former laws of Egypt
> until the 44th year [526 BCE] of Pharaoh Amasis. Let them
> bring here the law of Pharaoh, of the temple, and of the
> people.

The papyrus continues to note that it took sixteen years for them to record all of these laws, which were then sent to Darius in two languages, Egyptian (Demotic) and the common language of the empire (Aramaic).

There is no record of such an order having been sent to Israel, but it is certainly plausible. Darius may have sought to assemble the local laws of each province in his vast empire, to which he could add the imperial laws that applied everywhere and then send the combination back to the respective provinces, where they then served as the law of the land. We have no way of knowing how many laws Israel already had in writing from the period before the exile—perhaps a good number, perhaps none. It is possible that an imperial order from Darius gave the Judeans the impetus to draft collections of their laws—the laws of the kingdom, the laws of the religious centers, and the laws of the common people. These laws were not the laws now retained in the Pentateuch, but they represented an effort to compile laws according to a somewhat orderly structure. It probably took the Judeans another century or two to follow suit with their own assemblage of laws, which now appears in the Hebrew Bible.

Ancient Southwest Asia

The Persian period is thus the likely time of the greatest written activity for the biblical laws, even if some of them are based on legal traditions transmitted orally from earlier times. During this period as well as in the Neo-Babylonian period prior to the Persians, the Judeans had the opportunity to become acquainted with legal traditions from elsewhere in ancient Southwest Asia. Many of these laws from neighboring cultures were much older, but the Israelites did not have much chance to learn of them until they had the cultural contact resulting from exile and commerce. A number of legal collections predating this period, mostly from the Mesopotamian area, have now come to light, including:

Sumerian

Ur-Namma	ca. 2100 BCE
Lipit-Ishtar	ca. 1930 BCE

Old Babylonian

Eshnunna	ca. 1770 BCE
Hammurabi	ca. 1750 BCE
Hittite	ca. 1650–1500 BCE
Middle Assyrian	ca. 1300–1075 BCE
Neo-Assyrian	744–612 BCE
Neo-Babylonian	612–539 BCE

The Code of Hammurabi is by far the most famous, but the existence of the others shows the importance given to written law in the wider region. Geographically they stem from the various parts of Mesopotamia as well as what is now Turkey (Hittites). The two Sumerian lists are incomplete: 37 laws in the Ur-Namma collection, and 44 in Lipit-Ishtar. Eshnunna contains some 60 laws. Hammurabi is the longest with 282 laws as well as perhaps another 29 restored from other sources to fill in a gap in the stele. The Middle Assyrian collection is also fragmentary but includes at least 95 laws, some of them quite lengthy. The Hittite laws are about 200 in number. In addition, thousands of contracts, edicts, and other texts carrying legal weight have been found from these and other cultures.

There is a definite monumental character to the form of some of these collections. Most striking is the Code of Hammurabi, engraved on a black diorite stele nearly 8 feet high, now preserved in the Louvre. At its top is a depiction of the sun god and god of justice, Shamash, seated on a throne, with King Hammurabi standing in front of him. It is not clear from the image whether Hammurabi is giving Shamash the laws or Shamash is dictating them to Hammurabi. Whichever may be the case, the two are linked in the giving of the laws, much as is the case for Moses and God in the Hebrew Bible. Under the picture is a densely inscribed text with all of the laws.

Several of the collections (Ur-Namma, Lipit-Ishtar, Eshnunna, and Hammurabi) include a prologue and, in some cases, also an epilogue. The Hammurabi stele goes into great detail extolling both the gods and Hammurabi, giving some general history, and calling down the wrath of the gods on those who do not obey the laws. Even with the difference between the polytheistic background of these other texts and the monotheism evident in the Hebrew Bible, parallels exist between the prologues and epilogues of the Southwest Asian law codes and parts of the biblical legal texts. For example, Hammurabi's epilogue includes the following:[*]

> I am Hammurabi, noble king. I have not been careless or
> negligent toward humankind, granted to my care by the
> god Enlil, and with whose shepherding the god Marduk

---

[*] Translations of this epilogue and of the Mesopotamian laws are from Martha T. Roth, *Law Collections from Mesopotamia and Asia Minor,* 2nd ed. (Atlanta: Scholars Press and Society of Biblical Literature, 1997).

charged me. I have sought for them peaceful places, I removed serious difficulties, I spread light over them. Let any wronged man who has a lawsuit come before the statue of me, the king of justice, and let him have my inscribed stela read aloud to him, thus may he hear my precious pronouncements and let my stela reveal the lawsuit for him. May any king who will appear in the land in the future, at any time, observe the pronouncements of justice that I inscribed upon my stela. May he not alter the judgments that I rendered and the verdicts that I gave, nor remove my engraved image. (But) should that man [a future ruler] not heed my pronouncements, which I have inscribed upon my stela, and should he slight my curses and not fear the curses of the gods, . . . may the god Enlil, the lord, who determines destinies, whose utterance cannot be countermanded, who magnifies my kingship, incite against him even in his own residence disorder that cannot be quelled and a rebellion that will result in his obliteration; may he cast as his fate a reign of groaning, of few days, of years of famine, of darkness without illumination, and of sudden death; may he declare with his venerable speech the obliteration of his city, the dispersion of his people, the supplanting of his dynasty, and the blotting out of his name and his memory from the land.

This verbose excerpt represents only a small portion of the whole epilogue, which continues in the same vein.

Similar texts promising reward for obedience and punishment for rebellion are plentiful in the biblical literature, such as this statement in Exodus 34:6–7:

YHWH, YHWH, a God merciful and gracious, slow to anger, and abounding in steadfast love and faithfulness, keeping steadfast love for the thousandth generation, forgiving iniquity and transgression and sin, yet by no means clearing the guilty, but visiting the iniquity of the parents upon the children and the children's children, to the third and the fourth generation.

In addition, the book of Deuteronomy conforms to the general format of the Code of Hammurabi. It begins with a long prologue (Deut. 1–11) in which Moses recounts God's acts of delivering and aiding the Israelites and exhorts them to respond with obedience. The lengthy section of laws follows in Deuteronomy 12–26, concluding with a type of epilogue in Deuteronomy 27–34, which reminds the people of the consequences of obeying and disobeying the laws. Finally, Moses launches into two long songs, one praising God and the other blessing Israel (Deut. 32–33). As is typical in the appropriation of literary traditions, Deuteronomy conforms in part to the genre of lawgiving, while also including some creative differences, such as the two songs of Moses. This genre was known across Southwest Asian cultures, and it is not surprising that Israel made use of it, probably after becoming acquainted with it following the Neo-Babylonian conquest and exile.

These texts, structured in this manner, are literature or literary pieces. We cannot know whether any of Hammurabi's laws were actually practiced, just as we cannot be sure whether or when any of the biblical laws circulated widely among the Israelites. Even though these "legal" texts have the form of laws, they may represent idealized precepts developed by those with the power and the means to compose them in written form. Whether they were practiced as "living laws" among the general population is not the same as having them in writing. The majority of the Israelites, living in the hundreds of villages throughout the land, were more likely to have developed their own customary laws, retaining and transmitting them in oral form.

Rhetorical Forms

Beyond the literary genre of lawgiving, another stylistic similarity between biblical laws and ancient Southwest Asian laws is their rhetorical form. The most common form in both contexts is termed *casuistic* law, otherwise known as case law. It follows the structure "if . . . then" or "when . . . then." The first part of the law specifies the violation or charge, and the second part indicates the consequence or punishment. For example: "When someone borrows an animal from another and it is injured or dies, the owner not being present, full restitution shall be made. If the owner was present, there shall be no restitution; if it was hired, only the hiring fee is due" (Exod. 22:14–15; Tanakh 22:13–14).

This kind of statement identifies first a specific actionable occurrence and then the judicial ruling it deserves. We also see in this example another common phenomenon—a nesting of related provisions, each one raising a new circumstance or condition that could yield a different judicial outcome. It makes a difference whether the animal's owner is present or not and whether the animal is rented or borrowed. Many other examples of nesting are present in both biblical and other ancient Southwest Asian laws, as in this case from the Code of Hammurabi: "If a man steals an ox, a sheep, a donkey, a pig, or a boat—if it belongs either to the god [i.e., to the temple] or to the palace, he shall give thirtyfold; if it belongs to a commoner, he shall replace it tenfold; if the thief does not have anything to give, he shall be killed" (n. 8).

Again various conditions produce different judgments. Modern lawyers and judges may perceive various problems in these laws (e.g., vagueness of terms, too broad a scope, excessive and unequal penalties), just as ancient administrators of justice may have confronted. For those in ancient Israel or in surrounding cultures, however, these casuistic laws provided the means to differentiate between faults and their remedies. In fact, the nested laws reveal the flexibility of the judicial process in adjusting to new considerations that arise in the process of dealing with legal conflicts.

A second form is *apodictic* law, sometimes called categorical or principle law. Its classic and best-known examples are in the Ten Commandments: "You shall not. . . ." Rather than giving a violation and its remedy or punishment, an apodictic law pronounces a global prohibition: "Do not kill," "Do not commit adultery," and so on. This type also usually has the verb in the singular: it seems to address an individual, not a community. This rhetorical device—and an effective one at that—makes each person obligated to comply.

The global aspect of apodictic laws, however, makes it difficult to know how they could have been enforced. The laws about murder serve as a good test case. The Ten Commandments proclaim: "You shall not commit murder" (Exod. 20:13; Deut. 5:17). However, this injunction does not define "murder." The KJV renders it "Thou shalt not kill," which could include capital punishment and killing in battle as well as voluntary and involuntary manslaughter. However, the Hebrew verb is *ratzach*, which normally denotes homicide even though it can also refer to an act for which the killer is not culpable (e.g., it is found in the laws about the cities of refuge in Num. 35). So the word "murder" is a better translation in Exodus 20:13 than the word "kill." But when we get to the casuistic laws, we see an effort to address some of the variable circumstances that make killing anything but a clear-cut case. Thus the next chapter of Exodus, immediately after the Ten Commandments, states that motive can play a role in determining the application of the law: "Whoever strikes a person mortally shall be put to death. If it was not premeditated, but came about by an act of God, then I will appoint for you a place to which the killer may flee. But if someone willfully attacks and kills another by treachery, you shall take the killer from my altar for execution" (Exod. 21:12–14).

Here the lawmakers recognize the need to distinguish between a brazen, premeditated murder and an act for which the killer should not be held criminally liable. Thus an apodictic pronouncement is effective in conveying a general principle, but casuistic laws consider various conditions that can affect adjudication.

The origin of apodictic laws is anything but certain. Contrary to some earlier notions, the form is not unique to ancient Israel, nor is it mainly religious in nature. Rather, this form of expression is extremely common in everyday life. Probably all parents, at some time, have spoken to their children in apodictic form: do not lie, do not bother your siblings, do not talk to people like that, do not be unkind. Although this form of expression is rooted in the family, it lends itself effectively to religious, legal, and governmental use as well.

A third kind of law is *participial* law. It is recognizable in Hebrew because it begins with a participial verb, commonly translated into English as "Whoever does *x* . . ." or "He [or she] who commits *x*. . . ." Exodus 21:12, quoted above, provides an example: "Whoever strikes. . . ." By beginning with a verb this legal form parallels the apodictic form, which also starts with a verb, sometimes preceded by the negative. But like casuistic law it specifies the offense and the penalty. Exodus 21:15–17 contains three participial laws in a row, the final one of which is: "Whoever curses (or JPS: He who insults) father or mother shall be put to death."

A variant of the participial laws is the curse. Deuteronomy 27:15–26 contains twelve curse statements in rapid succession, reminiscent in their rhetorical effect of the concise pronouncements in the Ten Commandments. Cursed is anyone engaging in idolatry, dishonoring a parent, violating a neighbor's property, misleading a blind person, depriving the powerless of justice, engaging in incest or bestiality, causing injury to a neighbor, taking a bribe, or failing to observe the laws. The list reads like a condemnatory version of prohibitions; instead of "Do not do . . ." they say "Cursed are you if you do. . . ." No specific punishment is detailed. "Cursed" is more than enough, for it means that the violator is completely undone, condemned in his or her own community. Thus, each of these twelve curses ends poignantly with the refrain: "All the people shall say, 'Amen!'"

Finally, quite a few laws contain what is called a *motive clause,* a rhetorical device that aims to motivate hearers to comply. The fifth commandment in the Decalogue illustrates one type of motive clause, which is used to encourage compliance via a benefit offered: "Honor your father and your mother, so that your days may be long in the land that YHWH your God is giving you" (Exod. 20:12). A second type warns persons of undesirable consequences—not just the specific punishment, but larger or vaguer results. For example, Leviticus 19:29 mandates: "Do not profane your daughter by making her a prostitute, that the land not become prostituted and full of depravity." Or again, following two laws about lending money there is an implicit threat that God will heed complaints lodged by the borrower: "If your neighbor cries out to me, I will listen, for I am compassionate" (Exod. 22:27; Tanakh 22:26).

A third version of the motive clause invokes God's supreme authority for giving the law. The imprimatur of divine authority becomes motive enough for obedience: the law is to be followed *because* it is divinely given. Most clauses of this type occur in the Holiness Code. Opening a section on incest laws is: "None of you shall approach anyone near of kin to uncover nakedness [i.e., to have sexual intercourse]: I am YHWH" (Lev. 18:6).

Finally, there are the motive clauses that seek to enhance compliance by pointing to occurrences in Israel's past that should induce the people to act properly. A few examples: "You shall not wrong or oppress a resident alien, for you were aliens in the land of Egypt" (Exod. 22:21; Tanakh 22:20); "Observe the month of Aviv by keeping the passover to YHWH your God, for in the month of Aviv YHWH your God brought you out of Egypt by night" (Deut. 16:1); "You shall not abhor any of the Edomites, for they are your kin" (Deut. 23:7). The text clearly recognizes not only the need for laws but also the importance of trying to motivate the Israelites to obey them.

Administering Justice

The book of Ruth (4:1–12) contains an intriguing anecdote that provides us with an inkling of how the community reached a decision when confronted with a legal problem. The background is the story of Ruth, a foreigner from Moab, who had married an Israelite (already a complication since marriages were ideally to be endogamous, within the husband's clan). Her husband, Mahlon, dies, as does his brother, Chilion. Their two widows, Ruth and Orpah, thus become widows like their Hebrew mother-in-law, Naomi. Widowhood is a socially and legally precarious condition if the woman does not have adult children to care for her, for she cannot count on her deceased husband's relatives or even her own birth family to offer her shelter and sustenance. Naomi decides to leave Moab and return to Bethlehem in Israel, and Ruth opts to accompany her, even though she will then become, as both widow and foreigner, doubly vulnerable. (Chapter 9 will revisit the Ruth story to focus on these issues of intermarriage and the status of non-Israelites.)

Ruth eventually attracts the attention of Boaz, a wealthy relative of her father-in-law, Elimelech, Naomi's deceased husband. Boaz decides to act as next of kin to Ruth, meaning that he is willing to marry her and assume responsibility for her since her husband had been his relative. The problem, though, is that there is a closer relative than Boaz. At the root of the legal dilemma in this story is the institution of levirate marriage, whereby the nearest kin is expected to marry the widow of his deceased relative, should the dead man have no son and heir. It is spelled out with reference only to a brother in Deuteronomy 25:5–10. Another vivid story about the levirate is the tangle involving Judah, Tamar, Er, Onan, and Shelah in Genesis 38.

Boaz needs to resolve the legal issue of kinship duties. He goes to the gate of Bethlehem, where commercial and apparently also judicial activities of the town are often transacted. Soon after he takes his seat there, the man who is the nearest living kin passes by. Boaz invites him to sit down with a rather odd phrase, *peloni almoni*, translated in the NRSV with the neighborly touch of "friend," but in the JPS as "So-and-so!" It seems a rather dismissive way of speaking to a relative. A better translation connects *peloni almoni* to the word "here": "Come over, and sit here somewhere." To complete the cast of characters, Boaz assembles ten elders to hear the case.

Boaz then addresses his relative with a clever, self-serving strategy. He informs him that Naomi wants to sell some land belonging to her dead husband. It is the first we readers—and apparently also the man who is next of kin—hear about it. The latter immediately responds that he will buy it (the Hebrew has "redeem" because it is a kinship duty). Boaz then wastes no time in reminding him and the panel of elders that if the next of kin redeems Naomi's land, he must also take Ruth, whose well-being depends in part on the produce of that land. No biblical law requires the next of kin to marry the widow if he redeems the land, but it is a plausible legal custom that might have prevailed among the people, even if it was not included in the Bible. Boaz may have known of his relative's circumstances and thus created this classic setup. The next of kin begs off on the grounds that his own inheritance could be at stake. By declining the whole package, the land and Ruth, he leaves Boaz free to obtain both.

Then the text provides a parenthetical clarification of what it says is an old custom: that the one selling or not redeeming a property takes off his sandal or shoe and gives it to the person who is acquiring it. Only a few other biblical texts attest to this practice. According to Psalm 60:8 (Tanakh 60:10) God says, "On Edom I hurl my shoe," apparently indicating ownership of that land. Amos accuses the wealthy of selling "the needy for a pair of sandals" (2:6), another transaction, though not of land.

Especially close to the symbolism of the sandal in Ruth is Deuteronomy 25:9–10, which follows the law about levirate marriage. According to the text, if the brother refuses to marry his widowed sister-in-law, then the widow "shall go up to him in the presence of the elders, pull his sandal off his foot, spit in his face, and declare 'This is what is done to the man who does not build up his brother's house.'" The symbolism of a sandal as evidence of a transaction, including the duties of next of kin, is all the more suggestive in this passage because of the sandal's association with feet, a euphemism for genitalia—hence the levirate duty to produce an heir for the deceased. In the book of Ruth, Boaz takes on the duties of next of kin. The elders and the people present pronounce themselves to be witnesses to the decision and the transaction. The book ends with a genealogy showing that Boaz and Ruth become the great-grandparents of King David.

This description in Ruth of a trial to adjudicate a civil matter is too small a basis on which to generalize about the manner in which legal proceedings actually occurred in ancient Israel. Some trials may well have followed this model, especially in the context of village life. The "gates" denote the place through which most residents of a town or village pass every day, leaving to tend their fields and returning, and it is a convenient setting for assembling judges, witnesses, and an audience. During the time of the monarchy, cities had formalized court settings presided over by judges presumably appointed by the king, as Deuteronomy 16:18 intimates: "You shall appoint judges and officials throughout your tribes, in all your towns that YHWH your God is giving you, and they shall render just decisions for the people." Furthermore, there were religious courts conducted by the priests. Deuteronomy 17:8–13 indicates that, if a case at a local level is too difficult to decide, it should be brought to the priests at the capital for adjudication. All such trials must have included a statement of the issues by the disputing parties (probably not as staged as the trial in Ruth appears) together with presentation of evidence and witnesses, on the basis of which the judge or elders would make a decision.

Yet there could also be complications. Boaz devised a ploy that worked in his favor, and all of Israel could find satisfaction in it since, according to the story, it ultimately resulted in King David's ancestry. Other cases also had winners and losers, but sometimes the losers were dealt an injustice. Biblical laws warn against perverting justice through bribery ("You shall take no bribe, for a bribe blinds the officials, and subverts the cause of those who are in the right," Exod. 23:8; similarly Deut. 16:19), partiality ("You shall not deprive a resident alien or an orphan of justice; you shall not take a widow's garment in pledge," Deut. 24:17), or perjury ("You shall not spread a false report. You shall not join hands with the wicked to act as a malicious witness," Exod. 23:1). In fact, evenhandedness is due for all sides ("You shall not side with the majority so as to pervert justice; nor shall you be partial to the poor in a lawsuit," Exod. 23:2b–3). The perversions of justice mentioned in these and other biblical texts are probably not unrealistic, given the substantial inequities of power and wealth in ancient Israelite society during much of its history.

Using dramatic language, several of the prophets also rail against wholesale injustices. Amos, operating in the northern kingdom not long before its fall in the eighth century BCE, uses the phrase "in the gate" to refer to the courts of law: "For I know how many are your transgressions, and how great are your sins—you who afflict the righteous, who take a bribe, and push aside the needy in the gate" (5:12). The reference is to those who use the legal system to exploit the poor. Micah views the problem as part of a larger system of oppression:

> Hear this, you rulers of the house of Jacob and chiefs of the
> house of Israel, who abhor justice and pervert all equity,
> who build Zion with blood and Jerusalem with wrong! Its
> rulers give judgment for a bribe, its priests teach for a price,
> its prophets give oracles for money; yet they lean upon
> YHWH and say, "Surely YHWH is with us! No harm
> shall come upon us." (3:9–12)

The prophets sense the vulnerability of people not only in the social and economic spheres but also in law courts, where judgments can be skewed in favor of the wealthy and the powerful.

Several principles underlie Israel's system of judicial procedure, whether the cases involve physical injury to others, violations of property or contracts, other actions for which a person is considered legally liable, or religious infractions. We cannot know that these principles were applied throughout Israelite society, and the prophetic texts imply that miscarriages of justice occurred all too often, just as can happen today. Some of the following ten characteristics or ideals are resonant in modern laws, while others have minimal or no afterlife in our times.

1. *Trial without delay.* Even though a speedy trial is considered a right in many modern countries, all too often individuals charged with a crime are held in custody for months, if not years, before they have benefit of trial. Not so in ancient Israel or among its neighbors. Any prisons that existed in these countries largely served the special interests of the king, who could confine and release at will. The Hebrew Bible mentions prisons infrequently, generally only in conjunction with the monarchy.

When the wife of Joseph's Egyptian master falsely accuses him of making advances toward her, Joseph is thrown into "the place where the king's prisoners were confined" (Gen. 39:20). The prophet Jeremiah is imprisoned by officials who charge him with treason, and the king also confines him to the court of the guards (32:2–3; 37:13–16, 21; 38:6–13). In the Persian period Ezra sets imprisonment as one of several forms of judicial punishment (7:26). Prisons did not exist throughout the country, as is the case in modern countries. They were primarily used for state offenses, not for common crimes, and they did not serve to hold persons for extended periods who were waiting for trial.

Legal texts in the Hebrew Bible give the impression that trials for most crimes and torts (a wrong or injury done to a private party, for which a court can assess damages) were conducted almost immediately, as soon as the crime was detected or the civil dispute occurred. In the case involving Boaz and Ruth, the trial (a civil hearing with legal force for resolving a claim or obligation) is held the day after their threshing-floor episode. If an offense involved a personal injury, a theft or destruction of property, a violation of social norms, or similar charges or evidence of legal transgressions, the people may well have organized a trial without delay—*really* without delay, probably the same day the offense came to light.

The case of adultery is a good example. Called a "great sin" or "great guilt" in Genesis 20:9 as well as in ancient Egypt and in Ugarit to the north of Israel, adultery was widely regarded as sexual activity between a married or engaged woman and any man not her husband or fiancé. Using a series of casuistic laws, Deuteronomy 22:13–29 describes several different circumstances in which adultery may be charged. If the charge is determined to be true, the parties are immediately tried, and the guilty are taken to the town gate and stoned, presumably immediately after the finding is established. No story in the Hebrew Bible describes a case of adultery adjudicated and punished. In Genesis 38 when Tamar's pregnancy (by her father-in-law, Judah) is discovered, Judah unilaterally orders that she be burned to death—until Tamar confronts him with the evidence that he is the father. David is not punished with death for his act of adultery with the married Bathsheba, although the death of their child seems to be some sort of punishment (2 Sam. 11–12).

The book of Susanna, regarded as canonical in the Catholic and Orthodox traditions but not in the Jewish and Protestant scriptures, contains the only explicit trial for adultery in the Old Testament. In the story, set not in Israel but in Babylon, two Jewish judges—suggesting that the community had a fair amount of autonomy—conspire to seduce the beautiful Susanna, but are rebuffed by her. They charge her with adultery, take her to trial, secure a capital sentence, and are almost successful in having her executed before the hero, Daniel, exposes their lie and causes them to suffer the death they had planned for Susanna. Both the trial and execution occur speedily—the trial on the day after the judges make the charge, and the capital punishment apparently directly following the trial.

2. Testimony of witnesses. As a rule, witnesses need to be present at a trial, and Deuteronomy 19:15 takes particular care to spell out that more than one witness is required: "A single witness shall not suffice to convict a person of any crime or wrongdoing. . . . Only on the evidence of two or three witnesses shall a charge be sustained." Deuteronomy 17:6–7 clarifies that multiple witnesses are needed for capital cases and that the witnesses are to be the first to stone the accused. The kangaroo court arranged by Queen Jezebel to dispense with Naboth, whose vineyard Ahab wants, proceeds with trumped-up charges delivered by two false witnesses, described in the text as "scoundrels" (1 Kings 21). This problem of false witnesses is also confronted directly in laws: "If the witness is a false witness, having testified falsely against another, then you shall do to the false witness just as the false witness had meant to do to the other" (Deut. 19:18b–19a). The importance of witnesses in a trial is also commonly treated in law collections from other ancient Southwest Asian cultures. Not only free men but also women and slaves can testify as witnesses.

3. *Evidence.* The testimony of witnesses was sufficient for determining a conviction in many cases, but other forms of evidence could make the difference in other instances. Two types of evidence were possible, only the first of which would be credited in most courts today. The first is physical evidence, something that could establish the truthfulness of one party's claim—at least in the eyes of the ancients. The nested laws in Exodus 22:10–13 (Tanakh 22:9–12) regulate the claims and protections in the case of someone who has received for safekeeping another person's donkey, ox, sheep, or other animal. If it dies because it was attacked by wild animals, the person guarding it must bring the mangled carcass "as evidence" and will be exonerated. The Hebrew word for "evidence" here is *ed*, the same term used for a human witness. In another case (in Deut. 22:13–21), a woman marries a man who subsequently claims that she was not a virgin when they were married. Her parents then have the chance to present to the elders the cloth showing blood from the bridal night, and the cloth serves as evidence to dispute the charge. If the parents cannot provide such evidence, then the bride is to be stoned to death. We could find all sorts of problems with such evidence, but the text in Deuteronomy suggests that it was sufficient for adjudication.

The second kind of evidence, focusing on divine judgment or communication, would be much less conclusive in our courts today—although the American practice of swearing on a Bible may share some common ground with ancient religiosity. One form of divine evidence is the sacred lots, the Urim and Thummim. Some type of small objects, they apparently signaled a simple "yes" or "no" to a question posed to God. Biblical tradition specifies that they are to be kept in the breastpiece of Aaron's priestly vestments (Exod. 28:30; Lev. 8:8) or those of later priests.

The story in 1 Samuel 14:24–46 demonstrates their use in indicating the guilty party. Prior to a battle against the Philistines, King Saul rashly swears an oath to kill any of his soldiers who eat food before evening. Not having heard of this oath, his son and likely successor, Jonathan, eats some honey. When Saul seeks word from God about the impending battle and receives no response, Saul calls for the Urim and Thummim to help determine who is at fault. In the end the lot falls on Jonathan, who confesses and is saved from death only through the intervention of the people. A form of lottery is used in other instances as well, as in Samuel's choosing Saul to be king (1 Sam. 10:20–21) and in Joshua's selection of Achan as the one who violated the prohibition against taking booty after a battle (Josh. 7).

The other form of divine evidence, the oath, is a more common means in the Hebrew Bible for invoking God's judgment when other forms of enforcement or punishment are unavailable. In Solomon's prayer dedicating the temple, he mentions God's role in ensuring judgment: "If someone sins against a neighbor and is given an oath to swear, and comes and swears before your altar in this house, then hear in heaven, and act, and judge your servants, condemning the guilty by bringing their conduct on their own head, and vindicating the righteous by rewarding them according to their righteousness" (1 Kings 8:31–32).

In addition to this type of self-sworn oath, a curse against another is a form of oath. For example, after the conquest of Jericho, Joshua swears: "Cursed before YHWH be anyone who tries to build this city—this Jericho! At the cost of his firstborn he shall lay its foundation, and at the cost of his youngest he shall set up its gates!" (Josh. 6:26). According to 1 Kings 16:34, this curse is fulfilled when the city is rebuilt during King Ahab's reign.

The so-called Mizpah benediction, "May the LORD watch between you and me, when we are absent one from the other," recited at the close of some Christian worship services today, is more of a curse than a blessing in the biblical text. Laban and Jacob have had their tensions, and now Jacob is leaving with his large family, including his wives, Rachel and Leah, Laban's daughters. Laban seems not at all happy about it, and at Mizpah he says to Jacob: "May YHWH watch between you and me, when we are absent one from the other. If you ill-treat my daughters, or if you take wives in addition to my daughters, though no one else is with us, remember that God is witness between you and me" (Gen. 31:49–50). Jacob is to abide by their agreement, and Laban invokes divine sanctions on him if he breaks its terms.

The final form of divine evidence is the ordeal. The history of witch hunts in sixteenth- and seventeenth-century Europe and America reminds us that this practice does not belong to just the ancient past. Ordeals can be set up in two ways: in one, the accused either dies and is thus proven guilty or survives and is pronounced innocent; in the other, the accused dies and, being innocent, is believed to be rewarded in the afterlife. The former is the ancient Southwest Asian custom. In Mesopotamia the ordeal took place at the Tigris or Euphrates River, which the Babylonian laws sometimes refer to as "Judge River." The Code of Hammurabi mandates: "If a man's wife should have a finger pointed against her in accusation involving another male, although she has not been seized lying with another male, she shall submit to the divine River Ordeal for her husband" (n. 132). In another law involving an accusation of witchcraft, the accuser acquires the accused's estate if he dies, but if he does not, then the accuser is killed for making a false charge (n. 2).

Only one ordeal is mentioned in the Hebrew Bible, and it parallels the Hammurabi law, though without the river. Numbers 5:11–31 begins by describing a case in which a wife has had intercourse with a man other than her husband, but is not caught *in flagrante*. The husband suspects that his wife is guilty, but he has no witness. The ordeal can be triggered even if she were not unfaithful but he is jealous and suspicious. In either case, the husband brings his wife to the priest, who conducts the ordeal. The priest mixes a potion of water and dust from the tabernacle floor; this concoction is called the "water of bitterness." He then places her "before YHWH" (i.e., in the tabernacle), dishevels her hair (the symbolism suggests that she has just emerged from a sexual tryst), and places her husband's grain offering in her hand. The priest pronounces that, if she is innocent, she will be immune to the water of bitterness; but if not, then:

> Let the priest . . . say to the woman, "[May] YHWH
> make you an execration and an oath among your people,
> when YHWH makes your uterus drop, your womb dis-
> charge; now may this water that brings the curse enter your
> bowels and make your womb discharge, your uterus drop!"
> And the woman shall say, "Amen. Amen."

It is not clear what physically is to happen to the woman, and translators have struggled to understand the terms. In comparison with the NRSV, the JPS renders the Hebrew more literally: "May this water that induces the spell enter your body, causing the belly to distend and the thigh to sag." One possible interpretation is that the result of the test is a prolapsed uterus, a condition in which the muscles and ligaments supporting the uterus weaken, causing the uterus to descend into the vaginal canal. Another is that the ordeal effects a miscarriage, which raises the question of whether the husband's jealousy resulted from his wife's becoming pregnant. We have no way of knowing how often or even if this "water of bitterness" test was practiced in ancient Israel. In case there should ever be criticism of the husband (and there is no reason to think that only modern people would be aghast over the ordeal), the text concludes by attempting to forestall it: "The man shall be free from iniquity, but the woman shall bear her iniquity." The wife is physically at risk, but her husband is not culpable.

4. *Intent and premeditation.* The Hebrew Bible typically does not consider the motivation of the offending party. If a crime, tort, or breach of contract has occurred, then it must be punished or remedied, regardless of intentionality or mitigating circumstances. Only a few cases seem to accommodate such conditions. The law in Exodus 21:13 regarding killing makes a special provision for an act done without premeditation. The Hebrew phrase commonly translated "by an act of God" uses the rare word *innah*, indicating that God causes it to happen, which apparently reflects the notion that everything has to have a cause—if not by humans, then by God. Differentiating between someone who "lies in wait" to kill another and someone who accidentally causes the death is the subject of a longer set of laws in Numbers 35:16–34. Deuteronomy 19:5 offers the following scenario, which considers mitigating circumstances: "Suppose someone goes into the forest with another to cut wood, and when one of them swings the ax to cut down a tree, the head slips from the handle and strikes the other person who then dies; the killer may flee to one of these cities [of refuge] and live" (19:5). We will return shortly to this subject of the cities of refuge.

A case potentially involving adultery seeks to determine whether the woman was a willing participant. According to Deuteronomy 22:23–27, if a man has sexual intercourse with a woman engaged to another man and their activity occurs in a town, the law prescribes stoning both of them because the woman could have cried for help. But if they have intercourse in the open countryside, then only the man will die. The law allows for the possibility that the woman may have cried for help but was not heard because they were too far from other people, so she is exonerated in this case. Although this second scenario represents a merciful concession, the law does not allow for the possibility that the woman in the city may have been raped without a chance to summon help or may have been threatened to remain silent for fear of her life or that of others. The legal reasoning in this case goes a decent distance, but not all the way.

5. *Proportionate punishment in cases of personal injury and death.* A basic principle of biblical law is that the punishment should fit the crime. The full form of the *lex talionis* (Lat., "law of retaliation," or the talionic law)— "an eye for an eye"—occurs in Exodus 21:23–25: ". . . life for life, eye for eye, tooth for tooth, hand for hand, foot for foot, burn for burn, wound for wound, stripe for stripe" (see also Lev. 24:17–21; Deut. 19:21). Although this principle of punishment may strike us as brutal and barbaric, in biblical times it probably represents a deliberate move to limit excessive revenge and punishment: no more than *one* life for a life, no more than *one* eye for an eye. It reins in the inclination toward the excessive use of force in retaliation, averting a spiral of violence.

Early Christian and Jewish traditions went in different directions with the principle. In the Sermon on the Mount Jesus directs his followers to counter aggression or loss with acts designed to undo the aggressor: when struck, turn the other cheek; when deprived of your coat, give your cloak as well; when pressed to go one mile, go an extra mile also. However, Jesus does not elaborate on physical injury. Jewish interpreters, on the other hand, noted that an exact measure-for-measure system would be impossible to satisfy. No two eyes are identical; if the person to be punished has only one good eye, then taking it is an excessive penalty; or taking the eye will also result in loss of blood, which exceeds the limit of just the one eye. In light of such considerations, the early authorities (Mishnah *Bava Kamma* 8:1; Babylonian Talmud *Bava Kamma* 83b–84a) substituted a system of monetary compensation according to the injury or loss.

At the local level of village and tribal life in ancient Israel, the goal for punishments and remedies falls on setting an appropriate response that will be balanced against the original offense, thus restoring the victim (if still living) to his or her prior state or giving the relatives of the victim (if dead) a sense of justice and closure. At the national level, the state (the monarch and administrators) has the power to claim whatever it will of the people, although the Bible is critical of exploitative and oppressive actions against the populace.

Biblical laws usually do not specify who is to enforce these punishments. We know of no state apparatus to ensure that justice is done at the local levels, although we can be relatively certain that the state's own interests were always protected. In all likelihood, the local communities conducted their own legal affairs, both in trials and in punishments. Nonetheless, many offenses may have occurred with impunity, especially if a power imbalance existed between two contending parties. The fact that the majority of the biblical laws are never again mentioned in biblical narratives may indicate that they were not enforced, or that they constitute ideals rather than real laws, or that they were put into practice in general and simply not referenced again.

Personal injury, short of death, generally results in a payment of restitution to the injured party or, in the case of a slave, to the slave's owner. Biblical laws do not cover many cases—unlike Babylonian laws, which distinguish between the classes of the offender and the victim. Exodus 21:18–19 considers injury resulting from a brawl. If the victim dies, the death is presumably treated as a homicide, though this is not explicitly stated. But if an injury results, then the question is whether or not the injured party is able to get up from bed and walk with the aid of a cane. If so, there is no penalty for the injurer other than to pay for the loss of time from work.

A variation of this law about fighting considers a pregnant woman who is injured while two men are fighting (Exod. 21:22–25). If she miscarries, the one who harmed her is obligated to pay a fine set by her husband. If the woman herself is injured beyond suffering the miscarriage, then the law of an eye for an eye applies. An additional case involves an injury inflicted by a slave owner on a slave: the owner is punished (the details are unstated) if the slave dies, but not if the slave survives "a day or two," because "the slave is the owner's property" (21:20–21). But if the slave's eye is destroyed or a tooth is knocked out, the slave is to be freed (21:26–27).

6. *Proportionate punishment in cases of property damage or loss.* When loss or damage to either movable or immovable property occurs, biblical law usually ordains compensation to cover the loss. The case of the goring ox presents an intriguing example, especially since a close analogue occurs also in eighteenth-century BCE Babylonian laws (Eshnunna, nn. 53–57; Hammurabi, nn. 250–252). It is the kind of string of laws that scribal students in Babylonia probably copied and recopied not only to become

proficient in writing, but also to learn legal reasoning regarding both personal injury and property damage. The biblical counterpart is in Exodus 21:28–32, 35–36, an elaborate nest of related laws considering different conditions. There are two base points, one involving ox on ox and the other an ox that kills a person.

The first starting point is as follows: "If someone's ox hurts the ox of another, so that it dies, then they [presumably the two owners] shall sell the live ox and divide the price of it; and the dead animal they shall also divide." The underlying principle is that an animal's actions cannot always be controlled, though an owner has a special responsibility for the animal once it has exhibited aggressive behavior. Here the biblical law stipulates that the owner of the goring ox should not suffer excessively with the first instance of goring. Both owners will take half of the sale price brought by the living ox, and each will get half of the carcass of the dead ox. However, the next verse goes to the issue of liability: "But if it was known that the ox was accustomed to gore in the past, and its owner has not restrained it, the owner shall restore ox for ox, but keep the dead animal." So the owner of the ox with the rap sheet will suffer monetarily, while the other owner will receive full restitution. Yet the second owner should not benefit from the incident by keeping the carcass as well. Instead, the owner of the goring ox gets the full carcass, in addition to keeping the living ox and buying a new ox for the other owner.

The second starting point is more severe: "When an ox gores a man or a woman to death, the ox shall be stoned, and its flesh shall not be eaten; but the owner of the ox shall not be liable." The meat of the goring ox is apparently considered tainted because the ox has killed a person, and the owner's liability is limited because it was the ox's first offense. But in the next verse the law calls for much more severe punishment for the goring ox's owner if he knew it could be violent and had not restrained it sufficiently: not only is the ox to be stoned to death, but the owner is as well. Another provision specifies that the consequence is the same if it is a boy or girl, not an adult, who is killed; apparently there might have been a lesser punishment if not spelled out. However, if the ox kills a slave, then the ox's owner must compensate the slave owner with thirty silver shekels, and the ox is to be stoned. The Babylonian laws handle a case of a biting dog the same way as that of a goring ox. However, the Babylonian cases result only in monetary restitution, not in the death penalty for the owner.

7. *Capital punishment, blood vengeance, and cities of refuge.* The Hebrew Bible prescribes capital punishment for a variety of offenses, not all of them related to personal injury or death: intentional homicide and kidnapping (e.g., Exod. 21:12, 16), adultery, certain religious violations (e.g., blasphemy, Lev. 24:10–23, although the definition of blasphemy is not clear), and certain other specific crimes. However, unlike the situation in neighboring cultures, destruction or theft of property is not a capital offense in biblical law.

Capital punishment for personal injury can result from negligence in constructing a house: the homeowner who has not built a parapet on a flat roof can be liable for the death of someone who falls from it (Deut. 22:8). In this text the form of execution is not specifically named; instead, there is a reference to "bloodguilt" (*damim*, the plural form of the word for blood), a term that indicates that the perpetrator must die, without specifying whether the community or God will carry out the execution. The Code of Hammurabi has a parallel case: the builder hired to construct a house (probably for the upper classes since peasants generally built their own homes) is liable, life for life, for damages caused by a collapse (nn. 229–231). If the collapse kills the owner, his child, or his slave, then, respectively, the builder, his child, or his slave is to be killed.

Biblical laws also consider circumstances in determining punishments. If a homeowner kills a burglar who breaks and enters a home at night, it is not a capital crime, but it will bring the death penalty against the owner if the break-in occurs during the daytime and the burglar is killed (Exod. 22:2–3; Tanakh 22:1–2). The Old Babylonian law code from Eshnunna, just shortly before Hammurabi's rule, includes a similar distinction: a burglar caught in the daylight must pay a fine, but will be executed if apprehended in the house during the night (n. 13). Laws in many jurisdictions today also prescribe a more severe punishment for burglary at night than during the daytime.

Other grounds for execution are related to social structures. Illicit sexual behavior, particularly adultery and incest, is especially threatening to clan relations and is therefore punishable by death or expulsion (e.g., Lev. 20:10–17; Deut. 22:20–27). There is also a provision (in Deut. 21:18–21) for stoning to death a "stubborn and rebellious" son—not a child in the "terrible twos," but an adult who is "a glutton and drunkard," probably disobeying elderly parents and neglecting the duty to provide for them. It is hard to imagine parents' filing such charges against their children if stoning them to death could be the outcome, and the Hebrew Bible contains no indication that this law was ever applied.

The biblical law of retaliation—an eye for an eye—has its extreme form in the practice of blood vengeance. When one person is killed by another, the family members of the deceased are permitted, even expected, to slay the murderer, and no punishment of the avenger will ensue (Num. 35:16–21). Various texts from the region both before and during Israel's existence indicate that vengeance was condoned elsewhere as well. The practice still exists in some societies today.

The Hebrew Bible provides a loophole for those cases in which the killing may have been accidental or unintentional. It designates six "cities of refuge" at places well spaced throughout the land, three on the west side of the Jordan River and three on the east side. According to the biblical account, God first instructs Moses to establish them (Num. 35:9–28; also Deut. 4:41–43; 19:1–13), and Joshua carries out the directive once the people are in the land (Josh. 20). Anyone who has killed someone unintentionally or accidentally can flee to one of these specified cities and find sanctuary there from the blood avenger. The city is essentially a safe zone until a trial can be organized to rule on the killing. If the act is judged to be intentional, then the murderer will be turned over to the avenger. But if not, the person who caused the death is allowed to remain in the city of refuge until the high priest dies and then can return home. Until that time, if the person leaves the city of refuge, the avenger can take vengeance with impunity (Num. 35:24–28).

The fratricide committed by Cain against Abel, the first heinous crime reported in the Bible, is a case where legal and social values conflict. On the surface of the story, the murder occurs before laws and courts have been established, so God has to intervene to determine the crime and punish it. But at a deeper level, this text is part of the mythic prehistory of Genesis 1–11 (see Chapter 7), reflecting realities and tensions that exist among the Israelites of a period much later than the story seems to describe. Thus issues of kinship, crime, and punishment converge in this narrative. The storytellers and the audience know that Cain must be executed for his murderous act, and the blood avenger or, lacking a family member to avenge Abel, the community must carry out the death penalty on Cain. On the other hand, they also know that kinship ties require that family members protect each other. The parents, Adam and Eve, are put into the impossible position of both executing and protecting. God's solution is for the murderer to be banished. Cain is thus allowed to live, but without the life-giving support of his family.

8. *Maiming.* Mesopotamian laws provide often for monetary compensation if a person loses use of a body part because of someone else's action, but blinding, severing limbs, and other forms of maiming are also used as punishments. For example, according to the Code of Hammurabi, a physician could have a hand amputated for botching a medical procedure (n. 218); another law prescribes that "if a child should strike his father, they shall cut off his hand" (n. 195).

The only case of maiming in the Bible is set in the context of a fight between two men (Deut. 25:11–12). If, in the middle of the skirmish, the wife of one of them reaches out and grabs the genitals of the other, her hand is to be cut off. It seems a rather odd punishment and does not follow the symmetry of the retaliation principle ("eye for an eye, hand for a hand"). The Hebrew word translated "genitals" is *mebushim*, derived from *bosh*, which means "shame"—thus "his privates"; this is the sole occurrence of this word in the Hebrew Bible. Perhaps the idea is that the woman has violated the man's male dignity. More likely, though, the law reflects the Israelites' view of reproduction, in which the man's genitals are seen as his means for gaining posterity and thus prestige. Another text showing the symbolic significance of male genitalia is Genesis 24:2–4, in which Abraham tells his servant, whom he is dispatching to find a wife for his son Isaac, to place his hand under Abraham's "thigh" and swear an oath that he will not select a Canaanite wife for him.

Bodily mutilation may have been a common way to treat the conquered enemy, especially the king. According to Judges 1:6–7, the Israelites defeated the Canaanite and Perizzite armies and captured their king, Adoni-bezek; they cut off his thumbs and big toes, considered a just punishment since Adoni-bezek had previously done the same to seventy other kings. Second Kings 25:7 reports that after taking Jerusalem in 586 BCE the Neo-Babylonian king Nebuchadnezzar captured Judah's king, Zedekiah, slaughtered his sons before him, and then gouged out his eyes before taking him prisoner to Babylon.

Leviticus 24:19 describes maiming in conjunction with the law of retaliation, but no specific examples are given: "Anyone who maims another shall suffer the same injury in return." As often as maiming is described and prescribed in ancient Southwest Asia, its sole case as a punishment in biblical law, the instance of a woman interceding in a brawl, stands out as a rare exception.

9. *Purging evil.* Although biblical laws seek to forestall criminal acts and punish those who commit them, their import can extend beyond the individual to the concerns of the broader community and even the land. Several laws, all from the book of Deuteronomy, prescribe a punishment and then end with the phrase: "so you shall purge [literally, 'sweep away'] the evil from your midst." Cases with this statement deal with punishing a false witness (19:19b), a stubborn and rebellious son (21:21b), adultery (22:21, 22, 24), and kidnapping (24:7).

A scenario described in Deuteronomy 21:1–9 sheds light on the urgency to respond in some way to especially pernicious violations. If a person's body is found in the open country and the murderer cannot be identified, then the elders are to measure the distance from the body to nearby towns to determine which is closest. (Babylonian and Hittite laws [Hammurabi, nn. 23–24; Hittite, n 6] also treat a comparable dilemma.) The elders in that town are then to take a heifer "that has never been worked, one that has not pulled in the yoke," and break its neck; no mention of sacrifice is included. With levitical priests participating, those elders wash their hands over the heifer and declare: "Our hands did not shed this blood, nor were we witnesses to it. Absolve, YHWH, your people Israel, whom you redeemed; do not let the guilt of innocent blood remain in the midst of your people Israel." This ritual exculpates them of bloodguilt: "So you shall purge the guilt of innocent blood from your midst, because you must do what is right in the sight of YHWH."

10. *Appeals.* Biblical law provides for an appeals process, but one that is very different from that with which we are familiar today. Rather than allowing for a convicted person to appeal the verdict to higher judicial levels, the appeal is initiated by the judges or elders themselves, the ones who are responsible for adjudicating the case. If any judicial body (e.g., the group of village elders) reaches a verdict, it is final and not appealable—except, perhaps, to God if the convicted person feels an injustice has been done. Such is the case in the above mentioned trial of Susanna. However, Deuteronomy 17:8–13 describes what is to be done when the elders or other judges are stymied by the case:

If a judicial decision is too difficult for you to make
between one kind of bloodshed and another, one kind of
legal right and another, or one kind of assault and another—any such matters of dispute in your towns—then
you shall immediately go up to the place that YHWH your
God will choose [Jerusalem], where you shall consult with
the levitical priests and the judge who is in office in those
days; they shall announce to you the decision in the case.

There may have been some levels of jurisdiction in between: from village or clan elders, to tribal elders, to regional city judges, to judges in the
capital city, and finally to the high priest (for religious cases) or the king
(for all other cases, and perhaps even for some religious issues). At any
point along the way, a judgment could be reached that would essentially
stop any continuation of the appeals process.

A very well known case shows the result of this appeals procedure. In
1 Kings 3:16–28 we hear of two unnamed women who present a legal co-
nundrum that could confound lesser minds than Solomon's. Two women
living together each give birth to a son, one of whom dies in the night.
The mother of the dead child claims the live baby. The two women confront King Solomon, each insisting that the living son is hers. Solomon
famously calls for the living child to be cut into two parts, with half going
to each woman. Immediately one woman, out of compassion, begs Solomon
not to do so but to allow the other woman to take him, while the other
woman is content to see the process through. Solomon discerns that the
compassionate woman is the true mother, and he orders that the infant be
returned to her.

As with so many other texts in the Bible, a number of issues are at
work here. The story is one of several in 1 Kings 1–10 that glorify Solomon
and his kingdom (before it unravels in 1 Kings 11). In particular, he is
praised for his legendary wisdom and cleverness. This particular dilemma
shows the complexity marking some legal cases—and thus the need for
a central authority to adjudicate what local institutions cannot manage.
Whether two women with a private conflict could have had access to the
country's king is probably as unlikely as the chance that Solomon could
have understood the psychology of the women. In addition, this story may
not be about a legal case at all, for the division of the baby into two parts

expresses metaphorically the division of the kingdom into northern and southern halves, which is precisely what happens directly after Solomon's death according to 1 Kings 12.

Yet the story does describe a conflict that needs to be resolved legally, and it is believable that local groups of elders sitting in judgment may not always have had the capacity to find a solution that the community could affirm. For knotty conflicts needing a "Solomonic judgment" they had the option to appeal to broader levels of society, although we have no way of knowing whether or how often they ever did so. The royal ideology typical of ancient Southwest Asia regards the monarch as the supreme judicial adjudicator, and kings probably did issue rulings for especially contentious cases and, above all, for those affecting state interests.

Although portions of these ten principles may strike us as quaint, excessive, or even cruel, they spring from contexts in which ancient Israel's society tried to maintain order and minimize behavior that could tear apart the social fabric by depriving parties of the justice they deserved. Biblical laws aim to accomplish the same goal, expressing it in the context of divine justice and human obedience. When people become obstinate and intractable in their unjust and disobedient ways and when punishment seems to have no lasting effect, the ultimate recourse is that presented by Jeremiah, quoting God as saying: "I will put my law within them, and I will write it on their hearts" (Jer. 31:33). It is an incursion that would change human nature itself.

Chapter 5

The Divine

Following the creation of the world, the "LORD God" (Heb. YHWH Elohim) creates "the *adam*," the earthling, and places him—better "it," but Hebrew has only masculine and feminine nouns—in the Garden of Eden to till it and keep it. To this earthling, the deity says, "You may freely eat of every tree of the garden; but of the tree of the knowledge of good and evil you shall not eat, for in the day that you eat of it you shall die" (Gen. 2:16–17).

Shortly thereafter, a snake, the most crafty of creatures that this "LORD God" had made, approaches the man's partner—not yet named Eve, but called "the woman"—and asks: "Did God (Elohim) say, 'You shall not eat from any tree in the garden'?" (3:1). The woman, who had not yet been created when the *adam* received the injunction, adds some words to the initial charge when she replies: "God said, 'You shall not eat of the fruit of the tree that is in the middle of the garden, nor shall you touch it, or you shall die'" (3:3). The deity said nothing about touching. Perhaps the *adam* added this warning; perhaps the woman added it herself.

The subtle snake disagrees: "You will not die; for God knows that when you eat of it your eyes will be opened, and you will be like God (or gods [*elohim*]), knowing good and evil" (3:4–5). The woman and the *adam* eat, but they do not die. Rather, they gain knowledge of their nakedness, recognize shame, and leave the innocence of childhood behind. The snake was right.

What kind of God would so tempt humanity with forbidden fruit? Why threaten death, but not carry out the threat?

Escaping with his wives, children, and substantial goods from the household of his father-in-law, Laban, Jacob arrives at the Jabbok River. In the morning he will meet his twin, Esau, whom decades before he had cheated out of birthright and blessing. After sending his family across the river, Jacob is "alone," and "a man wrestled with him until daybreak" (Gen. 32:24). The opponent injures Jacob's hip, but is unable to prevail. Finally, he urges, "Let me go, for the day is breaking." But Jacob says, "I will not let you go, unless you bless me." The blessing is a renaming: "You shall no longer be called Jacob, but Israel, for you have striven with God (Elohim) and with humans, and have prevailed." Then Jacob asks him, "Please tell me your name." But he replies, "Why is it that you ask my name?" Right after that question, the text says, "And there he blessed him." So Jacob calls the place Peniel (i.e., "face of God") saying, "For I have seen God (Elohim) face to face, and yet my life is preserved."

How is Jacob both "alone" and with a man? Was the opponent human, an angel, or God? Or was the opponent Jacob's conscience—was the patriarch wrestling with, and wounded by, his own shame and guilt? Or yet again, are such questions too modern to be applied to an ancient text?

Having escaped Egypt after murdering a slave master who had been beating an Israelite slave, Moses marries the daughter of the local Midianite priest and takes up the low-income, low-status task of shepherding. Meanwhile, in Egypt, the Israelites "groaned under their slavery. . . . God (Elohim) heard their groaning, and God remembered his covenant with Abraham, Isaac, and Jacob" (Exod. 2:23–24). Instead of directly liberating the Israelite slaves, God commissions this fugitive murderer.

On Mt. Horeb, the "mountain of God," Moses sees a bush ablaze, and "the angel of the LORD (YHWH) appeared to him in a flame of fire out of a bush" (Exod. 3:2). "When the LORD (YHWH) saw that he had turned aside to see, God (Elohim) called to him out of the bush" (3:4), commissioning him to tell Pharaoh to free the Israelite slaves. Moses asks, "If I come to the Israelites and say to them, 'The God of your ancestors has sent me to you,' and they ask me, 'What is his name?' what shall I say to them?" (3:13). In other words, "Which God are you?" The answer he receives (3:14) is, "I WILL BE WHAT I WILL BE" (*ehyeh asher ehyeh*).

What sort of God shows up in a bush? What sort of God appears not to royalty, but to a fugitive murderer? What kind of a name is "I will be what I will be"?

On Mt. Sinai, "the LORD (YHWH) descended in the cloud" and passed before Moses. In the previous chapter, we saw the following quote, here in a slightly more literal translation. The Lord (YHWH) proclaimed:

> The LORD, the LORD (YHWH), a God (El) merciful and
> gracious, slow to anger, and abounding in loving-kindness

and truth, keeping loving-kindness for the thousandth generation, forgiving iniquity and transgression and sin, yet by
no means clearing the guilty, but visiting the iniquity of the
parents upon the children and the children's children, to the
third and the fourth generation. (Exod. 34:6–7)

Is this the stereotypical "Old Testament God of wrath," or is it a pronouncement that humans are morally accountable and that justice will
prevail? How does this proclamation of generational guilt (see also Exod.
20:5; Deut. 5:9) comport with the Bible's insistence that "a child shall not
suffer the iniquity of a parent" (Ezek. 18:20; cf. Deut. 24:16)?

These portraits, distinct and complex, can be multiplied: the God who
regrets creating humanity and so cleanses the earth with a flood (Gen. 6);
the God who listens to Abraham plead that the city of Sodom be spared, if
ten righteous people can be found within its walls (Gen. 18); the "God who
gave you birth" (Deut. 32:18) and who promises, "Even to your old age I am
he, even when you turn gray I will carry you. I have made, and I will bear; I
will carry and will save" (Isa. 46:4); the God who showed Isaiah the heavenly throne room, where the seraphim call to each other, "Holy, holy, holy is
YHWH of hosts; the whole earth is full of his glory" (Isa. 6:3).

The God of the Bible, although systematized, psychoanalyzed, narrativ-
ized, and otherwise sized up, remains beyond any simplistic categorization:
imminent and transcendent; personal and unknowable; omnipotent and suffering; merciful and yet by no means clearing the guilty—the biblical deity
refuses categorization. The God of Israel is free, as the self-identification
"I will be what I will be" announces. But this free God graciously interacts
with humanity: "I am YHWH, and I will free you from the burdens of the
Egyptians and deliver you from slavery to them. I will redeem you with an
outstretched arm and with mighty acts of judgment. I will take you as my
people, and I will be your God. You shall know that I am YHWH your
God, who has freed you from the burdens of the Egyptians. I will bring
you into the land that I swore to give to Abraham, Isaac, and Jacob; I will
give it to you for a possession. I am YHWH" (Exod. 6:6–8).

Four Stumbling Blocks to Talking About the Biblical God

Whenever we talk about God—whether the God of the Bible or any interpretation of the God of the Bible—we can only approximate a descrip-

tion. We choose which books to feature, which events to highlight, which adjectives to use. The Bible refuses to provide a single view or center to its theology, despite the hope of biblical theologians and canonical critics that a center can be found. The biblical God is too mysterious, too magisterial, and too much interested in a relationship with humanity to be stuffed into a theological box.

These diverse pictures should challenge the idea that the God of this text is a changeless, unmoved mover, "the same yesterday and today and forever" (Heb. 13:8, in reference to Jesus Christ). Perhaps our own sense of personal chaos leads us to project onto the text an image of a changeless and predictable being. But the biblical God is primarily a relational deity, and in true relationship both parties can change. This God can be surprised and delighted, pained and angry, far distant and too present, often mysterious, and always, always free.

A second concern comes with the question of the existence of God. This approach, popular on the raging secular front, claims we invented God. We humans could not control nature, did not understand the mystery of birth, and feared death, so we invented a power greater than ourselves, a power that brought order to chaos, purpose to life, and comfort in death. Next, we invented religion to explain the power that we invented to explain our fears of what we could not control. Then, we wrote the Bible to control the religion that explains the power that we invented. . . . Next came clergy, to interpret the Bible that we wrote. . . . And today we have academics to challenge the clergy who interpret the Bible that we wrote to control the religion that explains. . . . And this is the house that Jack, or Moses, or Ezra built. But these are not issues the Bible addresses.

For the Bible, the existence of God is presupposed; atheism does not even occur in ancient Southwest Asian texts. The question the Bible poses is not, "Is there a God?" It asks, instead, "What kind of God is there?" "How do we relate to this God?" and "Where is God when we are in dire need of divine help?" As Psalm 89:46 laments, "How long, O YHWH? Will you hide yourself forever?"

Given that the text is an anthology, the answers to these questions will vary. To the skeptic who says, "I don't believe in God," the anthology responds, "Tell me about the God you do *not* believe in, and I will agree with you." In one book, the Hebrew version of the book of Esther, the deity is absent or at least is not explicitly present. Traditional interpretation suggests that Mordecai, in exhorting his cousin Queen Esther to act on her people's behalf, evokes God: "For if you keep silence at such a time as this, relief and deliverance will rise for the Jews from another place (*maqom*), but you and your father's family will perish" (4:14). The Hebrew *maqom* can be a circumlocution for God. The first-century Jewish historian Josephus thought so, as he paraphrases: "If she now neglected this opportunity, there would certainly arise help to them from God some other way" (*Antiquities* 11.227). The Septuagint goes out of its way to insert explicit references to God in the book of Esther. If one wants to find God in the text, or in the world, one will. But the story, all the stories, work regardless of whether there is a transcendent deity to which it points.

Even the nontheist can regard the Bible as "inspired" in the same way one can speak of a painting or a concerto as inspired. To claim a work of art is inspired does not mean that a supernatural power held the paintbrush or the violin. Nor does "inspired" mean perfect; the Bible is necessarily limited, because it is communicated through our limited language. Even New Testament claims regarding inspiration limit the application of the term. Second Timothy 3:16 states, "All scripture is inspired [*theo-pneustos*, literally, 'God-breathed'] by God and is useful for teaching, for reproof, for correction, and for training in righteousness." This does not say that the text is the *only* source of teaching, and it does not explain the sort of "teaching" for which scripture would be helpful (instruction in theology is not the same thing as instruction in biology or physics).

Whether the text is *divinely* inspired is a question that cannot be answered by history—that is a matter of faith. For those who read through theistic lenses, the Bible is God's story for humanity. For those who have a secular approach, the Bible is the expression of humanity's hopes and fears as understood through the experiences of ancient Israel. The artistry of the narrative, the morality of the law, the pathos of Lamentations, and exultant joy of the Song of Songs offer much, regardless of one's theology. To read the text in light of theological questions should mean, for the theist, to be challenged by the diverse presentations of the deity. For the atheist or agnostic, the text raises other challenges: What is the purpose of life? Where is justice to be found? How does the human spirit respond to suffering, inequity, violence? Is there a power—call it conscience, or nature, or God—that transcends the selfish will of the individual?

A third stumbling block to understanding the biblical deity is "the Old Testament God of wrath vs. the New Testament God of love" configuration. This approach not only misreads the theology of both Testaments;

it results in anti-Jewish propaganda and misguided Christian apologetic. The canard is easily dismantled by select citations. For example, the "Old Testament" insists, "The LORD is my shepherd" (Ps. 23:1), whereas the New Testament condemns people to "the outer darkness, where there will be weeping and gnashing of teeth" (e.g., Matt. 8:12). If the flood story seems bad, the book of Revelation, in which the world is destroyed one and a third times, is worse. If the ten plagues inflicted on the Egyptians for failing to free the Israelite slaves seem harsh, so does the punishment of the unforgiving servant in Matthew 18:32–35: "His lord handed [the servant] over to be tortured until he would pay his entire debt. So my heavenly Father will also do to every one of you, if you do not forgive your brother or sister from your heart."

According to the church, the God of creation, of Genesis and Isaiah and Psalms, is the God to whom Jesus taught his followers to pray, "Our Father" (Matt. 6:9). There is no personality shift between the Testaments. The Jewish tradition recognizes the God of the Tanakh as loving and compassionate, so the God of wrath stereotype tends not to be a problem for Jews informed about their own tradition.

Notice of tradition brings us to the fourth stumbling block to appreciating the Bible's presentation of the deity. Many people impose their own religious beliefs onto the text. Reading from the New Testament or rabbinic sources back to Genesis or Isaiah is a legitimate theological move, but it should serve to complement, rather than substitute for, the meaning the text would have had to its original audience. For example, certain Christian readers may well find the Trinity in Genesis 1:26, "Let *us* make humankind in our image" and see Jesus in Isaiah's suffering servant, who "was wounded for our transgressions, crushed for our iniquities; upon him was the punishment that made us whole, and by his bruises we are healed" (53:5). People who first heard Genesis 1 and Isaiah 53 were not thinking of Jesus. But meaning is not restricted to authorial intent or the impressions of the first audience. Those who read through Christian lenses will see Christian concerns. The Pontifical Biblical Commission put the point well when it stated, in *On the Jews and Their Scriptures in the Christian Bible*, that one should not be expected to find Jesus in the pages of the Old Testament unless one presupposes he is there.

The issue is not, "What is the right reading?" It is, rather, "What do we seek to know when we read the text?" Some readers will seek the answers to theological questions, others to historical or literary ones. Some read for guidance, others for pleasure, still others for historical interest. Different agendas yield different results.

Similarly, there are Jewish understandings of God as revealed in the Tanakh. To eliminate Christian readings would require eliminating Jewish readings as well. One famous *midrash* (an "investigation" or "study") offers the following interpretation of Exodus 15. When the Egyptian chariots, in pursuit of the fleeing Israelite slaves, become caught in the mire of the Reed Sea, the charioteers drowned. "The prophet Miriam, Aaron's sister, took a tambourine in her hand; and all the women went out after her with tambourines and with dancing. And Miriam sang to them: 'Sing to YHWH, for he has triumphed gloriously; horse and rider he has thrown into the sea'" (15:20–21). The midrash says that the angels took up the song, but God did not join the celebration. Searching, the angels found God weeping. When they inquired, God responded, "My creatures are drowning in the sea and you want to sing praises?" (Babylonian Talmud *Megilla* 10b). To appreciate the biblical view of the deity, then, means recognizing that the picture is colored not only by which texts are cited, but also by the lenses through which they are read and by the questions that readers bring to the text.

The Names of God

The generic term for "god" throughout the Semitic language groups is *el* or *eloah*, the latter related linguistically to the Arabic *allah*. The designation El referring to the biblical God appears in the Bible 238 times, often in compound names. For example, Isra-el, "strives with God," is the name Jacob receives at the Jabbok River. But El is also the proper name of the principal god of the Canaanite pantheon. Biblical references to El and the related terms El Elyon, El Shaddai, El Olam, and even Elohim bear linguistic connections to their Canaanite context. Each of the names attributed to the deity attests different powers, different manifestations, and different origins. To understand fully the biblical portrait of the God of Israel, we must also understand the Canaanite as well as Egyptian, Babylonian, and Persian contexts in which biblical theology took shape.

Information on Canaanite traditions comes primarily from literary remains of the ancient city of Ugarit, discovered in 1929 at Ras Shamra, on Syria's Mediterranean coast. Along with temples and a palace, archaeologists found texts primarily dating around 1400 BCE, written in the West

Semitic language of Ugaritic as well as in Akkadian, Hurrian, Egyptian (script and hieroglyphic), Hittite, and Cypro-Minoan. The religious texts describe the head god, El, as an old man with a white beard; he sits surrounded by his heavenly court. Over a millennium later, the prophet Daniel offered a similar picture: "As I watched, thrones were set in place, and an Ancient One took his throne, his clothing was white as snow, and the hair of his head like pure wool. . . . A thousand thousands served him, and ten thousand times ten thousand stood attending him" (7:9–10; see also 1 Kings 22:19; 2 Chron. 18:18; Ps. 102; Job 36; Isa. 40).

For the Bible, El appears frequently with epithets: El Shaddai, El Elyon, and so on. Each may have been a separate deity or the same deity attached to distinct locations or events (as one might talk about the Virgin Mary as "Our Lady of Guadalupe" or "Our Lady of Czestochowa"): same god, different titles and different stories. For the biblical editors, all these references are to the same deity. For the biblical historian, each epithet may indicate a distinct god with a distinct geographic center and a distinct cultic apparatus.

El Shaddai appears thirty-one times in the book of Job. Like *eloah*, the generic name that also occurs mostly in Job, El Shaddai likely seemed to the author of Job a designation appropriate on the lips of a Gentile. Outside of Job, El Shaddai is often paired with the name YHWH, a connection masked by most English translations. For Genesis 17:1 (and see Exod. 6:3), the NRSV reads: "The LORD (YHWH) appeared to Abram, and said to him, 'I am God Almighty.'" Behind "God Almighty" is the Hebrew El Shaddai.

The translation "God Almighty" is not without some justification. Job asks, "What is *shaddai* that we should serve him?" (21:15). The Septuagint translates *shaddai* as *ikanos*, meaning "strong, sufficient, or able," and from "strong" it's an easy step to "almighty." Job 8:5 reads in the Hebrew, "If you will seek *el* and make supplication to *shaddai* . . ."; in Greek *el* becomes *kyrios* (Lord) and *shaddai* becomes *pantokratora*—literally, "all mighty."

In ancient Hebrew, El Shaddai may have meant "God of the Mountains" or "God of the Breasts" (i.e., "twin peaks"). Jacob's blessing to Joseph includes the following wordplay: "By the God of your father, who will help you, by *shaddai* who will bless you with blessings of heaven above, blessings of the deep that lies beneath, blessings of the breasts (*shadayim*) and of the womb" (Gen. 49:25). Although the terminology is masculine, the attributes are feminine. That deities would be represented as combining genders should not be unexpected, as we shall shortly see.

El Elyon, usually translated "God Most High," is like the other El identifications assimilated to the singular biblical deity. Here the focus is on geography rather than power; whereas El Shaddai can be seen to focus on might, El Elyon focuses on height. Numbers 24:16 shows a triple conjunction of divine names: "The oracle of one who hears the words of *el,* and knows the knowledge of *elyon,* who sees the vision of *shaddai.* . . ." "Most High" as a translation of *elyon* is faithful to the Hebrew—the root *alah* means to "go up" (and is a cognate to the term *aliyah,* which today refers to Jews who immigrate, or "go up," to Israel). The Septuagint recognizes the connection by translating YHWH Elyon as *kyrios hypsistos,* "Lord Most High" (Ps. 47:3, LXX 46:3).

In a passage revealing an earlier tradition in which this integration of titles had not become secure, Deuteronomy 32:8–9 appears to distinguish Elyon from YHWH. "When Elyon apportioned the nations, when he divided *bene adam* [humankind], . . . YHWH's own portion was his people, Jacob his allotted share." Here, YHWH may have been originally conceived as one (very powerful) god within the royal pantheon; Israel was given to YHWH, who in turn expected Israel's complete loyalty. Other nations had their own gods.

El Elyon, which appears fifty-seven times, is, like El Shaddai, connected to non-Israelite biblical figures. Genesis 14:18–20 identifies the mysterious figure Melchizedek as the "priest of God Most High," the *kohen l'el elyon.* His name means "king" (*melech*) of "righteousness" (*tzedek*), and he is also the "king of Salem" (in Hebrew, without vowels, the words *salem* and *shalom,* "peace," are identical). Thus he is also "king of peace." Melchizedek says to the patriarch Abraham: "Blessed be Abram by God Most High (*el elyon*), maker of heaven and earth; and blessed be God Most High (*el elyon*), who has delivered your enemies into your hand!" Abraham, impressed (and perhaps a wee bit concerned about Melchizedek's power), "gave him one tenth of everything." Psalm 110:4 brings Melchizedek into a Yahwistic framework: "YHWH has sworn and will not change his mind, 'You are a priest forever according to the order of Melchizedek.'" The New Testament (Heb. 5–7) applies the verse to Jesus.

El Olam. A third epithet of El, along with Shaddai and Elyon, is Olam. The Hebrew means "eternity," and thus El Olam means "eternal God" or "everlasting God." Genesis 21:33 associates the name with Beersheva. The Septuagint offers *kyriou theos aionios,* the last word of which comes into English as "eon."

Also likely having localized connection is *El Berit*, the "God of the covenant," whom Judges 9:46 associates with the city of Shechem. This particular epithet did not catch on; perhaps the Shechemite connections were too strong.

El Roi, "God who sees," has an etiology associated with Hagar, another non-Israelite. Having fled her abusive owner, Sarah, the pregnant Hagar encounters an angel in the wilderness. He sends her back to her mistress, saying: "Now you have conceived and shall bear a son; you shall call him Ishmael [from *shema*, "to hear"], for YHWH has given heed to your affliction" (Gen. 16:11). Genesis 16:13 reports, "So she called the name of YHWH, the one who spoke to her, 'You are *el roi* [God who sees].'" The verse plays on the relationship of the senses of hearing and sight. Hagar explains the etymology: "Have I really seen God and remained alive after seeing him?" It also creates a disjunct: the narrator speaks of an angel; Hagar believes she has seen the deity directly. The theological conclusion depends, literally, on the eyes that do the seeing.

As these titles are related to particular locations, so the epithets of God associated with the patriarchs may reflect separate tribal groups. The "shield" of Abraham (Gen. 15:1); "the fear [or kinsman]" of Isaac (31:42); and the "mighty one," "shepherd," and "rock" of Jacob (49:24) may be the titles used by those who traced their ancestry to these figures. As Deuteronomy associates YHWH with El Elyon, so the patriarchal narratives place Abraham, Isaac, and Jacob in genealogical relation and assimilate their distinct gods into one God. But the view that the titles respect distinct tribal affiliations must remain hypothetical.

This one God is then distinguished from its Canaanite neighbors by the more familiar names Elohim (used 2,600 times in the Bible) and YHWH (used 6,828 times). Elohim is technically a masculine plural (as in *cherub-im* and *seraph-im*), probably of the generic *eloah*, but when referring to the God of Israel it takes masculine singular verbs and adjectives: the form is plural, the use is singular. English Bibles translate Elohim as "God." This fits the Septuagint, which translates Elohim as *theos* (whence "theology"), "God."

Regarding Elohim's origins, Exodus 18:12 posits a Kenite or, more broadly, Midianite connection: "Jethro, Moses's father-in-law, brought a burnt offering and sacrifices to God (Elohim); and Aaron came with all the elders of Israel to eat bread with Moses's father-in-law." Offering limited support to this connection is 1 Chronicles 2:55, which associates the Kenites with the Rechabites, a group known for strict personal piety (see Jer. 35:18). The term is associated with the Elohist source, which many have dated to the ninth century BCE, but which may not be so old. The Elohist uses the name Elohim to refer to the deity up to the story of the burning bush (Exod. 3), where it assimilates the names Elohim and YHWH.

The name YHWH, also referred to as the Tetragrammaton, or "four letters," appears in the Bible 6,828 times; it is missing only from Ecclesiastes, Esther, and the Song of Songs. The Septuagint typically translates this consonantal cluster as *kyrios,* or "Lord," and most English translations offer "LORD" (in small caps, a good mnemonic device, since both YHWH and LORD have four letters).

The Tetragrammaton is also encoded into numerous personal names, recognizable in English by the prefix "Jo," such as Jochebed, the mother of Moses, whose name means "YH(WH) is glory," or Jonathan, the son of Saul, whose name means "YH(WH) has given." Another theomorphic clue is the suffix "iah" (YH), as in Isaiah, meaning "YH(WH) is salvation," or Jeremiah, meaning "YH(WH) exalts." The Hebrew term *hallelujah* is, literally, "(you all) praise YH(WH)." The name is certainly old. Archaeological investigation in Jerusalem recently yielded two small silver scrolls from the sixth century BCE with the Tetragrammaton inscribed in Hebrew.

In answer to Moses's request for the God's name, Exodus provides the formal introduction to the Tetragrammaton: "God said to Moses, 'I AM WHAT I AM (I WILL BE WHAT I WILL BE, *ehyeh asher ehyeh*). . . .' Thus you shall say to the Israelites, 'I AM (*or* I WILL BE, *ehyeh*) has sent me to you'" (Exod. 3:13–14). The name of God, on the lips (metaphorically speaking) of God, is *ehyeh,* "I am," the first-person singular of the irregular (as might be expected) Hebrew verb "to be." Elsewhere in the Bible and subsequent Hebrew literature the term is not in the first person, but in the third, "He will be," or *yihyeh.* YHWH is thus comprised of the consonants of the verb meaning "he will be." The tense of YHWH is the "imperfect," which connotes not imperfection, but rather incomplete, open, or future action. "I will be what I will be" is one possible translation; others include "I cause to be," "I make exist," and "I make happen." The future orientation, with its connotation of freedom, is emphasized in Exodus 6:6–9: "I am YHWH, and I will free you from the burdens of the Egyptians and deliver you from slavery to them. I will redeem you with an outstretched arm and with mighty acts of judgment. I will take you as my people, and I will be your God. You shall know that I am YHWH."

The Septuagint translates Exodus 3:14 as *ego eimi ho on*, "I am the one who is," thereby presenting a more static identity. For the New Testament, Jesus's "I am" statements, as in "I am the true vine" or "I am the way, and the truth, and the life" (John 15:1; 14:6), echo the Septuagint's version of the divine name.

Although both the Hebrew and the Greek derive YHWH from the Hebrew verb "to be," other etymologies are possible. Suggestions include the verb "to fall" (like a meteor) or "to cause to fall" (like rain). Another is that "Yah" was a battle cry or a cultic shout. The Song of Moses, the ancient poem preserved in Exodus 15, exclaims: "My strength and my song YH is, and he has become to me salvation. This is my God (El) and I will praise him, Elohe [i.e., "God of"] my father, and I will exalt him" (15:2). Or perhaps the four letters were seen as having magical or mystical properties (as one might regard certain numbers, such as 7, 12, and 13, as having special power), since they mimic the sound of inhaling and exhaling.

These suggestions presume that the etymology offered in Exodus 3 is later than the name. The Bible has a tendency to play with names, and words in general, and sometimes to provide false etymologies. For example, although Exodus 2:10 states that Moses receives his name because Pharaoh's daughter "drew" him (Heb. *mashah*) from the water, the name is most likely an Egyptian term designating one belonging to a god, like Ra-*messes* or Thut-*mose*. However, this Egyptian connection does not mean that the biblical deity derives from the Egyptian monotheism promoted by Pharaoh Akhenaten in the second millennium BCE. The greater influences on the biblical text are from Ugarit and Babylon.

This deity, whose name is a verb, is appropriately found not primarily in the cyclical and (relatively) predictable aspects of nature; this is a God who is manifest not only in mythic time, but also in the "here and now" and in relation with the covenant community. Nor is this God attached to one place, despite the importance of the "promised land." Because this God operates in history, the divine presence is not restricted; Israel encounters its God at home or in exile, in Jerusalem and Egypt, Babylon and Persia.

The biblical editors insist that it is the same God encountered in all these locations. Exodus 3:15 makes the connection among the names of God: "Elohim also said to Moses, 'Thus you shall say to the Israelites, "YHWH, Elohe (God of) your ancestors, Elohe Abraham, Elohe Isaac, and Elohe Jacob, has sent me to you": This is my name forever (*le'olam*), and this my title from generation to generation.'" Exodus 6:2–3 reinforces the connections: "Elohim spoke to Moses and said to him: 'I am YHWH. I appeared to Abraham, to Isaac, and to Jacob as El Shaddai, but by my name YHWH I did not make myself known to them.'" Yet Genesis 4:26 states: "To Seth [Adam and Eve's son] also a son was born, and he named him Enosh. At that time, people began to invoke the name of YHWH." Here one of the Bible's editorial seams is evident: the J source uses YHWH prior to Exodus 3, the E source does not, and the P source puts the terms together.

YHWH presents a problem not only in translation—should it be rendered phonetically as a proper noun or translated as "Be/ing" (as some theologians do)?—but also in pronunciation. Early Christian writers offered their own guesses. Theodoret of Cyprus, writing in the first half of the fifth century, claimed that the Samaritans pronounced the divine name as *iabe;* then again, taking into consideration Theodoret's accent and that of the Samaritans, the pronunciation is necessarily suspect. A century earlier, Epiphanius stated that an early Christian group had a similar pronunciation. Clement of Alexandria, a century earlier still, offered two possible pronunciations: *iaoue* and *iaouai*. In ancient spells, recorded in what are now called the Magical Papyrii, the name is listed as *iaooue*. And in some versions, it is pronounced *pipi*, as in "Longstocking" or, more accurately, as in the sound that early Egyptians attributed to chickens. The reason for this permutation is easily located. The Tetragrammaton, written in Hebrew letters and read right to left, would make no sense to a Greek speaker. However, the *h* that is the second and fourth letter looks somewhat like the Greek *p*. The *y* that begins the term and the *w* that is the third letter can look like the Greek *i*. Read backward (i.e., left to right) and in presumably Greek script, the Hebrew YHWH looks like the Greek *pipi*, the colloquial term for "chicken" (in today's English "peep-peep").

This name that is to be praised for all generations is, according to traditional Judaism, ineffable. One legend has it that the sacred name came to be recited, once a year, on Yom Kippur, the Day of Atonement, by the high priest in the Holy of Holies, the inner sanctum of the Jerusalem temple. The Babylonian Talmud (*Yoma* 39b) suggests that around 30 CE, a generation before the destruction of the temple, after the high priest Simeon the Righteous died, the priests in the temple no longer pronounced the divine name. One later Jewish mystical tradition suggests that if the name could be correctly pronounced, the Messiah would be summoned. A less attractive Jewish tradition, from the early days of Christian Rome when the church began to persecute Jews, suggests that Jesus was a magician who was able to work signs because he had the name of God sewed into his thigh.

Despite the lack of vowels—and Torah scrolls to this day contain only Hebrew consonants—the Tetragrammaton has to be pronounced, given readings of the Torah in the synagogue. In Jewish prayer books, the Tetragrammaton is printed with vowels derived from, but not exactly the same as those of, the word *adonai*, which means "my lord(s)" (the name of the Greek god Adonis is a cognate); the plural form is, like Elohim, treated as a singular. Thus readers are cued, when seeing the Hebrew letters Y-H-W-H with odd points (or vowels), to say Adonai. Readers of the Torah will, upon seeing the Tetragrammaton, say Adonai as well. And, since Adonai is thus intimately associated with the sacred, religious Jews will not use this word outside of a worship context. Thus a circumlocution is needed for the ineffable name. To refer to the deity, religious Jews might use *adoshem* ("lord" + "name") or simply *ha-shem*, "the name" (see Lev. 24:11 for a very early use of this designation).

This special visual treatment of the Tetragrammaton antedates the time of Jesus. In several of the Dead Sea Scrolls, written in Hasmonean and Herodian script, the Tetragrammaton appears in paleo-Hebrew. For a modern analogy, one might imagine a text in New Times Roman font with "GOD" printed in Gothic. In the Targums, early common era Aramaic translations of the Tanakh, the Tetragrammaton is depicted as two *y*s, with a *w* over them; the letters *y* (10, twice) plus *w* (6) add up numerically to 26, which is the same number obtained by adding the numerical equivalents of Y-H-W-H. All Hebrew letters have numerical equivalents; adding up the letters of a word or phrase, finding the total, and then interpreting the word or phrase in terms of other words and phrases with the same numerical equivalent is known as *gematria*. This type of numerology is perhaps best known from the New Testament. The book of Revelation's "beast whose number is 666" (13:18) presents the numerical equivalent of the Hebrew letters spelling the name "Neron Caesar."

Although the Hebrew for "he will be" is *yihyeh*, the more common English pronunciation is Yahweh. The pronunciation likely stems from the work of Wilhelm Gesenius (1786–1842), a German biblical scholar, who suggested *Yahveh*. The Anglicized version turned the *v* into a *w*. Some Protestant churches use the name Yahweh to identify the God of the "Old

Testament"; the problem with this well-intentioned usage, well-intentioned since it respects the Hebrew text, is that it sometimes leads congregations to thinking that Yahweh is the God of the Old Testament, but not the God of the New Testament. Conversely, in 2008 the Roman Catholic Church suggested that the faithful avoid the name "Yahweh" in worship and thus maintain the name's sanctity. And still other churches speak of "Jehovah." The origins of this composite term come from early English translators who saw the Tetragrammaton with the vowels of *adonai* in Hebrew manuscripts and read the word literally. The *Y* of YHWH was pronounced as a *J* (as, e.g., Johann), and the *W* as a *V* (as, e.g., *Wehrmacht*), thus yielding JeHoVaH. The term appears a few times in the KJV, including Exodus 6:3.

For the heirs of this scripture, the synagogue and the church and the mosque as well, the God attested by the Bible is a single God; there is none other. The various names are regarded as titles, and to those titles are added more epithets: the Merciful, the Compassionate, the Redeemer, Father, and so on. Islamic tradition attributes at least ninety-nine names to the divine; the Jewish mystical tradition (Kabbalah) offers names spelled with forty-two and seventy-two letters, each combining several of the names and epithets found in the Tanakh.

Religious Competition and Co-optation

In the Canaanite pantheon as presented in the Ras Shamra texts, El has a son, Baal (meaning "lord" or "husband"); he is a warrior and a lover, god of storm, rain, and fertility. Baal dies and rises annually, and his story thus ties into the agricultural cycle. The following passages, set in different periods of Israel's history and different parts of Israel's literature, show the ongoing appeal of Baal worship to Israel's population and the writers' insistence on the worship of YHWH alone.

Numbers 25:1–3 describes how the wilderness generation "yoked itself to the Baal of Peor, and YHWH's anger was kindled against Israel." Twenty-four thousand Israelites die in the resulting plague, which is stopped when Phineas the priest, in an act the narrator hails as epitomizing fidelity, "pierced . . . through the belly" an Israelite man and a Midianite woman engaged in sexual intercourse.

In Judges 6, Gideon (from whom the society that places Bibles in hotel rooms takes its name) pulls down an altar to Baal. When the townspeople threaten to execute him, his father responds: "Will you contend for Baal? Or will you defend his cause? Whoever contends for him shall be put to death by morning. If he is a god, let him contend for himself, because his altar has been pulled down." Therefore, we are told, "Gideon was called Jerubbaal, that is, 'Let Baal contend against him,' because he pulled down his altar" (6:31–32). However, this account appears to be an apologetic etiology explaining how an Israelite judge had a name honoring Baal. What the writers promote and what the people do are not necessarily equivalent.

It turns out that numerous Israelites had a Baal component in their names, although in many instances the Hebrew scribes did a bit of editing. According to 1 Chronicles 8:34; 9:40, Saul's son Jonathan had a son named Merib-baal, or "Baal's beloved." In 2 Samuel 4:4 and elsewhere, this son is renamed Mephibosheth, "exterminator of the shameful one." The Hebrew of 2 Samuel 11:21, part of Joab's instructions to the messenger who will report the death of Uriah the Hittite to David, reads: "Who killed Abimelech son of Jerub-boshet?" (*boshet* means "shame"). The Septuagint, reflecting what is likely an earlier version than the extant Hebrew texts, reads "Jerubaal," and most English translations follow the Greek. The same practice occurs with Ishbaal ("man of Baal"), one of Saul's sons mentioned frequently in 2 Samuel. The Hebrew reads *ish-boshet*, "man of shame." For a variant on this process, David's son Baaliada ("Baal knows"), mentioned in 1 Chronicles 14:7, becomes Eliada ("my God, or El[ohim], knows") in 2 Samuel 5:16 and 1 Chronicles 3:8. Along with personal names, numerous locations bore the name "Baal": Baal-gad (Josh. 11:17; 12:7; 13:5), Baal-hamon (Song of Sol. 8:11), Baal-hazor (2 Sam. 13:23), Baal-hermon (Judg. 3:3; 1 Chron. 5:23), Baale-judah (2 Sam. 6:2; cf. Josh. 15:60; 18:14), Baalah (Josh. 15:9; 1 Chron. 13:6), and so on. As with other locations named after deities—for example, Athens, named for Athena—the name remained even when the worship of the god ceased.

First Kings 18 depicts a contest between the prophet Elijah and the priests of Baal. When Baal does not miraculously ignite the sacrifice his priests had prepared, Elijah taunts: "Surely he is a god; either he is meditating, or he has wandered away [likely a euphemism for, to use another euphemism, 'relieving himself'], or he is on a journey, or perhaps he is asleep and must be awakened" (18:27). The "fire of YHWH" then consumes Elijah's sacrifice, and Elijah orders the execution of Baal's prophets. Completing this anti-Baal polemic is Elijah's experience, in the next chapter, on Mt. Horeb, the site where Moses encountered the burning bush. Fleeing Queen Jezebel, who supported Baal worship, Elijah hides in a cave on Horeb. There the "word of YHWH" commands him: "Go out and stand on the mountain before YHWH, for YHWH is about to pass by." Then we are told: "Now there was a great wind, so strong that it was splitting mountains and breaking rocks in pieces before YHWH, but YHWH was not in the wind; and after the wind an earthquake, but YHWH was not in the earthquake; and after the earthquake a fire, but YHWH was not in the fire; and after the fire a sound of sheer silence" (19:11–12). Baal, the storm god, would be expected in wind, earthquake, and fire; here the God of Elijah comes in the peace after the storm.

The Baal worship that thrived under Jezebel ended, according to 2 Kings, when Jehu, the coup leader who displaced the queen and her husband, Ahab, executed all the worshipers of Baal after tricking them to come to a public sacrifice. Jehu and his companions "demolished the pillar of Baal, and destroyed the temple of Baal, and made it a latrine to this day. Thus Jehu wiped out Baal from Israel" (10:27–28).

The prophets tell a different story. Ahab reigned in the mid-ninth century, and Jehu shortly thereafter. But Hosea, who prophesied in the northern kingdom about a hundred years later, still yearns for the day when YHWH will say to Israel, "You will call me, 'My husband' (*ishi*), and no longer will you call me, 'My Baal' (*baali*). For I will remove the names of the Baals from her mouth, and they shall be mentioned by name no more" (2:16–17; Tanakh 2:18–19).

Kings could demolish and prophets could inveigh, but Baal worship along with other forms of worship disapproved of by the Bible's editors continued. Canaanite traditions were adopted into Israel's worship practices, with descriptions of Baal, who rides on the clouds and the wind—the image of a god as a cloud rider occurs in Ugaritic literature as early as the fourteenth century BCE—ascribed to the biblical God (see, e.g., Pss. 18:8–10; 68:33; 104:3). Writing in the late seventh century, on the eve of the Babylonian exile, Jeremiah could blame the destruction of Jerusalem on the people's worship of foreign gods: "When your people say, 'Why has the LORD our God (YHWH Elohenu) done all these things to us?' you shall say to them, 'As you have forsaken me and served foreign gods in your land, so you shall serve strangers in a land that is not yours'" (5:19).

The Divine Feminine

Hebrew is a gendered language. Nouns are masculine or feminine; there is no neuter as there is in Greek, the language of the Septuagint and the New Testament. Both grammatically and metaphorically, the biblical God is depicted as male. The God who rescues Israel "by a mighty hand and an outstretched arm" (e.g., Deut. 4:34) is a (male) divine warrior. The "LORD of hosts" (1 Sam. 1:3; and 246 other times) is a military image; the "hosts" are an angelic army.

However, the biblical God is not constrained by categories of masculine and feminine. Genesis 1:26–27 reads: "God (Elohim) said, 'Let us make humankind in our image, according to our likeness. . . .' So God created humankind in his image, in the image of God he created them; male and female he created them." The text uses anthropomorphic images, but it demurs from descriptions of a distinctly male or female body. Moses sees a vision of God, but what he sees is sexually indeterminate: "You shall see my back; but my face shall not be seen" (Exod. 33:23). Ezekiel describes his vision: "There was . . . something that seemed like a human form. Upward from what appeared like the loins I saw something like gleaming amber, something that looked like fire enclosed all around; and downward from what looked like the loins I saw something that looked like fire, and there was a splendor all around" (1:26–27).

Although called "father," but not "mother," the biblical God does have female attributes. As we have seen, the patriarch Jacob blesses his son Joseph "by the God of your father, who will help you, by the Almighty (*shaddai*) who will bless you with blessings of heaven above, blessings of the deep that lies beneath, blessings of the breasts (*shadayim*) and of the womb (*rakham*)" (Gen. 49:25). Along with the birthing image of Deuteronomy 32:18 is Psalm 22:9, where God is both midwife and nurse: "Yet it was you who took me from the womb; you kept me safe on my mother's breast." Isaiah 42:13–14 combines traditional masculine and feminine images: "YHWH goes forth like a soldier, like a warrior he stirs up his fury. . . . I [YHWH] will cry out like a woman in labor, I will gasp and pant." Maternal images continue in Isaiah 46:3 ("Listen to me, O house of Jacob, all the remnant of the house of Israel, who have been borne by me from your birth, carried from the womb") and 66:13 ("As a mother comforts her child, so I will comfort you").

More cynical readers might see these attributes as a co-optation of the woman's body. However, given the positive attention the texts pay to mothers in both narratives and the law code (e.g., the commandment to "revere your mother and father," in Lev. 19:3, where the mother is listed first), it is more likely that the maternal images show a valuation of childbirth and the maternal role.

For some Israelites, this valuation was theologically insufficient; they required more material recognition of the divine feminine. Both archaeological and textual material attests to an interest in goddess worship. Excavations have yielded numerous female images: recumbent on a bed and standing; with extended arms or holding snakes; with hands holding the breasts; as pregnant or as holding a child. However, we cannot determine if these artifacts—totaling in the thousands from Israel and Judah in the Iron II period—were primarily associated with matters of fertility, whether for families or for agriculture. They could have served as symbols of the divine, talismans, dolls, or good-luck charms; they were also likely objects of worship

The Bible indicates that women "wept for Tammuz"—another fertility god, like Baal, who dies and rises annually—at the Jerusalem temple (see Ezek. 8:14–16; Ezekiel is by no means happy about this practice). Jeremiah 7:18 describes how "children gather wood, the fathers kindle fire, and the women knead dough, to make cakes for the queen of heaven; and they pour out drink offerings to other gods." According to Jeremiah 44:15–19, they pursue this worship because they believe that their previous abandonment of it had caused the loss of blessings from the goddess. Judges 10:6 notes the worship of Astarte, a consort of Baal, and numerous texts speak of the "sacred pole" or grove, called an *asherah,* and dedicated to the goddess of the same name. For example, Judges 6:30, the people's call for Gideon's death, mentions not only that he pulled down the altar of Baal, but also that he "cut down the *asherah* beside it" (see also Isa. 27:9). Both the goddesses Asherah and Astarte occur in earlier, Late Bronze Age Ugaritic literature. The Bible tends not to distinguish between them, and it sometimes includes in its general category of "goddesses the writers don't like" Baal's consort Anat.

For the official line espoused by the biblical editors, there was no "goddess," nor was there need of one. But to the question, "Did God have a wife?" the answer is not a simple no, but rather "Not usually" and "It depends on whom one asks." Papyri from a fifth-century BCE Jewish military community in Elephantine, Egypt, attest the worship of the God of Israel, whom they called "Yahu" (YHW), as well as a deity called "Anat-YHW," colloquially, "Mrs. Yahu." Closer to home, a pottery jar from the eighth century BCE turned up in 1975–76 at an ancient caravanserai (or perhaps a shrine complex) at Kuntillet 'Ajrud in the northern Sinai desert, bearing a blessing "by Yahweh of Samaria and by his Asherah." Drawings of three figures from the same find may depict the deities. Even closer, an inscription at Khirbet el-Qom, about eight miles west of Hebron, includes another reference to "Yahweh" and "his Asherah."

More often, traits associated with the feminine divine become in Israel's tradition transferred to Wisdom (Heb. *chochmah;* Gk. *sophia*). In Proverbs 8 she says: "YHWH created me at the beginning of his work, the first of his acts of long ago. Ages ago I was set up, at the first, before the beginning of the earth. . . . I was beside him, like a master worker; and I was daily his delight, rejoicing before him always" (8:22–23, 30; see Prov. 1–9; Wis. 6–10; Sirach, *passim*). In the postbiblical Christian tradition goddess imagery reappears in some depictions of both the Virgin Mary and the Holy Spirit (the Spirit is grammatically feminine in Hebrew and Aramaic, although grammatically neuter in Greek). In the Jewish tradition, Wisdom is associated with the Shekinah (from the Hebrew root meaning "to dwell, to camp," related to the *mishkan*, the "tent of meeting"), the feminine manifestation of the divine. Some Targums express the sanctity of the name Elohim by substituting Shekinah for it.

Father God, Children of God, Angels

The biblical God does not officially have a wife; nor does he, again unlike his other divine counterparts, engage in sexual intercourse. However, this deity is described with marital metaphors. Hosea analogizes his marriage to Gomer, a prostitute and adulteress, to the faithful deity's marriage to unfaithful Israel; Ezekiel 16 extends this metaphor in a manner that may justly be considered, by today's standards, pornographically violent.

More often the biblical deity is depicted as a father. Deuteronomy 32:6b asks, "Is not he your father, who created you, who made you and established you?" Isaiah 64:8 proclaims: "Yet, YHWH, you are our Father; we are the clay, and you are our potter; we are all the work of your hand." Jeremiah 3:4 has the deity reminisce, "Have you not just now called to me, 'My Father, you are the friend of my youth.'" And Malachi 2:10 pleads with the people: "Have we not all one father? Has not one God created us? Why then are we faithless to one another, profaning the covenant of our ancestors [literally, 'fathers']?" It is a commonplace in some Christian circles to suggest that Jesus invented the idea of calling the deity "father" and established an intimacy not known in prior or contemporary Jewish sources. Those who make such a claim have, obviously, not read their Old Testament.

Other relational metaphors include "brother" (1 Sam. 14:3) and "redeemer" (*go'el*), referring to the close relative who would protect the family, as Leviticus 25:25 mandates: "If anyone of your kin falls into difficulty and sells a piece of property, then the *go'el* shall come and redeem what the relative has sold." Redeemer language appears in the famous line from Psalm 19:14, "Let the words of my mouth and the meditation of my heart be acceptable to you, YHWH, my rock and my redeemer (*go'el*)."

Both by words, as noted above, and by plot, the biblical God is also a friend to humanity. Exodus 33:11 states: "YHWH used to speak to Moses face to face, as one speaks to a friend." Abraham argues with the deity as one would argue with a friend. The approachability presumed by friendship also underlies the arguments that Job and Moses bring to the divine, and it underlies as well the psalms of lament, such as Psalm 44:24–25: "Awake, why do you sleep, Lord? . . . Why do you hide your face and forget our sufferings and oppression?" Despite suggestions that to see God's face would bring death (Gen. 32:30; Exod. 33:20), people do experience this direct encounter and live, as the many statements about seeing God "face to face" attest (not only Gen. 32:30; Exod. 33:11, but also Num. 14:14; Deut. 5:4; Sir. 45:5).

As God is imaged as father, so members of the covenant community are his children. Exodus 4:22 insists: "Thus says YHWH: Israel is my firstborn son." Hosea 11:1 offers the same idea: "When Israel was a child, I loved him, and out of Egypt I called my son." As the Hebrew "children of God" refers to those of Israel, so the New Testament uses the Greek equivalent, *huioi theou*, to refer to those who have accepted Jesus as Lord (e.g., Rom. 8:14, 19; Gal. 3:26). The singular "son of God" refers to Jesus, except in Luke 3:38, where it refers to Adam and therefore to all humanity.

The term for "son" in Hebrew is *ben;* the plural is *banim,* and the construct state (the genitive) indicating "sons of" is *bene* (an alternate transliteration is *b'nai*). Hence the name of the Jewish organization B'nai B'rith means "sons of the covenant." Today, "sons" is frequently translated as "children." The Aramaic term for "son" is *bar,* as in the term *bar mitzvah,* literally, "son of the commandment," or the names Barabbas ("son of the father") and Bar Cochba ("son of the star").

The term "son of God" typically referred to the king, whether the man on the throne or a future, idealized ruler. The so-called royal psalms or enthronement psalms develop this idea; here the king is depicted as adopted by the deity. Psalm 2, for example, uses "son" language in the context of a symbolic adoption: "I will tell of the decree of YHWH: He said to me, 'You are my son; today I have begotten you'" (2:7). The Dead Sea scroll 4QFlor 10–14 reads this text messianically, as does the New Testament in reference to Jesus (Acts 13:33; Heb. 1:5; 5:5).

When the plural, "sons of God" (*bene elohim*) appears, the reference is to titanlike figures, heavenly courtiers, or, in the early biblical material, other gods. According to Genesis 6:1–4, the "sons of God" mated with the "daughters of men/humankind" and produced a race of giants called the Nephilim, "fallen ones." The idea and the name "sons of God" may come from Ugaritic traditions that mention "children of El" or "sons of El." Genesis 6 is the prompt for later traditions that speak of fallen angels. According to a third-century BCE text known as *1 Enoch* and attributed to Enoch, who is seven generations down from Adam, these "sons of God" were supposed to watch over, and so protect, humanity, but the "Watchers" looked a bit too closely at human women. They taught humanity the arts of war and cosmetics and otherwise corrupted them. This tradition, although not recognized today as biblical, did have authoritative status for many in antiquity and was retained in the Ethiopian Orthodox canon. In the New Testament, the letter of Jude (14–16) refers to this tradition.

Ugaritic influence also lies behind Psalm 29:1. The English reads: "Ascribe to the Lord (YHWH), O heavenly beings, ascribe to the Lord glory and strength." The Hebrew, which is chanted in the synagogue on the Sabbath when the Torah scroll is brought out to the members of the congregation, reads not "heavenly beings," but "sons of God" (*bene elim*). For Job 38:7, the "sons of God" (*bene elohim*) are compared to the "morning stars"; again, the NRSV provides the less theologically threatening "heavenly beings." A similar hesitance on the part of English translators appears in Psalm 89:6 (Tanakh 89:7), where the NRSV offers, "Who among the heavenly beings is like the Lord (YHWH)"; the Hebrew is, again, *bene elim*, "sons of God."

For *bene elohim* in Job 38:7, the Septuagint offers "all angels." The same formulations can be found in Daniel 3:25, where in the Hebrew the fourth figure who accompanies Daniel's three friends, Shadrach, Meshach, and Abednego, in the fiery furnace is, in the Aramaic, "Like a son of the gods" and, in the Greek, "like an angel of God." Job 1:6 and 2:1 identify the satan as one of these "sons of God"; again the Septuagint reads "angel." For Psalm 82, the opening line in the NRSV reads: "God has taken his place in the divine council; in the midst of the gods he holds judgment." Here the English gets the right intent, although the Hebrew is even more striking to those who hold to a monotheistic view: "Elohim (God) stands in the congregation of El, among Elohim (gods) he judges." The polytheistic idea continues in vv. 6–7: "I say, 'You are Elohim (gods), and you all are children of Elyon; surely, like *adam* (humanity) you will die."

Eventually, these "sons of God," or, for the gender-inclusive aficionados, "children of God," become understood as angels. They are first connected to the nameless "messengers" (Heb. *malachim;* Gk. *angeloi*) who convey the divine word. Jacob, for example, sees the angels ascending and descending on the ladder (ramp) to heaven (Gen. 28:12). The wilderness generation was told that "an angel" would guard them on their way to the promised land (Exod. 23:20). Joshua sees the "commander of the army of YHWH" (5:14). However, the term *malach* in Hebrew as well as its Greek counterpart could simply indicate a "messenger." The name Malachi, which is associated with the last book in the prophetic corpus, literally means "My messenger." Thus the final book in the prophetic corpus is by a writer who remains anonymous.

Just as the biblical text unevenly equates the various names of the divine, so it unevenly equates the messenger/angel with the divine. In Genesis 16, an "angel" appears to Hagar, but Hagar, as we have seen, perceives that she saw God, El Roi, directly. Exodus 3:2 states that an angel (*malach* YHWH) appeared to Moses in the flame of the burning bush; v. 4 states that "God" (Elohim) called to him from the bush. For a more literarily complex example, in Genesis 22, God (Elohim) calls to Abraham with the command to sacrifice his son, but it is an "angel of the LORD" (*malach* YHWH) who stays the father's hand. Perhaps the text seeks to associate Elohim with transcendence and sacrifice, while YHWH represents immanence and compassion; perhaps the story is comprised of two sources; perhaps the reference to the angel suggests that the deity does not want to converse with Abraham directly. Indeed, following this account, Abraham and God no longer converse.

Yet the text also suggests that angels look like human beings. The divine messengers who join Abraham for lunch, who promise the birth of a son to Sarah, and who protect Lot and his daughters while Sodom and Gomorrah are destroyed are in human form (Gen. 18–19). Jacob's wrestling foe may have been an angel, or a person, or God. Samson's mother states that the "man of God" she encountered had an appearance "like that of an angel of God, most awe-inspiring" (Judg. 13:6).

According to Isaiah 6:1–3, the famous "throne vision," each of the seraphim who called to one another, "Holy, holy, holy is YHWH of hosts," had six wings: a pair for flying, a pair for covering their faces, and a pair for covering their feet (the last term is likely the standard euphemism for genitals). In Isaiah 14:29, the seraph is serpentine and fiery, as are the seraphim of Numbers 21:6–8. The etymology of the term suggests something "fiery" or "burning."

Connected to the seraphim are cherubim, but the biblical cherub is not a chubby toddler. Mentioned ninety-two times in the text, they appear as composite beings who attend the heavenly chariot. Ezekiel 10:14 mentions the "face of the cherub," but distinguishes it from the "face of a human being." Ezekiel 41:18 suggests that cherubim have two faces.

By the late Persian and early Hellenistic periods, angelic beings become mediators of heavenly secrets. In Daniel and other early apocalyptic literature, angels explain the divine plan to the visionary; in folktales they are rescuers in disguise, and they can work miracles for the faithful. The Septuagint, by translating "sons of God" as "angels," adds to this development, as in, for example, the story of the faithful Israelites who escape Nebuchadnezzar's fiery furnace (Dan. 3:25, 28). It is also an angel who aids Daniel in the lions' den (6:22).

Eventually, the angels receive names and, later, personalities. Michael, whose name means "who is like God?" is one of the "chief princes" (Dan. 10:13) and the "protector" of Israel (12:1). According to these passages, Persia and Greece also have guardian angels (an idea that will develop into the notion of patron saints). According to the book of Jude (9) and the book of Revelation (12:7–9), Michael is the leader of the heavenly hosts who defeat Satan and his angels.

Gabriel, the "man of God," serves as Daniel's heavenly mediator who explains the bizarre visions, and he gives Daniel the news that he must wait "seventy weeks of years" before divine justice will prevail (8:16; 9:21). He makes another appearance in the New Testament to announce to Mary her forthcoming pregnancy (Luke 1:26–28).

In the deuterocanonical book of Tobit, the angel Raphael (Heb., "God has healed") disguises himself as a human, serves as the hero Tobias's guardian and tutor, and explains the means by which Tobit can be cured of his blindness. Tobit 12:15 mentions the "seven angels who stand ready and enter before the glory of the Lord," and from here comes the idea of seven arch (or chief) angels: Raphael, along with Michael, Gabriel, Uriel (who appears in *1 Enoch*), and three others whose names vary from tradition to tradition. Qumran's "Angelic Liturgy" contains a similar list, as does the Zoroastrian list of seven *amesha spentas* ("bounteous immortals"): Holy Spirit, Good Mind, Truth, Right Mindedness, Kingdom, Wholeness, and Immortality. According to the Qumran scrolls, the "prince of light" will fight the "angel of darkness" and the "sons of darkness" (1QM 13; 1QS 3).

Although part of Jewish, Christian, and Muslim theology, angels were not accepted by all Jews through the first century. The New Testament (Acts 23:8) indicates that the Sadducees, one Jewish movement, rejected the idea of angels. On the other hand, Josephus mentions not only that the Essenes believed in angels, but also that they kept secret a list of angelic names (*War* 2.142); here the mystical attributes of the divine name extend to other heavenly creatures. By the fourth century, Christianity had added to the ranks: archangels, cherubim, seraphim, virtues, powers, principalities, dominions, and thrones. Islam, although strictly monotheistic, also recognizes other supernatural beings. One tradition suggests that there are four bearers of Allah's throne, symbolized by a man, a bull, an eagle, and a lion. These symbols match iconographic images for the four canonical Gospels: Matthew as a human being, Mark as a lion, Luke as an ox, and John as an eagle. Islamic tradition also records four archangels, Jibril (Gabriel), the revealer; Mikal (Michael), the provider; Izra'il, the angel of death; and Israfil, the angel of the last judgment; as well as various guardian angels.

Polytheism, Henotheism, and Monotheism

References to other gods or "sons of God" suggest that the ancient Israelites, at least in their earlier history, acknowledged that other gods existed—their distinction was that, of the many gods, the Israelites were only supposed to worship one. This idea is known as *henotheism* (the worship of one god among many) as opposed to *monotheism* (the belief that there is only one God, period). A perhaps early passage attesting to this view is in the Song of Moses. Moses sings, "Who is like you, YHWH, among the gods (*elim*)?" (Exod. 15:11). English translations sometimes render the text as "among the mighty." Judges 2:12 laments that the people had abandoned YHWH, the God of (Elohe) their ancestors, and followed "gods of (Elohe) the people"—with no indication that these gods do not exist. Psalm 86:8 praises YHWH: "There is none like you among the gods." Had the author not thought that other gods existed, the praise would lose its force.

Henotheism is also suggested by the famous verse known as the Shema, from its opening exhortation, "Hear" or "Listen up!" Deuteronomy 6:4 reads: "Hear you, Israel, YHWH our God, YHWH is one (*or* YHWH alone)." Israel was not the only nation to have a primary deity; the Moabites had Chemosh, and the Ammonites had Milcom. In Torah scrolls, the last letter of the word *Shema* (*ayin*) and the last letter of *echad*, the term for "one" or "alone" (*dalet*), are written in letters larger than the rest of the text: *ayin* and *dalet* comprise the word *ed*, "witness," and thus this verse serves as "witness" to the text's primacy in Israel's theology. Jesus would have agreed; according to Mark 12:29, the Shema is the "first commandment."

But for the Israelites, their God deserved their sole loyalty, for this God had rescued them from the hands of their oppressors *and their oppressors' gods*. Exodus 12:12 states: "For I will pass through the land of Egypt that night, and I will strike down every firstborn in the land of Egypt, both human beings and animals; on all the gods of Egypt I will execute judgments: I am YHWH" (see also Num. 33:4). Joshua 24:15 even presents the worship of one God as the Israelites' choice: "Now if you are unwilling to serve YHWH, choose this day whom you will serve, whether the gods your ancestors served in the region beyond the River or the gods of the Amorites in whose land you are living."

By the mid-sixth century, the time of the Second Isaiah, the allure of these other gods ceased being a real threat and became something to be satirized. Instead of Elijah's fierce denunciations, Isaiah (44:9–17) shows through humor the folly of idol worship: "Who would fashion a god or cast an image that can do no good?" Isaiah describes the workman who uses part of a log as fuel and fashions the other part into a god that he then worships.

It is at this time as well that the idea of the biblical God's universalism begins to become a prominent theme. If the God of Israel is the God of the world, then no other heavenly beings could have power. Whereas the texts of the exilic and postexilic periods do not expect the gentile nations to become part of Israel, they do expect these nations eventually to worship this one all-powerful and merciful God. At the same time, the biblical editors expect complete loyalty of the people Israel.

Seeing the Portraits Again

Anyone can appreciate a painting, make observations on the colors or the brushstrokes, talk about how much or how little the depiction approximates its subject, and explain how the painting makes one "feel." The same configurations hold for the Bible. One can look at a particular depiction of the deity and draw various conclusions. Yet to see those depictions as part of a larger exhibit, to see the presentation of the same scene through the eyes of different artists, to look again after learning more about the sources of the paint, the type of the canvas, even the goals of the patrons allows the viewer to appreciate the creation in greater depth and with more enjoyment. The same should hold true for the study of the Bible and thus of the biblical God.

The God of Genesis 2–3 can be viewed in several ways. One way, associated with the so-called Gnostic groups of the early Christian era, sees this deity as inept and clueless, as wishing to keep people from having knowledge, and as creating an obviously flawed world.

A second way is to read Genesis 2–3 as the continuation of the story begun in Genesis 1, the story that offers the first commandment: "Be fruitful and multiply, and fill the earth" (1:28). The first couple are placed initially in the garden, but they must make their own fate; they must choose to leave the garden, or the nest, and make their way in the world. God, like a parent, offers them the opportunity of displaying their free will, and so of making their own choices.

Yet a third way is to see God as offering the first couple an opportunity to choose the right, since a life without choice of whether to obey or disobey is a life of slavery, not freedom. With humanity's choice, the deity, although disappointed, does not abandon his creation. Instead, when the man and his wife are banished from Eden, God goes with them. There is no irreparable breach between humanity and divinity, for divine mercy and compassion prevail.

Yet another view proclaims a breach, an original sin, that destroys the relationship between heaven and earth, but in this interpretation divine mercy rectifies the breach through the obedience, death, and resurrection of the "son of God," Jesus of Nazareth. The story opens to multiple interpretations, as any good story should, and the God can be seen in multiple ways, as any true deity not constrained to a single view will.

Jacob, wrestling at the Jabbok, encounters distinct manifestations of the divine: as external force, in the face of another, in the conscience of his heart. One does not come away from such an encounter unchanged, and Jacob, who will limp the rest of his life after this encounter, continues to show its impact. From this liminal encounter, Jacob learns, or at least appears to learn, that his fortunes come in part from the grace of the divine. He urges his brother, Esau, "Please accept my gift that is brought to you, because God has dealt graciously with me, and because I have everything I want" (Gen. 33:11). The sincerity of his claim seems to be demonstrated by his building an altar in Shechem, which he calls El Elohe Israel, "God, the God of Israel" (33:20). In this encounter, he is also able to see the face of the divine even in his twin: "For truly to see your face is like seeing the face of God—since you have received me with such favor" (33:10).

Finally, from this encounter he learns that he is not all-powerful, that he will continue to struggle, that deceit can lead not only to birthright and blessing, but to loss and death. At Shechem, Jacob's daughter, Dinah, is seduced or raped by the prince of the territory, and Jacob's sons take revenge by destroying the Shechemites. Jacob is forced again to relocate his family: "Jacob said to Simeon and Levi, 'You have brought trouble on me by making me odious to the inhabitants of the land, the Canaanites and the Perizzites; my numbers are few, and if they gather themselves against me and attack me, I shall be destroyed, both I and my household'" (Gen. 34:30). On the road, Rachel will die in childbirth. To be in relationship with this mysterious deity does not mean that all is milk and honey; it means being aware that actions have consequences, that easy answers are not forthcoming, and that divine support does not compromise free will.

Like Jacob, Moses is no saint. In this Testament, no one is. The text does not expect the covenant community to be perfect in thought and deed; rather, it especially hails those who reorient their lives to fulfill divine will. God makes a habit of choosing not the elite, but the marginal. The first annunciation comes not to Abraham, but to the Egyptian slave Hagar; the Law and the Prophets express divine concern for the disenfranchised and the condemnation of power; Psalms speaks of divine forgiveness.

According to Deuteronomy, Moses teaches the people that they too have been called by God:

> Although heaven and the heaven of heavens belong to the
> Lord your God (YHWH elohecha), the earth with all
> that is in it, yet the Lord (YHWH) set his heart in love
> on your ancestors alone and chose you, their descendants
> after them, out of all the peoples, as it is today. . . . The
> Lord your God (YHWH elohechem) is God of gods
> (*elohe ha-elohim*) and Lord of lords (*adone ha-adonim*), the
> great God (El), mighty and awesome, who is not partial
> and takes no bribe, who executes justice for the orphan and
> the widow, and who loves the strangers, providing them
> food and clothing. (10:14–18)

This is the God who, in freedom, chooses to be in covenant with Israel and chooses to forgive "our transgressions" when "deeds of iniquity overwhelm us" (Ps. 65:3). This is a God who demands much, but who remains faithful when those demands are not met.

As the portrait of God in Exodus 34:6–7 shows, the biblical God is both forgiving and demanding. This God demands individual responsibility, but teaches that the sins of one generation will impact the next. The crimes of adultery and murder committed by David impact the next generation. Amnon, the crown prince, rapes his half sister Tamar, and Absalom, another of David's sons, kills Amnon and wages civil war against his father. We see that same generational sin on the national and global levels, from the destruction of the environment to the outcomes of arming one group in order to fight another. The Bible insists on both personal responsibility and recognition that what we do inevitably impacts the generations to come. We are not guilty of the sins of past generations, but we nevertheless suffer their repercussions.

The biblical text refuses to offer a single portrait of the deity; instead, it offers complementary views of mercy and demand, compassion and condemnation. To recognize the import of free will and moral responsibility, the text in select places poses questions to its readers. Three examples conclude this study of the biblical God.

First, the question of God's presence, or absence, is often palpable. Genesis 34, the story of Dinah and Shechem and the slaughter that ensues, ends with a question. To Jacob's assertion that his sons' attack will make him "odious in the land," Simeon and Levi respond, "Should our sister be treated like a whore?" (34:31). In this chapter, God does not appear. And thus the text permits readers to ask: "Where is God when women are raped and men are killed?" Who will give voice to the justice that the biblical God demands?

This same question of absence and presence besets Job. Job both demands the divine presence to explain his suffering and seeks to escape from it: "Will you not look away from me for a while, let me alone until I swallow my spittle? If I sin, what do I do to you, you watcher of humanity? Why have you made me your target? Why have I become a burden to you?" (7:19–20). Ecclesiastes (Qohelet) takes the question one step farther: "What do people gain from all the toil at which they toil under the sun? . . . For who knows what is good for mortals while they live the few days of their vain life, which they pass like a shadow? For who can tell them what will be after them under the sun?" (1:3; 6:12).

The Hebrew text allows its readers to rail against injustice, to demand its God respond with compassion and righteousness, to express their despair. It may not provide a definitive description of the divine, but it does provide guidelines on how to approach the divine—with honesty, with emotion, with demand.

The book of Jonah, which describes the repentance of the city of Nineveh, the capital of the Assyrian empire, ends with a question. Jonah has regretted this repentance and the consequent reprieve of the city, whether because it means that his own prediction of destruction will not be fulfilled or because he presciently knows that Nineveh, here spared destruction, will later destroy the northern kingdom, Israel. Yet God responds, "Should I not be concerned about Nineveh, that great city, in which there are more than a hundred and twenty thousand persons who do not know their right hand from their left, and also many animals?" (4:11). The God of the Bible is concerned with, and in relationship with, not only Israel, but also the nations.

Conversely, the prophet Nahum celebrates the destruction of Nineveh. Here the final question accentuates not divine mercy, but divine punishment: "There is no assuaging your hurt, your wound is mortal. . . . For who has ever escaped your endless cruelty?" (3:19). The text reinforces the claim from Exodus that YHWH is "slow to anger but . . . will by no means clear the guilty" (1:3): for this God, enough is enough. In the opening poem (1:2–10), Nahum, prophesying in the early years of the reign of King Josiah (ca. 640–20), anticipates the fall of Nineveh, the Assyrian capital; he also expects that this destruction will lead the people of Judah to repentance.

In times of crises, the prophets recognize divine mercy and steadfastness; in times of plenty, the prophets insist that God's standards for righteousness be maintained. As the fortunes of the nation and of its members change, so does the prominent depiction of the deity. Never imaged and yet described by anthropomorphic terms, unable to be seen and yet in relationship face-to-face, ever merciful and yet condemning the guilty, the biblical God remains free, enigmatic, and, for those who hold the text sacred, a protective ruler, a caring, compassionate parent, and a worthy subject for worship.

Chapter 6

The Cultus

Today the term "cult" has negative associations. "Religions" are what *we* have, but "cults" are what *they* do; "religions" have normal traditions, but "cults" are weird. Therefore, when biblical critics use the term "cult" to refer to ancient Israel's sacrificial system or to biblical codes concerning how the people were to sanctify their land, houses, or bodies, many readers rankle. Their reaction is comparable to what happens when biblical interpreters use the term "myth" to describe Genesis 1–11. Like "myth," "cult" is technical vocabulary in biblical studies. "Cult," from the Latin *cultus*, meaning "adoration" or "care," as one would care for a shrine, indicates formal forms of worship: sacred space such as temples and shrines; rituals such as sacrifice, dietary restrictions, and ablutions; and religious professionals such as priests and temple singers. Otherwise put, the cultus is the public expression of religion; it signifies communally recognized orthopraxy rather than idiosyncratic or individualistic religious activity.

Freud diagnosed religion as a neurosis and ritual practices as the obsessive acts of neurotic people fearful that, if they do not follow the ritual exactly, disaster will strike. But Freud's classification is not how the biblical text regards cultic activity. Through rituals and their attendant time and place, practitioners hallow time and space, draw closer to the divine, solidify communal bonds, and sanctify their bodies. The concern is not the divine wrath that follows if rituals are not followed precisely; on the contrary, in biblical teaching disaster comes when *moral* precepts are ignored. Hosea, addressing the northern kingdom, Israel, in the early eighth century BCE, says that God desires "steadfast love and not sacrifice, the knowledge of God rather than burnt offerings" (6:6). Amos, speaking to the same audience just a bit earlier, is more sarcastic when he parodies the people's showy rush to two old shrines: "Come to Bethel—and transgress; to Gilgal—and multiply transgression; bring your sacrifices every morning, your tithes every three days; bring a thank offering of leavened bread, and proclaim freewill offerings, publish them; for so you love to do, O people of Israel!" (4:4–5).

Rather than regard cultic activity as the neurotic manifestation of arbitrary regulations—eat this, don't eat that; offer this sacrifice; do this ablution—it would be more appropriate to see these practices as the way ancient Israel told its story of origin, brought the presence of the divine into daily life, resisted assimilation, and allowed all community members to participate in religious life. Cultic practices establish continuity where there might be chaos, meaning where there might be emptiness, and belonging where there might be alienation. Rather than as signs of an obsessive-compulsive disorder, they might just as accurately be regarded as actions designed to prevent neurosis. Such a generous view would also help people understand their own cultic practices today, such as the myth and rituals associated with Thanksgiving and the Fourth of July in the United States and comparable festivals in other countries.

The descriptions of tabernacle-based practices are, in the Torah, related to a wilderness context, where all Israel lived in the neighborhood of the sacred. To apply these practices to the pre- or postexilic Jerusalem temple requires enormous caution. Among the problems besetting the history of the text, three stand out. First, how much of the Torah is later material, dating not simply to monarchic times, but even to the Persian and Hellenistic periods, and retrojected back? Second, how much of it is prescriptive (what the editors thought people should do) and how much descriptive (what people actually did)? Finally, for what purpose or purposes were the commandments relating to the sanctuary or the temple instituted?

The "Domestic Cult"

Ancient Israel's cultic practices began not with a centralized temple and formal priestly staff, but in the home and in localized sacred spaces, or "high places." What the home-based practice "looked" like cannot be determined. Although archaeologists have located the remains of homes— amazing itself, given the mud-brick construction—furnishings were not preserved. We do not know if homes had spaces dedicated to worship or wall-niche shrines. Although numerous artifacts, including animal and human figurines, amulets, and incense holders, seem to indicate cultic functions, "seem" is a necessary hedge. An excavation, three millennia from now, of a twenty-first-century home might yield small figurines with impossibly perky breasts and conclude they were fertility objects. Barbie collectors would know better. The blue equine statue with wings could be a god, or it could be "My Little Pony." One shudders to think of what these anthropologists would make of "Hello Kitty." Amulets can be jewelry, or incense holders can be ancient air fresheners. Complicating the question of determining a cultic object even more: a sacred symbol to one group is a false idol to another (as any adult who has attempted to separate "My Little Pony" from a four-year-old knows).

Complicating the question of understanding cultic practices as well is formulating any secure distinction between "religion," defined narrowly as worship of the transcendent, and "magic," defined narrowly as the manipulation of the supernatural. Thousands of figurines dating from around 1000–600 BCE and depicting women with their hands either holding their breasts or covering their genitalia could be sacred symbols, comparable in "religious" terms to a crucifix, or they could be good-luck or fertility charms, comparable in "magical" terms to a rabbit's foot. That the presence of such figurines increases in the late eighth century in northern Israel and in the late seventh century in Judah may indicate that people went into religious high gear when facing pressure from, respectively, the Assyrians and the Babylonians. Alternately, the proportions of artifacts may be related to the conquests; massive destruction, particularly when the postdestruction settlement is lighter, may preserve more artifacts than gradual erosion.

If these artifacts were used in cultic functions, such practices would be seen as "heterodox" (i.e., "other belief") by the biblical authors, compared to the "orthodoxy" and "orthopraxy" (right belief and practice) they promote. However, these would not be the labels the ancient practitioners would have used, even if they spoke Greek. A practice is only heterodox if it is so labeled by the historical winner. At the times these artifacts were used, the majority of the population may have seen them as entirely acceptable. For example, 1 Kings 14:23, set immediately after the reign of Solomon (ca. 900), states that the Israelites "also built for themselves high places, pillars, and sacred poles on every high hill and under every green tree." Jeremiah 44:17, set in early sixth-century Egypt, quotes members of the population of Judah who escaped Babylon's attacks on Jerusalem as saying, "We will . . . make offerings to the queen of heaven and pour out to her libations, just as we and our ancestors, our kings and our officials, used to do in the towns of Judah and in the streets of Jerusalem."

What priests and prophets proclaim was thus not always commensurate with what the people did. Given the diversity of practices, especially before the centralization of the cult under King Josiah in the late seventh century, it is thus more appropriate to speak of ancient Israelite religions, rather than of a single set of beliefs and practices.

Archaeological and other textual evidence supports the presence of such diverse traditions. Local temples provided cultic means of addressing local needs, such as agricultural and personal fertility, and their legitimacy was associated with the local manifestations of deities (e.g., El Shaddai, El Berith). From the monarchic period, or Iron II, comes evidence of cultic facilities, usually on "high places," in Arad, Megiddo, Hazor, Dan, Jezreel, Gezer, and Lachish. Preserved from a temple in Arad in the Negev are an altar, incense stands, an outer building, and an inner chamber that probably functioned as the place the deity was encountered. Regarding such places, Deuteronomy is not a model of interfaith tolerance. Moses exhorts the Israelites about to enter Canaan: "Break down their altars, smash their pillars, hew down their sacred poles, and burn their idols with fire" (7:5).

The biblical picture of sacrifice suggests that it was gradually limited from anyone offering a sacrifice anywhere to a professional practice by priests in temples. Genesis recounts the sacrifices made by Cain and Abel (Gen. 4), Noah (Gen. 8), Abraham (12:7–8; 13:18; 22:13), Isaac (26:25), and Jacob (28:18; 35:14). Gideon (Judg. 6:24) and Samson's father, Manoah (13:19), offer sacrifices, as do Saul (1 Sam. 13:9) and Elijah (1 Kings 18). Judges 17:5 indicates that an Ephraimite named Micah built himself a shrine, made cultic objects (an ephod, an embroidered linen girdle; teraphim, carved images perhaps used for divinatory purposes; Judg. 18:17–18 adds an "idol of cast metal" to the cultic accoutrements) and then installed one of his sons as priest. However, for the period of the judges, the Bible casts these independent shrines and independent priests as undesirable.

Priests and other religious professionals, especially those not connected to shrines, could and did freelance, as seen with the Levite of Judges 17. Similarly, Saul is prepared to pay Samuel for help—"providing a prophetic oracle" in religious terms—in locating his father's lost donkeys (1 Sam. 9:3–10). Prior to Josiah's cultic reforms in the seventh century, and possibly after, Levites could be hired by well-to-do families; having one's own Levite was likely a status symbol. As Micah in Judges 17:13 puts it, "Now I know that YHWH will prosper me, because the Levite has become my priest." This particular Levite is strongly encouraged—a tribe outfitted for war presents an offer difficult to refuse—by the Danites to leave Micah's house and become priest to the Danite community at their temple in Dan. The northern sanctuary is thus again condemned, along with Levites, by the southern-based writer.

As the scattered Israelite communities of the premonarchic period were brought together into a centralized state ruled by a monarch, the authority of any regional shrines such as at Shiloh and Dan decreased while the authority of the national one increased. In ancient Southwest Asian society, any good centralized government, whether on the regional level or the national one, had its cultic apparatus. The centralized cultus legitimized the king and so royal policies. It could serve as the personal shrine of the royal household and so represent the close connection between God, recognized as dwelling in the temple or at least more associated with it than with the field or the market, and government.

Tabernacles and Temples

According to Exodus 25, the Israelites constructed a "tabernacle" (Heb. *mishkan*) corresponding to divine blueprints. Cultic objects included the "altar of incense, with its poles, and the anointing oil and the fragrant incense" (35:15), a six-branched "lampstand" (*menorah;* 25:31 and forty-one other times) with a central stem, a table for the "bread of the Presence" (25:30), and, behind a curtain in the center, the ark (*aron*), in which rested the commandments Moses received on Sinai (Exod. 25).

No remains of this portable shrine or its objects have been preserved. The descriptions of this sanctuary and of associated practices may reflect historical memory, they may be projections of later practices back into Israel's ancient past, or they may be what the later writers imagined happened during this period.

Whether historically accurate or not and whether actually used or not, the tabernacle and its items served a role in Israel's self-identity. Hearing the description, the population living later than the wilderness generation could picture the tabernacle; their memories could be created and reinforced by the narrative. Moreover, for a population that had lost its own sacred site, as Israel did with the destruction of one temple by the Babylonians in 586 BCE and then again with the destruction of the second temple by the Romans in 70 CE, the description served to remind them that the divine was with them as God traveled with them in the wilderness. What was important was what the tabernacle represented—the presence of God—not its location (Exod. 35–40). Anywhere it stood became sacred space. For the New Testament, refocusing the memory, the ideal tabernacle is projected into heaven (Heb. 8–9).

As the story progresses from the Torah to the Deuteronomistic History and as it recounts Israel's entry into the land promised to Abraham, the tabernacle comes to rest. Joshua 18:1 names Shiloh as the place where, once having entered the land, the Israelites "set up the tabernacle" and then determined the tribal distribution of the land.

The stories in 1 Samuel of the family of Elimelech making annual pilgrimage to Shiloh, offering sacrifice, and praying may have a historical core, but they also serve an etiological function. Unlike the temple sacrificial system, where specific cuts of meat set aside for the priests were codified, at Shiloh the priest received whatever "the fork brought up" (1 Sam. 2:13–14). This system was open to abuse, as 1 Samuel 2:15–16 explains. The priest's servant would tell the worshiper, "Give meat for the priest to roast; for he will not accept boiled meat from you, but only raw." If the command were refused, the servant would respond, "No, you must give it now; if not, I will take it by force." Such abuses become the explanation for the priesthood being stripped from Eli's family and given to another.

There are also no definitive remains of an early Iron Age temple in Jerusalem, the one Solomon purportedly built. However, absence of evidence is not the same thing as evidence of absence. Put another way, if there were a King Solomon, he would have had a temple. Evidence of this temple may exist, but political problems and religious sensitivities regarding excavating Jerusalem's Temple Mount may prevent the discovery.

First Kings 6–8 (and 2 Chron. 2–4) describes Solomon's temple with less detail than is given elsewhere to the wilderness sanctuary, but with enough to show that the temple was the "house of (*bayit*) God," the place where the divine presence could be particularly experienced. A similar "experience" can occur with the reading of Ezekiel's projected temple described in chapters 40–42. "Houses" of deities included not only the Jerusalem temple, but also the "house of Baal-berith" (Judges 9:4; cf. 9:6), the "house of Dagon," the Philistine god (1 Sam. 5:2, 5), and the "house of Ashtaroth," the Canaanite goddess (1 Sam. 31:10). Genesis 28:19 indicates that Jacob renamed the city of Luz "Bethel," literally, "house of God." The architecture needed to befit the status of the resident.

According to the Deuteronomistic narrator, the temple is a rectangular structure, but determining its size depends on the modern equivalent of the cubit, and that is difficult since antiquity had several forms of the cubit. A good guess is that the temple as described in 1 Kings 6:2 was 105 feet in length, 35 in width, and 52 in height, or 3,675 square feet. On the other hand, the temple's measurements suggest a larger building than some other cultic sites in the Iron II period. Idealizing the building, 1 Kings 6:7 states that all materials were worked at the quarry before transfer, so that, in a move that would please urban residents to this day, "neither hammer nor ax nor any tool of iron was heard in the temple while it was being built."

In front of the temple stood two hollow pillars of cast bronze named Jachin and Boaz (1 Kings 7:21; 2 Chron. 3:17). The names—Jachin likely means "may [God] establish" and Boaz means "power"—and the pillars' architectural prominence signal both divine and political authority. That the temple was built by imported labor using imported goods also bespeaks its political role. The king who built it had the funds to secure the best in construction, and imported elements suggest that the temple is the world's center, with all goods flowing toward it.

Temples were not simply houses of worship; they were political symbols, economic producers, and national banks. Cuneiform records of the Sumerian city of Girsu dating around 3000 BCE attest that, in a population of a hundred thousand, over a third were connected to the temple. As houses of the divine, temples needed everything an estate needed: food handlers, a cleaning staff, managers, advisers (e.g., prophets and prognosticators), textile and ceramic producers, security personnel, hospitality workers, and so on. Postexilic texts mention a group of people called Netinim, from the Hebrew root *n-t-n*, meaning "to give," who are "given" to temple service. First Chronicles 9:2 mentions them as returning from Babylon along with "Israelites, priests, and Levites," and Ezra 8:20 describes them as people "whom David and his officials had given (*n-t-n*) to attend the Levites." Postbiblical tradition associates this group with the Gibeonites, a tribe that avoided execution by tricking Joshua into thinking they were travelers from a far distance (Josh. 9). The chapter ends with the etiology that "Joshua made them hewers of wood and drawers of water for the congregation and for the altar of YHWH, to continue to this day, in the place that he should choose" (9:27). Although often regarded as slaves, it may be more accurate to think of them as a guild of cultic officiants, matching evidence of such guilds in Ugaritic texts.

Ancient temples also served as banks, with the resident deity as banker (or at least guarantor of funds) and the staff engaged in what modern bankers do: obtaining securities, making investments, distributing loans, and so forth. Unlike most modern banks and investment firms, however, they also supported the poor. The ancient shrine is, to some extent, comparable to a diversified corporation or, for that matter, a modern church with real estate holdings, a stock portfolio, and weekly donors.

Records from Assyrian and Babylonian temples during the time of Israel's early monarchy show loans of both money (in the form of silver) and seeds. The interest rate was around 20 percent, lower than private contracts of the same period, which ran around 33.3 percent. Judges 9:4 recounts that Abimelech obtains seventy pieces of silver from the temple of Baal-berith as a campaign contribution.

Babylonian texts dating around 1750 BCE, the time of Hammurabi, record temples as owning over twenty-five hundred acres; real estate was a relatively safe investment, and the real estate served to produce crops and feed livestock and so serve the temple's economic base. Records of the temple of Ur around 2000 indicate herds of almost seventeen thousand animals; even given possible inflation, that's a lot of beef. That worshipers, whether through religious zeal, desire for the honor gained through benefaction, or concern to please the king or high priest, made donations to the temple did not hurt the institution's economic situation either.

According to Leviticus 27:9–33, donors dedicated land, houses, animals, and other offerings, which they could then redeem at the price the priest established, plus a one-fifth markup. Numbers 7 records that tribes and family groups made gifts of silver. Individuals would also, according to these texts, offer various forms of sacrifice: animals, grain, fruits, and the like. Telling here is the observation that the coin or, more accurately, metal weight mentioned most often in the Bible is the "holy shekel" (sometimes translated "sanctuary shekel," e.g., Exod. 30:13, 24; 38:24). The temple may have been the institution to determine the true weight; monarchies can be and often are replaced, but the temple institution remains permanent and thus is a better guarantor of monetary issues.

According to Leviticus 27:30, the temple also gained income from tithes of food products: "All tithes from the land, whether the seed from the ground or the fruit from the tree, are YHWH's; they are holy to YHWH"; v. 32 includes within these tithes every tenth animal from "herd or flock." According to Numbers 18:21, the tithes were used to support the Levites "in return for the service that they perform" in the sanctuary, and the Levites in turn gave a tenth of what they received to the priests. Deuteronomy 14:22–29 offers an alternate system, in which the people set aside foods to be tithed, bring them to Jerusalem, and eat them in the temple. Every third year, these foods are given to Levites (who, once the high places had been closed, as Deut. 12 mandates, had no freelance opportunities), resident aliens who own no land, widows, and orphans. Nehemiah 10:37–38 assigns tithe collection to Levites; Nehemiah 12:44 adds optimistically that "Judah rejoiced over the priests and the Levites who ministered." Conversely Malachi 3:8–10 laments that not everyone tithed.

With the Deuteronomistic reform, the tithing system supported Jerusalem's economy. People were to bring sheep and cattle along with grain and wine to Jerusalem; there they were still required to eat tithed products (so, e.g., Deut. 12:17, which reflects Josiah's interest in centralization: "Nor may you eat within your towns the tithe of your grain, your wine, and your oil, the firstlings of your herds and your flocks, any of your votive gifts that you vow, your freewill offerings, or your donations").

Such tithing practices were part of ancient culture. Abraham gives a tithe of his property to Melchizedek, the priest (and king) of Salem (Gen. 14:20). Jacob vows a tithe to God at Bethel, which means to the cultic establishment there (28:22). Political advantages to such tithing are extensive. King Hezekiah stored the temple tithe (2 Chron. 31:5, 6, 12), and Ezekiel 45:17 suggests that the king would collect the tithed goods and then contribute them to the temple.

Another means of institutional support was the "temple tax." The etiology, recorded in Exodus 30:12–16, connects the half-shekel tax enjoined on all men age twenty and up to a census. The biblical text does not much approve of the census; whereas today a population count is used to determine social services and governmental representatives, in antiquity it was used primarily to determine taxation rates for districts. This point is demonstrated by biblical spin: 2 Samuel 24:1 states that David took a census; 1 Chronicles 21:1 rephrases, "Satan stood up against Israel, and incited David to count the people of Israel." Exodus 30:12 explains that the census is "a ransom" for the people's lives, and registration protects them from plague. Exodus 38:26 suggests that the funds were used for temple construction. On the positive side, the census allows all members a place in the institution; on the negative, it is another means of obtaining funds and indeed support for the central institution. The points are not mutually exclusive.

National temples and local shrines could function in a complementary manner. Shrines served to bond smaller villages or tribal groups or focused specifically on agricultural needs; the national temple united the population and focused on political issues such as war. But the two institutions could also be antithetical. The localized shrine could promote the interests of the locals at the expense of the nation. What is often called "popular religion" celebrated regionally distinct traditions, which the temple would clamp down on in favor of a united whole.

National temples were to serve the interests of the population, but they also served the interests of the monarchy. The case is made strikingly in the account of Jeroboam, who led ten northern tribes in their secession from Rehoboam's rule. To solidify his power base, Jeroboam built shrines at Dan and Bethel, with their own "golden calves" (e.g., 1 Kings 12:29–30; 2 Kings 10:29); these cultic centers served as alternatives to Jerusalem and so reoriented the northern population's religious loyalty. Judges 18:31, likely a retrojection reflecting an antinorthern perspective, anticipates these shrines by describing the altar that the tribe of Dan set up in the eponymously named city.

Jeroboam also "appointed priests from among all the people, who were not Levites" (1 Kings 12:31), a move that might have seemed to the locals as populist, although for Jeroboam this move suggests a savvy patronage system. Finally, Jeroboam set up his own festivals, perhaps on the model of, or even as a replacement for, the Festival of Booths (Sukkot, Tabernacles; 1 Kings 12:32–33). Thus he used the cult to solidify his political base.

In the late seventh century, according to 2 Kings 23:5–9, King Josiah closed down cultic sites throughout the country and established Jerusalem as the only place where sacrifice could be offered. His motive was the discovery in the temple of a scroll of the law, which he authenticated by the word of the prophet Huldah (whose husband, conveniently, happened to be a member of the royal staff). Hailed by the Deuteronomistic historians as religious reform, the action allowed Josiah to consolidate his power both by restricting religious influence and by ensuring that all donations would flow into the Jerusalem temple's coffers.

This centralized system had its political advantages and social benefits, but like any institution it was subject to abuse by both rulers and priests who sought to use it for private benefit rather than public sanctity.

The Deuteronomistic historian dryly notes that, although it took Solomon seven years to build the temple (1 Kings 6:38), it took him thirteen to build the palace (7:1). Other kings felt free to use the temple deposits as their own personal banks. According to 1 Kings 15:18–20, King Asa of Judah took gold and silver from the temple treasury to buy military assistance; 2 Kings 16:8–9 reports that his successor, Ahaz, did the same. Such abuses continued into the first century, when Pontius Pilate dipped into the temple treasury to build an aqueduct in Jerusalem.

The treasury into which Pilate dipped belonged to what is called the Second Temple. The first was burned down by the Babylonians in 586 BCE (2 Kings 25:8–17). When those exiled to Babylon and their families returned to what was now the Persian province of Yehud in 538, they did not immediately rebuild the temple. Construction began around 520, with the prodding of the prophets Haggai and Zechariah and the support of both the Davidic descendant Zerubbabel (a nice Babylonian name) and the high priest, Joshua. Official support, which made the project practically and politically possible, came from the Persian emperor Darius, who shrewdly strategized that the best way to keep his colonies happy was to allow them to function according to their own traditions, in which religious practices were central. However, the times in Yehud during 520–515 were so filled with poverty, insecurity, and instability—especially in the area of the Jerusalem ruins—that building a temple must have been anything but a straightforward enterprise.

Haggai complains about the Second Temple's less-than-glorious appearance, especially compared to its past: "Who is left among you that saw this house in its former glory? How does it look to you now? Is it not in your sight as nothing?" (2:3). Ezra 3:12 confirms the comparative disappointment: "Many of the priests and Levites and heads of families, old people who had seen the first house on its foundations, wept with a loud voice when they saw this house, though many shouted aloud for joy." The size may have been comparable, but missing were opulent materials and highly skilled artisans. King Herod the Great, beginning around 30 BCE, began the task of temple renewal, and it was Herod's temple, purportedly rivaling the "Solomonic temple" in opulence and majesty, that Rome burned down in 70 CE.

Priests

All ancient Israelites could serve in a cultic capacity. The women who wove garments for the goddess Asherah (2 Kings 23:7) were just as much cultic agents as the women who dedicated to the tabernacle "what they had spun in blue and purple and crimson yarns and fine linen" and the "women whose hearts moved them to use their skill (*chachamah*, the same word used generally in the Hebrew Bible for 'wisdom') [to spin] the goats' hair" (Exod. 35:25–26). All people can bring sacrifices; all people can participate in pilgrimage, prayer, and personal piety.

However, permanent cultic institutions need permanent personnel. As roadside altars gave way to buildings and personal stories of religious experience became the bases for communal piety, priests associated with these shrines became essential; they preserved the memory of the cult's origins and the know-how to perform its rites. The priest (Heb. *kohen*) first surfaces in the Bible with reference to Melchizedek, the priest-king of Salem (Gen. 14:18–20) associated with El Elyon. The royal-priestly combination, seen in biblical history only in the later books of the Maccabees when the Hasmonean rulers took over the high-priesthood, prevented the possibility of a system of checks and balances or, more likely, prevented a situation where power could not be fully consolidated in one institution. Convenient for the ruler, the consolidation of roles portends possible abuses both political and cultic.

The Torah establishes the Levites, the sons of Jacob and Leah's third son, Levi, as the order of priests. From this tribe descend both Aaron and Moses, and it is to Aaron and his descendants that a special role of priest is assigned. The monarchy is to be of a different line, the family of Judah.

Numbers 3:12 explains that Levites serve as substitutes for all Israelite firstborn sons, who, like all animals "that open the womb," belong to God (see Exod. 13:2). However, although the Levites take on the special role these sons had, the sons still require what amounts to a buyout from sacerdotal duties. Numbers 18:16 states: "Their redemption price, reckoned from one month of age, you shall fix at five shekels of silver, according to the shekel of the sanctuary." This redemption ceremony, called the *pidyon ha-ben* ("redemption of the son"), is still practiced in Judaism, with the ancient shekel at the conversion rate of (usually) five dollars or some multiple thereof paid to a *kohen* and then dedicated to charity.

As religious professionals, priests were to be in a ritually pure state (a priest who suffered from leprosy or who recently had a genital emission could not serve at the altar) and to be unblemished (see Lev. 21:17–23). In 40 BCE Antigonus, the Hasmonean ruler, mutilated his uncle Hyrcanus by cutting off his ears (Josephus says he "bit" them off) and so prevented him from serving as high priest. Priests who were drunk (Lev. 10:9) could not serve, and they had to be appropriately dressed (Exod. 28:40–3), including wearing linen undergarments.

Because priests serve God, they should not, according to the biblical text, hold day jobs and they "shall have no allotment in their land" (Num. 18:20; see Deut. 12:12; 14:29; 18:7); in modern terms, they can't own real estate for farming save for restricted areas (Num. 35:2–7; Josh. 21:3). Instead, they receive tithes from the members of the other tribes "in return for the service that they perform, the service in the tent of meeting" (Num. 18:21), leftovers from grain offerings (Lev. 2; 6), and select portions of meat from sacrifices (Lev. 7:31–36; 10:12–20; cf. Deut. 18:1–8). Given that meat was more expensive than what most people could afford, priests serving in the temple did very well. Providing an etiology for the Levites' lack of property, Genesis 49 indicates that Jacob deprived Levi of his land grant because of the massacre he and his brother Simeon perpetrated on the Shechemites in response to the local prince's sexual relations with their sister, Dinah (Gen. 34).

For Levites and priests who lived away from Jerusalem, poverty and even starvation were real possibilities. Matters for Levites became dire in the late seventh century when King Josiah closed the high places. Ezekiel, writing during the Babylonian exile, locates the Levites as demoted, because of their "going astray after idols," to temple workers whose tasks included maintaining order in the temple, serving as doorkeepers, and slaughtering burnt offerings (44:10–14). A similar division between priests and Levites is recorded in Numbers 18:2–6, which may also reflect exilic or postexilic concerns. Conversely, the Chronicler, who tends to enhance levitical roles, states that the Levites were "more conscientious than the priests in sanctifying themselves" (2 Chron. 29:34). These diverse comments likely reflect not only cultic power struggles in the Second Temple period, but the attempts by the writers to solidify present position by writing past history.

Textual ambivalence about Levites and priests indicates that they are not the only ones responsible for the composition of the text. In fact, these priestly groups receive quite a lot of criticism, of which Jacob's condemnation in Genesis 49 is only the start.

Not only is the Levite associated with Micah and then the Danites condemned; even more so is the Levite from the hill country of Ephraim who permits his concubine to be gang-raped, hacks her (still living?) body into twelve pieces, and prompts a civil war because of the outrage done to *him* (Judg. 19–20). The Levite along with the priest in the New Testament's famous parable of the good Samaritan (Luke 10:30–35) follows suit: instead of aiding an injured man, he passes by, not because he was following any cultic law, since no law prevents a Levite from coming into contact with a corpse in order to maintain a state of ritual purity, but because he was *not* following the law, he was *not* "loving his neighbor as himself" (Lev. 19:18).

Aaron and his family too receive substantial criticism. According to Exodus 32:1–6, the Israelites had camped at Mt. Sinai while Moses received the Torah. But law takes time, and Moses delayed. Approaching Aaron, the people demand that he "make gods" for them. Aaron instructs them to donate the gold jewelry of their wives and children—perhaps hoping that the family members would balk?—and out of it he molds a golden calf. The Israelites, in a staggering moment of forgetfulness, announce, "These are your gods, O Israel, who brought you up out of the land of Egypt!" Aaron then builds an altar and proclaims a day of feasting and sacrifice. This behavior does not go over well with Moses, who upon seeing the calf and its worship, smashes the first set of the tablets of the law.

Criticism of Aaron, again in the context of a rivalry with Moses, continues in Numbers 12. There he speaks out, together with his sister Miriam, regarding Moses's marriage to a Cushite woman. One question about this text is whether the challenge to Moses comes from both Miriam and Aaron or only Miriam, since the Hebrew verb in 12:1 has the singular feminine form. The NRSV translation presumes both were involved: "Miriam and Aaron spoke against Moses because of the Cushite woman whom he had married." In all likelihood, both sister and brother are involved, since Hebrew syntax permits a singular feminine verb for a female and male compound subject when, as in the Hebrew word order here, the verb precedes the subject (see Gen. 33:7).

In Numbers 3, the critique of Aaron extends to his first two sons, Nadab and Abihu. These young men offer "unholy fire" (3:10) to God and for this action are immolated. The warning of their death extends to all priests: do only what is required; don't innovate; don't let personal religious enthusiasm get in the way of your representative role of offering sacrifice on behalf of the people.

Priests are advised not to become too involved with the monarchy either. In a series of cautionary tales, the Deuteronomistic historian shows the dangers. First, Saul arranges for the deaths of eighty-five priests "who wore the linen ephod" (1 Sam. 22:18) for their support of David. From this massacre at Nob, the single survivor, Abiathar, becomes one of David's priests. But Solomon deposes him for supporting the rival claimant to the throne, Adonijah (1 Kings 1). Solomon tells the priest, "Go to Anathoth, to your estate; for you deserve death. But I will not at this time put you to death, because you carried the ark of the Lord YHWH before my father David, and because you shared in all the hardships my father endured" (2:26).

The execution would not have well served the new king, since the old priestly regime still had its supporters. Abiathar came from the house of Eli, the priest of Shiloh (see 1 Kings 2:27), and the Shiloh shrine remained influential. Abiathar's home, Anathoth, was also the home of Jeremiah, who half of a millennium later would issue his own challenges to Solomon's descendant, the king of Judah at the time of the Babylonian exile.

According to 1 Kings 2:26, 35, Solomon appoints Zadok in Abiathar's place. This story provides the later group known as the Zadokites an eponymous ancestor. Ezekiel, writing in the mid-sixth century, states that the priests (*cohanim*) are not just the descendants of Aaron, but also the descendants of Zadok; Ben Sira, writing in the early second century, celebrates the "sons of Zadok" chosen by God to be priests (Sir. 51:12). Zadok may also serve as the eponymous ancestor of the Sadducees (the origins of the name are not clear), known in the Gospels and Acts as opponents of both the Pharisees and the early Jesus movement.

In the absence of the monarchy in the early years of the postexilic period, the priests took over the government, with Ezra epitomizing the new system. Priests had the institutional structure; they also had a hereditary role, which helped to preclude either the chaos that comes with charismatic leaders or military coups. The ancient world was not a democracy, and electing a leader was not an option.

The priests worked to solidify their rule in what was then called the province of Yehud by enhancing the role of the temple. The "Songs of Ascents" (e.g., Pss. 120–134) may represent an effort by the priests to encourage the population to make a pilgrimage to Jerusalem. Psalm 84, another ascent psalm, serves both to enhance the temple's value and express the community's heartfelt belief:

> How lovely is your dwelling place,
> O LORD of hosts!
> My soul longs, indeed it faints
> for the courts of the LORD;
> My heart and my flesh sing for joy
> to the living God.
> Even the sparrow finds a home,
> and the swallow a nest for herself,
> where she may lay her young,
> at your altars, O LORD of hosts,
> my King and my God.
> Happy are those who live in your house,
> ever singing your praise. *Selah*
> Happy are those whose strength is in you,
> in whose heart are the highways to Zion. (84:1–5)

Both art and music served to make the temple an impressive and a welcoming place. The Levites provided instrumental music and singing for the services (1 Chron. 16:4–6), and Asaph and Korah, to whom psalms are attributed, represent levitical families.

Yet priests could not rule alone, and other elites with ties to the Persian system filled the leadership vacuum in both Yehud and Samaria. Nehemiah 13:28 records that among the grandsons of the "high priest Eliashib was the son-in-law of Sanballat," one of the rulers of Samaria; marrying into a high-priestly family was a way up the success ladder. Colonial powers could appoint local leaders, such as the Persian appointee Nehemiah; they could also depose and appoint high priests, as did Antiochus IV Epiphanes in the second century BCE in the period leading up to the book of Daniel.

For the earlier part of this postexilic period, priestly authority was also checked by the role of the prophet. Malachi, writing in the fourth century to the Judean population under Persian rule, laments:

> A son honors his father, and servants their master. If then
> I am a father, where is the honor due me? And if I am
> a master, where is the respect due me? says the LORD of

hosts to you, O priests, who despise my name. You say,
"How have we despised your name?" By offering polluted
food on my altar. And you say, "How have we polluted it?"
By thinking that the LORD's table may be despised. When
you offer blind animals in sacrifice, is that not wrong?
And when you offer those that are lame or sick, is that not
wrong? Try presenting that to your governor; will he be
pleased with you or show you favor? (1:6–8)

Here the prophet notes the collaboration of priestly and political authority, even as he hopes that the government can keep the cultic functionaries in check.

Purity

The Bible presents three categories of relationship to the sacred: holy, profane, and impure. Holiness (Hebrew root *q-d-sh*) indicates that which is set apart; the closer one comes to the sacred, the more set apart one needs to be. Thus the temple has concentric circles of sacrality: an outer court where men, women, Israelites, non-Jews can meet and pray, an inner court for Israelite men, then the court of the priests, and then the innermost court entered only by the high priest on the Day of Atonement. Similarly, holiness radiates outward: the temple's holiness extends to Jerusalem, the holiness of Jerusalem impacts the neighboring cities, and so on.

The profane is defined in relation to the sacred, since holiness, that which is set apart, has to be set apart from something. Finally there is the impure (Heb. *tame*, which rhymes with *lame*). To be impure means that one cannot approach the sacred; the point is ritual, not moral status. An evil high priest can be ritually pure; a saintly widow can be impure.

The major sources of impurity concern life and death: birth (Lev. 12); menstruation, ejaculation, and irregular genital discharge (Lev. 15); corpses (Num. 19) and animal carcasses (Lev. 11); and skin disease (Lev. 13). Contact with such matters is not to be easily dismissed. For the Bible, one cannot come into the presence of death and then lightly offer a sacrifice; normal, profane life has been interrupted, and such interruptions require recognition. The focus on life and death, rather than "blood" per se or bodily discharges, is clear. A bloody nose or a cut on the arm does not render one unclean. Nor do tears, breast milk, urine, and sweat. The concern for life may also explain why leavened bread (Lev. 2:4) and honey (2:11) cannot be offered as a sacrifice; bread rises and honey ferments and thus both have a quality of "life."

It would be stretching the evidence to claim that the biblical category of "unclean" (*tame*) is to be associated with the repugnant, and it is certainly stretching to claim that the state of uncleanness in all cases indicates removal from the community. The community is not defined by its proximity to the sacred; if it were, then all nonpriests would be less a part of the community than Levites and the *cohanim*, who have to maintain higher degrees of ritual purity.

Anthropological study has attempted to determine a grand scheme to explain purity regulations. They could have their origins in the human need to respond to real or imagined dangers, or to address the abnormal or "out of place," or to show respect for what is outside human control. A number of commandments—that a field not be planted with more than one kind of seed (Lev. 19:19; Deut. 22:9); that garments not mix linen and wool and that animals not be cross-bred (Lev. 19:19); that men and women keep distinct gender roles (18:22; 20:13) and avoid sexual contact with animals (18:23; 20:16)—do reflect concerns for order and completion; holiness avoids admixture. Yet other explanations for these and other laws can also be offered. For example, the concern for planting a field with only one crop might betray the interests of a central economy for specialized agriculture and thus be based not on holiness but on economic profit; the same commandment could indicate the need for community cooperation and the attempt to prevent any landholder from being self-sufficient.

The texts and the practices do not tell us their rationale for placing items in various categories, other than to insist that the origins are divine commands and the result is the status of holiness. The Holiness Code, a group of chapters (Lev. 17–26) many scholars see as reflecting earlier material incorporated into the Torah, states that Israel is to be holy—by diet, sexual behavior, communal ethics, observance of holidays, agricultural practices, and so on—because God, who is holy, commands it. Holiness practices particularly mark the community as distinct. Israel's neighbors also had purity laws and sacrifices; all had feast and fast days. The Holiness Code grounds Israel's distinct practices in the holiness of the deity: "You shall be holy; for I YHWH your God am holy" (19:2).

People who talk about "purity taboos" suggest that the biblical laws would hamper individuals from fully participating in community life.

Those who are unfamiliar with purity-based behavior as seen in, for example, Orthodox Judaism, Islam, and Hinduism, often dismiss the practices as primitive, retrograde, and oppressive. Biblical purity laws do not hamper most individuals from participating in daily life: a menstruating woman can cook, engage in textile work and ceramics, walk in the streets, or work in the fields.

The purity system is not designed to marginalize women. Given that men are more likely to have discharges than women are to menstruate, especially at a time when the age of menarche was later than at present, when pregnancy and lactation were frequent, and where menopause set in comparably earlier than it does today, women were not, contrary to stereotype, perpetually unclean or regarded as such. Third, purity was not a means to promote social hierarchy. A poor woman can be pure, a rich man can be impure (which is how, for example, he would be able to produce heirs to inherit his estate).

The major impact of purity laws concerns access to the site of the sacred, be it the wilderness tabernacle or the Jerusalem temple. A ritually impure person cannot eat meat offered in sacrifice (Lev. 7:20), but since eating meat was for most people a rare event, the daily impact of the injunction is negligible. Nor can a ritually impure person enter the sanctuary. Leviticus 12:4 states in regard to a woman who has just given birth: "Her time of blood purification shall be thirty-three days; she shall not touch any holy thing or come into the sanctuary until the days of her purification are completed." The next verse doubles the time if a baby girl is born. Whether such legislation was perceived by mothers as a hardship or a blessing cannot be determined. Some may have wanted to go to the temple to express gratitude; some may have appreciated the month or two months of separation from cultic activities, or sexual ones for that matter.

Regaining a state of purity was generally easy. Most processes require ritual bathing and washing of clothes (the hygienic value of these activities need not be their rationale, but rather a beneficial effect). For example, Leviticus 15:16 states: "If a man has an emission of semen, he shall bathe his whole body in water, and be unclean until the evening." Leviticus 15:18 adds that if he "lies with a woman and has an emission of semen, both of them shall bathe in water, and be unclean until the evening." Given the specificity of the second law, the first would refer to emissions not occasioned by heterosexual intercourse, from nocturnal emissions to masturbation. In cases of irregular discharges, men and women have to wait an extra week past the cessation of the discharge, and then both bathe and offer a sacrifice (Lev. 15:2–15, 25–30).

The "ritual bath" or "bathing pool" (Heb. *miqveh*) begins to appear in the archaeological record in the second century BCE; at the time of Jesus, there are hundreds of them. In earlier times and concurrent with the rise of the formal bath—likely itself influenced by Greek and especially Roman bathing practices (a Roman stepped pool looks like a *miqveh*)—people had access to lakes, rivers, and the Mediterranean.

Two special forms of impurity, corpse contamination and "leprosy," required additional rituals. Corpses are the most extreme source of impurity, for here the contagion does not require direct physical contact. To be in a tent with a corpse or even in a tent where someone has died within the past week renders a person impure (Num. 19:14). To regain purity after corpse contact, Numbers 19 prescribes the sprinkling of the ashes of a red heifer that have been mixed with cedar, hyssop, and pure water. Anyone who fails to participate in this ritual is to be "cut off" from Israel. Yet the text fails to indicate how this extirpation is accomplished—there are no purity police who discharge public functions.

Cases of "leprosy" (Heb. *metzora* or *tzara'at*), which is not Hansen's disease (modern leprosy) but a variety of skin-related disorders such as psoriasis or allergic reactions, were to be diagnosed by the priest. Much like an umpire's calling of balls and strikes in baseball, the disease is only a problem if the priest says it is. The diagnostic process is extensive (Lev. 13–14), which already suggests that people with such conditions were not barred from the community. Only when very selective symptoms have been confirmed does the question of isolation emerge: "The person who has the leprous disease shall wear torn clothes and let the hair of his head be disheveled; and he shall cover his upper lip and cry out, 'Unclean, unclean.' He shall remain unclean as long as he has the disease; he is unclean. He shall live alone; his dwelling shall be outside the camp" (13:45–46).

Once again, the law code and the narrative are at odds. The texts function not descriptively, but prescriptively. The Torah, set in the wilderness period, states what the people in the land of Israel *should* do, not necessarily what they *did* do. According to the biblical narratives, those suffering from *metzora* do not remove themselves from society or walk around announcing their unclean state. In 2 Kings 5, Naaman, the commander of the Aramean army, is not socially hampered by his affliction. Although he would not be under Mosaic law, it is nevertheless notable that the biblical authors do not find his contact with Israelites to be a problem. Second Kings 7 mentions four people suffering from leprosy located "outside the city gate"; the point could be social isolation, but this view is compromised by the fact that many, if not most, people lived outside the city gate, since that is where the fields were located. Second Kings 15:5 (2 Chron. 26:19) recounts that King Azariah (called Uzziah in 2 Chron.) suffered from a leprous disease and subsequently lived in a separate house; there is nothing about his removal from the community (he's still in Jerusalem) or proclaiming himself "unclean."

The most famous narrative test case for leprosy concerns Miriam, the sister of Moses and Aaron, who is struck with leprosy for her role in questioning Moses's marriage to the Cushite woman and, more broadly, his leadership (Num. 12). Miriam is "shut out of the camp" for a week, but not because of Torah regulations. Rather, this is a specific commandment direct from God.

A skin eruption diagnosed as *metzora* did mean removal from the proximity of the sacred. However, what the Torah mandates for life in the wilderness period does not always translate into life in settled Israel; the farther away from the center of holiness, which eventually was the Jerusalem temple, the less likely it is that laws directly related to the issue of proximity to the sacred were upheld. Even in the New Testament, people with leprosy are not barred from the community and do not proclaim themselves unclean (see Mark 1:40–45; Matt. 8:2–4; Luke 5:12–14; 17:12–19).

In contrast to the person with leprosy was the person under a Nazirite vow (Num. 6). This vow was ancient Israel's means for expressing personal religiosity. Nazirites, both men and women, were prohibited from alcohol consumption, from coming into contact with impurity, and from cutting their hair or shaving. The vow was for a limited period—Samson, consecrated as a Nazirite from birth, was an exception. At the completion of the vow, the Nazirite performs a sacrifice to mark return to profane status. The popularity of this practice in the first century is noted in the New Testament, where the book of Acts hints that Paul himself was under a Nazirite vow (18:18) and that he redeemed (i.e., paid for the concluding sacrifices of) four Nazirites (21:23).

Dietary Concerns

Among the most familiar biblical laws are those concerning diet. The popular term for food that can be consumed is "kosher," which derives from a Hebrew root meaning "proper" or "fit." The term is not biblical; rather, the three uses of the root *k-sh-r* in the Bible refer to success (Eccl. 10:10; 11:6), as in Queen Esther's success in winning the king's approval (Esther 8:5). Used for more than food, the term can be applied to Torah scrolls and *tefillin* (phylacteries), to people (as in acceptable witnesses), and colloquially to just about anything; that is, the use of "kosher" to describe something fit or appropriate is kosher.

The dietary laws, detailed substantially in Leviticus 11, are another cross-cultural phenomenon. Most cultures and religious traditions have practices not only of feasting and fasting, but of avoiding certain foods and exhorting the eating of others (turkey at U.S. Thanksgiving, ham on Easter, with the latter an alimentary signal to the church that with the coming of Jesus, those Mosaic dietary laws are no longer applicable).

These regulations do not function the same way as purity laws do. First, impurity cannot be avoided (menstruation, ejaculation, and death happen), and in fact the Torah does not warn people away from such events, but the consuming of nonkosher foods can be avoided. Second, impurity can be removed by certain ritual acts, but the Bible offers no mechanism for responding to consuming nonkosher food. The point is, rather: just say no.

Kosher animals fit for consumption by Israelites—as presented the laws aim to keep Israel "holy" and make it distinct from the nations, and thus they do not apply to non-Israelites other than resident aliens—must have a split hoof and chew the cud. The pig is out, as are camels and rabbits (Lev. 11:6 errs in regarding bunnies as ruminants).

Although from the late Second Temple period the eschewal of pork becomes a major marker of Jewish identity, the Hebrew text rarely mentions pigs. Leviticus 11:7 and Deuteronomy 14:8 repeat the command that pork is not to be consumed, because pigs neither chew the cud nor have a split hoof; Proverbs 11:22 comments on the pig's appearance, negatively ("Like a gold ring in a pig's snout is a beautiful woman without good sense"); and Isaiah 66:17 condemns eating pork, vermin, and rodents. The greater focus on pork in later texts may well come from the use of pig in the Greek sacrificial systems.

Both archaeological and textual evidence from the Middle Bronze Age suggests that pigs were a major part of ancient Southwest Asian economies; they were included in royal herds, used in sacrifices (especially by Hittites), and killed for both meat and hide. But the Late Bronze and early Iron Age sites attest a decline in both domesticated pigs and wild boars, and this decline continues until the rise of Hellenism under Alexander the Great in the late fourth century. In Israel, pig bones are found primarily in Philistine cities (Ashkelon, Ekron, Timnah), but not in cities associated with a primarily Israelite population. But lack of access need not translate into prohibition.

Another suggestion for the forbidding of pork was that in Egypt the pig was associated with lower classes and therefore the elitist lawmakers copied the cultural repugnance of their Egyptian models. This point is weak as well, since the Egyptian evidence is unclear and since Egyptian, as opposed to Canaanite and Babylonian, influence on the biblical cult is minuscule.

In the first century, the Jewish philosopher Philo of Alexandria suggested in his *Special Laws* (4:17–18) that pigs were forbidden on the model of analogy: pigs are lazy and they scavenge; by avoiding swine we remind ourselves not to behave like swine. Philo also notes that pigs eat human flesh, and therefore people would do well to avoid pork, lest they be contaminated that way. Modern critics are apt to cite the problem of trichinosis, although in antiquity those Hittites and Greeks knew that meat should be sufficiently cooked.

Clearer motivations can be ascribed to those laws forbidding animals that consume carrion, such as vultures. Here Philo's analogous model is more plausible. Also forbidden is anything containing blood (Lev. 17:10–14; 19:26). Genesis 9:4–6, God's post-flood instructions to Noah, offers a modest etiology for this prohibition: "You shall not eat flesh with its life, that is, its blood. For your own lifeblood I will surely require a reckoning: from every animal I will require it and from human beings, each one for the blood of another. . . . Whoever sheds the blood of a human, by a human shall that person's blood be shed; for in his own image God made humankind." The comparison to the divine image is strained: if the basis of the law is the divine image, then flesh rather than blood would be proscribed. Another possible etiology is from an earlier text, Genesis 4:10, where the blood of Abel calls out to God. Here, the structural motivation again seems to be the concern to mark off the categories of life and death.

Rarely, etiologies for dietary regulations appear. For example, Genesis 32:32 states that "Israelites do not eat the thigh muscle that is on the hip socket, because [the 'man' Jacob encountered at the River Jabbok] struck Jacob on the hip socket at the thigh muscle." And, as with many such etiologies, the story may be a ex post facto explanation of a tradition whose origins were lost with the passage of time.

No single explanation fits all the laws. One can claim that camels were prohibited for economic reasons. Domesticated in the early Iron Age, camels were the ancient equivalent of the sports cars, as compared to the donkey, the slow clunker, but this point doesn't hold for the happily replenishing rabbit. Nor does distinction from Canaanite practice explain the laws, for Canaanite diets also included sheep and cattle, which are kosher for Israelites. Although these laws could have, and in certain periods of history did have, health benefits, this concern also does not explain all the injunctions. Water-dwelling creatures to be eaten must have fins and scales, so shellfish are forbidden, but shellfish do prompt difficulties ranging from allergic reactions to red tide. Undercooked pork can cause trichinosis, and eating vermin, which is also forbidden, brings a host of diseases. But there is no hygienic reason to avoid rabbit or camel.

The reason the Bible gives for these laws is one of holiness: people are to be holy as the divine is holy. The arbitrary aspect of the commandments may encourage a form of discipline or self-control: one chooses to be holy and thus sanctify the body. By keeping the laws, one chooses to resist assimilation and chooses to proclaim a particular community affiliation.

Sacrifice

For many today, the idea of animal sacrifice seems primitive, brutal, superstitious, and, for those who have studied Marxist history, a mechanism by which priests exploit peasants and the elite can control the masses by limiting their access to the holy. Missing in such configurations is attention to how the ancients, who hadn't read Marx but who did perceive the workings of the divine in their lives, understood sacrifice. For the ancient world and for those who still practice ritual sacrifice today, the offering is an efficacious means of uniting humanity and divinity. It takes seriously that animals are slaughtered for human consumption and so respects life (temple sacrifice is not agri-farm slaughter), it recognizes the preciousness of life, and it provides one of the few opportunities the majority of the people had to eat meat.

The efficaciousness of the sacrificial system was not something people in antiquity questioned; everyone knew that it worked. To some degree, it is comparable to the Internet. It is mysterious and yet necessary; it has priests (called "technicians" or "geeks") who facilitate the communication between self and other; it sets up a social mechanism for defining community (the Mac user vs. the PC user); it is costly, and yet it is worth what is spent.

Deuteronomy offers slightly different versions of the sacrifices detailed in Exodus, Leviticus, and Numbers, with a major difference being one of geography. The earlier books speak of the wilderness camp around the tabernacle; Deuteronomy posits a settled community with a singular worship center: "When you cross over the Jordan and live in the land that YHWH your God is allotting to you, . . . then you shall bring everything that I command you to the place that YHWH your God will choose as a dwelling for his name: your burnt offerings and your sacrifices, your tithes and your donations, and all your choice votive gifts" (Deut. 12:10–11). "The place" is left unspecified in Deuteronomy, but no one would miss that it was Jerusalem and its temple—though Jerusalem is not explicitly mentioned in the Bible until Joshua 10:1.

Animal sacrifice in the temple was distinguished from profane slaughtering by several cultic requirements. The person wielding the knife had to be a priest, the animal unblemished, and the altar made of unchiseled stones (Exod. 20:25; Deut. 27:5; cf. Josh. 8:31). The blood was to be dashed against the sides of the altar or placed on the altar's horns. Although Leviticus 17:3–4 mandates that all animals to be consumed be offered as sacrifices, this commandment appears from the rest of the chapter to refer to slaughtering done for sacrificial purposes (see Lev. 17:8–9). Deuteronomy 12:15 clarifies the concern by permitting consumption of meat not offered as sacrifice.

The most common sacrifice was the "burnt offering," a term that first appears in Genesis 22:2, God's commandment to Abraham to take his son Isaac and "go to the land of Moriah, and offer him there as a burnt offering." The Hebrew term is *olah,* which is related to the verb meaning "to go up"; the connection is that the smoke from the sacrifice will ascend heavenward. The Greek equivalent is the origin of the term "holocaust." Second Chronicles 3:1 notes that "Solomon began to build the house of YHWH in Jerusalem on Mt. Moriah, where YHWH had appeared to his father David" and thus also presents Genesis 22 as an etiology for the Temple Mount.

Burnt offerings generally served to give thanks and to purify. The specific peace or "well-being" offering gave thanks for such matters as safe travel, release from prison, and recovery from illness (see Ps. 107). Votive offerings repaid vows, and freewill offerings were exactly that.

The term usually translated "sin offering" (e.g., Lev. 4:1–5:13) does not primarily refer to sacrifices made for atonement of moral or civil transgressions. Sins against other people required restitution or punishment; they were covered by the judicial rather than the sacrificial system. Nor do sin offerings atone for crimes "with a high hand" (see Num. 15:30–31) against God; apostasy and blasphemy do not fit into the atonement system. Despite its name, the "sin offering" primarily removed impurity from the sanctuary and the impurity to be cleansed concerned unwitting violations of a commandment (see Lev. 4:2), the postpartum mother (12:6), the cessation of skin disease (14:19, 22), the end to a genital discharge (15:15, 30), or the completion of a Nazirite vow (Num. 6:14, 16). Such events are by no means sins.

Although holidays such as the Sabbath and Passover require special sacrifices of the same forms as general burnt offerings, the Day of Atonement, Yom Kippur (from a root meaning "to cover or cover over" or, more broadly, to wipe out), requires additional ritual practices. According to Leviticus 23:28, on this day, like the Sabbath, work is forbidden. Leviticus 25:9 mandates the sounding of the *shofar* (a hollowed-out ram's horn; most English translations render the term "trumpet"). Leviticus 16 mandates two purification offerings, one for the priest and his family and one for the people. The high priest brings the sacrificial blood into the inner sanctuary of the tabernacle to be sprinkled on the "mercy seat" (Heb. *kapporet*), which sits atop the ark and perhaps "covers" part of it (Exod. 25:21). Like the "sin offering," the issue is one of purification, here of both ritual impurity and repentance from moral transgression.

The priest is also to take two goats and then cast lots—"One lot for YHWH and the other for Azazel" (Lev. 16:8)—regarding their fates. The Hebrew Azazel is often left untranslated in English versions, since the meaning is debated. Biblical dictionaries offer "scapegoat," which is a definition based on the animal's function. The goat dedicated to YHWH is sacrificed as a sin offering. As for the other: "Aaron shall lay both his hands on the head of the live goat, and confess over it all the iniquities of the people of Israel, and all their transgressions, all their sins, putting them on the head of the goat, and sending it away into the wilderness. . . . The goat shall bear on itself all their iniquities to a barren region; and the goat shall be set free in the wilderness" (Lev. 16:21–22). Numerous etymologies are possible; none is definitive. As good as any other: *azel* means "go away, disappear," and an *az* is a "goat." Later tradition understood Azazel to be a demon; in the third-century BCE book of *1 Enoch* Azazel is the leader of a group of rebellious angels.

Child Sacrifice

Although the biblical tradition forbids human sacrifice (e.g., Lev. 18:21), ancient Israelites sacrificed their children, as did their neighbors to the east, west, and south. The rationale was to give to the deity what one found most precious. Child sacrifice was a recognized response to national crisis. The sacrifice indicated to the gods and the population the dedication of the parent making the offering, and the child in turn was seen to serve as the protector of the people or city. For example, 2 Kings 3:27 records that the King of Moab "took his firstborn son who was to succeed him, and offered him as a burnt offering on the wall. And great wrath came upon Israel, so they withdrew from him and returned to their own land." The suggestion is that the act was efficacious. Something similar may be hinted at in 1 Kings 16:34: "Hiel of Bethel built Jericho; he laid its foundation at the cost of Abiram his firstborn, and set up its gates at the cost of his youngest son Segub"—which is taken to be a fulfillment of Joshua's curse after the fall of Jericho (Josh. 6:26).

The site for some of this practice by ancient Israelites was the "valley of Hinnom," southwest of Jerusalem. The Hebrew term is *ge hinnom*, which is the source of the Greek and through Greek the English "Gehenna" known from the Gospels (Matt. 13:42, 50; 25:41; Mark 9:43). In Gehenna was a high place called Tophet—a name whose origins remain debated. Perhaps it derives from an Aramaic term meaning "fireplace"; perhaps it derives from a Scythian goddess. The Masoretes gave the term *tophet* the vowels of the term for "shame" (as seen in names such as Mephibosheth and Ishbosheth). There Ahaz and Manasseh, two kings of Judah, reportedly offered their sons (2 Kings 16:3; 21:6; 2 Chron. 28:3; 33:6). According to 2 Kings 23:10, Josiah, as part of his Deuteronomic reform, defiled the altar at Tophet that Manasseh had revived.

Ezekiel 20:25–26, in a very enigmatic passage, even suggests that God commanded child sacrifice to cause the people, if they practiced it, to show how evil they were: "Moreover I gave them statutes that were not good and ordinances by which they could not live. I defiled them through their very gifts, in their offering up all their firstborn, in order that I might horrify them, so that they might know that I am YHWH." This odd admission may allude to the law in Exodus 22:29b, "The firstborn of your sons you shall give to me," which becomes replaced when Moses designates the dedication of the Levites as substitutes for the firstborn children (Num. 3:11–13; 8:16–18).

With regard to early narrative, Genesis 22, the story of the "binding" of Isaac, is often read as an injunction against human sacrifice. Though not an incorrect interpretation, this is not the text's most obvious reading. The sacrifice here is specifically in relation to Isaac, not a general practice. The idea of substituting the ram is Abraham's and is not part of a heavenly command. On the other hand, the judge Jephthah does sacrifice his daughter, according to Judges 11. Jephthah likely knew that his daughter would meet him at the door; explanations that suggest he was expecting the household pet are apologia, not history. Yet readers of the book of Judges familiar with the Isaac story also knew that the deity could refuse the sacrificial offering. Indeed, given the time period in which the story of Jephthah was likely first told, human sacrifice was not unknown: it was not a common practice; it was done only in cases of national emergency; it involved the child of the king. Jephthah, as far as the book of Judges is concerned, is not a monster, but a tragic figure.

In Micah 6:7–8, the prophet uses the image of child sacrifice to show the import of a morally upright life. In the first part, child sacrifice, along with excessive sacrificing, represents the "absolutely not"; the second part explains what is mandatory:

> Will YHWH be pleased with thousands of rams,
> with ten thousands of rivers of oil?

Shall I give my firstborn for my transgression,
the fruit of my body for the sin of my soul?
He has told you, O mortal, what is good;
and what does YHWH require of you
but to do justice, and to love kindness,
and to walk humbly with your God (Elohim)?

Chapter 7

Chaos and Creation

The first eleven chapters of the Hebrew Bible describe a time before time. Here we read of the creation of the world and all life in it. We are introduced to God, whom we see strolling in the Garden of Eden and later nearly destroying the whole of creation with the flood. Although all is declared "good" in Genesis 1, two chapters later the first wrongdoing occurs, and shortly thereafter evil takes on the abhorrent form of fratricide. As humanity increases, so does wrongdoing until wickedness is seemingly obliterated by forty days and forty nights of rain, only to reappear a short time later. Again humanity multiplies, conspires to build a tower to the heavens, and is summarily fragmented as God creates languages to separate people from each other. By the end of Genesis 11, the world is essentially as we know it to be, having moved from primordial chaos to pristine order and then to new forms of chaos triggered by human actions.

Other narratives about the origins of the world are also found in the Bible and elsewhere in ancient Southwest Asia. Yet the Genesis account is so well known as to have become virtually synonymous with the word "beginning." We will begin with Genesis before moving to the other texts for comparison.

Creation Today

Genesis 1–11 has drawn an enormous amount of attention—especially in areas dominated by Christianity. Many take it to be a historical account, a literal description of how the world came to be. In this view Adam and Eve were a flesh-and-blood couple living in a real Garden of Eden. A talking snake actually tricked Eve. People like Methuselah really lived to the age of 969. A universal flood nearly obliterated all living beings, and Noah's remarkable ark should still be discoverable if we look in the right place. The multiplicity of languages is God's punishment for the people's arrogance in trying to build a tower to heaven. This literal interpretation of Genesis 1–2 is now evident in the creationist movement, a political and religious effort to promote the teaching of the Genesis account rather than evolution. An early case, celebrated in literature and film, occurred in 1925 in Dayton, Tennessee, when schoolteacher John T. Scopes was tried and convicted of violating a state law that forbade instructors "to teach any theory that denies the story of the Divine Creation of man as taught in the Bible, and to teach instead that man has descended from a lower order of animals." While this so-called monkey trial now lies in the past, other forms of creationism continue to appear on the modern scene.

Because Genesis 1–11 is told in a straightforward manner that makes it appear as if its events happened in the real world, a cottage industry of sorts arose in the Middle Ages to calculate the date of the world's creation. In the seventeenth century, the period when the new interest in science appeared as a potential threat to religion, another surge of interest in such calculations emerged. Modern methods of genetics, geology, and astrophysics were unavailable at the time, and so the calculations were based on the ages of ancestors and kings as well as other lengths of time provided in the Hebrew Bible. Of the many attempts made, no two results are identical, although two have survived and are still in use.

One, with some variations, stems from early Jewish tradition and sets the date of creation on 7 October 3761 BCE. Early rabbinic discussions did not show agreement on this date, but by the twelfth century CE this date became generally accepted. The Jewish calendar now in use counts forward from that year.

Another date, still widely used in Christian circles, was suggested in 1658 by James Ussher, archbishop of Ireland. According to him, creation began at sunset preceding Sunday, 23 October 4004 BCE. This date was subsequently adopted in several printed versions of the Bible, especially the Scofield Reference Bible (1917), which the American minister Cyrus Scofield produced with notations and references that many have regarded as divinely authoritative as the surrounding text. With less focus on the year 4004 BCE, but still believing that God's creative acts occurred recently and not billions of years ago, a sizable number of people today subscribe to the notion of a "young earth," by which they mean that the earth and all life on it are less than ten thousand years old.

In stark contrast, scientists set the origin of the universe at more than

13 billion years ago, the age of the earth at some 4.5 billion years, and the first appearance of life forms approximately 1 billion years later. With a somewhat ironic stroke, geneticists have dubbed the earliest hypothesized common matrilineal ancestor "Mitochondrial Eve," who first appeared in Africa some two hundred thousand years ago, according to current estimates. Her male counterpart, "Y-chromosomal Adam," did not follow until more than fifty thousand years later. Keyed to the story in Genesis 2–3, these two singular, hypothetical figures denote a type set during the origins of human history.

Genesis 1–11 offers no calculations about when its events occurred. The prescientific notions mentioned above miss the point of the biblical narratives, and we should not view this primeval period as straightforward history. Although the stories from Genesis 4 (Cain's murder of Abel) forward seem to give an impression of realism, the accounts of creation and the Garden of Eden are timeless, set in an unspecified period before history begins.

Despite their realistic cast, the narratives and genealogies in Genesis 4–11 also belong to this primordial period, when life as we know it is still in the process of being established. No archaeological age or historical period corresponds to the events as described; Genesis 1–11 is suspended in time or before time. The primeval period also has limited significance in the biblical tradition, and with the slightest exceptions the persons named in Genesis 1–11 (aside from Abraham's line at the end of Genesis 11) never reappear in the Hebrew Bible. The only exceptions are in 1 Chronicles 1, where Adam, Noah, and other ancestors of that period occur in a genealogy list but without any stories about them, and in Isaiah 54:9 and Ezekiel 14:14, 20, where Noah is mentioned briefly. Although the theme of creation itself figures into later biblical texts, these characters do not. In contrast, several early Jewish and Christian writings from the Hellenistic and Roman periods, such as Sirach (Ecclesiasticus), *1 Enoch, Jubilees, 2 Baruch, 4 Ezra* (2 Esdras), and the New Testament, do incorporate references to a number of these figures.

The stories of creation, the Garden of Eden, Cain and Abel, the flood, and the Tower of Babel are myths. The term "myth" does not mean that its contents are false or fictitious. Literary scholars, anthropologists, and religion scholars use the term "myth" to describe a story that conveys a "truth" transcending time and the empirical world. It is normally set in primeval times or in conjunction with the beginning of a culture, and the myth explains how the essential traits of the world or of that culture came to be. Thus, far from being fictional, these myths are true in a fundamental, essential manner. The question is not: Did Adam and Eve really exist? Rather, it is: How are we like Adam, and in what ways does Eve represent us? What in their story explains us to ourselves in a way that a story set in our own real time cannot do as effectively? Focusing on a literal interpretation of these stories, as if there were a real Adam and Eve or Noah's flood really covered the earth, diverts us from plumbing the depths of the meanings the narratives convey. The originators of myths remain elusive; what is significant is not that the texts stem from some identifiable author, but that they articulate "truths" about reality as experienced by that culture.

There are also etiological elements in these stories—not scientific, but popular explanations of how something came into being. The Garden of Eden story offers a reason for why snakes have no legs, why women suffer labor pains, and why men have to work hard. In fact, this whole primeval story in Genesis 1–11 amounts to an etiology of all Western etiologies since it defines the nature of life, the character of social living, humanity's relation to the natural world, and the nature of God. It reflects a very natural, widespread curiosity about origins, the kind of question perennially asked by children—"Why?" It does not describe the way things have to be, but it does offer an explanation for why things are the way they presently are.

Together with Genesis 1–11, other biblical texts containing descriptions of creation, especially Psalm 104, Job 38–41, and Isaiah 40–45, contribute to a complex picture of creation, much more intricate and multileveled than that present in Genesis 1–3 alone. In addition, a variety of other creation stories, some with parallels in the Hebrew Bible, arose in Mesopotamia, Egypt, and the Levant. All these source materials figure in the following discussion.

Cosmic Architecture

The Bible opens with a big bang, or actually a double bang. The first two chapters of Genesis tell two different stories of creation. The first account is Genesis 1:1–2:4a, and the second is Genesis 2:4b–24. The accounts differ from each other in several distinctive ways. For example, stylistically Genesis 1:1–2:4a is highly structured, following a seven-day pattern with substantial repetition from day to day, while Genesis 2:4b–24 has more of a narrative flow. In the first account, the creation occurs mostly by fiat ("Let there be light," etc.), while in the second God actively forms the creatures. The seven-day chronology in the first is matched by no chronology in the second, where everything could have been created on the same day or over an indefinite time period. The first has the whole cosmos as its physical environment, while a garden is enough in the second. The main actor in the first is "God" (Elohim); in the second it is "the LORD God" (YHWH Elohim). The first includes a positive command to eat of all plants and trees (1:29), while the second prohibits eating from one specific tree, the "tree of the knowledge of good and evil" (2:17). The first story culminates in the sanctifying of the seventh day; the second ends with the primeval couple naked and unashamed of it.

For all of these differences, the two accounts are not necessarily in conflict with each other; they can be seen, rather, as stories stemming from distinctive perspectives. Genesis 1:1–2:4a seems to reflect an urban point of view, where everything should be ordered and in its place, much as in Israel's royal cities, which were planned by central authorities from the capital. God functions as a cosmic architect, ordering the work to be done according to plan, and it all turns out "good." Genesis 2:4b–25, on the other hand, has more of an agrarian feel—or maybe an urban rendition of it—with its up-close focus on soil, water, crops, animals, and helpers, culminating in the next chapter with the description of Adam toiling in the field (3:17–19). More than the second, the first story also evinces an interest in religious practices, exemplified by the seventh day sanctified as a day of rest. Because of these distinctions, scholars who follow the source-critical hypothesis for the origin of the Pentateuch associate the first story with the Priestly source because of its cultic interests, and the second account with the Yahwistic source because of its more populist and less institutional leanings.

The very first words of Genesis 1 present us with a dilemma that may have been as puzzling in ancient times as it is today: Did anything exist before God's first act of creation or, for us, before the big bang? The ancient Israelites may have harbored some curiosity about it, for Genesis 1:1–2 intimates that some amorphous substance existed before creation. Unfortunately, the precise meaning of the text is not clear. The chief problem lies with the very first word in the Hebrew Bible, *bereshit*, which is usually translated "in the beginning." There are, however, two main ways to interpret the term.

Modern translations have generally understood this word as a prepositional phrase, followed by a verb in the past tense: "In the beginning God created." The ancient Greek and Latin versions both read it in this manner. According to this reading, God's first act of creation was to form the heavens and the earth, and the earth as God created it was initially formless, with a wind sweeping over the waters. Alternatively, *bereshit* can be read as the beginning of a dependent temporal clause, with the independent clauses in v. 2 describing the state of affairs existing before God's creative act: "When God began to create the heavens and earth, the earth was formless and empty." In other words, before God began creating, a formless and empty earth already existed as well as waters with wind blowing over them, and the first act of creation was to form light.

This problem cannot be resolved on grammatical or linguistic grounds alone, since both readings of the Hebrew are possible. The notion called in Latin *creatio ex nihilo*, or creation out of nothing—a notion that supports the first reading—developed into a theological doctrine in the patristic period of Christian history, but it seems to be implied in the second-century BCE Greek text of 2 Maccabees 7:28, where a mother implores her son to remain faithful to their God in the face of the threat of torture: "I beg you, my child, to look at the heaven and the earth and see everything that is in them, and recognize that God did not make them out of things that existed (*or* God made them out of things that did not exist). And in the same way the human race came into being."

However, *creatio ex nihilo* is not a developed theme in 2 Maccabees, and neither is it a key theological doctrine in the Bible. It is more likely that the ancient Israelites shared with their neighbors from Mesopotamia to Egypt the concept that unformed primordial matter preceded the acts of creation. For them, water, earth, and time are the most common prime materials out of which all else eventually arises. The chaos myth takes the form either of a battle between opposing deities or of sexual reproduction, and in both cases the world emerges from the original chaotic substances. Genesis 1 does not use the imagery of combat or sex; in a sovereign manner God creates order out of chaos. To express this process and also to acknowledge the larger mythic world in which Israel shared, the better opening of the text is: "In the beginning, when God created the heavens and the earth, the earth was a formless void."

The Hebrew phrase denoting the chaotic mass is memorable for its rhyming sounds: *tohu vavohu*, two words meaning "wasteland" or "emptiness," together reinforcing each other along the lines of "a formless void." The phrase appears elsewhere only in Jeremiah's terrible imagery of a desolate land after a war, when all seems to have returned to a primeval chaos: "I looked on the earth, and lo, it was waste and void (*tohu vavohu*)" (4:23). The prophet's message is clear: creation had to overcome desolation and disorder, but life can easily slip back into chaos if the people are disobedient.

The phrase usually translated "and darkness covered the face of the deep" is a fragment also shared with neighboring cultures. In Genesis 1:2 the Hebrew word for "deep" is *tehom*, a linguistic cognate to Tiamat, the Babylonian goddess of the salt seas. She represents the great abyss, the endless seas around and under the earth. English translations rendering *tehom* as "the deep" are in effect watering it down, demythologizing it into a commonplace word. *Tehom* here and in its nineteen other biblical occurrences never has the article "the," but is a simple noun, almost as if it were a proper name. Thus a better translation that preserves the personal, mythic aspect of the Hebrew idiom is: "and darkness covered the face of Deep."

Numerous creation myths from ancient Southwest Asian cultures have come to light during the past 150 years—from Sumer, Babylonia, the Levant, and Egypt. The *Enuma Elish*, the Babylonian creation epic, ranks—along with the other great Babylonian epics, *Gilgamesh* and *Atrahasis*—among the supreme literary finds from the region. Known since its first partial publication in 1876 and found in additional fragments over the course of the next several decades, the *Enuma Elish* fills seven cuneiform tablets and dates well back into the second millennium BCE, thus predating the biblical story in Genesis by several centuries. It is named *Enuma Elish* after the first two words, meaning "When on high. . . ."

The epic begins with a theogony, the creation of the gods, well before the world and humanity appear. At the very beginning are Tiamat, goddess of saltwater, and Apsu, god of freshwater. Their commingling produces two more gods, and other divine generations follow. The younger deities proceed to make so much noise that Apsu resolves to slay them, but Apsu is instead killed by one of them, Ea, who supplants Apsu as god of freshwater. His son is Marduk, the hero of the epic. When Tiamat seeks to avenge the death of Apsu and quell the unrest, she engages in mortal combat with Marduk, the champion of the younger generation. Backed by an army of demons and monsters led by her consort, Kingu, she advances on Marduk, who challenges her to do battle alone with him. In the fearsome struggle, Marduk subdues Tiamat by driving a wind into her mouth until she becomes bloated, and he then kills her. Splitting her watery corpse in two, he places one half in the sky, with the firmament to hold it back, and the other half around and under the earth as rivers and the oceanic abyss. After creating the stars and the moon and establishing the annual calendar, Marduk assumes the throne as king of the gods. He slays Kingu and from his blood creates humanity to serve the gods. The epic ends with a litany of Marduk's fifty names, which denote various aspects of his life and works.

This remarkable myth differs from Genesis 1–11 in several fundamental ways, such as the multiplicity of gods, the creation of the gods, the internal dissension and finally war within the divine ranks, and the creation of humans from the blood of a rebellious god. But other features are tantalizingly similar. Water plays a key role in both, as does the separation of land from water. Wind is blowing over the water of chaos in Genesis 1:2, and it serves as Marduk's decisive weapon in battle. A pantheon of gods is not present in Genesis 1, but some kind of divine plurality is implied in the statement, "Let *us* make humankind in *our* image, according to *our* likeness" (1:26). The location of the halves of Tiamat's watery body above and below the earth compares with the sources of Noah's flood: "All the fountains of the great deep [again "Deep," without "the"] burst forth, and the windows of the heavens were opened" (7:11). The *Enuma Elish* includes references to the food offerings and the incense that the people are to present to the gods, not unlike the sacrifices and "pleasing odor" offered to God by Noah (8:20–21). Yet even with these common elements, the overall message of the biblical story differs from that of the Babylonian myth in two fundamental ways: Genesis 1 depicts a sovereign God, one not in competition with other deities, and humanity is created in God's likeness, not as a slave.

Biblical Hebrew does not have a single word for "cosmos" or all physical reality; it uses such expressions as "the heavens and the earth" (Gen. 1:1; 2:4), "the heavens, earth, and sea" (Exod. 20:11; Ps. 69:34), or simply "all" or "the entirety" (Isa. 44:24; Jer. 10:16). Allusions culled from Genesis 1–11, Job 38–41, and Psalms 33, 74, and 104 indicate that the ancient Israelites had a view of the cosmos quite similar to the cosmological understandings evident in other Southwest Asian texts.

They conceived of a closed, three-storied universe with the flat earth in the middle, held up by pillars sunk deep in the abyss, the "waters below." The dry land is interspersed with freshwater bodies, and in the heart of the earth is Sheol, the abode of the dead—all the dead (there is no differentiation between good and bad; this is not hell). Over the earth is the firmament, a semipermeable dome held up by the pillars of the sky, the mountains. Under this canopy are the sun, the moon, and the stars. The "waters above" are located above the dome, and the "windows of the sky," sluices in the dome, let down water to fall as rain. This firmament was perhaps even considered transparent, permitting the blue of the celestial waters to show on sunny days.

God dwells above the firmament but can also be present on the earth and even in Sheol (Ps. 139:8). Job envisions a foundation and cornerstone of the earth, doors holding back the sea, houses for the light and the darkness, storehouses for the snow and the hail, gates to the netherworld (Job 38). In another image Job pictures the earth hanging over nothingness (26:7). Such descriptions in the books of Job and Psalms are poetic and colorful, not much different from the picturesque images and motifs given narrative form in Genesis 1–11.

In this primordial context, Genesis 1 depicts God overcoming the chaos of the formless void through a series of acts that separate like from unlike, distinguishing species from each other and assigning each to its proper space and role. More items are created than match the seven-day pattern, so they must double up on certain days. They follow a sequence of creative acts and consequences:

Day	Creation of	Consequence	Genesis
1	Light	Separation of day from night	1:3–5
2	Firmament	Separation of waters above from waters below	1:6–8
3	Dry land	Separation of land from seas	1:9–10
	Vegetation	Vegetation	1:11–13
4	Sun, moon, stars	Light, days, seasons, years	1:14–19
5	Sea life, birds	Sea life, birds	1:20–23
6	Land animals, insects	Land animals, insects	1:24–25
	Humanity	Dominion over all animals, fish, insects; vegetation for eating	1:26–31
7	[end of creating]	Consecration of the Seventh Day	2:1–3

The overall intention of the story is to establish an orderly world according to roles and boundaries. The first three creative steps and the final one involve acts of separating: the light distinguishes day from night; a firmament or dome separates the waters above and below; dry land means that the seas are in their own designated places; the seventh day is different from all the other days as a day of rest. All other creative acts involve populating various domains with appropriate physical forms: plants and trees for the soil; heavenly bodies for the sky; aquatic life for the waters; birds for the air; animals and creeping things for the land; and humans to have dominion over all that lives.

The purpose of creation in Genesis 1—to establish order out of chaos—fits well with the worldview elsewhere in ancient Southwest Asia. For example, Egyptian texts, especially from the New Kingdom (1550–1069 BCE), indicate a key role for the goddess Ma'at, who personifies harmony, correctness, truth, and order—thus cosmic, legal, and moral stability. The daughter of the sun god Re (or Ra), Ma'at was present at creation and continues thereafter to ensure an orderly structure to existence. Her symbol is the ostrich plume, a common motif in Egyptian art, often pictured in paintings and reliefs as a symbol of the essential need for all humans to act in harmony with the divine order of the world. In Egyptian, Mesopotamian, and Israelite literature, this order originates in creation itself and undergirds all reality.

Creation thus involves much more than simply bringing the physical world into existence. Without being ordered, all that exists can fall into a state of disorder, of chaos. At its heart creation sets an order to reality. In Genesis 1, when at the end of each day God pronounces creation "good," the word is not primarily an aesthetic or moral descriptor but a functional characteristic: the new creation works, runs smoothly, fits with the rest. Two chapters later, in Genesis 3, the humans' act in disrupting the order is the mythic counterpart to real-life acts of sin and injustice, which disturb the social, moral, and religious world. Later texts in the Hebrew Bible, especially in the book of Job, confront the problem of theodicy, the appearance that God is not maintaining the order established at creation according to which the righteous are to be rewarded and the wicked are punished. This short story of creation in Genesis thus presents a grand plan, and the Israelites are to conform their actions and practices to the orderly structure of all that is created. The long history of political and religious failures, detailed in the Pentateuch and the Deuteronomistic

History, demonstrates the disasters that follow when the leaders and the people act counter to the harmony ordained by God.

Light is the first to be created on Day 1, but the sun, moon, and stars do not appear until the fourth day. The ancients may not have understood that all light on earth stems from solar energy. When they observed light in places where no heavenly body was directly shining, for example, in a room or under cloud cover, they may have concluded that light could exist on its own and was not dependent on the sun. The creation of light functions as the first act of ordering, in which light and darkness are separated from each other, thereby producing day and night—essential for this narrative organized on a night-and-day sequence.

When the sun, moon, and stars are later brought into existence, traces of the astral worship common in neighboring cultures are slightly evident. The text avoids referring to the sun and moon by name, calling them instead the "greater light" and the "lesser light." The normal Hebrew words would have conjured up images of deities in earlier cultures: *shemesh* for "sun" (cognate of Shamash, the Babylonian deity) and *yerach* for "moon" (cognate of Yarikh, the Ugaritic moon god). Yet even in Genesis these heavenly bodies are personified in their roles as rulers of the day and night. As difficult as it is to craft a creation story free of all associations with other religious beliefs and practices, Genesis 1 concedes no divine power or status to any beings other than God.

The creation of humans occurs on the sixth day as God's last formative act according to the first narrative, whereas the story in Genesis 2:4b–25 situates it prominently at the outset. The two stories differ also in their stylistic form here. Genesis 1:26–30 consists mostly of divine speech, while Genesis 2:7 contains no speech, only action. A closer look at the nature of this created human being follows in the next section, where we discuss the second creation narrative. Here in the first story the distinctive element is the "image" of or "likeness" to God, a theme that goes unmentioned in the second narrative. The account begins with Genesis 1:26: "Then God said, 'Let us make humankind in our image, according to our likeness; and let them have dominion over the fish of the sea, and over the birds of the air, and over the cattle, and over all the wild animals of the earth, and over every creeping thing that creeps upon the earth.'"

The meaning of the two terms "image" (*tzelem*) and "likeness" (*demut*) is not clarified in the text, but they have drawn considerable attention in later circles. In early Christian thought, for example, St. Augustine (fourth–fifth centuries CE) saw in the "image of God" a reference to the soul. Others after him tried to distinguish substantively between the two terms in line with the Vulgate's renderings: "image" (Lat. *imago*) and "similitude" (*similitudo*). For their part, Jewish medieval commentators, Maimonides (twelfth century) among them, stressed that these terms were not meant to be taken literally since God possesses no corporeal being and is absolutely not to be rendered in images.

An alternate interpretation looks to the rest of the biblical verse. Humans are to "have dominion over" all other created beings—fish, birds, cattle, wild animals, and "creeping things." The words "image" and "likeness" are thus understood with regard to humanity's role: humans are God's representatives, ones who are to act on God's behalf in the world. The imperial politics of the biblical period reinforces this understanding. Numerous texts from Babylon and Egypt refer to the king or pharaoh as the "picture" or "image" of the deity. For example, one Neo-Assyrian letter reads: "The father of the king, my lord, was the very image [Akkadian *tzalmu*, related to Hebrew *tzelem*] of Bel [title of a Babylonian god, similar to Baal], and the king, my lord, is likewise the very image of Bel."* The king or pharaoh was thus, if not a god himself (as in Egypt), then the agent of the gods (as in Babylonia and Israel). Similarly, when an emperor wanted to ensure allegiance in the far reaches of his empire, he could erect a statue or image of himself there to remind subjects that their imperial administrators acted on his behalf.

However, this reference to "rule" or "have dominion over" does not necessarily denote crass exploitative power—which is how a despotic king could function if he desired. Rather, the royal ideology present in Mesopotamia, Egypt, and also Israel held just rule as the ideal—treating subjects in a manner responsive to their needs and their due.

Although the motif of ruling is more evident in the first than it is in the second creation story in Genesis, it appears also in a distinct form in Genesis 2. There God creates animals, birds, and other living creatures and commissions the *adam* to name them (2:19–20). To give something a name implies having power over that being. In the Hebrew sense, a name is more than just a handle; it expresses something essential about the one carrying it, just as the given names for humans in the Hebrew Bible often have mean-

---

* I. J. Gelb et al., eds., *The Assyrian Dictionary of the Oriental Institute of the University of Chicago*, vol. 16 (Chicago: Oriental Institute, 1962), 85.

ings that express a fundamental trait or experience. Israel is "God strives" (or "the one who strives with God"), Isaac is "he laughs," Jacob is "heel" or "supplanter," and Joseph is "he adds" or "may [God] add." The *adam* is thus pictured as the superior or most powerful of all created beings.

Although nothing destructive is necessarily implied in the concepts of dominion and naming, people have taken these texts as legitimation for exploiting the natural world. They have viewed the created order as having no purpose other than to serve the greater interests of humankind; because they were made "in God's image," everything in the physical world was thought to be at their disposal. Some today locate the fault for much of the modern ecological crisis in this interpretation of the Genesis creation stories by those who feel entitled by the Bible to exploit nature excessively. However, the Genesis creation stories do not grant humans this entitlement. To "rule over" the natural world means, according to these texts, to care for what could be (or those who could be) victimized and weakened by the powerful.

According to this first story in Genesis, the sixth day brings an end to all creative acts: "Then the heavens and the earth were finished, and all their multitude. And on the seventh day God finished the work that he had done, and he rested on the seventh day from all the work he had done" (2:1–2). The Hebrew root *sh–b–t* (whence Shabbat, or Sabbath) means "to stop" or "to cease," as in to stop working. Instead of doing further creative work on this day, God "blesses and consecrates" the seventh day. "Consecrate" or "make holy" (from *qadash*) has a basic meaning of setting something apart, that is, separating it from the commonplace—in this case from the other six days. The day is not called the "Sabbath" (*shabbat*) here; that designation is first used when the Israelites are in the wilderness after their escape from Egypt (Exod. 16:23). Nor are the first humans, or anyone else, enjoined in these verses to rest as God does. We simply hear that the deity rests after the labors of creation, and Jewish and Christian traditions later see in this act one of the grounds for setting aside a day of the week for rest from work.

Hands-on Artisanship

In comparison to the first account of creation, the second (Gen. 2:4b–25) differs at several points. It is more of a narrative than a report; it involves interactions rather than mainly actions alone; there is conversation rather than only commands; intimacy substitutes for distance; and only a few creative acts occur explicitly:

Creation of	Purpose	Genesis
The first human	To till the garden	2:7
Garden of Eden	Home for the human	2:8
Vegetation	Food for the human	2:9
Animals and birds	Partners for the human	2:19
Woman (and thus the differentiation between the two sexes)	Partner for the human	2:21

Even the sequences of these creations vary in comparison with each other:

Genesis 1:1–2:4a	Genesis 2:4b–25
	The first human
Vegetation	Garden of Eden
Birds	Vegetation
Land animals	Animals and birds
Humanity, male and female	Woman

What is missing from the first account is equally significant: the creation of light, firmament, dry land, sun, moon, stars, sea life, and insects.

These differences indicate different foci: cosmic and terrestrial order in the first story, and immediacy in the divine-human relationship in the second. The Garden of Eden serves as an ideal and idyllic setting in Genesis 2, a microcosm in contrast to the macrocosm of Genesis 1. The garden is created directly after God forms the first human, and Genesis 3 ends with the man and woman expelled from the garden forever. Genesis 2–3 relate a poignant drama of idyll, rebellion, and loss, all of which are more effective when presented up close and personal than against the backdrop of the cosmos. The two creation accounts in Genesis cannot easily be collapsed into a single story. They stand alongside each other as complementary mythic pictures of the complexities of reality and life.

The theme of chaos resonates in the second story as it did in the first. Here, however, the chaos is dry, not wet. Genesis 2:5–6 describes an arid land, rainless and untended: "In the day that YHWH God made the earth and the heavens, when no plant of the field was yet in the earth and no herb of the field had yet sprung up—for YHWH God had not caused it to rain upon the earth, and there was no one to till the ground; but a stream would rise from the earth, and water the whole face of the ground."

In both myths the chaos may well symbolize a perceived fundamental threat to the respective culture responsible for the given story. In Genesis 1 the chaotic abyss represents the absolute opposite to a structured urban, monarchic, cultic order, whereas in Genesis 2, with the agrarian economy more at stake, it is a drought that evokes a sense of disorder and loss. In Genesis 1 the unruly water is controlled by establishing boundaries between bodies of water and dry land and between the waters above and the waters below; here in Genesis 2, however, water is lacking and needs to be supplied. Unlike Egypt and Mesopotamia, Israel does not have rivers that annually flood to irrigate the soil in areas where most of the agricultural population lives. So in Genesis 2:10–15, four rivers are explicitly named to water the nearby regions. The first two, Pishon and Gihon, are unknown to us, but the lands of Havilah and Cush mentioned in this text are in the vicinity of Egypt. The other two rivers are well known—the Tigris and the Euphrates in Mesopotamia. These four rivers stem from a source in the Garden of Eden, according to Genesis 2:10, but the story goes no further than to mention them and their connection to the garden—itself a telling point since they foster the development of major cultures in Southwest Asia.

As mentioned in an earlier chapter, a source for considerable confusion is the meaning of the word *adam*. Since ancient times the term has been interpreted to refer to the male sex alone and has been translated either as "man" or as a proper noun, "Adam." From this interpretation an enormous tradition has developed. It is safe to assume that ancient Israelite society was based on a patriarchal system in which males, especially adult males, enjoyed the primary privileges and power in the society. Many interpretations of Genesis 1–3 over the past two thousand years and into the twenty-first century have seen and still see in these stories the legitimation for continuing this male privilege and status. Since God created a man first—so the reasoning goes—men deserve to be dominant in society, and since the woman was the first to do wrong, women are ultimately more liable for the ills of the world and deserve their secondary status.

The Hebrew conveys quite a different meaning, at least in most cases. In twenty-two out of the twenty-five occurrences of *adam* in Genesis 1–3, the form used is *ha-adam;* the first syllable, *ha-*, is the definite article "the," thus literally, "the *adam*." This *adam* is not exclusively male, and its best translation is "human being" or "humankind." Genesis 1:27 thus reads: "So God created humankind (*ha-adam*) in his image, . . . male and female he created them." First humanity in general is mentioned, and then the text goes on to indicate that humankind is divided between males and females.

If the authors of Genesis 1 and 2 had wanted to make it clear that a male was created first, other words were available in Hebrew to refer exclusively to males, such as *ish* (used later in Gen. 2 and appropriately translated "man"), *zakar* ("male"), and, more colorfully, *mashtin beqir*, which the KJV translates literally as "he that pisseth against the wall" (1 Sam. 25:22, 34; 1 Kings 14:10; 16:11; 21:21; 2 Kings 9:8; the NKJV waters the phrase down to "male"). To speak of humans individually rather than as a whole, biblical Hebrew has such phrases as *ben adam* (literally, a "son of humankind"; e.g., Ezek. 2:1, translated by the NRSV as "mortal," but more often rendered "son of man") and *benot ha-adam* (literally, "daughters of humankind"; Gen. 6:2–4). A good example of the generic use of *adam* is Psalm 8:4 (Tanakh 8:5): "What are humans (*enosh*) that you are mindful of them, mortals [*ben adam*, singular in Hebrew] that you care for them?"

In the second creation story *ha-adam* occurs in a sense similar to its sense in Genesis 1:27, but with additional details that make its meaning even clearer, although modern versions rarely translate the terms in a manner that makes the nuances apparent. Both the NRSV and the JPS follow the KJV almost word for word: "And YHWH God formed man of the dust of the ground (*or* earth)" (2:7). The Hebrew text, however, has the word *ha-adam* where these versions translate "man," so a better reading is "YHWH God formed the human being (*or* humankind) from the dust of the earth." The Septuagint in both Genesis 1:26–27 and 2:5–7 also uses the generic term in Greek for "humankind" or an individual "human," *anthropos*, as opposed to the Greek term designating a man or a male, *aner*. Thus, the first human creation was not a male person, but a human of unstated sex. In this sense the word *adam* functions similarly to our word "human," which also does not indicate sexual identity. The division between the sexes is not evident until the end of the chapter when God forms a woman from the first human's side. We will revisit the matter of sex in more detail, including its depiction in Genesis 1–3, in Chapter 10. Here we focus on the creation of *ha-adam*.

In only a few instances does *adam* (without the definite article) function as a proper noun referring to an individual named Adam. Genesis 4:25 reports that Adam and his wife have a son named Seth, and Genesis

5:1, 3–5 and 1 Chronicles 1:1 list Adam in a genealogy. Also in Genesis 2:20; 3:17, 21, *adam* lacks the definite article and could be interpreted either as the proper noun or as a generic term. All six other occurrences in the story in Genesis 3 have *ha-adam*, which is better translated as "the man" rather than as "Adam" to identify the pair "the man and his wife (*or* woman)" (Heb. *ishshah* can be translated either "wife" or "woman") as in v. 8: "The man and his wife hid themselves from the presence of YHWH God among the trees of the garden."

Two folk etymologies stand out in the second creation narrative, and we will look at one here and leave the second (Gen. 2:23) for Chapter 10. As a branch of linguistics, etymology seeks to trace the history of a word and determine its origin or root, usually in a different language or at an earlier stage of the same language. By comparison, a folk or popular etymology springs from a similar interest but is generally carried out by nonspecialists who refer only to other words in the same language on the basis of similar sounds. Genesis 2:7 states: "YHWH God formed the human (*adam*) from the dust of the ground (*adamah*)." English counterparts might be "human" from the "humus" or "earthling" from the "earth." Though scholars discredit many folk etymologies as too fanciful to be true (which is the case for Gen. 2:23), this case for *adam* and *adamah* has been largely, although not completely, supported by historians of the Hebrew language. Both words probably stem from the root *adm* meaning "red," as in the reddish color of skin and of ground. This connection between *adam* and *adamah* to express the origin of humans also explains the reverse—that at death we return to the earth: "By the sweat of your face you shall eat bread until you return to the ground (*adamah*), for out of it you were taken; you are dust (*afar*), and to dust you shall return" (3:19).

The notion of creating humans from the earth is not unique to Israel. The god Khnum, whose cult was based from the third millennium BCE at Elephantine in Upper Egypt, is pictured as a potter forming gods, humans, and animals at the potter's wheel. He fashions not just the first human but all persons who are born. A later text from the Roman period, "The Great Hymn to Khnum" is a long hymn expounding on the creativity of this beneficent deity. It details his accomplishments as a potter:

> He made hair sprout and tresses grow,
> Fastened the skin over the limbs;
> He built the skull, formed the cheeks,

To furnish shape to the image.
He opened the eyes, hollowed the ears,
He made the body inhale air;
He formed the mouth for eating,
Made the [gorge] for swallowing.
He also formed the tongue to speak,
The jaws to open, the gullet to drink.*

A detail in the creation story in Genesis 2 sets the stage for the dramatic conflict in the following chapter. Of all the trees and plants placed in the Garden of Eden, two specific ones are identified: the "tree of life" and the "tree of the knowledge of good and evil." Genesis 2:17 provides an ominous foreshadowing when God tells the human being that all of the vegetation is good to eat, but not "the tree of the knowledge of good and evil" or death will follow. Of these two trees, the tree of life might seem more desirable because it represents immortality. In the great Babylonian *Epic of Gilgamesh*, the hero nearly succeeds in his long quest for immortality when he obtains the plant of life, but later in an incautious moment he allows a snake to steal it from him. In another Babylonian story from at least around 1400 BCE, the mortal Adapa is summoned to a hearing before the gods for a wrong he had committed. When he pleases them, they offer him the food of life, but he declines on the prior advice of his own benefactor and with that loses his chance for immortality.

The tree of life in Genesis 2 is not the tree from which the couple eat, but it reappears at the end of Genesis 3 when God bans them from the garden; the entrance to the garden is guarded by an angel with a flaming sword, and Adam and Eve, for now they are so named, will have no opportunity to eat its fruit and thereby become immortal. Rather, the tree of the knowledge of good and evil plays the key role in this story. What the "knowledge of good and evil" means remains unresolved, and several interpretations are possible: an awareness of moral distinctions, an understanding of the feeling of shame, the ability to judge what is right or wrong, or absolute, total knowledge, the last of which the snake suggests: "Your eyes will be opened, and you will be like God (*or* like divine beings)" (3:5). Or it is very possible that the emphasis falls not so much

---

* Miriam Lichtheim, *Ancient Egyptian Literature: A Book of Readings*, vol. 3, *The Late Period* (Berkeley: Univ. of California Press, 1980), 112.

on "knowledge" as on "good and evil," a theme that starts in this story and runs through the remainder of the primeval history, ending in Genesis 11.

Disorder and Estrangement

Genesis 3 carries the two creation stories in Genesis 1–2 forward, but in a new direction. The first account in Genesis 1:1–2:4a functions well as a general backdrop to Genesis 2–3, but no explicit linkage occurs between it and Genesis 3. On the other hand, the second account, in Genesis 2:4b–25, is closely connected to Genesis 3 in setting, characters, and the motif of the forbidden fruit. Genesis 2–3 probably originated together as a complete story independent of Genesis 1, but in its present position in the book Genesis 3 continues while also countering both creation stories. If not for the events in Genesis 3, readers would be left in the pristine world of Genesis 1 and 2; with the third chapter the mythic idyll becomes threatened.

In the Garden of Eden of Genesis 3 we are introduced to the problem of evil. This element adds a somber note to the repeated affirmation of goodness in Genesis 1. As with the creation of the physical world, the meaning of "evil" and its larger implications for human relations are ideal topics for the narrative world of myth. The carefully structured and organized creation and the hospitably tended garden now become compromised—not because of some flaw in the created world but due solely to human decision and action. Genesis 3 is not a story about humanity's "fall," a term known from theological discussions but not present in this narrative. The word for "sin" also does not occur here. In Genesis 3 the couple disobey or rebel. Even the snake is not ultimately at fault, as the humans could have chosen differently than they do in the story. In the remainder of this chapter we will follow this theme of evil and disorder, noting the role it plays throughout the primeval history in Genesis 1–11. These stories are dense with details and literary features, and other chapters in this book, particularly those on literature, the divine, sex, and theodicy, will take up issues not addressed here.

Genesis 3 has a political dimension as well. The human players assert themselves by deliberately violating the single prohibition given them by God. In both of the creation stories God is sovereign and supreme, and the humans are not defiant. Now in Genesis 3 they resist the limit placed upon them and suffer the consequences, but they have made their own choice. A political reading of these chapters reveals a power imbalance, especially with

God over the two humans, but also with the humans over the animals and eventually the man over the woman. The Lord is also the lord over the man, who at the end is compelled to till the soil in order to survive.

As Genesis 2 closes, the Garden of Eden seems pristine and idyllic. The couple have all they could want—including each other. The very first Hebrew word in Genesis 3 is *ha-nachash*, "the snake," which for many both in antiquity and today would be intimation enough that something will soon change. This snake, the shrewdest of all the animals, can even talk, and it confronts the woman regarding the tree God declared off-limits. There is no explanation why the snake converses with the woman and not the man—a circumstance that has given interpreters ample room to speculate. When the woman hears the tantalizing message that eating its fruit will make them (plural in the Hebrew) godlike and realizes that the fruit looks delicious, she eats it and shares it with the man. (The Hebrew word for fruit is a generic term, not specifically an apple. It could just as well be a pomegranate, fig, or banana.) With that bite, they become aware of their nudity and arrange some fig-leaf cover.

The next we hear, God is taking an evening stroll in the garden and cannot find the couple. They come out of hiding and admit, when interrogated, that they ate some of the knowledge-of-good-and-evil fruit. The man passes the buck to the woman, who passes it to the snake, at which point God delivers the damning curses. The word "curse" is explicitly applied only to the snake and to the ground, not to the woman or the man. God makes the man and the woman clothing out of animal skin (the Hebrew word *or* does not mean "fur"; it occurs in the Hebrew Bible only in the sense of skin: Lev. 13:2; Exod. 25:5; 29:14; Job 40:31). God bans the couple from the garden, placing cherubim and a flaming sword to block access to the tree of life.

The snake in Genesis 3 is one of God's creatures, just craftier (*arum*) than all the others—much as we imagine the fox to be cunning. The snake suits this story ideally because of its double significance in Israel and elsewhere in the region: it can deliver lethal venom, but it is also worshiped in Egypt as the goddess Wadjet and stylized as the uraeus, the raised hooded cobra seen frequently at the forehead of the pharaoh's crown to signify protection of the ruler. The snake, cross-culturally often regarded as a chthonic deity, can also represent healing and fertility. The story in Numbers 21:4–9 combines both the deadly and the curative aspects: when the Israelites rebel in the wilderness, God sends poisonous snakes against them, but then instructs Moses to make a bronze image of a snake and place it atop a pole; when the people look at it, they are healed. Even the practice of translating the Hebrew word *nachash* as "serpent," the English word derived from Latin *serpens,* rather than "snake," derived from Anglo-Saxon *snaca,* perpetuates the exotic, pernicious, and mythic elements of this narrative figure.

Nothing in Genesis 3 indicates that the snake is Satan, the Arch-Evil One, although later Christian and Jewish sources make the connection. The snake in the story plays only a supporting role in demonstrating graphically the biblical understanding of evil. The snake draws attention to the possibility of disobeying God's single prohibition and presents it as a tempting option. The woman and the man alone make the decision to eat the fruit; they are not forced to do so. As a mythic device, the snake symbolizes the lure of transgression, the appeal of crossing boundaries, the willingness to risk all for the possibility of extraordinary gain. The point is not the snake but the disobedience performed by the woman and man. Humans alone are responsible for introducing evil into the world.

To cast the wrongdoing as "original sin" is valid primarily in a mythic, not historical sense. The narrative does not aim to recount some past event, as if there were two flesh-and-blood humans who ate a real fruit forbidden by God at some theoretically recoverable moment in history. Rather, the story pertains to all times, and the actions of these two human characters are not just their actions, but the doings of all of humanity. These are not sex-specific doings; *all* humans are the woman, and *all* humans are the man. The snake is talking to both Eve and Adam, and everything it says uses second-person plural verbs—in fact masculine verbs, even though it seems to be addressing the woman. Eve answers, and Adam, who does not dissent, may be standing right there alongside her.

The kind of wrong committed in the story is distinctive in its seeming pettiness—just a matter of eating a forbidden fruit, a cookie out of the cookie jar. However, this peccadillo, this ostensibly minor misdeed, violates an essential command, the only prohibition reported so far in the Bible: do not eat the fruit of the tree of the knowledge of good and evil. The fruit is not forbidden because it is ritually impure; the usual term for "unclean" (*tame*) does not occur here. Rather, the snake indicates that it will make them like God or like divine beings (either reading of Gen. 3:5

is possible) in knowing good and evil, and the man and the woman seem to aspire to this divine knowledge. This seemingly simple act of disobedience thereby assumes enormous significance.

Creation does not end with Genesis 1–2; the story of the Garden of Eden and the rest of the primeval history in Genesis 1–11 continue to configure the world as we know it. God's pronouncements against the snake, the woman, the ground, and the man represent a turning point in the larger creation narrative, a shift from the innocence of the primordial condition to a state of conflict (between snakes and humans), labor (for both women and men), and dominance (husband over wife). However, the narrative describes this disruptive state of affairs as the status quo after Genesis 3, not as the original goal of creation in Genesis 1–2, according to which the good world is characterized by both order and intimacy. Even though the humans are told not to eat of the tree of the knowledge of good and evil, no rupture has occurred by the last verse of chapter 2, and it is the two humans who introduce the disorder and estrangement evident by the last verse of chapter 3. The suffering humanity experiences stems from humans' own doing, and the story of disobedience in the garden conveys this message effectively and poignantly. The curses describe the world as it is, not as it should be. It is therefore appropriate to set our own moral goals toward recovering the harmony pictured in Genesis 1–2, not perpetuating the tensions and struggles of Genesis 3.

According to Genesis 1–3 and the rest of the Hebrew Bible, evil does not exist in the fabric of reality nor in the form of an "evil one," Satan, as we will discuss further in Chapter 14 regarding theodicy. Biblical monotheism does not tolerate a competitor to God. Divine dualism probably did not come into the picture until the people had contact with the Persians, whose Zoroastrian religion envisioned two opposing forces, the good Ahura Mazda and the evil Angra Mainyu, each with legions of lesser deities. Such a stark opposition between good and evil is foreign to the Israelite religions of earlier periods, when the Israelites were more likely to think in terms of a multiplicity of deities than a simple dualism. The figure of *ha-satan*, "the satan," in Job 1–2 is very different from Angra Mainyu. Later apocalyptic thought, evident in Qumran, in the New Testament, and in other early Jewish and Christian writings, presupposes an evil Satan, but the snake in Genesis 3 is not it. Evil "exists" in human actions, and the rebellion in the garden portrays it dramatically.

From Cain and Abel to Noah and Babel

The drama intensifies after the primeval couple enters the "real" world—not fully real yet, but getting closer to it than was the pristine Garden of Eden. Immediately Eve gives birth first to Cain and then to Abel. Cain becomes a farmer, and Abel a shepherd—a classic opposition in both literature and history that in this case becomes the next step in the increase of evildoing stretching from Genesis 3 to 11, the end of the primeval history. Each of the two brothers brings to God an offering of his fruits—the harvest from Cain and the first sheep from Abel. God is pleased with Abel's offering but pays no regard to Cain's, although no reason is given for the difference. Cain's "face falls," the Hebrew idiom denoting displeasure or chagrin, to which God then answers, "Sin is lurking at the door; its desire is for you, but you must master it" (4:7)—the first mention of sin in the Bible. Nonetheless, Cain kills Abel and, when asked by God about Abel's whereabouts, answers with the now famous line: "Am I my brother's keeper?" (4:9), or "Do I take care of my brother?"

With this fratricide, sin has taken on major proportions. The move from the seemingly small thing of eating the forbidden fruit to the heinous crime of murder—and, at that, the murder of a sibling—represents an enormous and sudden increase in the severity of wrongdoing. Typical of biblical literature, much is left in the background for hearers or readers to ponder. We learn of no response from Adam and Eve, other than Eve's laconic statement that Cain killed Abel (Gen. 4:25). God banishes Cain—presumably from Adam and Eve, as to this point no other humans on the earth beyond his parents have been mentioned. Nor is the decision to ban and brand him explained. As mentioned above in Chapter 4, the situation may reflect a conflict between two opposing legal or customary principles: on the one hand, to punish a murderer with death and, on the other, to protect one's own family members from actions by others. Banning offers a third alternative, a way to punish severely without executing. The family or clan is the primary building block of Israelite society, and to be exiled from one's own home and land meant harsh deprivation, both physical and emotional. Cain was a farmer, and now God condemns him to a life of wandering. Cain considers it a most severe punishment, since wandering without his family's protection he will be vulnerable to anyone who wants to kill him. God shields him by marking him in some unexplained way and pronouncing a curse on anyone who does him harm.

The narrative then digresses to populate the world with people and professions. Cain heads east of Eden and marries (Gen. 4:17), though the story gives no account of the origin of his wife. He builds a city, though there is no mention of its inhabitants or further details about the nature of this city. One of Cain's descendants becomes the ancestor of tent dwellers and herders, another is the father of musicians, and yet another is the first of the metalworkers. Despite his crime, Cain seems to have achieved status as progenitor of portions of later society. However, from the perspective of agriculturalists in Israel, none of these professions was particularly favored: nomadic or seminomadic tent dwellers circulated on the fringes of settled society; professional musicians served the elite; and metalworkers often practiced their esoteric craft outside towns and cities.

The rest of the primeval history recounts, in dramatic or prosaic forms, the proliferation of humanity and wickedness, sometimes explicitly but often quite subtly. The steps along the way evince a movement between small-scale and large-scale events:

1:1–2:4a	Creation of the cosmos and all life
2:4b–25	Creation of life in a garden
3:1–24	Disobedience in the Garden of Eden
4:1–15	Cain and Abel
4:16–26	Beginnings of civilization
5:1–32	Genealogy: Adam to Noah's sons
6:1–4	Divine sons and human daughters
6:5–8:22	Noah's flood
9:1–17	Covenant with Noah
9:18–29	Curse on Canaan
10:1–32	Genealogy: Table of Nations
11:1–9	Tower of Babel
11:10–32	Genealogy: Shem to Abram

The genealogies in Genesis 5, 10, and 11, usually regarded as tedious to read, are more than mere fillers in the primeval history. At one level they span long time periods between the major events related in these chapters. From Adam, Eve, and their children to the story of the divine sons and human daughters and then the flood, a substantial number of years elapse. Rather than simply stating "After *x* number of years . . . ," the narrative tracks the generations as they unfold in formulaic fashion. By the end of the genealogy we can sense that the world's population has increased exponentially and a long period has passed before the next event occurs. The same happens after the flood, building up the population once again and spreading it geographically until the episode with the Tower of Babel. Finally, another genealogy serves as the bracket connecting the Babel story with the birth of Abram/Abraham, whose history and offspring will then become the subject of the rest of the book of Genesis.

In addition to showing the passage of time and the increase in population between key events in the narrative, the genealogies demonstrate the degradation of humankind. The ancients in Southwest Asia apparently associated human longevity with legendary figures. The Sumerian King List, dating from 2000–1700 BCE but referring to kings in southern Mesopotamia during the third millennium BCE, names eight kings who ruled from 18,600 to 43,200 years each; variants of this text claim even longer reigns. After these kings a flood occurred, and then another thirty-nine kings are listed with reigns of much shorter duration, the longest being 1,560 years and the shortest only 6 years. A comparable drop in age at death is also present in the Genesis genealogies:

Adam to Noah: between 969 (Methuselah) and 777

Adam: 930

Enoch: did not die, but "walked with God" at age 365

Noah: 950

Shem (Noah's son) to Terah (Abraham's father):
  between 600 and 148

Abraham: 175

Sarah: 127

Isaac: 180

Joseph: 110

As in the Sumerian King List, the flood serves as a dividing line, and after it the astronomical ages gradually recede into the past. The biblical figures show a steady though not consistent decline in ages, with no explanation provided other than God's statement in Genesis 6:3 ordaining that human life should be limited to 120 years. By comparison, Psalm 90:10 lowers it even more: "The days of our life are seventy years, or perhaps eighty, if we are strong." The ancient Israelites knew of the frailty of life, and their average life expectancy must not have been much over 35, judging from the archaeological record of burials as well as from comparisons with other cultures in a similar environment and without benefit of modern medicine. Death in childhood was especially common. Evidence from a burial cave at the Galilean site of Meiron during the Greco-Roman period reveals 197 skeletons; 95, or almost 50 percent, of the persons died before the age of 18, and of those 70 percent during their first five years of life. According to the ages reported in the books of 1–2 Kings in the Hebrew Bible, the Israelite kings, more pampered than the commoners, averaged a life span only in the forties.

Genesis 1–11 describes two parallel developments—an increase in wrongdoing and a decrease in longevity. The linkage between the two is indirect but effective: people die earlier because they have become more sinful. The spread of wrongdoing thus has the ravaging effect of a pandemic upon a population, and it reaches a peak in the stories of the flood and the Tower of Babel.

The brief tale in Genesis 6:1–4 (discussed in Chapter 5), immediately prior to the flood, demonstrates further that something is going awry. Divine beings (the Hebrew phrase *bene ha-elohim* means literally "the sons of the God" or perhaps "the sons of the gods") spy human females (*benot ha-adam*) and consort with them, producing the Nephilim (literally, "fallen ones"), apparently giants or fearsome warriors; the only other appearance in the Hebrew Bible comes in Numbers 13:33, the report of the Israelite scouts about the terrifying residents of Canaan. This mingling of the divine and the human worlds prompts God to limit human life spans to 120, an explicit instance of connecting wrongdoing and shortened lives.

The flood story in Genesis 6–9 begins ominously: "YHWH saw that the wickedness of humankind was great in the earth, and that every inclination (*yetzer*) of the thoughts of their hearts was only evil continually. And YHWH was sorry that he had made humankind on the earth, and it grieved him to his heart" (6:5–6). There is little in the primeval history to this point to demonstrate this "great wickedness" beyond the three anecdotes of disobedience in the garden, Abel's murder, and the mingling of divine and human beings. Genesis 6:11–12 refers also in general terms to corruption and violence.

An opaque word occurs in the first verse just quoted—*yetzer*, usually translated as a person's "inclination," "intent," or "plan." Genesis does not indicate whether God has created this "inclination" as an inherent human characteristic or whether humans spawn or choose it themselves. Genesis 8:21 identifies this *yetzer* as evil and says it is with people from their childhood, though not from birth. The Babylonian language has a cognate, *etzeru*, with the meaning of drawing a plan for a building or other structure. Although the Hebrew Bible does not develop this notion of the *yetzer*, early Jewish thinkers debated its meaning. For example, the book of *4 Ezra* (2 Esdras), a late first-century CE Jewish apocalyptic writing, takes up the motif of the evil *yetser* and proposes that it stems from the original creation of Adam: "For a grain of evil seed was sown in Adam's heart from the beginning, and how much ungodliness it has produced until now— and will produce until the time of threshing comes!" (4:30). Later rabbinic thought developed this notion further, distinguishing between the *yetzer ha-ra* and the *yetzer ha-tov*, the "evil inclination" and the "good inclination," the human propensity to do wrong and the countervailing desire to control the evil inclination and do good.

Stories of catastrophic floods are known from many cultures, although there is no physical evidence of a universal flood, only of local floodings. Anthropologists and literary historians have tallied more than three hundred different flood stories, taken from every continent except Antarctica. They cannot all be traced back to the Genesis account since there are differences among them in details, geography, and historical periods. Basically, they all have only two ingredients in common, water and survivors, one of whom usually becomes a culture hero.

Not only is the flood account in Genesis one of a type found broadly, but its details also make it implausible. For example, a ship of the size 450 feet long, 75 feet wide, and 45 feet high (6:15, assuming an 18-inch cubit) could never contain a pair of every species on the globe. Moreover, forty days and forty nights of rain, even at the torrential rate of 1 foot per twenty-four-hour period, would not be enough to cover a tall tree, let alone engulf all the mountains.

As with many of the other stories, Genesis 6–9 fits into the larger creation myth in that it nearly undoes the earlier creative acts, returning the world to the watery chaos out of which it originated. In effect, then, an act of re-creation follows the flood—dry land emerges again as it did in Genesis 1, animals and humans repopulate the world, and a pristine world devoid of human wickedness again constitutes the new beginning—even though human strife and wrongdoing will again appear only a few verses later. God commits never to repeat the destructive flood (8:22): "As long as the earth endures, seedtime and harvest, cold and heat, summer and winter, day and night, shall not cease."

God gives the rainbow as a sign of the divine covenant with humans (Gen. 9:12–17). This selection of the rainbow is poignant because, except for its occurrence here and in Ezekiel 1:28, the Hebrew word translated "bow" always means the device that shoots arrows. God is turning this weapon of war into a feature of nature so God will remember the covenant of preservation (9:8–11).

The Genesis flood story is actually a composite of what were originally two independent traditions, one matching in style the Priestly creation account (Gen. 1:1–2:4a) and the other similar to the Yahwistic creation story (2:4b–25). This hypothesis of double narratives also helps to account for some of the duplications and differences within the story: The waters come from rain (7:4, 12, Yahwistic) or from "the deep" (*tehom*, "Deep") and the "windows of heaven" (7:11, Priestly). Flooding continues for 40 days and nights before Noah opens the window and sends out the bird (7:12; 8:6, Yahwistic), or it floods for 150 days and the high waters last more than one year before Noah and family can disembark (7:11, 24; 8:14, Priestly). The Priestly interest in chronology in Genesis 1:1–2:4a recurs in the flood story's details about time (8:3–5, 13–14). Noah takes on board seven pairs of all clean animals and birds and only one pair of all unclean species (7:2–3, Yahwistic), whereas in the other story he saves one pair of all species (7:8–9, Priestly).

Flood stories from other ancient Southwest Asian cultures have parallels at too many points to suggest that the connections between the biblical version and those of neighboring cultures are coincidental. Most of these stories come from Mesopotamia; so far Egypt has yielded nothing comparable, even though the Nile River floods annually. Although some fragments of flood myths have appeared from third-millennium BCE Sumer in southern Mesopotamia on the Persian Gulf, most of them are from Babylonian and Assyrian settings farther north in the area of the Tigris and Euphrates, where flooding also occurs every year. The two longest accounts are the *Epic of Gilgamesh* and *Atrahasis,* both from the second millennium BCE and discovered in the nineteenth century. As mentioned above, the Gilgamesh epic describes Gilgamesh on a quest for immortality, and during his odyssey he visits Utnapishtim, the flood hero who along with his wife received immortal status from the gods after surviving the deluge. Other versions of the flood story have Atrahasis, not Utnapishtim, as the hero of the flood.

In the *Epic of Gilgamesh,* Utnapishtim recounts the story of his flood, which shares a number of striking similarities with Noah's flood. From the divine world comes the impetus to send the flood, and the god Ea urges Utnapishtim to prepare for it by constructing a large boat. He does so, coating it with bitumen or pitch. He then boards the boat along with his family and animals, "the seed of all living things" (no mention of loading them in pairs or of clean vs. unclean animals). The fearsome storm rages for 7 days, not 40 or 150 as in Noah's case. The ship grounds on a mountaintop. Three times Utnapishtim sends out a bird—first a dove, then a swallow, and finally a raven, which does not return as it has found a resting place; Noah's order of birds is first a raven and then twice a dove. After their floods, both Utnapishtim and Noah offer a sacrifice, and in both cases the deities savor the pleasing odor. In the biblical story YHWH resolves not to cause such destruction again; in the case of Utnapishtim the god Ea remonstrates with Enlil, the god who had caused the destructive flood, that he should not have sent it when more limited means of punishment were available.

The story of Gilgamesh seems to have been fairly widespread in Southwest Asia during the second millennium BCE; a fragment, stemming from another part of the epic than the flood story, was even discovered at the site of Megiddo in northern Israel, dating from about the fourteenth or thirteenth century BCE. At the latest, Israelites became acquainted or reacquainted with *Gilgamesh* and the *Enuma Elish* during the eighth and seventh centuries BCE when the Assyrians, who knew the Utnapishtim story, had conquered Israel, or later during the Babylonian exile when Judahites lived in Babylonia.

The remainder of the primeval history reflects the Israelites' recognition of other cultures in the region. First is the short episode (Gen. 9:18–29)

involving Noah's drunkenness and his three sons, which ends with a curse
of Canaan and a blessing of Shem—that is, an elevation of the S(h)emites
over the Canaanites (not a curse of African populations, as it was interpreted
during the days of American slavery and segregation). Next, in Genesis 10,
comes the Table of Nations, a listing of the descendants of Noah's three sons,
describing their dispersion throughout the known world and their founding
of cities and population groups. Some of the descendants' names are associated with places or groups known in later times: Ashkenaz, Kittim, Cush,
Egypt, Canaan, Babel, Sidon, Elam, Asshur, Aram, and Sheba. The post-
deluge world is now repopulated as the ancient Israelites knew it to be.

The final incident described in the primeval history involves the Tower
of Babel (Gen. 11:1–9). As Noah's descendants migrate, many settle in
Mesopotamia and proceed to build a city, including a very high tower.
Towers, called ziggurats, are known from that region from at least as early
as the third millennium BCE—massive structures, not exceptionally high,
but usually complex, tiered, pyramidal edifices intended for cultic purposes
or as dwelling places for the gods. In this story the people's collaboration
with each other may be more of a problem for God than the prospect of
their building it to heaven. To stop the project, God causes them to speak
different languages so they cannot communicate with each other, and the
people scatter in language groups over the earth. Not only does this story
serve as an etiology for the existence of diverse languages, but we also find
here one more folk etymology: the name Babel (Babylon) is associated
with the Hebrew *balal*, meaning to "confuse [their languages]" (11:9).

Into the ordered, congenial world created by God, humans have thus
introduced disorder and estrangement. The prehistory in Genesis 1–11, in a
sense the preface to the Bible, has brought us to the point where we can now
follow the story of one particular lineage, Abraham and his descendants.

Other Biblical Creations

Other creation accounts exist in the Hebrew Bible besides these in Genesis 1–11. Of three that stand out, Psalm 104 is especially distinctive for
its apparent ties to "The Great Hymn to the Aten." This beautiful Egyptian song is directed to the Aten, the sun disk and manifestation of the
sun god, Re. Discovered on the wall of a fourteenth-century BCE tomb
in Egypt, it expresses the "monotheistic" beliefs of pharaohs Amenhotep
III (1390–1352) and Amenhotep IV Akhenaten (1352–1336), the im-

mediate predecessors of Pharaoh Tutankhamen (1336–1327). Abandoning the common polytheistic religion, they developed a concept of the sole god Aten, creator and sustainer of the world, and sought to direct Egyptian religion toward this monotheism. The change was short-lived, and under Tutankhamen the priests and followers of the many gods and goddesses reasserted themselves and returned to traditional religious practices.

Psalm 104 contains numerous statements and allusions close to those in "The Great Hymn to the Aten." They may stem not directly from the Aten hymn but from a common tradition, especially since astral and solar worship seems to have taken hold in various Southwest Asian countries including Israel, as attested in 2 Kings 23:5, referring to Josiah's reform in deposing the priests "who made offerings to Baal, to the sun, the moon, the constellations, and all the host of the heavens" (see also 17:16). A few of the creation-related verses in Psalm 104 with similarities in the Aten hymn* include:

The Great Hymn to the Aten	Psalm 104
O Sole God beside whom there is none!	O YHWH my God, you are very great. (1a)
How many are your deeds. . . . You made the earth as you wished, you alone, All peoples, herds, and flocks.	O YHWH, how manifold are your works! In wisdom you have made them all; the earth is full of your creatures. (24)
When you set in western lightland, Earth is in darkness as if in death. . . .	You make darkness, and it is night, when all the animals of the forest come creeping out.

---

* Miriam Lichtheim, *Ancient Egyptian Literature: A Book of Readings*, vol. 2, *The New Kingdom* (Berkeley: Univ. of California Press, 1976), 96–99.

The Great Hymn to the Aten	Psalm 104
Every lion comes from its den,	The young lions roar for their prey,
All the serpents bite.	seeking their food from God. When the sun rises, they withdraw and lie down in their dens. (20–22)
When you have dawned they live,	When you hide your face, they are dismayed;
When you set they die;	when you take away their breath, they die
You yourself are lifetime, one lives by you.	and return to their dust. (29)
You set every man in his place, You supply their needs; Everyone has his food.	These all look to you to give them their food in due season. (27)
The entire land sets out to work.	People go out to their work and to their labor until the evening. (23)
The fish in the river dart before you, Your rays are the midst of the sea.	Yonder is the sea, great and wide, creeping things innumerable are there, living things both small and great. (25)
Birds fly from their nests,	By the streams the birds of the air have their habitation;
Their wings greeting your *ka* [vital force].	they sing among the branches. (12)

The Great Hymn to the Aten	**Psalm 104**
He makes waves on the mountains like the sea, To drench their fields and their towns.	You make springs gush forth in the valleys; they flow between the hills, giving drink to every wild animal. . . . The trees of YHWH are watered abundantly. (10–11a, 16a)

Both poems convey a belief that God/Aten alone created all that exists and is worthy of praise because of it.

A second biblical text filled with creation language is Job 38–41. In the chapters leading up to this point, Job has been arguing with his friends about his suffering, maintaining against them that he has done no wrong, does not deserve such treatment, and needs a response from God to explain his unjust afflictions. Evading Job's question, God explains instead that Job cannot even understand how the world was made, which God then proceeds to describe. These images of creation are normally left aside by those who argue for a literal interpretation of Genesis 1–11, perhaps because a literal interpretation of the language in Job 38–41 cannot be defended. However, there is no textual basis for treating the creation descriptions in Genesis and Job differently—they are both mythic and poetic.

Job 38–41 speaks of creation and cosmology in vivid language, set mostly in the form of questions God poses to Job. God "laid the foundation of the earth" and "its cornerstone," "shut in the sea with doors when it burst out from the womb" (whose womb is unspecified), and made "thick darkness its swaddling band," setting "bars and doors" to contain the ocean (38:4, 6, 8–10). God can cause the dawn to "take hold of the skirts of the earth" (probably meaning the earth's edges or corners) and shake the wicked out of it (38:12–13). There are "gates of death," a "way to the dwelling of light," "storehouses of the snow . . . and the hail," and a "place where the light is distributed" and where "the east wind is scattered upon the earth" (38:17, 19, 22, 24). The ice and frost are also born from a womb, and the surface of Deep freezes (38:29–30; here is the word *tehom* again, the waters of the abyss, as in Gen. 1:2; 7:11). God is in control of the stars—the Pleiades, Orion, the Bear (the dipper), and the signs of the zodiac—and can also "send forth lightnings, so that they may go and say to you, 'Here we are'"; there are also "waterskins of the heavens" that can tilt to water the earth (38:31–33, 35, 37–38). God provides food for baby birds and observes the birthing of mountain goats (38:41; 39:1–4). Who else can control the wild ass, the ox, the ostrich, the horse, the hawk, and the eagle—let alone Behemoth and Leviathan, perhaps representing the hippopotamus and the crocodile (40:15–41:34; Tanakh 40:15–41:26)? All of these striking images, colorful and dramatic as they are, give literary voice to the theological affirmation of divine superiority and creativity, part of the message also underlying Genesis 1–11.

The final example of the biblical accounts of creation occurs in the book of Isaiah, especially chapters 40–45, 48, and 51. Often called Second Isaiah or Deutero-Isaiah, Isaiah 40–55 stems from an unnamed prophet active in the waning years of the Babylonian exile, about 545–540 BCE. The work of this prophet follows in the tradition of the prophet behind Isaiah 1–39, but Second Isaiah differs markedly in its message and tone of comfort and encouragement, in contrast to the strong social and religious criticism present in First Isaiah. Drawing on creation rhetoric, Second Isaiah reinforces the image of YHWH as creator in the past: God "measured the waters in the hollow of his hand and marked off the heavens with a span . . . and weighed the mountains in scales and the hills in a balance" (40:12). God "sits above the circle of the earth, . . . stretches out the heavens like a curtain, and spreads them like a tent to live in" (40:22), bringing out "their host [the stars] and numbers them, calling them all by name" (40:26). YHWH "made the earth, and created humankind (*adam*) upon it" (45:12).

But the distinctive feature in Isaiah 40–45 pictures God not only as a creator at the beginning of time, but also as a creator of new things in the future, which is precisely the message the Babylonian exiles want to hear. The contrast between past and present parallels the juxtaposition of the old creation to the new creation: "Do not remember the former things, or consider the things of old. I am about to do a new thing; now it springs forth, do you not perceive it?" (43:18–19).

The new creation will manifest itself physically in a reformed earth. For the exiles eager to return from Babylon to Judah God will make the wilderness route passable, leveling the terrain and straightening the road, providing water in the desert, turning darkness to light, and guarding against wild animals (40:3–4; 41:17–20; 42:16; 43:19–20). The trip from Babylon evokes memories of the exodus from Egypt, when the waters parted and the enemy was overwhelmed (43:2, 16–17; 51:10). With explicit references to the creation language of Genesis 1, Second Isaiah affirms that God did not create chaos; in Isaiah 45:18–19 the word *tohu*, meaning "chaos" or "emptiness," is the same word used in the phrase *tohu vavohu*, "formless void," in Genesis 1:2. Rather, YHWH conquered "Deep" (*tehom*, Isa. 51:10; Gen. 1:2), used here in the sense of both the primordial abyss and the Reed Sea, which was parted for the exodus from Egypt. Another proper noun without the definite article, Rahab, meaning "raging" or "surging," is a mythical monster also associated with the sea: "Was it not you (YHWH) who cut Rahab in pieces, who pierced the dragon? Was it not you who dried up the sea, the waters of great Deep; who made the depths of the sea a way for the redeemed to cross over?" (51:9b–10). God formed the people of Israel (43:1) and now is calling the Persian emperor Cyrus to free the Israelites so they can return to their homeland (44:28–45:8).

In the biblical tradition creation is both an episode of the past and a process continuing in the present and the future. Various biblical texts, not just those at the beginning of the Bible, describe creation with an array of images, rhetoric, and plots, and from this assemblage comes no single account that incorporates all. From Sumer to Egypt, long before and during ancient Israel's existence, came many other descriptions of creation, some of them with striking similarities to biblical expressions. All stemmed from an understandable human curiosity to know about beginnings. At the same time the individual accounts embody and express a given culture's vision of itself and the world. Yet creation is not an end point, as the ensuing drama of life demonstrates again and again.

Chapter 8

Continuation and Completion

The biblical story not only of ancient Israel but also of humanity follows the effort, after dislocation, to find or make a home. Adam and Eve are exiled from Eden; the way back to paradise is blocked by the cherubim and a flaming sword (Gen. 3:24). Nevertheless, the first couple immediately begin the process of securing continuity by producing their sons Cain and Abel (4:1–2). Life outside the garden will be harsh, yet it will prevail. If human beings are to find immortality, they will do so, according to most of the Bible, through the memories they create and through their children.

The pattern of exile and the search for stability continues. Cain kills Abel and becomes "a fugitive and a wanderer on the earth" (Gen. 4:12). Rather than wandering, however, Cain settles in the "land of Nod, east of Eden" (4:16), and with his wife—her origins are of no interest to the biblical authors—conceives a son whom he names Enoch. Then Cain builds a city, which he names after his son. His name and posterity are ensured; even the flood does not wipe out his memory. The story suggests that for the biblical authors, cities are places of some ambivalence. The first one is founded by a murderer, they are able to be destroyed, and they cannot provide the security humanity so desires.

The search for stability continues with the generation of Noah. He and his family are displaced from their home, wherever it was, when the waters below the earth and the waters above combine to destroy creation. From this second formless void, the dry land again appears, and the ark lands on "the mountains [plural] of Ararat" (Gen. 8:4)—a notice that should give pause to any still insisting that the ark can be found on a singular mountain. Noah and his family receive the same blessing issued to the first humans in Genesis 1: "God blessed Noah and his sons, and said to them, 'Be fruitful and multiply, and fill the earth'" (9:1). The descendants of the sons Shem, Ham, and Japheth and their unnamed wives become the eponymous ancestors of the nations that "spread abroad on the earth after the flood" (10:32).

The next chapter, the final chapter in the primeval history, complicates this global notice. Genesis 11 opens with the statement that "the whole earth had one language and the same words" (11:1). Nor had all the descendants of Noah followed the commandment and "spread abroad"; the people gather in the land of Shinar (or Babylon), where they again seek a home and immortality. They want to build "a city and a tower with its top in the heavens," so they are not "scattered abroad upon the face of the whole earth" (11:4). What God offered as a blessing they regard as a threat. The city is humanity's attempt to re-create Eden, the location where they wish to remain, despite the command to "fill the earth." Like Eden, where human and animal conversed, in Babel no boundaries impede human communication. In Eden, the divine concern was ensuring that the people not become "like the gods"; YHWH expels Adam and Eve lest they "take also from the tree of life, and eat, and live forever" (3:22). At the tower, YHWH voices similar concern to keep humanity human and, so, limited: "Look, they are one people, and they have all one language; . . . nothing that they propose to do will now be impossible for them" (11:6).

In Eden, human disobedience leads to expulsion; at Babel, the diversity of language leads to the inability to forge common cause. The story ends with the notice that "YHWH scattered them abroad over the face of all the earth" (Gen. 11:9). Twice commanded to "fill the earth" and encouraged several more times, humanity finally fulfills the command because of divine intervention. The attempt to establish immortality cannot be accomplished by human endeavor. And yet, ironically, even though the place will not be permanent and the names of those who attempted to build the tower are not recorded, the stories remain.

Abraham's Search for a Home

The end of Genesis 11 opens another story of displacement. Shem's descendant Terah "took his son Abram and his grandson Lot son of Haran, and his daughter-in-law Sarai, his son Abram's wife, and . . . went out together from Ur of the Chaldeans to go to the land of Canaan; but when they came to Haran, they settled there" (11:31). Terah, who lives 205 years, does not complete his journey; he dies in Haran (11:32). It will be Abram's charge to move to Canaan.

Conveniently (or ironically), YHWH then orders Abram to do what he had been in the process of doing: "Go from your country and your kindred and your father's house to the land that I will show you. I will make of you a great nation, and I will bless you, and make your name great, so that you will be a blessing" (Gen. 12:1–2). Abram had already left the great city of Ur; his father had already died; the "land I will show you" turns out to be Canaan, the original destination. Abram takes his infertile wife, Sarai, and his nephew Lot and completes the interrupted journey. When Abram comes to the Oak of Moreh at Shechem, YHWH states, "To your offspring I will give this land" (12:7). The "promised land" does not here belong to Abraham, but to his posterity.

Abram and his family remain in Canaan for an entire six verses (Gen. 12:5–10), and then a famine hits. Like any Southwest Asian patriarch in the late Bronze Age, Abram knew that in times of famine, Egypt—whose agriculture was dependent not only on local rainfall, but on the annual flooding of the Nile—would have grain. He and Sarai head south. Displacement continues.

Entering Egypt, the patriarch tells his no doubt exhausted, aged, but nevertheless gorgeous wife, "I know well that you are a woman beautiful in appearance; and when the Egyptians see you, they will say, 'This is his wife'; then they will kill me, but they will let you live. Say you are my sister, so that it may go well with me because of you, and that my life may be spared on your account" (Gen. 12:11–13). On the one hand, Abram's first recorded words to Sarai are complimentary; on the other, one might wonder why he does not explicitly consult with her about leaving Ur or Haran. On the one hand, Abram asks Sarai to help him; on the other, his concern is with his own safety: "so that it will go well with *me*." Sarai's response goes unrecorded.

Abram was not exaggerating about his wife's beauty. The Egyptian officials praise her, and Pharaoh takes her into his "house," or more likely his harem. Whether Sarai was content to be pampered in the palace as opposed to living as a sojourner (or resident alien) in a tent in Canaan, or whether she longed for her husband and despised her position as sexual slave is, again, not recorded. Because the biblical text typically fails to record motivation or interior thought, readers must provide these details. As for her husband, it does "go well with" him: Pharaoh gives him "sheep, oxen, male donkeys, male and female slaves, female donkeys, and camels" (Gen. 12:16).

We can only imagine what occurred in Pharaoh's house as well. The next time Abram "sojourns" outside of Canaan and passes his wife off as his sister, to King Abimelech of Gerar (Gen. 20:1–18), the king receives a warning dream that he has taken a married woman into his household. Thus he stays away from Sarai. Pharaoh received no such dream, and Sarai no such explicit protection. Some scholars have explained this difference by attributing the two stories to two different sources. The account in Genesis 12 is part of the Yahwistic source, which is earthy and colorful and pictures God in anthropomorphic language, similar to the story of the creation and the Garden of Eden in Genesis 2–3; the second account, in Genesis 20, however, is Elohistic—more cautious, protective of the matriarch (there is no danger of Sarai getting approached by the king), and divinely indirect, as God communicates not in person, but through dreams.

Unexpressed as well is how Abram and Sarai expect to fulfill the commandment to settle in Canaan or even how—indeed, if—they expect to extricate themselves from this awkward situation. Abram is in no position to say to Pharaoh, "Oh, by the way, this woman whom I identified as my sister is also my wife." Nor, once taken into Pharaoh's house, is Sarai in a position to explain that her husband had withheld the truth of their relationship. The note in Genesis 20:12, where Abram explains to Abimelech that that Sarai is his *half* sister, is an insufficient corrective to the implicit lie, namely, that she is his sister and therefore not his wife.

Rescue can come only from above. And it does, although the prompt for Sarai's liberation is not clear. Most English versions translate Genesis 12:17 as, "But YHWH afflicted Pharaoh and his house with great plagues because of Sarai, Abram's wife." In this translation, Sarai is the object of divine pity. The translation "because of Sarai" is plausible, as the Hebrew *devar* can mean "thing" or "case," thus, "because of the case of Sarai" or simply, in colloquial English, "because of Sarai." But *devar* literally means "word." Therefore, the phrase can also be translated, "because of the word of Sarai" (*al devar Sarai*), which may indicate that Sarai had prayed for her rescue. In this translation, it is Sarai's own cry for liberation that prompts divine action.

Abram and Sarai leave—better, are expelled—from Egypt; the trip was profitable, as they return to Canaan with the property Pharaoh had bestowed on Abram. But their descendants will return to Egypt, and to an even more desperate situation. The promise of the land will not be fulfilled in Abram's generation or that of his son or grandsons. Generations will pass before the promise is realized.

Sarai's consignment to Pharaoh's house, Abram's economic benefits, and their divinely facilitated extrication from Egypt set the pattern for the opening chapters of the book of Exodus. YHWH tells Abram: "Know for certain that your descendants shall be aliens in a land that is not theirs, and shall be slaves there, and they shall be oppressed for four hundred years; but I will bring judgment on the nation that they serve, and afterward they shall come out with great possessions" (Gen. 15:13–14). The book of Exodus confirms the prediction. YHWH promises Moses: "I will bring this people into such favor with the Egyptians that, when you go, you will not go empty-handed; each woman shall ask . . . for jewelry of silver and of gold, and clothing, and you shall put them on your sons and on your daughters; and so you shall plunder the Egyptians" (Exod. 3:21–22; the prediction is confirmed in 12:35–36).

In Canaan, the pattern of sojourning and exile, slavery and liberation continues. First Sarai, unable to conceive a child, places her Egyptian slave Hagar into Abram's bed. Thus Sarai does to Hagar what Abram did to her. Like Sarai, Hagar was taken from her homeland, dragged across the desert, and placed into the bed of an elite man so that someone else could benefit from the "services" she provided. The rabbinic compilation known as *Genesis Rabbah* (45) recognizes the connection between the two women by identifying Hagar as Pharaoh's "daughter." Thereby she matches Sarai, whose new name in the next chapter, Sarah, means "princess." The two women, although they never speak to each other and refer to each other only as "mistress" and "slave," function as mirror images.

However, unlike Sarai in Pharaoh's household, Hagar conceives. Her pregnancy, and the resultant possibility of her advancement in Abram's household now that she is carrying a child, brings her to self-awareness. Genesis 16:4 in the NRSV, "When she saw that she had conceived, she looked with contempt on her mistress," misses the Hebrew pun. Literally, the text reads: "Her mistress became light [that is, 'light' in the sense of lightweight] in her eyes." The narrator's comment emphasizes both Hagar's personal sense of gravity and Sarai's relative lack of importance and calls attention to the pregnancy; as the pregnant Hagar becomes larger and literally gains weight, Sarai becomes "light" in her eyes, both personally and physically.

The next displacement is prompted not by exile but by flight. Sarai, unable to accept this turn of events, abuses her slave, and Hagar flees into the wilderness. There she encounters an angel, whose question reinforces her subordinated position: "Hagar, slave-girl of Sarai, where have you come from and where are you going?" (Gen. 16:8). The angel's address keeps the slave in her subordinate position, and Hagar's response indicates that she still recognizes her servile role: "I am running away from my mistress Sarai." But Hagar doesn't answer the second part of the question; she knows that she has fled a house of slavery, yet pregnant and alone, she has no place to go. The angel sends her back to "her mistress" (16:9), but with the promise that God will "so greatly multiply [her] offspring that they cannot be counted for multitude" (16:10). The promise continues: "You shall bear a son; you shall call his name Ishmael, because YHWH has heard your affliction" (16:11). The name, meaning "El hears," comes from the same root as the term *shema,* the opening of Judaism's statement of faith, "Hear, O Israel. . . ."

Hagar returns to Sarai, whether to ongoing abuse or not, the Bible again is silent. Thirteen years later, and three years after Sarah has given birth to her own son, Isaac, Hagar is again driven into the wilderness. This time the cause is not Sarah's abusive hand, but her tongue. She demands of Abraham: "Cast out this slave woman with her son; for the son of this slave woman shall not inherit along with my son Isaac" (Gen. 21:10). The prompt for Sarah's concern is ambiguous. The NRSV, following the Septuagint, offers, "But Sarah saw the son of Hagar the Egyptian, whom she had borne to Abraham, playing with her son Isaac" (21:9). However, the Hebrew lacks "with her son Isaac"; it only notes that Sarah sees Ishmael "playing." The Hebrew term, *metzacheq,* is a cognate of the name Isaac, which means "laughter." The Greek could indicate child abuse, as the parallel use of the term in Genesis 26:8 can indicate an intimate relationship. The Hebrew suggests a more psychological reaction: Sarah sees Ishmael as taking the place of her son, as being the one to bring laughter to the household, perhaps as taking her place as the center of Isaac's world.

Although Abraham is troubled by Sarah's command "on account of his son" (the reference is to Ishmael; he expresses no concern for Hagar), he obeys Sarah because God tells him to do so. Genesis 21:12 in the NRSV reads: "Whatever Sarah says to you, do as she tells you"; the Hebrew reads, "listen to her voice." A faint echo of the expulsion from Eden can be heard, where God had said to Adam, "because you have listened to the voice of your wife . . ." (3:17). That term for "listen," *shema,* again evokes the name Ishmael.

The story of Hagar and Ishmael, like that of Sarai's sojourn in Pharaoh's house, also foreshadows Israel's years in Egypt. Hagar's descendants, the Ishmaelites, will sell Sarah's great-grandson Joseph into Egyptian slavery (Gen. 37:25–28). Joseph will settle his family in Egypt, where they will be "strangers in a strange land" (see Exod. 2:22; 18:3). The name Hagar most likely is related to an Old South Arabic word meaning "splendid." However, the Hebrew letters *h-g-r* can also spell "the stranger." As the Egyptian slave and her child are expelled from Abraham's household to face death in the wilderness (Gen. 21:14), so the Israelites will leave Egypt to face death in the wilderness. The only ones to enter the promised land are Joshua and Caleb.

The story of the ancestors continues the movement between home and exile, sojourn and the search for permanence. Isaac is, like his parents, forced to leave Canaan because of a famine—the "promise" of the promised land is not encouraging. Isaac takes his family "to Gerar, to King Abimelech of the Philistines" (Gen. 26:1). This is the same Abimelech to whom Abraham had passed off Sarah as his sister. Then, YHWH forbids Isaac from entering Egypt, although Isaac had expressed no plan to do so. Finally, YHWH commands Isaac to do what he had planned on doing: remain in Gerar as a sojourner. The command recollects Abram's initial commission, the mandate to go to the land where he had already been heading. There may also be a subtle wordplay in these details. Gerar is from the Hebrew root *g-r-r*, which means "to drag away," but it evokes both the name Hagar and the idea of a "stranger," *ger*. Genesis 20:1 says Abraham *vayagar bigrar*, "and he lived as a stranger (*or* resident alien) in Gerar." Isaac's sojourn portends later possession. YHWH promises him, "Reside in this land as an alien, and I will be with you, and will bless you; for to you and to your descendants I will give all these lands, and I will fulfill the oath that I swore to your father Abraham" (Gen. 26:3).

These are the circumstances that lead to the third "wife/sister" ruse. This time, the same Abimelech of Gerar who had taken Sarah into his harem does not receive a warning dream, and no fertility problems beset his kingdom. Instead, as the NRSV translates: "When Isaac had been there a long time, King Abimelech of the Philistines looked out of a window and saw him fondling his wife Rebekah" (Gen. 26:8). Abimelech takes the cue and determines that Isaac and Rebekah are married. Like his father, Isaac has no plan to rescue his wife; unlike Abraham with Sarah, however, Isaac's relationship with Rebekah seems to be one of genuine love. The term for "fondling" in Hebrew is again *metzacheq*, the same term that appears in the expulsion of Ishmael. The text could be understood as suggesting that Isaac was being most himself when he was with his wife, in a way that people in love have with each other.

After retrieving his wife from Abimelech, Isaac settles down and, like his father, does well. "He prospered more and more until he became very wealthy. He had possessions of flocks and herds, and a great household" (Gen. 26:13–14). But this wealth provides no security, for "the Philistines envied him." Abimelech suggests (in the imperative): "Go away from us; you have become too powerful for us." The comment can be understood as Abimelech's attempt to protect Isaac lest envious Philistines kill him. A similar scene emerges in the opening chapter of Exodus, where Isaac's descendants have also, in a foreign land, become "powerful." There the ruler, rather than seeking to preserve the lives of the sojourners, instead states "to his people, 'Look, the Israelite people are more numerous and more powerful than we. Come, let us deal shrewdly with them'" (Exod. 1:9–10). In Egypt, power and success lead not to peaceful separation, but to enslavement.

Isaac and Rebekah settle in Canaan, but there is no peace in their household. The sojourning motif continues with their son Jacob. Escaping his brother Esau, from whom he had taken both birthright and blessing, Jacob spends twenty years with his father-in-law in Paddan-aram where, like his father, he prospers. Jacob occupies himself not only with creative forms of animal husbandry that yield him large flocks; he also with his four wives produces twelve sons and at least two daughters (Gen. 34:9, 16, 21; 37:35; 46:7). Even the jealousy expressed by brothers-in-law (Gen. 31:1) does not motivate his return to Canaan. Instead, the prompt comes two verses later, from YHWH: "Return to the land of your ancestors and to your kindred" (31:3).

Like his father and grandfather, Jacob returns to Canaan, only to leave again. The enmity between Jacob and Esau, perhaps encouraged by the favoritism shown by Rebekah to Jacob, reappears in the story of Jacob's sons. Joseph, Jacob's favorite son of his favorite wife, Rachel, incurs his brothers' jealousy. Joseph does not need to steal birthright or blessing; instead, he already has his father's special love, indicated by his long robe with sleeves (Gen. 37:3; LXX: "a coat of many colors"). He may even have been feminized by his father: the "long robe with sleeves" is the same garment worn by Tamar, David's daughter, who was raped by her brother, the crown prince Amnon; 2 Samuel 13:18 notes that "this is how the virgin daughters of the king were clothed in earlier times." Joseph also has divine backing, as indicated by his dreams of dominance. The brothers, none too happy with Joseph's dreams, favorite treatment, and his spying on them on his father's behalf, sell the youth to the Ishmaelites, who in turn sell him to Potiphar, Pharaoh's officer.

When, years later, a famine again strikes Canaan, Joseph's brothers follow their great-grandfather's pattern—they journey to Egypt for grain. There, instead of finding a matriarch in the harem, they find that Joseph, favored son and former slave, is in charge of the government. Joseph convinces his family to relocate to Egypt, and he settles them in the fertile land of Goshen. They will remain for four hundred years, according to the story. The land promised to Abram remains *promised*, and the story of exile and the search for a home takes another iteration.

From Slavery to Liberation

The story of the exodus both reflects other biblical narratives and addresses other biblical themes, including life under evil or callous rulers, diaspora existence, theodicy, charismatic leadership, and communal sin. The story is both eternal and specific to Israel's story. In Chapter 1, we discuss the historicity of the exodus; here we focus on the narrative.

The book of Exodus begins with the appearance, in the language of the KJV, of "a new king over Egypt, which knew not Joseph" (1:8). As with the various Egyptian rulers of Genesis, from the one who took Sarai into his household (Gen. 12:15–20) to the one who elevated Joseph over the kingdom (Gen. 40–50), this one goes unnamed. That Exodus opens with a reference to "a new king" rather than a "new pharaoh" allows the chapter to speak across the generations. This king can stand for all rulers, whether benevolent, pragmatic, or despotic. The Bible's general stance is distrustful of any human ruler. As each earthly government, whether headed by Israel's own rulers such as Saul, David, and Solomon or the nameless pharaohs along with Nebuchadnezzar of Babylon, Ahasueros of Persia, and Antiochus IV Epiphanes of Greece, fails to establish universal peace, Israel increasingly looks to divine rule.

The term "Pharaoh" appears first in Exodus in 1:11, the note that the Egyptians set taskmasters over the Israelites to "oppress them with forced labor. They built supply cities, Pithom and Ramesses, *for Pharaoh*." The verse connects the title not only with oppression but also with the quest for permanence; the cities are monuments to the king's immortality. The term "Pharaoh" itself speaks to this need as well. Derived from two Egyptian words meaning "great house," it referred initially to the palace complex. With Thutmose III in the early fifteenth century BCE, the name becomes a metonymy (as in the expression, "The White House says . . ."). By the tenth century, it is a title, as in Pharaoh Hophra (589–570; Jer. 44:30) and Pharaoh Neco (610–595; Jer. 46:2).

In Egyptian theology, Pharaoh is divine, the son of the sun god, Ra (or Re). Thus Exodus depicts a theomachy: the lordship of Pharaoh, who enslaves, versus the lordship of YHWH, who liberates. Exodus 7:1 makes the point explicit. YHWH tells Moses, "I have made you like God to Pharaoh, and your brother Aaron shall be your prophet." The two pharaohs of the Exodus—the one who "knew not Joseph" and enslaved the Israelites and the one who contested with Moses—show that although human rule is transient, divine rule is permanent. The pharaoh of Exodus 1 does not remember Joseph, but Israel's God "remembered his covenant with Abraham, Isaac, and Jacob" (2:24; cf. 6:5).

The contrast between God and Egypt's rulers is made even starker by the first pharaoh's ineptitude. Not only does he not know his own history, which is never a good sign, but also his proclamations, as the Bible recounts them, indicate at best a lack of political savvy. He begins with the observation: "The Israelite people are more numerous and powerful than we (*atzum mimmennu*)." Had he been prudent, he would have taken the course of Abimelech of Gerar and advised the Israelites, "Go away from us; you have become too powerful for us" (*atzamta mimmennu*—the same term, in the second person; Gen. 26:16). Instead, he advises: "Let us deal shrewdly with them, or they will increase and, in the event of war, join our enemies and fight against us and escape from the land" (Exod. 1:9–10). Enslaving a population is a poor way of discouraging that population from siding with enemies.

Pharaoh's comment does raise the question of why the Israelites do not resist this slavery, especially if they are "more numerous and powerful" than the Egyptians. The text leaves this speculation to readers. Perhaps the generations in Egypt have lost their memory of the promises to Abraham; perhaps they have lost their faith in YHWH and in themselves. Perhaps Pharaoh's statement was a bluff designed to encourage the Egyptian population to accept the enslavement of their neighbors. Or perhaps the Israelites were not as numerous as Pharaoh suggests. This would not be the first time in history or, sadly, the last that a subject population accepts its servitude. The text, as usual, offers only the dialogue; readers must determine the interpretation.

Suggesting that Pharaoh is more inept tyrant than Machiavellian campaigner is his next commandment. He orders the midwives assisting the Hebrew women in childbirth: "If it is a boy, kill him; but if it is a girl, she shall live" (Exod. 1:16). To keep the population down, the smarter move would have been to kill the girls. To presume that girls, or women, would not engage in political activism is naive. The midwives, who "feared God," disobey the commandment. The narrator provides their names, Shiphrah and Puah, and thus ensures their immortality. Of the characters in the story of Moses's infancy, they are the only two who are named. The NRSV also states that God "gave them families" (1:21), but the Hebrew reads, "made for them *houses*," probably in the sense of "households." Pharaoh, the "Great House," will see his line cut off by the tenth plague, but the houses of the midwives endure.

Finally, Pharaoh commands "all his people": "Every boy that is born you shall throw into the Nile, but you shall let every girl live" (Exod. 1:22). The commandment indicts the Egyptians who obey it even as it highlights the righteous refusal of the midwives. The command also again highlights the ineptitude of this ruler as pictured by the biblical authors. The Hebrew text mandates the death of *every boy;* Pharaoh has, through this command, foreshadowed the death of the Egyptian sons. The Septuagint and, following it, most English versions add "to the Hebrews" after "that is born." These translations give the sense of Pharaoh's intent, but they also lose the subtlety of the Hebrew, as we mentioned in Chapter 2.

Moving from the palace halls to the slave quarters, the next chapter turns to an unnamed couple from the priestly tribe of Levi. (Only later, in Exod. 6:20, are they named Jochebed and Amran.) Just as Pharaoh can stand for governmental authority, these unnamed parents represent the nameless, faithful slaves who defy unjust rule. The parents hide their newborn son for three months, and when the child is too big to hide any longer, the mother constructs an "ark" (*tevah*, the same term used for Noah's boat), places her son in it, and sets it upon the Nile. Like Noah's ark, the boat has no rudder; like Noah, its inhabitant will save his people from a watery death while the wicked drown in the waves. The baby's sister, also unnamed, stays in the reeds to watch.

The story would have been familiar to ancient readers. Zeus, Perseus,

Romulus, and Cyrus of Persia were also endangered infants who grew up to save their people; the Gospel of Matthew, depicting Jesus as a new Moses, describes how he too is saved when children around him are slaughtered. The Sumerian legend of King Sargon of Akkad (or Agade) provides the closest parallel with regard to both details and geographical proximity. In this account, the royal baby is born in secret, placed in a basket of rushes by his mother, and floated down the Euphrates, where a water drawer finds him and raises him. This motif replaces the pattern of infertile mothers established in Genesis with Sarah, Rebekah, and Rachel and repeated with the stories of the wife of Manoah, the mother of Samson (Judg. 13), Hannah, the mother of Samuel (1 Sam. 1–2), and the Shunammite woman (2 Kings 4) as well as Elizabeth, John the Baptist's mother (Luke 1). The "baby in danger" pattern serves not only to predict Moses's future; it also anticipates the exodus story. The baby in the water is saved; the children of the Egyptians will die in the final plague; the Israelites will pass through the waters safely on foot while the Egyptian charioteers drown.

Not a water drawer or a she-wolf but a group of unnamed women collaborate to rescue the child. Pharaoh's daughter sees the child floating in his ark and states, in what need not be a preternatural insight, "This must be one of the Hebrews' children" (Exod. 2:6). The princess pulls the baby from the water, and his sister arranges for his mother to be his nurse. These three women—mother, sister, and daughter—complement the two midwives in disobeying Pharaoh's command. Pharaoh's assumption that the female children will prove no threat appears increasingly misguided.

Likely the original birth story lacked the names of all the participants. In Exodus 15:20, Miriam is identified as Aaron's sister, and Aaron had already emerged as Moses's brother. Only in Numbers 26:59 is Miriam explicitly identified as Moses's sister. This final text reads: "The name of Amram's wife was Jochebed daughter of Levi, who was born to Levi in Egypt; and she bore to Amram: Aaron, Moses, and their sister Miriam." These gaps suggest that accounts of Aaron and Miriam circulated independently of the Moses stories, and an early editor combined them, just as separate sagas of the patriarchs were combined in Genesis and as accounts of the judges will be combined in the book bearing that name.

The narrative passes over Moses's childhood and resumes when he, as an adult, goes out to "his brothers" (Exod. 2:11; the NRSV's "his people" misses the more intimate and gender-determined nuance). Not only does

Moses see their oppression—perhaps indicating that he had been sheltered from, or oblivious to, the suffering around him—he murders a taskmaster he sees beating a Hebrew slave. The next day, as Moses attempts to break up a fight between two Hebrew slaves, the one in the wrong asks, "Who made you a ruler and judge over us? Do you mean to kill me as you killed the Egyptian?" (2:14). The answer to the first question will turn out to be God; the answer to the second goes unstated. Pharaoh also learns about the murder and resolves to kill Moses, so Moses flees. The book of Exodus thus establishes its own pattern of exile and return. It also establishes the pattern of self-criticism for which the Hebrew text is known. The recalcitrant slave anticipates the rebellious nature of the wilderness generation; they are unable to accept Moses's leadership; they are unable to take personal responsibility.

Moses flees to Midian. There, like Abraham's servant and Jacob, he meets a woman at a well. The marriage is forthcoming. He also, in the wilderness of Midian, encounters the burning bush and gains his brother, Aaron, as his more eloquent representative. By chapter 5, he has returned to Egypt with the refrain, "Let my people go" (Exod. 5:1; 7:16; 8:1, 20, 21; 9:1, 13; 10:3, 4). Performing signs for the Israelites, he begins their transformation: "The people believed; and when they heard that YHWH had given heed to the Israelites and that he had seen their misery, they bowed down and worshiped" (4:31).

Pharaoh's reaction is less positive. Having no desire to free his workforce and no reason to attend to Moses's God, he rejects Moses and Aaron's dissembling request: "Let us go a three days' journey into the wilderness to sacrifice to YHWH our God, or he will fall upon us with pestilence or sword" (Exod. 5:3). Instead, he increases the workload. The same pattern reappears in the Deuteronomistic History, but this time with an Israelite king. Solomon's son Rehoboam increases the demands on the population: "My father made your yoke heavy, but I will add to your yoke; my father disciplined you with whips, but I will discipline you with scorpions" (1 Kings 12:14). The result is mutiny. The Israelites in Egypt, expectedly, protest to Moses, and Moses protests to YHWH: "Why have you mistreated this people? Why did you ever send me? Since I first came to Pharaoh to speak in your name, he has mistreated this people, and you have done nothing at all to deliver your people" (Exod. 5:22–23). The protest resembles Abraham's concern for the righteous in Sodom (Gen. 18); it resounds in the wilderness as Moses protests God's plan to annihilate

Israel; it is the hallmark of the book of Job. The people Israel "struggle with God"; the protests are a major response to the problem of theodicy.

Moses and Aaron's next gambit to convince Pharaoh to free the people, the display of magical signs, also fails to impress. The court magicians easily match Aaron's trick of having his staff turn into a snake; that Aaron's staff gobbles theirs is no reason to dismantle the workforce. These magicians will also match the first two plagues by turning more water into blood and multiplying more frogs. Given that these are *plagues,* the magicians are not the sort of people one wants on the payroll. Pharaoh, his heart hardened, refuses to release the slaves. The scene is set for more plagues (Exod. 7–12), for more questions of history, and for more debates over theodicy.

Determining the historicity of the plagues is thwarted not only by lack of external attestation, but also by internal contradiction. Exodus mentions ten plagues; Psalms 78 and 105 mention seven plagues, and not the same ones. Arguments that the plagues are natural phenomena fuel speculation. Bacteria in the Nile could have prompted the belief that the water had turned to blood, even as it destroyed the balance of the ecosystem, which led to frogs and gnats. The problem for the religious conservative is that these explanations do not confirm the biblical account: red tide is not blood.

The divine hand is also present in the description of Pharaoh's response to such devastation. YHWH hardens Pharaoh's heart in Exodus 9:12; 10:20, 27 as well as in 14:8 after the Israelites flee Egypt. Yet other passages state that Pharaoh caused his own spiritual sclerosis. YHWH announces that he will loose Pharaoh's heart only after the tenth plague, that is, following the death of all the firstborn of Egypt (11:5). Source critics are sometimes wont to explain away the discrepancies: one source attributes the hardening to God; the second to Pharaoh's own inclination. This conclusion, however, requires an inept editor who stitched together an incoherent narrative. It is more likely that the changes between God's hardening Pharaoh's heart and Pharaoh's own responsibility create variations for narrative effect. Nevertheless, the question of theodicy will come in the wake of these shifts.

In the vacillating between a focus on Pharaoh's self-interests and the divine hardening that works against those interests, the text accurately presents both psychological dilemma and the problem of theodicy. That Pharaoh would act in a manner contrary to what is best for himself and for his kingdom—freeing slaves is preferable to suffering plagues—fits human nature; pride and stubbornness can be as uncontrolled as angina. Any nation that has kept its troops in battle when the war is lost has experienced this reaction. From a theistic perspective, this stubbornness can easily be seen as having a divine, or satanic, catalyst; no sane person would behave in such a manner.

This theistic reading should then evoke questions of theodicy, a theme already prompted by Exodus 1. God's remembering of the covenant can be celebrated, but unexplained is how God happened to forget this covenant and leave Israel enslaved for four centuries. The means by which their freedom will be obtained exacerbates the question of divine justice. Exodus 10:1–2 (cf. 9:15–16) explains: "I have hardened [Pharaoh's] heart and the heart of his officials, in order that I may show these signs of mine among them, and that you may tell your children and grandchildren how I have made fools of the Egyptians and what signs I have done among them—so that you may know that I am YHWH."

There are many ways to demonstrate power other than creating suffering. Already in antiquity, readers addressed this question of theodicy. In Romans 9:17–19, Paul paraphrases Exodus 9:16: "For the scripture says to Pharaoh, 'I have raised you up for the very purpose of showing my power in you, so that my name may be proclaimed in all the earth.'" He then interprets: "So then he [God] has mercy on whomever he chooses, and he hardens the heart of whomever he chooses." Paul is not saying that humans are sock puppets; he allows for free will along with divine sovereignty. At the same time, he suggests the relationship between fate and free will is a mystery not to be questioned: "Who indeed are you . . . to argue with God?" (9:20). Abraham, Moses, and Job might here beg to differ, although on the plagues Moses offers no argument.

Other readers find in the hardening not moral ambiguity, but satisfying justice. As Pharaoh revoked the freedom of the Israelites by enslaving them, so now God revokes Pharaoh's free will, and the biblical story presents the plagues as justly deserved punishment for the abuses inflicted on Israel, from the Egyptians' participation in the benefits of slavery to their participation by commission or omission in the death of the Israelite sons.

For an oppressed community, the recounting of the ten plagues can, like the similarly violent book of Revelation, provide comfort. These stories ensure that the oppressors will be punished and that those who endured will be rewarded. Moreover, the punishment of evil rests not with the oppressed community. Neither Exodus nor Revelation enjoins violence. Rather, they provide the good news that the desired type of justice will come.

Finally, readers disturbed by such vengeful fantasies—for that is one legitimate reading of the plagues, Revelation, and various apocalyptic scenarios of the destruction of their enemies—can choose to distance themselves. For example, at the Passover *seder*, the meal at which the Jewish community commemorates the liberation from Egypt, participants spill ten drops of wine in recognition of the plagues. One major interpretation of this ritual is that it serves to temper Israel's joy by the recognition of Egyptian suffering.

The *seder*, like the book of Exodus, focuses more on the redemption of Israel than on the plagues. The Hebrew term *pesach*, whence the English "Passover," refers to the events described in Exodus 12. In anticipation of the tenth plague, Moses instructs the Israelites to sacrifice a lamb and place the blood on the doorposts of their homes. The blood functions apotropaically; YHWH announces: "When I see the blood, I will pass over you, and no plague shall destroy you when I strike the land of Egypt" (12:13). For the prophet Isaiah the verb *pesach* carries the connotation of "spare" or "protect." Isaiah 31 makes reference to the exodus event. In 31:3 the prophet alludes to the perishing of the Egyptians; in 31:5, he speaks of how YHWH will "spare (*pasoach*)" Jerusalem.

Exodus 12 goes on to mandate the annual celebration of the Passover, including the offering of the sacrifice and the eating of unleavened bread for seven days. Exodus 12:39 offers an etiology: "They baked unleavened cakes of the dough that they had brought out of Egypt; it was not leavened, because they were driven out of Egypt and could not wait, nor had they prepared any provisions for themselves." The extent to which this festival was celebrated in the First Temple period remains unknown. Second Kings 23:22–23 (see also 2 Chron. 35:1–19), describing Josiah's reforms, attests, "No such Passover had been kept since the days of the judges who judged Israel, or during all the days of the kings of Israel or of the kings of Judah."

Explanations for what next happens, and where, also vary. The famous "parting of the Red Sea" is not in the Hebrew text. "Red Sea" comes from the Septuagint. The Hebrew term *yam suf* is better translated "Sea of Reeds," which makes a lovely allusion to the reeds (*suf*) of the Nile (Exod. 2:5) from which Pharaoh's daughter rescued Moses. In the book of Jonah, another story about a dangerous encounter with the sea, the prophet laments, "The waters closed in over me; the deep surrounded me; weeds (*suf*) were wrapped around my head" (2:5; Tanakh 2:6). His experience is the exodus in reverse: Jonah sought to escape his commission to warn Nineveh to repent and is trapped in the sea; the Israelites sought to escape Egypt to worship God, and they pass, dry-footed, through the water.

The parting of the sea functions symbolically as Israel's rebirth, and not simply by the obvious parturition imagery. The story repeats the third day of creation: "And God said, 'Let the waters under the sky be gathered together into one place, and let the dry land appear'" (Gen. 1:9). In their movement from slavery to freedom, from the chaos of life in Egypt to the order of the Sinaitic covenant, Israel is "created" anew.

The exodus then becomes the paradigm for Israel's orthodoxy and orthopraxy. The Pentateuch thirteen times refers to the God who "brought [Israel] out of the land of Egypt." In Exodus 20:2 the phrase begins the Ten Commandments: by releasing Israel, the deity establishes a relationship with the covenant community. The exodus is also the rationale for the keeping of the Sabbath. As Deuteronomy 5:15 enjoins: "Remember that you were a slave in the land of Egypt, and YHWH your God brought you out from there with a mighty hand and an outstretched arm; therefore YHWH your God commanded you to keep the sabbath day." Exodus 22:21 (see also Deut. 23:7) commands: "You shall not wrong a stranger (*ger*) or oppress him, for you were strangers (*gerim*) in the land of Egypt." Deuteronomy 24:17–18 proclaims: "You shall not deprive a resident alien or an orphan of justice. . . . Remember that you were a slave in the land of Egypt and that YHWH your God redeemed you."

As the Passover is one model for Israel's vision of universal redemption, so Moses is one model for the leader who will bring about this redemption. Moses himself represents the promise, and humanity's participation in it, even when the fulfillment remains in the future. Like Adam and Eve, he is cast out of his natal home. He is then, like Cain, exiled because of his crime of murder. Like Noah, he floats in his ark down the waters to land in a new place of both safety and danger. Like the inhabitants of Babel, he will move the people away from constructing buildings designed to immortalize human endeavor. Moses combines the roles of lawgiver, military leader, judge, prophet, and miracle worker. According to God's words to Moses in Deuteronomy: "I will raise up for them a prophet like you from among their own people; I will put my words in the mouth of the prophet, who shall speak to them everything that I command" (18:18).

For the Christian community, Jesus is the new Moses. The Gospel of Matthew, recounting the story of the origins of the church, alludes to the exodus story in general and Moses in particular. Matthew identifies the father of Joseph as Jacob, and thus reminds readers of that original Jacob and his son Joseph, who go down to Egypt. That Matthew's Joseph dreams dreams reinforces the connection to the Joseph of Genesis. Jesus's baptism recollects the parting of the sea; the temptation in the wilderness for forty days recalls Israel's forty-year sojourn in the wilderness; the Sermon on the Mount renews the laws given from Mt. Sinai. Conversely, the Jewish tradition both exalts Moses and ensures that he will not be seen as divine. He is absent from the Passover narrative, the Haggadah, recited at the *seder;* he is not expected to serve a messianic role.

Prophets like Moses continue to arise, and the exodus is repeated. The story, with its promise of liberation, gave hope to the Africans enslaved in the United States, as the spiritual "Go Down Moses" eloquently sings. The "new Moses," Harriet Tubman, led her people to freedom through dangers as great as those facing the original Moses. Such appropriation may seem to ignore Exodus 2:24–25, which states that the reason YHWH took notice of the Israelites was that he "remembered his covenant with Abraham, Isaac, and Jacob." However, that covenantal promise also became a blessing for non-Israelites. The fleeing slaves are joined by a "mixed multitude" (12:38). YHWH had promised Isaac, "All the nations of the earth shall gain blessing for themselves through your offspring" (Gen. 26:4). The multitudes who also gained their freedom may well see themselves as a partial fulfillment of this promise.

Following the release of the Israelites from slavery, Moses will lead the people for forty years in the wilderness. Yet he never enters the land promised centuries before to the patriarchs. YHWH tells him: "This is the land of which I swore to Abraham, to Isaac, and to Jacob, saying, 'I will give it to your descendants'; I have let you see it with your eyes, but you shall not cross over there." Then, as the next verse states, "Moses, the servant of YHWH, died there in the land of Moab, at YHWH's command" (Deut. 34:4–5). The leader who spoke to God "face to face" (e.g., Exod. 33:11; Deut. 34:10) has died; the site of his grave is unknown; the promises remain unfulfilled.

New Exodus: From Prophecy to Apocalyptic

Leviticus 26:44–45, set in the wilderness period, uses the image of the exodus as the promise of future liberation: "When they are in the land of their enemies, I will not . . . break my covenant with them; for I am YHWH their God; but I will remember in their favor the covenant with their ancestors whom I brought out of the land of Egypt in the sight of the nations, to be their God." Their temple destroyed, Jerusalem devastated, and their freedom taken away, the people needed these stories to give them hope. If freedom from Egyptian slavery could come, then liberation from Babylonian captivity could come.

The promise would be repeated, and so would alienation from the land and the search for home. Through displacement and sojourning, slavery and freedom, exile and return, conquest and resettlement, annexation and independence, the covenant community continually retold its story of liberation.

The Judahite community in Babylon shared with the exodus generation exile from the promised land, but unlike the slaves in Egypt, the elite from Judah lived well in Babylon. When Cyrus of Persia exhorted the Judahites to return home, many stayed, and that generation gave rise to the Jewish community, a millennium later, that composed the Babylonian Talmud. Yet others, encouraged by the words of the prophet known as the Second Isaiah, prepared to return.

"Second Isaiah"—the author of Isaiah 40–55—does not, like his prophetic predecessors, threaten destruction as the consequence for sin. Regarding the sins of Israel as expiated by their sufferings, he begins with gentle exhortations: "Comfort, O comfort my people, says your God. Speak tenderly to Jerusalem, and cry to her that she has served her term, that her penalty is paid" (40:1–2a).

This optimism is prompted not only by his theological views but also by his awareness of the political scene. The Neo-Babylonian empire is being pressured by Persia, and Isaiah, reading the signs of the times, identifies the Persian emperor Cyrus as God's "anointed" or "messiah," in Hebrew *mashiach* (45:1). The time of redemption seemed at hand; the promises would be fulfilled.

Second Isaiah's optimism matches the promises of his preexilic predecessors. The eighth-century prophet known as First Isaiah (2:4) as well as the prophet Micah (4:3) anticipated a time when "they shall beat their swords into plowshares, and their spears into pruning hooks; nation shall not lift up sword against nation, neither shall they learn war any more." Obadiah 21 simply states, "The kingdom shall be YHWH's." Consistent with Deuteronomy's view that righteous behavior would lead to a life of blessedness and the converse, that mistreatment of the poor and disloyalty to the deity would lead to evil and exile, the prophets exhorted the people to proper living and proper worship, lest punishment be meted out to them. Human action determined the future.

Second Isaiah's message of comfort proved, on the surface, correct. Cyrus did encourage the Jews in Babylon to return home. For Isaiah, this is a sign of the emperor's divine commission as "God's anointed"; for Cyrus, it was likely political expedience, as he needed a buffer on the Mediterranean to counter any threats from Greece.

However, Second Isaiah's comfort proved hollow to many who returned to Judea in 538. Awaiting them was not the glorious city of Jerusalem, but a ruined state. Rather than finding a pure tradition preserved, they encountered the descendants of the Jews who remained in the land, including many who had intermarried with women from local populations also displaced by the Babylonians and had, in the returnees' view, watered down Israelite identity. Despite the encouragement of Haggai and Zechariah, the new settlement could not match the glory of the old. By 515, the temple was rebuilt, but the reconstruction could not match the grandeur of the original. Haggai asks bluntly: "Who is left among you that saw this house in its former glory? How does it look to you now? Is it not in your sight as nothing?" (2:3).

But the postexilic prophets had nothing left to threaten. The people had witnessed the destruction of their city and endured exile. The age of the prophet, connected to the monarchy and serving as a balance of power against the king and the priests, had passed. When evil—whether real or perceived—appears to outstrip any sense of justice, when time is emptied of sacrality, and when meaning cannot be found in this world, prophecy has no more force. Second Isaiah's successor, the prophet today called Third Isaiah (Isa. 56–66), anticipates the shift from prophecy to the genre known as apocalyptic in speaking of "new heavens and a new earth" (65:17; 66:22; cf. 2 Pet. 3:13; Rev. 21:1). God would bring about this new creation, for human ability could not. And only in this new creation would the promises of the patriarchs be fulfilled, of a time when the "wolf shall live with the lamb, the leopard shall lie down with the kid, the calf and the lion and the fatling together, and a little child shall lead them" (Isa. 11:6). Zechariah 14:9 echoes, in a verse that is part of the synagogue liturgy, "And YHWH will become king over all the earth; on that day YHWH will be one and his name one."

Apocalyptic elements in texts such as Joel, Isaiah 24–27 and 56–66, Zechariah 9–14, and Daniel 7–12 accomplished through rhetoric what they lacked in realia: assurance that world and time were ordered rather than chaotic, that suffering would soon end, that those who persevered would be rewarded with resurrection and eternal life. Such works, despite their terrible images of destruction, respond to the human desire to understand the future, locate their readers at history's culmination, proclaim that a guiding hand controls history, and assure that justice will be done.

The term "apocalyptic" derives from *apocalypsis,* a Greek word meaning "to uncover" or "to reveal"—as in the New Testament's book of Revelation, also known as the Apocalypse of John. This new genre drew upon Israel's traditional prophetic and wisdom writings as well as the influences of foreign domination. From prophecy it took an interest in the future; from wisdom came its focus not just on Israel, but on the fate of the world, from creation to the eschaton (end times). From the Zoroastrianism that came with Persian rule (539–331) apocalyptic developed its sense of dualism, of good and bad, God and Satan; from the Hellenism that arrived in the wake of the conquests of Alexander the Great in 331, it appropriated stories of the afterlife, with rewards and punishments.

Books are classified as apocalypses based on several features, including those just listed, but none is a sine qua non of the genre. Complicating the determination of genre even more is that in the Bible apocalyptic sections are typically connected to other forms of literature: apocalyptic moments in Isaiah and Zechariah are placed within the context of prophecy; Daniel 7–12, the apocalyptic chapters, are appended to a series of folktales.

One major marker of apocalyptic literature is bizarre symbolism that requires angelic interpretation. The motif of a sign needing interpretation comes from prophecy. For example, Amos 8:1–2 offers the image of a basket of "summer fruit" (Heb. *qayitz*) and explains that the sign means the "end (*qetz*) has come upon my people Israel." The sign is a normal image, and the interpretation is based on an understandable wordplay. In apocalyptic, the signs are supermundane. Daniel 7:2–3 classically displays the genre: "I, Daniel, saw in my vision by night the four winds of heaven stirring up the great sea, and four great beasts came up out of the sea, different from one another." This is not a basket of summer fruit or a walk in the park. An angel, as is typical in apocalyptic, explains these beasts: "As for these four great beasts, four kings shall arise out of the earth" (7:17). For Daniel, the beasts represent Babylon, Media, Persia, and Greece, but any reader can fill in other countries. The symbols remain open for reinterpretation, and thus the book remains always viable.

Daniel 7 and much of the remaining apocalyptic chapters (8–12) present the apocalyptic motif of prophecy after the fact. Ostensibly writing immediately after the fall of Babylon, "Daniel" predicts the fall of Persia to Greece in 331, the division of Alexander the Great's empire, Israel's possession by the Ptolemies of Egypt and its transfer in 198 BCE to Syria's Seleucid rulers, and even the rise of the tyrant Antiochus IV Epiphanes and his profanation of the temple in 167. After this last date the book was composed. Apocalypses date to the time when the historical accuracy breaks down. However, because these events are recounted in symbols, as with the "four beasts," the rest of the text is open to later interpretations.

Using the books of Daniel and Revelation coupled with references from Isaiah, Ezekiel, Zechariah, and other texts, the second-century church father Irenaeus, the medieval mystic Hildegard of Bingen, Martin Luther, Sir Isaac Newton, and numerous others have insisted that the apocalyptic texts were speaking about their own time. Arnold Schwarzenegger, whose filmography does have a sense of the apocalyptic, made *End of Days* (1999), in which he attempted to stop the beginning of Satan's rule. Told by a priest (Udo Kier) that Satan (Gabriel Byrne) will come at midnight to impregnate the future mother of the antichrist, Schwarzenegger's character poses the well-taken question: "Eastern Standard Time?"

The point of apocalyptic texts is not to predict the future; it is to provide comfort in the present. The Bible is not a book of teasers in which God has buried secrets only to be revealed three millennia later. This view turns the deity into a trickster, ignores the context of the Bible's original readers, who would have taken no comfort in knowing that in thousands of years the sufferings they presently were enduring would end, and reflects a hubris that insists that the Bible is addressed *only* to present readers.

It is the assurance of justice that can remain eternal. This moment, whether called the "day of YHWH" (e.g., Isa. 13:6, 9; Jer. 46:10; Ezek. 13:5), the messianic age, the eschatological age (from Gk. *eschaton*, "end"), the "world to come," or the "kingdom of God," will have universal rather than national import, and it will be brought about by divine fiat rather than human effort. Its timing is known only to God; the Bible emphasizes *that* it will come, not *when*.

Amos, speaking in the eighth century, knows that the people anticipate the "day of YHWH" as a time of great joy, and he warns, "It is darkness, not light" (5:18). The book of Zephaniah, ostensibly written at the time of Josiah in the late seventh century but more likely an exilic or postexilic text, continues the proclamation: "The great day of YHWH is near . . . a day of wrath, a day of distress and anguish, a day of ruin and devastation, a day of darkness and gloom, a day of clouds and thick darkness" (1:14–15). This is the origin of the *dies irae* (Lat., "day of wrath") tradition of the Requiem Mass. Echoing the flood narrative, the prophet quotes: "I will utterly sweep away everything from the face of the earth, says YHWH" (1:2). The prophet thus responds to those who think that the deity is removed from history; lack of belief, with its attendant lack of righteousness, marks those who "say in their hearts, 'YHWH will not do good, nor will he do harm'" (1:12).

Also likely postexilic, the book of Joel mentions the cosmic implications of the "day of YHWH" (1:15): "The earth quakes before them, the heavens tremble. The sun and the moon are darkened, and the stars withdraw their shining" (2:10). Joel also anticipates a motif that will become an apocalyptic trait, the relation of the time of the Garden of Eden to the end time (or, in the German technical terminology of biblical studies, from the *Urzeit* [pre-time, primal time] to the *Endzeit* [end-time]).

Postbiblical apocalyptic texts often mark the end point of history, and thus the time of the readers, by an eschatological battle in which the heavenly host along with the faithful remnant (i.e., the group around the author) defeat the forces of evil. The *War Scroll* (1QM) from Qumran depicts the war of the "Sons of Light" against the "Sons of Darkness." Resembling the ten plagues and the destruction of the Egyptian army, scenes of the punishment of the wicked are also a familiar apocalyptic motif. Concerning the wicked, Isaiah 66:24 states: "Their worm shall not die, their fire shall not be quenched, and they shall be an abhorrence to all flesh." Daniel 12:2 speaks of those who will rise from the dead "to shame and everlasting contempt."

The primary biblical emphasis, however, is not on the punishment of the wicked, but on righteous humanity's gift of eternal life. Adam and Eve forfeited the chance of eating from the tree of life; created mortal, they lost the opportunity for immortality. Yet the related concepts of resurrection and life after death appear throughout the biblical texts. Taking a metaphorical approach that connects the fruit of immortality to wisdom, Proverbs 3:18 exclaims, "She [Wisdom] is a tree of life to those who lay hold of her; those who hold her fast are called happy." Psalm 133:3 states that on the mountains of Zion, "YHWH ordained his blessing, life forevermore."

Other traditions depict immortality granted to especially saintly individuals. Second Kings 2:11 notes Elijah's ascension to heaven with "a chariot of fire and horses of fire" and "a whirlwind," hence "Swing Low, Sweet Chariot." He is like Enoch, who "walked with God; then he was no more, because God took him" (Gen. 5:24). In later biblical tradition, Elijah returns to earth in anticipation of the messianic age (Mal. 4:5; Tanakh 3:23); in *1 Enoch*, the antediluvian hero has messianic functions.

Along with Elisha, the prophet who literally picks up his mantle (2 Kings 3:13–14), Elijah also contributes to the theme of ongoing life by resuscitating children (1 Kings 17:22; 2 Kings 4:34–35). Jonah as well contributed to postbiblical views not only of the exodus, but also of resurrection; his survival in the fish became regarded as symbolic of emergence from the tomb. This connection is already made in the New Testament, where Matthew 12:40 states, "For just as Jonah was three days and three nights in the belly of the sea monster, so for three days and three nights the Son of Man will be in the heart of the earth."

The ability of God to resurrect is expressed poetically in 1 Samuel 2:6: "YHWH kills and brings to life; he brings down to Sheol and raises up." According to Psalm 89:48, all people will descend to Sheol, which is synonymous with death; conversely, Isaiah 25:8 insists that God "will swallow up death forever," and Psalm 49:15 proclaims, "God will ransom my soul from the power of Sheol, for he will receive me." In the restored Jerusalem, "one who dies at a hundred years will be considered a youth" (Isa. 65:20). Isaiah 24–27, the latest oracle in the Isaianic collection, extends this prediction: "Your dead shall live, their corpses shall rise. O dwellers in the dust, awake and sing for joy! For your dew is a radiant dew, and the earth will give birth to those long dead" (26:19).

Ezekiel 37 recounts a vision of a valley filled with bones. The prophet watches as sinews and flesh covered the bones, the four winds breathed upon the bodies, and "they lived, and stood on their feet, a vast multitude . . . the whole house of Israel" (37:10–11). The vision then takes on the language of bodily resurrection, "I am going to open your graves, and bring you up from your graves, O my people; and I will bring you back to the land of Israel" (37:12).

This restoration is known as the "ingathering of the exiles." Jeremiah, on the eve of the Babylonian exile, promises: "He who scattered Israel will gather him, and will keep him as a shepherd a flock" (31:10). This ingathering includes the dispersed ten tribes of the kingdom of Israel and the residents of Judah sent to Babylon or escaped to Egypt.

This same chapter in Jeremiah speaks of a "new covenant" that will be made between God and "the house of Israel and the house of Judah." God says: "I will put my law within them, and I will write it on their hearts; and I will be their God, and they shall be my people. No longer shall they teach one another, or say to each other, 'Know YHWH,' for they shall all know me . . . for I will forgive their iniquity, and remember their sin no more" (31:31–34). In a complementary passage, Joel 2:28–29 depicts all Israel as prophets. The mundane world has been left behind; the perfected world, where people intuitively, naturally do the right thing and all have the gift of direct communication with God, will mark the messianic earth.

Finally, Daniel 12:1–3 predicts that at the culmination of history:

> Michael, the great prince, the protector of your people,
> shall arise. There shall be a time of anguish, such as has
> never occurred since nations first came into existence. But
> at that time your people shall be delivered, everyone who is
> found written in the book. Many of those who sleep in the
> dust of the earth shall awake, some to everlasting life, and
> some to shame and everlasting contempt. Those who are
> wise shall shine like the brightness of the sky, and those
> who lead many to righteousness, like the stars forever and
> ever.

For this chapter, the angel Michael serves as the catalyst who ushers in the eschaton.

Other texts associate Israel's redemption—geographical, political, and spiritual—with a human agent. The Hebrew text applies the term "messiah," from a Hebrew word meaning "anointed" (Gk. *christos*, whence "Christ"), to kings such as Saul (1 Sam. 9:16), David (2 Sam. 2:4; cf. Ps. 89:20), Solomon (1 Kings 1:39, 45), and even Cyrus of Persia, who serves as God's agent in ending the Babylonian exile (Isa. 45:1). Also "anointed" are priests such as Aaron and his descendants (e.g., Exod. 40:15). Psalm 105:15 (paralleled by 1 Chron. 16:22) connects the term to the patriarchs. In Habakkuk 3:13, "anointed" describes Israel. Daniel 9:25 uses the term "messiah" in parallel with the term "prince," but it is not clear that this messiah or anointed one refers to a figure who inaugurates the end time or to a figure in Daniel's own history.

The Bible generally envisions this "messianic" figure, whether or not the term is used, as a king in the Davidic line. In 2 Samuel 7:12–13, God promises David: "When your days are fulfilled and you lie down with your ancestors, I will raise up your offspring after you, who shall come forth from your body, and I will establish his kingdom. He shall build a house for my name, and I will establish the throne of his kingdom forever." There is nothing mentioned about a supernatural birth or a sinless king. This same passage continues: "I will be a father to him, and he shall be a son to me," but "when he commits iniquity, I will punish him with a rod such as mortals use" (7:14).

The anticipation of an ideal Davidic king appears in postexilic texts such as Isaiah 9:7 and 11:1–5. The latter begins, "A shoot shall come out from the stump of Jesse, and a branch shall grow out of his roots," and continues to describe the anticipated ruler: "He shall not judge by what his eyes see, or decide by what his ears hear; but with righteousness he shall judge the poor, and decide with equity for the meek of the earth; he shall strike the earth with the rod of his mouth, and with the breath of his lips he shall kill the wicked." Despite the common perception that the "Old Testament" anticipates a militaristic messiah, this ideal king is armed with authority and justice, not cannons or swords. Ezekiel 34:23–24 and 37:24–26 envision the Davidic king not as a warrior, but as a shepherd.

The last Davidic descendant named in the scriptures of Israel is Zerubbabel, who appears in the oracles of Haggai and Zechariah. The New Testament depicts Jesus in the line of King David (via Joseph), but the two genealogies in the Gospels (Matt. 1:1–17; Luke 3:23–38) do not match.

The promised Davidic king is one messianic image, but it is not the only one. Moses's prediction of a "prophet" (Deut. 18:15–18) is adopted by the *Community Rule* of Qumran, which speaks of the prophet along with the "Messiahs of Aaron and Israel" (1QS 9:10–11). The messiah of Aaron is likely a priest, and of Israel a Davidic king.

Isaiah's suffering servant (the Hebrew term also means "slave") hymns (42:1–4, 5–7; 49:1–6; 50:4–9, 10–11; 52:13–53:12) came to be regarded by some Jewish and Christian traditions as messianic prophecies. For the Targums and a few Dead Sea Scrolls, the servant is a messianic figure. For the church, the servant is Jesus of Nazareth, a point 1 Peter 2 establishes by quoting Isaiah 53.

A third possible messianic image is the mysterious "son of man" mentioned in Daniel 7. In this first vision, the seer describes the heavenly throne room (cf. Isa. 6) in which an "Ancient of Days" sat; "his clothing was white as snow, and the hair of his head like pure wool" (7:9). He sees "one like a son of man coming with the clouds of heaven" and to this figure the ancient one gives "dominion and glory and kingship, that all peoples, nations, and languages should serve him. His dominion is an everlasting dominion that shall not pass away, and his kingship is one that shall never be destroyed" (7:13–14). "Son of man" means "human being," as seen throughout Ezekiel's oracles, where the NRSV translates the Hebrew *ben adam* as "mortal," and in the famous Psalm 8:4: "What are human beings that you are mindful of them, mortals (*ben adam*) that you care for them?"

For Daniel, this human being—like Isaiah's suffering slave—symbolizes Israel. When Daniel asks one of the heavenly hosts to explain his vision, he is told, "The kingship and dominion and the greatness of the kingdoms under the whole heaven shall be given to the people of the holy ones of the Most High" (7:27a). In postbiblical tradition, Daniel's son of man evolves into a redeemer figure. The *Similitudes of Enoch* (*1 Enoch* 37–71), probably dating from the mid-first century BCE, describes the "son of man" as a "messiah" (48:10; 52:3); in the Gospels, "Son of Man" is both Jesus's self-designation and an apocalyptic figure who will "come on the clouds of heaven with power and great glory" (Matt. 24:30).

When the messiah or the messianic age arrives, the search for home, and for immortality, will be complete; the promises made to Abraham will be fulfilled; the exiles will return to the land, and nations shall learn war no more. Eden remains an ideal, the exodus proves the divine ability to redeem from oppression, apocalyptic texts promise a new heaven and a new earth. And the Bible speaks its promises to each generation anew.

Part 3

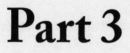

Part 3

Chapter 9

Self and Other

The identification of the covenant community varies across texts and times. Abraham receives the covenant, but his son Ishmael does not inherit it. Isaac receives the covenant, but his son Esau barters away his birthright and is cheated of his blessing. Jacob receives the covenant, and through him his sons, who become the progenitors of the twelve tribes of Israel. And yet those tribes are not comprised only of Israelites: Joseph marries the Egyptian Asenath, the daughter of the priest of Heliopolis; Judah has twin sons with Tamar, a woman likely to have been a Canaanite; and Moses marries first a Midianite woman named Zipporah. According to Exodus 12:37, the Israelites who left Egypt numbered "about six hundred thousand men (*gevarim*) on foot, besides children"; the women, alas, go uncounted and unidentified. But the next verse notes that "a mixed crowd" also went with them. Thus the people who made the exodus were not only descendants of Jacob; the wilderness population was never ethnically homogeneous.

As Israel expands from a predominantly clan-based, tribal, or ethnic group to a nation, it continually redefines itself and its relationship to others. The borders between Israel and the nations can be porous; intermarriage, resident aliens, trade, and alliances all challenge Israel's identity. Challenges are also posed by archaeological investigation, as the material culture of ancient Israelite villages looks very much like that of ancient Canaanite villages, to the point where some scholars claim that many early Israelites were actually Canaanites. From its start, then, Israel—to be a kingdom of priests, a holy nation, and God's possession—had to distinguish itself from the surrounding nations. Who this people Israel was and what it claimed to be "chosen" for remain perpetual questions, and the answers, necessarily, vary across time and text.

Hebrews

The origin of the term "Hebrew" comes from the Hebrew word *ivri*, for which Genesis 10:24 (cf. 11:14–15; 1 Chron. 1:18–19) offers the following unhelpful etiology: "Arpachshad became the father of Shelah; and Shelah became the father of Eber [the root of *ivri*]." In other words, Genesis regards the Hebrews as descended from a Mr. Eber, the same way that Egyptians are descended from a Mr. Egypt, and the Moabites and Ammonites from Mr. Moab and Mr. Ben-Ammi. Unfortunately, Genesis tells us nothing more about this Mr. Eber, and the connection of the name "Hebrew" to the name of this otherwise unknown character is linguistically insecure. Biblical scholars thus look elsewhere for Hebrew origins.

One plausible suggestion, already made by the Septuagint, is that the name derives from the Hebrew root *ebr*, which means to "cross over." The Hebrew of Genesis 14:13 mentions: "Abram *ha-ivri*," which is typically translated "Abram the Hebrew"; the Septuagint offers "Abram, the one who wandered." This rendition fits the Genesis story of Abraham's wanderings from Ur of the Chaldees to Haran to Canaan. Joshua 24:2–3 confirms this peripatetic ancestry: "Long ago your ancestors—Terah and his sons Abraham and Nahor—lived beyond the Euphrates and served other gods. Then I took your father Abraham from beyond the River and led him through all the land of Canaan."

Deuteronomy 26:5 offers an alternative narrative that also speaks to the idea of the patriarch as traveler, as one who crossed over from one location to another: "A wandering Aramean was my father; he went down into Egypt and lived there as an alien, few in number, and there he became a great nation, mighty and populous." There are at least two candidates for this particular Aramean. Abraham was originally from Ur, although he did sojourn briefly in the Aramean area around Damascus. More likely, this Aramean in Deuteronomy 26 is Jacob, because of his connection and that of his wives to Laban, who lived in Aramea, north of Damascus. For this verse, the Septuagint offers not "wandering Aramean," but "my father cast off (*or* abandoned) Syria." Complicating this passage from Deuteronomy, the Hebrew word for "wandering," *oved*, has the same consonants as the term for "destroy" or "perish," *ibed*. Since there are no vowels in the earliest scrolls, early translations ranged from "a Syrian ready to perish" (so the KJV; some modern commentators take the description to refer to Israel, ready to perish from the famine in Canaan) to "an Aramean sought to destroy my father." The Targumic tradition as well as the great medieval Jewish commentator Rashi (1040–1105) preferred this final rendition and identified the Aramean as Laban, the father of Leah and Rachel. That is the version of Deuteronomy 26:5 presented in the Haggadah, the "story" that is read at the *seder* meal with which Jewish families celebrate the Passover.

One popular etymology for "Hebrew" relates the origins of the people to a group called the Apiru (sometimes spelled Hapiru or Chapiru). Some cuneiform texts from the end of the third millennium through the Late Bronze Age (e.g., the time of the judges) describe the Apiru as outlaws or displaced persons. In the Amarna tablets, the fourteenth-century BCE letters written by Egyptian colonizers in the area of Jerusalem to pharaohs Amenhotep and Ahhenaton, the Egyptian overlords complain about Apiru raiding the king's territories and helping the local rulers of the city of Shechem expand their territorial holdings. For the Amarna texts, the Apiru are on the fringe of society from Egypt to Mesopotamia, including Canaan, and some aspects of early Israelite history, such as that depicted in the book of Judges, fit such a scenario. Other texts indicate the Apiru were a more heterogeneous group; some were poor, migrant workers, mercenaries, thieves, or former slaves, but others were princes, priests, and urban administrators. Ugaritic texts include the Apiru on taxation lists.

Although the discovery of the Amarna letters led to the positivistic claim that the Apiru could be matched up with the Israelites under Joshua, the claims were overstated. The linguistic connection between the Apiru and the Hebrews is not secure; the connection is at best a vaguely similar sound to the names.

"Hebrews" for the biblical text indicates a group sharing the same ancestry or, in modern terms, a national or ethnic group, distinguishable from—and distinguished from—members of other nations. For example, Mrs. Potiphar refers to Joseph as "that Hebrew slave" (Gen. 39:17), and Genesis 43:32 states that "Egyptians could not eat with the Hebrews, for that is an abomination to the Egyptians" and so suggests identifiable differences. Exodus 1:19 records the midwives' excuse for disobeying Pharaoh's orders to kill the sons of the Hebrew women as: "The Hebrew women are not like the Egyptian women; for they are vigorous and give birth before the midwife comes to them." By suggesting the Hebrew women are somewhat animalistic, distinct from the "civilized" Egyptian women, the midwives draw on the kind of negative stereotype Pharaoh would accept.

The biblical authors, whose own self-designation is usually "Israelites" and not "Hebrews," nevertheless make clear the connection between the two groups. Exodus 5:3 equates the "God of the Hebrews" with "YHWH, the God of Israel" mentioned in Exodus 5:1. This same pattern of equation appears frequently in 1 Samuel. For example, 1 Samuel 4:5 reads, "When the ark of the covenant of YHWH came into the camp, all Israel gave a mighty shout." The name shifts to "Hebrews" in the next verses: "When the Philistines heard the noise of the shouting, they said, 'What does this great shouting in the camp of the Hebrews mean?'" (4:6–9). In like manner 1 Samuel 13:3–4, continuing the description of the battles with the Philistines, records that after Jonathan had defeated a Philistine garrison, Saul "blew the trumpet throughout all the land, saying, 'Let the Hebrews hear!'" The narrator then states, "When all Israel heard that Saul had defeated the garrison of the Philistines. . . ." Finally, 1 Samuel 14:21 says: "The Hebrews (*ha-ivrim*) who previously had been with the Philistines . . . turned and joined the Israelites who were with Saul and Jonathan." The enigmatic verse could suggest that the Hebrews were of a different nationality or ethnic group than the Israelites, but the text is just as likely to be a pun indicating that some of the Israelites who had "crossed over" (*ivrim*) had returned. When they are with the Philistines, they are seen as "Hebrews"; when they are among their own people, they become, again, Israelites.

Indeed, the Bible normally uses "Hebrew" to distinguish Israelites from non-Israelites. The term "Hebrew" is used by non-Israelites (e.g., by Pharaoh or the Philistines) to refer to Israelites, and Israelites use "Hebrews" mainly when talking (according to the text) to non-Israelites. Another notable point is that all but four of the occurrences of "Hebrew" in the Hebrew Bible apply to persons in the premonarchic period; the four later references are in Jeremiah 34:9 (twice) and 34:14 and Jonah 1:9.

Circumcision

The seventeenth-century rationalist philosopher and Dutch Jew Baruch Spinoza—who had the distinction of both being banned by his own Jewish community and having his writings placed on the Vatican's *Index Librorum Prohibitorum*—states in his *Tractatus Theologico-Politicus:* "Such great importance do I attach to the sign of the covenant [circumcision] that I am persuaded that it is sufficient by itself to maintain the separate existence of the [Jewish] nation forever."

According to Genesis 17, when Abraham was ninety-nine years old, God established with him and his descendants a perpetual covenant. Abraham was to receive "all the land of Canaan, for a perpetual holding" (17:8) and, in turn, he and his male descendants would practice circumcision as a "sign of the covenant" (17:11). Sons born into Abraham's family were circumcised at the age of eight days, a practice that continues in Jewish families to this day (see Lev. 12:3). Today, the ceremony in Judaism is most often performed by a professional circumciser (sometimes a medical doctor; in some communities, this is also the family business, with seven or eight generations of professional circumcisers). The traditional blessing is: "Blessed are you, Lord, who has hallowed us by your commandments and has commanded us to make our sons enter into the covenant of Abraham our father."

Genesis 17 marks the seriousness of the ritual with the announcement that any "uncircumcised male who is not circumcised in the flesh of his foreskin shall be cut off from his people" (17:14). This covenantal sign does not apply exclusively to Abraham's offspring. Slaves born into his household and slaves purchased are also to be circumcised (17:12). Thus the "family of Abraham" extends beyond biological connection. Cutting back on this generous definition is the second factor determining group membership: the mother.

Immediately following the commandment concerning circumcision, God (Elohim) announces that Abraham's wife, Sarah, will have a son. The covenant with Abraham will only extend to this child and his descendants, not to Ishmael, the son of Abraham and Hagar, despite Ishmael's being circumcised at the age of thirteen. Nor will the covenant pass to Abraham's other children by Keturah, the woman he marries after Sarah's death.

The story of Shechem's "defiling" Dinah, Jacob and Leah's daughter (Gen. 34:5), and the resulting attack by Dinah's brothers demonstrates that circumcision alone does not determine in-group membership. In Genesis 34, the sons of Jacob insist that the men of Shechem receive circumcision in order to intermarry with the Israelite women, but instead of setting up weddings, they engineer a slaughter when the Shechemite men, in pain following the surgery, are in no shape to fight back. Indeed, other nations also practiced circumcision. In ancient Egypt, priests were marked by a dorsal incision on the foreskin itself. Jeremiah 9:25–26, for example, speaks of the days when God will respond to "all those who are circumcised only in the foreskin: Egypt, Judah, Edom, the Ammonites, Moab, and all those with shaven temples who live in the desert."

However, Israel defined itself over and against its neighbors who did not observe this rite. The concern for differentiation expressed in Genesis 34 receives emphasis in the early Deuteronomistic History, which consistently refers to the Philistines as "uncircumcised" (see, e.g., Judg 14:3; 15:18; 1 Sam. 14:6; 17:26). In like manner, Ezekiel 32:20–21 distinguishes between the circumcised and the uncircumcised.

The odd passage in Exodus 4:24–26 also speaks to the importance of circumcision:

> On the way, at a place where they spent the night, YHWH
> met him [Moses? Gershom, the firstborn son of Moses and
> Zipporah? Eliezer, their second son?] and tried to kill him.
> But Zipporah took a flint and cut off her son's foreskin,
> and touched his [Moses's? one of the son's?] feet [a euphe-
> mism for genitals? actual feet?] with it, and said, "Truly
> you are a bridegroom of blood to me!" So he [YHWH] let
> him [Moses? one of his sons?] alone. It was then she said,
> "A bridegroom of blood by circumcision."

The passage is notoriously difficult to interpret, and not simply because of the vague pronouns and its abrupt appearance in the narrative. The translators of the Septuagint were so concerned by this passage that they substituted "an angel of the LORD" for the reference to YHWH.

Some commentators, starting already in the rabbinic period, suggest that Moses himself was circumcised but that he neglected to circumcise his son (Targum Jonathan suggests the son was Gershom; Rashi, following Talmudic interpretation [*Nedarim* 31b], proposes Eliezer). So Zipporah performs the covenantal act and touches the foreskin to Moses's feet, here meaning, probably, "penis." In this reading, Moses could not appropriately lead the Israelites out of slavery if he himself did not see the importance of the sign of the covenant within his own family. Some, citing Akkadian antecedents, propose that "bridegroom of blood" conveys the sense of protection; in this configuration, the bloody foreskin has an apotropaic aspect—it will protect Moses from divine wrath. In this reading, Moses can also be regarded as uncircumcised, and the touching of his "feet" (here, the euphemism is in place) functions as a vicarious circumcision.

Still others suppose the phrase "bridegroom of blood" was a common term used in reference to a puberty rite, and the text redefines the expression in relation to Moses. Thereby, it reinforces the idea that circumcision should be performed on an infant and not as part of prenuptial planning.

The concern with circumcision continues in Joshua 5:2–7. As with Exodus 4:24–26, the text does not provide today's readers the details needed to make sense of the passage. On the one hand, Joshua 5:5 states: "Although all the people who came out had been circumcised, yet all the people born on the journey through the wilderness after they had come out of Egypt had not been circumcised." On the other hand, 5:2 depicts YHWH as commanding Joshua, "Make flint knives and circumcise the Israelites a second time." This Joshua does: "[He] circumcised the Israelites at Gibeath-haaraloth" (5:3). The best explanation for this apparent discrepancy is that the wilderness generation had been circumcised, but not fully. Circumcision can take various forms, from the complete removal of the foreskin to a small, dorsal incision in it. The former is the Israelite practice; the latter, an Egyptian one. Thus Joshua's "second" circumcision consists of the full removal of the foreskin. The sense of this more complete operation may be conveyed by Joshua 5:8: "When the circumcising of all the nation was done, they remained in their places in the camp until they were healed. YHWH said to Joshua, 'Today I have rolled away (*galoti*) from you the disgrace of Egypt.' And so that place is called Gilgal to this day."

For the Priestly Code, only circumcised men and their families could eat the Passover offering, but these men were not limited to those whose ancestors came out of Egypt. Thus the operation is not only, or not even, for the P source an ethnic identity marker. Israelite masters may circumcise foreign slaves, and these slaves may then celebrate the Passover (Exod. 12:44). Resident aliens may circumcise themselves, and doing so allows them also to participate in the Passover meal (Exod 12:48, which adds that the "foreigner" [*ger*] is to be "regarded as a native of the land").

The term also gains the metaphoric sense of conformity to divine will as well as aesthetic elegance. Moses, at the burning bush, describes himself as a man of "uncircumcised lips" (Exod 6:30; the NRSV gives the poor alternative of "a poor speaker"). The phrase could indicate someone who was not fully integrated into the covenant community (with an allusion to the bloody bridegroom of Exod. 4) or, less drastically, to someone lacking the maturity required to speak publicly. Leviticus 19:23 mentions "uncircumcised fruit trees" (NRSV: "fruit as forbidden"); here the reference is clearly to the matter of maturity; as the child waits until the eighth day before circumcision, so trees wait three years. Multiple texts describe the "uncircumcised heart" (Lev. 26:41; cf. Jer. 9:25; Ezek. 44:7, 9). Jeremiah speaks of the "uncircumcision of their ear" (6:10; the NRSV offers the more prosaic or phimotic "their ears are closed"); the references are not to purity matters but to the denial of the covenant (so again Gen. 17:14: the uncircumcised is "cut off from his people; he has broken my covenant").

For Isaiah 52:1, neither the unclean nor the uncircumcised shall enter the redeemed Jerusalem. Technically, purity concerns only Israelites (since Gentiles are not under the purity codes, they are neither pure nor impure), and "uncircumcised" is a plausible description of Gentiles. Therefore, this verse may run counter to the universalism with which Isaiah is generally credited (e.g., Isa. 56). Conversely, both terms may function here metaphorically: those who are excluded are those who do not show respect for the sanctity of the city and the covenant established between God and Israel.

Circumcision as the sign of the covenant applied only to men; women in the family of Israel and women such as Ruth who affiliated with them were seen, and saw themselves, as members of the community. Since they did not have the organ on which to carry the mark, they were not seen as needing it. Although later Jewish tradition developed various explanations for why women did not need to be circumcised—from a hyperpositive view that suggests that women, inherently righteous, do not need a sign to remind them of their identity, to the suggestion that the blood drawn in circumcision is comparable to the blood of menstruation and childbirth—the Bible does not address the matter. As with the law code's ignoring of lesbian sex, no penis, no problem.

Although not bearers of this sign, women did function as facilitators. We have already noted the case of Zipporah in Exodus 4, who in the nick of time circumcises her son to save her husband. During the Hellenistic period, when circumcision became a central divider between pro-Greek factions and nationalist factions, mothers disobeyed the law prohibiting circumcision (1 Macc. 1:48, 60–61). Those who had circumcised their sons were arrested; the children were murdered, the corpses hung around the mothers' necks, and the mothers then were thrown to their deaths from the temple parapet (1 Macc. 1:48). Reflecting the importance of circumcision in Second Temple times, the noncanonical book of *Jubilees* (15:6) mentions circumcision as the marker that distinguishes the saved from the damned, and a major debate in the movement formed in the name of Jesus of Nazareth was whether Gentiles in church communities needed to be circumcised. Paul's gospel, which argues against this practice, became the historical winner. Paul's view was, in fact, consistent with the dominant Jewish view at the time—most Jews did not think Gentiles needed to convert to Judaism in order to be in a right relationship with God.

Non-Jewish writers, such as Horace (*Satires*) and Martial (*Epigrams*), as well as Josephus (*Antiquities* 12.5.1), 1 Maccabees 1:15, and maybe even Paul (1 Cor. 7:18) suggest that the mark of circumcision could be removed. Some men used little "hats" to cover their circumcised penises; others practiced an operation called epispasm, which involved pulling what was left of the foreskin forward.

Today, circumcision is still practiced by Jews as well as by Muslims. In Judaism, boys are circumcised on the eighth day after birth (unless health reasons would prevent the operation). The ceremony is called the *brit* (or *bris*) *milah*, "covenant of circumcision" (the term itself does not appear in the Bible). Jewish tradition holds that the prophet Elijah, who claimed that he was the only faithful Israelite left (1 Kings 19:10, 14; Paul quotes Elijah in Rom. 11:3), attends every *bris*, and the ceremony demonstrates to him that he is not alone among the faithful.

The health benefits of circumcision—an issue the Bible does not consider—continue to be debated. Circumcision became moderately popular outside of Jewish contexts in the West when Christian pastors and medical doctors suggested that it would be a deterrent to masturbation (it wasn't). Then, during the trench warfare of World War I, circumcision responded to a concern for personal hygiene. Today many physicians regard circumcision as cosmetic rather than medically necessary. Although some studies suggest a lower rate of HIV/AIDS among circumcised men and a lower rate of cervical cancer among their women sexual partners, other studies dispute the correlation of circumcision, as opposed to other factors, to these findings.

Endogamy

The first example of an "intermarriage" or, more precisely, a pairing of individuals from distinct communities, occurs in Genesis 6:1–2 when the "sons of Elohim" (Heb. *bene ha-elohim*) notice that the "daughters of humankind" (*benot ha-adam*) are "good" (i.e., beautiful) and take them for wives. The verses evoke the well-known mythological pattern of divine beings mating with humans—Isis, Zeus, Aphrodite, and Apollo, for example, all had mortal lovers. Early interpreters of Genesis 6, such as *1 Enoch*, develop the story into that of fallen angels. Genesis 6:4 (see also Num. 13:33) indicates its disapproval with these matches by identifying the children of these human-divine couples as "Nephilim" (literally, "fallen ones"; KJV: "giants"). Their generation is wiped out by the flood.

In contrast to this divine-human relationship, Genesis promotes what is, at least initially, extreme endogamy. Although the close relationship of Adam and Eve will not be repeated, that of Sarah and Abraham shows a similar familial connection. Abraham tells Abimelech of Gerar that Sarah is "indeed my sister, the daughter of my father but not the daughter of my mother" (Gen. 20:12a). Leviticus 18:9 and Deuteronomy 27:22 prohibit sexual relations with one's sister, "the daughter of your father or the daughter of your mother."

Abraham's other marriages are not incestuous, but they are also not endogamous. Hagar, Sarah's Egyptian slave, becomes Abraham's "wife" (Gen. 16:3). Although some translations suggest she is a concubine, the Hebrew is direct. The first part of the verse speaks of "Sarai, wife of (*eshet*) Abram"; the second part states that Sarai gave Hagar to Abram "for a wife" (*l'ishah*—from the same root as *eshet*). Hagar herself knows the value of endogamy; she found an Egyptian wife for her son Ishmael (21:21). Following Sarah's death, Abraham—when he is "old and well advanced in years" (24:1)—takes another wife, Keturah, and with her has six more sons (25:1–4). He also had additional children with unnamed concubines (25:6). Abraham sends these children off with economic resources, and Ishmael will become the father of twelve tribes, but only Isaac inherits the covenant. First Chronicles 1:32 ties up the loose ends by insisting that Keturah was not Abraham's wife, as Genesis 25:1 puts it, but his concubine. Early Jewish tradition cleans up the story even more by suggesting that Keturah is another name for Hagar, and that following Sarah's death the two reconcile, after Isaac matches them up (*Midrash Rabbah* on Gen. 25:1).

Despite his exogamous relationships, Abraham insists that Isaac marry a woman from the home country. Keeping Isaac safely at home, the patriarch sends for his trusted servant and makes him swear that he will find Isaac a wife from Abraham's family rather than from among "the daughters of the Canaanites" (Gen. 24:2–4). The servant swears this oath by placing his hand underneath Abraham's "thigh"; the symbolism suggests that the oath involves not only Abraham, but also his posterity.

Abraham's servant serendipitously finds in Aram-naharaim Rebekah, daughter of Bethuel, the son of Milcah and Nahor, Abraham's brother. Rebekah is Isaac's only spouse—of all the patriarchs, he is the only monogamous one.

The question of appropriate marital partners again arises with Isaac and Rebekah's twins, Esau and Jacob. Readers generally remember Esau as the schlemiel who barters his birthright for a bowl of pottage and who is tricked out of his blessing by his mother and brother. Less familiar is the detail that he married two Hittite women, Judith and Basemath, who created a "bitterness of spirit" for Isaac and Rebekah. This familial difficulty could not have been predicted. Abraham got along well with local Hittites, including Ephron, who sold to him the Cave of Machpelah, which became the family tomb (Gen. 23:1–20; 25:9; 49:30; 50:13). Today that site, in Hebron, is also known as Haram el-Khalil (Arabic, "the sacred area of the friend"). Ezekiel follows Genesis by picking up the negative example of Hittite intermarriage: the prophet condemns Jerusalem: "Your mother was a Hittite and your father an Amorite" (16:3, 45).

According to the Bible, the Hittites were, along with the Canaanites and the Amorites, resident in Canaan at least since the time of Abraham (see Gen. 15:20; Exod. 23:28); Genesis 10:15 lists Canaan as the father of Heth, the Hittites' eponymous ancestor. External sources, which are numerous, attest that the Hittites, at least by the second millennium BCE, had a powerful presence in central Turkey and throughout Syria and Lebanon, but their early presence in Canaan is not confirmed either by external text or artifact. Around 1280 BCE, the Hittite king Hattusilis III signed a peace treaty with Ramesses II of Egypt, which solidified the Hittite presence in Syria and Lebanon, but the Hittites eventually lost their hold over the Philistines around 1200, about the same time in which the book of Judges is set. Nevertheless, the Assyrians continued to refer to the area between the Euphrates and northern Lebanon as the "Land of Hatti," and the Assyrian king Shalmaneser III (858–824) groups Ahab, king of Israel, among the Hittite rulers. It is likely from these first-millennium BCE descriptions that the biblical text derives its references to the Hittites in Canaan. Further, all individual Hittites the Bible mentions, including Uriah, have Semitic rather than Hittite names, such as Ephron, Beeri, and Ahimelech. By explicitly noting that these assimilated figures—by name, by religious practice, by political affiliation—retain their Hittite identity, the Bible thus preserves Israel's distinction.

Back in Genesis, when Rebekah realizes that Esau, none too pleased with his loss of blessing and birthright, plans to kill Jacob, she uses the Hittite daughters-in-law as an excuse to protect her favorite. She next explains to Jacob that his brother is planning murder and advises him to leave town. But to Isaac she says: "I am weary of my life because of the daughters of Heth [i.e., Hittites]. If Jacob marries one of the daughters of Heth such as these, one of the daughters of the land, what good will my life be to me?" (27:46). Isaac, on cue, summons Jacob and commands him not to take a wife from the "daughters of Canaan"; instead he should go immediately to Paddan-aram and find a wife from his mother's family (28:1–3). Jacob, wisely, complies. He will never again see his parents, but he will survive Esau's threat.

Meanwhile, when "Esau saw that the Canaanite women did not please his father Isaac (or the daughters of Canaan were bad in the eyes of Isaac his father), he went to Ishmael and took Mahalath, the daughter of Abraham's son Ishmael," for a wife (Gen. 28:8–9). Esau, despite his mother's deception and his father's failure to reserve the blessing, still seeks to please them. His plan was to marry endogamously, given that Ishmael is also part of the family of Abraham. But it would not be inappropriate to see his attempt as pathetic rather than as persuasive, for the text has already and will continue to exclude Ishmael and his family from Hebrew identification. Ishmael is the son of an Egyptian and the husband of an Egyptian; his daughter therefore is foreign. The Ishmaelites and the descendants of Esau, who will be called Edomites, are in the family, but they are not party to the promise. Genesis does not recount whether Rebekah and Isaac accepted their new daughter-in-law.

Genesis 34, which provides one of the major examples of the Bible's concern for circumcision, similarly provides another discouraging take on endogamy. Shechem, prince of the city by the same name, falls in love with Jacob and Leah's daughter Dinah and seeks to marry her. For Jacob, the offer is appealing; it is better to have intermarriage and the protection that comes with it than enmity with the neighbors. Since Shechem and Dinah had already consummated their relationship, Jacob could also marry off his daughter without worrying about her lack of virginal status. Hamor, Shechem's father, sees the intermarriage as an opportunity for his community to prosper: "Will not we get their livestock, their property, and all their animals?" (34:23a). But Dinah's brothers, who refuse the marriage and who perpetrate the ruse about the necessity of circumcision, have the last word: "Should our sister be treated like a whore?" (34:31). Later tradition ironically has Dinah involved in exogamous relationships. One account records her as the wife of Potiphera the Egyptian priest (41:45) and thus the mother of Joseph's wife Asenath; a second considers Asenath the daughter of Dinah and Shechem; and a third regards her as Job's second wife.

The next exogamous relationship also fares poorly. Jacob's son Judah, from whom the name Judea and therefore "Jew" derives, had separated himself from his brothers and married a Canaanite, Bath-shua or "Shua's daughter" (Gen. 38:2). Her name is not recorded, and the text offers no details on the relationship, other than it produced three sons. God kills the first, Er, for being "evil"; again, no details are provided. Jacob then calls upon the second, Onan, to marry Er's wife Tamar and produce an heir to inherit the dead brother's name and estate. The underlying practice here is levirate marriage (see Deut. 25:5–10; Ruth 4:10). The text is silent concerning Tamar's background.

Knowing that were Tamar to remain childless, his own children would inherit Er's portion, Onan practices birth control by "spilling his seed upon the ground" (Gen. 38:9). This action also displeases God, and another son is dead. Judah's third son, Shelah, is still too young to marry Tamar, so Judah sends the daughter-in-law back to her father's home to wait for Shelah to grow up.

Years pass, and Tamar realizes that Judah is not about to risk losing a third son; it is easier for him to blame the daughter-in-law than to acknowledge his two sons had sinned. Tamar takes off her widow's clothes, wraps herself up in a veil, and heads to "the entrance to Enaim, on the road to Timnah" (Gen. 38:14) to meet the recently widowed Judah, who is off to go sheepshearing. Geographical cues add literary nuance to the account. "Enaim" means "eyes," but Judah is unable to "see" his daughter-in-law. Instead, he takes her for a prostitute. The road to Timnah will resurface in Judges 14, where Samson, another exogamous Israelite, sees his first wife, a Philistine.

Judah, like Samson, is more interested in personal satisfaction than in covenant commitment. Attempting to reach an appropriate fee with the presumed prostitute, Judah agrees to send her a lamb (this is a high-end tryst) and, for his IOU, he gives her his staff, cord, and signet. True to his word, Judah later sends his friend Hirah the Adullamite to collect his items and drop off a sheep, but Hirah is unable to find the "holy lady" (NRSV: "temple prostitute"; the title is an upgrade from "whore") by the roadside. A few months later, Judah learns that Tamar is "pregnant as a result of whoredom" (Gen. 38:24) and commands that she be burned alive. Tamar then produces the staff, cord, and signet, and Judah, showing his honesty and honor, acknowledges that they, and the child she is carrying, are his. He even proclaims her "more righteous" than himself in that he had withheld his youngest son from her.

Tamar gives birth to twins (which run in the family), one of whom, Perez, will be David's ancestor. The book of Ruth mentions Tamar in David's genealogy, and the Gospel of Matthew mentions her as the first woman in Jesus's genealogy. Thus she can be, and has been, regarded as the "righteous" woman through whom Judah, and not Bath-Shua's sons, continues the covenantal line. Tamar's motives are, however, never given. Perhaps she wanted to further the family line; perhaps she wanted to kill Judah for sending her home. Judah thinks she is dangerous; perhaps she thinks the same thing about herself. Perhaps in everyone's best interests she and Judah never again have sexual relations.

The account of Judah and Tamar in Genesis 38 interrupts the story of Joseph and so another story of exogamy. Joseph's brothers, who despise him because of his dreams of preeminence over them, sell him to the Ishmaelites (Gen. 37), who in turn sell him to an Egyptian officer (Gen. 39). Because of his ability to interpret dreams, Joseph is elevated by Pharaoh to be Egypt's second-in-command. He receives not only wealth, but also an Egyptian name, Zaphenath-paneah, and an Egyptian wife, Asenath, the daughter of Potiphera, priest of On (41:45). Later on, only when he admits to his brothers, "I am Joseph, your brother" (45:4), do they recognize him. Membership in the family is determined not by dress or language, but here by self-identification and an acceptance of that identification by the majority.

Joseph's exogamous marriage is a major problem for later commentators. As noted above, one early Jewish tradition identifies Asenath as the child of Dinah, Jacob's daughter. An alternate tradition in the ancient text known as *Joseph and Asenath*—the document's origins, whether Jewish or Christian, have not been settled—makes Asenath a proselyte.

Intermarriage along with the broader question of determining identity recurs in the book of Exodus. Although the biblical record suggests that the enslaved population practiced endogamy—and so remained as an identifiable people for four hundred years in Egypt—Moses leaves the community after fleeing from his murder of the Egyptian taskmaster, arrives in Midian, and marries Zipporah, the daughter of the local priest.

This relationship also yields problematic offspring. Their first son is Gershom, for which Exodus 2:22 gives the etymology "stranger there" (Heb. *ger shom*), hence the expression "stranger in a strange land." But the name may rather reflect the Hebrew word *garash*, meaning "to drive out" or "to expel," a term used in Exodus 2:17. Either derivation suggests alienation. Gershom's son, Jonathan, becomes the idolatrous priest to the equally idolatrous Danite tribe. As Judges 18:30 puts it: "Jonathan the son of Gershom, son of Moses, and his sons were priests to the tribe of the Danites until the time the land went into captivity." Another translation, prompted by a calligraphical anomaly in the Masoretic text, is "Jonathan son of Gershom, son of Manasseh. . . ." Likely, the ancient scribes did not want this blot on Moses's family's reputation and so added the mark that causes this verse to read "Manasseh." Without it, the name of Gershom's father is "Moses," and "Moses" is how the Septuagint understands the verse. Thus, we have another reason for why Joshua, rather than Moses's son, inherits the community leadership. The major problem with the family is not exogamy, however; it is apostasy. The biblical text's dislike of political dynasties other than that of the Davidic house—and even in this case there is some ambivalence—may also underlie these depictions. Nevertheless, the exogamous origins serve to taint the family.

Reinforcing the impression that Israelite fathers and gentile mothers (such as the Midianite Zipporah) produce idolatrous children, elsewhere the Torah portrays Midianite women as a snare to the Hebrews. Numbers 25 recounts the wilderness plague occasioned by the relationships between Hebrew men and Moabite and Midianite women at Baal Peor. Phinehas, who kills the Hebrew man and his Midianite wife likely while they are in the midst of a sexual act (Num. 25:8), even receives an eternal priesthood.

In Numbers 12, an intermarriage serves as the pretext for Miriam and Aaron's complaint about Moses's leadership. The text begins with the somewhat redundant verse, "Miriam and Aaron spoke against Moses because of the Cushite woman whom he had married (for he had indeed married a Cushite woman)." The reference could be to Zipporah, since Habakkuk 3:7 places Cush and Midian in parallel construction. More likely, Cush here refers to Ethiopia or a proximate North African area. Jeremiah 13:23 asks, "Can the Cushite change his skin [NRSV: 'Can Ethiopians change their skin']?" The question presumes that the Cushites have a different skin color than that of Jeremiah's readers. The English translation follows the Septuagint, which consistently renders the Hebrew *cushi* as "Ethiopian." That Miriam's punishment for questioning Moses's authority is that she suffer from a skin disease that turned her "white as snow" (Num. 12:10) makes a fitting contrast to her complaint.

Whether Miriam and Aaron spoke out against her or on her behalf—the Hebrew can be translated either way—remains unclear. If *against* her, perhaps the two were concerned that she would take Moses away from his religious duties, which would have required him to be in a state of ritual purity. Honeymooning and face-to-face conversations with the deity are mutually exclusive. If *for* her, perhaps the two were concerned that the bride was not receiving her conjugal rights, given Moses's required state of ritual purity. In either case, Moses's marriage is a problem, and the generally negative view the Pentateuch takes toward exogamy exacerbates it.

At the end of the Pentateuch, Moses warns the Israelites against intermarriage with the seven nations of the land they are about to enter: Hittites, Girgashites, Amorites, Canaanites, Perizzites, Hivites, and Jebusites. He exhorts: "Do not intermarry with them, giving your daughters to their sons or taking their daughters for your sons" (Deut. 7:3); Exodus 34:16 explains that such intermarriage will lead to the worship of foreign gods.

Yet the exhortations do not fit the narrative. The first incursion into Canaan brings Israel to Jericho, where Joshua sends two spies on a reconnaissance mission. Instead of scouting military posts, the spies seek to ascertain the lay of the land by going immediately to visit Rahab, the prostitute (Josh. 2; 6). When the king of Jericho becomes aware of the spies, he sends messengers to Rahab, but she hides the spies, lies to the messengers, and secures her future by having the spies promise that when Jericho falls they will protect her and her family. Whether Rahab's recitation of Israel's salvation history shows her theological fidelity to the God of Israel or whether she is a realist who acts in order to preserve her family cannot be determined. As is often the case with biblical narrative, motives, especially those of women, remain suppressed. The story ends with the fall of Jericho's walls and the notice that Rahab's family "has lived in Israel ever since" (Josh. 6:25).

The story is an etiology explaining the ongoing presence of Canaanites in Israel, despite Deuteronomy's insistence on their eradication. Whereas the book of Joshua does not indicate intermarriage with Rahab—to the contrary, the editors note that her family remains distinct within Israel—the Gospel of Matthew locates her as the mother of Boaz (Matt. 1:5), the husband of Ruth, and thus in the genealogy of David and Jesus.

Intermarriages continue in the book of Judges; the story of Samson's involvement with a Philistine woman is the most notable. Samson's parents despair over his relationship. Their plea: "Is there not a woman among your kin, or among all our people, that you must go to take a wife from the uncircumcised Philistines?" Samson's response: "Get her for me, because she pleases me (*or* looks good in my eyes)" (Judg. 14:3). The relationship does not last. Samson tricks the bride's relatives, the bride is given to the best man, Samson destroys the Philistines' fields, and the Philistines burn the bride alive. Samson's later relationship with Delilah, likely a Philistine although the Bible does not give her ethnic identity, has similarly unfortunate results.

Under the monarchy, Israelite men continue to marry non-Israelite women. Kings require political alliances, which are most easily accomplished via intermarriage. David marries several foreign princesses; for example, his son Absalom is the "son of Maacah, daughter of King Talmai of Geshur" (2 Sam. 3:2).

As for David's most famous wife, Bathsheba, her first husband was Uriah the Hittite (2 Sam. 11), and thus she had participated in an intermarriage. Alternatively, were Bathsheba originally a Jebusite (the text is not clear on her origins), then her marriage to David is an intermarriage. David and Bathsheba's son Solomon was, like his father, invested in international alliances, and not only that. "King Solomon loved many foreign women along with the daughter of Pharaoh: Moabite, Ammonite, Edomite, Sidonian, and Hittite women, from the nations concerning which YHWH said, . . . 'You shall not marry with them, neither shall they with you; for they will incline your heart to follow their gods. . . . Among his wives were seven hundred princesses and three hundred concubines, . . . and his wives turned away his heart [after other gods]" (1 Kings 11:1–8).

For the Deuteronomistic historian, Solomon's idolatry prompts disaster. Solomon's heir, Rehoboam, the son of "Naamah the Ammonite" (1 Kings 14:21), witnesses the splintering of his kingdom when the northern tribes secede. According to Genesis 19:30–38, the Ammonites are, along with the Moabites, the descendants of the incestuous relationship between Lot and his daughters. Deuteronomy 23:3 insists that, because they failed to display hospitality to the Israelites in the wilderness, neither

Ammonites nor Moabites should enter the covenant community, "even to the tenth generation." Later commentators, noting the problem of Ruth the Moabite and Naamah the Ammonite within the Davidic household, suggest that the law referred only to Ammonite men. Yet the book of Judith records the conversion to Judaism of an Ammonite general. Again, law and narrative conflict, or "what the law says" and "what people do" are not always equivalent.

The southern kingdom, ruled by Davidic descendants, becomes known as Judah, named after the largest of the tribal groups. The northern kingdom, ruled by a succession of non-Davidic dynasties, is known as Israel, but it also takes the name Ephraim, from the younger son of Joseph and Asenath. Described primarily by Judahite writers, the story of Israel, epitomized by the Israelite king Ahab and his Tyrian wife, Jezebel (1 Kings 16–22), serves as a lesson in what happens when Israelite identity is compromised: foreign wives have foreign gods, foreign gods lead to apostasy, and apostasy leads to divine punishment.

Stories of dangerous foreign women—Delilah, Solomon's wives, Jezebel, and others—to some degree reflect the perspective of the biblical editors, writing in the wake of the Babylonian exile. Under the leadership of the priest Ezra, those who returned from Babylon found that the population left behind, "the people of Israel and the priests and the Levites," had not "separated themselves from the peoples of the lands with their abominations, from the Canaanites, the Hittites, the Perizzites, the Jebusites, the Ammonites, the Moabites, the Egyptians, and the Amorites. For they have taken some of their daughters as wives for themselves and for their sons" (Ezra 9:1–2). Their concern is both that intermarriage leads to unfaithful worship and, now, something new, that "the holy seed" has been compromised (9:2). Nehemiah states: "Half of their children spoke the language of Ashdod, and they could not speak the language of Judah, but spoke the language of various peoples" (13:24). His concern is that the gentile mothers will pass on gentile culture and values to their children. The solution is to divorce the foreign wives.

Time and again, the biblical text warns against the loss of identity because of intermarriage. However, it also depicts occasions when intermarriage works for the betterment of the community. Israel depicts itself not only as distinct from other nations, but also as welcoming through affiliation or, in the later part of its history, conversion, the best from among them.

Likely written as a counter to Ezra and Nehemiah, the book of Ruth establishes for King David a Moabite great-grandmother. Although Christian canons place her story chronologically between the book of Judges and 1 Samuel, Jewish canons locate the volume among the Ketuvim, Writings, which suggests the book's comparably later date.

The story opens with the emigration of Elimelech, his wife Naomi, and their two sons from Bethlehem in Judea to Moab. That the sons are named Mahlon and Chilion—"sickness" and "consumption"—does not auger well. In Moab they take Moabite brides, and then they and their father die. Naomi convinces one daughter-in-law, Orpah, to return to her Moabite family, but the other daughter-in-law, Ruth, insists, "Where you go, I will go; where you lodge, I will lodge; your people shall be my people, and your God my God" (1:16–17). Ruth "clings" (Heb. *davaq*) to Naomi—this is the same term used for the relation of the couple in Eden (Gen. 2:24): Naomi and Ruth, like the first man and woman, form a new family. And, resembling Abraham, Ruth accompanies an old, childless woman to a land she does not know.

In Bethlehem, Ruth marries Boaz, Elimelech's relative and the richest man in town, and so becomes a member of the community. The townspeople connect her to "Rachel and Leah, the two who built the house of Israel" (Ruth 4:11; cf. Gen. 35:23–26), as well as Tamar, Judah's daughter-in-law (Ruth 4:12; cf. Gen. 38). This latter connection may even be a sly allusion to Ruth's Moabite background—for Tamar tricked the older Judah into sex just as Ruth set up the older Boaz. Ruth and Boaz have a son, Obed, who will become the grandfather of King David, and thus the Moabite woman becomes the ancestor of Israel's king and, according to both Jewish and Christian tradition, the ancestor of the messiah (see Matt. 1:5).

The Bible commends such intermarriage in which the gentile partner, typically a woman, gives up home, family, and religious practice. For ancient Israel, the stories encourage the welcome of wives who show such loyalty, and they counter the negative portrayals of foreign women found elsewhere. However, stories of happy affiliations, such as Rahab's, and happy intermarriages, such as Ruth's, do create problems for later readers. These stories to this day are used by a few Christian missionaries to encourage women, especially in Asia and Africa, to be like Rahab and Ruth, to leave their religious tradition, in order to be "saved."

The Bible's final major story of intermarriage is not hailed as an ideal by anyone. Esther's marriage to the King of Persia may be part of a fictional story, but it is no fairy-tale romance. Instead, the king spends most of the book drunk, engages in massive fiscal waste, and has no clue about policies being conducted in his name. Esther's marriage is of no personal value to her; its value is that it allows her to save her people from genocide. For a full discussion of this book, see Chapter 12 on diaspora life.

The Tribes of Israel

Although the Bible conventionally speaks of the "twelve tribes of Israel" named after the twelve sons of Jacob, the number is artificial. All counted, the Bible lists more than twenty tribes, including Gileadites, Calebites, Kenites, and Gibeonites. By presenting the tribes as related, the narrative provides a common past that serves to unify the people of the present.

Genesis offers several etiologies for each tribal group. For example, by depicting Reuben's indiscretion with Bilhah, Rachel's slave and Jacob's wife, Genesis provides the rationale for the disappearance of the tribe of Reuben and its absorption into the tribes of Judah and Gad (see Gen. 35:22). In his testamentary address, Jacob notes that Issachar "became a slave at forced labor" (Gen. 49:15). The Amarna Letters mention that the king of Megiddo forced people from the city of Shunem near Mt. Tabor—the area assigned to Issachar—to serve as porters. In this same speech, Jacob also alludes to the story of Dinah to condemn Simeon and Levi, the two sons who initially attacked the men of Shechem, with loss of land. Simeon was absorbed into the larger, stronger tribe of Judah; instead of receiving land, the tribe of Levi became the priests, supported by tithes from the other tribes. Both tribes go unmentioned in the Song of Deborah (Judg. 5); by the time of the song's composition—yet another interpretive crux, for the archaic Hebrew may well be deliberate archaizing—perhaps they no longer existed as separate entities.

Jacob's speech next suggests that the tribe of Dan lacked an original connection to Israel. "Dan shall judge his people as one of the tribes of Israel" (Gen. 49:16) is an odd statement if Dan is already among those tribes. The books of Joshua and Judges also describe Dan's distinct identity. Joshua 19:40–48 connects the Danites with the Philistine settlements on the Mediterranean coast; Judges 5:17, the Song of Deborah, asks why Dan "abided with (or lingered by) the ships"; and Judges 18:1 remarks that "the tribe of the Danites was seeking for itself a territory to live in," since "until then no territory among the tribes of Israel had been allotted to them." Were these details not sufficient to indicate that the Danites were latecomers to the Israelite confederacy, external sources refer to a group of Sea Peoples called variously the Denyen, the Danaoi, and the Danuna.

A number of other tribes have names that suggest something other than what the biblical etiologies announce. Asher receives his name, according to Genesis 30:13, when Leah, overjoyed that she has given birth to another son, announces, "Happy am I (*ashri*)!" that is, to have given birth to another son. However, the name may come from Assur, the Assyrian god, or Asherah, the Canaanite goddess. The tribe's origins thus may rest not in Abraham's family, but in Canaanite culture. According to Genesis 30:11, when Leah's slave Zilpah gives birth to a son, "Leah said, 'Good fortune!' (*gad*) so she named him Gad." Yet Gad is also the name of a Canaanite god. Similarly, Genesis 30:20 records: "Leah said, 'God has endowed me with a good dowry; now my husband will honor me, because I have borne him six sons'; so she named him Zebulun." The Hebrew *zebul* can mean either "gift" or "honor"; both would fit the context. However, Zebulun, which can also mean "of the prince," is an epithet of Baal, the Canaanite god.

Earlier scholarship suggested that the number twelve indicated that ancient Israel was organized into a twelve-tribe league, or an "amphictyony." This confederation, usually based around a central shrine, existed among the Etruscans, early settlers of Italy. More likely, the tribes were originally autonomous, as the book of Judges suggests. They banded together for mutual aid, and common worship came to support those bands. The stories of Jacob's twelve sons suggest that the six "Leah" tribes—Reuben, Simeon, Levi, Judah, Issachar, Zebulon—may have had stronger connections with each other than they did with Dan, Naphtali, Gad, and Asher, the tribes descended from Zilpah and Bilhah. The Joseph tribes, Ephraim and Manasseh, along with Benjamin may have had their own initial identity, in rivalry with the Leah tribes.

The formal uniting of the tribes happens, according to the biblical story, under Joshua. The covenant-making ceremony of Joshua 24:2–13 includes the recitation of the people's common history—or what henceforth will be their common history: the call of Abraham; the births of Isaac and Jacob; the descent to Egypt and the exodus under Moses and Aaron; the years in the wilderness; and the possession of Canaan. However, missing is any mention of Sinai. Perhaps the various tribes that comprised Israel had different experiences and thus different memories: some were connected to the patriarchs; others experienced slavery in Egypt; others the Sinai theophany; still others had Canaanite origins. Behind the concise summary of Joshua 24:1–28 thus lies a long and complex historical process.

By the end of the eleventh century BCE, the tribes found common cause in resisting the pressure from the Philistines, and so the shift from loose confederacy to monarchy, from a tribal to national identity began. Tribal identity did not disappear—such listings are recorded in the New Testament, and Jews today retain the distinctive descent from the tribe of Levi. But over time the people gained new identities as well, not only as Israelites, but as Judeans and Samaritans, and, in the Second Temple period, as Jews.

The Samaritans

In 722 BCE, the Assyrians conquered the northern kingdom, Israel. They moved out substantial portions of the local population, and they moved in people from other conquered territories. The new population group created takes its name from Samaria, the capital of Israel that Omri built in the early ninth century. The location is the same as ancient Shechem, the site of Dinah's rape (Gen. 34), Abimelech's grab for power (Judg. 9), and Jeroboam's capital (1 Kings 12). First Kings 16:24 states that "Samaria"— *shomron* in Hebrew—derived from a man named Shemer, who owned the hill Omri purchased. However, the Samaritans themselves trace the name to the Hebrew term *shomrim*, which means "guardians" or "keepers" (of the law).

Because the history of Israel was compiled primarily by editors from Judah, descriptions of Samaria tend to be less than positive. Elijah condemned the northern king Ahab and his Phoenician wife, Jezebel, another intermarriage that was bad for Israel. Hosea, the only prophet from the north, condemns "the calf of Samaria" (8:4–6), a reference to the shrine at Bethel. Amos, from Judah, went north to condemn the "king's sanctuary" in Bethel (7:13) and more broadly Samaria for exploiting the poor (3:9–12; 4:1–3) and luxuriating in its wealth (6:1–7). Amos's condemnation of "those who lie upon beds of ivory" (6:4) is supported by archaeological discovery of ivory pieces, mostly of furniture or wall-panel inlays, from Samaria.

Samaria remained the capital of the northern kingdom until the Neo-Assyrians conquered it in 722. Second Kings 17:1–6 describes the siege as led by Shalmaneser V; Assyrian records credit the victory to his successor, Sargon II. Assyrian records also claim a deportation of approximately twenty-seven thousand people, and 2 Kings 17:6 adds that the exiles were moved to "Halah, on the Habor, the river of Gozan, and in the cities of the Medes," a verse that, as we will see in the chapter on diaspora, gives rise to the legend of the ten lost tribes.

Second Kings 17:24 states that the Assyrians relocated to the cities of Samaria people from Babylon, Cuthah, Avva, Hamath, and Sepharvaim, people who did not worship YHWH. When a pride of lions attacks these idolaters, the Assyrian king orders one of the exiled priests to return to Samaria to teach the population "the law of the god of the land" (17:27). His efforts proved unsuccessful. "To this day," says the Deuteronomistic historian, "they continue to practice their former customs" (17:34).

Samaritans tell a different story. Their sources report that they are the descendants of the two Joseph tribes, Ephraim and Manasseh, and that until the 1600s their priests were descended from Aaron. They had been united with the other tribes of Israel until Eli the priest—known in 1 Samuel as the man to whom Hannah entrusted care of her son Samuel—moved his shrine from Shechem to Shiloh.

The Babylonians, after conquering Jerusalem in 586 BCE, took control over Samaria; the Persians, who conquered Babylon in 539, separated the two districts. Regardless of imperial rule, relations between Judeans and Samaritans did not recover. According to the book of Nehemiah (2:9–20; 4:1–9; 6:1–14), Sanballat, the governor of Samaria, attempted to prevent the Judeans returning from exile from rebuilding Jerusalem's walls. Ezra 4:1–5 speaks of "the adversaries of Judah and Benjamin," that is, the two tribes comprising the southern kingdom. The text does not identify the adversaries with the Samaritans, but with the "people of the land"; that group would have included the Samaritans, but others as well. The text continues: when the Samaritans heard that the returned exiles were building a "temple to YHWH, the God of Israel," they petitioned the Persian-appointed ruler and Davidic descendant Zerubbabel: "Let us build with you, for we worship your God as you do, and we have been sacrificing to him ever since the days of King Esar-haddon of Assyria who brought us here." Zerubbabel and his allies refuse the offer, and in response the "people of the land" (again, including the Samaritans) discouraged the "people of Judah" (here, the returning exiles), made them "afraid to build," and even bribed officials to prevent the rebuilding.

The Samaritans identify the place "that YHWH your God will choose" for the temple (Deut. 12:5) as Mt. Gerizim; by the fourth century BCE, if not earlier, the Samaritans had their own temple there. Josephus (*Antiquities* 11.342–346) states that around 330 BCE Alexander the Great rebuilt the Samaritan capital as a Greek polis. The Maccabean ruler John Hyrcanus destroyed the city in 108 BCE, and Herod the Great rebuilt it around 30 BCE.

But enmity is not the Bible's only story of the relationship between Judea and Samaria. According to 2 Chronicles 28, the "people of Israel" (i.e., the Samaritans) took two hundred thousand Judeans captive, but a "prophet of YHWH" named Oded condemned the Samaritans for having attacked "relatives." Second Chronicles 28:15 states that a number of the Samaritans "got up and took the captives and . . . they clothed all that were naked among them; they clothed them, gave them sandals, provided them with food and drink, and anointed them; and carrying all the feeble among them on donkeys, they brought them to their kindred at Jericho." This passage underlies Jesus's parable of the good Samaritan.

Judeans and Jews

The southern kingdom, Judah, after eighteen months of siege by the Babylonians, was conquered in 586 BCE. The Babylonians burned down the Jerusalem temple and took the court as well as many of the elite citizens into exile. At this point, the Judahites began to change into Judeans and, eventually, "Jews." In exile, the Judahite population learned how to maintain its identity apart from its land, its temple, its independent government. Because it put into place identity markers that could function anywhere in the world, it helped turn the land-based ethnic group into a universal religious one.

The term "Jew" implies not only an ethnic or biological descent, but also, and often primarily, a religious and cultural worldview. The Greek term *ioudaismos*, living in the Jewish or Judean manner, first appears in 2 Maccabees 2:21, in a reference to those who "fought bravely for Judaism." The cognate Greek term *ioudaioi*, related to the Hebrew *yehudim*, can be translated "Judeans" or "Jews." "Judean" has a geographical focus: it refers to a person from the geographical area where the returnees from

Babylon settled. The Persian term for this community was Yehud, from the Aramaic, and it comes into Greek as Judea. "Jew" places emphasis less on the geographical specificity and more on the religious belief and practice. Thus "Jews" denotes both an ethnic group and a religion; Jews are a people, as are, for example, Egyptians or Ethiopians, but Judaism is also a religion to which one, from the Second Temple period onward, can convert.

Keeping the community identity coherent was a common story and a set of common practices. In the postexilic period, the people's stories and statutes were compiled into a single book—the Torah. Their histories were inscribed into the books of Joshua, Judges, 1–2 Samuel, and 1–2 Kings. The prophetic texts were collected and organized. Thus the people preserved a version of history that linked them to each other, tribe to tribe, back to common ancestors and common experiences of the exodus, Sinai, and the Davidic monarchy.

Along with a common story, they also had common practices. They sacralized time with the institution of the Sabbath and with the relationship of the seasonal harvests to events in their history. Thus they could celebrate their identity regardless of where they were living. In addition, new festivals were added such as Purim (Esther 9:20–22) and the Festival of Dedication (Hanukkah; cf. 1 and 2 Maccabees; John 10:22–23), so new sacred days continued the practice of hallowing time.

The mark of circumcision kept their males distinct from many others, as did their distinct diet. Only in the Second Temple period does the eschewal of pork become a primary marker of Jewish identity, as revealed by archaeological evidence. Jewish sites in Hellenistic times lack pig bones; gentile sites are replete with them. In the postexilic period, practices connected with ritual purity—regarding menstruation, childbirth, ejaculation, and corpse contamination; the use of stone vessels that do not convey impurity; the use of *miqva'ot,* or ritual baths; and so on—become increasingly popular. Such practices allowed the people to resist assimilation, mark their identity on a daily basis, and celebrate their relationship to each other and their God.

Some of the men wore ritual fringes with blue cords (*tzitzit;* see Num. 15:37–41) and phylacteries (*tefillin*), although ancient non-Jewish sources do not to mention these. Likely in the diaspora, Jews were indistinguishable by language and appearance from their non-Jewish neighbors. Living in Jewish neighborhoods, whether in Babylon or Rome, paying the half-

shekel temple tax for the upkeep of the Jerusalem temple, having an affiliation with the local synagogue, keeping the Sabbath, refraining from consuming food or wine offered to idols—all also served to preserve Jewish
identity. But no single marker identified the Jew as a Jew, then or now.

To support Jewish identity, a new institution was developed in the
Second Temple period: the synagogue. The term derives from the Greek
expression for "to gather together." Synagogues—which need not have
been distinct buildings but could have been public spaces such as rented
rooms—served not only as places of prayer but also as community centers
and houses of study. People would gather at the synagogue on the Sabbath
to pray and to hear the scriptures of Israel read (most people were illiterate)
and interpreted. As time passed, and especially after the destruction of the
Second Temple in 70 CE, the synagogue not only supplemented but also
replaced the temple. Although the priesthood, carried on in the paternal
line, continued among the people, sages or rabbis replaced the priests as
the religious leaders. It is from this post-70 Judaism, with its new religious
texts such as the Talmud and the Midrashim, that most forms of today's
Judaism descend. One can, with caution, reconstruct ancient Israelite religion and early Second Temple Jewish tradition from the scriptures of
Israel, but one cannot move from Leviticus or Ezekiel to contemporary
Jewish belief or practice. The texts are continuously interpreted in the light
of history and in the interests of each Jewish community.

In the Second Temple period, with settled Jewish presence in the diaspora as well as the continued Gentile presence in the land of Israel, Gentiles became increasingly attracted to the covenant community, its laws
and practices, values and stories. The First Temple period accommodated
resident aliens; in the Second Temple period conversion became possible.

Although Ruth is frequently seen as a convert, she undergoes no ritual
to mark her transition from Moabite to Israelite, and she is never identified
as a member of the people Israel. Her profession of faith and loyalty was
sufficient to make her welcomed by the people of Bethlehem; her marriage
to Boaz solidified this welcome. For Ruth, the affiliation was relatively
easy; she was not required to submit to circumcision, and the text mentions nothing about specific practices, such as ritual immersion, dietary
regulations, or Sabbath observance.

The first mention of what might signal "conversion" appears in the
book of Esther. As Esther "passes" as a Persian by hiding her identity,
so the Persian population, fearful of the Jews' right to defend themselves

from the genocidal edict passed against them, seek to "pass." By the king's command (and at Esther's instruction), the diaspora community slaughters over seventy-five thousand of "those who hated them." According to 8:17, "many of the peoples of the land made themselves Jews because fear of the Jews had fallen upon them." The Septuagint develops the point by reading: "Many of the nations circumcised themselves and lived like Jews." The community definition was extending from that of an ethnic group to what we would, today, call a religion, and thereby the borders of the community became more porous.

From Affiliation to Conversion

The book of Judith, written during the late second or early first century BCE following the Maccabean revolt, depicts the conversion of the Ammonite general, Achior. The fluid boundary Achior crosses appears in a volume that itself attempts to offer a self-definition for the covenant community. Within the Hellenistic world created in the wake of Alexander the Great, Jews faced two major challenges to their self-identification. First, they needed to define themselves in a world marked by Greek language and culture. Second, they had to determine how to understand foreigners who wanted to join their group.

Their response to Hellenistic society appears in the volumes that fall into the category of the deuterocanonical literature (Old Testament Apocrypha). This collection of texts written originally in or quickly translated into Greek witnessed increasing attention to the novella form, to women as main characters (Judith, Sarah and Anna in Tobit, the martyred mother of 2 and 4 Maccabees, Susanna), expressions of personal piety, and the development of characterization through descriptions of emotion. Like Greek novellae such as Chariton's *Chaereas and Callirhoe* and Achilles Tatius's *Adventures of Leucippe and Clitophon*, these Jewish stories of heroic characters, intrigue, and adventure captured the popular imagination. Through adopting and adapting Greek story forms, the Jews maintained and celebrated their identity.

The book of Judith, which is clearly fictional (the opening would in today's terms describe "President Obama, who rules over Iran from his capital in Pago Pago"), depicts a gentile general, Holofernes, who is smitten with the beautiful widow Judith; her name means "Jewish woman." Judith, to save her people from the invading army, seduces the general by speaking of the desires of "her Lord." Holofernes, mistaking the double entendre, is so encouraged that he loses his head to Judith—she chops it off with his own sword.

This volume shows how the covenant community also adapted its own history. Judith, who has the longest genealogy in the "Old Testament" canon, is a descendant of Simeon, Dinah's brother. Although Jacob's testament condemns Simeon for his attack on Shechem, Judith hails her ancestor and prays that she can rescue the "virgin" as Simeon rescued Dinah (Gen. 34); the name of her city, Bethulia, evokes the Hebrew term *betulah*, "virgin."

The stories of Judith and her sisters—Esther according to the septuagintal Additions, Susanna, Sarah of the book of Tobit—stories of beautiful, desirable, loyal, and pious Jewish woman, were a literary means hellenized Jews used to express their cultural values. As Holofernes's soldiers say of Judith: "Who can despise these people, who have women like this among them?" (10:19).

Resident Aliens and Foreigners

The frequent biblical injunctions regarding aliens or strangers (e.g., Lev. 17:12; 18:26; Num. 15:14–15) suggest that throughout their history the Israelites were neither a homogeneous nor a xenophobic society. As noted in Chapter 8 on the exodus, Israel's experience as resident aliens in Egypt provides the rationale for its treatment of sojourners in its midst. Exodus 22:21, 23:9, and Leviticus 19:33–34 mandate that Israelites must not oppress aliens—rather, aliens shall be treated as citizens—because the Israelites were aliens in Egypt. Numbers 15:15 and Deuteronomy 10:19 repeat the point. According to Exodus 12:49 and Leviticus 24:22, Israel's legal system applies to the native and the sojourner equally. Exodus 20:10 and 23:12 extend the Sabbath rest to slaves, to livestock, and to resident aliens, and Leviticus 16:29 extends the Yom Kippur moratorium on work to aliens as well.

Even the sacerdotal system is open to non-Israelites. As we have seen, Exodus 12:48 (cf. Num. 9:14) opens the celebration of the Passover to aliens, provided males are circumcised (the presumption is that women in the family would gain access with males). Confirming this openness is Numbers 15:14, which permits aliens to offer sacrifices. In turn, no resident alien is permitted to consume blood (Lev. 17:12).

Frequently the law code combines proper treatment of aliens with that of the poor and widows. Leviticus 19:10 requires that vineyards be open for gleaning by the "poor and the alien"; Deuteronomy 24:19 extends the benefit to the alien, orphan, and widow. This strong mandate continues into the Prophets and Writings. Jeremiah condemns the oppression of the alien, orphan, and widow (7:6; 22:3); Zechariah extends the list by including the poor (7:10); and Psalm 94:6 equates the widow, the stranger, and the orphan as in need of care. Judith 4:10 describes the resident alien, hired laborer, and slave as joining the Israelites in Bethulia in their fasting and wearing sackcloth. Certainly not all widows were poor, and neither were all foreigners or orphans. But they were the most vulnerable members of the community. Rather than leave their care to the moral compass of those who were better off or to the compassionate individual, the law insists that all members of society bear responsibility for the care of its neediest members.

The law codes do, however, distinguish between the "foreigner" (*nokri*), that is, someone who is not committed to living in Israel, and the "resident alien" (*ger*). Animals belonging to foreigners are unfit for sacrifice (Lev. 22:25), foreigners could be charged interest on loans (Deut. 23:19–20), and their debts were not forgiven in the sabbatical year (15:2–3). They were not permitted to eat the Passover sacrifice (Exod. 12:43).

Solomon's prayer in 1 Kings 8 anticipates that foreigners will worship in the temple he will construct. It speaks of foreigners who come from distant lands because of the name of YHWH and knowledge of his deeds, foreigners who will pray "toward this house" (8:41–43). Solomon exhorts God to hear and heed these prayers, so that all the nations will know of the divine power. Then again, his downfall is because of "foreign" women, as 1 Kings 11:1–8 recounts. The description of Solomon's apostasy, prompted by his foreign wives with their foreign rites, anticipates the commands in Ezra and Nehemiah mandating that Israelite men divorce their foreign wives. Conversely, the book of Ruth's titular heroine, the ideal wife and daughter-in-law, identifies herself as a "foreigner" (2:10).

When the prophets occasionally offer a different view of foreigners, their inclusive rhetoric suggests an eschatological vision rather than a present reality. Isaiah 56:3–5 speaks of foreigners who are joined to YHWH, "to minister to him, to love the name of YHWH, and to be his servants." In contrast, Ezekiel condemns "admitting foreigners, uncircumcised in heart and flesh" into his version of the temple (44:7, cf. 44:9). Ezekiel's more xenophobic view comports with that of Nehemiah, who records that "those of Israelite descent separated themselves from all foreigners, and stood and confessed their sins and the iniquities of their ancestors" (9:2).

The prophetic oracles frequently speak about the nations surrounding Israel as the means of condemning Israel for its own injustices. Amos
begins the pattern in the first chapter: "For three transgressions of Damascus, and for four," YHWH will punish the transgressors (1:3). The condemnation includes Gaza (1:6), Tyre (1:9), Edom (1:11), the Ammonites
(1:13), and Moab (2:1), the countries that circle Israel and Judah. Then
Amos condemns his own nation: "For three transgressions of Judah, and
for four, I will not revoke the punishment. . . . For three transgressions of
Israel, and for four, I will not revoke the punishment" (2:4, 6).

Other texts balance oracles against foreign nations by positive depictions of those same nations. The best examples of such pairing are the
books of Nahum and Jonah, the only books in the Hebrew canon that end
with a question. Each issues an oracle against Nineveh, the capital of the
Assyrian empire, but whereas Jonah evokes Exodus 34 in remarking that
God is "gracious and merciful, slow to anger" (4:2; see Exod. 34:6–7),
Nahum 1:3 quotes the next verses in Exodus 34, which describe God as
"by no means clearing the guilty."

Nahum, who spoke his oracles sometime between 663 (the date of the
fall of Thebes, mentioned in 3:8) and 612 (the date Babylon conquered
Assyria), predicts Nineveh's destruction. His final, rhetorical question
speaks to Nineveh's destruction; no one will pity the city; all will rejoice
at its fall: "There is no assuaging your hurt, your wound is mortal. All
who hear the news about you clap their hands over you. For who has ever
escaped your endless cruelty?" (3:19).

According to 2 Kings 14:25, Jonah the prophet was active in the north
during the reign of Jeroboam II (786–746). However, the book written in
his name is likely postexilic and, like Ruth, a reaction to the ethnocentrism
and xenophobia of Ezra and Nehemiah. Although Jonah is the only "prophet"
mentioned in the Qur'an (4:163), the book ascribed to him is not a collection
of oracles such as is found in Nahum; instead, also like Ruth, it is a short story.

The fictional nature of the story of Jonah is indicated not only by the
"great fish" that swallows the prophet and after three days vomits him
up on dry land or by the exaggerated rhetoric (the word "great" occurs
fourteen times), but also by the city's surprising repentance: the entire
population, and the cattle, repent after hearing a five-word (in Hebrew)
sermon: "Forty days more, and Nineveh shall be overthrown!" (3:4a). The
fiction also has an ironic twist. Had Jonah ben Amittai of 2 Kings 14 been
the Jonah of this short story, his efficacious prophecy would have doomed

his own country: Nineveh's repentance prevented its destruction, and so allowed it later to destroy Israel. One ancient Jewish commentary, noting this irony, proposed that Jonah tried to drown himself rather than provide Nineveh the chance to repent and so be spared.

Jonah opens with YHWH's call, "Go at once to Nineveh, that *great* city, and cry out against it; for their wickedness has come up before me" (1:2). Jonah, however, refuses the commission. The text does not give his reasons, but explanations are readily adduced. The Ninevites, with their imperial goals and their pagan ways, would not likely welcome an Israelite prophet. Nor do prophets in general seek their commission; to be a prophet is to proclaim to the people news they do not want to hear. The refusal of the commission is also conventional: Moses hesitated to issue his demands to Pharaoh; Jeremiah exclaims that he does not know how to speak, for he is only a boy (1:6). But Jonah's refusal outdoes them all. Rather than protest the commission, he flees from it.

Jonah books passage on a ship to Tarshish, descends to the hold, and promptly falls asleep. When a *great* storm threatens the ship, the sailors learn by casting lots that Jonah is the cause of their imminent demise. Waking the sleeping prophet, they question him about his identity. "I am a Hebrew," he replied. "I worship YHWH, the God of heaven, who made the sea and the dry land" (1:9). The statement shows the folly of Jonah's flight; one cannot flee from a God with universal rule. It also highlights the text's self-critique. While Jonah is sound asleep, the sailors cry out "each to his god" (1:5)—the non-Israelites display appropriate worship; Jonah does not.

The prophet then advises the sailors, three times, to toss him overboard. Perhaps he has a death wish; perhaps he has full confidence that his God will save him; or perhaps he wants to prove to himself that these pagan sailors are capable of murder. Yet these righteous Gentiles—like Abimelech of Gerar, Pharaoh's daughter, and Uriah the Hittite—pray that they not be "guilty of innocent blood" (1:14).

But the sailors have no choice. They throw Jonah into the sea (Jonah himself refuses to jump) and immediately the seas calm. The sailors, continuing to demonstrate their piety, offer sacrifices and make vows. Their worship contrasts with Jonah's ironic prayer from the fish: "Those who worship vain idols forsake their true loyalty, but I with the voice of thanksgiving will sacrifice to you" (2:8–9a).

Arriving in Nineveh, the *great* city, Jonah offers his sermon. The people repent. This makes Jonah the Bible's only fully successful prophet.

But Jonah sulks; he had wished for the destruction of the city, for that would have proved the legitimacy of his prophecy. To teach the prophet a lesson in compassion, God causes a plant to shelter Jonah from the sun, but then sends a worm to kill the plant. When Jonah complains, YHWH responds: "You are concerned about the bush. . . . Should I not be concerned about Nineveh, that *great* city, in which there are more than a hundred and twenty thousand persons who do not know their right hand from their left, and also many animals?" (4:10–11).

In Judaism, the book of Jonah is read on Yom Kippur, the Day of Atonement (see *B. Megilla* 10b). In its role in the Bible, the book of Jonah shows how Israel can be a blessing to the nations, counters the xenophobic pronouncements of Ezra, and uses the story of the Gentiles' conversion to encourage Israel's own repentance.

Chosen People

In planning the destruction of Sodom and Gomorrah—cities, like Nineveh, infamous for wickedness—YHWH says, "Shall I hide from Abraham what I am about to do, seeing that Abraham shall become a great and mighty nation, and all the nations of the earth shall be blessed in him? No, for I have chosen him, that he may charge his children and his household after him to keep the way of YHWH by doing righteousness and justice" (Gen. 18:17–19). The NRSV takes "I have known him" in the Hebrew and renders it "I have chosen him," and that is a correct nuance. The covenant means that Abraham and his posterity are chosen to be moral exemplars. Abraham demonstrates his reception of this commission by pleading that justice guide the divine hand: Sodom should not be destroyed lest righteous people suffer.

The idea of Israel as God's special possession appears in Exodus 19:4–6, where YHWH commissions Moses to proclaim to the Israelites: "You have seen what I did to the Egyptians, and how I bore you on eagles' wings and brought you to myself. . . . If you obey my voice and keep my covenant, you shall be my treasured possession out of all the peoples. Indeed, the whole earth is mine, but you shall be for me a priestly kingdom and a holy nation." The biblical text sees no reason to detail the reasons for this choice; love does not detail its rationale.

The term "chosen" appears in Deuteronomy 7:6, which reads: "YHWH your God has chosen you out of all the peoples on earth to be his people, his treasured possession." The same idea reappears in Deuteronomy 14:2, Psalms 33:12 and 105:6, Isaiah 41:8, Ezekiel 20:9ff., and elsewhere. This special relationship is based on divine grace, not on Israel's worth. Deuteronomy 7:7–8 goes on to state, "It was not because you were more numerous than any other people that YHWH set his heart on you and chose you— for you were the fewest of all peoples." Rather, "It was because YHWH loved you and kept the oath that he swore to your ancestors."

The New Testament picks up this same language—"You are a chosen race, a royal priesthood, a holy nation, God's own people" (1 Pet. 2:9)— and applies it to "the exiles of the Dispersion in Pontus, Galatia, Cappadocia, Asia, and Bithynia, who have been chosen and destined by God the Father and sanctified by the Spirit to be obedient to Jesus Christ and to be sprinkled with his blood" (1:1–2).

This elect status does not preclude the universality of the divine. To the contrary, divine protection is not restricted to Israel, and neither is the divine warrant for justice. That is why the text depicts God as consulting Abraham about Sodom and Gomorrah, sending Jonah to Nineveh, and allowing the nations to witness both the humiliation and the redemption of Israel, the suffering servant. Similarly, the biblical text consistently points to the righteous Gentile—from Noah to Abimelech of Gerar to Pharaoh's daughter to the palace eunuchs of Daniel and Esther to Job. To be elect does not give Israel the moral high ground, any more than King David, a "man after God's own heart" (1 Sam. 13:14), is without flaw. The Israelites are chosen out of love, but with this love comes responsibility. They are to remain a people "holy" to God and to bear witness to the nations. They can only do so if they reciprocate that initial love.

William Norman Ewer, British journalist and Soviet spy, is reputed to have coined the couplet, "How odd of God to choose the Jews." At the covenant renewal ceremony at Shechem, Joshua says to the people, "You have chosen YHWH, to serve him" (Josh. 24:22). The text provides an answer to the couplet: "It's not so odd—the Jews chose God."

Chapter 10

Sexuality

Questions of the Bible's view of sexuality—often questions that presuppose the Bible has only one view, rather than a series of possibilities—also tend to presume that the Bible has a single definition of "sex"; it does not. Neither does contemporary culture. "Sex" can concern what is legally permitted or encouraged or forbidden. Topics can include acts—homosexuality, abortion, intercourse out of wedlock, lust, marriage, polygamy, divorce, rape, incest, adultery, prostitution, concubinage, masturbation—as well as metaphors, gender roles, and attitudes. The topic of the Bible and sexuality is a broad one, and there are no simple answers. Law and narrative inform each other; communal welfare and personal needs clash; ancient values and modern ones are not always in harmony.

People of goodwill and personal integrity, with theological concerns backed by careful biblical study, will find themselves on the opposite sides of many of the issues that fall, directly or elusively, under the rubric of the Bible and sexuality. Those who state that the Bible is against homosexual intercourse do not necessarily proceed from an initial homophobia and then find biblical support; they have read the biblical text correctly. In turn, those who criticize the biblical text as homophobic, sexist, patriarchal, and so on are not necessarily dismissing the text. To criticize is not to dishonor or dismiss; to struggle with the text is to be "Israel" in the literal sense, to "wrestle with God." Alas, readers on different sides of sexuality issues tend, rather, to hunker down and, instead of using argument, choose invective. It's easier to insult the person holding the opposite view than it is to have a civil conversation.

To start the conversation on the Bible and sexuality, we begin, as is appropriate, in the beginning.

Revisiting Eden

Despite its reputation as a book of rules or an instruction manual on sexual activity, with the emphasis on the prohibitions, the Bible itself begins with a positive view of the human body and so of the body's gifts, including those of procreation, physical intimacy, and sexual response. A healthy and happy sexual attitude begins with a healthy and happy view of the human body, and this the Bible provides. Genesis opens with the point that human flesh is not dirty. To the contrary, according to Genesis 1:26–28: "God said, 'Let us make humankind (*ha-adam*) in our image, according to our likeness. . . .' So God created humankind in his image, in the image of God he created them; male and female he created them."

The details of "image" and "likeness" begin with visual form: to look at a human being is to see the image and likeness of the divine. The point is not only one of anthropology; it is also one with religious and even political import. The biblical term for "image," *tzelem*, means a model or duplicate; in Greek it is *ikon*. The term for "likeness," *demut*, also suggests a similarity or analogy and thus reinforces the first description. For example, Genesis 5:3 states that Adam fathers "a son in his likeness (*demut*), according to his image (*tzelem*)." All human beings are in this image: the rich are no more a reflection of the divine than the poor; the Gentile no less in the image of God than the Israelite. If we consider humanity to resemble the divine, then to attack another is to attack the image of the divine. Similarly, to fail to see that image of the divine in another—to dehumanize, to demonize—is to deny the biblical message of creation.

Compared to other ancient cultures that attributed divine resemblance to kings, the biblical text can be seen as regarding all humanity as royal. Since all humanity, male and female, is in the image of the divine, no sex, height, race, or hair or eye color can take priority. This point is subtly introduced throughout the rest of the biblical text, which rarely gives physical descriptions of the characters. For example, Rachel is gorgeous (Gen. 29:17), and Jacob falls in love with her at first sight, but whether she is four foot eleven and a size 20 (which would fit, in proportion, some ancient Southwest Asian goddess figurines) or six foot two and a size 0 (which would fit some contemporary images) goes unstated.

To humankind, created in the divine image and likeness, God issues the first commandment. "God blessed them, and God said to them, 'Be fruitful and multiply, and fill the earth . . .'" (Gen. 1:28a). Thus sexuality is part of God's initial blessing. This commandment also serves to distinguish humanity from divinity. God creates by the word (Gen. 1) and then by fashioning humanity from dirt and bone (Gen. 2). Humanity reproduces itself via personal intimacy. However, the text does not suggest that the *only* reason to engage in intercourse is to produce children.

On the other hand, the text does offer numerous examples of infertile women conceiving. Sarah, the wife of Abraham, is infertile (Gen. 11:30), but later gives birth to Isaac. Rebekah, the wife of Isaac, suffers the same physical circumstance, but Isaac intercedes on his wife's behalf, and Rebekah conceives (25:21). Other examples in the Hebrew scriptures of this literary convention, the infertile wife who conceives, include Rachel, Jacob's favored wife (30:1); Samson's mother, the wife of Manoah (Judg. 13:2–3); Hannah, the mother of Samuel (1 Sam. 1); and the Shunammite woman (2 Kings 4:14–16). The story is found in the New Testament in connection with the birth of John the Baptist (Luke 1), and it appears again in the second-century *Protevangelium of James,* an early Christian account of the birth of Mary, the mother of Jesus, to elderly, righteous parents.

For the Bible, the plight of women who are unable to bear children— Sarah; Rebekah; Rachel; Manoah's wife; Hannah; the Great Woman of Shunem (and, for the New Testament, Elizabeth)—is not caused by sin, and its solution is not dependent on righteousness; it is God who opens and closes wombs. On occasion, God has help. Genesis 30 explains how Rachel purchases mandrakes that Reuben, Leah's son, had found, as a fertility enhancement. The purchase price, which she paid to Leah, was a night with Jacob.

In more apocalyptic settings, biblical prophets announce that God will also restore potency to eunuchs. In Isaiah 56:5, to eunuchs who keep the Sabbath and hold fast to the covenant, God says: "I will give, in my house and within my walls, a monument and a name better than sons and daughters; I will give them an everlasting name that shall not be cut off." The term "monument" is, in Hebrew, literally "hand," likely a euphemism for "penis." This passage also speaks to the eschatological role of injured priests, for "no one whose testicles are crushed or whose penis is cut off shall be admitted to the assembly of YHWH" (Deut. 23:1).

The second creation account, Genesis 2:4b–3:24, reinforces the positive view of the human body. The name "Eden" is related to the Hebrew term for "pleasure"; this agricultural paradise reflects both the dreams of subsistence farmers and the romanticized view the authors of the story had of the pastoral countryside. The deity then gives the earthling its job description of tilling and keeping the garden, forbids the consumption of the fruit from the tree of the knowledge of good and evil, and then, in contrast to Genesis 1, finds something that is "not good": "It is not good that the *adam* should be alone; I will make him a helper as his partner (*ezer kenegdo*)" (Gen. 2:18).

The verse raises at least two questions in regard to the broader category of sexuality. The first concerns the relation of this story to the first creation narrative in chapter 1, in which male and female are created together, both in the image and likeness of God. If male and female exist together, why is this human being, this *adam*, alone in the garden? The second relates to the status of this "helper." What sort of help is needed, and who would best provide it?

The biblical text does not answer the first question. Source critics quickly point out that Genesis 1 comes from circles of Priestly scribes, who composed during or after the Babylonian exile (some date it in the sixth century BCE, others a century or more later), while Genesis 2–3 come from the perhaps earlier J (Yahwist) writers. Medieval Jewish readers, noting the possible discrepancy between the equal creation in Chapter 1 and the staggered creation of man-animals-woman in Genesis 2, posited that there was an earlier woman prior to Eve.

In this legend, the original, egalitarian creatures were Adam and his first wife, Lilith. Her name derives from an Akkadian word, either *lilatu*, meaning "night" (like the Hebrew word *laylah*), or *lilu*, meaning "demon" or "phantom." Isaiah 34:14 mentions the name explicitly: "Wildcats shall meet with hyenas, goat-demons shall call to each other; there too Lilith shall repose, and find a place to rest." There the term *lilith* may refer to a screech owl; it later takes on the connotation of "night demon."

As the story goes, Adam and Lilith lived peacefully together until Lilith insists that she wanted to be "on top" (when Smith College celebrated its centennial, it produced T-shirts that proudly read, "A Century of Women on Top"; this is as good an analogy as any). Adam refuses and engages God's support. Whether banished or whether she packs up on her own, Lilith leaves Adam, moves to Egypt, and sets up residence as the world's first succubus. Desperate to have children but unable to do so, she kills human infants out of jealousy. To ward her away, the story suggests that Jewish women should follow the laws of family purity (e.g., avoiding sexual contact with their husbands during menstruation), light the Sabbath candles, and toss a bit of dough into the oven before baking in remembrance of temple sacrifice. Meanwhile, desperate to conceive, Lilith visits men at night and causes nocturnal emissions. The folktale thereby provides an etiology the Bible missed.

Compared to Lilith, the helper in the garden, eventually to be named "Eve," may appear submissive and subordinate. But this is not the case according to Genesis. "Helper" is sometimes predicated of God, as in Psalm 33:20: "Our soul waits for YHWH; he is our help (*ezer*) and our shield." Moses names his second son Eliezer, literally, "My God is help." The second part of this job description in Genesis 2:18, *kenegdo,* has the sense of "appropriate to" or "opposite of" (as in a mirror image).

Although readers are now prepared for the creation of the woman, this is not what happens. First, YHWH Elohim forms the animals from the ground and brings them to the *adam* to see what he would call them. This parade yields no appropriate helper, but it does leave the question: What does the partner do to "help"? The most crass answer is that although the animals do not make fit partners because they cannot procreate with the *adam*—they cannot help him "be fruitful and multiply"—the woman does. Therefore, the "help" the woman provides is procreative.

To reduce the role of the "helper partner" to a baby machine ignores the role of human companionship, devalues infertile women, and denies the claim that women as well as men are in the divine image and likeness. With a sheep or a goat, poodle or pig, a person can still be "alone"; most people require another person to love and to be loved by, who challenges and inspires, to transcend the solitary life.

The woman is literally a part of the man, and without her he is both alone and incomplete. Genesis 2:21–22 states, according to most English translations: "So YHWH Elohim caused a deep sleep to fall upon the man, and he slept; then he took one of his ribs (*tzela*) and closed up its place with flesh. And the rib that YHWH Elohim had taken from the man he made into a woman and brought her to the man." However, the piece he contributes is not necessarily a "rib." The Hebrew term *tzela* is better translated "side"; in its forty-nine other biblical appearances "side" is the preferred translation. The majority of uses concern architecture, specifically the construction of the wilderness tabernacle and the Jerusalem temple.

The account of this "rib" may also be an etiology to explain not only woman's creation, but also the "closed up" place in male anatomy. Genesis states that following the *tzela*'s removal, God "closed up its place with flesh." It would have occurred to the biblical authors or anyone else familiar with the skeletal structure of animals that the human male lacks one major bone found in other vertebrates. Called technically the baculum and known colloquially as the "penis bone," this piece of male equipment facilitates erection. Human males, however, function according to what might be called a hydraulic system. They do not have a baculum, but they do have a seam on the underside of the penis. Thus, the story about the rib explains more than simply woman's origin: it both explains what the human male lacks compared to his mammalian cousins and fulfills that lack.

Complementing this interpretation, other ancient accounts of human origins depict a similar interest in an original connection between men and women. The *adam* can be seen as giving birth to the woman and thus as compared to male gods who give birth: Dionysius is born from Zeus's thigh, and Athena springs from his head. With this comparison, the male not only assumes the woman's role; he does her one better. The birth of the woman from the man in Genesis is clean and painless; for women pregnancy and birth are painful and difficult. Then again in this first parturition scene, Adam slept through the birth.

Upon waking, the *adam* sees the woman and exclaims: "This at last is bone of my bones and flesh of my flesh; this one shall be called woman (*ishshah*) for out of man (*ish*) this one was taken" (2:23). The connection is more than partnership and more than the possibility of procreation—the recognition is one of fulfillment and completion. Supporting this view is another ancient midrash that suggests that the woman was created from the man's "side," so that she would be his partner. Had she been created from his head, she would have dominated him; had she been formed from his feet he would have walked over her. Instead, she is created from his side, to be by his side, as his partner; the midrash also suggests that she is to be modest, domestic, and passive.

Genesis 2:24 describes this relationship: "Therefore a man leaves his father and his mother and clings to his wife, and they become one flesh." The statement is not an ordinance of what people must do; to the contrary, in many biblical stories, such as those of Rebekah, Rachel and Leah, and Zipporah, the wife leaves her parents and follows her husband. In other accounts, the man cleaves not just to one wife, but to many; in the case of Solomon, to hundreds. Thus to "become one flesh" is not limited to the sexual union and need not have a sexual connotation at all.

It, rather, means to be in a committed relationship, whether to another human being, to the king (so 2 Sam. 20:1), or to YHWH (Deut. 11:22). The term "cling" (Heb. *davaq*) is, as we have seen, the same term used for the establishment of a new family in the book of Ruth (1:14), when Ruth, rather than returning to her mother's house, "clung" (*davaq*) to her mother-in-law Naomi and returned with her to Bethlehem.

Concluding Genesis 2 is the observation that "the man and his woman were both naked, and were not ashamed." Eden represents a state of innocence, perhaps epitomized by little children, who feel no shame when nude. But the observation speaks also to sexuality. The ability to stand nude before a full-length mirror and say, "This is the image and likeness of God"—regardless of age, weight, or scars—is one possibility opened by Genesis 1. The ability to stand naked before a loved one and not feel shame is a possibility opened by Genesis 2. Both possibilities remain available, even after the expulsion from Eden.

Whether this primeval pair did anything more than stand before each other, the biblical text does not record. Later commentators, applying their own religious and cultural values, offer no consensus. For some, the pair remained celibate, just as they imagined that the resurrected body would also be celibate. Others, who equated sexuality with desire that cannot be controlled and so with the fallen nature of the human body, suggest that any intercourse the couple may have had would have been as natural, and as uninteresting, as lifting a finger. As far as the Bible makes explicit, sexual activity takes place only after the expulsion.

Nevertheless, the account of the snake, woman, man, and deity in Genesis 3 has received, in the history of interpretation, substantial commentary regarding prelapsarian sexual advances. For example, the idea that the woman sexually "tempted" the man remains a commonplace, although the text portrays no such "temptation": "So when the woman saw that the tree was good for food, and that it was a delight to the eyes, and that the tree was to be desired to make one wise, she took of its fruit and ate; and she also gave some to her man (*ish*), who was with her, and he ate" (3:6). Rather than a temptress, the woman could be regarded as a royal food taster. Whether the man is seen as implicitly trusting the woman or as a dolt who neither stops her from eating nor questions her motives will depend on readers' presuppositions.

Ancient commentators typically blame the woman for being a temptress, even as they seek to exonerate the man. The early Jewish commentator (and misogynist) Jesus ben Sira, writing in the early second century BCE, insists "From a woman sin had its beginning, and because of her we all die" (Sir. 25:24). The legend of Pandora, whose curiosity allowed evil to escape into the world, may be a partial influence on this approach. In 1 Timothy in the New Testament the points are extended: "For Adam was formed first, then Eve; and Adam was not deceived, but the woman was deceived and became a transgressor" (2:13–14). In this reading, the man nobly gives up his place in Eden to face damnation with his wife.

The church fathers Ambrose and Augustine took the next step by indicating that because of the sin of the first couple, humanity suffered a physical loss. The sperm of Adam became "vitiated," and thus all people conceived bore the taint of this "original sin." Recognizing the theological problem of having Jesus housed in a womb thus tainted, the Roman church concluded that his mother, Mary, was conceived without this taint, and so her conception was "immaculate." The Immaculate Conception became doctrine for the Roman Catholic Church in 1854.

The idea of a change in humanity's constitution is not inconsistent with the Genesis account. Upon eating the forbidden fruit, "Then the eyes of both were opened, and they knew that they were naked; and they sewed fig leaves together and made loincloths for themselves" (Gen. 3:7). The snake had promised the woman that she would become "like the gods, knowing good and evil." The knowledge she gained was that of shame. She and the man had been like toddlers, comfortable in their nudity. Now they have become mature; they lose their primeval innocence. But loss of innocence also creates a gain with regard to sexuality. Eden can be recovered, at least for a time, in an act of love between adults who are together and are not ashamed and who have an intimacy that is not shared with the rest of the world.

Not only do the first humans experience shame; they also face alienation from both the earth and their bodies. The deity condemns the snake to crawl upon its belly and then turns to the woman. The first part of the comment is typically translated: "I will greatly increase your pangs in childbearing; in pain you shall bring forth children" (Gen. 3:16a). However, the phrase "pangs in childbearing" can also be read "your labors and your pregnancies." The word for "pangs" (Heb. *etzev*) is the same term used in the next verse, typically translated, "Cursed is the ground because of you; in *toil* you shall eat of it all the days of your life." The term in 3:16 for "in childbearing" means "conception." Finally, instead of "in pain you shall bring forth children," the Hebrew can read, "along with toil you shall bear children." Woman's burden is not, or not only, pain in childbirth. The curse is what sociologists call the "second shift": she will be responsible for pregnancy, childbearing, lactation, and child care, and she will also have to labor in the workforce.

Genesis 3:16 is not, however, as we note in our chapter on Creation, a pronouncement of the way things need to be. It, rather, is the way things were and, in many settings, still are. The wife's subjugation to the husband was not God's original intention. The pronouncement concerning the woman is not a curse—the term is not used—but an etiology. To insist, as some literalists do, that a woman in labor should not receive analgesics because to do so is to deny the role given her in Genesis is to misread the text. Just as farmers have always sought ways to help the land yield its crops, despite the fact that the ground is "cursed" (3:17), so too humanity should find the means to ease women from the burden of the "second shift."

The comments to the woman end with a sexual notice: "Your desire shall be for your husband, and he shall rule over you." Again, the notice is etiological. Women will die in childbirth, as do the beautiful Rachel (Gen. 35:16–19) and the unnamed wife of Phinehas (1 Sam. 4:19–22). Yet many if not most women want to bear children. The etiology can be regarded as a continuation of Genesis 1: not only should humans be fruitful and multiply; they should enjoy the process. Bluntly put, ancient Israelite women did not have to lie back and think of Torah.

The best example of this positive sexual response in Genesis occurs when the menopausal Sarah, hearing that she is going to conceive a child, "laughed to herself, saying, 'After I have grown old, and my husband is old, shall I have pleasure?'" (18:12). The term for "pleasure," *ednah,* is a cognate of "Eden." The matriarch is thinking of the pleasure of conceiving a child. The more modest Septuagint omits this reference.

Conversely, the naturalization of this heterosexual response does not express the views of those who do not find their desire to be "for their husbands." Given that marriage in antiquity could be arranged, made for alliance and not necessarily for love, polygynous, and other variations, not all wives were likely to find their desire so focused.

The etiologies concerning the woman end with the notice that the man shall "rule over" his wife. The Hebrew term translated "rule" does suggest mastery. The same term describes the sun as "ruling" over the day and the moon over the night (Gen. 1:18); and God advises Cain to "master" his desire for sin (4:7). For Isaiah, civilization is in ruin when women "rule over" men (3:12). Then again, the biblical text does not prohibit women from holding public office, teaching, judging, prophesying, or using their own funds. Genesis 3 explains how things are, not how things should be.

Sexual Seduction, Response, and Potency

Hollywood, rather than the Bible, has provided the ancient tales with a sense of romantic passion. Exodus offers no record of anyone exclaiming, as did Anne Baxter's Nefretiri to Charlton Heston, "O Moses, you stubborn, splendid, adorable fool! . . ." Nevertheless, the Bible is not lacking in sexual dialogue. For woman's sexual response, and man's as well, the story of Eden is re-created in the Song of Songs (Song of Solomon, Canticles). Replete with garden imagery, the poems in this collection do not merely recount human physical desire; they celebrate it. Despite the Jewish and Christian traditions that interpret the text allegorically—as a love song between God and Israel or between Jesus and the church—for the earliest readers it was a love song between a man and a woman.

The title Song of Solomon may have helped the text gain inclusion in the canon, although ancient manuscripts do not ascribe the text to the king. The Song mentions Solomon, but generally as a lover who should not compete with the male singer: "My vineyard, my very own, is for myself; you, O Solomon, may have the thousand [pieces of silver], and the keepers of the fruit two hundred!" (8:12). Nevertheless, Solomon was renowned not only for his wisdom, but also for having, along with seven hundred wives, three hundred concubines (1 Kings 11:3).

The attribution of this biblical book to Solomon, or any man, is also inaccurate—much of the Song is not sung by a man, but by a woman. No demure debutante, this woman expresses her desire forcefully: "I will rise now and go about the city, in the streets and in the squares; I will seek him whom my soul loves" (3:2). When the lovers come together, the woman poetically, and graphically, describes her response: "My beloved thrust his hand into the opening, and my inmost being yearned for him. I arose to open to my beloved, and my hands dripped with myrrh, my fingers with liquid myrrh, upon the handles of the bolt" (5:4–5).

Even the more sober book of Proverbs, also attributed to Solomon, encourages sexual enjoyment: "Let your fountain be blessed, and rejoice in the wife of your youth, a lovely deer, a graceful doe. May her breasts satisfy you at all times; may you be intoxicated by her love" (5:18–19). Like "myrrh" in the previous reference, "fountain" is here a euphemism.

Proverbs extends this sexual imagery to describe the call that Wisdom issues. Like her sister in Song of Songs, Wisdom sings of her own actions. She takes her stand in public, "on the heights, beside the way, at the crossroads" (8:2; cf. 1:20–21) where she calls out, "My fruit is better than gold, even fine gold, and my yield than choice silver" (8:19; cf. 3:14). In contrast, she warns her young male readers: "Drink water from your own cistern, flowing water from your own well" (5:15) and stay away from the neighbor's wife, who says, "Come, let us take our fill of love until morning; let us delight ourselves with love. For my husband is not at home; he has gone on a long journey" (7:18–19). Epitomizing this adulterous lust is the wife of Potiphar, the Egyptian officer (Heb. *saris*) who purchased Joseph as a slave (Gen. 39:1). *Saris* means both "eunuch" and "officer"; were Potiphar a "eunuch," then the desperate Mrs. Potiphar receives another possible motive for her approaches.

A possible seduction appears in the book of Ruth. Having accompanied her Israelite mother-in-law, Naomi, to Bethlehem, Ruth takes up gleaning in fields belonging to Boaz, the richest fellow in Bethlehem, a bachelor, and Naomi's relative. The older woman advises her daughter-in-law, "Wash and anoint yourself, and put on your best clothes and go down to the threshing floor [where Boaz is winnowing barley]; but do not make yourself known to the man until he has finished eating and drinking." In other words, dress up, put on the good perfume, wait until the man is drunk, and then, "when he lies down, observe the place where he lies; then, go and uncover his feet and lie down; and he will tell you what to do" (3:2–4). That Amos locates prostitutes on the threshing floor (9:1) adds to the sexualization of the scene.

When at midnight Boaz awakes, he is shocked to find "there, lying at his feet, was a woman!" (3:8). Ruth calmly announces, "I am Ruth, your servant; spread your cloak over your servant, for you are next-of-kin." According to this version of levirate law, the nearest male relative of a deceased husband is responsible for marrying the widow and providing her a child who will inherit the dead husband's name and estate. Boaz, quite happy with the arrangement, praises Ruth for not having "gone after young men" (3:10).

That this is a seduction scene is indicated not only by the plot, but also by the euphemisms and its intertextual allusions. The Hebrew word *mar-*

gelot, here translated "feet" (the more common term for "feet" is *raglayim; margelot* technically suggests "the place of the feet") is a euphemism for genitals. Sometimes feet are simply feet, to be placed in shoes; occasionally the expression takes on this additional nuance. English translations sometimes find a euphemism for the euphemism. First Samuel 24:3a reads, in the NRSV, "Saul went in to relieve himself." The Hebrew text literally says, "And Saul came to cover his feet." Isaiah describes the seraphim, heavenly creatures, as having six wings: "With two they covered their faces, and with two they covered their feet, and with two they flew" (6:2). Again, the euphemism is likely in place. Finally, Isaiah also offers the charming expression, "the hair of the feet" (7:20); the reference is to pubic hair.

Readers unfamiliar with biblical euphemisms but knowledgeable about biblical plots would also see in Ruth 3 another basis for the seduction. Ruth is a Moabite, and the Moabites, according to Genesis 19, decended from incest. In a cave outside Sodom, Lot's older daughter advises her sister: "Our father is old, and there is not a man on earth to come in to us after the manner of all the world. Come, let us make our father drink wine, and we will lie with him, so that we may preserve offspring through our father" (19:31–32). The child of the older daughter is Moab; the Septuagint explicitly makes the name an etiology, "This one is from my father." The Hebrew *me'av* can mean "from [the] father." However, Moab (*mw–i–b*) is already attested on a Luxor temple wall from the time of Ramesses II (ca. 1275 BCE). Thus what the Bible does here is create a negative etiology for this population group. The younger daughter names her son Ben Ammi, which the Septuagint explains as "son of my people"; again, the etiology fits the Hebrew. This child becomes the eponymous ancestor of the Ammonites. Ruth thus evokes her Moabite origins: she uncovers the genitals of an older man and arranges to have a child with him. But what is perverse and incestuous in Genesis is for Boaz a blessing. He and Ruth will become King David's great-grandparents.

Legislating Sexuality

Legislation concerning who is permitted to have intercourse with whom, when, and how does not suggest that the biblical authors regarded sexual expression as innately shameful or dirty. The Sabbath and the temple are also surrounded by laws, and the laws keep the times and the places from becoming either profane or mundane. Further, the sexual laws suggest that humans have the capacity to act self-consciously; to follow biblical laws on sexual matters means to think before one acts.

Not all laws regarding sexuality are prohibitions. Deuteronomy 24:5, for example, mandates: "When a man is newly married, he shall not go out with the army or be charged with any related duty. He shall be free at home one year, to be happy with the wife whom he has married" (or otherwise translated, "to make his wife happy").

Other legislation that brings together war and sex is less sympathetic to the participants. Deuteronomy 21:10–14 states that an Israelite who desires to marry a woman he has taken as a war captive is to bring her into his home for a month; there she shall "shave her head, pare her nails, discard her captive's garb," and "mourn for her father and mother." Only after this period—when the soldier has seen the woman daily, when she has made herself unattractive, and when his initial lust may have abated—is he permitted to marry her. Should the marriage fail, he must set the woman free. The situation is no ethical ideal, but it does improve upon the scenario in which a captive woman is raped and enslaved.

The majority of sex laws focus less on the woman than on the man who has claims on her sexuality. Leviticus 18 (repeated in Lev. 20) details via language evoking both personal shame and personal possession prohibitions based on familial connection. For example, Leviticus 18:7a states, "You shall not uncover the nakedness of your father, which is the nakedness of your mother." The prohibition forbids mother-son incest, but the basis is not the mother's maternal role; the law is premised on the father's sole sexual access to the mother. The next prohibition forbids access to the "father's wife," since, especially in a polygynous society, one's "father's wife" may not be one's mother. For narrative material, the relationship between Jacob's wife Bilhah and his eldest son, Reuben (Leah's son), demonstrates this case (Gen. 35:22). Also prohibited are sexual relations with one's sister, niece or grandniece, aunt, daughter-in-law, or sister-in-law. Father-daughter incest, as represented (although blaming the daughters) in the story of Lot (Gen. 19), is not explicitly prohibited; the logic of the omission may be that the daughter's body belongs to the father, and the laws relate to exclusive access. The cultural expectation was that the father would guard his daughter's virginity.

Should illicit relationships occur and produce children, Deuteronomy 23:2 enjoins: "Those born of an illicit union shall not be admitted to the assembly of YHWH. Even to the tenth generation. . . ." The law suggests that violations of the prohibitions happened. The concern for the children establishes an additional warning to the parents: their actions can have repercussions for the lives of their children.

The levitical prohibitions then move from matters of property to matters of propriety. Leviticus 18:17 forbids a man from having sexual relations with both a woman and her daughter or her granddaughter; the next verse forbids the taking of two sisters as cowives, despite the marriage of Jacob to Rachel and Leah.

These laws fall neatly into the categories of sexual exclusivity or ownership, but the next several laws in Leviticus 18 extend the discussion from exclusivity to purity. Leviticus 18:19, which prohibits intercourse with a menstruating woman, likely reflects the priestly interest in marking off areas of birth and death. Menstruation represents a nonconception and thus a birth that did not occur. With intercourse resuming at the completion of the woman's period, she is more likely to conceive. This concern for life and death may also explain why Leviticus 18:21, which forbids the sacrificing of children to Molech (see also Lev. 20:2–5; 2 Kings 23:10; Jer. 32:35), is placed here.

The next two laws, the final items in the list, draw in part upon matters of taxonomy. Like a number of the commandments regarding food and agriculture, the laws forbidding male homosexual relations and bestiality (by either men or women) relate to a concern for categories. Human beings are not to have sex with animals, for that would create a category confusion. The prohibition of male same-sex relations fits into this consideration because of the language it uses: "You [male person] shall not lie down with a male (as) the lyings down [plural] of a woman," or, more colloquially, "You male person shall not treat another male sexually as if he were a woman" (Lev. 18:22). The prohibition is repeated in Leviticus 20:13, with the addition that "both of them have committed an abomination; they shall be put to death." For the law code, men are to act as men, women as women. Thus Deuteronomy 22:5 mandates: "A woman shall not wear a man's apparel, nor shall a man put on a woman's garment."

Likely the levitical prohibitions are meant to forbid homosexual anal intercourse, with the underlying presupposition that men are the ones who penetrate and women are the ones who receive penetration. However, the plural "lyings" may well extend the commandment to any form of sexual relations a man would have with a woman. Lesbian sexual relations go unmentioned in the law code, although Paul's Letter to the Romans in the

New Testament does extend the prohibitions to women (1:26–27). For the Hebrew text, the sexual laws relate to the presence of a penis.

Given the etiology in Genesis 3 concerning the woman's subordination to the man, a subordination expressed in terms of physical desire, and given the Bible's taxonomic concern for distinguishing men from women, the prohibition against male same-sex relations should also be seen as speaking to a concern for male honor and status. For a man to be feminized, then and even now (as any boy who has ever been accused of "crying like a girl" knows, with all the negative views of women such a comment connotes), was seen as a gross insult, an abomination.

Other explanations beyond the taxonomic have been proposed for the prohibition of male homosexuality, although several of these are less convincing. The claim that the injunction seeks to keep Israel distinct from Canaanites, who not only engaged in homosexual relations but also sacralized them, fails from lack of evidence. Leviticus 18:24 does offer, as a catchall explanation for the preceding injunctions, the notice that it was "by all these practices the nations [in the land of Canaan] I am casting out before you have defiled themselves." However, casting sexual aspersions against one's enemies is standard maladicta; no data suggest that Canaanites themselves sanctioned incest, adultery, or the other activities Leviticus prohibits.

Although the biblical text is interested in taxonomy, the view that the law seeks to prevent the mixing of semen and excrement also fails. Had that been the issue, the text would have forbidden heterosexual anal intercourse, just as it forbids bestiality for both men and women. It does not. Nor does it forbid the mixing of semen and saliva.

Also common is the explanation that the Bible forbids homosexual intercourse (as well as sexual relations with a menstruating woman) to preserve semen and so to keep the population up. Since same-sex relations do not lead to conception and since a menstruating woman is not at the peak of her fertility, so this argument goes, the law ensures that every sexual action can lead to conception. This explanation fails as well. No biblical law forbids any of the various forms of sexual expression enjoyed by heterosexual couples that do not lead to conception. Nor is there any prohibition against birth control, masturbation, intercourse with an infertile or menopausal person, or intercourse with a pregnant woman (who is not going to get pregnant again).

Poor Onan (Gen. 38), from whom we receive the term "onanism," meaning "masturbation," was not punished for engaging in self-gratification; his misdeed was a primitive form of birth control at the moment he was to fulfill his levirate duty to his deceased brother's widow. The closest the text comes to a reference to masturbation is Leviticus 15:16–17: "If a man has an emission of semen, he shall bathe his whole body in water, and be unclean until the evening. Everything made of cloth or of skin on which the semen falls shall be washed with water, and be unclean until the evening." The cause of the emission—masturbation, nocturnal emission—is not stated. The next verse mentions such an emission in the context of heterosexual intercourse. But the result is the same: the concern for an emission of semen, which, like menstruation, falls into the category of "life and death" issues since it relates to conception, has no negative connotation.

Yet another explanation suggests that the Bible forbids male sexual relations since the major place such activities occur is during war, where the homosexual act is an act of violence, of rape. The case can be made on the basis of the stories of Sodom and Gomorrah (Gen. 19) and the rape of the Levite's concubine (Judg. 19).

In the former account, the people of Sodom seek to "know" the two strangers who have found hospitality at the home of Lot, Abraham's nephew. Recognizing that the mob plans to rape his guests, Lot offers them his two virgin daughters: "Let me bring them out to you, and do to them as you please; only do nothing to these men, for they have come under the shelter of my roof" (Gen. 19:8). Lot recognizes that the people of Sodom are interested in sexual violence. However, there is no reason to presume the issue is explicitly *homosexual* violence. Genesis 19:4 mentions "all the people of the city" gathered at Lot's door; it is translators who choose to describe the people there as "men." The Hebrew term for "men," *anashim*, here means "people." And "all the people"—men, women, and children—will die when Sodom is destroyed. Nevertheless, many commentators continue to speak of homosexuality as the sin of Sodom, rather than condemn the violence of the townspeople and the abuse that Lot suggests, even if he is seen as bargaining with the townspeople he would permit to come upon his daughters.

In the reception history of the Genesis account, the "sin" of Sodom was not initially seen as homosexuality. The first commentator to detail the city's sins, Ezekiel, condemns Sodom for "pride, excess of food, and prosperous ease, but [it] did not aid the poor and needy" (16:49). Ezekiel thus extends the focus on sexual violence to other forms of violence against the neighbor.

The replay of the scene of Sodom in Judges 19 indicates that the intent of the crowd is not homosexual desire, but violence. In this version of the story, where the perpetrators are not the alien citizens of Sodom but members of the tribe of Benjamin, the visitor offered hospitality does not, as did Lot's guests, blind the local residents and permit the escape of the faithful. In this perversion of an already perverse scene, the host tosses the visitor's unnamed concubine to the mob. The woman is gang-raped until dawn.

The text, with pathos, records: "In the morning her master got up, opened the doors of the house, and when he went out to go on his way, there was his concubine lying at the door of the house, with her hands on the threshold. 'Get up,' he said to her, 'we are going.' But there was no answer" (19:27–28a). The Levite puts the concubine—dead? alive?—on his donkey, takes her home, chops up her body into twelve pieces, and sends the parts to the tribes of Israel. His call is to war, and the ensuing battle almost wipes out the Benjaminites. To protect the tribal identity, the remaining tribes permit the Benjaminites—whose women must have been killed in the battle, although the text makes no mention of them—to abduct other women. The violence is exponentially increased, tribal life is reduced to chaos, and the rape of the concubine represents how far the tribes have fallen from establishing a peaceful kingdom under Mosaic law. The crime, again, is one of violence, not one of "homosexuality."

However, the suggestion that "violence" lies beneath the injunctions against homosexual relations does fit with the concern for gender roles. The man who is attacked and defeated is also "feminized"; he is the one who is "ruled over" (Gen. 3:16).

It is possible that legislation against same-sex sexual intercourse appears elsewhere in the law code, but biblical metaphors prevent firm determination. The KJV translates Deuteronomy 23:17–18: "There shall be no whore of the daughters of Israel, nor a sodomite of the sons of Israel." However, the Hebrew offers neither "whore" nor "sodomite"; it says "holy one" (first in the feminine and then in the masculine). The term "holy one" (*qedashah*, feminine) is the same term that appears in Genesis 38:21–22, when Hirah the Abdullamite explains to his friend that the townspeople knew of no "holy woman" to whom Judah owed a sheep. The missing "holy woman" is Judah's daughter-in-law, Tamar, who is neither a prostitute nor connected to a temple. "Holy woman" may, on the lips of

Hirah, be a euphemism for the Hebrew *zonah*, "prostitute." Complicating the connection of Deuteronomy 23 to the levitical prohibition, there is no evidence that Canaanites practiced "sacred prostitution." Job descriptions for these "holy ones" are not provided.

Another text frequently cited as alluding to homosexual desire is the relationship between David, whom the prophet Samuel had anointed to be king of Israel, and his friend and brother-in-law Jonathan, the son of the reigning king, Saul. The relationship is certainly homosocial, as were most relationships in that society. Jonathan expresses his love for David by giving him the accoutrements of military and royal privilege: "Then Jonathan made a covenant with David, because he loved him as his own soul. Jonathan stripped himself of the robe that he was wearing, and gave it to David, and his armor, and even his sword and his bow and his belt" (1 Sam. 18:3–4). David, however, waits until Jonathan's death to proclaim his love. After the battle that takes the lives of both Jonathan and Saul, David publicly laments: "I am distressed for you, my brother Jonathan; greatly beloved were you to me; your love to me was wonderful, passing the love of women" (2 Sam. 1:26). David may be sincere, or he may be engaging in a bit of shrewd political rhetoric, given that with Jonathan's death his way to the throne is clear. Their relationship may have had a sexual component, but to insist upon this component denies the true and deep feelings people can have for each other apart from physical desire.

The converse of the story of David and Jonathan is that of Ehud, the left-handed charismatic leader of Judges 3, and his victim, King Eglon of Moab. The account plays upon negative stereotypes of same-sex attraction with puerile potty humor. The pattern is the standard scene that marks the book of Judges. Israel had sinned, and YHWH punished the community by delivering it into the hands of the Moabite ruler (connections to the putative incestuous origins of the Moabites should be read into the story). When Israel then cries out, YHWH raises up Ehud, a trickster who would be at home with the Native American figure of Coyote or the Greek god Pan.

Ehud prepared for his encounter with Eglon by constructing a very long two-edged sword, which he attached to his right thigh. The placement is where his penis would normally rest, but this left-handed judge has things "backward." So girded, Ehud presented himself to Eglon, whom the text describes as a "very fat man" (that his name means "fatted calf," with the diminutive *-on* ending to the name perhaps suggesting "fat little calf," adds to the picture). When the king cleared his cool roof chamber in order to hear Ehud's "secret message," "Ehud reached with his left hand [the hand traditionally used to hold the penis], took the sword from his right thigh, and thrust it into Eglon's belly. The hilt went in after the blade, and the fat closed over the blade . . . and the dirt came out" (i.e., the king defecated). The scene is one of a perverse intercourse: there is "entry" and there is "ejaculation." Ehud escapes down the back staircase, and the Israelites rout their enemies.

For the biblical texts, whether law code or narrative, the focus is not on intent or desire, but on the act itself. Thus the Bible says nothing about "homosexuality" with regard to disposition or genetics. This fact alone provides some readers warrant to dismiss the levitical legislation; they argue that, had the biblical authors known about genetics, they would not have included the prohibition. Other readers, taking a historical-literal approach, conclude that Leviticus prohibits anal intercourse, but not other forms of sexual expression between males. Still others find the biblical warrant against homosexual practice not in the law codes, but in the New Testament, in Romans 1:26–27, 1 Corinthians 6:9–10, and 1 Timothy 1:9–10. One revisionist reading suggests that the commandments in Leviticus 18 and 20 prohibiting one man treating another man sexually as if he were a woman be understood as saying that gay couples need not correspond to heterosexual norms. Neither male should play the "woman's role." Still others note God's observation that it is "not good" for the human being to be alone and therefore resist any teaching that would condemn gay people to lives of singleness or celibacy.

How today's readers assess these texts will depend on numerous factors: the weight given to historical context, views concerning gender roles, traditional teachings of church or synagogue, personal experience, and so on. Those who claim the text speaks against male homosexuality should not immediately be seen as homophobic bigots; they are reading the text faithfully. And those who seek religious sanction for marriage between same-sex couples or ordination of gay men and lesbians should not be seen as dismissing the biblical text. Debates will continue. It is our hope that the debates be informed by both historical-critical work and the respect and love the Bible demands we accord our neighbors.

Marriage, Divorce, and Adultery

There is no technical Hebrew term for "marriage," and the major words for "husband" and "wife" are, respectively, "man" (*ish*) and "woman" (*ishshah*). After God creates the woman out of a body part from the first human, the text reads: "This at last is bone of my bones and flesh of my flesh; this one shall be called Woman (*ishshah*), for out of Man (*ish*) this one was taken" (Gen. 2:23). It makes for a clever pun and works as a folk etymology, as we have noted, but linguists maintain that neither word actually derives from the other. The origin of *ish*, which means "male person" and occurs over twenty-one hundred times in the Hebrew Bible, is highly uncertain, but may come from a root meaning "to be strong." With a completely different linguistic history, *ishshah* ("woman") is most likely connected to the Akkadian word *ashshatu* meaning "wife" or "woman." A nice English analogy is the word pair "male" and "female." Although the two words appear to derive from the same root, they have completely separate origins—"male" from the Latin *mas* ("male person" or "male animal") and "female" from Latin *femina* ("woman"), which in turn stems from the root *felare* ("to suckle").

Nor does the text offer much in the way of legislation concerning marital arrangements. Some marriages were arranged by parents; others were decided upon by the individuals. Some marriages were based in love; others in economics or convenience. Biblical narratives occasionally mention that a relationship begins in love; the most notable example is Jacob and Rachel's. Jacob "loved Rachel" at first sight; the seven years he served her father "seemed to him but a few days because of the love he had for her" (Gen. 29:18, 20). His father, Isaac, also loved his bride (24:67); we are not told if Rebekah returned the love. Samson "loved a woman in the valley of Sorek, whose name was Delilah" (Judg. 16:4), but there is no notice of their marriage. The name Delilah likely stems from *dalal*, "to hang," as in loose hair, perhaps thus "flirtatious"; this is a good name for a lover, less so for a wife. The lovers in the Song of Solomon are not, as far as the text reveals, married.

Genesis 34:12 mentions a bride-price ("marriage present") paid by the groom's family to the father of the bride. According to 1 Samuel 18:25, King Saul set for his daughter, whom David sought to marry, a bride-price of one hundred Philistine foreskins. David, surviving the death this price intended, produces two hundred. Conversely, Genesis 30:20 and 1 Kings 9:16 speak of a "dowry" that the bride brings to the new family. Later texts, such as Tobit 7:13, mention that the wife has a "marriage contract," and copies of such contracts are preserved from the fifth-century BCE Jewish colony in Elephantine, Egypt. These contracts protect the wife in case of divorce. How early they existed in Israelite society cannot be determined.

Should the husband wish to take a second (or third or fourth) wife, no mention is made of consultation with the first wife. Husbands could also take women as concubines. This is a contractual arrangement whereby a woman reserves her sexuality for one man alone, but any child conceived in the relationship does not inherit equally with the children of the wives. Thus a concubine was not a wife, but neither was she a prostitute.

Legal regulations concerning divorce are equally sketchy. Deuteronomy 24:1 states: "Suppose a man enters into marriage with a woman, but she does not please him because he finds something objectionable about her, and so he writes her a certificate of divorce, puts it in her hand, and sends her out of his house; she then leaves his house." Since marriage is a contractual relationship, sealed with bride-price or dowry, a legal document is needed to sever the relationship.

The "objectionable thing" is vague, and perhaps deliberately so. This law is less interested in the technicalities of the bill of divorce than it is in the correct disposition of the former wife's sexuality. The law code goes on to note that were the divorced wife to remarry, were that second marriage to end in divorce or the death of the second husband, and were she to seek to return to her first husband, she is forbidden to do so. Here again, narrative does not necessarily correspond to law. Isaiah 50:1 and Jeremiah 3:8 compare the relationship of God and the covenant community to that of a husband and wife; the relationship had been dysfunctional, and YHWH had given Israel a "bill of divorce." Yet, with her sins atoned for in Babylonian exile, Israel is taken back as the wife of God.

Marriages could also be ended in cases of a fraudulent betrothal, although whether and how the instructions for doing so were put into practice remain disputed. Our discussion of law included the case of a man who enters into a marriage, but then, after consummation, decides that he does not like his wife. Were he to slander her by saying, "I married this woman; but when I lay with her, I did not find evidence of her virginity . . .'" (Deut. 22:13–14), the father and mother of the bride were to present the "evidence of the young woman's virginity" to the elders. That the evidence—blood from the wedding sheets—would be in the hands of the bride's parents seems like a loophole—the parents would likely present whatever would be needed to exonerate their daughter. For his "slander" the groom was to pay 100 shekels to the bride's father, and he was forbidden from divorcing his wife. It's hard to believe any groom would put himself through this process. Nevertheless, the text does state that if the charge is found to be true, the bride is to be stoned.

The text gives us no narrative examples of divorces under these circumstances. Instead, Malachi 2:16 is explicit: "I hate divorce, says YHWH, the God of Israel." Sirach 7:26 agrees: "Do you have a wife who pleases you? Do not divorce her." Ezra mandates divorce in the case of Judean men married to foreign wives, for they were in violation of the commandment prohibiting marriages with the "peoples of the land" (9:1, 11; 10:2); here the issue is not sexual misdemeanor, but a postexilic emphasis in some circles on endogamy.

Should a man not be satisfied with his wife, he had other options. Along with polygamy and concubinage, men could, and did, visit prostitutes. The widowed Judah thought his daughter-in-law, Tamar, was a prostitute (Gen. 38:15) when he found her by the side of the road. The veil in which she had wrapped herself would not necessarily indicate her profession; before she greeted Isaac for the first time, Rebekah also wrapped herself in a veil.

The spies Joshua sends into Jericho go immediately to the home of Rahab the prostitute. For all the commentaries that insist that the spies went to Rahab's home since there strangers would not be out of place or since there they could get information on local munitions, the men's only interest appears to be in the business Rahab promotes. But the prostitute engages in no sexual act. Rahab protects the spies from the king's soldiers, recites to her countrymen Israel's salvation history, and arranges for protection for both herself and her family. Rahab is a survivor. Should Jericho prevail, her business will remain open; should Israel prevail, she has the protection of the spies. Her story ends with the notice that the spies brought Rahab and all of her kindred out of Jericho, and "her family has lived in Israel ever since" (Josh. 6:23–25).

For the Deuteronomistic History, prostitution appears normative but is not commended. Jephthah the judge is the son of a prostitute (Judg. 11:1), but he is rejected by the sons of his father's wife. Samson goes to a prostitute in Gaza (16:1), but his track record with women is not to be emulated. Two prostitutes, both recent mothers, present themselves to King Solomon for his judgment about which is the mother of the one living baby

(1 Kings 3:16). The situation of the women and the child portends the division of the country.

Prophetic texts also regard prostitution as a given. Jeremiah (5:7) laments that the people "trooped to the houses of prostitutes," and Amos is one of several prophets who compares Israel's infidelity to the trade of a prostitute (17:7). The principal uses of the image of Israel as prostitute and/or unfaithful spouse—for the prophetic texts, the two images bleed into each other—appear in Hosea, the northern prophet of the mid-eighth century, and in Ezekiel, the southern prophet of the mid-sixth century in Babylonian exile. Each depicts Israel as a wayward wife who has gone after other lovers (international alliances, foreign gods) and betrayed her husband, God.

Hosea not only laments Israel's faithfulness; he shows in his own life both the effects of infidelity and God's desire to reunite with the wayward spouse. The prophet obeys the divine command, "Go, love a woman who has a lover and is an adulteress, just as YHWH loves the people of Israel, though they turn to other gods and love raisin cakes" (3:1). He marries a prostitute named Gomer, laments her infidelity, but, speaking in the persona of God, anticipates the time when he and his wife will reunite in love, when Israel will no longer refer to God as her *baal* ("master," with the connotations of the Canaanite storm deity), but as her *ish* ("man," "husband"). The prophet's extreme distress over Israel's infidelity becomes heightened when the Torah is considered: the command to love a woman guilty of adultery clashes with the Decalogue's prohibition of adultery, the commandment against prostitution (Lev. 19:29), and Deuteronomy's insistence (22:22) that adultery be punished by stoning. Hosea's divine mandate contradicts the Torah, just as does Israel's behavior. That God will take Israel back shows that compassion and covenant determine how the Torah is to be implemented.

Ezekiel brings the image of Israel as a prostitute or adulteress to a rhetorical nadir that some have termed "pornoprophetics." Chapter 16 begins an extended metaphor by describing how God, seeing Israel when she was "at the age for love" (16:8), pledged himself to her and "entered into a covenant." He bathed and anointed her body, provided her exquisite clothing and jewelry, and offered her delectable food. But Israel "played the whore" (16:15) with foreign lovers, sacrificed her own children, and betrayed the divine trust. Worse than an adulteress, worse than a prostitute, the covenant community even paid others to be her paramours. God's threatened punishment of her is severe. To her God says: "I will gather all your lovers. . . . They shall strip you . . . and leave you naked. . . . They shall bring up a mob against you, and they shall stone you and cut you to pieces with their swords. They shall burn your houses and execute judgments on you in the sight of many women; I will stop you from playing the whore, and you shall also make no more payments" (16:37–41). Only after this debasement will God's anger be appeased.

The scene replays, with more horror, in chapter 23. There Ezekiel describes two sisters, Oholah (Samaria) and Oholibah (Jerusalem), each of whom "played the whore" (23:3). The threats he mounts against the women are visceral. Ezekiel says God declares to Jerusalem: "I will rouse against you your lovers. . . . They shall cut off your nose and your ears, and your survivors shall fall by the sword. They shall seize your sons and your daughters, and your survivors shall be devoured by fire. . . . They will leave you naked and bare, and the nakedness of your whorings shall be exposed" (23:22, 25, 29). The extreme imagery cannot be taken as indicative of how adulterous wives were treated. To the contrary, Ezekiel is engaging in rhetorical shock, and he succeeds.

The imagery of Israel as unfaithful spouse and as prostitute and the exceptionally positive image of Rahab the prostitute overshadow in the Bible the lives of real prostitutes. Proverbs 6:26 hints at the economic difficulties facing women in the sex business, especially compared to the wife who, protected economically in a marriage, chooses infidelity: "A prostitute's fee is only a loaf of bread, but the wife of another stalks a man's very life."

Confirming the lack of social sanction for, although not the illegality of, prostitution are the law codes. Leviticus forbids a father to make his daughter a prostitute (19:29), forbids priests to marry either a prostitute or a divorced woman (the concern is at least to ensure priestly paternity for the offspring; 21:7, 14), and mandates that a priest's daughter who prostitutes herself should be burned to death (21:9). The law codes can give the impression that only non-Israelite women would become prostitutes, and the stories about Tamar, Rahab, and the Gaza prostitute support the view. But Israelite women too would have turned to this trade.

For the Bible, as the notice in Proverbs suggests, the major concern of authors is not prostitution, but adultery. Set among the Ten Commandments, "Thou shalt not commit adultery" (Exod. 20:14, cf. Lev. 20:10; Deut. 5:18) is one of Israel's major values. The sanctity of the marital relationship—which in this case means the husband's exclusive sexual access to the wife—is for Israel paramount. As the term is understood in the Bible, adultery does not apply equally to both spouses in a marriage. If a husband has intercourse with a woman not his wife, he has not become an adulterer; only a wife who steps outside the bounds of marriage commits adultery. On the other hand, if a husband has sexual relations with another's wife, both that woman and the man are liable for punishment, because both have violated the rights of the woman's husband. Israelite women are not their husband's "property" per se, but the sexuality of a married woman belongs to her husband.

Adultery, with connotations ranging from crimes against the husband and the family to idolatry, is known in Israel as "the great sin." In Genesis 20:9, after Abraham passes off his wife, Sarah, as his sister and she is taken into King Abimelech's palace, the king confronts Abraham with the charge that Abraham almost brought upon him "a great sin," that is, almost caused him to commit the sin of adultery. The other biblical occurrences of the phrase "great sin" refer to idolatry, conventionally condemned with the language of adultery as seen in the account of Aaron and the golden calf (Exod. 32:21, 30, 31) and the incident involving Jeroboam and his golden calves (2 Kings 17:21, referring to 1 Kings 12:25–33). Four marriage contracts from ancient Egypt and at least one text from fourteenth-century Ugarit also use "the great sin" to refer to adultery.

For Israel, adultery is a capital offense. Leviticus 20:10 mandates: "If a man commits adultery with the wife of his neighbor, both the adulterer and the adulteress shall be put to death." Whether this law was put into practice is another matter. In the famous story of David and Bathsheba, it is not.

The story does, however, detail the devastation adultery causes. Bathsheba becomes pregnant, David attempts to get Uriah home from the front to provide a cover story, and when Uriah refuses to be with his wife, David sends the soldier back, with sealed orders to Joab, the commander, to place Uriah "in the forefront of the hardest fighting" (11:14). Joab complies, although he does place skilled warriors by the doomed man in order to give him the proverbial fighting chance. Uriah is killed, as are a number of other brave men. The adultery has led to murder, not just of Uriah, but of his colleagues as well.

And the adultery is known. The court prophet Nathan condemns David for both the adultery and the murder. Speaking for God, he announces to David, "Now therefore the sword shall never depart from your house, for you have despised me, and have taken the wife of Uriah the Hittite to be your wife" (2 Sam. 12:10). The child conceived in adultery dies; David's son Amnon will rape his sister, David's daughter Tamar; and then Tamar's brother, Absalom, will have intercourse with David's concubines on the roof of the palace, before all Israel. The civil war that Absalom begins results in the deaths of thousands in Israel. The Bible's point is that adultery impacts not only the couple directly involved; it impacts families and communities, in this generation and the next.

Yet adultery is not the end of the story. Following Uriah's death, David brings Bathsheba into the palace and marries her. Their first child dies, but their second child, Solomon, gains the throne.

The Bible presents no examples of the stoning of an adulterous couple; to the contrary, the law code's requirements for conviction of a capital crime would make the prosecution of adultery difficult at best, unless the couple were remarkably careless. Deuteronomy states that "a person must not be put to death on the evidence of only one witness" (17:6b); "only on the evidence of two or three witnesses shall a charge be sustained" (19:15). These details are among the many that complicate the famous New Testament passage (John 8:1–11) concerning the "woman taken in adultery," which says, "Let anyone among you who is without sin be the first to throw a stone at her" (8:7). No witnesses appear, and the woman's lover is absent as well. Had stoning been the standard procedure in the first century, the question the "scribes and Pharisees" ask Jesus, "Now in the law Moses commanded us to stone such women. Now what do you say?" (8:5) never would have been asked.

Should a husband nevertheless suspect his wife, the law code does offer him an option. Numbers 5:11–31 explains that a man can bring his wife to the priest to have a test administered in which she drinks the "water of bitterness," which we discuss in Chapter 4. As appalling as the law is, it may never have been put into practice. It requires a man to admit that he believes his wife to have been unfaithful, and this would put him in the humiliating position of having been cuckolded.

Abortion

Reference to the "water of bitterness" test brings up the topic of abortion. Like the subject of homosexuality, abortion receives far more attention by people who read the Bible than by the Bible itself. The bottom line is that the Bible does not talk about abortion in the sense of legislating whether or not a pregnancy can be legally terminated.

This lack of legislation is striking, since other ancient Southwest Asian cultures do weigh in on this question. According to Middle Assyrian law, women who attempt to abort will be impaled, and their bodies will be denied an honorable burial. Other codes come closer to the Bible's interest, which is in the recompense due in cases of an injury to the fetus. The famous Code of Hammurabi states that if a member of the elite class strikes another elite male's daughter and she miscarries, the assailant must pay the woman's father ten silver shekels. If the daughter dies, the assailant's daughter is to be put to death. For people of lesser status, the compensation is decreased. In this scenario, the fetus is not regarded as having the same worth as a "life." In Hittite legislation, the fine for causing a woman to miscarry because of a blow increases as the pregnancy comes closer to term.

It is in this context that Exodus 21:22–25 best fits: "When people who are fighting injure a pregnant woman so that there is a miscarriage, and yet no harm follows [i.e., the woman does not die], the one responsible shall be fined what the woman's husband demands, paying as much as the judges determine. If any harm follows, then you shall give life for life, eye for eye, tooth for tooth. . . ." Thus the *lex talionis* applies only if the mother dies. On the question of whether the fetus is alive, the texts about the pregnant woman hurt in a brawl indicate that the answer is no.

When this Hebrew text is translated in the Septuagint, the legislation shifts: "If two men fight and they strike a woman who is pregnant, and her child comes out while not yet fully formed, he will be forced to pay a fine; whatever the woman's husband imposes, he will pay with a valuation. But if it is fully formed, he will give life for life, eye for eye, tooth for tooth. . . ." Philo, the first-century Jewish philosopher, agreed with the Greek text (it is not known if Philo could read Hebrew). The Mishnah (*Niddah* 5:3) follows the Hebrew: it does not regard the fetus as a "person" until it is born (i.e., the head emerges).

Since the law code is unclear on abortion, proponents of the pro-life view will often cite texts that speak of the fetus as of value, even as commissioned by God. For example, Psalm 139:13 states, "For it was you who formed my inward parts; you knit me together in my mother's womb." Since the fetus is fashioned by God, just as was the original *adam*, it should, in this reading, be seen as sacred. The same Psalm also speaks of the divine eyes beholding the "unformed substance" (Heb. *golem*, 139:16), embryonic matter. Jeremiah proclaims a prenatal commission: "The word of YHWH came to me saying, 'Before I formed you in the womb I knew you, and before you were born I consecrated you; I appointed you a prophet to the nations'" (1:5). Therefore, some pro-life advocates argue that to abort a fetus is to abort the plans God had for that fetus.

The pro-choice argument, when it does cite the Bible, is more apt to state that the Bible offers no definitive legislation regarding abortion and that metaphors should not be used as legal arguments. A few will note that "life" begins with the first breath, as Genesis 2:7 indicates: "Then YHWH Elohim formed the *adam* from the dust of the ground, and breathed into his nostrils the breath of life; and the *adam* became a living being."

Sexual Abuse

Biblical Hebrew has no word for "rape," but the Hebrew text does have laws that concern what today would be identified as rape as well as numerous accounts of women forced into sexual relations. Deuteronomy 22:23–29 (see Chapter 4) states that if a man forces a married or engaged woman (i.e., a woman who is sexually available only to her husband or fiancé) into intercourse in the open country, then only he is to be punished. The law presupposes that the woman would have cried for help, but given the setting, no help was available. However, if the act occurs in a town, then both are to be stoned to death—on the assumption that the woman could have cried for help if she had wanted (an assumption that may not be warranted).

Further, if a man is caught having had intercourse with a virgin who is not betrothed, he is to pay the woman's father fifty shekels of silver, and he and the woman are to be married, with no possibility of divorce. On the one hand, the law condemns a woman to be married to her rapist. On the other, the law may have aided couples in cases where the woman's father refused to sanction the relationship.

Bathsheba may have gone to David willingly; David's concubines, raped by Absalom, did not. The pathos of their lives is marked by the notice in 2 Samuel 20:3 that, after Absalom's death, when David returned to Jerusalem, he "took the ten concubines whom he had left to look after the house, and put them in a house under guard, and provided for them, but did not go in to them. So they were shut up until the day of their death, living as if in widowhood."

In the three major incidents—the attack upon Jacob's daughter Dinah (Gen. 34), the gang rape of the Levite's concubine (Judg. 19–20), and the rape of David's daughter Tamar (2 Sam. 13)—the stories express both the horror of the crime and the difficulty of finding a just response to it. The story of the attack upon Dinah raises numerous concerns regarding sexuality, politics, and justice. In Chapter 9, we briefly noted this story in relation to exogamy; here we focus on its depiction of sexuality.

The account begins when "Dinah, the daughter of Leah" goes out "to visit the women of the region" (Gen. 34:1). This anomalous, female-only setting, to be repeated only in the book of Ruth, breaks down immediately. Shechem, the prince of the region, sees her, "seizes her," and "lays with her by force." However, rather than present the prince as a sociopathic monster, the next verse shifts perspective: "His soul was drawn to Dinah; . . . he loved the girl, and spoke tenderly to her" (34:3). He seeks to wed Dinah, and his father agrees that an alliance with Jacob would be profitable.

Jacob, although aware that his daughter had been "defiled" (34:5), refrains from taking any action until he can consult with his sons. From his perspective, an alliance might have been the better course of action than an attack on Shechem, and the possibility that Dinah could have a life with the prince might have seemed a better option than having her remain single. The brothers disagree. They are furious that Shechem "committed an outrage," although whether their anger stems from concern for their sister, their own personal loss of honor, or a combination is not detailed. The brothers deceitfully agree to the planned intermarriages between the Shechemites and Israelites, on the condition that the Shechemite men all submit to circumcision.

"On the third day, when they were still in pain," the Shechemites are massacred by Dinah's brothers Simeon and Levi. As Dinah had been sexually attacked, so the brothers had wounded their targets through circumcision before killing them. The other sons of Jacob then pillage the city and bring back to their camp not only their sister, but also "all [the Shechemites'] wealth, all their little ones and their wives, all that was in the houses" (34:29). The wives and female children will likely be taken as wives or concubines and thus forced into intimacy with the men who killed their fathers, husbands, brothers, and sons. One attack leads to more death and to more rape. Jacob curses Simeon and Levi for bringing trouble upon him; he will now have to relocate, lest others seek revenge for the Shechemites. On the road, his beloved Rachel dies in childbirth. Yet the brothers end the story with the question, "Should our sister be treated like a whore?" (34:31). Revenge is no solution, since it leads to more violence, but the question of justice remains. Dinah, whose name means "judgment," is silent. The last the text records of her, she went down to Egypt with Jacob and his family.

In the story of the Levite's concubine, the justice sought by the Levite leads to a similar massacre, but on a larger scale. The tribe of Benjamin is almost wiped out, and to repopulate it will require the capture of innocent women. That such women are needed indicates that, in the war between the tribes, the women of Benjamin were killed.

Second Samuel 13 repeats the scene of Dinah and Shechem, this time with David's son and daughter. Amnon, the crown prince, announces, "I love Tamar, my brother Absalom's sister" (13:4); he arranges to get Tamar alone in his bedchamber, rapes her despite her pleas that he marry her with David's consent, and then hates her with a "loathing even greater than the lust he had felt for her" (13:15). For Shechem, the rape preceded the love; for Amnon, the rape killed it. Yet Tamar pleads with her brother not to send her away, as that would be worse, she says, than what he has already done to her (13:16). Amnon, refusing to listen, has Tamar removed from his chamber and bolts the door after her. Reading Genesis 34 in light of 2 Samuel 13, one could conclude that, for royal women, marriage to a rapist was preferable to being shut up in the palace.

Like Jacob, David refuses to take action. His rationale is not self-protection from the local populations; rather, "he would not punish his son Amnon, because he loved him, for he was his firstborn" (2 Sam. 13:21). Like Simeon and Levi, Tamar's brother Absalom does take revenge. Not only does he kill his brother and rival Amnon; he begins his plans for civil war.

The rapes serve as metaphors for the state of the community. Dinah's attack shows the breakdown between Jacob and his sons, and so it anticipates the further dissension in the family over the role of Joseph. The Levite's concubine symbolizes the twelve tribes, hacked into pieces and unable to find peace. Thus she represents, according to the book of Judges, the need for a king, for without a centralized leadership, "every man did what was right in his own eyes" (Judg. 21:25). Tamar's rape, which leads to civil war, shows the corruption within the Davidic household.

These stories of rape, incest, and abuse refuse to silence what "polite society" would prefer to ignore. The self-critical aspect of the text recognizes that abuse occurs not only "to them" but also "by us"; the moral aspect indicates that violence is no solution to a crime of violence, and at the same time it recognizes the suffering of the victims.

The possible rape of male victims is precluded in both Genesis 19, the story of Sodom, and Judges 19, the account of the Levite's concubine. Lot's daughters can be regarded as raping their father, although the story can be, and has been, read as a Freudian screen to protect fathers who commit incest by blaming the action on the daughters.

Innuendo

Judges 4–5 depicts the story of Deborah, a female judge who, with the aid of her general, Barak, routs the army of King Jabin of Hazor and its leader, Sisera. When Deborah summons Barak, he refuses to enter the battle unless she accompanies him. His response could be seen as a good tactical move. He is not going to risk his life unless the judge provides some surety of success. Or it could be seen as a mark of cowardice. Deborah agrees, but advises that YHWH "will sell Sisera into the hand of a woman" (4:9). The Israelite general is thus outmanned by a female judge and a yet unnamed female accomplice.

The accomplice turns out to be Jael, the wife of a Kenite who had broken his trust with Israel and gone over to the Canaanite side. Sisera, routed in battle, on foot, and seeking shelter, arrives at Jael's tent. Her husband, Heber, is nowhere to be found. Jael, like the spider to the fly, greets the general: "Turn aside, my lord, turn aside to me; have no fear" (4:18). She covers him with a rug and gives him some milk. The general, before nodding off, advises her: "Stand at the entrance of the tent, and if anyone comes and asks you, 'Is there a man here?' say 'No'" (4:20). Indeed, there is no "man" in the tent, for the general has given up the role.

When Sisera nods off, "Jael wife of Heber took a tent peg, and took a hammer in her hand, and went softly to him and drove the peg into his temple, until it went down into the ground—he was lying fast asleep from weariness—and he died" (4:21). She then exits the tent to welcome Barak—he too is unmanned by her action, for she, not he, had killed the general. One wonders about the missing Heber.

The Song of Deborah, preserved in Judges 5, retells the story, but here Jael dispatches Sisera while he is still standing, and the text recounts his detumescence: "She struck Sisera a blow, she crushed his head, she shattered and pierced his temple. He sank, he fell, he lay still at her feet; . . .

there he fell dead" (5:26–27) The song ends with an image of Sisera's mother, behind the lattice, awaiting her son's return. When she worries about his delay, she reassures herself: "Are they not finding and dividing the spoil?—A girl or two for every man . . ." (5:30a). The Hebrew reads, literally, "A womb or two for every man." The NRSV, bowdlerizing the text, offers, "a girl or two"; similarly, the JPS translates: "a damsel or two." The image is one of sexual spoil, but it is made doubly perverse by having it placed on the lips of a mother, and the irony exacerbated is in one more iteration, since the poem is itself spoken by a woman, Deborah, a "mother in Israel" (5:7).

The book of Judith, from the deuterocanonical collection, retells this story with Judith serving in the position of both Deborah and Jael. Like Deborah, she is a leader of her people, and she celebrates her victory in song. Like Jael, she dispatches the enemy general, Holofernes, with his own sword no less, as he lies dead drunk in his tent. As Deborah had promised Barak that the general would be delivered into the hand of a woman, so Judith prays, "Crush their arrogance by the hand of a woman" (9:10b).

This Greek text does more than recapitulate the accounts of Judges 4–5; it also provides one answer to the question asked at the end of Genesis 34: "Should our sister be treated as a whore?" Judith offers the following response in her prayer:

> O Lord God of my ancestor Simeon, to whom you gave a
> sword to take revenge on those strangers who had torn off
> a virgin's clothing to defile her, and exposed her thighs to
> put her to shame, and polluted her womb to disgrace her;
> for you said, "It shall not be done"—yet they did it; so you
> gave up their rulers to be killed, and their bed, which was
> ashamed of the deceit they had practiced, was stained with
> blood, and you struck down slaves along with princes, and
> princes on their thrones. You gave up their wives for booty
> and their daughters to captivity, and all their booty to be
> divided among your beloved children who burned with
> zeal for you and abhorred the pollution of their blood and
> called on you for help. O God, my God, hear me also, a
> widow. (9:2–4)

Thus the story of Judith retells the story of Dinah's attack, and it repeats the story of Jael and Deborah.

The Bible's treatment of "sexuality" broadly defined is complex, open to multiple interpretations, sometimes inconsistent, and not always definitive. It is nevertheless a topic that interests not only historians, but members of Jewish and Christian communities today who seek to live according to scriptural teachings. The church interprets the Old Testament's sexual laws through the New Testament and, for some communions, later church tradition. The synagogue reads these materials in light of rabbinic teachings and then through its understanding of those teachings. Different churches and synagogues thereby interpret these texts in different ways.

The question of the Bible and sexuality remains as vital today. The wide range of responses, both within the Bible and during its reception history, underscores both the complexity of the issues and their impact on human lives.

Chapter 11

Politics and the Economy

The extent to which a country's government should play a role in shaping or limiting the choices, freedoms, and protections of its citizens is a hotly contested issue today, yet it is by no means new. In a democracy the citizens expect the government to be responsive to their needs and wishes. The political system of ancient Israel was no democracy, and a substantial division existed between the rulers and the ruled, between the powerful and wealthy few and the vast majority living at or near a subsistence level. We know from our own situation that stark inequalities in power and privilege can easily provoke ill will and even hostility until the disparities are ameliorated, and ancient Israel had its own parallels to our antagonisms and antipathies, even despite the differences in government. The biblical literature reveals various and sometimes conflicting expectations of those in power.

Politics and economics course through the biblical literature, just as they do through society. Some texts affirm political hierarchies and economic benefits, while other biblical passages focus on denouncing as wicked those who oppress and exploit. Even for individuals who aim to improve the lot of others, proper morality and religious faithfulness do not guarantee positive outcomes, as the books of Job and Qohelet (Ecclesiastes) are quick to point out. The Hebrew Bible thus contains a mixed message about wealth and power, interpreting them in places as blessings for faithfulness, but in other texts as indications of wrongdoing. To understand the reasons for these differences in the biblical materials, we need to incorporate social analysis, watching for indications of how power and wealth became established and then how they benefited or exacerbated the situation of those who were disadvantaged and powerless.

Politics and economics do not occur in a vacuum but attach to specific structures and institutions in society. In ancient Israel, six social constellations stand out, three at the local and three at the central or national level. The three in the local context—the *household*, the *clan*, and the *tribe*—represented fundamental social organizations that lasted throughout most of biblical history, even as they adjusted to changes from the outside. The three at the central or national level—the *city*, the *state*, and the *empire*—were more short-lived, being less flexible in accommodating change. For example, a city may be well fortified and comfortably inhabited, but an incoming army can devastate it to the point that no two stones remain in place; however, the surviving inhabitants can reorganize themselves into the traditional structures of households and perhaps also clans and tribes, redeveloping their own internal arrangements of power and resources.

Chapter 1 takes a chronological look at developments in politics and economics from the earliest point in Israel's history to the Hellenistic period. In this chapter we consider these topics more on a horizontal plane, viewing economic and political structures and issues that cut across the breadth of Israelite society. According to modern political and economic thought, every social entity, from the household to the empire, has a political and an economic dimension, and all such entities tend to be interconnected. For this reason, a discussion of politics and economics needs to include all six social constellations in Israel, from the three overarching settings with direct national and international significance, to the local settings of household, clan, and tribe. Chapter 13 will focus on the intense criticism that politics and the economy receive at the hands of the biblical prophets and historians.

The Nation-State

An enormous amount of the biblical literature—most of the books of 1 and 2 Samuel, all of 1 and 2 Kings, most of 1 and 2 Chronicles, and much in the prophetic books—deals explicitly with the monarchy and its effects on the populace, and much of the rest of the Hebrew Bible, including the Pentateuch, indirectly reflects conditions and powers under the state. Hierarchies, oppressive means, and exploitation existed in the society and economy prior to the onset of the kingdom, but the centralized state introduced new structures of control with extraordinary reach and impact. How the general population regarded the monarchy and the upper class cannot be fully known, yet some of their sentiments seem to come through various biblical stories.

The book of Judges describes happenings during the prestate period, well before Saul becomes king. According to one story, Gideon's son Abimelech aspires to the kingship of what may have been a city-state at Shechem. He kills his seventy brothers so they would not contend for the throne; only the youngest brother, Jotham, survives. Jotham then addresses the people with a parable: The trees once sought a king. They first approached the olive tree, which declined because it produced oil that honors gods and humans. Next they went to the fig tree, which preferred the sweetness of its fruit to political power. Then they asked the vine to rule over them, but the vine took more pleasure in producing the wine that delights gods and people. So finally they approached the bramble, and it responded: "If in good faith you are anointing me king over you, then come and take refuge in my shade; but if not, let fire come out of the bramble and devour the cedars of Lebanon" (9:15).

The authors of the parable clearly did not hold kingship in high esteem. Their narrative recounts that Abimelech is crowned king and rules for three years, at which point his kingdom begins to fall apart. In the end a woman throws a millstone from a tower he is besieging and strikes a mortal blow to his head; he orders his armor bearer to kill him so it cannot be said that a woman killed him. With him also dies the monarchy until the time of Saul, David, and Solomon. The book of Judges describes the prestate period as the time when "there was no king in Israel; all the people did what was right in their own eyes" (17:6; 21:25)—not necessarily an anarchy, since many controls operate at the local levels, but certainly an absence of the royal controls of later times. Some incipient form of alliance among tribes may have existed in this early period, but without the trappings and power of a monarchy.

The books of 1–2 Samuel, 1–2 Kings, and 1–2 Chronicles tell the story of the Israelite monarchy. As indicated in Chapter 1 above, most of the details cannot be verified in contemporaneous records from nonbiblical sources. The colorful stories of the feats and failings of the forty-one kings and one queen reported in the Hebrew Bible largely stand on their own, without external corroboration. Yet even if they may be less than factual in the actions they describe, they reveal the sentiments circulating in the country, some supportive and others critical of the monarchic state's political and economic impact. In particular, each of the first three sovereigns, Saul, David, and Solomon, has an auspicious beginning in line with pro-monarchic visions, but the latter parts of their reigns show the reality of antimonarchic sentiments.

King Saul is a king without capital city, palace, or governmental administration. He musters an army of unbelievable size (370,000, according to 1 Sam. 11:8; 210,000, according to 15:4) and at first succeeds in several battles against the neighboring Ammonites, Philistines, Amalekites, Moabites, Edomites, and others (1 Sam. 11–14). But the Deuteronomistic narrative also attributes to him several grievous mistakes. He violates cultic protocol by offering a sacrifice himself rather than letting the prophet Samuel do it for him, for which Samuel declares that he will not have a dynasty after his death (10:8; 13:1–15). Soon thereafter, Saul makes the intemperate oath that almost brings about the death of his son Jonathan (14:24–46). Against the divine command delivered by Samuel he spares the life of the Amalekite king (15:1–35).

Samuel anoints David to be Saul's successor even though Saul's son Jonathan, presumed to follow him on the throne, is still alive (1 Sam. 16:1–13). From this point forward the portrait of Saul as a tragic figure becomes increasingly distinct. David bails Saul out of a crisis with the Philistines by killing their hero, the giant Goliath (1 Sam. 17). The people herald David as their deliverer, for which he becomes a target and near victim of Saul's wrath (18:10–16 and throughout the following chapters).

After Samuel's death Saul consults a medium and conjures up Samuel's spirit (Heb. *elohim*, "a god," 1 Sam. 28:13) much to its displeasure. Saul had previously "expelled the mediums and the wizards from the land" (28:3), so this act of seeking out a medium indicates his desperation and estrangement from the normal priestly means of receiving an oracle from God. It also shows that Saul's command had been ineffective: his soldiers readily locate a medium, despite the order of expulsion. In the end, Saul takes his own life on the battlefield, along with his armor bearer—two of only five suicides reported in the whole Hebrew Bible (31:3–6; for the other three, see Judg. 16:30; 2 Sam. 17:23; 1 Kings 16:18—none of them described as a "sin"). Despite his exploits and devotion to YHWH, Saul's leadership unravels in the Deuteronomists' account, demonstrating succinctly the political realities of a monarchy—political machinations, vagaries of the army, erratic behavior possible by a king, and the consequences all such behavior can have for the subjects.

When David succeeds the failed king Saul, he is already on his way to becoming the greatest, most revered king in Israel's history, and the Deuteronomistic narrative helps to explain the high esteem he enjoys in other parts of the Bible. He begins a dynasty that continues without interruption from his traditional dating in the tenth century BCE until the fall of Jerusalem in 586. During the early Persian period Zerubbabel, also in David's line, is appointed by the Persians to serve as governor, and much later the messianic king is crafted in David's image. The biblical account is filled with stories, many of them positive. David shepherds, sings, plays the lyre, and slays bears and lions with his bare hands. In one-on-one combat he defeats the Philistine giant Goliath with just a sling and a stone (1 Sam. 17). For this act, he acquires rock-star adoration as the women dance and sing of him: "Saul has killed his thousands, and David his ten thousands" (1 Sam. 18:7).

He and Saul's son Jonathan become intimate friends (1 Sam. 18–20; 2 Sam. 1), and David marries Saul's daughter Michal. Saul tries to hunt down and kill David so he will not succeed him on the throne, but David eludes capture and twice even refrains from killing Saul when he has the opportunity (1 Sam. 24; 26). After Saul's death and David has become king, he shrewdly establishes his capital in the old Jebusite city-state, Jerusalem, positioned near the border between the north and the south (2 Sam. 5:6–10). Even in the face of the contenders to his throne and the battles he must wage, David receives from God an unconditional promise of a dynasty without end: "When your days are fulfilled and you lie down with your ancestors, I will raise up your offspring after you, who shall come forth from your body, and I will establish his kingdom. . . . Your house and your kingdom shall be made sure forever before me; your throne shall be established forever" (2 Sam. 7:12, 16). Although this approbation probably stems from the Deuteronomists closer to the time of the exile, a stronger legitimation of his reign and his dynasty is scarcely thinkable. And to confirm his support from God, David continues to win battle after battle.

Some negative, or at least questionable, details accompany David as well. His followers include "corrupt and worthless fellows" (1 Sam. 30:22). He uses plunder to bribe elders around Judah to gain their support (30:26–31). He amasses wives in strategic places (18:27; 25:39–44; 2 Sam. 3:2–5; 5:13). After David has become well established as king, the Deuteronomists' critical report picks up, producing a sad string of misfortunes often, but not always, of David's own doing. A long strife between Saul's backers and David's supporters results in considerable bloodshed (2 Sam. 2–4). In a move that clears the way of possible contenders to the throne, he allows the Gibeonites to avenge themselves on Saul's family by impaling seven of Saul's sons and grandsons (21:1–14). David has a falling out with his wife Michal, Saul's daughter, who disapproves of his dancing scantily clad (perhaps nude; the text states he is wearing a "linen ephod," a cultic garment) before YHWH and the people (6:14–23). The dance is ritualistic in nature, not entertainment. With no clear explanation, God denies him his wish to build a temple (7:1–17); 1 Chronicles 28:3 states that all of his warring and bloodletting have made him unsuitable for the task.

David's kingship begins to unravel in the long prose section known as the Succession Narrative (2 Sam. 9–20; 1 Kings 1–2). His adultery with Bathsheba and manipulated murder of her husband, Uriah, are consistent with the powers that monarchs in ancient Southwest Asia could exercise, but David receives a resounding condemnation by God in the prophet Nathan's parable about the rich man and the poor man. And the child born to Bathsheba dies (2 Sam. 11–12). Further disarray within his family follows as his oldest son, Amnon, rapes his half sister and David's daughter Tamar and afterward turns on her with loathing. Upon hearing of the rape, David does nothing because Amnon was his firstborn (13:15, 21). Absalom, another son and Tamar's brother, kills Amnon in revenge, and later Absalom usurps the throne, forcing David to flee the capital. In an action laden with symbolism, Absalom has intercourse with his father's ten concubines "in the sight of all Israel," publicly claiming David's royal power (16:20–22). Absalom's death comes in striking contrast to his aspirations: he is riding his mule under an oak tree when his heavy shock of hair (alluded to in 14:26) gets caught in the branches, leaving him dangling in the air, where David's army commander, Joab, finds and kills him (18:9–15). Further revolts and bloodshed mark David's later years (2 Sam. 20–21).

One of David's final acts is to take a census of the people. According to 2 Samuel 24, YHWH is angry at the Israelites, although the reason is not clear in this text, and incites David to make the count. Such a census normally serves the purpose of military conscription or taxation. After the census is completed, YHWH prepares to punish by giving David a choice of three consequences, two against his people and one against David: three years of famine in the land; three months being chased by his enemies; or three days of pestilence in the land. When David chooses to avoid his own suffering (the second option), YHWH sends a pestilence that strikes down seventy thousand Israelites (2 Sam. 24), but then stops the angel of destruction from entering the city of Jerusalem. David offers a sacrifice and diverts the plague from spreading farther, but the whole episode casts a sad light on the last stages of his kingship.

At the end we find the great king David old and cold, in need of another body to keep him warm in bed. A search of the kingdom turns up the young Abishag, "very beautiful . . . but the king did not know her sexually" (1 Kings 1:4). It is a poignant closing to a chapter in monarchic history in which the king amasses royal power, establishes a central government, and wages wars successfully. Unlike Saul's rule, David's is not a failed kingship, and yet this exemplary king's reign was extremely troubled. Power maneuvers and internal conspiracies were normal among neighboring kingdoms, but they do not make for a satisfying reign. The stories of this exemplary king are fascinating, but they also become dispiriting as David abuses power and squanders his initial promise by taking ill advantage of his charisma and position. He does not even function well as a father.

For the Deuteronomists, David, like Saul, has personal and political accomplishments as well as personal and political failings. Saul becomes irrationally jealous and full of rage, while David's lust leads to raw abuse of power. Both seem humble at the outset but become prideful and obstinate by the end. Yet as leaders they do not violate the Deuteronomists' two negative criteria—worship of other gods and oppression of the people. Thus David can become the ideal king that later monarchs should emulate. With David's son and successor, Solomon, however, oppression moves to center stage, and apostasy emerges from the wings.

David's son Solomon takes the throne with power and bloodshed, eliminating possible contention and insurrection (1 Kings 2:13–46). He is excessively pious, offering one thousand sacrifices at a time on the altar (3:3–4). When God invites him to name whatever he most wants, he piously asks for "an understanding mind to govern your people, able to discern between good and evil" (3:9). Impressed with this response, God promises him everything—wisdom, riches, honor, fame, and a long life (3:10–14). Solomon immediately demonstrates shrewdness with his "Solomonic judgment"—adjudicating the difficult controversy between two women who each claim the same baby (3:16–28).

Solomon's reign appears to be idyllic. His subjects in Judah and Israel are "as numerous as the sand by the sea; they ate and drank and were happy" (1 Kings 4:20); the promise of countless citizens recalls God's pledge to Abraham (Gen. 22:17), while the happy eaters are the exact opposite of the wilderness generation under Moses. The food consumption of the royal court is staggering: for one day "thirty cors [about 14 bushels each] of choice flour, and sixty cors of meal, ten fat oxen, and twenty pasture-fed cattle, one hundred sheep, besides deer, gazelles, roebucks, and fatted fowl" (1 Kings 4:22). He also has forty thousand stalls of horses. The biblical narrative reports—though again we cannot verify any of it—that Solomon expands the kingdom's territory to the Euphrates River in the northeast and to Egypt in the southwest, builds a thriving commercial fleet of ships and a trade network, constructs a palace and temple, and generally establishes a wealthy and influential kingdom in the region. According to 1 Kings 6:37–7:1, construction of the temple took seven years while the palace took eleven—a subtle clue to Solomon's personal excesses for which he will, in the end, be criticized.

Solomon's wisdom becomes legendary: "His fame spread throughout all the surrounding nations. He composed three thousand proverbs, and his songs numbered a thousand and five," and he can converse about the plant and animal worlds (1 Kings 4:31b–33)—a shorthand message to glorify his wisdom and reputation. His renown spreads, and he receives visits from the queen of Sheba (location unknown, but perhaps on the Arabian peninsula) and other monarchs, all bearing lavish gifts (1 Kings 10). His harem embraces one thousand women, many the result of political marriages (11:1–3); for example, the Egyptian pharaoh gives his daughter to Solomon and throws in the Canaanite city of Gezer as her dowry (9:16). And Solomon fulfills David's dream: he builds a magnificent temple to YHWH in Jerusalem, appointed with all the fineries of the region (1 Kings 5–8).

The Hebrew Bible attributes to Solomon three developments essential to the power and operation of the central state. First, he organizes the country into twelve administrative districts, which vary substantially from Joshua's division into twelve tribal areas; it is an open question whether the government's districting or a traditional tribal structure came first historically. Solomon then appoints an official over each district to collect taxes from the people. In addition, he forms a cabinet of high officials: priests, secretaries, recorder, army commander, minister over the district officials, counselor ("king's friend"), manager of the palace (perhaps including all royal affairs), and superintendent of the forced labor (1 Kings 4:1–19). In comparison, David's cabinet was sparser, lacking the counselor, the palace manager, and the head of all the district officials as well as the district officials themselves (2 Sam. 8:15–18; 20:23–26).

The second development of considerable import for the security and expansion of the kingdom is the military. Saul had gathered what appears to be a rather limited army around him (despite the implausible number of soldiers claimed in 1 Sam. 11:8 and 15:4). David began with a guerrilla band of some four hundred (1 Sam. 22:2) while he was on the run from Saul. As king, David increased his army to fight his many battles and slew tens of thousands of enemy. The number of 1,300,000 soldiers in Israel and Judah (2 Sam. 24:9) is inflated; on the basis of available evidence, archaeologists calculate a total population of only about a third of that number in the country during the height of the monarchic period in the eighth century. Solomon then develops a professional army built around not only foot soldiers, but chariotry (purportedly twelve thousand horses, fourteen hundred chariots, and twelve thousand horsemen) stationed around the country (1 Kings 4:26; 10:26). The military plays a key role in later monarchic history, and villagers feel the brunt of its buildup since they are routinely conscripted into the army.

Third, Solomon is associated with the development of one of the most onerous aspects of the monarchy—forced labor, also called the corvée or labor gangs. Palaces, temples, city walls, and roads did not build themselves, and the elites who benefited most from them did not carry out the actual construction. The king expected all subjects to serve the crown whenever ordered, just as the state could at will conscript able-bodied men into the army. Edifices from antiquity that impress us today with their beauty and size were constructed not by laborers earning a living wage and not only by slaves and war captives, but generally by peasants and farmers who were compelled to spend months away from their families and fields for state building projects and receive, at best, only enough food to survive. Israel did not have an extensive slave economy on the order of that in ancient Egypt and Greece; the "free" but usually impoverished population was recruited whenever Israel's kings decided to build.

David reportedly had a foreman over the forced labor (2 Sam. 20:24), but Solomon increases the corvée to an unprecedented extent to carry out his lavish, much-lauded building projects, especially the temple and palace. According to 1 Kings 5:13–15 (Tanakh 5:27–29), Solomon presses thirty thousand Israelites into forced labor to haul the cedar logs from

Lebanon, plus another seventy thousand to work with eighty thousand stonecutters in the hill country, plus thirty-three hundred supervisors. He also uses forced laborers to build cities, "Hazor, Megiddo, Gezer . . . as well as all of Solomon's storage cities, the cities for his chariots, the cities for his cavalry, and whatever Solomon desired to build, in Jerusalem, in Lebanon, and in all the land of his dominion" (9:15, 19). Named in Solomon's cabinet are Adoniram, in charge of the corvée, and thirteen other officials (twelve for Israel in the north and one for Judah in the south) to collect the taxes (4:1–19).

Corvée and taxation were commonplace in Southwest Asian monarchies, and 2 Samuel 20:24 indicates that David used forced labor as well. But the Deuteronomists blame Solomon for expanding it to such a degree, which fulfills Samuel's prediction that the kings will lay oppressive burdens on the people (discussed in more detail in Chapter 13). Eventually, this forced labor becomes the tipping point in the division of the kingdom into two separate states.

Ten chapters in 1 Kings (1–10) detail Solomon's wonders, and in one quick chapter (11) we see his undoing. It is blamed on his having taken seven hundred wives and three hundred concubines, many of them in political marriages with various peoples in the region: the Egyptians, Moabites, Ammonites, Edomites, Sidonians, and Hittites. The wives have brought with them their own religions, and according to 1 Kings 11:1–13 Solomon in his old age erects shrines and worships their gods Astarte, Milcom, Chemosh, and Molech. Deuteronomy 17:17 warns that the king "must not acquire many wives for himself, or else his heart will turn away." Solomon's apostasy, a harbinger of the practices of later kings such as Ahab and his Phoenician queen, Jezebel, becomes the grounds for YHWH to announce that the land will be split after his death and only the tribal area of Judah in the south will remain for David's dynasty (11:12–13, 26–40). The magnificence of Solomon's kingdom at its height stands in striking contrast to the dissension at its end (11:14–40). Solomon's death notice is terse: "Now the rest of the acts of Solomon . . . are they not written in the Book of the Acts of Solomon? The time that Solomon reigned in Jerusalem over all Israel was forty years. Solomon slept with his ancestors . . ." (11:41–43). David's reign also lasts forty years (1 Kings 2:10–12)—a conventional number to indicate a long period. The mention of the Book of the Acts of Solomon is one of several biblical references to nonbiblical sources that, if they ever existed, are no longer extant.

During the period of the divided kingdom, not much difference existed between the two states with regard to political and economic practices. Both were hierarchical in structure, with an administrative machine to match. Both tended toward dynastic succession, without much success in the northern kingdom. Both were centered in cities and used outlying royal cities and local administrative cities to manage internal affairs, as we will see shortly. Both relied on the religious establishment to give them the ideological legitimacy and divine blessing they coveted. Both used militaries for defense and domestic control. Both interacted with foreign states that were sometimes in greater and sometimes in lesser positions of power than they. Both sought alliances to improve or secure their geopolitical position. And both prided themselves in their construction projects.

In addition, both states were involved in land ownership for farming, raising livestock, and supplying themselves with other products. The bounty of produce envisioned in Deuteronomy 8:7–9 is impressive: "A land with flowing streams, with springs and underground waters welling up in valleys and hills, a land of wheat and barley, of vines and fig trees and pomegranates, a land of olive trees and honey. . . ." All of these crops and resources were indeed present in the land, but by no means in all locales. Most peasants were able to scratch only certain crops out of their parcels of land. The only groups who could realistically have enjoyed the full panoply of resources and produce were the wealthy and the powerful—those living in the cities, managing their estates and their laborers and slaves.

Some wealthy landowners may have lived closer to their estates than the nearest city would allow, as in the case of Nabal, owner of large herds of sheep and goats and resident of the town of Maon, near his property in Carmel, according to 1 Samuel 25. The royals and the elites were in a position to collude in ensuring sufficient supplies of desirable goods for themselves. Both the palace and the temple, each with substantial landholdings throughout the country, instituted a command economy, requiring tenant farmers and others producing food for the cities to specialize in certain types of crops and livestock, such as grains, grapes, olives, sheep, and goats, according to areas propitious for each crop or herd. An individual peasant family living in a village needed to diversify in order to guard against loss of a single crop, but a centralized state could order other strategies to produce dietary variety for those who could afford it. If the local peasants suffered as a result, so be it.

With more arable land, the northern state of Israel was considerably wealthier than its southern counterpart. The north also benefited from the major east–west trade route that ran through the Jezreel Valley, north of its capital. In addition, it was considerably more populous: some three hundred fifty thousand inhabited Israel compared with a hundred thousand in Judah during the eighth century BCE. With its wealth and size came more political power, all of which explains why the Neo-Assyrian empire chose to conquer the northern kingdom and obliterate its leadership structure, while merely forcing the southern kingdom into vassalage.

The Cities

Cities in ancient Israel served as the political and economic arms of the kingdoms, both in the north and in the south. Although Canaanite and Philistine city-states had existed prior to 1000 BCE in border regions and some interior areas of the country, urbanization among the Israelites did not begin until the Iron II Age. After the Neo-Babylonian conquest of Jerusalem and other major cities in the land, urban culture declined during the sixth century and was only gradually restored in the course of the next several centuries of first Neo-Babylonian and then Persian and Hellenistic imperial rule.

During Israel's monarchic period four main types of cities existed, the first three of which were the direct outcomes of the centralized government's needs for security and administration. The most powerful and most impressive were the two *capitals*, Samaria in the northern kingdom until its fall in 722 BCE and Jerusalem in the southern kingdom until 586 BCE. Both were fortified and well appointed with impressive buildings, monuments, and open ceremonial spaces. According to archaeologists' estimates, roughly 75 percent of the total walled-in area served governmental or religious purposes, and not much more than 25 percent was residential. During the eighth century BCE Samaria exceeded Jerusalem both in size (up to 150 acres compared to Jerusalem's 75 acres) and in population (some twelve thousand compared to six thousand). Jerusalem swelled to about thirteen thousand inhabitants in the seventh century BCE after refugees from the conquered northern kingdom fled to the south and took up residence in Jerusalem or just outside its walls.

The second type of urban settlement in the hierarchy of power is commonly called a *royal city*. Basically alternative royal centers, they possessed massive walls, monumental architecture, military headquarters, administrative buildings, a temple or other cultic installation, and a royal residence to accommodate the king when he traveled to the area. There were only a handful of them spaced strategically around the country—Hazor, Megiddo, and Dan in the north, Gezer and Lachish more in the center and south, and perhaps others not yet identified. Not many more than five hundred residents found their permanent homes here. One distinctive feature in several of the cities is the six-chambered city gate, constructed with three small rooms on either side of the entrance. The function of these rooms has long eluded satisfactory explanation, but a new proposal makes a convincing case that they served as hitching spaces for horse and chariot. These and other structures suggest that the royal cities were centrally planned, probably by urban architects operating out of the capital cities.

The third type of governmental settlement is the local *administrative city*. Probably several were established in each geographical region under the jurisdiction of the nearest royal city. Built according to urban plans, as were the capitals and royal cities, they served state interests in taxation, military conscription, recruiting labor for building projects, and general control of the population. Beersheva in the south is a prime example from the eighth century BCE. Only about 2.5 acres in size, it boasted a fortification wall, an orderly network of streets, a four-chambered city gate, plazas, several administrative buildings, grain silos, storehouses, an efficient water-collection system using most of the city's horizontal surfaces, and about seventy-five houses holding between three hundred and three hundred fifty residents. Although Beersheva figures into various ancestral and prophetic stories, it occurs most frequently in the Hebrew Bible in the formulaic phrase, "from Dan to Beersheva," to indicate the northernmost and southernmost reach of the country.

The last type of urban settlement is the *residential city*, which does not play as direct a governmental role as the others. The inhabitants were primarily agriculturalists or artisans producing pottery, textiles, and other basic objects. Storehouses, wine presses, and other such installations served the common needs of nearby villagers. The residential cities show little evidence of urban planning, and houses and paths appeared randomly as each settlement grew. Most were not fortified, and they held few if any public buildings. These cities, more plentiful than the other city types, tended to be 5–12 acres in size and to have a population of between three hundred and two thousand persons.

Thus through most of this period of the kings, the cities were remarkable in two respects. First, in population size they were very small, each with typically only five hundred to two thousand inhabitants. The two capital cities were larger, but only relatively so—not many more than thirteen thousand residents, a far cry from our modern cities with millions of inhabitants.

Second, the social makeup of the first three types of cities in ancient Israel varied sharply from the demographics of modern cities. Archaeologists have so far not been able to uncover enough of the residential areas to characterize the inhabitants in detail, but all indications suggest that the cities were not filled with middle class and urban poor. Rather, the urban dwellers were elite, well-to-do, and powerful—royalty, large landowners, wealthy merchants, administrative officials, military leaders, and central priests, along with the slaves who ensured their comfort. Jerusalem of the seventh century BCE, after the rather sudden arrival of northern refugees, probably had some poorer sections, but with that exception the pattern followed by the two capitals, the royal cities, and the administrative cities was to house mainly the political and economic power of the country. To use a modern analogy, the cities of ancient Israel were gated communities.

These urban enclaves also served as the bases for the primary institutions with substantial reach throughout the country—governmental agencies and administration, business interests, military headquarters, and the religious establishment. Here worked the bureaucrats, retainers, merchants, priests, scribes, slaves, and others. No middle class such as ours today existed in ancient Israel, which had basically a two-tiered society: the rich and powerful formed only 1–2 percent of the total population, and the masses of poor agrarians made up 80–95 percent, depending on the historical period. The remaining group of attendants, administrators, and service personnel, who enjoyed more comfort than did the peasants in the countryside, served at the pleasure of the elites and could lose their positions on a whim. Each urban population group associated mostly with others of their class—elites with elites, bureaucrats with bureaucrats, priests with priests. The stories in 1–2 Samuel and 1–2 Kings, showing little interaction with commoners by name, mainly follow the doings of the kings and the well-to-do or well-placed.

The move of power toward the urban centers is evident in Deuteronomy's theme of the centralization of the cult. Set in the wilderness before the people enter the land under Joshua, the text of Deuteronomy never mentions Jerusalem by name but refers repeatedly to "the place that

YHWH your God will choose" (e.g., Deut. 12:5), to which the people are to bring their sacrifices and gifts. The Israelites are also commanded to tear down all other cultic sites in the land, which King Josiah obediently attempts to do in his religious reform during the latter part of the seventh century BCE (Deut. 12:2–4; 2 Kings 23:1–25). With this move, the central priesthood, based in Jerusalem and supported by the monarchy, asserts control over all other cults, even though archaeological evidence points to the ongoing widespread distribution of cultic sites, paraphernalia, and presumably personnel in places other than Jerusalem alone.

The Empire and the Colony

The third political and economic setting is the empire. Ancient Israel was a tiny country buffeted by geopolitical forces it could scarcely repel. Armies came from all sides—Egyptians from the southwest, Neo-Assyrians and Neo-Babylonians from the northeast, Persians from the east, Greeks from the northwest, and Romans from the west. The little sliver of land that was Israel counted hardly as a destination spot for these forces, but more as a place en route. The Egyptians wanted to conquer Mesopotamia; the Mesopotamians and Persians wanted to control Egypt; the Greeks and Romans wanted it all; and Israel unluckily happened to be in the middle. A country of its size stood no chance against imperial armies. The hundreds of small villages, with no means of protection, could not resist any force that needed provisions, foot soldiers, or slaves. Fortified cities such as Megiddo, Lachish, and Jerusalem offered more of an obstacle to invading armies, but once an emperor determined to take them, they were doomed. Jerusalem, for example, managed to survive the Neo-Babylonian siege of 587–586 BCE for eighteen months, yet eventually its walls were breached and the city was obliterated for its resistance to the inevitable.

In the case of each empire Israel became a colony or province among many others. The extent of some of these empires is remarkable given that the armies traveled on foot or, for cavalry and officers, on horseback and by boat where they could. The Neo-Assyrian empire of the eighth and seventh centuries BCE, based in north-central Mesopotamia, stretched one thousand miles from the Persian Gulf to eastern Turkey and another thousand miles to southern Egypt. Two centuries later, the Persians, with their capital in modern-day Iran, managed to reach even farther, almost three thousand miles from the Indus River in the east to Greece in the west as well as Egypt and part of modern-day Libya in North Africa. Another two centuries later, Alexander the Great replicated this feat, in places extending its borders even farther. Again almost two centuries later, the Romans occupied most of this territory, plus Europe to the Iberian Peninsula in the west and England to the north as well as North Africa. In today's terms, their realm was comparable to the size of the forty-eight contiguous states in North America. In such a context Israel was a minuscule spot capable at most of becoming a minor irritant, as in the second and first centuries BCE when the Hasmoneans declared sovereignty from the Syrian Greeks.

As if they were competing with the accounts of these great empires, the biblical writers tell of expansive conquests by David and Solomon. David starts with a small militia and ends as the king of a nation-state. Not only does he claim the throne of Israel after Saul's death, but he also conquers Israel's perennial enemies on the other side of the Jordan River, the Moabites, the Edomites, and the Ammonites, as well as the Philistines along the Mediterranean coast, the Amalekites within the Israelite territories, and the Arameans north of Damascus (2 Sam. 8; 10). Solomon extends the kingdom, reaching all the way to the Euphrates River in the northeast and to the border with Egypt in the south (1 Kings 4:21; Tanakh 5:1). The Hebrew Bible even praises him with superlatives befitting a great emperor: "Thus King Solomon excelled all the kings of the earth in riches and in wisdom. The whole earth sought the presence of Solomon to hear his wisdom. . . . Every one of them brought a present, objects of silver and gold, garments, weaponry, spices, horses, and mules, so much year by year" (1 Kings 10:23–25). Such an image may have given the Israelites comfort during the long centuries when they were serving foreign masters, delivering to them their own tributes and fealty.

Leadership in the provinces depended entirely on the decisions made by whichever empire and emperor happened to be in power. After the fall of the north, for example, the Neo-Assyrian emperors kept the native Judahites Manasseh and Amon on the throne as puppet kings during the seventh century BCE. Second Kings 21 condemns both severely for worshiping other gods and, presumably, catering to the empire's wishes. In another instance, following the conquest of Jerusalem in 586 BCE the Neo-Babylonians moved the capital to nearby Mizpah in the Benjaminite territory and appointed Gedaliah, from Judah, as governor, but he was assassinated some four years later, according to Jeremiah 40–41. Governors were often not native to Judah; the Persian empire usually appointed a Persian to the position of satrap, the Persian term for governor of a province or satrapy.

The fate of the populace also lay in the hands of the emperor. Although the Neo-Assyrians tended to deport their captives and scatter them around their empire, the Neo-Babylonians moved theirs to discrete settlements in Babylonia and expected them to be productive there. In a politically expedient move, the Persians encouraged those already in exile to return to their home countries, sometimes with actual support to help them rebuild, as the books of Ezra and Nehemiah indicate.

The economic impact of empires on their colonies was as severe or even more severe than the political. Emperors instituted what is called a tributary economy, a system in which colonies were expected to send tribute to the imperial capital at whatever level demanded of them. According to 2 Kings 15:19–20, Menahem, king of Israel during the eighth century BCE, sent the Neo-Assyrian emperor Tiglath-pileser III (called King Pul in the biblical text) the sum of a thousand talents of silver, that is, approximately fifty tons (the precise weights are uncertain). The text adds: "Menahem exacted the money from Israel, that is, from all the wealthy, fifty shekels of silver from each one, to give to the king of Assyria," and these wealthy Israelites probably collected it from those under them. A later incident shows more explicitly how the burden was passed down to those at lower economic rungs. To raise one hundred talents of silver and a talent of gold, Jehoiakim, the king of Judah (end of the seventh century BCE), "taxed the land in order to meet Pharaoh's demand for money. He exacted the silver and the gold from the people of the land, from all according to the assessment, to give it to Pharaoh Neco" (2 Kings 23:35).

One-time demands could be less onerous than a recurring tribute expected every year or more often. Peasants working the land could barely survive in a subsistence economy, in which surpluses occurred seldom, if ever. To take from their meager produce for the benefit of a distant emperor or even for a homegrown tyrant resulted in extreme hardships. The prophets rail against those who "trample on the poor and take from them levies of grain" for their own benefit (Amos 5:11).

The Household

The empire occupies one end of the social and political spectrum in ancient Israel, and the family or household lies at the opposite end. Yet as different as they are from each other in size, both are saturated with power dynamics and economic concerns. They also intersect with each other, inasmuch as families are present at all levels of the empire and monarchy—from the ruler to the most remote of the ruled—and the actions of the government can affect the very survival and livelihood of all families. Both political and economic entities also figure prominently in the Hebrew Bible.

In both village and city the core social unit was the family. The story of Achan from the account of the conquest of the land under Joshua illustrates the layers of kinship, somewhat analogous to a *matryoshka,* a Russian nesting doll. According to Joshua 7, the Israelite troops attacked the city of Ai but were roundly defeated because some Israelite soldier had violated the holy war prohibition against taking booty from the enemy. In a process to identify the guilty party, Joshua first brings the people to YHWH tribe by tribe (*shevet*), and YHWH selects the tribe of Judah, perhaps by sacred lot. Then Joshua repeats the process clan by clan (*mishpachah*) within the tribe, and the clan of the Zerahites is indicated. The next stage is man by man (*gever,* apparently referring to the head of a household; JPS: "ancestral house"), and Zabdi is taken. The final selection process searches within Zabdi's household (*bet*) and settles on his grandson Achan, old enough to be a warrior and to have his own family. Joshua confronts Achan, who confesses to having taken the booty. The Israelites then stone and burn not only Achan but also his entire household—his children, livestock, tent, and belongings. In the biblical tradition, collective punishment is warranted here because of the close identification between a father and all under his authority.

The most common term in Hebrew for the entity lower than the clan is *bet av,* literally, "father's house." Only twice in the Hebrew Bible do we find *bet em,* "mother's house"—both spoken by a woman, once by Naomi (Ruth 1:8) and once by the female protagonist in the Song of Songs (3:4). Frequently the word "house" occurs alone but means household or family, not the physical building (e.g., Zabdi's "house," Josh. 7:18). There is not a single definition of "family" in the Hebrew Bible; three configurations stand out in the stories. Archaeologists, with the aid of ethnoarchaeologists, who compare ancient material remains with modern social traditions from the same or similar region, have contributed considerable information to complement the biblical picture of domestic settings in ancient Israel.

The *nuclear family* includes only the parents, their children, and any slaves they may have owned. In light of the size of houses and the uses made of the rooms, archaeologists have estimated that four or five persons per household typically resided in such homes. That figure seems plausible in light of other considerations: health and death. As detailed in Chapter 7, mortality rates, especially among infants, were extremely high, and the early death of family members due to childbirth, disease, and severe injuries affected the average size of the nuclear family.

The second configuration is the *extended family,* comprising the nuclear family along with other close relatives—elderly parents, unwed sisters or brothers of the main couple, and perhaps even a widowed sister, aunt, or uncle. Given the small size of most houses, the total rarely exceeded more than just a few beyond the nuclear family, perhaps only six or seven all together.

The *compound family,* or multiple-family household, is the third type, which is represented in the Achan story by the household of Zabdi. A three-generational household included the parents in a nuclear- or extended-family setup in one house and their married child or children living with their own children in an adjacent home. Another variation may involve two brothers who divided the land inherited from their parents and developed contiguous homes to house their families. Known as partible inheritance, this system of inheritance occurs in many cultures and can fit the archaeological evidence from Israelite sites. Although Deuteronomy's law of levirate marriage (25:5) does not necessarily depend on a compound-family arrangement, it does take this living situation as its point of departure.

Archaeologists have found houses that fit these types in both cities and villages—single-family dwellings, somewhat expanded homes with a second story providing extra space needed for relatives, and two houses clustered together, sometimes sharing a wall, a courtyard, and a cooking area. The familial narratives in Genesis depict all of these arrangements. Although Abraham and Sarah are wealthy enough to have needed several buildings or tents to house themselves and their slaves, the story in Genesis focuses on Abraham, his wife Sarah, and the slave/concubine/wife Hagar. The family expands with the birth of Ishmael to Hagar and the birth of Isaac to Sarah, and then contracts when Sarah presses Abraham to send Hagar and Ishmael away. It begins as a nice size for a nuclear family, but eventually increases along with their wealth and, after Sarah's death, the birth of six more children to Abraham's third wife, Keturah. Abraham's sole heir, Isaac, lives with his wife, Rebekah, and their twin sons, Esau and Jacob, as a nuclear family. Later Esau marries two women, and they apparently live in proximity to his parents since Genesis 26:35 states that Esau's two wives "made life bitter for Isaac and Rebekah." When Jacob takes up residence with his uncle Laban, Rebekah's brother, that household becomes an extended family until it turns into a multiple-family compound when Jacob marries Laban's two daughters and commences to produce twelve sons and an unspecified number of daughters (Gen. 37:35; 46:7) by his wives and their two slave women. Thus all three family configurations are evident in these stories, and they shift fluidly from one to the other as individuals are born, die, or leave.

The authority and power in family matters rested in the first instance with the parents, but the community also had an investment in the smooth running of local affairs and could intervene when needed. The term *paterfamilias*, Latin for the "father of a family," stems from law and tradition in ancient Rome according to which the father rules all family affairs without needing to share the decision-making process with others in his family. If a son is married and his family still lives with his parents, the son's father functions as the *paterfamilias* as long as he remains competent. Anthropologists have observed this institution of the powerful household head in a wide variety of cultures, and numerous biblical texts suggest that a similar status resided with fathers in ancient Israel as well.

For example, Noah is the family member with whom YHWH negotiates at the time of the flood. Abraham heads his family, has life-and-death power over his son Isaac, arranges his marriage, and decides that he will be his sole heir; Sarah exercises influence over her husband regarding Hagar and Ishmael, but Abraham makes the final decision. Isaac pronounces the final blessings on his son, although Rebekah deceives Isaac into blessing Jacob rather than Esau (Gen. 27:5–29). Rachel tricks her father, Laban, as she absconds with the household gods, and Laban explicitly states that he can punish his son-in-law Jacob and family who have been living in his household: "It is in my power to do you harm" (31:29). With no trial, Judah decrees that his daughter-in-law, Tamar, be burned to death for prostitution—until Tamar exposes him as the father of the twins she is carrying (38:24–26). Even in old age, Jacob determines to relocate his large household to Egypt (Gen. 46). Jacob's sons, but not his daughters, become the ancestors of the tribes of Israel. The decision of Korah, Dathan, and Abiram to rebel against Moses and Aaron leads to the execution not just of them but of their whole households (Num. 16). Joshua makes a commitment for his entire family: "But as for me and my household (*beti*), we will serve YHWH" (Josh. 24:15). Jephthah's oath leads to the death of his own daughter, his only child (Judg. 11:29–40).

Yet despite the power and authority residing with the male head of household, the mother's role was just as crucial for the survival of the family. In the hierarchy of family law and politics, the distance between parents and children was greater than the power differential between husband and wife. Both parents together are to bring a charge against a son who is "a glutton and a drunkard," shifting the responsibility for stoning him to the community (Deut. 21:18–21). One of the Ten Commandments explicitly states that children are to respect and attend to both parents: "Honor your father and your mother" (Exod. 20:12). Both father and mother must contribute fully to securing the family's sustenance, and each has specialized tasks in it, as do the children as soon as they are old enough to take on responsibilities.

In an ode to a skilled wife, Proverbs 31:10–31 praises the woman who is not just trusted by her husband and effective in raising their children, but who is proficient in conducting the affairs of the household—tirelessly procuring food and supplies, buying fields, weaving textiles and making clothes, providing for the poor, giving wise counsel to others, bringing prestige to the family. She receives fitting praise from her husband: "Many women have done excellently, but you surpass them all" (31:29).

The household formed the most fundamental and most ubiquitous economic entity in the country. Ancient Israel did not have a market economy, and coinage did not even appear in the country until the sixth century BCE under Persian rule. Families had to be self-sufficient in a situation that, for the vast majority, fluctuated between hard at best and dire at worst. Most of the people, between 80 and 95 percent of the whole population, clustered together in tiny villages and worked the land surrounding each. They continuously faced a subsistence economy and struggled to eke an existence out of the dirt and keep their livestock fed and healthy. Farming was labor-intensive, and the terrain and climate too often unforgiving. Surviving from harvest to harvest depended on a family's diversifying their efforts between small-time cultivation and animal husbandry. Strategizing seasonal crop rotations helped, so long as the weather cooperated. The crops raised most frequently—although the land everywhere was not conducive to all produce—included grains, grapes, lentils, cucumbers, melons, flax, spices, olives, dates, and figs. The small livestock were primarily sheep and goats. The most a family could hope for was a small plot of land, probably inherited, where they could raise their own food and perhaps some livestock. All too often they lost the land during hard times to large landowners; the palace and the temple were among the largest holders of property in the country. Without land of their own, peasants had to work as tenant farmers, hope for day labor, or sell their children or themselves into slavery (Exod. 21:7; Deut. 15:12; Lev. 25:39–46).

Although relatively few in number, the wealthy and privileged families possessed the means to have their land worked by tenant farmers, day laborers, and slaves, or their income from other sources allowed them to purchase their food as well as luxury items. Kings and emperors could command farmers to produce specific crops or livestock, which had an impact on the farmers' need to strategize for their own survival. Archaeologists have discovered an increase in pig bones during Hellenistic and Roman times, an example of a cultural shift in food preferences as the Greeks brought their taste for pork to the cities of the Levant and demanded that farmers satisfy them.

God's pronouncement to Adam before the expulsion from the luxuriant Garden of Eden poignantly describes the farmer's life: "Cursed is the ground because of you; in toil you shall eat of it all the days of your life; thorns and thistles it shall bring forth for you; and you shall eat the plants of the field. By the sweat of your face you shall eat bread until you return to the ground, for out of it you were taken; you are dust, and to dust you shall return" (Gen. 3:17b–19).

This description is quite a contrast to the image of the land "flowing with milk and honey." The general state of the peasants' life in ancient Israel can be termed brutish and short. Add to the natural obstacles the pressures exerted by human forces—military conscription, labor gangs for the king's building projects, exploitation by the elites, enslavement due to indebtedness, raids by marauding bands—and it is a wonder that the people living close to the land survived at all. The household structure provided them, however, with the most reliable means of support possible under these circumstances.

The Clan

Political and economic issues shift when we consider the next larger social group, the *mishpachah,* or clan, which is comprised of several related families. Although the word *mishpachah* in modern Hebrew and Yiddish is the general word for "family," in the Hebrew Bible it normally designates a kinship group embracing more than one household, as in the above story about Achan, who belongs to one of the households in the clan of the Zerahites. Unfortunately modern translations often vary in their renderings of *mishpachah*, sometimes using "clan," but in other places "family," "stock," or even "tribe." But then the word "family" in English usage can be just as flexible, ranging from a nuclear family to a larger, indistinct group of relatives and even nonrelatives.

A clan differs from a tribe insofar as the clan involves specific relations by blood or marriage that can be traced, whereas the tribe, a larger group comprising many clans, considers itself descended from some actual or imagined ancestor. Thus, for example, for an ancient Israelite male (wives usually live with their husband's clan), the household includes wife and children, his parents, his unmarried siblings, and possibly his brothers and their families. The clan, on the other hand, embraces also his father's brothers and their households, and probably even his grandfather's brothers and their households, thus also his second and even third cousins. We have no way of knowing where it ended, and different practices may well have existed around the country. Most members of a clan live close to each other, in the same small village or in nearby villages, while a tribe ranges over a wider territory. Both clan and tribe are greater than a single household.

In Judges 18:19 the tribe of Dan, in its migration to the northern part of the country, entices a priest serving the wealthy family of Micah to come along: "Is it better for you to be priest to the house(hold) (*bet*) of one person, or to be priest to a tribe (*shevet*) and clan (*mishpachah*) in Israel?" Since the Danites succeed in drawing the priest away from his patron, it seems that the answer to their question is that the clan and the tribe take precedence over a single household—or that the priest could not refuse their offer.

The pattern of leadership within Israelite clans cannot be known at this point. A single individual may have served as chief, perhaps by virtue of charisma or some other quality that gave that person more standing than others. More likely, though, the heads of the households within a given clan or within all the local clans deliberated together about matters of common concern. The elders described in biblical texts appear to be household heads, not leaders of clans. They convene as needed, whether the issue at stake is peculiar to one clan or crosses over clan lines. For example, Boaz corrals the elders as they exit the town en route to their fields in the morning, and they help to decide the transfer of the property and wife of one of their deceased kin (Ruth 4:1–12). The text states they are elders, not household heads; no clear definition of "elders" is present in the Bible, and we find no other set of leaders at the community level other than the heads of households. Frequently in the legal texts, as mentioned in Chapter 4, the elders—again presumably the household heads—serve as the judges of alleged violations, and they also carry out the punishments they decree. At an even wider level, elders instigate the decision to found the monarchy (1 Sam. 8:4).

A clan is not a tight economic unit such as a household, but linkages exist in three areas: inheritance, marriage, and redemption. An example of the first is the five daughters of Zelophehad, who bring to Moses, the priests, and the congregation (the story is set during the wilderness wanderings) the problem of inheritance when only daughters and no sons survive the father (Num. 27:1–11). YHWH instructs Moses to rule that the inheritance of a sonless father can indeed go to his daughters and only secondarily to someone else in the following order: his brothers, his paternal uncles, then his next nearest kin in the clan.

Then a few chapters later this decision is appealed by "the heads of the ancestral houses of the clan (*mishpachah*) of the descendants of Gilead son of Machir son of Manasseh, of the Josephite clans (*mishpechot* [plural])" (Num. 36:1). This second ruling specifies that, if no son survives, daughters can "marry whom they think best; only it must be into a clan (*mishpachah*) of their father's tribe that they are married, so that no inheritance of the Israelites shall be transferred from one tribe to another" (36:6–7). These household heads do not argue that the land must remain within the father's clan, as we might expect if they had stemmed from only that one clan, but rather within the father's tribe, which household heads from several clans would prefer. Conveniently, Zelophehad's brothers had enough sons of their own, and the five daughters married them, keeping the property within the clan.

Endogamy, discussed in Chapter 9, was probably the custom for most Israelites, even though not many stories depict it. Abraham sends his trusted slave to the family of his brother Nahor, some four hundred miles away near the Euphrates, to find a wife for Isaac (Gen. 24). Isaac's son Jacob retraces the slave's steps when he goes again to the same area and marries two daughters of his mother's brother. We have no idea how often long-distance marriages were arranged in this manner since only stories, not archaeological evidence, describe them. The cohesion expected within the clan made it the ideal context for finding marriage partners. It also ensured that inherited land remained within the clan or at least within the tribe. Although incest laws forbid marriage between a half brother and a half sister (Lev. 18:9, 11; 20:17; Deut. 27:22), that does not stop Abraham and Sarah (Gen. 20:12). Isaac's and Jacob's marriages to their first cousins are not considered among the incest prohibitions in the Pentateuch. Keeping the clan together is what matters for continuity and community.

Both kinship and economic issues lie at the heart of marriage and inheritance; they also form the basis for the practice of redemption, one of the key responsibilities of clan members according to the Hebrew Bible. If someone in a given clan becomes impoverished and needs to sell the ancestral property, the nearest relative in the clan is obligated to redeem it, that is, buy it back so it stays in the clan. The lengthy set of laws in Leviticus 25 covers numerous details. For example, special allowances are present in the jubilee-year law, which decrees that any ancestral land that had to be sold shall revert to the original clan in the jubilee year, which occurs every fifty years (25:8). Perhaps out of fairness to the person who buys the land from the owner in need, the law provides that the parties calculate the number of years between the redemption and the jubilee year and set the purchase price on a pro rata basis.

Next comes a puzzling codicil distinguishing between property in a city and property in a village (Lev. 25:29–31). If a person sells a house in a walled city, the house can be redeemed only within the first year, and thereafter it becomes the permanent possession of the purchaser and is not subject to the laws of the jubilee year. However, houses in unwalled villages are always eligible for redemption and jubilee return. We can only speculate on the reasoning behind this distinction. One possibility is that the cities are associated with Canaanite cities, and thus Israelite traditions of redemption and jubilee do not apply to them. Another interpretation sees the distinction as a class issue: the wealthy normally reside in the cities and would not tolerate such restrictive customs on themselves, whereas the poorer landowners in the villages benefit from the rights of redemption and jubilee return. Somewhat connected with the second reason, clans may not be commonplace in cities, the dwelling place of mainly the wealthy and the powerful, not of their poor relations, as discussed earlier.

The beneficiaries of the redemption custom may live mostly in the villages, while their redeemers are more likely found in the cities among other prosperous families.

Obligations to fellow clan members extend beyond property, according to Leviticus 25. When people become destitute, their kin are to lend what is needed and not take profit at their expense. If they become so impoverished that they must sell themselves into slavery, they are to be treated as hired laborers, not as slaves. If they are sold to a resident alien, then their kinfolk are to redeem them, with additional compensation prorated for the remaining years until the jubilee. Just as the adult children serve as the safety net for their aging parents, the clan—or at least its more well-off families—is expected to absorb the losses of its poorer members.

The Tribe

Although the Bible mentions tribes frequently, they are even harder to define than clans. Contemporary anthropologists have investigated the origin and nature of tribes, with various results. One notion, proposed in light of studies of some Native American tribes, is that a tribe comes into existence or reshapes its self-understanding mainly in response to a crisis, such as a political or environmental threat. Smaller groups, such as clans, find it expedient to coalesce to respond more effectively to the danger that they could not manage alone. Whether or not the Israelite tribes formed due to a crisis is hard to say, but we first meet them in the Hebrew Bible in conjunction with the people's sojourn in Egypt, their escape from slavery there, and then the conquest and settlement of Canaan—all crises of major proportion. The dangers seem to be overcome when Joshua assigns territory to each tribe (Josh. 13–21). Historically, though, the crises connected with forming a new identity and new social structure in a new setting only just began with the people's settlement of the land.

The tribes occupy a position in the social and political hierarchy above the households and clans and below the state. The most obvious characteristic of tribes is the territories with which they are traditionally associated, and these are far from equal in size. Judah and Manasseh occupy the largest areas, while Dan and Benjamin in the south and Zebulun and Issachar in the north have the smallest. The tribe of Dan relocates from the south to an area in the far north, and Simeon seems to disappear. Manasseh has the River Jordan running through it. Two and a half tribes are located east of the Jordan—Gad, Reuben, and half of Manasseh. Jerusalem is in Benjaminite territory. Ephraim and Judah become especially prominent; Ephraim often stands for the northern kingdom, Judah for the southern (e.g., Hos. 5:5).

Each of the twelve tribes bears the name of an eponymous ancestor, one of the sons of Jacob, except for the special adjustments involving Levi, Ephraim, and Manasseh. Joshua assigns to each a territory in Canaan—with one exception, the Levites, who are set aside for priestly duties and receive from Joshua not a territory but a total of forty-eight towns and surrounding lands scattered among the other tribes (Josh. 21). The Levites' special treatment leaves the twelfth territory unassigned, so Joshua compensates by allotting a territory to each of Joseph's two sons, Ephraim and Manasseh, rather than a single territory to Joseph alone. Genesis 48 provides an etiology for the unequal division between the two by recounting how Jacob, in blessing Joseph's two children shortly before his death, deliberately crosses his arms to place his right hand on Ephraim's head and his left on Manasseh's, indicating that the younger son's tribe (Ephraim's) will supersede the elder's (Manasseh's).

Genesis 49 continues with Jacob's lengthy blessing to his twelve sons, describing each in ways that suggest stereotypical notions about each tribe when the text was composed, probably during the monarchic period or later. Reuben is "unstable as water," Simeon and Levi are angry and violent, Judah will be prominent over others, Zebulun will be a haven for seafarers, Issachar will work like a donkey, Dan will strike like a snake, Gad will raid and be raided, Asher's food will be rich, Naphtali is like a doe set free, Joseph is strong and blessed, and Benjamin is like a ravenous wolf. In his final address to the people (Deut. 33), Moses again blesses the tribes with characterizations that are often quite different from Jacob's. Intriguingly, the tribe of Simeon is omitted in Moses's list. Assigned a space within the land of Judah, Simeon's tribe may over time have been absorbed into Judah's.

The book of Joshua outlines the borders of each, giving more details about the tribal boundaries in the south than those in the north; the discrepancy suggests that the authors lived in the south and did not know the topography of the north and east as well as they did their own region. The two and a half tribes living east of the Jordan have virtually no eastern borders, according to what is provided in the book of Joshua. In general, the boundaries of the territories are defined by topographical features—

rivers, mountains, valleys, or other distinctive markers. Bearing the name of Reuben's son, the "Stone of Bohan" (Josh. 15:6; 18:17) must have been an obvious landmark; in Hebrew *bohan* is similar to *bohen*, meaning "thumb" or "big toe," thus "Thumb Rock" or "Big Toe Rock." All villages and towns within each territory were likely counted as part of the tribe. How firm these regional identities remained is uncertain.

Tensions among the tribes are evident in several stories. One is based on the location of two and a half tribes (Reubenites, Gadites, and half of the Manassites) to the east of the Jordan River, while all the other nine and a half tribes (including the other half of the Manassites) live on the west side. These two and a half tribes are the only ones to which Moses himself assigns land (Num. 32)—on the strict provision that their men of fighting age join the other tribes first in conquering the land to the west. Joshua eventually apportions the western territories to the other tribes.

When the conquest is finished and Joshua directs the eastern warriors to return with all their booty to their homes on the other side of the Jordan, they stop en route at the Jordan and erect a massive altar. Alarmed, the westerners prepare to make war against the easterners. However, they first dispatch emissaries to charge the easterners with perfidy for having built the altar. The westerners think either that these two and a half tribes have built the altar to worship other gods or that they have contravened the command in Deuteronomy 12 against building any altars other than the central one (in Jerusalem). The easterners are appalled at this charge, calling three divine names twice in a row: "YHWH, God of gods! YHWH, God of gods!" (Josh. 22:22). Confronting the westerners, they say they built the altar as a memorial—to remind future generations of *western tribes* that they, the eastern tribes, belong as much to the followers of YHWH as do those west of the Jordan River. They intended the altar to be only a replica of YHWH's altar, not for actual sacrificial use but as a witness to future generations.

With that protestation the crisis is averted. Nonetheless, the easterners' concern that their contributions will be ignored is subtly confirmed. Throughout the book of Joshua the terms "Israel" and "Israelites" include all twelve tribes, but in this narrative in chapter 22 at least sixteen of the nineteen occurrences of "Israel" designate only those living west of the Jordan (the possible exceptions are in vv. 16, 18, 20). The easterners are excluded, just as they had feared when they built the altar to remind the westerners that they are all one community.

A second narrative of tribal tensions appears in Judges 12:1–6, a story that has resulted in a word now a part of English vocabulary. The Gileadite judge Jephthah leads the Gileadites, residents of the area overlapping parts of the two and a half tribes on the east side of the Jordan, in defeating the Ammonites. The Ephraimites, located directly to the west on the other side of the Jordan, confront Jephthah and threaten him because he did not recruit them in the war against the Ammonites. A battle ensues, and the Gileadites rout the Ephraimites, who flee in retreat toward their homeland. The Gileadites then take control of the fords of the Jordan. Whenever a warrior approaches to cross the Jordan, they demand that he speak the word "shibboleth." The word means either "flowing stream" or "ear of corn," but the meaning is irrelevant in the story. At issue is the word's pronunciation. If he answers "sibboleth," they will know he is an Ephraimite, whose Hebrew dialect pronounced the word with the *s* rather than the *sh* sound.

There are other instances of strife or suspicion among the tribes. The only loss in Joshua's conquest is blamed on a family from the tribe of Judah (Josh. 7). Later, Deborah accuses several tribes—Reuben, Gilead, Dan, Asher, plus the town or clan of Meroz—of not answering her battle cry to defend Israel (Judg. 5). In Judges 19–21, all of the other tribes attack and nearly extinguish the tribe of Benjamin because of the gang rape that occurred in Benjaminite territory. After the fall of the northern kingdom, Benjamin and Judah alone remain and blame the northern tribes for the apostasy that led to their defeat.

The political and economic structures of the tribes are elusive. There may have been a kind of confederacy of the tribes, but the evidence for it is sketchy at best. Tribes probably functioned independently, active mostly at the local level of their constituent clans or in response to some need—a legal dispute between clans, defense against an external enemy, cooperation in the face of an environmental threat. It is unlikely that a tribe possessed enough centralized power to amass funds and resources or to control behavior among villagers. In fact, a tribe may not have had much in the way of a formal presence or structure; rather, it embodied the interests of those living in its territory, facilitating their well-being to the extent possible.

The book of Judges uses the term "judge" to refer to individuals who function less as judicial figures than as leaders or deliverers of the tribes of Israel during the premonarchic period. The book identifies twelve such judges, divided evenly between two types, the "minor judges" and the "major judges."

The "minor judges" are mentioned very tersely. For example, in just five verses at the start of Judges 10 we hear of two who "judged" or led Israel: Tola, from the hill country of Ephraim, the leader for twenty-three years; and Jair, from the region of Gilead, the leader for twenty-two years. We hear nothing else about them, except for the detail that Jair had thirty sons who rode thirty donkeys and owned thirty towns. Three other "minor judges" are summarized in Judges 12:8–15—again with several round numbers: Ibzan had thirty sons and thirty daughters and "judged" Israel for seven years; Elon "judged" for ten years; and Abdon had forty sons and thirty grandsons, all of whom rode seventy donkeys. The sixth such judge is Shamgar, who killed six hundred Philistines with an oxgoad (3:31). Biblical use of numbers is often not accidental. Multiples of three and of four indicate completeness, and seven and its multiples symbolize perfection. In many cases the numbers simply stand for "many."

The six "major judges" represent the heart of the book of Judges. They are introduced in the context of the four-part cyclical pattern described in Chapter 1: disobedience and apostasy by the Israelites, followed by God's punishment by letting a foreign country conquer them, then the Israelites' cry to God for help, and finally the raising up of someone to deliver them. The description of Othniel in Judges 3:7–11 demonstrates the four-part cycle succinctly, while the other five deliverers all receive more elaborate narratives.

Some of the major judges are charismatic leaders, while others have character flaws. The left-handed Ehud uses his left hand to draw his sword unexpectedly and thrust it into the obese King Eglon's belly until "the hilt also went in after the blade" (3:22). Deborah leads the tribes to battle against the Canaanite army commander Sisera, and Jael is subsequently able to kill Sisera by driving a tent peg into his temple while he sleeps (Judg. 4–5). Gideon directs the Israelites in a surprise attack on the Midianites (Judg. 6–8). Jephthah also succeeds in battle, but at the tragic cost of his own daughter (Judg. 11–12). The mighty Samson has adventures and romances before his final act of destroying thousands of Philistines along with himself (Judg. 13–16). Similar to the rule of the minor judges, the major judges' tenure after their act of deliverance is usually reported in formulaic manner: Othniel for forty years, Ehud for eighty, Deborah for forty, Gideon for forty, Jephthah for six, and Samson for twenty before his death.

These stories of the major judges are popular traditions about heroes in early times. They cannot be historically verified, and they probably stem from a later period, during or after the monarchy, when the people looked back with longing to the period when "there was no king in Israel; all the people did what was right in their own eyes" (21:25). The patterns in the book of Judges—the four-step cycles of apostasy and deliverance, the formulaic treatment of the six minor judges, the focus on usually only one or two key dramatic stories for each major judge—point to editors who worked the traditions into a literary whole as a part of the Deuteronomistic History covering the period from Joshua's conquest to Jerusalem's fall.

Political and economic connections among tribes are unlikely during the premonarchic period because of the absence of any centralized powers or structures. The people who settled in each geographical region had contact primarily with others living in that same natural environment, and those contacts occurred most frequently at the clan level and, when mutually beneficial, with other clans and villages nearby. These clans had fairly equal status with each other, and no dominant leader or group took lasting control over any region until the founding of the monarchy. The royal government probably initiated the division of the territories into administrative districts, which the Deuteronomistic History projects back to Solomon's time (1 Kings 4), and only later did they become popularly identified as tribal regions named after ancestors. The government needed the country organized; the people did not. But the people could turn the status quo into folk narratives with religious and moral import. Without the governmental overlay and even despite it, the local level of village life, first developed during the settlement period on the basis of familial patterns, continued through all of Israel's history, adjusting as necessary to outside political and economic interests.

The political and economic makeup of Israel and Judah was as complex and varied as that of any culture that survives for many centuries. Much depends on where one lives—whether in the hamlets, in the relatively small but powerful cities, or in exile in a remote land. Much will also be dictated by the larger political scene—whether a central state is absent or present, whether sovereignty is lost to a distant emperor. Hierarchies exist in all contexts. Inequalities in land ownership, labor, sustenance, and resources affect the well-being of all parties. The Bible contains not only pictures favorable to most of these aspects of society, but it also engages in massive criticism as well. We return to the critique by the biblical prophets and historians in Chapter 13.

Chapter 12

Diaspora

Abraham and Sarah find themselves as sojourners in Egypt as well as in the land of the Philistines; Isaac and Rebekah temporarily settle in the kingdom of Gerar; Joseph relocates his family to the land of Goshen; Moses along with almost the entire exodus generation dies in the wilderness. The yearning for the land that marked the generations of the Pentateuch will mark their descendants as well, for Israel will again find itself outside the land of the promise. Yet the descendants of the ancestors, scattered by war to Babylon, to Egypt, to untold locations in Asia Minor, North Africa, and Europe, will express this yearning in different and distinct ways. Forming one of the world's oldest ongoing diaspora communities, these heirs of Abraham establish their identities apart from the land, but always in relation to the promise.

Initial Scattering and Return

The word *diaspora* comes from a Greek expression meaning "to scatter seed" (*spora* is, in English, "spores" or "seeds"); the English is "dispersion." The term, which was common in the Greek-speaking world of antiquity, referred to individuals who left their homeland when it was conquered and who generally settled in the territories belonging to their conquerors. Some left voluntarily; some escaped as refugees; some were resettled by the invading forces. The Septuagint uses the verb *diaspeiro,* "to scatter," sixty-seven times, and the noun twelve times. The noun also appears in the New Testament (John 7:35; James 1:1; 1 Pet. 1:1). It refers to the "sons of Noah" who repopulated the earth after the flood (Gen. 9:19) and to the people of Babel, dispersed "over the face of the earth" (11:8, 9), but in both Testaments, and subsequently in Jewish and early Christian history, the term usually refers to members of the covenant community living outside of the land of Israel. For example, James 1:1 addresses "the twelve tribes of the dispersion" (*diaspora*). Today, "diaspora" has come to refer to any national group outside its homeland, as in the broadly defined African diaspora or the more narrowly defined Korean diaspora or Cuban diaspora. In postbiblical Jewish culture, the term *galut,* meaning "exile," functions as a partial synonym for "diaspora." But whereas diaspora does not necessarily convey, in Jewish thought, a strong sense of alienation (one can be quite happy in the diaspora), *galut* retains a sense of loss and hope for return.

For the biblical worldview, diaspora is part of God's will: to be uprooted from one's home and taken into exile was, for antiquity, the worst conceivable threat, just as to be returned to the land was the greatest blessing. Regardless of what political motivations prompted the several ancient empires to attack and then disperse populations, for the Bible the process of conquest and resettlement was always a manifestation of the divine plan. Ezekiel, in his typically visceral way, explains the dispersion of the covenant community:

> When the houses of Israel lived on their own soil, they defiled it with their ways and their deeds; their conduct in my sight was like the uncleanness of a woman in her menstrual period. So I poured out my wrath upon them for the blood that they had shed upon the land, and for the idols with which they had defiled it. I scattered [LXX: *diaspeiro*] them among the nations, and they were dispersed through the countries; in accordance with their conduct and their deeds I judged them. (36:17–19)

But dispersion cannot be the end of the story. God said to Abraham: "To your offspring I will give this land [of Canaan]" (Gen. 12:7; 13:15; 15:7, 18; 17:8; 24:7; 26:3; 28:4, 13; 35:12; 50:24—the number of iterations shows the importance of the promise). For this promise to be fulfilled, the exiles in the diaspora will need to return. Isaiah announces that God will gather the "dispersed" (LXX: the participle form of *diaspeiro*) of Judah from the four corners of the earth (11:12). In one of the servant songs in Isaiah, God proclaims to the servant: "It is too light a thing that you should be my servant to raise up the tribes of Jacob and to restore the dispersed [LXX: *diasporan;* NRSV: 'survivors'] of Israel;

I will give you as a light to the nations, that my salvation may reach to the end of the earth" (49:6). Here the dispersion has a positive effect on the people among whom the covenant community lives; Israel's existence as an ongoing, distinct community eventually restored to its homeland witnesses to the nations the power of its God. As part of the extended hymn with the famous refrain, "Give thanks to YHWH, for he is good, for his mercy endures forever," Ben Sira proclaims, "Give thanks to him who gathers the dispersed of Israel, for his mercy endures forever" (Sir. 51:12), and Judith celebrates the restoration of the community from Babylonian exile: "They have returned to their God, and have come back from the diaspora (*diaspora*) where they were scattered (*diaspeiro*), and have inhabited Jerusalem, where their sanctuary is" (5:19).

Although some diaspora communities yearned for a return to the homeland, others preserved the memory and, often, the connection, but preferred to remain in their new location. Diaspora Jewish communities established in the sixth century BCE at the time of the Babylonian conquest and later in Asia Minor, North Africa, and Europe remained in contact with Jerusalem through letters, donations to the temple, pilgrimages, and ambassadors, but did not seek to return. Instead, they justified their diaspora existence theologically: their dispersion was predicted by God, and their dispersion allowed them to serve as witnesses to the God of Israel apart from the land of Israel. Thus the initial message that exile is a punishment became, for those in exile, transformed into a blessing. Since the promises to Abraham included the international point that in him "all the families of the earth shall be blessed" (Gen. 12:3), dispersion provided the means by which the family of Abraham could serve as a witness to the nations.

Therefore, when we think of diaspora, we should think not only of the scattering of seed, but also of its planting in a new location. As plants that grow from seed cultivated in one type of soil and one type of climate become modified when transplanted to a new location, with new climate, new fertilizer, and new care, so the covenant community itself changed. Barley does not become wheat—but the soil from which it draws its nutrients and the environment in which it grows create something different. Diaspora identity is realized in new pressures, new promises, and new purposes. It also faces new challenges, from the pressure to assimilate and therefore ultimately to lose distinct identity, to pressures from local governments whose laws may conflict with Israel's traditions. As the new state seeks to define its diaspora populations, so the populations themselves must determine who they are in relation to their new home.

Jacob, his children, and their families, who move to Egypt to escape famine in Canaan, become members of a diaspora community. They recognize their distinction from the Egyptians, and the Egyptians recognize that distinction as well. This initial community is able to retain its cultural cohesion in part because it settles in a distinct area, the "land of Goshen" (see, e.g., Gen. 45:10); in part, they stay together because Egyptian prejudices keep them distinct. When Joseph dines with his brothers before making his identity known to them, the table seating preserves ethnic boundaries. The Egyptians "served him by himself, and them by themselves, and the Egyptians who ate with him by themselves, because the Egyptians could not eat with the Hebrews, for that is an abomination to the Egyptians" (43:32). The biblical narrative suggests that, for the Egyptian diaspora community, social pressure along with and perhaps even rather than religious belief or practice, reinforced ethnic identity and kept the community intact.

Similarly, Joseph advises his family to explain to Pharaoh: "[We] are keepers of livestock from our youth even until now, both we and our ancestors" so that they may settle in the land of Goshen, "because all shepherds are abhorrent to the Egyptians" (Gen. 46:34). Such self-denigration remains a common ploy by diaspora communities. Self-denigration, one of the weapons of the weak, defuses any potential threat and can even evoke pity, whereas self-aggrandizement can evoke threat.

The diaspora community in Late Bronze Age Egypt does not continue past the exodus (if the story has a historical core). Whatever Israelite population did live there becomes lost to the historical record; the Bible gives the impression that all left with Moses. Its memories, however, remain with the community, regardless of its location. The ongoing celebration of the Passover in Jewish households recalls the slavery in Egypt, the escape from bondage, and the ongoing diaspora, for the Passover ritual meal, the *seder*, ends in the diaspora with the wish, "next year in Jerusalem." Leviticus 19 evokes Israel's diaspora context in mandating care for others who have been dispersed: "When an alien resides with you in your land, you shall not oppress the alien. The alien who resides with you shall be to you as the citizen among you; you shall love the alien as yourself, for you were aliens in the land of Egypt: I am YHWH your God" (Lev. 19:33–34).

The Ten Lost Tribes

The initial Israelite population in Egypt is not the only biblical diaspora community to lack material traces of its existence. In 722 BCE, Assyria conquered the northern kingdom, Israel (2 Kings 18:9–10). Like any good ancient Southwest Asian empire, Assyria protected its new holdings by taking the social elites of the defeated nation into exile. The courts and upper classes were moved out, and remnants of other conquered nations moved in. The mixing of the population groups, combined with the trauma of the attack and the presence of occupying forces, was designed to prevent the conquered population from achieving the cultural coherence needed for effective, organized revolt. Inside the land, the new kingdom—comprised of the Israelites who remained and the new peoples moved in by the Assyrians—became known as Samaria, a name taken from the northern kingdom's capital city.

As for the population taken into diaspora, 2 Kings 17:6 (cf. 18:11) reports, "The king of Assyria carried the Israelites away to Assyria. He placed them in Halah, on the Habor, the river of Gozan, and in the cities of the Medes." The cities of the Medes, for the author of 2 Kings, writing likely in the fifth century BCE or later, included the area extending from present-day Azerbaijan to Afghanistan, to northern Pakistan, to Iran. The Chronicler, writing in the fourth or third century BCE, notes that the "Reubenites, Gadites, and the half-tribe of Manasseh" are in "Halah, Habor, Hara, and the river Gozan, to this day" (2 Chron. 5:26). The names of the cities, cities otherwise unknown to history, sound more like folktale than road map. The river Habor mentioned in 2 Kings becomes for the Chronicler a city; "Hara," which sounds suspiciously similar to "Halah," is added to the list. Similarly, Obadiah—writing perhaps in the sixth century—speaks of the "exiles of the Israelites who are in Halah, [who] shall possess Phoenicia as far as Zarepath" (20a). This is one prediction that cannot come true, since Phoenicia no longer exists.

The northern tribes, wherever they landed, became lost to history, and where history is silent, imagination reigns. Bartolomé de las Casas, in the early 1500s, argued that the tribes had migrated to the West Indies, Peru, and Guatemala. Antonio de Montezinos, a century later, claimed he located a Jewish tribe in the Andes. James Adair, an eighteenth-century trader, proposed that the Cherokee were one of the ten lost tribes. Such "discoveries" were not merely ethnic curiosities; they related directly to some eschatological hopes. Menasseh ben Israel, a Dutch Jew, sent his "Humble Addresses" to Oliver Cromwell in 1655 to convince him to allow the Jews, barred from England since the thirteenth century, to return, now that the possibility of the ingathering of the Jews fully was at hand. This politically well-connected rabbi tapped into the Puritan millenarian view that the scattering of the Jews to every kingdom on the globe would permit the inbreaking of the messianic age. The proof-text for this view was Daniel 12:7: "And I heard the man clothed in linen, which was upon the waters of the river, when he held up his right hand and his left hand unto heaven, and sware by him that liveth for ever that it shall be for a time, times, and an half; and *when he shall have accomplished to scatter the power of the holy people,* all these things shall be finished" (KJV, italics added). Whereas one branch of Christian thought today believes that all Jews should return to Israel in order to bring about the return of Jesus, in the seventeenth century the approach was the opposite: let the Jews live in all the lands, so that the apocalyptic vision of Daniel 12 could be fulfilled and the messianic age can begin.

Claimants for the descendants of the ten tribes of this early diaspora continue to proliferate. Candidates include the Pashtun people of Afghanistan, the Lemba of Zimbabwe, and the Igbo of Nigeria, the Sefwi of Ghana, the Bene Ephraim, Bnei Menashe, and Nasranis from India, the Beta Israel (also known as Falashas) from Ethiopia, residents of Bukhara of Uzbekhistan, the Chiang Min from northwestern China, and the Japanese according to the Makuya sect. A movement known as British-Israelism supports the idea that the British, or the Anglo-Saxons, are the descendants of the ten lost tribes; some promulgate this teaching based on an etymological argument: since the Hebrew word for "covenant" in Sephardic (Mediterranean/Spanish) pronunciation is *brit* and the Hebrew for "man" is *ish,* hence "Brit-ish"—"man of the covenant." The etymology is false, but the argument still finds a number of wishful thinkers. In the United States, this idea is best known from the teachings of Herbert W. Armstrong, founder of the Worldwide Church of God (following Armstrong's death in 1986, the church repudiated this teaching).

Jewish mystical tradition suggests that God placed the faithful members of the tribes on an island surrounded by the river Sambatyon. The river rages six days a week, but is calm on the Sabbath. The lost tribes, of course observing the Sabbath, would not cross on that day. Thus they remain in their own diaspora, awaiting reunification with the other two tribes—Judah and Benjamin—at the dawn of the messianic age.

The idea of the ingathering of the exiles remains part of the Jewish tradition. Ezekiel's instructions from God predict the reunification: "Take a stick and write on it, 'For Judah, and the Israelites associated with it'; then take another stick and write on it, 'For Joseph (the stick of Ephraim) and all the house of Israel associated with it'; and join them together into one stick, so that they may become one in your hand" (37:16–17). And Jesus of Nazareth, by appointing twelve special followers, was symbolically reconstituting the tribes.

The Babylonian Diaspora

The ten tribes that comprised the northern kingdom lost their distinct identities and became lost to history. A similar loss was not the case when the Babylonians conquered the southern kingdom, Judah, in 586. How the exiles managed this remarkable preservation, politically, economically, and theologically, is the subject of this next section.

Politically, the southern kingdom had always been more stable than its compatriot to the north, at least according to the biblical narrative, as we describe in the next chapter. In the south, monarchs claiming descent from King David remained on the throne; dynastic consistency, with an attendant consistency among the ruling class, led to greater social stability than in the north, where numerous coups marked the rule. At least in the southern kingdom, the promise made to David of a house and a kingdom "made sure forever" appeared to have been fulfilled (2 Sam. 7:12–16).

When the northern kingdom was conquered, there was no recognized ruling family or permanent dynasty who could summon communal loyalty. The biblical text does not even record the fate of Hoshea, king of Israel at the time of the Shalmaneser's conquest of Samaria. The most 2 Kings 17:4 recounts is that Hoshea, despite Israel's vassal status to Assyria, refused to pay the tribute due, and Shalmaneser then imprisoned him. Yet for the southern kingdom, the political infrastructure of society remained more or less intact during the exile. Perhaps the three waves of exiles—in 597, when Jehoiachin was deposed; in 586, at the fall of Jerusalem and the end of Zedekiah's reign; and in 582, with the assassination of Gedaliah (see Jer. 41)—rather than a single, destructive attack, helped preserve Judahite identity. Second Kings 24:14–16 suggests that the royal

house and the community leaders retained some authority even in Babylon: "He [Nebuchadnezzar] carried away all Jerusalem, . . . Jehoiachin, the
king's mother, the king's wives, his officials, and the elite of the land, . . .
all the men of valor, . . . the artisans and the smiths." Babylon preserved
the royal household, and the returnees to Jerusalem in 538 had at their
head the Davidic descendent Zerubbabel; the name is Babylonian, but his
Israelite identity remained secure. That the Babylonian exile lasted for less
than half a century (586–538) whereas the Assyrian rule lasted more than
twice as long also suggests why the exiles from Judah in Babylon were,
unlike their northern counterparts, able to preserve their identity.

Kings alone do not maintain community coherence; economic placement and critical mass do as well. Rather than being dispersed throughout
the Babylonian empire—as their neighbors to the north were dispersed
in Assyrian lands—the ten thousand or so exiles from Judah (see 2 Kings
24:14) remained in the same area. The Babylonians not only allowed the
community to remain intact; they apparently also granted the diaspora
populations, eventually located in several sites (see Ezek. 1:1–3; 3:15;
Ezra 2:59; 8:17), substantial autonomy. For example, archaeologists have
pieced together the records of a Judahite family of commercial contrac-
tors, Murashu and Sons, who found economic prosperity in southern
Mesopotamia a century and a half after the Babylonian exiles began.
Indeed, when the exile formally ended with the conquering of Babylon by Cyrus of Persia in 539 BCE, a number of the Judahites remained
in Babylon. It is from this community that, a thousand years later, the
Babylonian Talmud was developed; today, there are only a handful of
Jews, if any, living in Iraq, but they trace their origins to the diaspora
community of the exile.

Finally, compared to their northern relatives, religiously the exiles
from the south were able to promote practices that would limit assimilation. Their religious coherence derived partially from the distinct practices
of the southern kingdom. In the north, the cult in the capital city of Samaria was the largest and most powerful in the land, but Israelite priests
served at other shrines, such as Dan and Bethel. The people's religious
loyalty had no single geographic focus and perhaps no centralization of
Yahwistic priests. The southern kingdom, following Josiah's reforms, had
a centralized cult and a centralized priesthood. Although Canaanite practices did continue in the south, as both archaeological remains of cultic
objects from the period and Jeremiah's invectives attest, the centralized

cult provided the south both a geographical focus and a comparably more coherent religious identity.

What could be transported, however, was the cultural legacy of the north, and that inheritance aided in the southern kingdom's survival. In 722, refugees fled southward, and they brought with them their stories: the version of the patriarchal narratives, accounts of kings, tales of Elijah and Elisha, the oracles of Hosea. The south used this cultural repository to enhance its own political and theological legitimacy; further, the south could learn from the mistakes the north had made.

Whereas Israel to the north had multiple shrines, the Deuteronomic reform of Josiah at the end of the seventh century reportedly sought to centralize southern worship in Jerusalem. The impetus for the reform, recorded in 2 Kings 22, is a serendipitous find by the high priest Hilkiah, who reports locating in the temple "the book of the law." King Josiah, desiring assurance that the book is genuine (or, more cynically, seeking to legitimize a politically opportune series of reforms), commands Hilkiah and his associates: "Go, inquire of YHWH for me, for the people, and for all Judah, concerning the words of this book that has been found; for great is the wrath of YHWH that is kindled against us, because our ancestors did not obey the words of this book, to do according to all that is written concerning us" (22:13).

Hilkiah and his associates go to Huldah, a prophet conveniently married to one of Josiah's court functionaries. Huldah not only proclaims the book to be legitimate; she also announces: "Thus says YHWH, 'I will indeed bring disaster on this place and on its inhabitants—all the words of the book that the king of Judah has read. Because they have abandoned me and have made offerings to other gods, so that they have provoked me to anger'" (22:16–17). The message "follow the teachings of this book" or suffer the consequences could not be clearer; the destruction of Israel in 722 alerted the people in Judah that the threat was real.

Josiah, who was attempting to break free of Assyrian vassalage, had much to gain from the implementation of this new law—so much so that a number of historians question the historicity of the account in 2 Kings 22–23. Josiah also had strong economic motives for centralizing the cultus: funds for the localized shrines would now all be channeled to Jerusalem.

According to the Bible's account, Josiah implements this law book, now known as Deuteronomy. The name comes from 17:18, which mandates that the king "shall have a copy of this law written for him in the presence of the levitical priests." The Septuagint translates "copy of this law" as *deuteronomion*, literally, "second law." In Hebrew, the book is called Devarim, "Words," for the opening phrase, "These are the words that Moses spoke to all Israel beyond the Jordan." Whether it was an ancient text ascribed to Moses that was accidentally discovered during temple repair work (it would be an odd thing to misplace) or an example of political machination that justifies innovation by attribution to a sacred source, the Deuteronomic tradition established practices that helped the community maintain its identity in diaspora.

Second Kings 23 reports that Josiah's Deuteronomic reform removed from the temple all items as well as personnel dedicated to Baal and Asherah, and it closed all of the public "high places." These moves by no means erased local practices; the increase in the number of figurines from the decades just prior to 586 tends to support Jeremiah's view of the ongoing apostasies in the land. Nevertheless, the centralization of the cult in Jerusalem led to a comparably stronger priesthood, albeit under the king's watchful eye, even as it led to the impoverishment of village Levites and priests.

The Deuteronomic tradition also promoted an insistence on education, and that too helps a community retain its identity in the diaspora. In a passage still recited as part of synagogue liturgy, Deuteronomy 6:7–9 insists: "You shall teach them [the laws] diligently to your children, and shall talk of them when you sit in your house, and when you walk by the way, and when you lie down, and when you rise up. And you shall bind them for a sign upon your hand, and they shall be for frontlets between your eyes; and you shall write them upon the doorposts of your house and upon your gates." The same idea occurs in Exodus 13:9, 16 and Deuteronomy 11:18. At least by the later part of the Second Temple period, Deuteronomy 6 was taken literally. During prayer, men (and perhaps women) wore on their left arms and foreheads two small, square leather boxes containing biblical verses related to the references: Exodus 13:1–16; Deuteronomy 6:4–9; 11:13–21. By the first century CE, the boxes are known as *tefillin* (Aramaic) or, in English from the Greek, *phylacteries*. Also taken literally was the commandment about the sign on the doorposts and gates. This reference gives rise to the practice of placing a *mezuzah* (Heb., "doorpost")—a case containing a parchment scroll inscribed with the words of Deuteronomy 6:4–9; 11:13–21—on the doors and gates of Jewish homes.

The diaspora communities themselves enhanced ritual practice by developing oracles and stories to explain their situation, to anchor their present circumstances to Israel's past, and to guide their future. From law code to prophecy to history, the text understands exile as God's righteous response to sin. In Deuteronomy, Moses reminds the people that preservation in the land is contingent upon loyalty to God. Apostasy prompts defeat at the hands of their enemies: "You shall become an object of horror to all the kingdoms of the earth" (28:25). The Septuagint renders the Hebrew term "object of horror" as, literally, "in diaspora." The Deuteronomistic historian focuses the blame for the exile on King Manasseh, and thus to some extent absolves the people of the personal guilt they might have faced: "Still YHWH did not turn from the fierceness of his great wrath, by which his anger was kindled against Judah, because of all the provocations with which Manasseh had provoked him" (2 Kings 23:26).

The prophet Ezekiel manages in one modestly convoluted couplet both to blame Judah for its exile and to show how the exile furthers divine concerns: "It is not for your sake, O house of Israel, that I am about to act, but for the sake of my holy name, which you have profaned among the nations to which you came. I will sanctify my great name, . . . and the nations shall know that I am YHWH" (36:22–23; cf. 39:21). Both the people's diaspora existence and, especially, their being gathered back to their land display divine power.

Second Isaiah (Isa 40–55) similarly sees diaspora existence as a means of religious testimony: "You are my witnesses, says YHWH, and my servant whom I have chosen" (43:10a; see also 43:12; 44:8). The result of the witnessing will be the acclamation by the nations: "God is with you only, and there is no other; no god besides him" (45:14). Unlike Ezekiel, however, Second Isaiah's oracles focus less on blaming Israel for the sins that led to the exile than on providing comfort; he says the exile will soon be over. For Second Isaiah, Israel had served the term of its punishment, paid double for its sins (the extra penalty in certain cases of civic misdeed), and is now released from the debt its sins incurred with God. Thus, Isaiah 40:2 records: "Speak tenderly to Jerusalem, and cry to her that she has served her term, that her penalty is paid, that she has received from YHWH's hand double for all her sins."

The servant/slave, mentioned in Isaiah 43, receives more extensive treatment in Second Isaiah's four "servant songs": 42:1–4 (with vv. 5–9 an interpretive elaboration); 49:1–6; 50:4–9; and 52:13–53:12. The identity of the slave in these passages is unclear, and the reception history of the passages further complicates any firm determination. The slave can be seen as the prophet himself; for example, in 49:5–6, the prophet describes himself as having been "formed in the womb" to be God's servant and describes his commission as bringing "Jacob back" to religious fidelity: "Is it too light a thing that you should be my servant to raise up the tribes of Jacob and to restore the survivors of Israel?" Or the figure could be an otherwise unidentified leader, such as a Davidic descendant in Babylon.

The Jewish community traditionally recognizes the servant as the covenant community, Israel. Isaiah 49:3 states: "And he said to me, 'You are my servant, Israel, in whom I will be glorified.'" Although some scholars claim that the word "Israel" in this verse disturbs the meter and therefore is probably a gloss, other passages also take a communal approach to the figure (41:8–9; 44:1–2, 21; 45:4; 48:20). For example, Isaiah 44:1–2 reads: "Now hear, O Jacob my slave, Israel whom I have chosen." In this reading, Second Isaiah shows how Israel's humiliation in exile—"despised and rejected by others" (53:3)—leads not only to its own redemption, but to the redemption of those who witnessed God's power in restoring the community: "But he was wounded for our transgressions, crushed for our iniquities; upon him was the punishment that made us whole, and by his bruises we are healed" (53:5). The Christian church would later associate this servant not with Israel in diaspora, but with Jesus of Nazareth.

But such theological proclamation did not replace the despair of the initial population taken to Babylon. The prophets Ezekiel and Isaiah do not dismiss the distress; instead, they share it, and yet they transform it by reminding the people that their God has not deserted them. If the people will repent, then God will respond to their desire for return and bring them home.

The book of Lamentations, ascribed traditionally to Jeremiah (and therefore positioned directly after Jeremiah in the Christian canon, but not in the Tanakh), retains rather than suppresses the pain of exile: "Cry aloud to the Lord! O wall of daughter Zion! Let tears stream down like a torrent day and night! Give yourself no rest, your eyes no respite!" (2:18). Lamentations continues to be recited by the synagogue on the 9th of Av (July/August), the anniversary of the destruction of the temple. It thereby calls the people home. Outside of Zion, the covenant community is, for most of the biblical text, incomplete. The point is reinforced by Psalm 137:

By the rivers of Babylon—
there we sat down and there we wept
when we remembered Zion.
On the willows there
we hung up our harps.
For there our captors
asked us for songs,
and our tormentors asked for mirth, saying,
"Sing us one of the songs of Zion!"
How could we sing YHWH's song
in a foreign land?
If I forget you, O Jerusalem,
let my right hand wither!
Let my tongue cling to the roof of my mouth,
if I do not remember you,
if I do not set Jerusalem
above my highest joy. (137:1–6)

Such articulation of grief and guilt, hope and longing became a means of encouragement. Unexpectedly, shockingly, the last line of the same psalm goes on to proclaim: "Happy shall they be who take your little ones and dash them against the rock!" The line is not an incitement to violence, but it does acknowledge how despair can yield to the desire for revenge. Here the psalmist reflects a response to Israel's own experiences. Second Kings 8:12 (see also Hos. 13:16) depicts Elisha weeping, knowing that Hazael will "kill [Israel's] young men with the sword, dash in pieces their little ones to the ground, and rip up their pregnant women." Those who suffer conquest and exile at times mimic their conquerors.

Second Isaiah does not merely predict Babylon's fall (46:1a) and the return of the exiles to Jerusalem; he encourages them to visualize the end of their exile: "A voice cries out: 'In the wilderness prepare the way of YHWH, make straight in the desert a highway for our God. Every valley shall be lifted up, and every mountain and hill be made low; the uneven ground shall become level, and the rough places a plain'" (40:3–4). The New Testament picks up this verse, but following the Septuagint repunctuates: "The voice of one crying out in the wilderness, 'Prepare the way of the Lord'" (Mark 1:3). The voice is that of John the Baptist.

Jewish cantillation marks also follow the Septuagint reading for Isaiah 40:3–4.

As the prophets encouraged repentance and promoted hope, the priests recounted the history of the people and promoted practices to keep the community intact. During the Babylonian exile, the priestly writers likely began to frame the history of the covenant community and established the laws that marked them as distinct. Their efforts, known as the Priestly Code, would take final shape during the Persian period.

Genesis 1:1 begins, in the Hebrew, not "In the beginning . . ." but, literally, "When, in the beginning. . . ." The opening is a temporal clause, and as such it represents an alternative to the Babylonian creation epic, the *Enumah Elish*, translated "When on High. . . ." For the Bible's opening chapters, the focus is not geographical, but temporal; the climax of creation is not the founding of a city but the establishment of the Sabbath: "So God blessed the seventh day and hallowed it, because on it God rested from all the work that he had done in creation" (Gen. 2:3). With this creation story, the diaspora population could celebrate their deity in any location. At the same time (literally), the Sabbath kept the community's identity distinct.

For Second Isaiah, the Sabbath symbolizes Israel's redemption as well as its gift to the nations: "And the foreigners who join themselves to YHWH, . . . all who keep the Sabbath . . . and hold fast my covenant— these I will bring to my holy mountain; . . . my house shall be called a house of prayer for all peoples. Thus says the Lord YHWH, who gathers the outcasts [LXX: the participial form of *diaspora*] of Israel, I will gather others to them besides those already gathered" (56:6–8; see also 58:13– 14). The Israelites remain Israelites, and the Gentiles remain Gentiles, but all come to worship Israel's deity. In the Gospel of Mark Jesus quotes: "My house shall be called a house of prayer for all the nations" (11:17). At the time of Jesus, the temple in Jerusalem had an outer court, called "the court of the Gentiles," where non-Jews were invited to worship with the covenant community.

The scribes also played their part in preserving communal identity. Whether during the exile or afterward, under Persian rule, they began compiling various sources—J, E, D, P, the Deuteronomistic History— into a continuous narrative that spoke of infidelity, punishment, and restoration. The Torah, with its depiction of Abraham outside of the promised land, with its stories of the patriarchs' sojourns in Gerar and Egypt, and with its final image of Moses looking into the land he would never enter, retells the story of the diaspora. From it the people outside the land knew that their children would return, that if the promise were not fulfilled in their own generation, it would be fulfilled in the future.

In 539, Cyrus of Persia conquered the Babylonian empire. The prayers of the Judahites were answered; the predictions of Ezekiel and Second Isaiah were fulfilled. Second Chronicles 36:20–23 provides both the explanation for the exile and the exhortation to return to Judah. The exile would last until the land had "made up for its sabbaths. All the days that it lay desolate it kept sabbath, to fulfill seventy years. In the first year of King Cyrus of Persia, in fulfillment of the word of YHWH spoken by Jeremiah, YHWH stirred up the spirit of King Cyrus," who declared, "YHWH, the God of heaven, has given me all the kingdoms of the earth, and he has charged me to build him a house at Jerusalem, which is in Judah. Whoever is among you of all his people, may YHWH his God be with him! Let him go up." This is the last line of the Tanakh, the Jewish canon. The last word comes from the same root as the Hebrew term *aliyyah*, which means both to "go up" to recite the blessings before and after the reading from the Torah in the synagogue and to "go up" or "immigrate" to Israel. The concern for the Sabbaths conveys the sense that Israel's exile served as its penalty for its sins, and the sins impacted not only the people, but the land itself. Now both would be redeemed.

Many returned to the land now known as the province of Yehud, a small part of the vast satrapy (district) called "Beyond the River [Euphrates]," which stretched from the Euphrates all the way to the border with Egypt. Referred to frequently in the books of Ezra and Nehemiah, it was one of twenty satrapies created by the Persian ruler Darius (522–486 BCE) to facilitate rule and collect taxes.

Others stayed in Babylon. Still others, such as those who took Jeremiah and Baruch with them to Egypt, found new homes on the Nile.

Postexilic Diaspora Communities

Located in southern Egypt at what is modern-day Aswan, a Jewish military colony on the island of Elephantine thrived in the sixth and fifth centuries BCE. Perhaps founded in the mid-seventh century when the Judahite king Manasseh provided forces to Pharaoh Psammetichus I, the colony attests to a diaspora existence that adapted, partially, to its new cultural environment. The Aramaic documents of this colony—business contracts, marriage and divorce decrees, manumission statements, and personal letters—resemble the texts produced by local Egyptians, but evidence of the distinct identity of the authors permeates the corpus. Notable is the presence of a temple dedicated to Israel's god. Among the papyrii, one reports that the Persian king Cambyses (529–522) did not damage their temple despite destroying "all the temples of the gods of the Egyptians." This temple promoted the worship of Israel's deity, called YHW, as well as Anat-YHW, or "Mrs. YHWH." Although in touch with the Jerusalem temple as well as the Samaritan community in the early postexilic period, the Elephantine colony practiced its own Egyptian-indigenous form of the traditions of its ancestors. Documentation of this group lasts until the mid-fourth century BCE.

Yet others originally from Judah followed new Persian rulers throughout the eastern diaspora. Although the tradition strongly insists that the true home of the Judahite population is the land of Israel, the combination of theological witness, new communal ties, economic opportunities, and personal familiarity kept many in the next generations at home away from home, in the diaspora. To explain their new positions of hybridity, of being once again strangers in a strange land, the community did what it had done in the past: it told stories.

Esther

As the eastern diaspora became a major center of Jewish life, new questions of self-definition arose. To what extent should community members acculturate themselves to Persian or Greek thought and practice, and what traditions would preserve their identity? What elements of their tradition would they emphasize, and what genres would best express their situation?

One response to these issues was the development of the court tale, seen in the stories of Esther and Daniel. The genre had already been established in the earlier diaspora stories of Joseph, the second-in-command in the court of Egypt, and Moses, raised in Pharaoh's household and familiar with court proceedings. By depicting Jews in intimate, prolonged contact with Gentiles, the writers explored the question of their national identity even as they encouraged their readers to maintain it. By presenting the Jews in the context of the court, and thus with access to political power, they offered an optimistic sense that one could thrive apart from

Judah and thereby witness to the nations. The court tales of Esther and Daniel combine the humorous and the macabre, the tragic and the joyous. They portray both the real threats to community existence and a remarkably healthy, robust sense of identity.

The book of Esther is today celebrated in the Jewish festival of Purim, when children (and quite a few adults) dress in costume and celebrate the sparing of the Jewish community from genocide. But the book of Esther is much more than a children's story. Through a combination of farce and tragedy, Queen Esther's narrative raises profound questions about politics, religious identity, ethics, and gender relations.

It also raises questions of date and provenance. Whether the text was actually written in the Persian diaspora remains a question. It contains a number of Persian loanwords, the names of the characters are plausibly Persian, and the Hebrew text does not evidence any Greek terms. Thus a date for the original story sometime in the Persian period (539–331) is plausible. Complicating the date, however, is the textual history of the book. The story is preserved in three ancient versions. First is the Hebrew text, which never invokes the name of God, which sees no explicit problem with the intermarriage between the Jewish Esther and the pagan king Ahasuerus, and which mentions no specific Jewish practices.

There is also a Greek version, which contains six major additions to the Hebrew. This text pays much greater attention to Esther's Jewish piety. She prays, and she explicitly notes her hatred of exogamy by exclaiming to God, "You know all things; you know that I hate the splendor of the pagan; I abhor the bed of the uncircumcised or of any Gentile" (14:15, LXX). The Greek text introduces the divine name (2:20; 4:8; 6:1; 6:13) and makes clear that God is the hero of the story. Whereas the Hebrew text presents a fully assimilated queen who could easily pass as a non-Jew, in the Greek she insists: 'I, your servant, have not eaten at Haman's table, nor have I graced a banquet of the king nor touched the wine of his drink offerings" (14:17, LXX). Finally, there is a second Greek version known as the "Alpha text"; whether this Greek text precedes the Hebrew and the Septuagint versions or whether it relies on both remains a question under scholarly debate.

The Septuagint records a colophon that dates the book to "the fourth year of the reign of Ptolemy and Cleopatra" (114 BCE, or possibly 77, or even 44). The book is in place by the date of 2 Maccabees, which mentions "Mordecai's Day" in 15:36. Not making matters any easier for the historian, the date of 2 Maccabees remains uncertain, although a first-century BCE date is possible. The book of Esther does not appear among the Dead Sea Scrolls, but its absence has multiple possible explanations, from a late date of composition to the fact that the Hebrew never mentions the name of God and thus may not have been considered canonical, or even worthy of being copied, by the Qumran community. Perhaps fragments of the scrolls, which continue to surface, might even have a line or two from Esther's story.

The story begins: "This happened in the days of Ahasuerus, the same Ahasuerus who ruled over one hundred twenty-seven provinces from India to Ethiopia" (1:1). "The same Ahasuerus" is an immediate clue that the text is reporting something other than history. The Hebrew name Ahasuerus has no clear Persian or Greek equivalents, and to pronounce it can make the speaker sound a tad intoxicated (much like the king himself, through most of the text). Nevertheless, the king was, even in antiquity, associated with the Persian ruler Xerxes I (485–465 BCE). The Septuagint provides the name Artaxerxes.

Although the story offers snippets of historical verisimilitude, much as does a present-day romance novel, problems with its historicity abound. For example, there is no record of Xerxes or any other Persian king having a Jewish queen, let alone one named Esther (Xerxes's queen was Amastris), or a Jewish prime minister, although there was a court functionary named Marduka under Xerxes I. Greek authors do mention Persia's famous banquets (Heb. *mishteh*, literally, "drinking party"), but none mentions a plot to kill Jews or a slaughter in which Jews killed tens of thousands of Persians. And though there is no mention in Persian records that Xerxes replaced his queen by holding an all-Persia beauty contest and then auditioning candidates on successive nights, Greek historians do remark that Xerxes was both impulsive and prone to anger.

Verisimilitude can account for a number of the book's details. For example, although the Persian capital was Persepolis, the court had a winter palace at Susa, the setting of the book. Xerxes was assassinated by two courtiers, and Esther 2:20–23 records an assassination plot hatched by Bigthan and Teresh, two palace eunuchs. It is their plot that Mordecai reveals to Esther and that will later bring Mordecai to the attention of the king. The Persians were known for having a highly efficient postal system, and the book does suggest that the king's commands were received, with great efficiency, throughout the empire. Although insisting that "all [the king's] acts of might and power, and the high dignities that he conferred on Mordecai, are recorded in the annals of the kings of Media and Persia" (10:2), the story of Esther is less a historical record than a tale of diaspora life designed to provide both instruction and entertainment.

The instruction opens with a concern for Jewish identity, especially as that relates to matters of gender. For Jewish men in the diaspora, various practices could distinguish them from the Gentiles around them, from the wearing of *tzitzit* or *tefillin* to the physical mark of circumcision. But for Jewish women, who have no distinctive marker on their flesh or on their clothes, diaspora identity is to some extent negotiable; one can "pass." According to Esther 2:10, Mordecai advises his beautiful young cousin, about to taken into the king's harem, to withhold mention of her people and her religion. Esther's Jewish identity becomes known only when she admits it to the king. The story thus alerts Jewish women readers that they might be able to pass, but their loyalty must ultimately be to their community. Its fate is necessarily their fate.

A second lesson concerns the relationship of the diaspora community to the local government. Esther's opening chapter makes clear that the king is, at best, a dolt. This ruler gives a banquet for "all his officials and ministers, the army of Persia and Media and the nobles and governors of the provinces" (1:3), in other words, the entire imperial infrastructure. He "displayed the great wealth of his kingdom and the splendor and pomp of his majesty for many days, one hundred eighty days in all" (1:4). The king had given orders "to all the officials . . . to do as each desired" (1:8). Thus, the government has taken a half-year vacation. The message to Jews in the diaspora is not good news—the local government may not be fair, or sane, or logical. Governmental malevolence is bad, but governmental stupidity may be equally dangerous.

The king, who is drunk through most of story, displays his political ineptitude not only by his excess, but also by his lack of concern for those around him. "Merry with wine" (his normal condition), he orders his eunuchs to "bring Queen Vashti . . . wearing the royal crown, in order to show the peoples and the officials her beauty" (1:10–11). Vashti refuses the command, perhaps because she is hosting her own party for the women of the court, perhaps because she refuses to be an object to be displayed— readers can develop a multitude of explanations. One rabbinic interpretation suggests she had a long spotted tail of which she was embarrassed; another proposes she was cursed with a skin disease; a third suggests that the king ordered her to appear *only* in the crown and she, with appropriate modesty, refused.

The king, infuriated, inquires into the Persian law concerning spousal disobedience; in this text, the Persians have a law for everything (the story may be offering a satire on the Jewish legal system itself). His advisers proclaim, "This deed of the queen will be made known to all women, causing them to look with contempt on their husbands" (1:18). They therefore advise the king to make a law preventing Queen Vashti from appearing before him (i.e., the law makes legal the queen's behavior; Vashti is prevented from doing what she does *not* want to do) and that he find a more worthy queen. Finally, they advise that he "proclaim throughout all his kingdom, vast as it is, all women will give honor to their husbands, high and low alike" and that "every man should be master in his own house" (1:20, 22). The king is a dolt, the courtiers are benighted, and at this point it's not clear that the new policies will be good for the Jews.

To replace the queen, the king arranges for all the beautiful virgins of the kingdom to be brought to the palace. Caught in this dragnet is Esther, a young woman descended from the exiles taken into Babylon. Esther 2:6 records that Mordecai was "taken into exile from Jerusalem . . . with King Jeconiah of Judah" (ca. 597 BCE), which would make him approximately 115 years old at the time of Esther's rise to power and thus, perhaps, a contemporary of Daniel.

Esther's name is a cognate of Ishtar, the Babylonian goddess, just as Mordecai's name evokes Marduk. Her Hebrew name, Hadassah, means "myrtle." But despite their names, their Jewish identity remains paramount. Esther's name is also connected to the Hebrew term for "to hide," and it will be her identity that she will hide, but only for a time. Her name also hints at the theology of the book and so of one way to understand theology in the diaspora. Although Mordecai's comment to Esther, "If you remain silent at such a time as this, relief and deliverance for the Jews will appear from another quarter; but you and your father's family will perish" (4:14), has been taken as a veiled theological reference, the text omits direct reference to God's presence in history. For life in the diaspora, at least according to this text, the third lesson is that the people have to rely on their own cleverness and fortitude.

Arriving in Susa, Esther and the other virgins are subjected to a "regular period of cosmetic treatment, six months with oil of myrrh and six months with perfumes" (2:12). After marinating, which should have eliminated any ethnic identification, each "girl" is taken to the king. "In the evening she went in, then, in the morning, she came back to the second harem" (2:14). For her turn, Esther "asked for nothing except what Hegai the king's eunuch, who had charge of the women, advised . . . [and] the king loved Esther more than all the other women; of all the virgins she won his favor and devotion, so that he set the royal crown on her head and made her queen instead of Vashti" (2:15–17). Jewish tradition says that she spent the night teaching him Torah, which is just as good an explanation as any other.

Meanwhile, keeping an eye on his ward, Mordecai also relocates to Susa, where he refuses to "bow down and do obeisance" to Haman (3:4). This slight leads to Haman's decision to wipe out Persia's Jews. Mordecai has no religious reason for refusing to honor the prime minister; nor is bowing to a ruler forbidden: Esther prostrates herself before Ahasuerus (8:3). Rabbinic tradition suggests that Haman wore an idol and thus Mordecai was expressing religious fidelity by refusing to bow, but the Hebrew text of Esther offers a more subtle, and more profound, point. Despite Mordecai's eventual replacement of Haman, the Hebrew text indicates that Jews could endanger themselves by refusing to pay honor where honor is due. The Greek text precludes this reading by indicating that Haman hates Mordecai because Mordecai revealed the regicidal plot in which Haman also had a hand.

Bent on revenging Mordecai's slight, Haman tells the king, "There is a certain people scattered and separated [LXX: *diaspeiro*] among the peoples in all the provinces of your kingdom; their laws are different from those of every other people, and they do not keep the king's laws, so that it is not appropriate for the king to tolerate them" (3:8). Ironically, Haman is also not a native Persian; he is an Agagite. He solidifies his insider status by using the Jews as a scapegoat. Indeed, Haman never tells the king, and the king never asks, who these "scattered" people are. He could just as easily be speaking of his fellow Agagites. Thereby the book issues another warning to the diaspora communities: they may serve the political purposes of others; their very difference makes them vulnerable.

In addition, those purposes might represent ancient rivalries. Mordecai is from the tribe of Benjamin; he is a descendant of a fellow named Kish, as was King Saul (Esther 2:1). Haman descends from Agag (3:1; 9:24), the Amalekite king whom Saul spared and because of whom Saul lost his throne (see 1 Sam 9:1; 15). Just as the book of Judith replays the story of Dinah (Gen. 34), so the book of Esther replays the story of Saul and Amalek (1 Sam. 15).

Despite diaspora dangers, the people have reason to hope. Zeresh, Haman's wife, insists: "If Mordecai . . . is of the Jewish people, you will not prevail against him, but will surely fall before him" (6:13b). By placing this reason on the lips of Haman's wife, the text reinforces the courage and resilience of its Jewish readers. It also, with some irony, shows that husbands would do well to listen to their wives and may suffer if they do not.

Mordecai—the only major figure in the book who is not married—does prevail, but only by prevailing upon Esther to show her loyalty. Whereas Vashti had refused to come when summoned, Esther—at the risk of her own life—approaches the king without an invitation. This court is so dangerous that to enter without an invitation is a capital offense. Welcomed by the king, "she won his favor and he held out to her the golden scepter" (5:2), Esther does not plead for her people; rather, she invites him and Haman to a dinner party. She then repeats this process (5:3, 7–8). Finally, the king, drunk again, asks, "What is your petition, Queen Esther? It shall be granted to you. And what is your request? Even to the half of my kingdom, it shall be fulfilled" (7:2; cf. 5:3, 6–7). This, once again, is a politically unwise promise.

Esther responds: "Let my life be given me—that is my petition—and the lives of my people—that is my request." Ahasuerus, clueless, demands to know what the problem is. Although he had sanctioned the genocide of Persia's Jews, Esther is not about to blame him. Rather, she exclaims: "A foe and enemy, this wicked Haman!" Hearing of Haman's plot, "The king rose from the feast in wrath and went into the palace garden." This is, once again, not the most politically adept move, but it does serve the purposes of the plot. In the king's absence, "Haman stayed to beg his life from Queen Esther, for he saw that the king had determined to destroy him" (7:7). Ahasuerus returns to find his prime minister having thrown himself on the couch where Esther was reclining. Thinking Haman is ravishing his queen (Esther does not disabuse him of this belief; the king does not recognize that Haman, under the circumstances, might have something other than sex on his mind), he orders the minister executed. Haman is hanged on the gallows he had prepared for Mordecai. The king, now out a minister, appoints Mordecai to Haman's position and bestows on him Haman's estate.

But the edict to carry out genocide is still in effect. Since the king is unable to change the irrevocable Persian law (1:19; 8:8, a motif that reappears in Dan. 6:8, 12, 15), he issues a new edict allowing the Jews to defend themselves. Diaspora readers thus learn that they may find themselves no longer welcome in the land they had made their home; even if the authorities wish to protect them, the local population may not. The "enemies of the Jews" gather to attack, but by the king's command (and at Esther's instruction), "the Jews struck down all their enemies with the sword, slaughtering and destroying them, and did as they pleased to those who hated them. In the citadel city of Susa the Jews killed and destroyed five hundred people" (9:5–6). "The other Jews who were in the king's provinces also gathered to defend their lives, and gained relief from their enemies, and killed seventy-five thousand of those who hated them; but they laid no hands on the plunder" (9:16). The final notice indicates that the people had engaged in holy war.

Maimonides, the great twelfth-century Jewish teacher, ranked the book of Esther as of utmost importance in the canon, second only to the Torah. The sixteenth-century Protestant reformer Martin Luther, disgusted by the book's lack of theology as well as promotion of the Jewish people, wanted the volume removed from the canon. In 1994, an American Jewish immigrant to Israel, inspired by Esther's story, massacred Muslim worshipers in the Hebron mosque. The fiction was taken for fact and the warning to an ancient diaspora community taken as warrant to engage in a preemptive strike. In synagogues today, when the book of Esther is read on the festival of Purim, the holiday that commemorates the preservation of Persia's Jewish community, the custom is to blot out the name of Haman; when the reader comes to this name, children especially will use noisemakers to drown out the sound. The custom draws from the comment in Deuteronomy 25:19, "You shall blot out the remembrance of Amalek from under heaven; do not forget." The commandment is impossible to fulfill, for the name Amalek is preserved in Torah; the more one attempts to blot out the name, or that of his descendant Haman, the more attentively one listens for it. Danger cannot be avoided; diaspora existence can never be ensured; the name of the enemy cannot be blotted out; and the community must remain ever vigilant.

Daniel

Fourteenth-century BCE Ugaritic sources mention a wise king named Dan'el, Ezekiel 14:14 associates a Daniel with Noah and Job, and Ezekiel 28:3 mentions a wise Daniel who knows heavenly secrets. But in the biblical book bearing his name, Daniel is a Jew taken into exile in Babylon. Like the book of Esther, the book of Daniel offers a complicated picture of Jews in a foreign court. Although the book was finally redacted around 165 BCE, during the later years of the reign of the Seleucid king Antiochus IV Epiphanes, the stories of Daniel and his friends in the Babylonian and then Persian court preserve earlier materials. And like Esther's adventures, these stories are less historical reports than tales of diaspora survival and encouragement.

Daniel 1:1 dates the story to the "third year of the reign of King Jehoiakim," which would be 606 BCE (2 Chron. 36:5–7), when the Babylonians supposedly besieged Jerusalem. However, the Babylonian king Nebuchadnezzar reigned 605–562 BCE and did not invade Judah until after 605 or besiege Jerusalem until several years later. Thus the book, which recounts the fate of Judahites in exile, suffers the type of chronological problem typical of a folktale. The opening of the book of Judith, "It was the twelfth year of the reign of Nebuchadnezzar, who ruled over the Assyrians in the great city of Nineveh" (1:1a), epitomizes such problems, for Nebuchadnezzar never ruled from Nineveh.

The folktales of Daniel 1–6, like Esther, depict an imperial ruler who is ignorant and dangerous rather than malevolent and a diaspora setting where Jews live in peace, even if not with a complete sense of security. Consequently, the tales are likely to be products of the Persian (539–331 BCE) or early Hellenistic (331–168 BCE) periods rather than of the time of Antiochus IV. Chapters 2:4b–7:28 are written in Aramaic, the common language of Southwest Asia from the Babylonian exile until the incursion of Hellenism; chapters 1, 8–12 are in Hebrew, which was experiencing a renaissance in the late second century.

Complicating the history of the book of Daniel are the Septuagint and Old Greek versions. Like the Septuagint version of Esther, the Septuagint version of Daniel adds to the story, but here the additions are freestanding tales: the story of Susanna, the Prayer of Azariah and the Song of the Three, and Bel and the Dragon. Still more books within the Danielic corpus surfaced in the documents discovered among the Dead Sea Scrolls.

One, the Prayer of Nabonidus (4QprNab), may be an earlier version of Daniel 4.

Both the Hebrew text and the Greek Additions raise questions of concern to Jews living under foreign rule. Should food offered to idols be consumed? Should idols be worshiped? Should one cease to pray to God according to royal decree? How is identity maintained? The major problem is assimilation; the major instruction is in resistance.

According to Daniel 1, Nebuchadnezzar took to Babylon young noblemen, Daniel, Hananiah, Mishael, and Azariah, to be instructed in Chaldean language, literature, and values. He gives the youths the Babylonian names of, respectively, Belteshazzar, Shadrach, Meshach, and Abednego (1:6–7); like Joseph, whom Pharaoh renames Zaphenath-paneah (Gen. 41:45), they are to be members of the new court and thus to shed their Judahite identities. The four youths, however, refuse to assimilate; they resolve not to eat the king's rations lest they "defile" themselves (1:8). Their focus is not primarily on finding kosher food, but avoiding meat offered to idols (an issue that concerned even early Christians, as 1 Cor. 8; 10; Acts 15, 21; and Rev. 2 attest) and wine poured in libation to foreign gods. On their diet of green vegetables and water they thrive, such that their appearance improves more than does that of other youths at the king's table. Following this show of fidelity, God imparts to them "knowledge and skill in every aspect of literature and wisdom; Daniel also had insight into all visions and dreams" (1:17).

Daniel's insight, recollecting Joseph's ability at dream interpretation, comes in handy for the next chapter. Nebuchadnezzar orders his "magicians and enchanters and sorcerers" to tell him not only the interpretation of his troubling dreams (2:1, cf. Gen. 41:8), but also the content of the dreams themselves. When the court magicians protest—interpretation is one thing; mind reading is another—Nebuchadnezzar orders "all the wise men in Babylon" executed. Daniel, one of the "wise men," obtains a temporary stay of execution; while his friends pray, he receives "the mystery" (2:19) in a night vision. Appropriately crediting his God, Daniel correctly recounts the dream and its meaning. Appropriately impressed, Nebuchadnezzar worships Daniel's God and appoints Daniel "chief prefect over all the wise men of Babylon" (2:48). His position is comparable to that of both Joseph and Mordecai.

But diaspora life remains precarious, as Nebuchadnezzar's dream indicates. In the dream, a stone strikes a giant with a golden head, silver chest and arms, bronze torso and thighs, iron legs, and feet of iron and clay; the stone then becomes a great mountain filling the earth. Daniel explains that the giant represents the kingdoms of Babylon, Media, Persia, Greece, and then the division of Alexander's empire—the present golden age to the period of clay and iron. The great mountain is the kingdom of God, but its arrival is in the far future. Empires come and go; the diaspora community will face increasing hardship.

The dangers of diaspora life reappear in the next chapter. Nebuchadnezzar builds a freestanding gold statue "sixty cubits by six" and, with pomp (and repetition), orders a fiery death for anyone refusing to worship it. Shadrach, Meshach, and Abednego of course refuse: "If our God whom we serve is able to deliver us from the furnace of blazing fire and out of your hand, O king, let him deliver us. But if not, be it known to you, O king, that we will not serve your gods and we will not worship the golden statue that you have set up" (3:17–18).

Tossed into a fiery furnace, the three youths, accompanied by a fourth figure "like a son of God" (3:25), walk unharmed through the flames. Impressed, Nebuchadnezzar again blesses Israel's God. Yet, like Ahasuerus, at best volatile, the king goes on to say that because the young men disobeyed his command "and yielded up their bodies rather than serve and worship any god except their own God . . . I make a decree: Any people, nation, or language that utters blasphemy against the God of Shadrach, Meshach, and Abednego shall be torn limb from limb, and their houses laid in ruins; for there is no other god who is able to deliver in this way" (3:28–29). Like the psalmist who can celebrate the murder of children, the storyteller has also been seduced by the ways of the empire: governmental edicts that promote paganism are condemned; edicts that promote the God of Israel are praiseworthy.

The prohibition against blaspheming the Jewish deity will find its way into Jewish tradition via the Noachide laws, commandments understood as given to Noah when he exited the ark and thus commandments for all humanity. Whereas Israel received 613 commandments, the gentile nations have only 7: prohibitions against murder, stealing, sexual crimes, idolatry, blaspheming the Jewish God, and eating the limb from a living animal along with the mandate to establish courts of justice.

By chapter 5, Nebuchadnezzar is no longer on the throne. The text identifies the new king, Belshazzar, as Nebuchadnezzar's son; he was in fact the son not of Nebuchadnezzar, but of the last Babylonian king

Nabonidus (555–539), during whose absence Belshazzar served as regent. The drunken Belshazzar, reminiscent of the drunken Ahasuerus, commands that the vessels Nebuchadnezzar had taken from the Jerusalem temple be brought to his dinner party so that he, his lords, his wives, and his concubines might drink from them. Responding to this irreverence, the fingers of a human hand begin writing on the wall (5:5). Court diviners have no interpretation, but the queen (mother) recalls Daniel's ability to interpret signs (5:11).

Summoned to the court, Daniel rehearses Nebuchadnezzar's life, from greatness to madness, and then condemns Belshazzar for not humbling himself, given this knowledge. He reads the handwriting on the wall: "*Mene, mene, tekel, u* ['and'] *parsin.*" *Mene* (*mina*), a large weight, indicates "counting." Daniel interprets: "God has counted the days of your kingdom and brought it to an end." *Tekel*, a cognate of *shekel*, is one-sixtieth of a *mene*. Its meaning: "You have been weighed in the balance [on the scales] and found wanting." *Parsin* are two coins, each equaling a half-shekel, and they represent division. Daniel interprets: "Your kingdom is divided, and given to the Medes and the Persians." That night Belshazzar is killed and Darius the Mede (actually a Persian who aided the Judeans in the rebuilding of the temple [see Ezra 6]) takes the kingdom (Dan. 5:30–6:1).

From a blaspheming king, the diaspora community passes into the hands of a relatively benign ruler with evil advisers. The scene will replay the book of Esther. Darius decentralizes the government with 120 provinces and plans to appoint Daniel over all; other rulers, jealous as was Haman over Mordecai, convince Darius to make it a capital crime to worship anyone but the king. Daniel disobeys. Three times daily, on his knees, in his upper room, facing Jerusalem, he prays to his God. This practice of thrice-daily worship becomes part of later Judaism (Mishnah *Berakot* 4:1) and Christianity (*Didache* 8). Daniel must, according to "the law of the Medes and the Persians, which cannot be revoked" (6:12, 15; cf. Esther 1:19; 8:8), be tossed into the lions' den. The plot recapitulates that of the book of Esther, but here salvation comes not through militarism, but through miracle.

Daniel, like his friends in the furnace, emerges from the den unscathed; his accusers are tossed in with less positive results. The king decrees that all people "should tremble and fear before Daniel's God" (6:26). The scene has occurred before, and it will appear again.

The three Additions to Daniel continue to document the dangers of diaspora life. For Susanna, the threat is internal and stems from faulty leadership; for Bel and the Dragon, the threat is the external allure of idolatry; for the Prayer of Azariah and the Song of the Three, the threat is also external, and it is the possibility of martyrdom. Yet all three of these Additions reflect a robust diaspora identity; their focus is not on returning to Judah, but on living well in their new homeland. Susanna's story only subtly critiques the diaspora setting. Verse 5b, in a description of the elders, reads: "Concerning them the Lord said, 'Lawlessness (*anomia*) came from Babylon, from elders who were judges, who were supposed to govern the people.'" The quotation is not found in any biblical book.

As for textual history, the Additions are preserved in two Greek versions. The Septuagint locates them at the end of the chapters that comprise the Hebrew/Aramaic materials found in the Masoretic text. The second-century CE Greek text known as Theodotion places Susanna at the beginning of Daniel's story, since the book presents the hero as a "young man," and then locates the other two Additions after Daniel 6. The Additions likely antedate the Maccabean revolt, as do the Hebrew and Aramaic folktales. Their first independent attestation is from the church father Irenaeus of Lyon, around 180 CE.

Susanna, whose righteous parents had trained her "according to the law of Moses" (v. 3), is like Esther of the Septuagint, Judith, and Sarah in the book of Tobit—beautiful, chaste, religiously faithful, and frequently depicted as praying. For diaspora Jews, she and her literary sisters can be seen as representing the covenant community as it would like to see itself: desirable, beautiful, rich, faithful, and ultimately protected from threats external and internal.

Instead of weeping by the waters of Babylon, Susanna, her husband, and children are doing so well that the young wife can plan an afternoon bath in her pleasure garden. There, no wicked kings or malevolent advisers threaten her. Instead, two community elders, who had for weeks been lusting after her, offer her an impossible choice: either have sex with them or they will accuse her of adultery. Echoes of David and Bathsheba—of a powerful ruler and a naked woman by the bath—can be heard; also in the background is the story of the righteous Joseph and the more powerful, lusty Mrs. Potiphar.

Like the youths in the furnace and Daniel in the lions' den, Susanna chooses conviction over capitulation. She prays—unlike Hebrew Esther, in this story everyone, including the narrator, mentions God—and, as she is brought to trial, "Through her tears, she looked up toward Heaven, for her heart trusted in the Lord" (v. 35). Instead of pleading her case to the court, she cries out: "O eternal God, you know what is secret and are aware of all things before they come to be. You know that these men have given false evidence against me, and now I am to die, though I have done none of the wicked things that they have charged against me" (vv. 42–44).

In answer to this prayer, God "stirs up the holy spirit" of Daniel, who comes to the rescue and so initiates one of the world's first detective stories. Cross-examining the elders independently, he proves that their accounts of the alleged adultery are inconsistent. The judges are then put to death, for Deuteronomy 19:16–21 mandates that those who bring false accusations should suffer the penalty they wanted imposed on their victim.

The paired tales of Bel and the Dragon combine the detective story genre with that of idol parody (cf. Isa. 44). In the first account, Daniel proves that the idol is not a god by demonstrating that the Babylonian priests had been sneaking into the temple at night and eating the food set out for it. In the second, Daniel proves that the giant snake is not a god by feeding it a noxious concoction that kills it.

Both accounts in turn may represent narrative developments of Jeremiah 51, which describe Babylon in alimentary terms, for example, "King Nebuchadrezzar of Babylon has devoured me, he has crushed me; he has made me an empty vessel, he has swallowed me like a monster; he has filled his belly with my delicacies, he has spewed me out. . . . I will punish Bel in Babylon, and make him disgorge what he has swallowed" (51:34, 44a). The texts again reflect a confidence in diaspora life: the ruling system can be parodied; the people are safe; idol worship or worship of any deity but the God of Israel is not alluring, but ridiculous.

The final Addition to Daniel, the Prayer of Azariah and the Song of the Three, often printed as Daniel 3:24–90, provides another example of the popularity of personal prayer in the Second Temple period. Here the threat, derived from the story of the furnace, is one of martyrdom. The young men reflect complete fidelity and confidence in their God, whom they "praise and exalt forever."

Tobit

Set amid the remnants of the tribe of Naphtali exiled to Assyria in the eighth century BCE, the book of Tobit—like Judith, Daniel and the Additions, and the Hebrew as well as Greek Esther—uses humor, adventure, and allusions to earlier biblical material to instruct its readers about life in a diaspora context. Fragments of one Hebrew and four Aramaic texts, dating to the late third or early second century BCE, were discovered among the Dead Sea Scrolls, but the version found in printed Bibles today comes from early Greek versions. Like Judith, the Additions to Daniel, and Greek Esther, the text is canonical for Roman Catholic, Anglican, and Eastern Orthodox churches.

The plot begins with Tobit's story. In exile, he displays his covenant loyalty both by speaking about his previous righteous acts, especially in regard to his charitable giving and his offering sacrifices at the Jerusalem temple (Tobit is hardly theologically modest), and by disobeying King Shalmaneser's orders to let the corpses of his enemies rot in the streets. Like Daniel, he will not obey an unjust law.

One night, while outside following yet another burial, this Jewish Antigone is blinded when a bird with an unfortunate aim evacuates in his eyes. Unable to work, Tobit is then supported by his wife, Anna. After several marital spats, Tobit resolves, against his wife's wishes, to send his son, Tobias, to collect funds deposited with a relative in Media. Meanwhile, Tobias's cousin Sarah is experiencing her own problems. Married seven times, she is unable to consummate the relationship because the love-sick demon Asmodeus continually murders her grooms.

These problems and others find their resolution when a man appears at Tobit's door, announces himself to be his long-lost cousin Azariah, and volunteers to serve as Tobias's guide and traveling companion. Azariah is actually the angel Raphael, whose name means "God heals." On the way to collect the funds, Raphael helps rescue Tobias from a ravenous fish and instructs him on how to preserve its heart, gall, and liver, for one never knows when fish guts will prove handy. Raphael next tells Tobias about Sarah and mentions that she is to be his bride. Tobias, understandably reluctant but fortified with faith, and fish, agrees.

The travelers find their way to Sarah's house, where, after a hasty introduction, Sarah's father composes a marriage contract for his unlucky daughter and groom number eight. Hedging his bets, the father also takes time that evening to dig a fresh grave. Meanwhile, entering the bedroom, Tobias follows Raphael's instructions and places the fish heart and liver on the grate. The smell drives Asmodeus to Egypt, where Raphael binds him. The demon exorcised and the marriage under way, the plot needs only to resolve the matter of Tobit's blindness. As expected, the young couple and the angel in disguise return home. Tobias makes a paste of the remaining fish parts, which he puts on his father's eyes. The scales (as it were) fall from them; the father opens his eyes to greet not only his son, but his new daughter-in-law.

At the end of the story, Tobit summarizes his advice for living in the diaspora. He repeats the Deuteronomistic view that sin leads to punishment and repentance to redemption, and he anticipates the ingathering of the exiles and the repenting of the nations. He places emphasis on endogamy: "Remember, my son, that Noah, Abraham, Isaac, and Jacob . . . took wives from among their kindred. They were blessed in their children, and their posterity will inherit the land" (4:12; see also 14:10). He also encourages fasting, concern for temple sacrifices, tithes, pilgrimages, almsgiving, sexual purity, and individual prayer.

Life in the diaspora remains precarious, but through such stories the covenant community preserved its identity, resisted assimilation, found renewed means of religious expression and, more than likely, shared many a hearty laugh.

Part 4

Chapter 13

Critique and Reform

One of the more remarkable characteristics of the Bible is its criticism of power. The biblical writers espouse the sovereignty of YHWH and the hierarchy of social power, especially the authority granted the kings and leaders. At the same time, however, they also advocate the imperative of social justice and the centrality of community and attack anyone—king, priest, elite, or commoner—who threatens these principles. Those in positions of authority and control have influenced the contents of the Hebrew Bible, but they are not immune to its censure.

The two main groups issuing these critiques are the biblical historians and the prophets. That they or anyone else dared to speak out against power is itself extraordinary. During the times of the monarchy, from the tenth to the early sixth century BCE, the kings and one queen held tight control over the country, in particular those aspects that affected their interests. As we have seen, they allowed the villagers to run their own affairs so long as they did not impinge on the wealth and power of the royal house, which meant that much in the everyday lives of the majority of the population did not come to the attention of the monarch. But whenever the rulers wanted labor forces, military conscripts, taxes, and comforts, then the masses were compelled to deliver. The elites, who owned lands, commercial interests, slaves, and other signs of wealth and privilege, also had the means to exploit and manipulate the peasants of the land. Even the priestly establishment knew that its own well-being was tied to the state's success, and its ability to express divine approbation gave the monarchy the legitimacy it craved.

During monarchic and imperial times, thus for most of Israel's history, the established powers formed a formidable force. They controlled the military, commerce, taxation, the cult, and the means of communication beyond the local settings. Writing on a professional level belonged to those with power or wealth: the monarchs had their archivists and correspondents; the wealthy and the priests, their scribes. Most of the texts that eventuated in the Hebrew Bible stemmed not from the largely illiterate populace but from circles that could both produce literature and preserve it over generations. We would not expect it to contain materials critical of royal rule, of upper-class exploitations, and of priestly privilege—nor of God's handling of affairs in this world, the theme of theodicy.

Nonetheless, strong criticisms are present throughout much of the Hebrew Bible. They arise out of the four primary streams of tradition that came together to form the canon—the Deuteronomistic, the prophetic, the priestly, and the sapiential (wisdom). Each was relatively distinguished from the others, and each had an institutional base. Although they at times experienced tensions with each other, for the most part each carried on rather independently, developing oral traditions and practices and transmitting them from generation to generation. Eventually these traditions became written and combined with each other into the emerging biblical text. All of them criticize political leadership, social injustices, and religious infidelity, with each tradition having a primary emphasis: the Deuteronomistic, on politics and religion; the prophetic, on social issues and religion; the priestly, on religious practices; and the sapiential, on practical and realistic observations about life. With parts oriented to the status quo and others to reform, the priestly tradition stands behind the cultic practices and religious laws described in Chapters 5 and 6. The sapiential stream of tradition engages broad theological and social issues with such intensity and insight that we will devote the entire final chapter to its critique. In this chapter, we focus on the Deuteronomistic and the prophetic critiques of politics, society, and religion.

Historians as Critics

The Hebrew Bible includes considerable stretches of historical accounts. The Pentateuch traces the family line from Abraham to Joseph, followed then by a description of the Israelites' escape from Egypt and wanderings in the wilderness. The Deuteronomistic History (Joshua through 2 Kings) picks up the story as the people cross the Jordan River to conquer and settle the land, and it then relates the history of the monarchy from Saul to the fall of Jerusalem in 586 BCE, along with a few notes about exilic times. The books of 1–2 Chronicles cover much of the same ground, ending with a reference to Persian emperor Cyrus's edict releasing the exiles in 538 BCE. The books of Ezra and Nehemiah are more limited in scope, focusing mainly on the early years after the exiles returned home and rebuilt the Jerusalem temple (538–515 BCE) and then on the period 458–430, when Nehemiah and Ezra report on their own involvement in rebuilding Jerusalem and dealing with the issue of intermarriage between Jews and non-Jews. Much of the material from 2 Chronicles 35–36 and the books of Ezra and Nehemiah is also present in the book of 1 Esdras, a second-century BCE text included in the Greek and Russian Orthodox canons.

Historians can scarcely function dispassionately. The notion that history must be told objectively and neutrally is now widely recognized as illusory, for all historians bring to the task values and perspectives that affect their selection and interpretation of details from the past. Biblical historians—here this term refers to the historians who wrote the historical accounts in the Bible, not modern historians who write about biblical times—also had their own values and perspectives, which inevitably show in their narratives. Unlike contemporary secular historians, they readily assume that the divine world intersects with the human world, and for them God becomes a primary actor in the events and situations they describe. More specifically, these biblical historians hold to such theological and moral principles as the supremacy of YHWH, the primacy of the Israelite people over other peoples, and the imperative to treat the powerless and disadvantaged with compassion.

As a result, the historical presentations in the Hebrew Bible reflect such principles. The biblical historians appraise their country's past very critically, holding individuals and groups to the high standards represented in these and other religious and moral principles. As critics, they target especially the period of the monarchy when, in their opinion, the leaders of the people make particularly bad decisions about the gods they worship and the practices they follow in treating their subjects. Even the people receive censure when they follow in the paths of their rulers. These historians' objectives point, however, beyond the mere retelling of history. They aim to instruct or reform their own and future generations, and they use the mistakes of prior generations to direct their readers and hearers in the proper course for the future.

These historical narratives are unlikely products of the times they describe since no monarch would have knowingly allowed such scathing critiques, let alone commissioned them. Royal archives can retain materials of which the rulers are unaware, and stories circulating in oral form among the wider public, outside governmental control, can transmit unflattering details. Yet it took biblical historians in a later period, drawing on all such materials at their disposal, to craft them into narratives that disparage the leaders so sharply. King Hezekiah, around 700 BCE, and King Josiah, three quarters of a century later, appear in this history as the only faithful and reform-minded rulers. Although the historians may have collected and edited their materials as a part of the reform during Josiah's time, it is more likely that these great historical works, both the Pentateuch and the Deuteronomistic History, stem from the postexilic period, the sixth to the fourth centuries BCE, when Israel's kings were no longer present to control the narrative. In such a setting, these history writers functioned free of monarchic—though not imperial—pressures, and they could look back to the times of the kings and earlier to trace the line of apostasy and oppression that, in their view, resulted in Jerusalem's capture and the people's exile.

Moses, Flawed but Unassailable

Political and religious leadership operates at the most basic levels of the household, clan, and tribe. However, the first leaders of the people as a whole emerge well before the founding of the state in the stories of the escape from Egypt, wanderings in the wilderness, and conquest of the promised land. A solitary law in the Covenant Code (Exod. 21–23) lays down a succinct principle: "You shall not revile God, or curse a leader of your people" (22:28; Tanakh 22:27). The Hebrew word for "leader," *nasi,* can designate both a tribal leader and a king, and in the canonical context of this law Moses is the most likely immediate referent. The NRSV translation "revile" is too soft; the Hebrew original means to "treat contemptuously" or "curse." Linking God and the leader so closely in this law functions as divine legitimation of the king/leader, at least ideally. It also sets the stage for the people's complaints, if not curses, against their leader Moses.

The stories about the wilderness wanderings have two primary political purposes: to portray the ideal leader as God's surrogate with legitimate authority and to show the people as recalcitrant. Several episodes depict the people complaining vociferously, on the verge of a rebellion against their primary leader, Moses, and his brother, Aaron, who heads the cult.

Two grounds for complaint occur in these stories: either the people face an actual physical need or they express a more broadly based dissatisfaction with Moses's leadership. In the first case the people complain to Moses that they lack drinking water: "Why did you bring us out of Egypt, to kill us and our children and livestock with thirst?" (Exod. 17:3). Or they have water, but no food, at least not the variety they remember enjoying back in Egypt: "If only we had died by the hand of YHWH in the land of Egypt, when we sat by the fleshpots and ate our fill of bread; for you have brought us out into this wilderness to kill this whole assembly with hunger" (16:3). God responds with a daily supply of manna and quails. According to early rabbinic interpretation, the manna had multiple tastes, so everyone would find it pleasing. But bored with that diet, the people demand more: "We remember the fish we used to eat in Egypt for nothing, the cucumbers, the melons, the leeks, the onions, and the garlic; but now our strength is dried up, and there is nothing at all but this manna to look at" (Num. 11:5–6). With a couple million people wandering together in the wilderness (purportedly 603,550 fighting men, according to Num. 1:46, plus women, children, and elderly), responding to these bitter complaints seems all the more daunting, but the people receive the food and water they need.

With the second type of complaint, the people challenge Moses and Aaron's leadership at a more fundamental level. In two instances they charge either ineptitude or something approaching tyranny, and both times the text interprets the people's charge as rebellion against God, who had appointed Moses and Aaron. The first instance, which sounds like the charge of ineptitude if not malice, occurs after the initial reconnaissance of the land of Canaan results in the disquieting news that it is inhabited by fierce giants (the Nephilim, the same term used for the mythological offspring of the "divine sons" and "human daughters" in Genesis 6:1–4). The Israelites confront Moses and Aaron in near mutiny: "Would that we had died in the land of Egypt! Or would that we had died in this wilderness! Why is YHWH bringing us into this land to fall by the sword? Our wives and our little ones will become booty; would it not be better for us to go back to Egypt? . . . Let us choose a captain, and go back to Egypt" (Num. 14:2–4).

The word translated by the NRSV as "captain" is not the word *nasi* ("leader") used in Exodus 22:28, but *rosh*, the usual word for "head." Moses and Aaron beseech the people not to rebel, but the Israelites respond by threatening to stone them. Although Moses in other stories exhibits a short temper, here he intercedes with YHWH who, on the verge of wiping out the people, says to Moses: "I will strike them with pestilence and disinherit them, and I will make of you [Moses] a nation greater and mightier than they" (Num. 14:12). In response to Moses's appeal, YHWH relents but decrees that the wilderness wanderings will last for forty years until those who had lived in Egypt, the exodus generation, have died. The people's complaint thus has consequences for them, but they do not receive a substantive response to their charge that Moses and Aaron have led them into danger.

The second instance goes to the heart of the issue of political leadership and power. In Numbers 16, Korah, Dathan, Abiram, and On gather 250 well-respected men and, without referring to any specific incident, approach Moses and Aaron with a general charge: "You have gone too far! All the congregation are holy, every one of them, and YHWH is among them. So why then do you exalt yourselves above the assembly of YHWH?" (Num. 16:3). Moses's immediate response is to "fall on his face," an act of humility and supplication, and he then summons them to appear the next day so YHWH can decide between them and Moses and Aaron. Moses does not yet defend himself but suggests one of the points of contention when he accuses the Levites of aspiring to the priesthood; earlier texts (especially Num. 1:48–54; 3:1–13; 4; 8) had detailed the duties of the priests and the Levites, with the Levites largely in the role of assistants to the priests. Instead, Dathan and Abiram (they are Reubenites, not Levites) defy him: "We will not come!" Moses, now furious, implores God not to accept the rebels' offering (which is the first we hear of an offering), and Moses even sounds somewhat defensive: "I have not taken one donkey from them, and I have not harmed any one of them" (16:15). Yet when God threatens, as in previous stories, to wipe out the whole community, Moses again intercedes, but only briefly: "Shall one person sin and you [YHWH] become angry with the whole congregation?" (16:22). It is an argument reminiscent, though in the reverse (the wicked few, not the righteous few), of Abraham's challenge to God before the destruction of Sodom and Gomorrah (Gen. 18:22–33).

Seeking to reassert his authority, Moses sets up a test to demonstrate which group God will find guilty—whether Moses and Aaron or the rebels. Immediately the ground opens up and swallows the rebels together with their wives, children, and infants, and fire consumes their 250 supporters. When the rest of the congregation accuses Moses and Aaron of killing the rebels, God sends a plague and kills 14,700 of the people before Aaron can avert further recriminations against the whole community. As in the previous case, Moses indicates that the revolt represents an attack not just against him and Aaron but against God: "You and all your company have gathered together against YHWH. What is Aaron that you rail against him?" (Num. 16:11; also 14:9a). The political message is clear: the leaders (Moses and Aaron) have divine backing and are not to be challenged.

In a confrontation that further reinforces Moses's unique leadership, his siblings, Miriam and Aaron, meet with a harsh response when they question their brother. According to Numbers 12, they criticize him for marrying a non-Israelite woman, a Cushite (possibly Zipporah, identified in Exod. 2:15–22 as a Midianite). The problem of intermarriage with foreigners, discussed in Chapter 9, resonates with later criticisms of kings, especially Solomon and Ahab, who marry foreign women, and Ezra and Nehemiah are especially critical of the practice in postexilic times.

But Miriam and Aaron's charge takes on a scope broader than the issue of marriage: "Has YHWH spoken only through Moses? Has he not spoken through us also?" Moses, we then learn, is "very humble, more so than anyone else on the face of the earth"—not exactly the impression given earlier of this dominant leader who can kill an Egyptian, face down Pharaoh, and lead a massive group of slaves out of bondage. God calls the three of them together and responds that Moses is different from all the prophets through whom God communicates only in dreams: "He [Moses] is entrusted with all my house. With him I speak face to face—clearly, not in riddles; and he beholds the form of YHWH" (12:6–8). The NRSV translation "face to face" is misleading; the Hebrew has "mouth to mouth," emphasizing verbal communication rather than physical viewing, which God has already stipulated is impossible: "You cannot see my face; for no one shall see me and live" (Exod. 33:20, in this case using the Hebrew word for "face").

For their insubordination, God strikes Miriam with a skin disease (*tzara'at*, not "leprosy," Hansen's disease, from which one cannot be completely healed). Aaron is left untouched, with no reason given for his escaping a similar punishment. Perhaps the tradition needed to preserve Aaron, the progenitor of Israel's line of priests, from this unclean condition since priests are to determine when a person has recovered from a skin condition (Lev. 13–14). Never mind that in an earlier story Aaron leads the people in erecting a golden calf for the people to worship (Exod. 32). In the end Moses appeals to God, and Miriam is restored after seven days.

The Pentateuch paints a portrait of Moses as a supreme, exemplary leader of the people. No other source from early times exists to offer another perspective on him. According to the Hebrew Bible, he possesses the attributes needed for the task—strength, purpose, compassion, resilience. He claims to be a poor speaker (Exod. 4:10), but it is unclear whether he means he suffers from a speech impediment or a lack of eloquence. Then again, having God on his side to quell any coups is no slight asset.

Moses also has weaknesses, in particular his quick temper and perhaps an inflated estimation of himself. God forbids him to enter the land of Canaan; he will get no more than a view of it from the top of Mt. Nebo, east of the Jordan River near the Dead Sea. The reason comes at the end of another incident in which the people quarrel with Moses about their hard trek and lack of food and water (Num. 20:2–13; the site will be named Meribah, which means "quarrel").

God tells Moses and Aaron to take their staff, assemble the people, and command water to spring forth from a nearby rock. Instead, Moses angrily tells the grumblers: "Listen, you rebels, shall we bring water for you out of this rock?"—suggesting that he thinks he and Aaron can miraculously produce the water by themselves. Rather than command the rock to issue water, Moses strikes it with his staff, and it produces abundant water. YHWH then tells Moses that he will not be allowed to lead the Israelites into the land of Canaan—on the rather unclear grounds that he "did not trust in me [YHWH], to show my holiness" to the people (20:12), which may mean that Moses claimed to have the power that belongs only to God. It seems a small infraction when compared to all Moses does throughout the expanse of Exodus, Leviticus, Numbers, and Deuteronomy.

A few other texts refer to this incident at Meribah, even calling it a rebellion by Moses (Num. 27:14; also Deut. 1:37; 32:51–52), but one exchange in particular shows God's anger and impatience with Moses over it. In Deuteronomy 3:25–26, Moses begs to be allowed to cross the Jordan River with the people, but YHWH responds: "Enough from you! Never speak to me of this matter again!"

The Pentateuch presents God as a deity with both a demanding and a compassionate side, and Moses as a paradigmatic leader with many successes but also failures. Others succeed him as the head of the people: Joshua, his immediate successor; the "judges" who lead the people during the rest of the premonarchic period; and finally the kings. Prophets and priests occupy key positions as religious leaders, but without the centralized authority of a singular ruler. Only with the monarchy does a system emerge that possesses the durability, economic means, administrative mechanisms, monumental architecture, and extensive power to control the populace and engage geopolitically with other countries. Such power and privilege can easily evolve into despotism, and the biblical accounts are critical of Israel's leaders when that happens. However, the Hebrew Bible falls short of calling into question the hierarchy inherent in monarchies. Indeed, Moses is the precursor of later kings, and YHWH is king of all: "For YHWH is our judge, YHWH is our ruler, YHWH is our king; he will save us" (Isa. 33:22).

As His Father David Did

Chapter 1 focused on the monarchy from the perspective of a modern historian following the trail of the kings, especially in light of any extrabiblical evidence of their existence and actions. In this chapter we shift the question to the *biblical evaluation* of the various regents. For modern historians, the decision of whether a given ruler was good or bad depends primarily on how that ruler performed geopolitically and domestically, whereas for the biblical writers the monarchs' allegiance to YHWH and treatment of their subjects receive foremost attention.

The purpose of the Deuteronomistic History is less to recount history than to judge it. Stretching from Joshua to 2 Kings, this long narrative carries the name "Deuteronomistic" because its approach to writing history takes its lead from the religious and moral principles enunciated in the book of Deuteronomy—worship of YHWH exclusively, centralization of the cult (in Jerusalem), obedience to the law, and humane treatment of others. There is no modern consensus about its date of composition. Some think it was compiled near the end of the sixth century BCE during the time of King Josiah's reform. Others place it in the exilic context, when those in exile may have examined their past to determine why they had suffered such a great loss. Still others argue that it was drafted after the exile during the period of restoration or realignment involving exiles who returned to Judah together with those who had not gone into exile or their descendants a few generations later.

The latter date, sometime between the late sixth and the fourth centuries BCE, has the most to commend itself for three reasons. First, writing during the monarchic period was controlled mainly by the rulers and the elites, the supporters not of reform but of the status quo and personal benefit. Second, the relentless criticisms of the monarchs in these books must stem from a period when the monarchy existed only as an ideal. And, finally, the Persian empire in this period encouraged its provinces to record their laws and cultural memories. Oral traditions passed down from monarchic times, enhanced with archival records and a zeal for religious faithfulness, served as the building blocks of this literature. Its critique of the royal lines in Israel and Judah, from Saul at the outset to Zedekiah at the end, runs like a scarlet thread through the narrative. Multiple persons were involved in compiling these traditions and editing the documents; hence, the plural term "Deuteronomists" or "Deuteronomistic historians."

Whatever its date and authors, the Deuteronomistic History stands out as a literary masterpiece, filled with stirring anecdotes, suspense, intrigue, conflicts between characters, touching interactions, hopeful developments, sad tragedies, and moral and religious commentary. Only summaries and allusions are possible in our discussion, and nothing takes the place of reading the full historical narrative as it has come down to us. The commentaries or editorial notes added by the Deuteronomists stand out in their content (the imperatives for the one people to worship one God in one place, Jerusalem; also the summaries of past history), their style (prosaic, exhortative, didactic, repetitive; Josh. 24:2–14, for example, as well as the summaries at the deaths of the judges and kings), and their formulaic phrases (e.g., "following/worshiping other gods," "the place that YHWH will choose/has chosen," "keep the commandments," "the land that YHWH gives you as an inheritance," Egypt as "the house of bondage," "YHWH alone is God," "for the sake of David, my servant"). These commentaries are interspersed among the traditional materials that the Deuteronomists inherited.

In Chapter 11 we described the kinds of monarchic powers gained by Israel's first three kings according to the biblical history; here we focus on the Deuteronomists' judgment of their reigns, beginning with a pair of stories that describes the founding of the monarchy. One promonarchic and the other antimonarchic, the accounts are interwoven in the present text but probably originated separately, much as did the two creation stories in Genesis 1 and 2–3.

According to the promonarchic version (1 Sam. 9:1–10:16), YHWH desires the monarchy and directs Samuel to anoint the man whom God will send, evident by his physical appearance: "handsome" and "head and shoulders above everyone else" (9:2). The candidate is Saul, who is not even familiar with Samuel, a local seer. Saul appears as predicted, and after some back-and-forth Samuel privately anoints him king somewhere in the hill country of Ephraim, not far from Gilgal, the site of a religious shrine. Saul then continues on his way, telling no one what has transpired. The story paints a positive picture of kingship inasmuch as YHWH freely initiates it by directing Samuel to anoint Saul.

The antimonarchic story (1 Sam. 8; 10:17–27) gives a very different impression. Here the initiative lies with the people, not with God. All the Israelite elders approach Samuel, who is depicted not as a little-known seer but as the recognized leader of the people, much like a "judge" in the book of Judges. They say to him: "You are old and your sons do not follow in your ways; appoint for us, then, a king to govern us, like other nations" (8:5). Samuel is extremely displeased, as is God, who tells Samuel: "They have not rejected you, but they have rejected me from being king over them. . . . Now then, listen to their voice; only—you shall solemnly warn them, and show them the ways of the king who shall reign over them" (8:7b, 9).

In harmony with the "law of the king" in Deuteronomy 17:14–20, Samuel relays YHWH's message to the people and launches into an ominous prediction in his "ways of the king" address (1 Sam. 8:11–18). He tells the people they will regret their choice because their future king will press them into serving him in the military, in farming his lands, and in preparing his food; he will take their crops, their slaves, their cattle and flocks and will even enslave the people themselves. And then the zinger: "And in that day you will cry out because of your king, whom you have chosen for yourselves; but YHWH will not answer you in that day." Undeterred, the people repeat their demand, and Samuel convenes them at Mizpah—a foreshadowing of sixth-century exilic times, when the Neo-Babylonian empire established Mizpah as the administrative center of the province. In a process of elimination apparently using sacred lots, Samuel chooses the tribe, the clan, and finally Saul himself, who is so shy that God has to tell them he has hidden himself among the baggage. Without an actual anointing ceremony, the people affirm his selection by acclamation, "Long live the king!" or literally in Hebrew, "May the king live!" (1 Sam. 10:24).

The promonarchic tradition is the type of account that kings affirm and likely keep in their archives as justification for their rule. The antimonarchic story, however, had no place in those archives. It reflects the sorry history of oppressive regimes as experienced by the vulnerable living outside the circles of power. The account represents a "prediction after the fact," that is, a statement based on later experience and projected back to an earlier time—here the founding of the monarchy—to appear as a prediction of later happenings. With this antimonarchic story the Deuteronomists introduce the line of criticism that carries forward throughout the rest of their history and into the prophetic literature.

The Deuteronomistic History spends almost twice as much space on Israel's first three kings, Saul, David, and Solomon, than on all the other thirty-nine monarchs combined. Two reasons for this imbalance stand out. First, the story of the monarchy's beginning dramatizes the devolution from optimism to cynicism, from the hopes and desires reflected in the promonarchic story to the oppressions and apostasies of the antimonarchic tradition. The first three kings all have their good points, and David later becomes revered as the ideal king against whom all other monarchs are measured. But according to the Deuteronomists, the first three reigns sow the seeds of trouble, which then come to fruition with most of the later rulers. Second, having made that point, the Deuteronomists can now deal in short order with the three centuries of monarchs who almost unfailingly follow the wrong lead of their predecessors. Chapter 11 describes Saul, David, and Solomon as the founders of the state's political and economic structures and as the initiators of the royal tradition of apostasy and oppression. Here we now see the Deuteronomists' critique of the rest of the monarchy.

The antimonarchic perspective dominates this narrative of the monarchy. It begins with the story of the secession of the ten northern tribes, leaving only Judah and Benjamin in the south. Rehoboam, Solomon's son, ascends to the throne after Solomon's death, and his first item of business, according to the Deuteronomistic historians, is the corvée and taxation. The northerner Jeroboam, who had started an insurrection against Solomon because of his apostasy and then had to flee the country, approaches Rehoboam at Shechem with a request on behalf of the people: "Your father made our yoke heavy. Now therefore lighten the hard service of your father and his heavy yoke, . . . and we will serve you" (1 Kings 12:4). Rehoboam consults his father's counselors, who advise that he grant the request. There was precedent for it among several ancient Southwest Asian rulers who extended special relief on their ascension to the throne. For example, we have edicts from two of Hammurabi's successors in eighteenth- and seventeenth-century Babylon, Kings Samsu-iluna and Ammi-saduqa, as well as others over the next thousand years, who remitted debts, released slaves, forgave tax obligations, and announced other forms of release when they became king.

But Rehoboam's younger counselors, with whom he had grown up, urge the opposite: "Thus you should say to them, 'My little finger is thicker than my father's loins. Now, whereas my father laid on you a heavy yoke, I will add to your yoke. My father disciplined you with whips, but I will discipline you with scorpions'" (12:10–11). Rehoboam follows his friends' advice, omitting the sexual innuendo but keeping the mention of scorpions, which probably refers to lashes with iron tips. Jeroboam and his followers revolt, slay Rehoboam's corvée master, and secede from the union, sending Rehoboam scurrying back to Jerusalem.

Two countries result from this division, the northern kingdom, Israel, first ruled by Jeroboam and comprising ten of the tribes, and the southern kingdom, Judah, under Rehoboam with only two tribes, Judah and Benjamin (1 Kings 12:20–24; the prediction in 11:29–36 mentions only one tribe—presumably Judah, which is much larger than Benjamin). The Deuteronomistic History from this point forward follows both kingdoms until the north falls to Neo-Assyria in 722, and it then tracks the south alone until its demise at the hands of the Neo-Babylonians in 586.

The Deuteronomists assess each king or queen according to the two negative criteria of apostasy and oppression—whether the monarch adheres to or abandons Yahwistic worship and whether the people benefit or are exploited during the reign. The introductory or concluding statements about each reign usually offer a summary statement on this order: "Ahab son of Omri did evil in the sight of YHWH more than all who were before him" (1 Kings 16:30), or "Asa did what was right in the sight of YHWH, as his father David had done" (15:11). Often a positive assessment appears, such as this one for Asa, followed then by another note that the given monarch has failed in some respect: "But the high places [local shrines] were not taken away" (15:14).

A clear pattern emerges in which the writers are extremely critical of the north but less so of the south. The northern kingdom, Israel, lasted for only 200 years, a much shorter period than the 336 years of the southern kingdom, Judah. The chart of rulers in Chapter 1 shows that the two countries had almost the same number of monarchs each: twenty in the

south, with an average reign of 16.8 years; and nineteen in the north, av-
eraging 10.5 years each, suggesting significantly less stability in the north.
Applying their two criteria, the Deuteronomists rate only two kings very
good, both from the south: Hezekiah and Josiah. The Deuteronomists
approve of several others, but not so unequivocally, and again all are from
Judah: Asa, Jehoshaphat, Jehoash, Amaziah, Uzziah, and Jotham. Jehu in
the north starts with approbation but ends on the bad side of the ledger,
and all the other northern kings are deemed bad. Six rulers are fully evil:
Ahaz, Manasseh, and Amon in the south and Jeroboam, Omri, and Ahab
in the north. The statistics for assassinations and suicides conform to this
pattern. Assassinations were commonplace in ancient Southwest Asia,
whereas suicides—except for those done under force—occurred much less
frequently. According to the Deuteronomistic History, almost a third of
all the monarchs, twelve out of thirty-nine, die in a coup, and all but two
(Jehoash and Amaziah in Judah) are either bad or evil. The north again
seems much more disruptive, with more such deaths than the south has
in nearly twice the length of time. The only suicide is the northern king
Zimri; Ahab's death from fighting in battle as a common soldier seems
reckless if not intentionally destructive (1 Kings 16:15–20; 22:29–37).

Since we lack external sources to confirm these judgments, we are left
only with biblical stories that fit the Deuteronomists' agenda—roundly
critical of the north and substantially unhappy with the south despite a
few bright lights. Because of their tilt toward the south, we can assume
that the Deuteronomists themselves either lived in the south prior to the
fall of Jerusalem or, as the descendants of southerners during the exilic or
postexilic periods, were steeped in this point of view.

The book of Judges ends with a statement that seems to denigrate the
period before the monarchy: "In those days there was no king in Israel; all
the people did what was right in their own eyes" (21:25). From the pictures
provided by the Deuteronomists, the monarchic system of government is not
much of an improvement. The regents continually get things wrong, and
the people suffer as a result. Even the reform efforts by Hezekiah and Josiah
are short-lived, as their successors undo any improvements. The Deuteronomists do not propose a new political alternative, although the above statement regarding the time when "there was no king in Israel" could be read
as wistful nostalgia by the oppressed subjects. Instead, the Deuteronomistic
History criticizes past leaders as a means of calling for reform to renew allegiance to YHWH and to lessen oppression of the people.

Stories of several monarchs during the divided kingdom demonstrate the Deuteronomists' interest in deriding most of the kings. King Jeroboam is the first monarch in the north and the leader of Israel's secession from Judah (1 Kings 12–14). The Deuteronomistic historians sympathize with the northern rebels because of the harsh treatment threatened by King Rehoboam, but the writers' summary statement after the revolt is more condemnatory: "So Israel has been in rebellion against the house of David to this day" (12:19; "to this day" is a commonly used formula to indicate some later point in the history of the tradition). The next we hear, Jeroboam, fearing that the people will continue to trek to Jerusalem to worship and then may decide to rejoin the southern kingdom, makes two golden calves and sets them up in the shrines he establishes at Bethel and Dan in northern Israel. Reminiscent of the golden calf built by Aaron during the wilderness wanderings (Exod. 32), Jeroboam's two calves symbolize either of two Canaanite gods—El, the supreme god at the head of the pantheon, or Baal, the god of thunderstorms and fertility. Jeroboam's act thus seeks to legitimate the northern kingdom by associating it with two of the most powerful competing deities worshiped by people of the region.

Three prophets appear to denounce Jeroboam for this perfidy (1 Kings 13:1–14:18). A prophet from Judah comes to the north and pronounces doom against the altar Jeroboam erected and the priests he appointed. When Jeroboam points toward the prophet, his hand withers, but it is restored when he entreats the prophet to intercede for him. Then an old prophet from Israel deceives the prophet from Judah into violating God's command, with the result that a lion attacks and kills the latter prophet on his way home. The lion and the prophet's donkey remain standing over the body so everyone will see the punishment, and the lion does so without eating the body or attacking the donkey. Finally the old Israelite prophet fetches the body and gives it a proper burial in his own grave. This incident is followed by another in which Jeroboam sends his wife to deceive a third prophet into healing their sick son, but at God's command the prophet pronounces death on the son, Jeroboam and his family, and all of his followers because of their apostasy. Altogether, these three stories of prophets severely condemn Jeroboam and all associated with him, and they include a reference to the northern kingdom's demise and exile: "YHWH will strike Israel, as a reed is shaken in the water; he will root up Israel out of this good land that he gave to their ancestors, and scatter them beyond the Euphrates" (14:15).

Another wicked king of the north, Ahab, and his wife, the Phoenician princess Jezebel, command more space in the biblical history than any other single reign during the divided monarchy (1 Kings 16–22; 2 Kings 9). Ahab's marriage to Jezebel is the first detail reported in this long account, ominous because of the Deuteronomistic sense that she is likely to promote the worship of other gods, as did Solomon's foreign wives. The second detail then pictures Ahab erecting an altar to Baal and a "sacred pole," in Hebrew *asherah*, representing the goddess who is Baal's consort. These acts rate Ahab a resounding censure: "Ahab did more to provoke the anger of YHWH, the God of Israel, than had all the kings of Israel who were before him" (1 Kings 16:31–33). The stories of Ahab and Jezebel are laced with a multitude of prophets, three by name (Elijah, Elisha, and Micaiah) as well as many other unidentified prophets of either YHWH or Baal (18:20–40; 22:5–28). The Yahwistic prophets figure prominently throughout the Deuteronomistic narrative as the conveyors of divine judgment on the monarchs; Samuel and Nathan are early prototypes during the time of Saul and David.

One of the most memorable incidents involving Ahab and Jezebel is the acquisition of Naboth's vineyard (1 Kings 21). Naboth owns a vineyard in Jezreel, and Ahab wants to annex it and use it as a vegetable garden. This shift in use is itself a subtle comment about Ahab's extensive landholdings since he is willing to tear down a vineyard, which takes years and even generations to develop into a productive crop. He offers to buy it or to exchange a better vineyard for it, but Naboth declines on the grounds that it is ancestral land he has inherited. Ahab then returns home pouting and depressed; "he lay down on his bed, turned away his face, and would not eat" (21:4). This Deuteronomistic belittling of Ahab's conduct contrasts with the political prowess attributed to Jezebel, who tells him sarcastically: "Do you now govern Israel? Get up, eat some food, and be cheerful; I will give you the vineyard of Naboth the Jezreelite" (21:7).

Naboth is no poor, vulnerable peasant, as some interpreters have viewed him; rather, he belongs to the upper class inasmuch as his valuable vineyard borders on the king's summer palace grounds. So Jezebel has to move carefully to achieve her goal. She organizes a sham trial with two false witnesses ("scoundrels") and with Naboth's peers as judges (1 Kings 21:8–14). The charge is not that Naboth has violated some personal or property law, but that he has blasphemed: "Naboth has cursed God and the king," a violation of the law "You shall not revile God, or curse a leader of your people" (Exod. 22:28; Tanakh 22:27). Predictably, Naboth is pronounced guilty and is stoned, and Ahab takes possession of the vineyard. The prophet Elijah then delivers God's judgment that, because of this act of injustice, Ahab and his family will die and dogs will eat their bodies. When Ahab then repents and appeals for mercy, God relents and postpones the destruction of Ahab's dynasty until a later generation (21:17–29).

Jezebel disappears from the narrative for seven years, reappearing in 2 Kings 9:30–37 for her violent death scene. Ahab has already died in battle after a confrontation with the prophet Micaiah (1 Kings 22). Now Jehu, the present king of Israel, arrives at the city of Jezreel, where the incident involving Naboth's vineyard occurred. Hearing of his arrival, Jezebel paints her eyes with kohl and coifs her hair for her formal audience with him. From her window she calls down to Jehu: "Is it peace (*shalom*), Zimri, murderer of your master?" Calling him Zimri is a snide reference to an earlier king of Israel, Zimri, who murdered King Elah and usurped the throne, only to commit suicide after a reign of just seven days (1 Kings 16:8–20). Jehu is a "Zimri" because he has already killed King Joram of Israel, Ahab and Jezebel's son. Jehu asks for anyone on his side to throw Jezebel out of the window, and two eunuchs, attendants in the king's harem, do so. Thus she dies, with "some of her blood spattered on the wall and on the horses, which trampled on her" (2 Kings 9:33). Jehu enters the city to eat and drink, eventually instructing someone to see to Jezebel's burial because she belongs to royalty—pointedly not as King Ahab's wife, but as the daughter of a Phoenician king. But when they arrive at the place where her body should be, "they found no more of her than the skull and the feet and the palms of her hands" (9:35). The Deuteronomists have Jehu interpret Jezebel's horrible death as the fulfillment of Elijah's prediction, which Jehu next completes by massacring the rest of Ahab's family (2 Kings 10).

The sole queen serving as head of either state is King Ahab's daughter, Queen Athaliah of Judah (2 Kings 11), who seizes the throne after Jehu kills her son Ahaziah. Athaliah seems especially vicious because of her efforts to kill all members of the royal family, but other monarchs such as Solomon, Zimri, and Jehu also murder possible contenders to the throne in their early years of rule. Queen Athaliah's plan is thwarted, though, when Ahaziah's sister conceals his son Joash (also called Jehoash) so he escapes the massacre. Several years later, when Joash is seven years old, the high priest at the temple rallies the soldiers, and they crown him king. Upon hearing the acclamation, Queen Athaliah goes to the temple, charges the people with treason, but is then assassinated at the priest's command. And with that stroke the seven-year-old Joash ascends the throne for a long and, according to the Deuteronomists, quite a good reign.

The fall of the northern kingdom in 722 BCE elicits categorical denunciation by the Deuteronomistic historians. They do not blame the defeat mainly on King Hoshea, who reigned at the time; according to their report, his predecessors were worse and more at fault: Hoshea "did what was evil in the sight of YHWH, yet not like the kings of Israel who were before him" (2 Kings 17:2). In a lengthy passage of pure Deuteronomistic prose (17:7–23), the historians describe how the kings and the people of the north had repeatedly abandoned Yahwistic worship and commandments. They "worshiped other gods and walked in the customs of the nations whom YHWH drove out," "set up for themselves pillars and sacred poles on every high hill and under every green tree," "served idols," "would not listen" to the prophets, "despised [YHWH's] statutes, and his covenant that he made with their ancestors," "made their sons and their daughters pass through fire" (a reference to child sacrifice), "used divination and augury," and "continued in all the sins that Jeroboam committed." The Deuteronomists express sharp criticism against the southern Judahites, but they have almost nothing good to say about the northern Israelites. Their appraisal ends simply: "YHWH removed Israel out of his sight, as he had foretold through all his servants the prophets. So Israel was exiled from their own land to Assyria until this day" (17:23).

Only two of the thirty-nine kings after Saul, David, and Solomon can be considered very good: Hezekiah (2 Kings 18–20) and Josiah (2 Kings 22–23). Hezekiah receives the accolade: "He trusted in YHWH the God of Israel; so that there was no one like him among all the kings of Judah after him, or among those who were before him" (18:5). Though inconsistent with this statement, another superlative affirmation goes to Josiah: "Before him there was no king like him, who turned to YHWH with all his heart, with all his soul, and with all his might, according to all the law of Moses; nor did any like him arise after him" (23:25). In this statement is an echo of Deuteronomy 6:4–5, the Jewish declaration of faith called the Shema: "Hear (*shema*), O Israel: YHWH is our God, YHWH alone. You shall love YHWH your God with all your heart, and with all your soul, and with all your might."

Hezekiah and Josiah parallel each other in several respects. Both stem from the southern kingdom, Judah. Hezekiah is the first king crowned under the Neo-Assyrian empire after the fall of the north, and he reigns some twenty-eight years as a vassal. Josiah is the last Judahite vassal under the Neo-Assyrians, ascending to the throne some forty-seven years after Hezekiah's death. He reigns during the protracted demise of the Neo-Assyrian empire, probably breaking free from it sometime during the 620s BCE along with other kingdoms in the region. Both resist foreign powers— Neo-Assyria and Philistia by Hezekiah, and Neo-Assyria and Egypt by Josiah. Both kings also launch the most significant reforms in their country's history, at least according to the Deuteronomists. Hezekiah "removed the high places, broke down the pillars, and cut down the sacred pole [*asherah*]" (2 Kings 18:4); both the pillars and the sacred pole were symbols of the Canaanite goddess Asherah. Josiah makes comparable reforms, reported in a text containing more details than we find for Hezekiah. Josiah eradicates the temple of the deities Baal, Asherah, and the astral symbols, deposes or slaughters idolatrous priests at the "high places," eliminates the practice of male prostitution at the temple, breaks down the shrines at the high places, brings an end to child sacrifices, and, like Hezekiah, "broke the pillars in pieces, and . . . burned the sacred pole (*asherah*)" (23:14–15). Both consult a prophet—Isaiah in the case of Hezekiah and Huldah by Josiah. Hezekiah and Josiah also follow in the footsteps of King David (18:3; 22:2).

According to the Deuteronomists, both also obey the Mosaic laws. Hezekiah "held fast to YHWH; he did not depart from following him but kept the commandments that YHWH commanded Moses" (2 Kings 18:6). After the long and wicked rule of Kings Manasseh and Amon (2 Kings 21), Josiah reportedly discovers "the book of the law" (*sefer hatorah*) during temple restorations (22:8–20), implying that he may not have been familiar with it previously. Whether or not such a discovery actually happened is impossible to know. The story has the earmarks of the Deuteronomists, who present the episode as a final high moment in what was too often a bleak history of the monarchy. "The book of the law" becomes a bracket connecting the two ends of their long historical narrative: the history begins with an explicit reference to "the book of the law" in Joshua 1:8, and near the end is the rediscovery of "the book of the law" in 2 Kings 22:8. In between those reference points lies the long history of disobedience and neglect of the Mosaic law.

The death stories about both Hezekiah and Josiah vary from the usual accounts of the demise of all other kings. Hezekiah is deathly ill and appeals to God on the grounds that he has been faithful, and the prophet Isaiah relays word that he will not die immediately but will recover and have an additional fifteen years to live (2 Kings 20:1–11). As a sign, God causes the shadow on the sundial to move backward ten intervals, reminiscent of the sun standing still for Joshua in battle (Josh. 10:1–15). The next we hear, Hezekiah receives an emissary from Babylon, which is seeking alliances against Neo-Assyria. Opposed to any such agreements with foreign powers, the prophet Isaiah reacts angrily, predicting that Hezekiah's wealth and descendants will eventually be taken to Babylon as plunder and captives. To this word, Hezekiah thinks, "Why not, if there will be peace and security in my days?" (2 Kings 20:19). No other account of Hezekiah's life during his fifteen-year reprieve is provided, and 2 Kings 20:20–21 simply reports Hezekiah's death. The Deuteronomists may not have wanted to give him further approval, for in their view the best king of all after David is Josiah.

If the reform efforts by Josiah occurred during the 620s, as is likely, the Deuteronomistic History follows it with a gap of more than ten years, except for the brief statement in 2 Kings 23:26–27 about YHWH's determining to cause Jerusalem's fall. For one so good and so highly praised during his earlier rule, Josiah dies abruptly and with virtually no comment (23:28–30). As the Neo-Assyrian empire gradually fell apart, the Neo-Babylonian forces moved into the Levant en route to Egypt, while Pharaoh Neco of Egypt marched northward through the Levant. In the battle of 609 BCE at Megiddo against Neco, Josiah is killed, and his servants take his body back to Jerusalem for burial. The Deuteronomists do not elaborate beyond this simple notice. Perhaps the lack of detail reflects a certain conspiracy of silence in their treatment. The Deuteronomists base their theological history on the principle that obedience to God will result in blessings and disobedience will produce doom. Josiah has been completely obedient, according to the Deuteronomists' own account, and he should therefore live a long and comfortable life. But having his life cut short at the age of only thirty-five does not fit this scheme, and the Deuteronomists may have simply decided not to reflect on the matter any further.

The remainder of Judah's monarchic history is told in short order (2 Kings 23:31–25:30). The last four kings are weak and bad, and the Neo-Babylonians have little trouble bringing Judah into their burgeoning empire. Jerusalem falls and is fully destroyed in 586 BCE, and Emperor Nebuchadnezzar carries off the royal family, the elite of the land, and the treasures of the palace and temple. Where one might expect an extensive moral and theological critique similar to the commentary about the defeat of the northern kingdom, there is only a terse, poignant statement: "So Judah went into exile out of its land" (25:21). Critique enough.

Prophets as Critics

Individual prophets appear frequently in our discussions, and now we step back to consider their general role as critics of the status quo. Prophecy as an institution stems from cultures that existed centuries before Israel appeared in history. One of the main sites is Mari, the Babylonian kingdom dating from the eighteenth century BCE, located in modern-day Syria near the point where the Euphrates River passes into Iraq. There a number of tablets have emerged that report prophets transmitting messages from the gods to the king. Other texts referring to prophets stem from ancient Egypt, the Hittites (fourteenth century BCE, in modern-day Turkey), and elsewhere. These prophets function in a variety of ways—as spokespersons for the gods, as seers, as ecstatics, and as agents of religious and social change. Prophecy in one form or another is found in many cultures and times around the world. In Israel prophets were probably present during the majority if not the entirety of the monarchic period and into the exilic and postexilic years.

A traditional division of labor among religious professionals existed in ancient Israel, at least according to a proverb-like statement quoted in Jeremiah 18:18—"For instruction shall not perish from the priest (*cohen*), nor counsel from the wise (*chacham*), nor the word from the prophet (*navi*)" (see also Ezek. 7:26). These three traditional roles are not firmly and exclusively delineated but are most evident with regard to function and source of knowledge. The priest deals with formal, recurring religious matters on the basis of ritual traditions; the sage treats informal, recurring, sometimes religious matters on the basis of a tradition of experience and reflection; and the prophet deals with particularized, not necessarily recurring, religious or moral matters that require a new oracle from God. Although overlap exists among these roles, each type of figure is rooted in a tradition or institution that provides identity and heritage.

A common notion about the prophets is that they preoccupy themselves with making predictions about the distant future. Had prophets wanted to peer down the corridors of history and, like Nostradamus, divine what was going to happen in faraway times, we might expect that they would give some indication of that intention, but they never do so. The prophets are engaged in their own times, and they address their own compatriots, not believers centuries later. They frequently make predictions, but with few and very general exceptions these predictions are meant for fulfillment in the immediate future. The prophets want the people in their own generation to heed their warnings and promises, and they predict that if the people do not comply, they will experience the consequences the prophets outline.

At the heart of prophecy is a message delivered from the divine world to the human world, often to a specific person such as a king, and the prophet is the one who delivers it. The most common term in Hebrew for prophet is *navi* (plural: *nevi'im*), stemming from a word that means "to call" or "to proclaim." Two less common terms refer to the prophet as a "seer" or as "one who has a vision." Suggesting that some development occurred in the language used of prophets, 1 Samuel 9:9 includes a parenthetical note clarifying that "the one who is now called a prophet (*navi*) was formerly called a seer (*ro'eh*)." In another anecdote, when Moses protests to God that he cannot speak well enough to deliver messages to Pharaoh, God arranges for Aaron to do the speaking: "See, I have made you like God to Pharaoh, and your brother Aaron shall be your prophet" (Exod. 7:1; also 4:16). Thus, instead of the usual sequence God to prophet to recipient, in this case it will be Moses to Aaron to recipient. However, prophets are not mere mouthpieces; they remain individuals with personalities of their own, which affects their relations both with God and with other persons. Jeremiah may be the best example: his audience maligns him and God does not adequately protect him, and Jeremiah protests vociferously.

Although this role of delivering messages is central, the prophets have other functions and characteristics as well. For example, ecstatic prophecy appears both in the Hebrew Bible and in other cultures. In this type of activity, the prophet is so grasped by God or so possessed by a spirit that behavior becomes frenzied. The best biblical example takes place immediately after Samuel anoints Saul as the first king of Israel. Samuel predicts that Saul, on his way home, will meet "a band of prophets coming down from the shrine . . . in a prophetic frenzy." He says that the spirit of YHWH will possess Saul, and he "will be in a prophetic frenzy along with them and be turned into a different person" (1 Sam. 10:5–6)—all of which then transpires. The Hebrew word translated in the NRSV as "being in a prophetic frenzy" or in the JPS as "speaking in ecstasy" is from the same root as *navi* and can mean not just "to proclaim" but also "to bubble up" or "to pour forth," as in uncontrollable excitement. Ecstatic prophecy must be observed or experienced; there will not necessarily be a verbal message. The account of Elijah in competition with King Ahab's 450 prophets of Baal may represent another example of ecstatic prophecy. To plead with their god Baal to light a fire under their altar, "they cried aloud and, as was their custom, they cut themselves with swords and lances until the blood gushed out over them" (1 Kings 18:28).

The prophets' effectiveness lies not just in their message but also in the power of their rhetoric and actions. They generally speak in a very direct manner, drawing images from the natural world and from the everyday life of farmers as well as urban residents. With just a few words they can evoke compelling, even frightening scenes, as in Jeremiah's description of the land after a terrible battle—suggestive of the landscape after a nuclear attack:

> I looked on the earth, and lo, it was waste and void;
> and to the heavens, and they had no light.
> I looked on the mountains, and lo, they were quaking,
> and all the hills moved to and fro.
> I looked, and lo, there was no one at all,
> and all the birds of the air had fled.
> I looked, and lo, the fruitful land was a desert,
> and all its cities were laid in ruins
> before YHWH, before his fierce anger.
> For thus says YHWH:
> The whole land shall be a desolation; yet I will not make
>   a full end. (4:23–27)

Such an oracle is all the more ominous and effective because it comes not after a battle but before, predicting the defeat lying ahead for the people when Jerusalem is captured and the land is devastated.

The prophets also master the art of the pun. One of many examples is in Isaiah 5:7b, where Isaiah rebukes the people for oppressing the powerless: "He [YHWH] expected justice (*mishpat*), but saw bloodshed (*mispach*); righteousness (*tzedaqah*), but heard a cry (*tze'aqah*)!"

More impressive, at least visually, is the prophetic sign, a symbolic action that dramatizes the message. According to Isaiah 20, Isaiah walks around naked and barefoot for three years to illustrate that the Egyptians and Ethiopians, who sought to rebel against the Neo-Assyrians, will be conquered and taken naked into captivity. His point is that the people of Judah must not imagine that forming an alliance with Egypt or Ethiopia will help them against the Neo-Assyrian forces. Jeremiah buys and dons a new linen loincloth, walks 450 miles from Judah to the Euphrates River, hides it there in the rocks, returns to Judah, and then many days later makes the trip again to bring back the loincloth, now ruined, to make the point that the Judahites will soon be taken in exile to the Euphrates region, that is, to Babylon (13:1–11). To symbolize the coming Neo-Babylonian siege of Jerusalem, Ezekiel takes a brick, sketches on it an image of Jerusalem under attack, and lies on his left side for 390 days, one day for each year that the northern kingdom will be punished; and then he lies on his right side facing the brick for 40 days, one for each year of Judah's exile (4:1–8).

The prophets occupied a distinctive position in their society, from which they could utter pronouncements to their leaders and the people. Not all of the prophets operated in the same circles, however. Isaiah and Ezekiel, for example, are at home in the capital of Jerusalem, probably their city of origin. Isaiah seems almost aristocratic in comparison with most other prophets. He has access to the king and other elites, and he preaches a message that praises the stature of Zion (Jerusalem) as YHWH's special abode and protectorate. At the same time, he addresses the political issues of the eighth century, the pressures first from the Syrian and northern Israelite coalition and later from the Neo-Assyrian empire. Ezekiel is raised in a family of priests and trains to be a priest himself. He lives and works in Jerusalem until 597, when the Neo-Babylonians take him and others into exile, and there in Babylon he continues as a religious leader among the diaspora community.

Both Amos and Micah, on the other hand, have rustic roots. Amos calls himself "a herdsman and a dresser of sycamore trees" (7:14), raised south of Jerusalem but then sent by God to proclaim justice in the north during the politically tumultuous eighth century. Also from the same period, Micah comes from the village of Moresheth-gath, some twenty-five miles southwest of Jerusalem, and he champions the cause of the poor and the vulnerable in scathing attacks on the rulers and religious leaders in Jerusalem, which he predicts will become "a heap of ruins" (3:12). Jeremiah grows up within eyesight of Jerusalem and reports having access to the king and the cult during the decades leading to Jerusalem's fall, but with his harsh criticism of the leaders and his strong sympathy for the oppressed he has the character of one who easily moves in and out of different sectors of society.

The prophets and the Deuteronomists share considerable common ground. Both apply the criteria of religious faithfulness and social justice, both are devout Yahwists, and both seek to address their own generation. They differ not in the substance of their message but in their métier and expression. We know nothing of any public role the Deuteronomists played. They may have stayed at their desks and written their theological history, although it is likely they discussed their analysis of history with others, perhaps even preached about it.

The prophets, on the other hand, functioned above all in public, speaking directly to the audiences that most needed to hear their message—in the royal court, in the marketplace, in judicial contexts, in the temple, and in other public and private settings. Their utterances, often as short as just a few verses at a time, may have been prepared in advance or delivered spontaneously—probably some of both. The prophets were primarily speakers, not pamphleteers or literary figures. There is no way of knowing if most of them were even literate; they may well not have been since advanced literacy was largely restricted to the professional scribes. Some of them may have had disciples, as suggested by Isaiah when he entrusts his spoken words to his followers: "Bind up the testimony; seal the teaching among my disciples" (8:16). Jeremiah describes dictating his messages to Baruch the scribe. The scroll reaches the king, who has a scribe read it to him, and the king cuts it up with a penknife and burns it. Jeremiah then dictates all his sayings again to Baruch, "and many similar words were added to them" (36:32).

This scenario may indicate the process whereby much of the prophetic literature came into being. Prophets may have first delivered their utterances in public to their target audience and then later dictated the prophecies to scribes, or perhaps disciples wrote them down after a prophet's death. The prophetic pronouncements that originated in written form, perhaps such as Second Isaiah (Isa. 40–55) during the exile, were unusual in that largely oral world. The prophets had urgent messages to deliver, and they proclaimed them most effectively in the flesh. Their criticisms focused on three general areas: politics, economics, and religion.

Politics

The prophets do not hesitate to criticize any sector of society, and the leadership and the institutions of the country come under heavy attack. The kings receive considerable attention from the prophets, although not as much as from the Deuteronomists—especially in the period after the conquest of Judah when the monarchy is only a memory. Following David's affair with Bathsheba and the arranged death of her husband Uriah, the prophet Nathan excoriates David for his abuse of power, using a parable to deceive David into condemning himself (2 Sam. 12:1–15). The prophet Elijah repeatedly confronts King Ahab, especially after the incident involving Naboth's vineyard, when Elijah predicts a shameful death for Ahab and his family (1 Kings 21:17–29).

Jeremiah finds himself in a period of political intensity and disaster— the decades leading up to the fall of Jerusalem and several years after it. Although Jeremiah 1:2 states that YHWH's word comes to Jeremiah in King Josiah's thirteenth regnal year (627 BCE), about the time of Josiah's reform, we have no prophetic utterances that clearly date to the period before Josiah's death in 609. From that point onward Jeremiah is active in speaking out against the kings for their policies and actions. In one particularly dense section (22:11–30) he first mentions Shallum (better known as King Jehoahaz II), Josiah's son and successor, who reigns for only three months before Pharaoh Neco captures him and exiles him to Egypt, and Jeremiah pronounces that Shallum will die there in Egypt.

Next the prophet delivers a long diatribe against King Jehoiakim, another of Josiah's sons and Jeremiah's chief nemesis for a full decade, 609–598—he is the king who burns Jeremiah's scroll. Jeremiah denounces Jehoiakim for constructing a luxurious palace while his subjects suffer as corvée labor: "Woe to him who builds his house by unrighteousness, and his upper rooms by injustice; who makes his neighbors work for nothing, and does not give them their wages. . . . Your eyes and heart are only on your dishonest gain, for shedding innocent blood, and for practicing oppression and violence" (22:13, 17). Jehoiakim, Jeremiah says, will die and receive the burial accorded a donkey, his body left outside the city to decompose or be eaten by scavengers.

Finally Jeremiah predicts that King Coniah (also known as Jehoiachin, Jehoiakim's son and successor) will be taken captive to Babylon and die there, childless. Jehoiachin is referred to in a Neo-Babylonian document, and 2 Kings 25:27–30 (also Jer. 52:31–34) reports that he is eventually released from prison and is allowed to dine regularly with the emperor. Zedekiah, the last king of Judah, is friendly toward Jeremiah, who counsels him against joining an alliance with Egypt and urges him to surrender to the Babylonians rather than face certain destruction (Jer. 27). Zedekiah protects Jeremiah against those who charge him with suspected treason (Jer. 37–38). Eventually the Neo-Babylonians storm the city of Jerusalem, capture Zedekiah, and deport him to Babylonia, leaving Jeremiah in Judah until he is later taken to Egypt.

The prophets were astute observers of the political scene, including geopolitical affairs that could affect Israel and Judah. Yet the prophetic literature retains mainly those assessments and predictions that came true, and we have no idea how often the prophets missed in their forecasts. A rare example of a failed prediction is Ezekiel 26:7–14, one of many "oracles against the nations" delivered by the prophets. Here Ezekiel announces that the Neo-Babylonian emperor Nebuchadrezzar (an alternative spelling for Nebuchadnezzar) will destroy the Phoenician island-city of Tyre, a leading commercial port on the Mediterranean coast in the first millennium BCE, and he adds that it will never be rebuilt. Nebuchadrezzar did lay siege to it for a thirteen-year period directly after the fall of Jerusalem (586–573), but he did not destroy it, probably signing a treaty with its leaders instead. Then in Ezekiel 29:17–20 the prophet acknowledges that the siege of Tyre had failed, and he states that in its place God will give Egypt to Nebuchadrezzar; Jeremiah predicts the same about Egypt (Jer. 43:8–13). The Babylonians attacked Egypt in 568 but did not conquer it. Most of the prophets' political predictions did, however, come true, at least those contained in the Bible.

Economy

Israel's economy, as described in Chapter 11, was based on a system of sharp inequalities, both economic and political. The palace, the temple, and the elites owned the majority of land and resources during the time of the monarchy, and a similar imbalance continued into Persian and Hellenistic times. The masses residing in the villages scattered around the countryside were largely powerless to resist exploitation and manipulation by the state and the elites. All too often they lost their ancestral lands to large landowners, both private individuals as well as the palace and the temple. When farmers borrowed heavily to plant their fields, they could fall into an interminable cycle of debt that forced them either to give up their lands or to sell themselves and their families into slavery. This dilemma is apparent in numerous biblical texts in all types of literature—historical, legal, prophetic, lyrical, and wisdom traditions. While apostasy was the single most addressed problem in the religious sphere, poverty was the most frequently treated problem in the social sphere. It was a real, not a theoretical issue.

The prophets are among the greatest advocates for the poor in the Hebrew Bible, a role they played readily because of their willingness to speak critically to the king, the priests, and the wealthy. Most striking, though, are the rhetorical power and vivid imagery they bring to their messages. Amos, who left the south to preach in the north during the eighth century, depicts the exploitation of the poor in terms of buying and selling: the powerful are "buying the poor for silver and the needy for a pair of sandals" (8:6). He goes so far as to equate the poor with the righteous, setting them parallel to each other: "They sell the *righteous* for silver, and the *needy* for a pair of sandals" (2:6). Here Amos does not give a romanticized view of the poor as persons who are in themselves righteous. Rather, he is suggesting that, if they are needy, then they must not be like the wicked who have exploited others to become wealthy. And again with brutal images: "They who trample the head of the poor into the dust of the earth, and push the afflicted out of the way" (2:7). He disdains the wealthy for their privilege and waste: "Hear this word, you cows of Bashan who are on Mount Samaria, who oppress the poor, who crush the needy, who say to their husbands, 'Bring something to drink!'" (4:1). This picture of the wealthy at leisure contrasts sharply with the poor at a subsistence level, who have no leisure and must work—everyone in the family—to survive economically. Amos turns these practices into a threat: "Therefore because you trample on the poor and take from them levies of grain, you have built houses of hewn stone, but you shall not live in them; you have planted pleasant vineyards, but you shall not drink their wine" (5:11).

Micah, also during the eighth century, confronts the rulers with a cannibalistic image: "You who hate the good and love the evil, who tear the skin off my people, and the flesh off their bones; who eat the flesh of my people, flay their skin off them, break their bones in pieces, and chop them up like meat in a kettle, like flesh in a caldron" (3:2–3). This image was viscerally powerful, especially given the prohibition against consuming blood, which in the Hebrew Bible is projected all the way back to Noah's time (Gen. 9:4).

Jeremiah, a century later, continues the attack on wanton oppression and prejudicial administration of justice in the courts:

> For scoundrels are found among my people;
> they take over the goods of others.
> Like fowlers they set a trap;
> they catch human beings.
> Like a cage full of birds,
> their houses are full of treachery;
> therefore they have become great and rich,
> they have grown fat and sleek.
> They know no limits in deeds of wickedness;
> they do not judge with justice
> the cause of the orphan, to make it prosper,
> and they do not defend the rights of the needy. (5:26–28)

It is impossible to know how effective the prophets actually were in their criticisms of kings, priests, and the wealthy. They obviously hit their mark in many cases, at least according to the later history of the monarchy. Jezebel reportedly tries to kill the prophets of YHWH, and one hundred are hidden and saved by a loyal worshiper (1 Kings 18:3–4). Jeremiah escapes an assassination plot and a capital trial, and he is put in the stocks after angering a priest (11:18–23; 20:1–6). The New Testament reports a tradition that the Israelites killed the prophets (Luke 11:47; Acts 7:52; 1 Thess. 2:15), but the Hebrew Bible has scarce record of it. Probably Jewish in origin, *The Lives of the Prophets,* a noncanonical text from the first or second century CE, describes the lives and deaths of twenty-three prophets of Israel, maintaining that Isaiah, Jeremiah, Ezekiel, Amos, Micah, and Zechariah son of Jehoiada (2 Chron. 24:20–23) died as martyrs; only Zechariah's death is recorded in the Hebrew Bible. The prophets may well have been in danger at times from those they attacked. However, even if they did not accomplish the reforms they sought, the Hebrew Bible places any blame squarely on the leaders and the people, not on the prophets. Their critique stands as an indictment of the exploitation and abuse of power in ancient Israel. At the same time, these prophets promote a vision of a society and cult oriented toward a model of justice, and this heritage of criticism and reform remains to this day.

Religion

The prophets frequently address both the religious establishment and religious practices. For the most part, prophets were not isolated individuals in ancient Israel, even though Isaiah, Jeremiah, Ezekiel, and the biblical prophets may appear to be loners. Many of them probably had followers, and they themselves may have begun by following senior prophets and learning the tradition and rhetoric in the process. Many, perhaps even most prophets were attached to the cult to respond to requests for an oracle from God or to intercede on the people's behalf, as in Amos 7:1–6, a prayer of intercession to stave off God's anger against the people. The 450 prophets of Baal who opposed Elijah in the contest of sacrifices (1 Kings 18) are an example, and the band of ecstatic prophets that Saul unexpectedly joined (1 Sam. 10:5–13) is another. When the priest Amaziah confronts Amos and tries to drive him away from the shrine at Bethel, Amos pointedly differentiates himself from such groups: "I am no prophet, nor a prophet's son" (7:14), that is, he is not a prophet by profession but has been specially called by YHWH to prophesy to the northern kingdom.

Prophet against prophet is a common trope in the Hebrew Bible. Jeremiah attacks fellow prophets most frequently, accusing them of prophesying in the name of other gods (2:8), of lying (14:14), of adultery (23:14), and more. False prophecy takes on an especially acute form, however, when two or more prophets declare opposite messages—not one from YHWH and the other from another god, but both from YHWH. According to 1 Kings 22:5–40, before his final battle King Ahab solicits advice from the four hundred prophets of YHWH about whether he should go to war against Aram, and all of them tell him, "Go up; for YHWH will give it into the hand of the king." Not trusting them, he calls for another prophet of YHWH, Micaiah son of Imlah, even though he dislikes him because, he says, "he never prophesies anything favorable about me, but only disaster." At first Micaiah says he will be victorious, and only when pressed further does Micaiah deliver the opposite message. Micaiah explains the confusion by indicating that YHWH had sent "a lying spirit" to confound the four hundred prophets into enticing the king to take to the field. When Ahab is killed in the battle, it becomes clear that Micaiah is the true prophet and the others had prophesied falsely.

Jeremiah confronts this dilemma of false prophecy as well. As the Neo-Babylonians threaten Judah, a claque of prophets purporting to speak on behalf of YHWH gives the people the comforting message: "It shall be well with you" (23:17). Jeremiah responds with a different word from YHWH: "I did not send the prophets, yet they ran; I did not speak to them, yet they prophesied" (23:21). Jeremiah finds evidence of false prophecy in the eagerness with which those prophets announce a message they claim they received in a dream. Again he delivers this word from God:

> I have heard what the prophets have said who prophesy lies
> in my name, saying, "I have dreamed, I have dreamed!" . . .
> They plan to make my people forget my name by their
> dreams that they tell one another, just as their ancestors
> forgot my name for Baal. Let the prophet who has a dream
> tell the dream, but let the one who has my word speak my
> word faithfully. What has straw in common with wheat?
> says YHWH. (23:25, 27–28)

Although it is easier to decide between true and false prophecy after the predicted event does or does not occur, uncertainty exists prior to that point. This difficulty in discerning the true from the false prophet may also explain the gradual decline of prophecy after the exile and the increase in the significance accorded priests, sages, and the apocalyptics during the Persian and Hellenistic periods.

The prophets denounce priests as well when they fail to carry out their teaching and ritual duties properly. The prophets speak of the kings more frequently than of the priests, but the priests are not protected simply because they, like the prophets, are religious leaders. The narrative describing Jeremiah's call to be a prophet explicitly names the priests in the list of opponents Jeremiah will have: "And I [YHWH] for my part have made you today a fortified city, an iron pillar, and a bronze wall, against the whole land—against the kings of Judah, its princes, its priests, and the people of the land" (1:18). Isaiah accuses priests and other prophets of intoxication: "The priest and the prophet reel with strong drink, they are confused with wine, . . . they err in vision, they stumble in giving judgment" (28:7). Hosea charges the priests with committing murder (6:9), and according to Jeremiah 26 the priests and prophets try to get Jeremiah killed as well. Micah accuses the priests of charging a fee for the instruction they are supposed to offer (3:11). Hosea indicts them for forgetting God's law (4:6). Especially grievous, they promote the worship of idols and other gods (Jer. 2:26–28).

The prophets criticized not only the priests and other prophets but also cultic activity that was wrongly directed, not complemented by moral action, or taken to excess. The prophets were not opposed in principle to the cult, no more than they fundamentally opposed the institution of kingship. They did not condemn sacrifice per se, even though the statement by God in Hosea 6:6 sounds close to it: "I desire steadfast love and not sacrifice, the knowledge of God rather than burnt offerings." This pronouncement, which is picked up in Matthew 9:13 and 12:7, is best understood as a rhetorical equivalent to "steadfast love more than sacrifice, knowledge of God more than burnt offerings." The prophets target the abuse and misuse of the sacrificial system, especially its practice without the moral actions to match it. Micah 6:6–8, cited at the close of Chapter 6, describes an escalation of sacrifices and asks rhetorically how much it takes to please YHWH. The prophet does not answer that no sacrifice is needed; instead, Micah exhorts the worshiper not to engage in excess but to realize that something entirely different will delight YHWH: justice, loving-kindness, and walking humbly with God.

The biblical historians wrote after the events they describe had taken place, perhaps even several centuries later. The prophets, when they could, spoke directly to the leaders and the people intended as their audience, who could reform or, just as easily, dismiss their pronouncements, as when the king burned Jeremiah's scroll (Jer. 36). Yet even when these historians and prophets failed to correct the troubled times they criticized, their evaluations have had an effect on later generations of readers and hearers who looked and look to the past for direction. The extensive historical and prophetic literature in the Hebrew Bible is a storehouse of insights, vivid in rhetoric and narrative style and effective in social and religious analysis. Other biblical authors attend to fundamental questions of the nature of the world and divine justice, to which we now turn.

Chapter 14

Wisdom and Theodicy

Challenges of one sort or the other are a constant in human experience, yet new issues emerge to confront each generation. The ancient world did not face many of today's most dire problems: overpopulation, global threats to our natural environment, the rapid spread of epidemics through modern means of transportation, threats of nuclear destruction, moral ambiguities arising from biomedical research, the challenges posed by the explosion of knowledge and communication innovations during the past century, and shared political and economic fate on a much broader scale than ever before.

At the same time, there are many points of commonality between the past and the present, both for individuals and groups. For millennia we have suffered from disease, accidents, violence, and negligence. We have seen massive inequalities of wealth and resources, imbalances in power among groups and races, corruption and dishonesty, genocides. Individuals experience hope and hopelessness, satisfaction and depression, handicaps and new opportunities, and always a quest for meaning in life. The Hebrew Bible, which seeks to represent the experiences of a select group of people over a millennium and more, incorporates materials reflecting these and other enduring concerns.

The sapiential or wisdom stream of tradition is not the only portion of ancient Israel's literary heritage that engages such issues, but in this stream we find the most concentrated form of inquiry and reflection on the nature of human existence in this world. During the past century many scholars considered the wisdom materials peripheral to the Bible, out of step with the divine acts in history so central to the Pentateuch and the Deuteronomists' and Chroniclers' narratives. Today we realize that the wisdom tradition records the essential groundwork for biblical thought: the notion of order, the relationship between cause and effect, the realistic confrontation with the world, and the place of the divine in human affairs. Far from being peripheral, wisdom offers indispensable perspectives that inform the other biblical traditions.

Who Is Wise?

When the deuterocanonical book of Sirach (6:34) raised the question, "Who is wise?" in the second century BCE, the wisdom tradition had already passed through two millennia of Southwest Asian development. With the arrival of Alexander the Great in the latter part of the fourth century, Hellenistic culture and philosophy introduced new ideas and styles that affected writers like Ben Sira. Hebrew wisdom traditions, however, imported concepts with Babylonian and Egyptian roots and combined them with distinctive Israelite experiences, and the result is the wisdom literature now preserved in the Hebrew Bible—the books of Proverbs, Job, Ecclesiastes (Qohelet), and scattered poems and aphorisms.

The Hebrew word for "wisdom," *chochmah* (Gk. *sophia*), has a variety of meanings, not all of which are religious in tone. In many cases it designates a professional skill. For example, artisans have *chochmah* (skill) for creating objects out of wood, stone, metal, and textiles (Exod. 31:3–11). Women display *chochmah* (dexterity) in spinning yarn (35:25). Tailoring involves *chochmah* (expertise, 28:3). Certain women show *chochmah* (adeptness) in keening at someone's death (Jer. 9:17–18; Tanakh 9:16–17). A magician may have *chochmah* (talent, Isa. 3:3). Sailors need *chochmah* (expertise) to traverse the seas (Ps. 107:27). Governing requires *chochmah* (competence, Gen. 41:33, 39). A good counselor in the royal court gives *chochmah* (advice, Isa. 19:11). All such usages have in common an ability specific to a task, ranging from physical and technical skills to the capacity for offering insight and guidance.

The word *chochmah* has another sense that extends the scope beyond the professional realm. A person who is *chacham* (the adjective form of *chochmah*) knows how to address people and circumstances in an effective manner and thus lives a life that today we might call meaningful, gratifying, and full. The "wise" person is knowledgeable and well spoken (Prov. 10:13–14; 15:7), but also capable of rebuking those who need it (Eccl. 7:5). He—and for most but not all of the wisdom literature the "wise person" is understood to be an elite male—teaches others, especially children (Prov. 1–7). And he himself is teachable (1:5; 15:14; 18:15;

21:11), not arrogant (3:7; 26:12) but receptive to advice (12:15; 19:20). The wise man is persuasive and judicious (16:21, 23), hardworking yet moderate in his desires (20:13; 23:20; 25:16), generous and humble (22:4, 9). He can defuse conflict (29:8) and is himself not easily irritated (16:32) or insulted (12:16). Old age brings him respect and deference (16:31).

Wisdom thus has a practical as well as a personal character, but it is rooted in a distinct, fundamental understanding of cause and effect, a conceptual tradition connecting Israel with Egypt and Mesopotamia. In Chapter 7 we describe the principle of order. At creation God sets the world in an orderly structure, with clear divisions between light and dark, land and sea, water above and water below, and living species assigned to their respective domains. The goddess Ma'at embodies this principle of harmony for the Egyptians; she was present at creation, and she effects order in human affairs by carrying out justice. In Egyptian, Babylonian, and Israelite wisdom traditions the notion of order takes the form of a strong connection between act and consequence: if a person does what is right, then blessing is supposed to follow; if a person contravenes accepted principles or rules, then punishment or suffering ensues.

On the basis of this simple, straightforward logic, people should expect certain results from their actions. The act–consequence connection is so tight, according to this worldview, that merely doing a given act triggers its necessary and inevitable consequence. This same assumption undergirds the legal concept of justice: punishment is the appropriate response for violating a law. The order built into creation means that all people must act in harmony with it, and not doing so leads to suffering and trouble. The book of Proverbs affirms this fundamental role of wisdom by describing its involvement with YHWH in the very creation of all reality:

> YHWH created me [wisdom] at the beginning of his
>   work,
> the first of his acts of long ago.
> Ages ago I was set up,
> at the first, before the beginning of the earth. . . .
> Then I was beside him, like a master worker;
> and I was daily his delight, rejoicing before him always,
> rejoicing in his inhabited world
> and delighting in the human race.
> And now, my children, listen to me:

> happy are those who keep my ways. . . .
> For whoever finds me finds life
> and obtains favor from YHWH;
> but those who miss me injure themselves;
> all who hate me love death. (8:22–23, 30–32, 35–36)

Wisdom is not simply a human possession or an attribute. As elsewhere in Southwest Asia, it is hypostatized, regarded as a part of reality with substance and even personality. It was the first of God's creations (also stated in Sir. 1:4); it assisted God in creating the rest of the world; it gave God delight; and now it instructs people, urging them to seek wisdom and be blessed or avoid it and suffer the consequences.

This theological principle of cause and effect is evident throughout biblical wisdom literature. The book of Proverbs often details the act–consequence connection with an extended section about either the act or the consequence, but a few examples of the principle in the shorter aphorisms demonstrate its use: "A slack hand causes poverty, but the hand of the diligent makes rich" (10:4); "Those who are kind reward themselves, but the cruel do themselves harm" (11:17); "Whoever walks with the wise becomes wise, but the companion of fools suffers harm" (13:20); "A false witness will not go unpunished, and a liar will not escape" (19:5); "If you curse father or mother, your lamp will go out in utter darkness" (20:20); "The clever see danger and hide; but the simple go on, and suffer for it" (22:3); "As pressing milk produces curds, and pressing the nose produces blood, so pressing anger produces strife" (30:33).

The act–consequence principle is at work elsewhere in the Hebrew Bible also. In his final address to the Israelites, Moses articulates it succinctly: "See, I am setting before you today a blessing and a curse: the blessing, if you obey the commandments of YHWH your God, . . . and the curse, if you do not obey the commandments of YHWH your God" (Deut. 11:26–28).

Wisdom influences reach widely in the thought world of the ancient Israelites, and the book of Deuteronomy and the historical principles underlying the Deuteronomistic History reflect its cause-and-effect view of people's actions. The wisdom literature does not, however, have the same emphasis on law and obedience as found in the Deuteronomistic stream.

Sages and Their Literature

The carriers of the wisdom tradition are the sages, those referenced second in Jeremiah's list of religious professionals (18:18). Although all Israelites are urged to be wise, the sages in Israel and their counterparts in the neighboring cultures steep themselves in the literature and the issues belonging to this tradition. They may have been attached to educational settings where children of the elites received training befitting their class, but we know very little about any such schools and their teachers until the Hellenistic period. The book of Proverbs contains numerous references to instruction without indicating clearly whether the teaching occurs in formal or informal settings: "My child, do not forget my teaching . . ." (3:1); "Hear, my child, and accept my words . . ." (4:10); "And now, my children, listen to me . . ." (8:32–33). Some of the teaching could be parental advice, but most of it fits better in a setting where someone schooled in pedagogy and the subject matter is the instructor.

Although sages mentored the young, they likely maintained a running discussion with their peers as well. It is impossible to know whether they constituted a loosely knit group or a more formal institution, but some type of context gave them a chance to explore wisdom themes together. How familiar the sages in Israel were with the substantial wisdom literary corpus in neighboring cultures is also unknown, but there is enough overlap of biblical wisdom with other Southwest Asian texts to indicate that they had access to some of them during the centuries of contact with Egypt, Neo-Assyria, Neo-Babylonia, and Persia. This wisdom tradition is considerably older, extending as far back as the third millennium BCE—more than four thousand years ago. From these civilizations come proverbs, instructions, and contemplative discourses, three of the primary wisdom genres found also in the Hebrew Bible: the first two in the book of Proverbs and the third in the books of Job and Ecclesiastes (Qohelet).

An additional source—harder to trace but nonetheless present—was folk wisdom, the insights generated by those living close to the land and outside the circles of power and education. Such groups expressed their experiences and reflections in catchy aphorisms, puns, metaphors, and ironies. A few examples preserved in the Hebrew Bible may well have stemmed from people at home with agriculture, nature, and deprivation: "Like the partridge hatching what it did not lay, so are all who amass wealth unjustly; in mid-life it will leave them, and at their end they will prove to be fools" (Jer. 17:11); "Some pretend to be rich, yet have nothing; others pretend to be poor, yet have great wealth" (Prov. 13:7); "'Bad, bad,' says the buyer, then goes away and boasts" (20:14); "Some give freely, yet grow all the richer; others withhold what is due, and only suffer want" (11:24); "One who winks the eyes plans perverse things; one who compresses the lips brings evil to pass" (16:30); "Even in laughter the heart is sad, and the end of joy is grief" (14:13); "The parents have eaten sour grapes, and the children's teeth are set on edge" (Jer. 31:29; Ezek. 18:2); and phrases like "apple of the eye" (Ps. 17:8) and "Like mother, like daughter" (Ezek. 16:44—not our usual version: "Like father, like son").

The wise may have existed as a discernible group throughout most of Israel's history, especially after the founding of the monarchy, but the wisdom books were produced in the period after the exile, from the fifth through third centuries BCE. During this period Israel's cultural memory was becoming concretized in literature. The sages were probably part of that process, especially as they reflected on the people's current situation as a colonized land. Such political and economic subservience to a foreign ruler, when contrasted to the visions of Israel's golden era of sovereignty and religious faithfulness, gave the sages more than enough substance to consider as they thought about the meaning of their collective existence.

The sages' interests ranged widely, both in Israel and in other cultures, and their primary source of authority was their own and their colleagues' observations and experiences. They pondered life's mysteries and dilemmas, as we will see shortly in the books of Job and Ecclesiastes and their Babylonian counterparts. The sages also observed nature and noted its peculiarities and ironies. Lauding Solomon's wisdom, 1 Kings 4:33 states that "he would speak of trees, from the cedar that is in the Lebanon to the hyssop that grows in the wall; he would speak of animals, and birds, and reptiles, and fish." Comparisons between animal and human behavior were especially prized, as in these numerical proverbs:

> Three things are too wonderful for me;
> four I do not understand:
> the way of an eagle in the sky,
> the way of a snake on a rock,
> the way of a ship on the high seas,
> and the way of a man with a young woman.
>   (Prov. 30:18–19)

> Three things are stately in their stride;
> four are stately in their gait:
> the lion, which is mightiest among wild animals
> and does not turn back before any;
> the strutting rooster, the he-goat,
> and a king striding before his people. (30:29–31)

Wisdom in such cases represents knowledge of nature and reflection on distinctive traits.

The sages also took delight in ironies and satires. In the Babylonian piece called "The Dialogue of Pessimism" (ca. 1000 BCE) a master repeatedly gives his slave an order and then promptly reverses it, and every time the slave affirms each option with a sound reason. At the end the master considers killing the slave, at which point the slave advises against it on the grounds that the master could not manage without him for three days. In the Egyptian "Satire of the Trades" (ca. 1300 BCE), the scribes denigrate all trades other than their own scribal profession. Another ironic text from Egypt, "The Eloquent Peasant" (from the first half of the second millennium BCE), is a rather lengthy tale in which a peasant who has been robbed makes such an articulate and moving appeal to the judge that the judge reports it to the king. Also impressed with the peasant's eloquent plea, the king instructs the judge not to rule on the case immediately but to record the peasant's continued appeals. The judge receives a total of nine petitions from the peasant and sends a copy of them to the king, who enjoys them and directs the judge to give the peasant the justice he is due. The Babylonian fable "The Tamarisk and the Palm" (first half of the second millennium BCE) is a wry example of excessive boasting, with each tree seeking to outdo the other in utility and appeal. Although entertaining, such wisdom pieces have the more serious intent of exposing human attributes, not all of them attractive.

The sages also developed a counterpart to such satires: instructions. To steer people, especially youth, from behavior deserving of ridicule or even punishment, the sages developed lengthy lists of instructions regarding all manner of conduct: etiquette, deference toward rulers and others of high rank, respect for elders, moderation in eating and drinking, care in managing one's household, warnings against speaking carelessly or critically, and much more. One list with biblical counterparts is "The Instruction of Amenemope," from Egypt around 1300 BCE. It contains instructions similar to those in Proverbs 22:17–24:22. Most striking is the statement in Proverbs 22:20–21 within this bloc of instructions similar to the Egyptian collection: "Have I not written for you thirty sayings of admonition and knowledge, to show you what is right and true, so that you may give a true answer to those who sent you?" "The Instruction of Amenemope" has thirty sections or chapters, making it likely that the author of Proverbs was acquainted with this Egyptian collection and is alluding here to its thirty parts.

Sirach and the Wisdom of Solomon

The tradition of wisdom thought in the late biblical period is responsible for two books of particular importance as they appear in the Septuagint and are included in the Roman Catholic, Anglican, and Orthodox canons: Sirach and the Wisdom of Solomon.

The book of Sirach is also known as the Wisdom of ben Sira (Sirach, in Greek) and as Ecclesiasticus. The latter, meaning "ecclesiastical" or "belonging to the church," is its Latin name in the Vulgate and should not be confused with Ecclesiastes, which is the book Qohelet in the Hebrew Bible. Stemming from the period around 180 BCE, Sirach was originally written in Hebrew by Jesus ben Sira and then, according to its prologue, translated into Greek by Ben Sira's grandson for the non-Hebrew-reading public. Although the Tanakh does not include the book, rabbinic discussions during the first millennium CE refer to it on occasion. The book represents an effort to draw on a variety of biblical traditions, including legal and prophetic materials as well as wisdom, and it virtually equates wisdom with the law, both of which need to be followed or obeyed fully: "Whoever holds to the law will obtain wisdom" (15:1b); "The whole of wisdom is fear of the Lord, and in all wisdom there is the fulfillment of the law" (19:20).

Probably belonging to privileged society, Ben Sira expects the student of law and wisdom to have leisure, access, and resources: "How different the one who devotes himself to the study of the law of the Most High! He seeks out the wisdom of all the ancients. . . . He serves among the great and appears before rulers; he travels in foreign lands and learns what is good and evil in the human lot" (38:34b–39:1a, 4).

The book of Sirach is intriguing not because of novelties and profundities, but because it venerates the wisdom tradition up to that point and seeks to replicate its instructions. In line with emphases in the book of Proverbs,

Sirach begins with a focus on wisdom and creation as well as on wisdom personified as a woman (Sir. 24). At the same time it has misogynistic comments, especially: "From a woman sin had its beginning, and because of her we all die" (25:24); "Better is the wickedness of a man than a woman who does good; it is woman who brings shame and disgrace" (42:14).

Sirach is no advocate of Greek philosophy, but he probably did feel most at home in prosperous and powerful circles of his Hellenistic era. Accordingly, the book advocates cautious use of one's financial holdings, strict treatment of slaves and children, property ownership, and such values as prudence, friendship, humility, moderation, self-control, charity, truthfulness, self-restraint, temperance, and good etiquette.

The book called the Wisdom of Solomon was written somewhat later, most likely during the first century CE or perhaps a few decades earlier. A Jew living in Egypt and writing in Greek was the likely author. Solomon gets credit for it in the title; it was commonplace at the time and earlier for books to be attributed to famous figures from the past, even though they had no role in authoring them. The book opens with a set of wisdom teachings about life, wickedness, the contrasting forms of afterlife for the righteous and the wicked, and the need for kings to rule according to the precepts of wisdom and justice, for which they will be held especially responsible: "For the lowliest may be pardoned in mercy, but the mighty will be mightily tested" (6:6).

In Wisdom 7–9, the king—presumably Solomon—speaks in the first person to describe his continual pursuit of wisdom, here personified as a woman: "I loved her and sought her from my youth; I desired to take her for my bride, and became enamored of her beauty. . . . For she is an initiate in the knowledge of God, and an associate in his works" (8:2, 4). Even though earlier wisdom books describe wisdom with the persona of a woman, in this case the tradition of Solomon as a lover of women—with reportedly one thousand wives and concubines in his harem—gives an ironic cast to his love of Woman Wisdom.

The last half of the book comprises a quick survey from Adam to Moses, including harsh descriptions of the "lawless" and "ungodly" Egyptians (17:2; 19:1), references to the trek through the wilderness, and teachings against idolatry and nature worship. The book on the whole is a paean to wisdom, described as a woman who was present at creation (9:9) and remains present in the laws, expressed here in a syllogism: "The beginning of wisdom is the most sincere desire for instruction, and concern for instruction is love of her, and love of her is the keeping of her laws, and giving heed to her laws is assurance of immortality, and immortality brings one near to God; so the desire for wisdom leads to a kingdom" (6:17–20).

Woman Wisdom

The Hebrew Bible refers often to sages, nearly all of them male and almost all unidentified, generalized figures. Two exceptions with a speaking role in a story are female, both of them especially notable due to their association with David, the ideal king in the Deuteronomistic History. The wise woman (*chachamah*, feminine form of *chacham*) of Tekoa, a town twelve miles south of Jerusalem, advises David at a crucial point in his reign. His son Absalom has killed his other son Amnon, who had raped Absalom's sister Tamar, and Absalom has fled Jerusalem to escape possible recrimination from David. Instead, David is despondent over the estrangement with Absalom. At the instigation of David's army commander Joab, the woman from Tekoa approaches David with a concocted story about a fratricide among her own sons, which David adjudicates in favor of the killer, as the woman had hoped. She then confronts David: "In giving this decision the king convicts himself, inasmuch as the king does not bring his banished one home again" (2 Sam. 14:13). David gets the point and restores Absalom. Sometime later, another wise woman negotiates a conflict involving David's army commander, preventing a battle as a result (20:14–22).

Three sets of contrasting images of women appear in the book of Proverbs: wisdom and folly personified; the faithful and the adulterous wife; and the good and the contentious wife. The first of these contrasts is related to the hypostatization of wisdom as God's first creation, as noted above. Proverbs 1–9 goes further in personifying wisdom as Woman Wisdom, together with her opposite, Woman Folly. We first meet Woman Wisdom as she tries to catch the attention of passersby:

> Wisdom cries out in the street;
> in the squares she raises her voice.
> At the busiest corner she cries out;
> at the entrance of the city gates she speaks:
> "How long, O simple ones, will you love being simple?

How long will scoffers delight in their scoffing
and fools hate knowledge?" (1:20–22)

The "simple" persons are young, inexperienced, naive, but teachable, while the "scoffers" and "fools" are more resistant, insolent, and intractable.

In dramatic contrast to Woman Wisdom, Woman Folly also solicits in public, but toward a very different end:

> The foolish woman is loud;
> she is ignorant and knows nothing.
> She sits at the door of her house,
> on a seat at the high places of the town,
> calling to those who pass by,
> who are going straight on their way,
> "You who are simple, turn in here!"
> And to those without sense she says,
> "Stolen water is sweet,
> and bread eaten in secret is pleasant." (9:13–17)

The sexual innuendo is unmistakable in Woman Folly's appeal but less so in Woman Wisdom's. Both speakers approach their audience directly; both use an insult in referring to the male audience as "simple"; both employ the language of persuasion; both have something to offer. Woman Wisdom presents the prospect of knowledge as well as a threat of punishment and disaster (in 1:23–33). Woman Folly, on the other hand, offers care-free pleasure and no negative consequences—although Proverbs quickly inserts the commentary after her speech that those who enter Folly's house "do not know that the dead are there, that her guests are in the depths of Sheol," the abode of the dead (9:18).

The second contrast juxtaposes two types of women in Israelite society. One is the ideal faithful wife. The negative character, from the perspective of Proverbs, is the adulterous woman or the prostitute, the one who "lies in wait" to capture "a young man without sense." She "seizes him and kisses him" and says, "Come, let us take our fill of love until morning; let us delight ourselves with love. For my husband is not at home; he has gone on a long journey" (7:1–27). This woman is also called the "foreign woman" (2:16; 5:20; 7:5; 22:14; NRSV: "loose woman"), a type on the order of Jezebel and Solomon's foreign wives, whom the Hebrew Bible regards as conduits for the worship of foreign deities. Some of this negative imagery could be allegorical of Woman Folly, but there are enough specifics in these descriptions to suggest that they reflect real women (e.g., prostitutes) or projections by males of women who do not meet the ideals of Israelite society.

The third set of contrasts, the good wife and the contentious wife, again represents generalized features. The contentious wife appears in Proverbs: "It is better to live in a desert land than with a contentious and fretful wife" (21:19); "A continual dripping on a rainy day and a contentious wife are alike; to restrain her is to restrain the wind or to grasp oil in the right hand" (27:15–16). The good wife, however, receives much praise: "He who finds a wife finds a good thing, and obtains favor from YHWH" (18:22). This message is elaborated in a long passage that ends the book of Proverbs: "A capable wife who can find? She is far more precious than jewels" (31:10). "Capable wife" is a common translation of *eshet chayil*, but the Hebrew word translated here as "capable" has a stronger set of synonyms such as "powerful," "wealthy," and "brave in battle." The poem continues with details about her faithfulness, hard work inside the house and out, entrepreneurial activities, and good repute, ending with a touching word directed to her: "Many women have done excellently, but you surpass them all" (31:29). The Hebrew word for wisdom, *chochmah*, indicates skillfulness, which is certainly present in this description of the capable wife, but here it is combined with strength and purposefulness, both attributes of wisdom as well. In traditional Judaism, husbands sing this song to their wives on Friday evening, the beginning of the Sabbath.

These texts raise other issues—at least for many today, if not for those in antiquity. The personifications allow the authors, who were most probably male, to attach stereotypes of women to each figure, Wisdom, on the one hand, and Folly, on the other. Wisdom in itself may not be seductive to younger and older persons in reality, but casting it as a woman gives it more appeal than it might otherwise have. By extension, Folly is denigrated by imaging it as a prostitute. Prostitutes were condoned in Israelite society but not normally included in the most fundamental social unit, the family, and in the process prostitutes suffer further estrangement by being considered dangerous figures to avoid. The prophets are fond of depicting apostasy in the images of adultery and prostitution, so here in these wisdom texts they are now all linked to Folly, the opposite of Wisdom. The male point of view thus controls the concept of wisdom, preempting the role of women, especially mothers, in their contributions to the upbringing of the young.

Job and Theodicy

It has been said that Job is the one figure in the Hebrew Bible whom readers know the best and understand the least. He is typically cast as a patient, long-suffering victim who endures the most horrendous loss and pain and yet maintains his faith and serenity. Though he does suffer grievously, in the bulk of the book he is scarcely patient or even-tempered about it. Quite the opposite, he protests vociferously and relentlessly because to his knowledge he has done nothing to deserve the tragic suffering inflicted upon him. With this response, he challenges the dual notions carried in the wisdom stream of tradition: that faithfulness will be rewarded and that a deed inevitably brings its appropriate consequence. Job's complaint articulates the problem of theodicy.

The word "theodicy" derives from two Greek words, *theos,* meaning "god," and *dike,* meaning "justice." The etymology suggests it is an effort to justify or vindicate God, but that explanation does not quite express the problem satisfactorily. Theodicy seeks to reconcile human suffering with the belief in a supreme deity that is seen to be both all-good and all-powerful. Two alternatives present themselves: either (a) God is all-good but not powerful enough to mitigate or remove the suffering and disorder; or (b) God is all-powerful enough to eradicate suffering and disorder but not good enough to want to do so. Simply attributing suffering and disorder to evil or to the devil offers an easy solution, but it does not escape the basic problem: either God cannot stop the evil or the devil, or God can but chooses not to. The problem of theodicy is not limited to moral issues of human wrongdoing. Natural disasters that destroy vast numbers of lives—hurricanes, earthquakes, epidemics—raise similar questions about the power and will of the deity, and a satisfactory answer is as elusive in such cases as it is with the suffering of a lone individual.

The biblical treatment of theodicy is usually keyed to the formula of cause and effect. The Deuteronomists maintain and the conventional wisdom tradition reinforces the principle that the righteous will thrive and the wicked will suffer. However, an endless number of cases exist in which these promised results do not match reality, and the story of Job serves as a prime example for the debate the sages wish to develop about the problem. They do not take their point of departure in challenging the traditional principle of cause and effect. For them Job represents one who has done nothing wrong and expects exoneration. Indeed, this act–consequence principle remains his continual basis for appealing to God. If God had disclosed to him that his suffering was the result of a test that God and "the satan" had agreed to apply to Job, we can only speculate how Job would have taken it.

Treatments of the problem of theodicy began early in ancient Southwest Asia, and the book of Job follows in their wake. "A Man and His God," a Sumerian poem from the first half of the second millennium BCE, relates the story of a righteous sufferer who is afflicted with various diseases and is treated poorly by his acquaintances. He appeals to his god for relief and is eventually granted it. The poem differs from the book of Job in that it lacks the dialogue section but includes prayers of petition and thanksgiving. Also this sufferer acknowledges some wrongdoing, which Job does not.

Another example, stemming from Babylon in the fourteenth to twelfth centuries BCE, is "The Poem of the Righteous Sufferer" (also called "I Will Praise the Lord of Wisdom"). A lengthy and elegant literary work, it is structured as a monologue by a nobleman who for no clear reason loses his belongings, social standing, and health. The god Marduk had caused his suffering and eventually brings him healing and restoration; the poem thus underscores the power of the gods. Unlike Job, the protagonist is not angry and argumentative but accepts whatever he receives from Marduk's hand, and he remains pious to the end.

A third poem, called "The Babylonian Theodicy," was crafted about 1000 BCE as a dialogue between a sufferer and a friend. The sufferer, weakened by illness and loss of assets, questions divine justice and seeks support and understanding from his friend. The poem ends with his appeal to the gods to have pity on him. These three texts do not resolve the theodical dilemma (nor does Job, for that matter) but aim primarily to describe the human condition of vulnerability, hoping for support from the deities.

A specific set of texts in the Hebrew Bible serves as additional background for Job's treatment of theodicy. The prophet Jeremiah, working just before Jerusalem's fall and during the first part of the exilic period, complains that YHWH has not protected him as promised in his call to be a prophet: "Do not be afraid of them [his opponents], for I am with you to deliver you, says YHWH" (1:8). As Jeremiah delivers his prophecies, however, he is personally attacked by his fellow Judahites, imprisoned, nearly killed, put in the stocks, and ridiculed. His response is recorded in the "confessions of Jeremiah"—not confessions of his sins, but "jeremiads," complaints against God. There are seven such confessions (11:18–23; 12:1–6; 15:10–21; 17:14–18; 18:18–23; 20:7–13; 20:14–18) in which the prophet describes feeling abandoned by God. The complaints become progressively more strident, and the penultimate charge is particularly confrontational: "O YHWH, you have enticed me, and I was enticed; you have overpowered me, and you have prevailed. I have become a laughingstock all day long; everyone mocks me" (20:7) The NRSV softens the language with "entice," as most translations try to do. The Hebrew word *patah* occurs in Exodus 22:16 (Tanakh 22:15) with the meaning of "seduce" (in the sexual sense); coupled with "overpower" and "prevail" in Jeremiah the image is one of assault, if not rape: "O God, you lured me and forced me against my will."

Jeremiah's final diatribe, which will have an echo in Job, is the strongest of the confessions. He does not consider suicide, nor does he curse God. Instead, he curses the day on which he was born, and he fiercely denounces the person who bore word of the birth to his father: "Cursed be the day on which I was born! The day when my mother bore me, let it not be blessed! Cursed be the man who brought the news to my father, saying, 'A child is born to you, a son'" (20:14–15). Jeremiah wishes the messenger had killed him while he was still in the womb. The complaint ends with a wail: "Why did I come forth from the womb to see toil and sorrow, and spend my days in shame?" (20:18). Jeremiah does not develop his complaint into a discussion of theodicy, but as well as anyone in the Hebrew Bible he presents material for such a discourse.

The book of Job stems from a much later period than the other Southwest Asian theodicies but not long after the time of Jeremiah. It was most likely written sometime in the fifth to the third centuries BCE by sages living in Yehud (Judea) during the period of the Persian empire. Scholars consider its Hebrew style to indicate the postexilic period. Few specific references provide a foothold for any close dating. One specific clue may lie in Job 19:24: "O that with an iron pen and with lead they [Job's words] were engraved on a rock forever!" A famous, imposing inscription was carved into a mountain face at Behistun (near modern-day Kermanshah in western Iran) by the Persian emperor Darius toward the end of the sixth century BCE, using iron and lead, and it still exists on that same site.

A few other details in the text point to this same general period. The fall of Jerusalem is well in the past; many who were in Babylonian exile have returned, and the rebuilding of cities has begun on a modest scale; the people still lack sovereignty, as they have to send tribute to the imperial capital when it is demanded; and in spite of these circumstances they have managed to retain a cultural memory, social and religious institutions, and a resolve to survive. These disasters and processes do not need to be addressed in the book of Job, yet they form the background of the sages' reflections on the larger problem of theodicy. The book of Job represents the efforts of sages in their community, trained in the old wisdom tradition, to reflect on the predicament of loss, suffering, restoration, and survival. In particular, they seek to reconcile these harsh situations with their belief in the all-powerful and compassionate YHWH.

The book does not directly engage the political and economic issues of the period. It is timeless in the sense that it speaks to the dilemma of unjust suffering in general without limiting it to one historical time frame. Job 1 opens with the simple statement: "There was once a man in the land of Uz whose name was Job." Uz is unknown to us, and the numerous speculations have not resulted in any consensus about its location. For our purposes, the story could just as well begin: "Once upon a time there was a man from the land of Oz." There are also no grounds in the text for dating the story to the ancestral times, as many have been inclined to do, thus interpreting it as an episode prior to the Mosaic law. Rather, it derives from the postexilic period, and its authors wrote with knowledge of the legal traditions, cultural experiences, and religious notions current at the time.

The book of Job comprises two distinct sections. A prose folktale forms the prologue and epilogue (Job 1–2; 42:10–17); in between, making up most of the book, is a series of poetic dialogues with epilogue (3:1–42:9). The patient and pious Job appears in the prose tale, but in the dialogues he rails against his friends and God for the injustice done to him. Very likely, the two parts had different origins and histories. Older than the dialogue, the folktale is not unlike the Sumerian poem "A Man and His God" in that both focus on suffering and recovery without the confrontation with friends or God. The sages could use such a story as the framework and insert into it their long dialogue about divine justice. The prose story presents a conventional view of suffering and piety, according to which one should not blame God for human afflictions and distress. As such, it serves as the perfect foil for Job's later arguments. In the monologue that ends the dialogues (Job

38–41), God is magisterial and all-powerful, another contrast with the prologue, where God takes on a problematic, pliable character.

Job 1–2 sets the stage for the rest of the book. It opens with a description of Job's wealth, abundance, privilege, and perfection. Job is "the greatest of all the people of the east" (1:3), with thousands of head of livestock, an abundance of slaves, and the ideal mix of children for that patriarchal context—seven sons and three daughters, who obviously enjoy themselves: "His sons used to go and hold feasts in one another's houses in turn; and they would send and invite their three sisters to eat and drink with them" (1:4). Job is so pious that he offers a prophylactic sacrifice for each of them after every party because "It may be that [his] children have sinned, and cursed God in their hearts" (1:5). In Hebrew body symbolism, the heart represents not the seat of emotions, but the mind.

The scene next moves to heaven, where YHWH is holding court with the heavenly beings (the "sons of God," the same term found in Gen. 6:1–4, where the "sons of God" come to earth and mate with the "daughters of humans"). And now we meet "the satan." The Hebrew word *ha-satan* literally means "the satan" (*ha* is the definite article "the"). *Ha-satan* is not a proper noun, "Satan," just as *ha-adam* in the creation story does not mean "Adam," but "the human." The Hebrew *satan* is a "prosecutor" or "accuser" in the forensic sense, the one whose office it is to test individuals and bring charges of wrongdoing; the word can also be used as a verb, "to indict" or "to accuse" (e.g., Ps. 109:4a, "In return for my love they accuse me"). The *satan* is a member of God's celestial council, not the Evil One who opposes God. In the book of Job, the *satan* acts on God's behalf and with God's full support.

The same figure reappears in 1 Chronicles 21:1; here *satan* (the proper noun without the definite article) incites David to take a census of the people; however, the figure is still God's functionary, not a hostile figure. The parallel story in 2 Samuel 24:1 has YHWH, not *satan*, inciting David to take the census. God is displeased when David lets himself be enticed (1 Chron. 21:7), just as God would likely have been displeased with Job if he had not remained faithful. The only other appearance of *satan* in the Hebrew Bible is in Zechariah 3:1–2, where YHWH rebukes the *satan* for preparing to accuse the high priest Joshua. Not until later texts outside the Hebrew Bible does one find "Satan" as the arch Evil One, the opponent of God (e.g., in *Jubilees* 23:29; *Assumption of Moses* 10:1; and frequently in the New Testament, as in Matt. 4:10; Luke 22:3).

So in the Job story, the *satan* joins the heavenly court. God asks where he has been, and the *satan* responds that he has been out and around in the world. God calls his attention to Job, "a blameless and upright man." Scoffing, the *satan* states that Job is pious because it pays off for him in earthly blessings, and that he would curse God were he to lose everything. God gives the *satan* carte blanche to test Job—with the sole exception that he not touch Job himself. The *satan* then proceeds to destroy Job's family and possessions.

The import of this understanding of *ha-satan* in Job 1–2 is that God is complicit in causing Job's suffering—the death of his children, the loss of all his belongings, and eventually the physical pain he suffers. In the biblical view, nothing in this world except for human rebellion happens without God's concurrence. As is clear in this story and elsewhere in the Hebrew Bible, the *satan* cannot act independently of divine command, but only tests and accuses someone whom God will ultimately judge.

After Job declines to blame God following the first set of disasters, the scene moves back to heaven, where God and the *satan* compare notes about Job's response. The *satan* increases the challenge, and God lets him afflict Job physically so long as he does not take his life. The next time we see Job, he is covered with "loathsome sores," scratching them with a potsherd and sitting on ashes. Job's wife urges him to curse God and die, but he refuses: "Shall we receive the good at the hand of God, and not receive the bad?" (2:10). The text states that Job does not "sin with his lips," an intriguing note that leaves unsaid whether he sinned in his heart—as he was afraid his children may have done after their feasting (1:5).

The role of Job's wife in this story is an enigma. Either she really thinks Job has every right to curse God, even if it means God will kill him, or she may be speaking out of empathy for him, thinking that he will be freed of his suffering if he curses God and dies for it. Whichever is the case, Job refuses, calling her by a hard word meaning "senseless" and "disgraceful" (2:10). Both Jewish and Christian traditions have considered Job and his wife parallel to Adam and Eve on the grounds that both men were urged by their wives to sin.

Finally, Job's three friends arrive—Eliphaz, Bildad, and Zophar. They intend to comfort and console him, and they go through a mourning ritual, tearing their robes, throwing dust on their heads, and sitting with him silently for seven days and nights. This is one origin of the Jewish mourning ritual of *shivah*, a word meaning "seven," as in "seven days" here in 2:13. At this point the prologue concludes with Job remaining consistently pious, unwilling to complain, at least vocally, about his losses and pains. In the remainder of the book the *satan* never reappears, and no mention is made of the test. Job's wife is also silent during the rest of the dialogues, but is referred to twice (19:17; 31:10). The focus shifts to Job and his friends.

Before the dialogue commences, Job changes the mood abruptly with a monologue in which he wishes he had never been born. The depth of Job's misery and anger stands in stark contrast to his earlier acquiescence in Job 1–2. Whereas the prologue pictures him as unwilling to curse God, here he curses his birthday with vehemence. In this calculated denunciation he does not violate a principle the sages would have known from their heritage: "Whoever curses father or mother shall be put to death" (Exod. 21:17). They also would have been familiar with Jeremiah's curse of his own birthday and patterned Job 3 on it, expanding it to almost three times the length of Jeremiah's utterance. Job's vitriol is palpable as he begins similarly to Jeremiah: "Let the day perish in which I was born, and the night that said, 'A man-child is conceived.' Let that day be darkness! May God above not seek it, or light shine on it. Let gloom and deep darkness claim it. Let clouds settle upon it; let the blackness of the day terrify it. . . . Yes, let that night be barren; let no joyful cry be heard in it" (3:3–5, 7).

He wishes he had been stillborn, his mother's womb had not opened, her breasts had not been there to suckle him, and he had never seen the light of day. The words contrast to his pious statement in the prologue: "Naked I came from my mother's womb, and naked shall I return there" (1:21)—one of the few texts in the Hebrew Bible suggesting the motif of Mother Earth. He ends his first complaint with foreboding: "Truly the thing that I fear comes upon me, and what I dread befalls me. I am not at ease, nor am I quiet; I have no rest; but trouble comes" (3:25–26). It is not clear whether Job anticipates more loss and suffering or if he expects his friends to offer him no comfort. Whichever may be the case, he has nothing left to lose.

Following Job's monologue cursing his birth, the dialogues that make up the largest portion of the book follow a fairly strict structure, which may seem wooden on the surface but which effectively serves the purpose of allowing all participants to speak. The sages who wrote the book opted for this type of conversation or debate rather than a more discursive essay. There are three cycles (Job 4–14; 15–21; 22–28), and each cycle contains an orderly give-and-take. First the friend Eliphaz speaks and Job answers;

then Bildad's speech is followed again by a response from Job; and finally Zophar addresses Job and receives a response from him. The second cycle follows the same sequence, as does the third cycle except that the final speech by Zophar is not evident unless it is present in 27:13–23. Job concludes the dialogues with a final defense of his case in chapters 29–31. Next is a lengthy monologue by a fourth friend, Elihu, of whom we have heard nothing until now (32–37), and his statement goes unanswered by Job. Instead, YHWH responds to Job with two speeches (38–41), each one answered briefly by Job (40:3–5; 42:1–6). The double epilogue in 42:7–17 concludes the book. The following summary restructures the material into three primary arguments presented by the friends.

The long dialogue section is filled with variety, passion, and literary power. It follows a crescendo of intensity as the speakers become increasingly direct and accusatory. Job appears progressively more sympathetic as his plight and options look dimmer and dimmer. Job and his friends parse the problem of theodicy in a variety of ways. The friends' arguments smack of conventional dogmas, reasons that were old and tired already by their time, but that are still heard today. Job will have nothing of them, and he refutes each argument.

The first and most basic conventional argument from the friends is a repeat the Deuteronomistic doctrine. Suffering is punishment for sinning or wrongdoing, and blessings await those who obey the law. In this scheme, there is no such thing as undeserved suffering, so Job must have sinned and is now being punished for it, as Eliphaz states early in the first round: "Think now, who that was innocent ever perished? Or where were the upright cut off? As I have seen, those who plow iniquity and sow trouble reap the same" (4:7). Those who do right are not punished; only the wicked suffer. With little sensitivity, Bildad adds that Job's children obviously died because of their own sins: "Does God pervert justice? Or does the Almighty pervert the right? If your children sinned against him, he delivered them into the power of their transgression" (8:3–4).

Job's response is clear and unequivocal. He is innocent of any wrongdoing, and God knows it (10:7). Job speaks adamantly: "Until I die I will not put away my integrity from me. I hold fast my righteousness, and will not let it go; my heart does not reproach me for any of my days" (27:5–6). One of his most forceful statements comes in Job 31, an asseveration of his virtue and integrity in never having done harm to others. In Job 13, using judicial language, he repeats again and again that he needs to present his case to God, even if it costs him his life: "I would speak to the Almighty, and I desire to argue my case with God. . . . See, he will kill me; I have no hope; but I will defend my ways to his face" (13:3, 15; see page 52).

God is his witness, says Job, the one who can vouch for him (16:19), though at the same time God is also the judge. Job's complaint is bitter (23:2) because of its urgency. He needs to be vindicated before he dies since justice means that things are set aright during one's own lifetime when others can witness it as well—although he recognizes that for him vindication may not come until after his death (19:23–27). As it is, he is suffering, and "there is no justice" (19:7). God crushes him, will not even let him catch his breath, can overpower him, and can discredit him and his case (9:16–21). "There is no umpire between us, who might lay his hand on us both" (9:33). Job pleads for an advocate: "Oh, that I had one to hear me!" (31:35).

The second charge from the friends is that Job is arrogant in questioning God's justice. Humans cannot understand God's greatness and the workings of the world (36:24–37:24), the friends maintain: "God is greater than any mortal" (33:12). Humans pale in comparison, as Bildad avers: "How then can a mortal be righteous before God? How can one born of woman be pure? If even the moon is not bright and the stars are not pure in his sight, how much less a mortal, who is a maggot, and a human being, who is a worm!" (25:4–6). Job's arrogance, they maintain, is leading him to commit further rebellions against God (34:37), and his wickedness affects others (35:8). He needs to back down!

Job responds to this argument at two levels. First, just as his friends use an ad hominem argument in calling him arrogant, Job offers an ad hominem rejoinder—what kind of "friends" are they anyway? He accuses them of "whitewashing with lies" (13:4) and "speaking falsely for God" (13:7). They are "miserable comforters" (16:2), not superior to him (13:2), and they only make his situation worse rather than better: "How long will you torment me, and break me in pieces with words? These ten times you have cast reproach upon me; are you not ashamed to wrong me?" (19:2–3). It is easy to preach dispassionately about suffering if one is not suffering: "Those at ease have contempt for misfortune, but it is ready for those whose feet are unstable" (12:5). So Job is not only the brunt of God's injustice, but he also becomes a "laughingstock" to his friends (12:4) and is mocked by others: "I am one before whom people spit" (17:6; see also 30:10).

Job also responds by redirecting their argument. When the friends claim that God is beyond human understanding, Job's retort is that God, not being human, cannot fully understand the human condition, and he directs his charge to God: "Do you have eyes of flesh? Do you see as humans see? Are your days like the days of mortals, or your years like human years?" (10:4–5). How, Job asks, can God empathize with us whose circumstances and life's course are so radically different? Unlike YHWH, humans have a hard and ultimately hopeless life (7:1–10), and Job describes its end with melancholy: "For there is hope for a tree, if it is cut down, that it will sprout again. . . . But mortals die, and are laid low; humans expire, and where are they? . . . Until the heavens are no more, they will not awake or be roused out of their sleep" (14:7, 10, 12). Although Job cries for vindication before he dies, he acknowledges that his spirit is now so broken (17:1) that death would come as a relief to him (6:8–13; 7:16).

The sages writing these dialogues make two notable reversals of past traditions, the first regarding God's compassion. Serving as a prophet in the northern kingdom before its fall in 722, Hosea announces that Israel deserves be to decimated because of its continued apostasies, yet YHWH will not act with vindictiveness toward humans but will spare Israel the punishment it should receive: "I am God and no mortal, the Holy One in your midst" (Hos. 11:9). Job finds it ironic that, unlike Hosea's claim, he is now being punished though he does not deserve it.

The second and even more stunning reversal for the sages is evident in a comparison of two texts. Psalm 8:4 (Tanakh 8:5) juxtaposes humanity to the vastness of the universe, which could command so much more of God's attention: "What are human beings that you are mindful of them, mortals that you care for them?" The psalmist is astounded that God, who has created so much on a grand scale, cares to attend to individual humans. Job, however, sees an ominous, disquieting aspect to God's attention: "What are human beings, that you make so much of them, that you set your mind on them, visit them every morning, test them every moment? Will you not look away from me for a while, let me alone until I swallow my spittle?" (7:17–19). Rather than seeing God's presence as a source for comfort and support, Job would prefer to be left alone. He is not arrogant, as his friends charge, but abused and to be pitied.

The friends' third argument pushes the basic principle of fairness one step further. Job's suffering, Eliphaz insists, occurs as God's way of disciplining him: "How happy is the one whom God reproves; therefore do not despise the discipline of the Almighty. For he wounds, but he binds up; he strikes, but his hands heal" (5:17–18). The Hebrew word for "happy," *ashrei,* appears frequently in Psalms and elsewhere. Often translated "blessed," it can introduce a formal word of blessing, as in the first line of the Psalm 1: "Happy (*or* blessed) are those who do not follow the advice of the wicked." So Job's friends are interpreting his sufferings as a sign of divine favor. The deity is disciplining Job for his own good and, in time, will bind up and heal Job.

Despite the anger and impatience Job shows when hearing the other rationales, he largely ignores this patronizing argument. At most, he expresses sorrow and caution that he is not dealing with reliable friends: "Those who withhold kindness from a friend forsake the fear of the Almighty. My companions are treacherous like a torrent-bed, like freshets that pass away. . . . Such you have now become to me; you see my calamity, and are afraid" (6:14–15, 21).

The last word reveals much. Job's situation may have shaken his friends' confidence in their position and produced fear in them. They do not acknowledge any legitimacy to his arguments, but they may find his case unsettling. All they can do is fall back on platitudes, as Job points out: "Your maxims are proverbs of ashes, your defenses are defenses of clay" (13:12). Of the three arguments, the friends' third effort is the weakest. Though Job might accept the idea that suffering is a form of discipline, the claim that all will be healed is, for Job—who has a very strong view of the permanence of death—patently false. His children are dead; nothing and no one can take their place.

It is not a matter of who won this round, Job or his friends, for the problem of theodicy is too urgent and monumental to trivialize as a contest among friends. The friends play a key role as dialogue partners, but Job's real argument is with God, whom he challenges for an explanation in his final summary of innocence (Job 31): "Let the Almighty answer me!" (31:35).

God's response comes with force—"out of the whirlwind" (38:1), an image associated with divine anger (Isa. 29:6; Jer. 23:19). It is an enigmatic answer, not a direct reply to Job's many specific questions and accusations, but also not a theodical theory to explain the existence of suffering and disorder. The first of God's two speeches (38:1–40:2; 40:6–41:34) addresses the matter of knowledge, power, and wisdom. God indicates that Job was wrong not in claiming innocence but in asserting his wisdom, and God proceeds with a series of ironical, impossible questions to demonstrate the limitations of Job's knowledge: "Who is this that darkens counsel by words without knowledge? Gird up your loins like a man, I will question you, and you shall declare to me" (38:2–3).

Many of the questions treat the process of creation and were discussed in Chapter 7. God asks where Job was at the time of creation, whether he can measure the sky, if he can shut up the sea, whether he can control the light, what he knows about the abode of the dead, if he has visited the storehouses of snow and hail, whether he can manage the constellations, if he can bring the rain and lightning. In addition to these creation images, God challenges Job to hunt with the lions, fly with the ravens, attend the birth of mountain goats and deer, tame the wild ox, change the behavior of ostriches, make the horse mighty, and soar with the hawk and the eagle. God ends this first speech bluntly: "Shall a faultfinder contend with the Almighty? Anyone who argues with God must respond" (40:2).

A new element here, not present in the introduction to God's first speech in Job 38:2–3, is the word "faultfinder"; the Hebrew term *yissor* refers to someone who admonishes, corrects, or disciplines someone else, often in a positive sense as when a parent corrects a child (e.g., Prov. 19:18; 29:17). So God is not accusing Job of wrongdoing, which Job considered the issue in the dialogues, but here is saying that if Job is going to try to correct or criticize God, he (Job) needs to prepare to defend himself. Job's reply to God's first speech is not transparent: "See, I am of small account; what shall I answer you? I lay my hand on my mouth. I have spoken once, and I will not answer; twice, but will proceed no further" (40:4–5). For one who has so energetically been demanding a trial with God to get justice, Job could mean one of two things. Either he is confessing his ignorance and his inability to answer God, or he defiantly refuses to get sidetracked by God's speech. The divine speech does not address substantively Job's complaint that he has been unjustly punished, and so Job, in response, does not reply directly to God's words.

Job is silenced but is not yet convinced. God issues a second speech. Job 40:8 articulates the key issue: "Will you even put me in the wrong? Will you condemn me that you may be justified?" Job may be convinced that he is righteous, but here God is accusing him of self-righteousness, trying to blame God so he (Job) will look better in comparison.

As in the first speech, God addresses Job's case only obliquely. Having established that Job lacks the majestic scope of the creator, God now argues that Job lacks the ability to rule the world. God demonstrates this point by elaborating the phenomenal strength of two animals, neither of which Job can master. The first is Behemoth, possibly the hippopotamus. The second is Leviathan, a sea monster or possibly the crocodile. Archaeologists have discovered bones of both the hippopotamus and the crocodile in swamps along the Levantine coast—the hippopotamus from the Iron Age and Persian period (twelfth to fourth centuries BCE) and the crocodile even until the twentieth century. Whether Job 40–41 intends real species or mythological creatures, they represent creatures of enormous strength that a human such as Job has no chance of capturing and controlling. God, on the other hand, treats them as mere playthings: "Will you play with it [Leviathan] as with a bird, or will you put it on leash for your girls?" (41:5; Tanakh 40:29). Leviathan reappears in apocalyptic literature as the primordial sea dragon that God will finally kill at the end of time (Isa. 27:1).

God's second speech also does not answer Job's specific charges. Job's second response follows in 42:1–6, and in it he again acknowledges his limitations but not any error in his challenge for justification: "I have uttered what I did not understand, things too wonderful for me, which I did not know" (42:3). God has persuaded him that the world is much larger and more complicated than he can grasp, and Job either finds this realization sufficient or he is resigned that he will get no further explication from God. His final statement is translated unfortunately in the NRSV: "Therefore I despise myself, and repent in dust and ashes" (42:6). The Hebrew word should not be understood as a reflexive verb ("despise myself") but as a normal transitive verb with an implied object ("reject" or "revoke"). Job is withdrawing his lawsuit against God, not admitting fault, not repenting of his attempt to find justice, and not submitting piously to God. Job retains his integrity.

The book ends with a double epilogue, the first concluding the long dialogue section and the second concluding the story begun in Job 1–2. The first (42:7–9) conveys a remarkable, revealing assessment of the dialogue. God says that the three friends (the fourth, Elihu, is unmentioned here) have erred in their pronouncements: "You have not spoken of me what is right, as my servant Job has done" (42:7–8). God finds fault in the conventional arguments they invoke—that a system of cause and effect explains human fate; that Job has been arrogant in protesting his undeserved suffering; and that suffering aims to discipline humans. Because of their errors, God directs them to offer a sacrifice of forgiveness, and Job will give a prayer of intercession for them, all of which transpires. It represents an ironic conclusion to the impassioned exchange between Job and his friends. Seen in the light of Job 1–2, this acknowledgment by God begs the question of divine justice. Moreover, God emphasizes in the whirlwind speech that Job does not know the divine plan (which is also one of the friends' arguments), but then by speaking out of the symbolic chaos of the whirlwind God leaves open the question of whether the deity is indeed trustworthy. For the sages behind this book, God's acknowledgment that Job, not his friends, has spoken rightly of God (42:9) is a weighty admission.

The second epilogue (42:10–17) returns to the end of Job 2, almost as if Job 3–41 did not exist. God restores to Job all that he had, plus some: double the number of livestock, friends and relations, wealth, and comfort. The same number and gender of children, seven sons and three beautiful daughters, are born to them, and all receive an inheritance, which is unusual in the customs of the time. There is no mention of Job's wife, but one specific detail represents another unexpected acknowledgment. Job is surrounded by his larger clan and all his acquaintances, and they comfort him "for all the evil that YHWH had brought upon him" (42:11). That God is capable of doing evil is an admission that returns to the beginning of the discussion of theodicy. Whether this "evil" refers to God's permitting *ha-satan* to "test" Job is left unsaid, but it is the most likely referent. The book simply concludes with a fairy-tale ending similar to its beginning: Job has reached an advanced age in comfort and with his family around him.

Qohelet (Ecclesiastes) and Realism

Job protests against undeserved suffering and so acknowledges the gap between conventional theology and real life. The same theme, expressed not through angry protest but through sober reflection, appears in the book of Qohelet, a candid but not cynical interpreter of life.

The Hebrew *qohelet* occurs in the book's first verse with the meaning of "preacher" or "speaker" (NRSV: "Teacher") of an assembly (the root *qahal* means "assembly"). The Septuagint provides the title Ecclesiastes, which means a preacher or member of the assembly. Qohelet 1:1 attributes the book to "the Teacher, the son of David, king in Jerusalem," implying Solomon, although he is not explicitly named in the book as he is in the first verse of the books of Proverbs and Song of Songs. A royal author is unlikely, however, as the person behind the book seems to be of moderate means, without royal authority himself, and indeed even critical of the monarch: "Better is a poor but wise youth than an old but foolish king, who will no longer take advice" (4:13); "There is an evil that I have seen under the sun, as great an error as if it proceeded from the ruler" (10:5). Moreover, another text identifies Qohelet as a *chacham*, a sage (12:9). Because the Hebrew of the book is characteristic of a late stage in the language, its date of composition is no earlier than the latter part of the Persian period or the early part of Hellenistic rule, thus during the fourth or third century BCE. It appeared after the book of Job and continues its scrutiny of conventional religious views. Two fragments dating from the second and first centuries BCE appear among the documents found at Qumran, indicating that the Qohelet manuscript had begun to be copied and circulated by that time.

The book of Qohelet belongs to the genre of contemplative discourse, but it is more in the form of an essay than a dialogic poem with a prose frame, as in the case of the book of Job. It is not primarily a discussion of theodicy. Instead of trying to explain the existence of suffering, Qohelet asserts that all life is vacuous and unstable. A term occurring thirty-five times in the book, *hevel* is translated "vanity" in some older versions, but its meaning goes more in the direction of "breath," "vapor," "nothingness," "emptiness," "transience," or "futility."

The book begins with this pronouncement according to the NRSV: "Vanity of vanities! All is vanity." Or better, following the JPS: "Utter futility!—said Kohelet—All is futile!" (1:2). A definite repetitiveness characterizes life. People work, but get little pleasure from it. The sun rises and sets, the wind blows from one direction or the other, water runs to the oceans but never fills them, our senses cannot get enough, individuals are forgotten after death (1:3–11). "There is nothing new under the sun"; the phrase "under the sun" is repeated twenty-six times in the book to underscore the cyclical patterns of life. We may try to find pleasure in wine or sex, acquire wealth and possessions, construct great buildings, enjoy our work—but it all amounts to nothing (2:1–11). Or we can hate life, grow weary of our work, despair over our efforts to become wise—but such negativity is also fruitless, and someone else will enjoy what we accomplish (2:15–23).

The theme of repetitiveness is nowhere clearer than in the well-known passage in Qohelet 3:1–8, which has been appropriated in literature, rhetoric, and song:

> For everything there is a season,
> and a time for every matter under heaven:
> a time to be born, and a time to die;
> a time to plant, and a time to pluck up what is planted;
> a time to kill, and a time to heal;
> a time to break down, and a time to build up;
> a time to weep, and a time to laugh;
> a time to mourn, and a time to dance. . . .

It continues for a total of fourteen pairs, juxtaposing opposites to produce a sense of rhythm, monotony, and futility. With fourteen binaries the text has twice the number seven, the number signifying totality—totality doubled, absolutely everything. Each type of event happens, and each has its proper time, which humans cannot control. Even though this pattern suggests an order consonant with the order of creation, it gives little satisfaction.

Qohelet is no atheist, and God crops up frequently in the book's discussions. The deity is responsible for all that happens, including assigning humans their tasks. In one of the text's most difficult passages, Qohelet states that God has put *ha-olam* in the hearts of humans (3:11). The word *ha-olam* is usually rendered "eternity"; the NRSV has it as "a sense of past and future," which is an appropriate rendering in this context. For Qohelet, this capacity of humans to transcend their own time frame is beneficial, but it can also be frustrating when one wants to know the past or the future, as Qohelet is quick to emphasize. We also cannot be sure of what happens after death: "For the fate of humans and the fate of animals is the same; as one dies, so dies the other. . . . All go to one place; all are from the dust, and all turn to dust again. Who knows whether the human spirit goes upward and the spirit of animals goes downward to the earth?" (3:19–21).

Qohelet is being realistic in this assertion. We may know the past, but we cannot change it. And eventually, we will all be forgotten. Similarly, we may wish or believe, but we cannot *know* what awaits us after death. God too is inscrutable. All that transpires may seem caprice or chance (8:10–17; 7:14), and we cannot even know if justice predominates, the problem that aggravates Job.

So what should we do in life? Qohelet has clear advice that affirms life. We should enjoy eating and drinking and working: "This is what I have seen to be good: it is fitting to eat and drink and find enjoyment in all the toil with which one toils under the sun the few days of the life God gives us; for this is our lot" (5:18; Tanakh 5:17). We should also enjoy love and marriage (9:9), and companionship is an essential component of our well-being: "Two are better than one, because they have a good reward for their toil. For if they fall, one will lift up the other; but woe to one who is alone and falls and does not have another to help. Again, if two lie together, they keep warm; but how can one keep warm alone?" (4:9–11). Above all, we should practice moderation, for extremism in any behavior will not bring satisfaction. This advice applies even to religious practice, according to Qohelet: "Do not be too righteous, and do not act too wise; why should you destroy yourself?" (7:16). And definitely relish your youth while you have it (11:9; 12:1).

Qohelet is not hostile toward religion or morality, but he expresses wistfulness that we cannot be sure they are effective. In this respect Qohelet levels a criticism against traditional Yahwism, which advocates continual religious and moral practice. Qohelet, however, represents a chastened and realistic approach to life: we do best to recognize our limits, avoid excess, and enjoy the good things of life—in moderation.

Like the book of Job, Qohelet also has an epilogue with contents that do not fully match the body of the text. The entirety of the book until this point is a frank, hard-hitting appraisal of conventional notions and practices in Israel's tradition. But after Qohelet's insistence that the search for wisdom must not be taken to the extreme, 12:9–11 affirms the work of sages: "The sayings of the wise are like goads, and like nails firmly fixed are the collected sayings that are given by one shepherd." Next comes the familiar line: "Of making many books there is no end, and much study is a weariness of the flesh" (12:12). It is almost as if to say that this book of Qohelet is just another publication, and we should be cautious not to take it too seriously.

And then the final lines: "The end of the matter; all has been heard. Fear God, and keep his commandments; for that is the whole duty of everyone. For God will bring every deed into judgment, including every secret thing, whether good or evil" (12:13–14). This affirmation offers an orthodox conclusion to an otherwise unorthodox treatise. In all likelihood a later writer added the last two sentences to bring the book more in line with accepted beliefs and practices. And this interpolation seems to have succeeded since, despite a controversy during the canonization process, the book became part of the canon. No doubt the ending of the book made it palatable, and the book's traditional attribution to Solomon confirmed its authority. In addition, Qohelet urges people to fear God, and despite the critical tone he seeks to understand the human condition within a religious framework. The book is one of the last in the Hebrew Bible to have been written and canonized. Qohelet is a provocative text that continues to speak to the modern sensibility in the same way as it must have moved the ancients.

Conclusion

At the end of this project, we find ourselves both marveling over how much material we have covered and frustrated that we could not adduce more. Every book of the Bible deserves, and has received, its own commentary; every major figure and many minor ones have been studied, in detail, in hundreds and hundreds of pages. For each passage, Jewish and Christian interpreters writing from within their religious communities have found moral teaching and theological understanding, and secular historians and literary critics have discovered meaning in ancient culture and narratives. For every verse we have discussed, numerous other readings can be presented. For every historical and cultural context we have proposed, new archaeological finds and anthropological theories will provide nuance or correction. There is not a sufficient number of pages to encompass all that could be said about this material.

The biblical story spans time from creation (Gen. 1) to Judaism's encounter with Hellenism in the wake of Alexander the Great (Daniel), and for each setting it provides a variety of literatures: cosmological myths and stories of origin (Gen. 1–11), sagas of heroes (e.g., Gen. 12–50, Joshua, Judges), laws (Exodus, Leviticus, Deuteronomy), oracles (Amos, Isaiah, Jeremiah, other prophets), court tales (the stories of Joseph, Esther, Daniel), cosmopolitan wisdom (Proverbs, Job, Qohelet, Sirach), apocalyptic images (Isa. 24–27, Zech. 9–14, Dan. 7–12), and magnificent love poetry (Song of Songs). Its authors include storytellers, bureaucrats, prophets, priests, scribes, sages, and visionaries. And its subjects address such diverse issues as self-definition and relation to others, politics and economics, law and justice, gender and sexuality, assessment of the present and hope for the future. With this diversity of approaches and responses, it is clear that the Bible is not a book of answers. It may be, however, a book that helps its readers ask the right questions, and then provides materials that can spark diverse answers. As long as readers continue to read, interpretations will continue to be generated. And that is a good thing.

This ongoing process of interpretation should serve to inform the frequently heard refrain, "The Bible says it and I believe it." Although we do not wish to dissuade people from their beliefs (or at least most of those beliefs—we do both teach in a university divinity school, and the majority of our students are Christian, many of them candidates for ministerial ordination), we want to see those beliefs enhanced by careful study and informed by the knowledge of the Bible's multiple perspectives. One can certainly read the Bible for personal inspiration (we have done that ourselves), but we also believe in enhancing the study by learning all we can about the texts in their contexts and by seeing the Bible's diverse approaches to the same issues.

Given the Bible's manifold approaches to the questions it asks and humanity's ever widening formulations of new questions and answers, there can be no fully satisfactory conclusion to the literature the previous fourteen chapters address. The biblical canon appropriately has different endings, whether in Malachi or 2 Chronicles, whether with the deuterocanonical literature or not. Readers will remember different points, find different approaches congenial, and seek more understanding of different texts.

From the Mishnah, a late second- or early third-century CE Jewish text, in a tractate called *Pirke Avot* ("Ethics of the Fathers" 5:26), Rabbi Ben (son of) Bag Bag is quoted as saying about the Torah, "Turn it and turn it again, for everything is in it. Pore over it, and wax gray and old over it. Stir not from it, for you can have no better rule than it." Today the Torah and by extension the rest of the canon of the Bible, however that canon be defined, remain a rule for many. It guides views on behaviors ranging from tort law to sexuality; its pages provoke debates and denominations; it continues to inspire artists and theologians. It is our hope that, at the very least, those who would cite this text when speaking of public policy or personal morality would attend to the diverse perspectives it offers and the likely cultural contexts of these perspectives. And it is our hope as well that readers who may have found this collection of texts daunting or incomprehensible, or dismissed it as ancient claptrap, or discredited it as inconsistent and therefore unworthy of study will turn to it again and will find new appreciation, ask new questions, and raise new interpretations.

Acknowledgments

Much of the material in this book took shape during years of teaching courses and presenting materials before academic, clergy, and lay audiences. The questions and responses of countless students, numerous faculty colleagues, and other conversation partners gave us the opportunity to think through many of the knottier problems the biblical texts pose and develop what we now think are appropriate interpretations. The volume also reflects major advances in the field of biblical studies; the bibliography at the back of the book represents only a small sample of the superb scholarship that has continually provided us both information and inspiration.

The Vanderbilt University Divinity School kindly granted each of us a sabbatical leave to complete the work on the book, as well as a fund to support the final stages.

Caryn Tamber-Rosenau, Vanderbilt graduate student in Hebrew Bible, assisted with fact-checking and proofreading. Lauren E. Kohut, Vanderbilt graduate student in anthropology, designed the maps.

The editorial staff at HarperOne has been especially supportive. John Loudon and Eric Brandt provided creative suggestions as we developed the concept and structure of the book. Michael Maudlin saw the project to its conclusion with his judicious advice about issues large and small. As production editor, Lisa Zuniga worked her magic in turning the manuscript into a finished product.

To all of these people, named and unnamed, we express our deep appreciation.

Douglas A. Knight
Amy-Jill Levine
Nashville
July 2011

Bibliography

Bible Versions

A New English Translation of the Septuagint (LXX). Edited by Albert Pietersma and Benjamin G. Wright. Oxford and New York: Oxford Univ. Press, 2007.

New Revised Standard Version (NRSV). New York: Division of Christian Education of the National Council of the Churches of Christ in the USA, 1989.

Tanakh: The Holy Scriptures: The New JPS Translation According to the Traditional Hebrew Text (JPS). Philadelphia and Jerusalem: Jewish Publication Society, 1985.

Study Bibles (with articles and notes on the text)

The Catholic Study Bible: New American Bible. Edited by Donald Senior and John J. Collins. 2nd ed. Oxford and New York: Oxford Univ. Press, 2006.

The HarperCollins Study Bible: The New Revised Standard Version with the Apocryphal/ Deuterocanonical Books. Edited by Harold W. Attridge, with the Society of Biblical Literature. Rev. ed. San Francisco: HarperOne, 2006.

The Jewish Study Bible: Jewish Publication Society Tanakh Translation. Edited by Adele Berlin and Marc Zvi Brettler. Oxford and New York: Oxford Univ. Press, 2004.

The New Interpreter's Study Bible: New Revised Standard Version with the Apocrypha. Edited by Walter J. Harrelson. Nashville: Abingdon, 2003.

The New Oxford Annotated Bible: New Revised Standard Version with the Apocrypha: An Ecumenical Study Bible. Edited by Michael D. Coogan. 4th ed. Oxford and New York: Oxford Univ. Press, 2010.

General Resources

Civilizations of the Ancient Near East. Edited by Jack M. Sasson. 4 vols. New York: Scribner, 1995.

The Anchor Bible Dictionary. Edited by David Noel Freedman. 6 vols. New York: Doubleday, 1992.

The HarperCollins Bible Commentary. Edited by James L. Mays, with the Society of Biblical Literature. Revised edition. San Francisco: HarperSanFrancisco, 2000.

The HarperCollins Bible Dictionary. Edited by Mark Allan Powell, with the Society of Biblical Literature. 3rd ed., revised and updated. San Francisco: HarperOne, 2011.

The Oxford Bible Commentary. Edited by John Barton and John Muddiman. Oxford and
    New York: Oxford Univ. Press, 2001.
Theological Lexicon of the Old Testament. Edited by Ernst Jenni and Claus Westermann.
    Translated by Mark E. Biddle. 3 vols. Peabody, MA: Hendrickson, 1997.

Commentary Series
Anchor Bible. New Haven, CT: Yale Univ. Press.
Berit Olam. Collegeville, MN: Liturgical.
Hermeneia. Minneapolis: Augsburg Fortress.
Interpretation: A Bible Commentary for Teaching and Preaching. Louisville, KY: Westmin-
    ster John Knox.
New Interpreter's Bible. Nashville: Abingdon.
Old Testament Library. Louisville, KY: Westminster John Knox.
Word Biblical Commentary. Nashville: Thomas Nelson.

Texts from Ancient Southwest Asia
Dalley, Stephanie, trans. and ed. *Myths from Mesopotamia: Creation, the Flood, Gilgamesh,
    and Others.* Rev. ed. New York: Oxford Univ. Press, 2000.
Foster, Benjamin R. *Before the Muses: An Anthology of Akkadian Literature.* 3rd ed.
    Bethesda, MD: CDL, 2005.
Hallo, William W. *The Context of Scripture: Canonical Compositions, Monumental
    Inscriptions, and Archival Documents from the Biblical World.* 3 vols. Leiden and Bos-
    ton: Brill, 2003.
Lichtheim, Miriam. *Ancient Egyptian Literature.* 2nd ed. 3 vols. Berkeley: Univ. of Cali-
    fornia Press, 2006.
Roth, Martha T. *Law Collections from Mesopotamia and Asia Minor.* 2nd ed. Atlanta:
    Scholars Press and Society of Biblical Literature, 1997.

For Further Reading
Ackerman, Susan. *Warrior, Dancer, Seductress, Queen: Women in Judges and Biblical Israel.*
    Anchor Yale Bible Reference Library. New Haven, CT: Yale Univ. Press, 1998.
Alter, Robert. *The Art of Biblical Narrative.* 2nd ed. New York: Basic Books, 2011.
Anderson, Cheryl B. *Ancient Laws and Contemporary Controversies: The Need for Inclu-
    sive Biblical Interpretation.* Oxford: Oxford Univ. Press, 2009.
Bach, Alice, ed. *Women in the Hebrew Bible: A Reader.* New York: Routledge, 1999.
Bailey, Lloyd R. *Genesis, Creation, and Creationism.* New York: Paulist, 1993.
Bal, Mieke. *Lethal Love: Feminist Literary Readings of Biblical Love Stories.* Indiana
    Studies in Biblical Literature. Bloomington: Indiana Univ. Press, 1987.
Berquist, Jon L. *Judaism in Persia's Shadow: A Social and Historical Approach.* Minneapo-
    lis: Fortress, 1995.
Birch, Bruce C., Walter Brueggemann, Terence E. Fretheim, and David L. Petersen.
    A Theological Introduction to the Old Testament. 2nd ed. Nashville: Abingdon, 2005.
Brettler, Marc Zvi. *How to Read the Bible.* New York: Jewish Publication Society, 2005.

Collins, John J. *Between Athens and Jerusalem: Jewish Identity in the Hellenistic Diaspora.* 2nd ed. Grand Rapids, MI: Eerdmans, 1999.

Crenshaw, James L. *Old Testament Wisdom: An Introduction.* 3rd ed. Louisville, KY: Westminster John Knox, 2010.

Dever, William. *Who Were the Israelites and Where Did They Come From?* Grand Rapids, MI: Eerdmans, 2003.

Eskenazi, Tamara, and Andrea Weiss, eds. *The Torah: A Women's Commentary.* New York: URJ, 2007.

Exum, Cheryl. *Fragmented Women: Feminist (Sub)versions of Biblical Narratives.* Library of Old Testament Studies. Sheffield: Sheffield Academic, 1993.

———. *Plotted, Shot and Painted: Cultural Representations of Biblical Women.* Journal for the Study of the Old Testament Supplement. Sheffield: Sheffield Academic, 1996.

Finkelstein, Israel, Amihai Mazar, and Brian Schmidt. *The Quest for the Historical Israel: Debating Archaeology and the History of Early Israel.* Atlanta: Society of Biblical Literature, 2007.

Finkelstein, Israel, and Neil Asher Silberman. *The Bible Unearthed: Archaeology's New Vision of Ancient Israel and the Origin of Its Sacred Texts.* New York: Free Press, 2001.

———. *David and Solomon: In Search of the Bible's Sacred Kings and the Roots of the Western Tradition.* New York: Free Press, 2006.

Friedman, Richard Elliott. *Who Wrote the Bible?* New York: Summit, 1987.

Fritz, Volkmar. *The City in Ancient Israel.* Sheffield: Sheffield Academic, 1995.

Gottwald, Norman K. *The Politics of Ancient Israel.* Louisville, KY: Westminster John Knox, 2001.

Grabbe, Lester L. *Ancient Israel: What Do We Know, and How Do We Know It?* London and New York: Continuum, 2007.

Gruen, Erich S. *Diaspora: Jews Amidst Greeks and Romans.* Cambridge, MA: Harvard Univ. Press, 2004.

Halpern, Baruch. *David's Secret Demons: Messiah, Murderer, Traitor, King.* Grand Rapids, MI: Eerdmans, 2001.

Heschel, Abraham Joshua. *The Prophets.* New York: Harper & Row, 1962.

Kessler, Rainer. *The Social History of Ancient Israel: An Introduction.* Minneapolis: Fortress, 2008.

King, Philip J., and Lawrence E. Stager. *Life in Biblical Israel.* Louisville, KY, and London: Westminster John Knox, 2001.

Kitchen, Kenneth A. *On the Reliability of the Old Testament.* Grand Rapids, MI: Eerdmans, 2003.

Knight, Douglas A. *Law, Power, and Justice in Ancient Israel.* Louisville, KY: Westminster John Knox, 2011.

Kugel, James. *Traditions of the Bible: A Guide to the Bible as It Was at the Start of the Common Era.* Cambridge, MA: Harvard Univ. Press, 1999.

Lemche, Niels Peter. *Ancient Israel: A New History of Israelite Society.* Sheffield: JSOT, 1988.

Levenson, Jon. *Creation and the Persistence of Evil: The Jewish Drama of Divine Omnipotence.* Princeton, NJ: Princeton Univ. Press, 1994.

———. *The Hebrew Bible, the Old Testament and Historical Criticism: Jews and Christians in Biblical Studies.* Louisville, KY: Westminster John Knox, 1993.

———. *Sinai and Zion.* New York: HarperCollins, 1985.

Matthews, Victor. *Studying the Ancient Israelites: A Guide to Sources and Methods.* Grand Rapids, MI: Baker Academic, 2007.

McNutt, Paula M. *Reconstructing the Society of Ancient Israel.* Louisville, KY: Westminster John Knox; London: SPCK, 1999.

Meyers, Carol. *Discovering Eve: Ancient Israelite Women in Context.* New York: Oxford Univ. Press, 1988.

Milgrom, Jacob. *Leviticus 1–16.* Anchor Bible 3. New York: Doubleday, 1991.

———. *Leviticus 17–22.* Anchor Bible 3A. New York: Doubleday, 2000.

———. *Leviticus 23–27.* Anchor Bible 3B. New York: Doubleday, 2001.

Miller, J. Maxwell, and John H. Hayes. *A History of Ancient Israel and Judah.* 2nd ed. Louisville, KY: Westminster John Knox, 2006.

Miller, Patrick D. *The Religion of Ancient Israel.* Louisville, KY: Westminster John Knox, 2000.

Page, Hugh R., Jr., ed. *The Africana Bible: Reading Israel's Scriptures from Africa and the African Diaspora.* Minneapolis: Fortress, 2010.

Perdue, Leo G., Joseph Blenkinsopp, John J. Collins, and Carol Meyers. *Families in Ancient Israel.* Louisville, KY: Westminster John Knox, 1997.

Smith, Mark S. *God in Translation: Cross-cultural Recognition of Deities in the Biblical World.* Grand Rapids, MI: Eerdmans, 2010.

———. *The Memoirs of God: History, Memory, and the Experience of the Divine in Ancient Israel.* Minneapolis: Fortress, 2004.

Sugirtharajah, R. S., ed. *Voices from the Margin: Interpreting the Bible in the Third World.* 3rd ed. Maryknoll, NY: Orbis Books, 2006.

Toorn, Karel van der. *Family Religion in Babylonia, Syria, and Israel: Continuity and Change in the Forms of Religious Life.* Leiden: Brill, 1996.

Trible, Phyllis. *Texts of Terror: Literary-Feminist Readings of Biblical Narratives.* Philadelphia: Fortress, 1984.

Westbrook, Raymond, and Bruce Wells. *Everyday Law in Biblical Israel: An Introduction.* Louisville, KY: Westminster John Knox, 2009.

Zevit, Ziony. *The Religions of Ancient Israel: A Synthesis of Parallactic Approaches.* London and New York: Continuum, 2001.

Index